Exercises in Psychological Testing and Assessment

Sixth Edition

Ronald Jay Cohen
St. John's University

McGraw Hill

Boston   Burr Ridge, IL   Dubuque, IA   Madison, WI   New York   San Francisco   St. Louis
Bangkok   Bogotá   Caracas   Kuala Lumpur   Lisbon   London   Madrid   Mexico City
Milan   Montreal   New Delhi   Santiago   Seoul   Singapore   Sydney   Taipei   Toronto

The McGraw-Hill Companies

Higher Education

2 3 4 5 6 7 8 9 0 QPD/QPD 0 9 8 7 6 5

ISBN 0-07-312910-0

www.mhhe.com

Brief Contents

Contents

Chapter 12   Personality Assessment Methods   198

Part 5: Testing and Assessment in Action

Chapter 13   Clinical and Counseling Assessment   214

Chapter 14   Neuropsychological Assessment   224

Preface

Students taking a course variously described as "psychological testing," "psychological assessment," and "tests and measurement" will find this book to be a useful, hands on supplement to in-class lectures and other reading assignments. Chapters in the book generally correspond to the order of the coverage of topics presented in *Psychological Testing and Assessment: An Introduction to Tests and Measurement,* Sixth Edition (Cohen & Swerdlik, 2005). And while it is heartily recommended that this workbook be used as a companion to that text, this workbook will enhance the student's academic experience even if used along with another measurement text.

Like its companion textbook, this book was designed to facilitate and enhance learning. Given this fact, readers may well raise questions about how the author conceptualizes learning and, more specifically, how learning can be facilitated through such books. My own response to such key questions begins with the observation that *learning* is both a noun and a verb. Sequentially in one's experience, learning may initially be a verb (as in "learning new material") and a noun later (as in "calling upon one's learning"). However, it is also true that old learning facilitates new learning, and so arguments about the prominence of new versus old learning take on a kind of chicken-or-the-egg impossibility of resolution. Regardless, learning is an active process that requires deliberate effort in both storing information and maintaining readiness for instant retrieval. In my view, one of the best ways to facilitate the process of learning is to mentally "work out" with the learning. This means, among other things, that one tries to link what is currently being learned to past learning, generate new and novel ideas related to the learning, and think critically about it.

Elsewhere, I have written about what I termed "generative thinking," or *the goal-oriented intellectual production of new or creative ideas* (Cohen, 1994, p. 13). As implied in this definition, there is little that is random about generative thought. Generative thinking may have different objectives, including a better understanding of a new concept. A philosophy guiding the development of the exercises in this book is that the best way to grasp measurement principles is to understand them and then apply them. Accordingly, each chapter herein begins with a crossword puzzle that surveys many of the key terms presented in the corresponding Cohen and Swerdlik (2005) chapter. The exercises that follow encourage the student to build on and enhance this basic understanding. This building and enhancement may take any of several forms—

for example, an essay, independent research with regard to a particular test, or preparation for an oral presentation or group discussion. Whatever the form, the objective of enhancing past learning and creating new learning by fostering generative thought is a common thread throughout.

In addition to providing stimuli for generative thought, seven objectives guided the development of this work. They are

1. to provide students with "do-able" laboratory exercises pertinent to basic measurement concepts, the better for them to achieve (a) a sense of personal mastery with respect to such concepts, (b) personal experience in relevant data manipulations, (c) the ability to understand and relate to technical terms in professional journals, test manuals, and test reports, and (d) the ability to develop an educated opinion about the psychometric soundness of any psychological test. In addition to step-by-step illustrations of the use of various statistics employed in the context of testing, there is also ample opportunity for students to be creative in developing applications of measurement principles;

2. to go beyond assisting the student in the acquisition of course content as presented in the primary text by stimulating depth of understanding of the theory and practice of psychological measurement;

3. to provide a person-oriented perspective on measurement by including biographical material on many past and present contributors to the field on our companion Internet site: *www.mhhe.com/psychtesting6;*

4. to blend theoretical and applied material in a way designed to provide the student with a rationale for (and a "hands-on feel" of) the assessment process. In the interest of maintaining the confidentiality of published materials, and in an effort to avoid "armchair analyses" and inappropriate generalization from data, all such exercises are accomplished using tests and test items constructed by students themselves or by other means (such as by the use of the mock personality inventory in Appendix A);

5. to provide case illustrations of the wide range of "real-world" contexts in which psychological tests are used;

6. to provide both in-class as well as out-of-classroom type tasks and exercises, many of which will be appealing to students who are at widely varying points along the continuum of experience and sophistication with psychological tests;

7. to help balance an appreciation of the science of psychological measurement as it exists today with a healthy, realistic degree of self-criticism and a vision of the challenges that lie ahead.

Some of the exercises can be completed in class by either independent or group work. Some of the exercises will require some out-of-class activity. For example, the "Pick-a-Test" exercise that is presented in some chapters requires students to select a test that they might like to learn more about and then do some library research.

In Chapters 3 through 7, many of the exercises entail the calculation of statistics commonly used in measurement. Step-by-step illustrations of the computations of many of these statistics are evident throughout these chapters, each such illustration designed to facilitate learning. While it is true that all the "real-world" user of virtually any statistic needs to know is how to select, run, and enter data into the right computer program, these step-by-step calculation exercises cannot help but lead to a better conceptual understanding of the process.

In some instances, an exercise might contain reprinted material from some article relevant to testing—the better to serve as a stimulus for thoughtful discussion. In other exercises, it is the students who are called upon to put their own experiences to work (along with what they have learned from the text) and, in essence, write an "article" relevant to testing.

Many students enjoy completing crossword puzzles. For this reason, the crossword puzzle was selected as the format to review key terms. Through the use of "free spaces" in each puzzle, terms that will be introduced in subsequent chapters are previewed. Many students also have an interest in movies. For this reason, the first exercise in each chapter, "Movies and Measurement," employs a film still as a point of departure for thinking and writing about some aspect of measurement. Subsequent exercises may draw on other stimuli designed to be equally engaging. In short, very deliberate efforts were made to make the exercises in this book appealing and challenging while still pedagogically valuable to students. Note here my hesitancy in using the word "fun" with reference to these exercises. This is due to an overlearned awareness of the limited extent to which students will attribute "fun" to most any task they sense to have pedagogical value. Still, despite such inclinations and preconceptions, I do believe that it is possible for students to have fun with some of these exercises—there, I said it—even while they enhance and extend their learning.

During the course of a semester, it is a safe assumption that the instructor will *not* assign every single exercise; there simply isn't time. The instructor's preference may be to concentrate attention on the psychometric foundations of testing, in which case the bulk (if not all) of time will be spent with Chapters 1 through 7. Alternatively, the instructor may focus the course more on applied phenomena and spend more time on the later chapters in this book. If, in skimming through this book, students find exercises that they think they might really enjoy—and find a valuable learning experience—they may want to bring such exercises to the attention of the instructor.

And now, three tips for all students using this book:

1. *Be prepared!* Know what will be required of you—a week or two in advance, if possible—and be ready. A sharpened pencil with an eraser, some unlined paper for calculations, some graph paper and a straight edge (6-inch ruler will do) for graphing, a pocket calculator, and lined, single-sheet paper suitable for essay-type writing are standard equipment for these laboratory exercises. Being prepared also means having read the chapter in your textbook that was assigned prior to the class meeting and being prepared to raise any questions that you have on the material.

2. *Maintain team spirit.* Many of the exercises require you to work with one or more of your classmates; root for them as you would like them to root for you. "Winning" in such team exercises is analogous with "learning," and it is essential for an atmosphere conducive to "winning" to be maintained from the start of the semester to the end.

3. *Take notes.* To maximize the benefit you derive from completing the exercises in this book, make a habit of jotting down any aspect of the exercise—or the concepts involved—for which a bit more explanation would be helpful. Don't hesitate to raise these notes in class; your instructor is there to help, and it's up to you to use that valuable resource to the fullest.

At the end of each chapter in this book, there is a four-question test on material from the corresponding chapter in Cohen & Swerdlik (2005). Referred to as the 4-Question Challenge, this test is designed to help students sample the degree to which they have retained the material in the chapter. In addition, this brief test can itself be employed in a firsthand exploration of how data from one test or series of tests (such as score on the 4-Question Challenge) relates to data from another test or series of tests (such as a midterm and/or final examination). As students learn more about numerically gauging the relationship between two or more tests, they may want to test the hypothesis that a strong, positive correlation exists between students' scores on the 4-Question Challenge and midterm and/or final course grade. Here's hoping that this hypothesis is confirmed and that students are greatly enriched for their efforts.

Answers keyed correct to all of the crossword puzzles, all of the 4-Question Challenges, and selected other exercises are presented at the end of the book, after the glossary. No peeking until the appropriate time!

ACKNOWLEDGMENTS

Thanks to my wife, Susan, for assisting in the development of the crossword puzzles that are presented at the beginning of each chapter. If you enjoy doing crossword puzzles, we hope that this type of exercise brings some fun into the process of learning about testing and assessment. Special thanks to Dr. Lisa L. Persinger for creating the *Figure This* questions and answers that are presented in Chapters 3 through 7. Thanks to April Wells-Hayes of Fairplay Publishing Service for her diligent copy editing and to our editor John Wannemacher at McGraw-Hill for all of his assistance.

Thanks to the Museum of Modern Art Film Still Archives and the courtesies extended by, in alphabetical order, Cinerama Releasing Corporation, Columbia Pictures Corporation, the Geffen Film Corporation, MGM, Orion Pictures, Paramount Pictures, RKO Pictures, Twentieth Century-Fox Film Corporation, United Artists, Universal Pictures, and Warner Brothers.

Finally, thanks to the many measurement instructors whose suggestions and comments have helped to continually enhance the quality of this workbook as a teaching tool for instructors and a catalyst for students' independent study and learning.

Ronald Jay Cohen, Ph.D., ABAP
Diplomate, American Board of Assessment Psychology

CHAPTER 1

Psychological Testing and Assessment

If you are reading this now, you are probably enrolled in a course that deals with tests and measurement, and you are probably using as your primary textbook, *Psychological Testing and Assessment: An Introduction to Tests and Measurement,* Sixth Edition (Cohen & Swerdlik, 2005). This workbook of exercises is a companion resource to Cohen & Swerdlik (2005), one designed to assist you in learning the material. The assistance comes in many forms ranging from exercises designed to gauge comprehension of chapter material, to exercises that require creative application of that material.

An effort has been made to make these exercises not only valuable from a pedagogical standpoint but also enjoyable. Many students enjoy completing crossword puzzles during leisure time, so crossword puzzles have been incorporated as a tool to both review some terms, and introduce new ones. Most students also enjoy movies and there is an exercise in each chapter that uses a movie still as a point of departure to raise a measurement-related question. To the extent possible, then, please have some fun with all of these exercises while you reinforce and expand your learning from the primary text.

Puzzle 1

Instructions Identify what is described, answer a question, or fill in the blank to complete this crossword puzzle based on material presented in Chapter 1 of Cohen & Swerdlik's *Psychological Testing and Assessment: An Introduction to Tests and Measurement* (6th edition). Some of the clues actually contain the answers in capital letters. These items usually provide you with a "sneak preview" of terms you will encounter in subsequent chapters. Consider these give-away items "free spaces" in the puzzle.

Across

2. A working relationship between the examiner and the examinee in the context of testing or assessment.
4 Common sources of it are test construction (including item or content sampling), test administration, test scoring, and test interpretation. It is error VARIANCE.
7. The process of assigning evaluative codes or statements to performance on tests, tasks, interviews, or other behavior samples.
8. A measuring device or procedure.
9. The assignment of numbers or symbols to characteristics of people or objects according to rules.
10. An online, electronic database maintained by the American Psychological Association designed to help users locate psychologically relevant journal articles and documents.
12. It's a judgment regarding how well a test or other measurement tool measures what it purports to measure. It's a reference to a test's VALIDITY.
14. An acronym for an organization that issues credentials of expertise in measurement to psychologists.
16. Records, transcripts, and other accounts made in written, pictorial, or other form, in any media, that preserve archival information, official and informal accounts, and other data and items relevant to an assessee. This describes _____ history data.
17. It's a tool of assessment involving a procedure wherein assessees are instructed to act as they would if they were placed in some sort of situation. It's a(n) _____ play test.
18. The process of measuring psychology-related variables by means of devices or procedures designed to obtain a sample of behavior.
21. In the tradition of true score theory, a statistic designed to estimate the extent to which an observed score deviates from a true score is the STANDARD error of measurement.
24. It could be a psychologist, an instructor, a counselor, an individual who works in human resources, or any of a number of other people. It's a test _____ .
25. It's a set of numbers or other symbols whose properties model empirical properties of the objects or traits to which numbers or other symbols are assigned.
27. It's used to monitor the actions of others or oneself by visual or electronic means, by recording quantitative and/or qualitative information about actions. It's _____ observation.
29. Don't expect to get completely unbiased descriptions of the virtues of tests by consulting test _____ .

30. The extent to which measurements are consistent or repeatable, this actually sets a limit on a test's validity.
31. It's almost anyone who has ever lived long enough to take the vapor test—that is, breathing on a mirror and seeing if the mirror gets fogged.

Down

1. Synonymous with the more antiquated term, *psychometry,* it's the science of psychological measurement.
3. The gathering and integration of data for the purpose of making an evaluation, accomplished through the use of tools such as tests, interviews, case studies, and behavioral observation.
5. It is a reconstruction of a deceased individual's psychological profile on the basis of archival records, artifacts, and interviews previously conducted with the assessee or people who knew the assessee, and it is called a psychological _____ .
6. An evaluation or diagnostic procedure or process that varies from the usual, customary, or standardized way a measurement is derived; it is referred to as _____ assessment.
11. It's the test performance data of a particular group of testtakers designed for use as a reference for evaluating, interpreting, or otherwise placing individual test scores in context. It's the test NORMS.
13. A description or conclusion reached on the basis of evidence and opinion through a process of distinguishing the nature of something and ruling out alternative conclusions.
15. A work sample.
19. In baseball it's a "no-no"; in measurement it's expected. It's ERROR.
20. Psychologists and other professionals do it. So do talk show hosts, typically with different objectives.
22. Phonetically it's pronounced like *a-bep,* and it's an abbreviation for the American Board of Professional Psychology.
23. This party to the assessment enterprise creates a test and is called a test _____ .
26. It's a source for learning about what tests a test publisher publishes.
28. Assigning numbers in accordance with empirical properties of objects or traits. Alternatively, a term frequently used with reference to Mount Everest.
29. The abbreviation for the brainchild of Oscar Buros, and a good *Consumer Reports* type of reference work on tests.

EXERCISE 1-1
MOVIES AND MEASUREMENT

Feeling faint?

OBJECTIVE

To verbalize some of your hopes and concerns as you begin your study of psychological testing and assessment

BACKGROUND

Was the overwhelmed actor in this 1926 Fritz Lang film (*Metropolis*) enrolled in a measurement course? Probably not. Still, matters regarding numbers, statistics, and measurement can seem a bit overwhelming. The key to mastery is quality study time and the thoughtful completion of exercises such as the ones found in this book.

YOUR TASK

Write a brief essay entitled, "Psychological Testing and Assessment: My Hopes and Concerns." In it, describe what knowledge and skills you hope to take away from this course. Also, describe some of your concerns and apprehensions regarding this course and how you plan to successfully deal with them.

EXERCISE 1-2
A NEW PERSPECTIVE

OBJECTIVE

To assume the role of a test user as opposed to that of a testtaker

BACKGROUND

Self-administered tests and quizzes have been a part of our popular-media landscape for as long as anyone living can remember. We note with some amusement, for example, tests published in the popular media purporting to measure a wide variety of skills and other characteristics, including the "sex" of one's brain (Moir & Jessel, 1992), children's "emotional IQ" (Barko, 1993), psychic ability (Woolfolk, 1992), communication style (Sandwith, 1994), healthy living habits (Derrow, 1993), "people smarts" and other supposed forms of intelligence (Clifford, 1992; Granat, 1990). But what do such tests actually reveal, if anything? In the box on pages 4 and 5 is a test along with excerpts of its accompanying text as published in a *Writer's Digest* article by Robyn Carr (1994) entitled "Do You Have What It Takes?" After you have self-administered it and tallied your score, think about what you have learned as a result of the exercise. And as you make your way through the rest of this book, think again about such self-administered tests in the popular media and the types of things their creators would have to do to make the test scores derived from them meaningful.

YOUR TASK

Commit to paper some of your thoughts about this test and about how much stock you think you would place in your score. Would you be in favor of using such a test as a tool in making important decisions about, say, college admission or the award of a scholarship? If you were a publisher seeking to retain authors to write books, do you think you might use such a test as a screening tool? If you were contemplating a career as a writer, how much stock would you place in such a test? Why did you answer each of the last three questions the way you did?

Perhaps your answers reflected some of the following concerns. This test does not measure the variety of skills people need to be writers. Is there any reason to believe that this test identifies people who will be good writers? Furthermore, no information is given about how the cutoff scores are established: Why is a score of 65 rated so much more highly than a score of 64? In a related vein, if a person took several of these kinds of tests, would the result be the same each time? Or could a person receive a "Nothing can stop you" rating on some of these kinds of tests, for example, then score low on others? Finally, some of the questions on this test could be confusing; perhaps some people get lower scores because of confusion about the questions being asked, not because of their interest in writing.

Psychometric techniques provide us with tools to address the practical questions raised above about the quality of tests. As we proceed in our study of psychometrics, we will come to view the tests published in the popular media as thought-provoking at best but seldom more than a form of entertainment.

DO YOU HAVE WHAT IT TAKES?

A *Writer's Digest* Article by Robyn Carr

Do you have what it takes? Put away your doubts, your worries, your fears. Take this simple quiz, and find out once and for all if you have the potential to succeed as a writer. . . . Pick the first answer that pops into your mind, and move on to the next question.

1. I am drawn to writing because
   a. I have an important message to share with the world.
   b. I have had many fascinating life experiences.
   c. I love to write, and the challenge excites me.
   d. I can do it in my underwear.

2. I work on my writing
   a. daily.
   b. most days.
   c. catch as catch can.
   d. I rarely have time.

3. I am writing
   a. a novel too complex to describe.
   b. the kind of novel I love to read.
   c. the kind of novel my mother would approve of.
   d. a novel that reflects what is most popular in the marketplace.

4. I read
   a. extensively.
   b. occasionally.
   c. rarely.
   d. for entertainment.

5. In my writing career, I plan to
   a. work in my underwear.
   b. be isolated and solitary; I enjoy my time alone.
   c. write fabulous stuff, be a great author, a star.
   d. get used to being a glutton for punishment.

6. When my work is criticized, I frequently
   a. have trouble understanding the problem.
   b. become depressed.
   c. really get into finding a solution.
   d. get angry.

7. When feedback on my project suggests major changes, I
   a. write something else and try harder to get it right.
   b. consider the changes and see how they work.
   c. ignore suggestions and keep gathering opinions.
   d. argue and explain.

8. When I finally type "The End," after much hard work,
   a. I send my manuscript by overnight mail to a publisher.
   b. I put it aside for a while, then review and revise.
   c. I keep working on it; it can never be too good.
   d. I stash it in the closet for a year or two.

9. When I get a rejection, I
   a. sink into depression.
   b. contact the editor and ask for "specifics."
   c. shelve the manuscript and move on to the next.
   d. mail the manuscript to another publisher.

10. After many rejections on a project, I
    a. suffer a grave depression.
    b. keep working on it until I finally get it right.
    c. put it aside and work on something else.
    d. take piano lessons.

11. Once I get that first publishing contract, I will
    a. drive something younger than I am.
    b. wave it in a few unsupportive faces around here.
    c. write what I really want to write.
    d. already have begun the next project.

12. The best way to achieve a successful writing career is to
    a. attend many conferences.
    b. study many how-to books and magazines.
    c. write and read compulsively.
    d. get to know editors personally.

13. I am fascinated by well-known authors'
    a. income.
    b. writing style.
    c. lifestyle.
    d. work habits.

14. I have to hurry and complete my current manuscript for
    a. an upcoming contest.
    b. an interested editor.
    c. extra money for something.
    d. I don't have to hurry for anything.

15. When I'm involved in my writing, I can be stopped by
    a. a call from my mother.
    b. my spouse's annoyance.
    c. parental responsibilities.
    d. blood. Lots of it. And screams. Loud ones. Nearby.

In Carr's (1994) scoring system, five points are awarded for each response keyed as correct, and two points for other responses. The responses keyed correct are as follows:

1 (c), 2 (a or b), 3 (b), 4 (a), 5 (b or c), 6 (c), 7 (b), 8 (b), 9 (d), 10 (c), 11 (d), 12 (c), 13 (a, b, c, or d), 14 (d), 15 (d).

(continued)

DO YOU HAVE WHAT IT TAKES? *(continued)*

Summing all points yields a total score that, according to Carr (1994), can be interpreted as follows:

65–75 points: You are gutsy, brazen, brave, and determined. You put the quality of your work and your learning ahead of everything else and yet are not afraid to dream, and dream big. Nothing can stop you—New York, take notice!

55–64 points: You stand a good chance of pulling it together; perhaps there are areas you need to work on, like saying *no* or reading with a new mission to learn. You have many of the qualities of successful writers, and such shortcomings as procrastination or rushing can be cured.

45–54 points: Don't worry—many writers have to *learn* to accept criticism, take rejection in stride, and write that sex scene even though Aunt Gladys will probably have a heart attack. Most writers are afraid of failure; many have trouble protecting their writing time. But if you want to make it as a writer, there are some things you must do; develop those disciplines and work habits required to do the job.

30–44 points: It's possible you want to be a writer more than you want to write, and probable that you have illusions about how writing is done. Maybe you're not willing to take criticism and rejection, not willing to read, study, and write as much as a successful writer has to in order to make it.

EXERCISE 1-3
ON MEASUREMENT

OBJECTIVE

To encourage generative thinking on the subject of measurement in general

BACKGROUND

Commodities of daily life are measured in familiar units. It is commonplace to measure, for example, gasoline by the gallon, fruit by the pound, and waistlines by the inch. Perhaps because we deal with these types of measurement so frequently, we tend to take measurement for granted. In the study of psychological testing and assessment, however, little about the process of measurement can be taken for granted. A variety of skills and knowledge must be brought to bear in the development of meaningful measures as well as in the administration and interpretation of those measures.

YOUR TASK

Write a brief essay on the subject of measurement. In that essay, discuss your thoughts on the subject of measurement in general—your essay need not relate to measurement in psychology. Give your imagination free rein, developing interesting concepts that have anything at all to do with measurement. Your essay can be well researched with references to the scholarly literature. You may choose instead to write an essay that is more informal, freewheeling, even humorous. Or, like the sample essay that follows, your essay may combine such features.

ON MEASUREMENT

Ronald Jay Cohen

Measurement? Simple. Well, not really.

The first tools used to measure distance were probably stones, branches, or parts of one's own body. For example, one widely used measure of distance was the *cubit*, defined as the length between an adult's elbow and the outstretched middle finger. For the purposes of "standardization," the length of some body part of a royal personage could be used. An Egyptian royal cubit, for example, is equal in length to seven palms and presumably was "standardized" on a pharaoh with very long arms. The standard measure of length in the United States—the foot—is based on the length of an English king's foot. One problem: it's difficult enough to get the cable guy to come when you need him, let alone a pharaoh or a king.

During the Renaissance in Italy, common units of measurement included the *passo* (pace), the *piede* (foot), and the *pollice* (the width of the thumb). The exact length of each of these measures might vary a bit not only from town to town but from trade to trade; an architect's *passo* might differ from that of an engineer's.

The metric system simplified all of that. . . . Well, yes and no.

How long is a meter? To provide a definitive, once-and-for-all answer to that (relatively simple) question, 17 nations met in 1875 to ratify a treaty at a meeting called the Convention of the Meter. The nations agreed that a meter would be equal in length to a platinum bar to be stored in a vault at the International Bureau of Weights and Measures in France. End of story. At least until 1960. . . .

Concerns about possible changes in an atom or two of the platinum bar standard led to a redefinition of the length of a meter in 1960. Another international meeting was convened, this one attended by representatives from 38 countries. A meter was defined as "1,650,763.73 vacuum wave-lengths of monochromatic orange light emitted by krypton atom of mass 86." The platinum bar idea was a lot simpler.

No, not even the measurement of simple things is as simple as it may appear at first blush. And measuring psychological variables such as intelligence, assertiveness, or aggression—well, that's a whole other story.

EXERCISE 1-4
THE PROCESS OF ASSESSMENT

OBJECTIVE

To enhance understanding of the tools of assessment as well as the roles of each of the parties in that process

BACKGROUND

The tools of assessment include the following:

- the test
- the interview
- the case study
- the portfolio or work sample
- behavioral observation
- computers as tools
- others

The parties to the assessment process include the following:

- the test developer
- the test user
- the testtaker
- society at large

YOUR TASK

Suppose that you are an independent distributor for a company that produces natural herbs that are represented to help students study more effectively by lessening debilitating anxiety. For the sake of example, let's call this natural herb company "Cramway." As a Cramway representative who also happens to be interested in psychological measurement, you design a study to measure the effect the Cramway product has on students' anxiety. Your study design is of the pre/post variety; anxiety will be measured before beginning the Cramway program and seven days after Cramway products have been ingested on the prescribed regimen. Now all you need is something to measure the construct of anxiety; something to measure how anxious a person characteristically is on any given day.[1]

[1]Technically, the construct being referred to here is the *trait* of anxiety—this in contrast to the more transient *state* of anxiety.

1. Of the tools of assessment available to you, which one (or more) do you think you would use? Which wouldn't you use? Why?
2. From what you've read in your text so far, and drawing on your own opinions and beliefs, explain the rights and responsibilities of each of the parties in the assessment process with respect to your anxiety assessment project.
3. This question, if assigned by your instructor, will require a bit of research in the university library. Using reference books, periodicals, and related sources of information about (as well as reviews of) tests and measurement procedures, decide on your top three selections for use as a measure of anxiety in your Cramway study. Explain why you chose the instruments or procedures you did.

EXERCISE 1-5
THE INTERVIEWER/INTERVIEWEE INTERACTION

OBJECTIVE

To better understand how an interviewer's personality can influence the conduct of an interview

BACKGROUND

Think of how various interviewers you have seen or heard on television or radio conduct their interviews; two interviews conducted with the exact same objectives in mind, sometimes even with much the same questions, might yield different data due to characteristics of the interviewer.

YOUR TASK

One student will volunteer to play an interviewee while another will volunteer to take on the role of any well-known celebrity interviewer. The more adept the latter student is at impersonating the celebrity, the more fun this exercise will be. Different teams of students, one playing the role of the celebrity interviewer, the other playing the role of the (student) interviewee, will get up in front of the class and execute an interview. The interviewer's initial prompt to the interviewee will be "Tell me about the happiest time of your life," and follow-up questions will probe the who, what, where, and how of whatever is described. The role of the "audience" is to note the differences in the interviewer's style of interviewing.

If you're having difficulty thinking of the role of a celebrity you'd like to play, how about one of these: David Letterman, Ted Koppel, Jerry Springer, Regis Philbin, Ellen DeGeneres, Barbara Walters, Larry King, Oprah Winfrey, Peter Jennings, Dan Rather, Tom Brokaw, Montel Williams, or Jay Leno.

EXERCISE 1-6
BEHAVIORAL ASSESSMENT

OBJECTIVE

To enhance understanding of, and promote generative thinking about, behavioral assessment

BACKGROUND

Deinstitutionalization and the placement of children and adult psychiatric patients into community-based facilities created a need for a means by which staff could monitor progress made in skills necessary for independent living. Behavioral checklists, such as the "Emptying Garbage" scale (Roth & Hermus, 1980, p. 89) in Figure 1-1 on page 8, can provide such a means. For this scale, note that the behavior of taking out the garbage has been broken down into a series of individual behaviors. "Goes to garbage can" and "Takes full bag from garbage can" are two short-range behavior objectives that, when both are attained, meet the long-range behavior objective of "Removing garbage."

YOUR TASK

After studying the "Emptying Garbage" behavioral programming scale, create your own behavioral programming scale. Your scale should take some relatively simple behavior necessary for independent living and then break it up into its component behaviors.

EXERCISE 1-7
PUTTING A TEST TO THE TEST

OBJECTIVE

To experience firsthand what is involved in gathering information and making decisions about a psychological test

BACKGROUND

Test catalogues, test manuals, test reviews, and published research on psychological tests can help prospective users make informed decisions regarding such instruments and procedures. To answer questions such as "Is this test appropriate for this use with this population?" test users need more than intuition; they need facts.

YOUR TASK

You are a psychologist employed in a university counseling center. The dean has decided that the university is going to build and operate a community child day care center. The dean has placed you in charge of hiring all of the caretakers at the center. Further, the dean wonders aloud whether all serious candidates for jobs at the new center should be screened for psychopathology with a test called the Minnesota Multiphasic Personality Inventory-2 (MMPI-2). The dean asks you to report back with your written opinion regarding the pros and cons of using the MMPI-2 for this purpose.

1. What sources would you use to gather information to respond to the dean's mandate?

2. What questions would you hope to have answered in your sources about the MMPI-2?

3. What other types of tests or assessment procedures might you wish to include in the process of hiring day care workers? Why?

4. Write your report to the dean.

EXERCISE 1-8
ADVENTURES IN CYBERSPACE

OBJECTIVE

To become familiar with the test-related resources available on the Internet

BACKGROUND

A number of test-related resources exist on the World Wide Web. For example, in your textbook, reference is made to the Web sites maintained by the Buros Institute at *http://www.unl.edu/buros*, Educational Testing Service *http://www.ets.org*, and a number of test publishers.

YOUR TASK

Select any psychology- or education-related variable that you are personally interested in. Then, explore the Internet to find out what tests or other assessment methodologies exist to measure that variable. Download the relevant resources, and prepare a five-minute presentation on your findings to share with your class.

REFERENCES

Barko, N. (1993, August). What's your child's emotional IQ? *Working Mother, 16,* 33–35.

Carr, R. (1994, April). Do you have what it takes? *Writer's Digest, 74,* 20–23.

Clifford, C. (1992, Spring). What kind of intelligence do you have? *YM,* pp. 34–39.

FIGURE 1-1 *The Taking-Out-the-Garbage Checklist*

Deinstitutionalization and the placement of children and adult psychiatric patients into community-based facilities created a need for behavioral checklists by which the facility staff gauges the progress of developmentally disabled individuals. Rudimentary skills necessary for independent living—such as taking out the garbage—are tracked via checklists such as the one below. This checklist came from the "Housekeeping Skills" section of a book of behavioral checklists, with other sections such as "Personal Management," "Kitchen Skills, " "Street Safety," "Travel Training," "Leisure Skills," and "Community Skills." (Source: Roth & Hermus, 1980, p. 89)

BEHAVIORAL PROGRAMMING SCALE

Name of Client _____ Instructor _____ Date _____

EMPTYING GARBAGE

LRO	SRO Behavior			Daily Recordings				
		M	T	W	Th	F	Weekly total	Criteria met? (Yes = +, No = –)
1. Removing Garbage		▓	▓	▓	▓	▓	▓	
	A. Goes to garbage can.							
	B. Takes full bag from garbage can.							
2. Disposing of Garbage		▓	▓	▓	▓	▓	▓	
	C. Takes bag of garbage to trash can.							
	D. Opens trash can.							
	E. Places garbage in trash can.							
	F. Closes trash can.							
3. Lining Can with New Bag		▓	▓	▓	▓	▓	▓	
	G. Goes to closet.							
	H. Takes new garbage bag.							
	I. Takes bag to garbage can.							
	J. Places bag in can.							
	K. Pushes bag into can.							
	L. Overlaps bag top over can top.							

LRO = Long-range behavior objective; SRO = Short-range behavior objective

Enter "1" through "7" in appropriate box to indicate client's level of skill. Criterion is met when a score of "7" is achieved four times out of five for two consecutive trial periods.

Derrow, P. (1993, June). Are your habits healthy? *Weight Watchers Magazine, 26,* 18–20.

Granat, D. (1990, September). What make you so smart? *Washingtonian, 25,* 134–141.

Moir, A., & Jessel, D. (1992, January). Discover your brain's sex. *Reader's Digest* (Canadian English Edition), *140,* 89–91.

Roth, M. R., & Hermus, G. P. (1980). *Developmental plan handbook for community skills training* (2nd ed.). New York: Developmental Press.

Sandwith, P. (1994, January). Building quality into communications. *Training and Development, 48*(1), 55–59.

Woolfolk, J. M. (1992, Spring). Are you psychic? *YM,* pp. 60–64.

THE 4-QUESTION CHALLENGE

In general, this self-administered test samples material from the beginning, middle, and end of each chapter in your textbook. The questions are very straightforward and in some instances represent verbatim excerpts from the book. This "Challenge" may help to serve as a rough gauge of how well you are attending to all of the material in each chapter.

After reading a chapter in your textbook, take the corresponding 4-Question Challenge. Give yourself one point for each correct answer. If all four items are answered correctly, your score will be 4. Do your best on these tests over the course of the term. Then note how your final grade in this course corresponds to your 4-Question Challenge average.

Here is your first 4-Question Challenge:

1. Which does not belong?
   a. dynamic assessment
   b. vocational assessment
   c. therapeutic assessment
   d. collaborative assessment

2. A television producer hires a director for a new show after viewing samples of the director's work on other television shows. Using the language of psychometrics, we could say that the director was hired on the basis of
   a. a portfolio assessment.
   b. a behavioral assessment.
   c. a case study evaluation.
   d. an interview.

3. Which is best associated with on-site scoring and interpretation of computer-administered tests?
   a. central processing
   b. teleprocessing
   c. local processing
   d. photo processing

4. If you needed a current, unbiased evaluation of a well-known psychological test, which would be the best source to consult?
   a. *Who's Who in Psychological Assessment?*
   b. the test's published manual
   c. the current edition of the test publisher's catalogue
   d. the current edition of the *Mental Measurements Yearbook*

CHAPTER 2

Historical, Cultural, and Legal/Ethical Considerations

Puzzle 2   **Instructions**   "Who am I?" Answer that question for each of the following items based on your reading of Chapter 2 of your textbook.

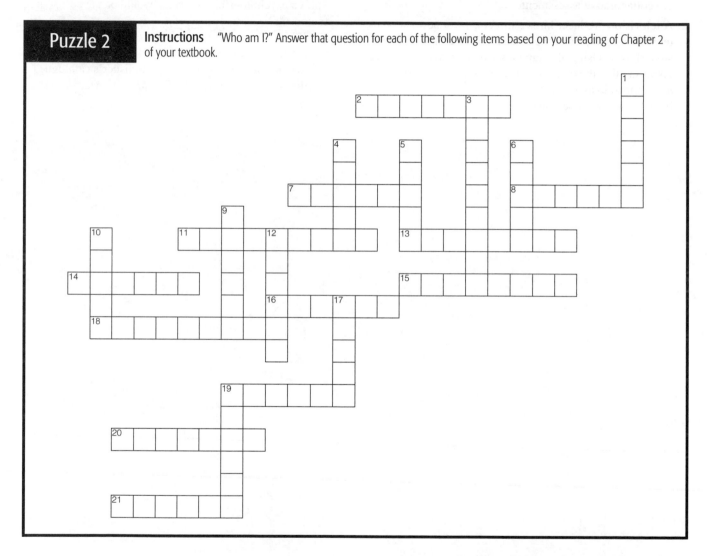

Across

2. My lawsuit against Merrell Dow Pharmaceuticals alleged that children were born with birth defects as a result of taking a drug called Bendectin during pregnancy. As the case was tried, a key issue before the Supreme Court concerned which expert testimony the trial judge could and should admit into evidence.

7. Although I have written quite a bit, I am probably still best known for my controversial 1969 *Harvard Educational Review* article entitled "How Much Can We Boost IQ and Scholastic Achievement?"

8. I worked at the Harvard Psychological Clinic in the 1930s experimenting with the use of stories told in response to pictures as a means of gaining insight into personality. Oh, and just for the record, I was originally the senior author of the Thematic Apperception Test (TAT). Nowadays, few people know that.

11. During World War I, I chaired a government committee on emotional fitness charged with the responsibility of developing a measure of adjustment that could be administered quickly and efficiently to recruits. To dis-

guise the true purpose of the test, the questionnaire was labeled a "Personal Data Sheet."

13. A lawsuit brought in my name against the Regents of the University of California has become virtually synonymous with the duty of mental health professionals to warn endangered third parties of their peril.

14. I was named as the defendant in a 1967 lawsuit involving the appropriateness of using a school ability tracking system that had the effect of inappropriately segregating students by race.

15. Preschoolers, older children, adolescents, and adults are tested with an intelligence test that bears my name.

16. I am a clinician and personality theorist who is perhaps best known for my work at the Harvard Psychological Clinic in the 1930s and 1940s, where I experimented with the use of stories in response to pictures to gain insight into personality. Today, I am best associated with the Thematic Apperception Test (TAT).

18. My name is that of a paper company that gained fame as a litigant in a landmark 1976 lawsuit involving allegations of racial discrimination in the workplace as a result of the use of a general ability test that predicted job performance.

19. I was the plaintiff in a 1971 lawsuit against Duke Power Company that charged discrimination in hiring on the basis of the tests and procedures used. The Supreme Court found in my favor, noting problems with "broad and general testing devices" and ruling that tests must "fairly measure the knowledge or skills required by a particular job."

20. "Mental test," you say? I am the psychologist who coined that term. My daughter, Psyche, is the author of a measure of infant intelligence. By the way, Raymond B., often thought of as a relative, is actually no relation.

21. You may have heard of my influential book, *On the Origin of Species by Means of Natural Selection,* first published in 1859. In it, I argued that chance variation in species are selected or rejected for survival according to adaptivity and survival value. On a less momentous note, my half-cousin is also in this puzzle; he is 19-Down.

5. In 1905, I and a colleague authored a 30-item "measuring scale of intelligence" designed to identify Paris school children with special needs. Hey . . . go know!

6. No, not Firestone, but the name of another tire company that was involved in litigation in 1999. The case resulted in the Supreme Court's expanding the principles of *Daubert* to all experts, whether or not the experts claim scientific research as a basis for their testimony.

9. In 1997, General Electric (GE) not only brought "good things to life" (as they say in the advertising), but they brought a lawsuit against me. The Supreme Court ruling in the case had the effect of modifying *Daubert;* the trial court had a duty to exclude as evidence unreliable expert testimony.

10. In 1970, I challenged the State Board of Education on issues regarding the testing of minority children for whom English was a second language. As a result of this landmark case, changes were made in the California Education Code. Placement in educable mentally retarded (EMR) classes would be made only on the basis of a comprehensive developmental and educational assessment, not merely on the basis of an intelligence test.

12. Is it any wonder why I have been called the "the little-known founder of clinical psychology"? In 1896, I founded the first psychological clinic in the United States at the University of Pennsylvania. In 1907, I founded a journal called *Psychological Clinic.* I also wrote the first article in that journal, which was entitled, appropriately enough, "Clinical Psychology."

17. Larry P. was the plaintiff, and I was the defendant in this 1979 case that involved the placement of minority students in EMR classes using intelligence tests. I always wondered what Larry's last name was.

19. "Genius!" That's what they called me. I studied issues of inheritance with sweet peas. In so doing, I sowed the seeds for what would later be known as correlation. I devised or contributed to the development of many tools of assessment. And I could go on. But I choose not to do so.

Down

1. Remember the case cited in 14-Across? I was the other litigant.

3. I am a Swiss psychiatrist, fascinated by projective measures of personality. You might imagine that, as a child, I was instructed not to cry over spilt milk but rather to talk about what I perceived in the resulting pattern.

4. At the University of Leipzig in Germany, I founded the first experimental psychology laboratory. My goal there was to formulate a general theory of human abilities using measures of reaction time, attention span, and the like.

EXERCISE 2-1

MOVIES AND MEASUREMENT

OBJECTIVE

To learn about the contribution of Charles Darwin to contemporary psychological testing and assessment

BACKGROUND

The work of Charles Darwin (1859) conferred new scientific responsibility on experimentation with animals—but not

Planet of Cross-Species Assessment

quite as much respectability as suggested in the film still above from (the original) *Planet of the Apes*.

YOUR TASK

Write a brief essay entitled, "Darwin's Influence on Psychological Assessment." In it, discuss how Darwin's writings on the subject of individual differences may have inspired the development of various tools of assessment. Feel free to use other authoritative source material in addition to your textbook when preparing this essay.

EXERCISE 2-2

GUIDELINES FOR USING PSYCHOLOGICAL TESTS

OBJECTIVE

To better appreciate the concerns of psychologists, educators, and others with responsibility for developing, selecting, administering, scoring, and interpreting psychological tests

BACKGROUND

The concern of the American Psychological Association (APA) with respect to the use of psychological tests dates at least as far back as 1895, the year the infant APA organized its first committee on mental measurement. Since that time, various guidelines regarding tests and testing have been published in numerous APA publications, including *Standards for Educational and Psychological Testing*.

YOUR TASK

1. Solely from what you know now, list the guidelines that you feel the profession should address with respect to all aspects of tests and testing. Include guidelines with respect to the following areas.
   a. test development and construction
   b. the publication of tests and accompanying technical manuals
   c. administration of tests
   d. scoring of tests
   e. interpretation of tests
   f. the use of tests in specific contexts such as clinical, educational, counseling, and employment testing
   g. the testing of linguistic minorities
   h. the testing of people who have disabling conditions

2. Write down your responses to each of the questions above. You may wish to save your answers at this stage in your learning about psychological testing and then compare your responses to these same questions as you near completion of the course. Should your responses to each of these questions be the same or very similar at both stages of the proposed pre/post design, it's a good bet that either (a) or (b) below is true:
   a. You exhibit a keen acumen for the field of psychological testing; you were aware of many of the issues in the field even at the initial stages of your measurement course.
   b. You were not very aware of the issues in the field of psychological testing in the initial stages of your measurement course, and you weren't that much ahead of the game by the end of the course.

   Of course if your responses are *not* the same or similar at both stages of the pre/post design, then a third alternative (c) may be applicable (particularly if your responses are demonstrative of a growing sophistication with the field):
   c. You have benefited from this course in ways that you now can't even anticipate, enriched your fund of information about tests and the process of testing, and made everyone around you (including your instructor) very proud.

EXERCISE 2-3

STANDARDS FOR TESTS: THEN AND NOW

OBJECTIVE

To obtain a historical perspective on desirable criteria for standardized tests by comparing a 1920s-era call for such criteria with the current edition of *Standards for Educational and Psychological Testing*

BACKGROUND

Over a half-century ago, measurement expert Giles M. Ruch proposed standards for tests that in many ways anticipated the current version of *Standards for Educational and Psychological Testing.* The original text of Ruch's (1925) article is reprinted below.

MINIMUM ESSENTIALS IN REPORTING DATA ON STANDARD TESTS

G. M. Ruch, State University of Iowa

With the increasing number of educational and mental tests, an already bewildering situation is daily becoming more aggravated. The writer refers particularly to the task of the superintendent, director of research, and the college teacher of tests and measurements, who is confronted with the problem of selecting and recommending the "best" test to use. Even if the cards were all on the table, the selection of the "best" test would present grave difficulties. These decisions must be made, and are being made daily, but it is an open question whether any living being possesses the exact knowledge required to make such decisions in anything approaching a scientific matter. Where does the difficulty lie?

The blame, to use a harsh term, lies primarily with the test authors, secondarily with the publishers of tests, and finally, to some extent, with the users of tests—the relative culpabilities showing wide individual differences within these groups.

The logic of the situation, viewed broadly, would seem to demand that two things be done at once: first, that a set of working *criteria* for test construction be established—and much progress has been made on this point; and second, that test authors, test publishers, test users, and test investigators adopt some fairly uniform practices in reporting on tests, at least to the extent of a few *minimum essentials.* Except in isolated cases, this has not been the regular practice. Although the second of these points is the primary consideration of this paper, a few statements about the first[1] will help to clarify matters.

Criteria for Evaluating Tests and Measurements

Validity—the general worth or merit of the test. A description of the validation of a test may well include such facts as the following:

1. The criterion against which the test was validated: analysis of courses of study, analysis of textbooks, recommendations of national educational committees, experimental studies (for example, word counts, analysis of social needs), age or grade rise in percent of successes, judgments of "competent" persons, correlation with an outside or independent criterion, or merely "armchair analysis" and "insight."
2. Statement of the exact details of all experimental work leading to the final forms of the test.
3. Statement of the diagnostic powers of the test, if any.
4. Statement of the exact field or range of educational or mental functions for which the test is claimed to be valid.
5. Statement whether the test is adequate for class measurement or pupil measurement. (This is largely a matter of reliability.)
6. Statement relative to equality of forms and how guaranteed. The same applies to equality of variabilities, namely, equal standard deviations for same groups.
7. Statement of the degree of correlation of the test with the criterion, or with school success, age, etc.; or statement of the agreement of test scores with the attainments of groups of individuals known to be widely spaced upon a scale of abilities.
8. Statement of the functions that the test can legitimately claim to serve; for example, prognosis, sectioning of classes, assignment of official grades, determination of passing or failing, efficiency of instruction.

These should be accompanied by summaries of the experimental evidence.

Reliability—the accuracy with which the test measures. This is independent of its validity, although high validity demands high reliability. Such facts as the following are absolutely essential:

1. Reliability coefficients, which are usually to be determined by correlation of similar forms. These are, however, practically meaningless unless accompanied by statements of (1) the range of talent involved in the determination—best stated in terms of the standard deviation of the test scores; (2) the population involved in the determination of the r's; (3) the age or grade groups involved and any evidence leading to judgments of the amounts of selection or systematic tendencies, or other factors militating against the representativeness of the sampling; (4) the order of giving the forms of the test; and (5) the mean scores on each form. These facts should be given in sufficient detail to permit a second investigator to reproduce the essential conditions of the experimentation at will.
2. Certain derived measures, which are relatively independent of (1) the range of talent employed and (2) the arbitrariness of the test units.

Ease of administration and scoring. The following facts might be given:

---

[1] Kelley, T. L. "The Reliability of Test Scores," *Journal of Educational Research,* 3:370–79, May, 1921.

Monroe, W. S. *The Theory of Educational Measurements.* Boston, Houghton Mifflin Company, 1923, pp. 182–231.

McCall, W. A. *How to Measure in Education.* New York, Macmillan Company, 1922, pp. 195–410.

1. Degree of objectivity of scoring. This influences markedly the reliability and hence the validity of the test.
2. Time for giving. This is of minor importance without supplementation by other facts, the popular opinion to the contrary, notwithstanding. The proper criteria should be: *Validity per unit testing time, reliability per unit testing time,* or some similar point of view.
3. Time needed for scoring. This is best stated in terms of the average number of papers scored per unit of time. That this is of secondary importance is shown by the fact that comparatively few standard tests exceed the ordinary written examination in the time or labor of scoring.
4. Simplicity of directions for pupil and examiner.

Norms. This should include:

1. Kinds of norms available (age, grade, percentile, mental age, *T* scores, etc.)
2. Statement of derivation of norms. This should cover, specifically, facts like those listed under "Reliability" above. The important thing is the *representativeness* of the sampling, *not the size.* Norms on one hundred thousand cases are not necessarily as accurate as those based on ten thousand, or even one thousand cases. *The validity of a norm is not determined by its probable error but by the principles and laws of sampling observed or violated.* Norms, at best, are doubtful devices;[2] and blind faith in numbers approaches "hocus pocus" at times. The most important thing that a test can do is to *place the pupil in accurate rank positions along a scale of true ability.* The common practice of pooling test-score tabulations voluntarily returned to the author, without a scrupulous program for the elimination of the almost inevitable selection effects incident to this procedure, is particularly to be regretted.

Cost. This has little or no theoretical interest but is a very practical consideration. The cost per pupil is practically valueless unless other facts are weighed. *Validity per unit cost* is the criterion to apply. A test may be a poor investment at one cent per pupil, while a second test would be cheap at ten cents per pupil. Costs of test vary with (1) the cost of experimental work (to the writer's knowledge, the variation on this point ranges from less than $100 to at least $10,000), (2) quality of printing, (3) length of test—

a very important factor in validity and reliability, and (4) profits to publisher and author.

With respect to all of the before-mentioned desiderata, no exact procedure can or need be recommended. It is merely the "spirit of the game" that is fundamental. There is, however, one very important question to be asked, Where should the above data be published? The best place, theoretically and practically, is in the manual of directions accompanying the test. This can well be expanded to four, ten, or even one hundred pages. The next best procedure is probably that of publishing abstracts of the complete description of the test in the manual of directions, reserving the details for articles in the standard journals or for publication in a separate monograph. The important thing is that full accounts be made accessible to the critical user or student of tests. To the user of tests should be extended the privilege of choice with open eyes, namely, with the "cards all on the table," to repeat an earlier statement.

If space permitted, the writer could at least entertain the reader by quoting numerous replies received from authors of secondary-school tests in response to an appeal for such data as have been outlined. Parenthetically it might be stated that fully 75 percent of test authors had made no systematic or critical study of their tests, and not a few did not comprehend the conventional test terminology. One responded to a question about the reliability of his test: "This is not an intelligence test." The correspondent must have been amazed at the writer's naïveté in expecting an educational test to possess reliability at all!

The Reporting of Reliabilities of Test Scores

The remainder of this discussion will be devoted to a single one of the criteria listed for the evaluation of tests, namely, *reliability.* Attention is directed to this topic partly because of its importance and partly because the data available on it are exceedingly meager. There has been a wide variety of practices in reporting test reliabilities— when, indeed, such have been reported at all—as follows:

1. The *reliability coefficient* [3] r_{12}

2. The *probable error of estimate,* [3]
$$P.E._{\cdot 1 \bullet 2} = 0.6745 \sigma_1 \sqrt{1 - r_{12}^2}$$

3. The *probable error of measurement,* [4]
$$P.E._{\cdot M} = 0.6745 \sigma \sqrt{1 - r_{12}}, \text{ where } \sigma = \frac{\sigma_1 + \sigma_2}{2}$$

4. The *index of reliability,* [4] $r_{1t} = \sqrt{r_{12}}$

---

[2] *See* Chapman, J. C. "Some Elementary Statistical Considerations in Educational Measurements," *Journal of Educational Research,* 4:212–20, October, 1921 for an excellent treatment of this question, and *Manual of Directions, Stanford Achievement Test,* Revised Edition; particularly the Appendix.

[3]*See* any standard textbook on statistics.

[4]Monroe, W. S. *The Theory of Educational Measurements.* Boston, Houghton Mifflin Company, 1923, pp. 206 ff.

5. $\dfrac{P.E._M}{M}$, where the $P.E._M$ is given by formula 3 above,[5]

   and M is the mean of the distribution of scores,

   and, presumably,[5] equals, $\dfrac{M_1 + M_2}{2}$

6. The *probable error of estimate of a true score by means of a single score of the same function*,[6]

$$P.E._{\infty \bullet 1} = 0.6745 \sigma_1 \sqrt{r_{12} - r_{12}^2}$$

Examination of the six procedures just listed will show at once that every one, except the first, in part, *calls for two fundamental facts*, namely, (1) the reliability coefficient; and (2) the standard deviations of the two distributions.

To these must be added, at least (3) the population on which r_{12} is based in order to calculate the probable error of *r*.

The following are most desirable and probably should always be reported: (4) a verbal description of the kind of talent involved in the calculation of *r*, for example, age or grade group, kind of school, and possible selective factors militating against the representativeness of the sampling; (5) the mean scores of the two distributions leading to *r*; (6) the order of giving the tests[7] and the conditions under which the testing was carried out.

It is greatly to be regretted that one further recommendation is not always practicable, namely, (7) the publication of the scatter diagrams for all *r*'s reported—this for its bearing on the lack of rectilinearity of the regressions and the possibility of faulty grouping. Both of these factors lower greatly the obtained *r* in comparison with the truth of the relationship.

Returning to our statements of the various methods of treating the reliability of test scores, it will be seen at once that our list of needed facts more than covers the needs of any or all of the six procedures, in fact, points (1) and (2) alone will suffice for the purely computational procedures. Granting this, the task of estimating the reliability of a test still would be a bit of a "leap in the dark" without the subsidiary data outlined in points (2) to (7), inclusive.

It is rather beyond the scope of this paper, and beyond the ability of the writer as well, to demonstrate the absolute superiority of any one of the six proposals. However, certain of these have grave defects that must be made apparent in the interests of their abandonment for the purpose. The six methods will be commented on briefly in turn.

What Is the Best Method of Stating Test Reliabilities?

The first method, the reliability coefficient, can be held to be almost valueless, per se, for two reasons: (1) it is a function of the range of talent (σ) and hence has no general stability, and (2) alone, it tells nothing about the behavior of the individual score. For Examiner A to report r_{12} as 0.85 for Test X and Examiner B to report 0.64 for Test Y *does not at all imply* that Test X is more reliable than Test Y. It would depend upon the range of talent employed. Assume the following facts for the case:

	Test X	Test Y
r_{12}	0.85	0.64
Group tested	500 pupils	500 pupils
	(Grades IV–XII)	(Grade VI only)
Standard deviation	40.4	10.1

It may readily be shown that Test Y, if applied to the group to which Test X was given, would show a reliability coefficient in the neighborhood of 0.98.[8]

The needed measure of reliability must be independent, in large part, of the influence of range of talent. The reliability coefficient, as we have seen, is not. The practice of reporting *r*'s unsupported by other facts should be discontinued.

The second proposed measure is the probable error of estimate,

$$P.E._{\cdot 1 \bullet 2} = 0.6745 \sigma_1 \sqrt{1 - r_{12}^2}.$$

This, however, does not serve the purpose. It helps little, or not at all, to obtain an estimate of the score in a second form of a test, when it is a simple matter to obtain a much better second score by actually giving the second test. An estimate of a *true* score is what is needed. The probable error of estimate does have a real value[9] as a measure of alienation from perfect prediction.

---

[5]Monroe, W. S. *A Critical Study of Certain Silent Reading Tests.* Urbana, University of Illinois, 1922, pp. 32 ff. (Bureau of Educational Research, College of Education, University of Illinois Bulletin Vol. XIX, Series, No. 8)

[6]Kelley, T. L. *Statistical Method.* New York, Macmillan Company, 1923, 212 ff.

[7]Because the order of giving the tests must necessarily be different for the determination of reliability coefficients than for the investigation of equivalence of difficulties from form to form. For the first purpose, all pupils should take the tests in the *same* order, e.g., Form A followed by Form B; for the second purpose, one half of the group should take Form A first and one half Form B first. In the first case we want the practice effects to be systematic; in the second, they should tend to be neutralized.

---

[8]See Kelley, T. L. *Statistical Method.* New York, Macmillan Company, 1923, p. 222, formula 178;

$$\frac{\sigma_1}{\Sigma_1} = \frac{\sqrt{1-R}}{\sqrt{1-r}}, \text{ or, } \frac{10.1}{40.4} = \frac{1}{4} = \frac{\sqrt{1-R}}{\sqrt{1-.64}} . \ R = 0.98 - .$$

It is assumed that both tests are scaled to the same units.

[9]Especially in the form recommended by Kelley, i.e., $k = \sqrt{1 - r_{12}^2}$.

The third proposal (by Monroe, apparently) of a probable error of a test score is a development of the same formula. It has been shown that the correlation of obtained scores with true scores of the same function is

$$r_{1 \cdot \infty} = \sqrt{r_{12}},$$

hence the probable error of estimate of true scores from obtained scores is

$$P.E._{\cdot 1 \cdot \infty} = 0.6745\, \sigma_1 \sqrt{I - r_{12}}$$

by substitution in the formula for the probable error of estimate. This, however, is not the needed formula but the reverse, for example, the probable error of estimate of a true score from an obtained score. Such a formula is number 6 in the list, namely,

$$P.E._{\infty \bullet 1} = 0.6745\, \sigma_1 \sqrt{r_{12} - r_{12}^2}.$$

The fourth proposal, namely, the ratio of $P.E._M$ to M, in the opinion of the writer, has no utility. Further comment is omitted here, because it has received an able criticism[10] since the first draft of this paper was written.

The fifth formula

$$r_{1t} = \sqrt{r_{12}}$$

is useful in evaluating certain correlation situations but would seem to have no particular reference to the problem of the reliability of test scores.

The last formula is probably the only one of the list that is entirely adequate to the problem at hand. It possesses the merits of being independent of the range of talent and of allowing for regression effects in test scores. The formula,

$$P.E._{\infty \bullet 1} = 0.6745\, \sigma_1 \sqrt{r_{12} - r_{12}^2},$$

gives us the probable error of estimating *true scores* from obtained or fallible scores, when the true scores are estimated by the formula,[11]

$$\overline{X}_{\infty \bullet 1} = r_{12} X_1 + (I - r_{12}) M_1$$

$\overline{X}_{\infty \bullet 1}$ may be regarded as the best estimate possible of a true score, such as would be obtained by the average of an infinite number of obtained (X_1) scores. It is the estimated true score and its probable error that are needed and not the reverse as in the case of the third proposal above. Kelley suggests further the use of the

$$\frac{P.E._{\infty \bullet 1}}{\sigma_1}$$

ratio[12] as a measure of the improvement due to the use of the test.

In conclusion, it will readily be seen that the real need in reporting reliability data on test scores is the publication of a minimum of four things:

1. The reliability coefficient
2. The standard deviations of the two distributions
3. The population involved in the calculation of the r's
4. The means of the two distributions

These four data will permit the treatment of reliability by any of the methods proposed to date, and in addition, estimates of true scores, and prophecies of changes in reliability with changes in the range of talent. The estimate of regression effects is implied as another possible procedure; and, in cases of intercorrelations of test scores, the application of correction formulas for attenuation is made possible in evaluating true relationships of the variables within the validity of the assumptions of such correction formulas.

Non-publication of such data as we have recommended is really a violation of the ethical codes of scientific procedures and not to be condoned by virtue of the fact that users of tests generally will not understand the technicalities. Rather, the teacher of tests and measurements should attempt to educate outgoing students to demand such confidences on the part of test authors. The alternative will certainly often be the refusal to recommend to school officials tests and scales upon which no critical facts are at hand. Such tests are not necessarily undependable, but the careful worker will not wish to assume responsibilities of proof, which in all fairness rest upon the author of the test. The test buyer is surely entitled to the same protection as the buyer of food products, namely, *the true ingredients printed on the outside of each package.*

This statement alone is offered as a sufficient justification for presenting facts that are in no sense original with the writer.

YOUR TASK

Compare the views of Ruch as expressed in the previous article with the contents of the current *Standards for Educational and Psychological Testing* (probably available in the reference section of your university library). In what ways did Ruch (1925) anticipate the *Standards*? In what ways could Ruch's views be informed by the *Standards*?

---

[10]Franzen, F. R. "Statistical Issues," *Journal of Educational Psychology,* 15:367–82, September, 1924.

[11]Kelley, T. L. *Op. cit.,* p. 214, formula 168.

---

[12]Actually, $\dfrac{\sigma_{\infty \bullet 1}}{\sigma_1}$ appears in Kelley's recommendation, but either ratio leads to similar interpretations (*Loc. cit.,* p. 215). The σ_1 cancels in numerator and denominator, leaving the expression under the radical; namely, $\sqrt{r_{12} - r_{12}^2}$ as the important measure.

EXERCISE 2-4
THE GREAT GALTON ROLE PLAY

OBJECTIVE

To allow one's creative imagination free rein in the service of devising a new psychological test

BACKGROUND

It is probably not an overstatement to assert that Sir Francis Galton (Figure 2-1) was one of the world's greatest scientists. Although this brilliant man's interests spanned a wide variety of areas (ranging from fashion to fingerprints to an experimental investigation of the efficacy of prayer) and his writings made contributions in many fields of human endeavor, we focus on those contributions that pertain to the field of psychological testing and assessment.

Galton was the ninth and last child in a large, wealthy, and influential British family. Galton's father was a banker, and at his insistence young Galton took up the study of medicine—study that Galton abandoned soon after his father's death. After travel, an award from the Royal Geographic Society for his account of his exploration of southern Africa, the publication of a guide for explorers, and the invention of some new instruments, including a teletype printer and instruments for charting weather, Galton's attention turned to the work of his half cousin Charles Darwin. Galton was intrigued with the implications of Darwin's theory of evolution, and he became increasingly intrigued—particularly with the social implications of the theory—as he grew older. Galton's (1869) study of heredity and genius pioneered the use of the statistical concept of correlation—a concept most integral to testing. Galton's scientific study of genetics led him to formulate various ways of measuring people, and he described these in his 1883 book, *Inquiries into Human Faculty and Its Development*. Some of the measurement techniques devised by Galton to gauge aspects of human perception included a tool to measure visual discrimination ability (referred to as the Galton bar), a whistle designed for use in measuring auditory discrimination of pitch, and a set of blocks that were similar in appearance but varied in weight in order to measure weight discrimination ability. Also included among the assessment instruments was a questionnaire—not a very revolutionary instrument by contemporary standards but certainly among the first formally used in psychological research when Galton introduced it.

At the International Health Exhibition in London (1884–1885) Galton exhibited the laboratory tools designed to measure people—his "anthropometric laboratory." After the Exhibition closed, the laboratory was reconstructed at London's Science Museum in South Kensington, where it continued in operation for six years. During its total period of operation, more than 9,000 people had measurements taken

FIGURE 2-1   *Sir Francis Galton (1822–1911)*

on 17 variables—leaving a mass of data that was still being analyzed long after Galton's death in 1911.

Much of Galton's work was used in support of the argument that genius ran in families and that the birth of more eminent people should be encouraged, whereas the birth of the less eminent (and, in Darwinian terms, "less fit") should be discouraged. Though he did not completely overlook the effect of environment on intelligence, Galton tended to minimize it—perhaps, as Schultz (1969) has suggested, because "he considered his own education for the most part a waste of time" (p. 92).

In general, Galton is perhaps best remembered for his systematic investigation of individual differences between people—an area of inquiry that has been referred to as a glaring "blind spot" in the field of psychology as it existed before Galton (Murphy, 1949). Despite views on the role of heredity and environment that in today's world would at best be highly controversial, we cannot deny that Galton was a great thinker of his day. As others (such as Flugel & West, 1964) have noted, one would be hard put to name another scientist who was so brilliant and versatile.

YOUR TASK

Pretend you are a great- great- great- (you get the idea) nephew of Sir Francis Galton. And while we are at it, let's say that your intellectual prowess and creative endowment may even exceed that of your great uncle. Inspired by reading Galton's works, you have come up with what you believe is a fabulous idea for a new psychological test. Now, all you need to do is convince the distinguished board of directors of a major publisher to fund the development of the test. Prepare a five-minute presentation designed to convince the board of the need for this test and its value to individual testtakers, test users, and society as a whole. Explain how the test you devised represents an extension of your great-uncle's vision. Present your idea to your fellow class members who will role-play the board of directors. Allow time at the conclusion of your presentation for a brief question-and-answer session with the board members, as well as some constructive feedback from them.

EXERCISE 2-5
THE COHEN CHICKEN SOUP ESSAY

OBJECTIVE

To provide a firsthand experience with the multicultural nature of contemporary society and illustrate the need for cultural sensitivity in test development

BACKGROUND

There are almost as many recipes for chicken soup as there are ethnic backgrounds. People from different Asian cultures may like to season their soup with soy sauce or curry. For many people from Arabic cultures, fresh lemon juice is an indispensable ingredient. Which recipe for chicken soup is best? It is all a matter of personal preference and taste. If you were the judge in an international chicken soup contest, you might choose the variety of soup that tasted most like the one you have traditionally been served. Then again, you might go for some wildly different entry from another culture.

YOUR TASK

Except for a panel of three students acting as judges, the entire class, or small groups within it, will hold a "Chicken Soup Challenge." Each participant will write down his or her recipe for chicken soup. Vegetarians may take an alternate form of this test by committing to writing their best recipe for vegetable soup. From all of the recipes, the panel of judges will select the best soup recipe. A spokesperson for the judging panel will explain why the winning recipe won. Then it's time for a debate between the judges and the rest of the participants—who may very well question why their recipe did not win top honors. The task for everyone will then be to come up with a set of culturally sensitive rules for judging essays in future contests. For the purposes of illustration, here is the recipe for Dr. Cohen's Chicken Surprise:[13]

---

[13]It is always a surprise to me when this soup comes out tasting the same way twice.

Ingredients

3 pound broiler-fryer chicken
2 quarts cold water
2 celery stalks with leaves (cut up)
2 carrots (cut up)
1 leek (cut up)
1 small onion (cut up)
1 sprig parsley
1 teaspoon salt (optional)

Place whole chicken, including giblets (except liver), and all other ingredients in a very large pot. [Reminder based on my own culinary experience: Don't forget to remove the wax paper envelope with the giblets from inside the chicken!] Heat to boiling, remove foam, and then reduce heat. Simmer for about 1½ hours or until meat parts easily from bone. Remove meat from bones and skin and place in separate container. Cover soup in a container and refrigerate for at least 12 hours. Skim congealed fat from soup prior to reheating, and add chicken.

EXERCISE 2-6
THE NONVERBAL INTERVIEW

OBJECTIVE

To sensitize students to the role of nonverbal factors in an interview

BACKGROUND

Many nonverbal behaviors "speak" even "louder" than spoken words about what an interviewee may be thinking or feeling. For example, sweaty palms may betray anxiety, as might hyperventilation.

YOUR TASK

Students will form teams of two, with one student playing the role of the interviewer and the other interviewee. The students will role-play any interviewer-interviewee they care to attempt (for example, psychologist-patient, news reporter-president, etc.) and work together to prepare in advance a list of a half-dozen or so interview questions. The questions should lend themselves to nonverbal as well as verbal responses. The team should also prepare in advance a list of the nonverbal answers that the interviewee will be trying to convey in response to each of the questions. The nonverbal response may be the same as or different from the verbalized one. Volunteer interviewer-interviewee teams will perform their interviews before the entire class. After each performance, the task for the rest of the class will be to guess the nonverbal response to each of the questions. After all of the interviews, a discussion on the role of nonverbal behavior during the interview will follow.

EXERCISE 2-7
THE TEST PURCHASER QUALIFICATION FORM

OBJECTIVE

To sensitize students to the position of test publishers and other distributors of professional psychological tests

BACKGROUND

In recent years, test publishing companies have voluntarily begun to make mandatory the completion of a test purchaser qualification form as a condition of the sale of certain tests. Currently, however, there is no one uniform test purchase form.

YOUR TASK

Design a "Uniform Psychological Test Purchase Qualification Form" to be used by all publishers of psychological tests. *Hint:* At a minimum, you will want to include on your form information about the prospective purchaser's education, licensure/certification, professional association memberships, and education, training, and experience with regard to testing and assessment. You may require the purchaser to make a statement regarding the intended use of the psychological test. After you have completed the form, write a brief message to the prospective purchaser explaining the reasons you require such information prior to selling the test.

EXERCISE 2-8
A LEGAL/ETHICAL ROUND TABLE

OBJECTIVE

To provide a forum for the debate of various ethical and legal issues attendant to the professional practice of psychological testing and assessment

BACKGROUND

Professionals in the field of psychology are presently grappling with a number of questions and issues regarding the use of psychological tests—questions and issues that will ultimately impact on (if not shape) the way psychological test-

ing and assessment are carried out in the future. Some of the topics under debate are listed below.

YOUR TASK

This exercise is an oral exercise, an in-class "round table." And, in the spirit of a round table, begin by moving the furniture so that all of your chairs form a large circle. If your classroom happens to be equipped with fixed-position chairs and desks, please do not attempt to execute the previous instruction.

Imagine now that you are all members of the State Board for Psychology and that you have assembled to come to some resolution regarding some outstanding issues. Your instructor is the chair of the committee, and he or she will read the questions below aloud and then ask follow-up questions as she or he deems necessary. Everyone in the class—everyone on the board, that is—should be given the opportunity to be heard on each one of the issues before the board. For this reason, the board chair may elect to select one board member to answer the question posed, and then, moving in clockwise fashion, listen to what, if anything, other board members have to add.

- Who should be allowed to purchase psychological tests? Why?
- Who should be allowed to use psychological tests? Why?
- How should rules regarding the purchase and/or use of psychological tests be enforced?
- What procedures in administering, scoring, and interpreting tests should be followed when testing people with disabling conditions?
- What procedures in administering, scoring, and interpreting tests should be followed when testing culturally or linguistically different people?
- What rights should be listed under the "Testtaker's Bill of Rights"? Why?

EXERCISE 2-9
ANOTHER LEGAL/ETHICAL ROUND TABLE

OBJECTIVE

To continue the discussion of issues related to the practice of psychological testing by focusing here on cases of alleged malpractice

BACKGROUND

Below is a sampling of actual legal cases as summarized in *Malpractice: A Guide for Mental Health Professionals* (Cohen, 1979).

YOUR TASK

Continuing the round table discussion as described in the previous exercise, one participant will read aloud one of the case summaries below. Immediately after each case is read, discuss in round-robin fashion some of the legal or ethical issues that you believe are important with respect to the case. What are the possible implications of these decisions for the practice of psychological testing?

TARASOFF V. REGENTS OF UNIVERSITY OF CALIFORNIA
118 Cal. Rptr. 129; 529 P.2d 553 (California, 1974)[14]

Tatiana Tarasoff was murdered by Prosenjit Poddar. Poddar had been in therapy with psychologist Dr. Lawrence Moore at the Cowell Memorial Hospital of the University of California at Berkeley. Two months prior to the murder, Poddar had made known to Moore his intention to kill an unnamed girl. After conferring with psychiatrists Gold and Yandell, Moore had written a letter to campus police chief William Beall requesting the assistance of the police department in securing Poddar's confinement. Dr. Harvey Powelson, the chief of the department of psychiatry at the hospital, asked Beall to return Moore's letter and directed that all copies of the letter and Moore's other notes on the case be destroyed. Powelson also "ordered no action to place Prosenjit Poddar in seventy-two-hour treatment and evaluation facility." After Tatiana was murdered, her parents brought suit against Doctors Moore, Powelson, Gold, and Yandell, Police Chief Beall, four campus police officers, and the Regents of the University of California as the employer of all of the other defendants.

The Supreme Court of California ruled that a psychotherapist has a duty to warn endangered third parties of their peril. The court recognized that many therapy patients make idle threats, and it acknowledged the need for privacy in therapist/patient communications. However, it ruled that screening the idle from the genuine threats was a matter of professional judgment and that the public interest superseded the individual patient's interest under certain conditions. It said:

> First, defendants point out that although therapy patients often express thoughts of violence, they rarely carry out these ideas. Indeed the open and confidential character of psychotherapeutic dialogue encourages patients to voice such thoughts, not as a device to reveal hidden danger, but as part of the process of therapy. Certainly a therapist should not be encouraged routinely to reveal such threats to acquaintances of the patient; such disclosures could seriously disrupt the patient's relationship with his therapist and with the persons threatened. In singling out those few patients whose threats of violence present a serious danger and in weighing against this danger the harm to the patient that might result from revelation, the psychothera-

pist renders a decision involving a high order of expertise and judgment.

> [5] The judgment of the therapist, however, is no more delicate or demanding than the judgment which doctors and professionals must regularly render under accepted rules of responsibility. A professional person is required only to exercise "that reasonable degree of skill, knowledge, and care ordinarily possessed and exercised by members of [his] profession under similar circumstances." (*Bardessono v. Michels* (1970) 3 Cal.3d 780, 788, 91 Cal. Rptr. 760, 764, 478 P.2d 480, 484.) As a specialist, the psychotherapist, whether doctor or psychologist, would also be "held to that standard of learning and skill normally possessed by such specialist in the same or similar locality under the same or similar circumstances." (*Quintal v. Laurel Grove Hospital* (1964) 62 Cal.2d 154, 159–160, 41 Cal. Rptr. 577, 580, 397 P.2d 161, 164.) But within that broad range in which professional opinion and judgment may differ respecting the proper course of action, the psychotherapist is free to exercise his own best judgment free from liability; proof, aided by hindsight, that he judged wrongly is insufficient to establish liability.

> In other words, the fact that a decision calls for considerable expert skill and judgment means, in effect, that it be tested by a standard of care which takes account of those circumstances; the standard used in measuring professional malpractice does so. But whatever difficulties the courts may encounter in evaluating the expert judgments of other professions, those difficulties cannot justify total exoneration from liability.

> Second, defendants argue that free and open communication is essential to psychotherapy (see In re Lifschutz (1970) 2 Cal.3d 415, 431–432, 85 Cal. Rptr. 829, 467 P.2d 557); that "Unless a patient . . . is assured that . . . information [revealed by him] can and will be held in utmost confidence, he will be reluctant to make the full disclosure upon which diagnosis and treatment . . . depend." (Sen. Committee on the Judiciary, comments on Evid. Code, §1014.) The giving of a warning, defendants contend, constitutes a breach of trust which entails the revelation of confidential communications.

> We recognize the public interest in supporting effective treatment of mental illness and in protecting the rights of patients to privacy (see In re Lifschutz, *supra,* 2 Cal.3d at p. 432, 85 Cal. Rptr. 829, 467 P.2d 557), and the consequent public importance of safeguarding the confidential character of psychotherapeutic communication. Against this interest, however, we must weigh the public interest in safety from violent assault. The Legislature has undertaken the difficult task of balancing the countervailing concerns. In Evidence Code section 1014, it established a broad rule of privilege to protect confidential communications between patient and psychotherapist. In Evidence Code section 1024, however, the Legislature created a specific and limited exception to the psychotherapist-patient privilege: "There is no privilege . . . if the psychotherapist has reasonable cause to believe that the patient is in such mental or emotional condition as to be dangerous to himself or to the person or property of another and that disclosure of the communication is necessary to prevent the threatened danger."

> [6] The revelation of a communication under the above circumstances is not a breach of trust or a violation of professional ethics; as stated in the Principles of Medical Ethics of the American Medical Association (1957) section 9; "A physician may not reveal the confidences entrusted to him in the

---

[14]The complete text of the significant decision in this case, including the majority opinion by Justice Tobriner and a dissenting opinion by Justice Clark, appears in the appendix to Cohen (1979). Also included in the appendix is an excerpt from Dr. Moore's letter to Police Chief Beall.

course of medical attendance . . . *unless he is required to do so by law or unless it becomes necessary in order to protect the welfare of the individual or of the community.*" (Emphasis added.) We conclude that the public policy favoring protection of the confidential character of patient-psychotherapist communications must yield in instances in which disclosure is essential to avert danger to others. The protective privilege ends where the public peril begins.

CLARK V. GERACI
29 Misc.2d 791; 208 N.Y.S.2d 564 (New York, 1960)

The plaintiff in this case was a civilian who worked for the Air Force as an accountant. He had taken off time from work owing to respiratory difficulties that stemmed from his alcoholism. In response to an official request for information concerning the causes of the plaintiff's absences, the defendant psychiatrist revealed that the plaintiff had a drinking problem (despite the fact that the plaintiff had explicitly objected to the revelation of that information). The plaintiff was subsequently fired from his job, and he brought suit against the doctor for breach of confidentiality.

The court recognized that breach of doctor-patient confidentiality is an actionable offense, but it declined to find in favor of the plaintiff in this case. The court held that the plaintiff had probably lost his job not because of the mere revelation of confidential material, but because of repeated absences from work. Furthermore, the court held the doctor's duty to the United States government to be above the doctor's duty to the patient.

BERRY V. MOENCH
8 Utah 2d 191; 331 P.2d 814; 73 A.L.R.2d 315 (Utah, 1958)

Berry was a patient seen by Dr. Moench, a psychiatrist, seven years prior to this litigation. Berry was about to remarry, and the father of his bride-to-be asked a Dr. Hellewell to write Dr. Moench to find out information about Berry. Hellewell wrote to Moench, specifically stating that the reasons he was soliciting information about Berry was to advise the father of the prospective bride-to-be. Dr. Moench's letter to Hellewell said that Berry had been diagnosed as "manic depressive depression in a psychopathic personality." Moench went on to offer the following advice in his letter:

> My suggestion to the infatuated girl would be to run as fast and as far as she possibly could in any direction away from him. . . . Of course, if he doesn't marry her, he will marry someone else and make life hell for that person.

Berry brought suit against Moench for breach of confidentiality. The court found in favor of the defendant, holding that the parents of the woman Berry was dating were concerned only with the welfare of their daughter and that that concern was a sufficient interest to protect legally. The court wrote that, according to generally accepted standards of decent conduct, "the privilege exists if the recipient has the type of interest in the matter, and the publisher stands in such a relation to him that it would reasonably be considered the duty of the publisher to give the information."

SCHWARTZ V. THIELE
242 Cal. App. 2d 799; 51 Cal. Rptr. 767 (California, 1966)

Judith Schwartz's suit against psychiatrist David A. Thiele alleged that they were strangers when they met in a restaurant parking lot about 9:30 in the morning. As stated in the court record, Judith and her sister "after having had breakfast at a restaurant in the city of Los Angeles, were walking to her automobile (when) the defendant, a total stranger to the plaintiff, and without her consent, purported to make an examination of plaintiff as to her mental illness." Exactly why Thiele had occasion to "examine" Schwartz or what, in fact, transpired in the parking lot is not clear from the court record:

> In the case at the bench, so far as it may be determined from the pleading, the defendant had some contact with the plaintiff, the exact nature of which is not disclosed.

After that contact, Thiele wrote a letter to the psychiatric department of the Superior Court of Los Angeles County stating that Schwartz was mentally ill and that she was likely to injure herself or others if not immediately hospitalized. After receiving the letter, a judge of the superior court signed an order appointing a physician to examine Schwartz. The court-appointed physician tried, through Schwartz's lawyer, to arrange an appointment for an examination. However, Schwartz was examined by her own physician, who did not find her to be mentally ill.

Schwartz's suit against Thiele claimed $100,000 in damages. She alleged that her right of privacy had been invaded and as a consequence of that invasion she had suffered "great mental pain and physical suffering, humiliation, annoyance, and mortification," and she had been exposed to "public ridicule and disgrace."

The court found in favor of the defendant, holding him immune from liability and noting that there was no publication of the letter. The court further stated:

> The restraint and treatment of persons who are mentally ill is a matter of public concern. If a person in good faith and for probable cause makes a written statement to an agency charged with the duty of enforcement of the law, designed to give such agency information upon which it can conduct an investigation, such a communication is not an invasion of the right of privacy of the person who is the subject of the communication.

CHAROULEAU V. CHARITY HOSPITAL OF NEW ORLEANS
319 So.2d 464 (Louisiana, 1975)

A patient was seen in a public hospital emergency room by a physician who referred the case to psychiatry. While a psychiatric resident was interviewing the patient, the patient took a revolver from her purse and pointed it at the resident. The resident took the gun from the woman, determined it was unloaded, and handed it back to the woman "to establish a rapport." The woman told the resident that she had previously been admitted to this hospital and that she was seeking admission now to rid herself of a drug abuse problem. The resident told the patient that she would not be committed to an institution against her will, and he proceeded within the patient's view to write a note stating that it was his opinion that the woman could benefit from prolonged hospitalization. The resident did not review the patient's chart, which could have been obtained from the records room, and he did not instruct anyone to keep an eye on the patient. He escorted her to the admission desk and instructed her to sit down and wait for the clerk to return. As well as can be determined, the patient took her chart sometime after the resident dropped her off, straying from the admission area. The patient was found dead the following morning in a hospital toilet, from a self-inflicted bullet wound.

The patient's husband brought suit against the resident and the hospital. The case against the resident was settled out of court, but the hospital contended that it could not be held legally culpable as the proximate cause of the patient's death. The plaintiff charged that the hospital negligently had a resident instead of a psychiatrist in the emergency room, that it did not have a procedure for direct admission into psychiatry, that it allowed psychiatric patients to stray from admission, that it did not prevent patients from seeing their own charts, and that it did not have a policy of reviewing the past records of potentially suicidal patients.

The court did not find the defendant hospital culpable, because as a matter of course previous records are not examined in emergency-room treatment, in order to expedite dispositions. The court found the admissions procedure used by the defendant hospital to be much the same as in comparable hospitals and did not find compelling evidence that the hospital was the proximate cause of the patient's death.

In Re Sterilization of Moore
221 S.E.2d 307 (North Carolina, 1976)

A director of a county's Department of Social Services requested the court to order authorization for the sterilization of a minor who, according to a psychological report, had a full scale IQ of under 40. The constitutionality of the order was challenged. Citing the opinion of the United States Supreme Court in *Buck v. Bell* (47 S.Ct. 584), the Supreme Court of North Carolina held that: A state does have the right to sterilize a retarded or insane person provided that the sterilization is not prescribed as punishment, the policy is applied equally to all persons, and notice and hearing are provided; according to mental health laws, the interest of the unborn child is sufficient to warrant the sterilization of a retarded individual; and, further, the People also have the right to prevent the procreation of children who will become a burden on the State.

REFERENCES

Cohen, R. J. (1979). *Malpractice: A guide for mental health professionals.* New York: Free Press.

Darwin, C. (1859). *On the origin of species by means of natural selection.* London: Murray.

Flugel, J. C., & West, D. J. (1964). *A hundred years of psychology: 1833–1933.* New York: Basic Books.

Galton, F. (1869). *Hereditary genius.* London: Macmillan. (Republished in 1892.)

Murphy, G. (1949). *Historical introduction to modern psychology* (rev. ed.). New York: Harcourt, Brace, & World.

Ruch, G. M. (1925). Minimum essentials in reporting data on standard tests. *Journal of Educational Research, 12,* 349–358.

Schultz, D. P. (1969). *A history of modern psychology.* New York: Academic Press.

Standards for educational and psychological testing. (1985). Washington, D.C.: American Psychological Association.

THE 4-QUESTION CHALLENGE

1. The historical significance of competitive examinations in China during the Chan dynasty has to do with
   a. cross-cultural and longstanding difficulties in hiring reliable postal workers.
   b. the perpetuation of nepotism in hiring for civil service positions.
   c. evidence of a reverse discrimination hiring policy in existence since 1115 B.C.
   d. evidence of concern for psychometric principles thousands of years ago.

2. Cultural sensitivity in test development is manifested by
   a. panels of experts who review test items for discriminatory content.
   b. test purchaser qualification forms that require statements of cultural background.
   c. behavioral evaluation of test scorers from different cultural backgrounds.
   d. strict adherence to guidelines set forth in *Tarasoff v. Regents of University of California.*

3. The Code of Fair Testing
   a. grew out of the work of a 1992 congressional subcommittee on test publisher practices.
   b. specifies obligations of test developers and test users with regard to various areas.
   c. specifies obligations of testtakers under statutory truth-in-testing laws.
   d. all of the above

4. According to the *Standards,* all of the following are rights of testtakers except:
   a. the right not to have privacy invaded.
   b. the right to be informed of test findings.
   c. the right to a nonstigmatizing diagnosis.
   d. the right of informed consent to testing.

CHAPTER 3

A Statistics Refresher

Puzzle 3

Instructions Identify what is described, answer a question, or fill in the blank to complete this crossword puzzle based on material presented in Chapter 3 of your textbook.

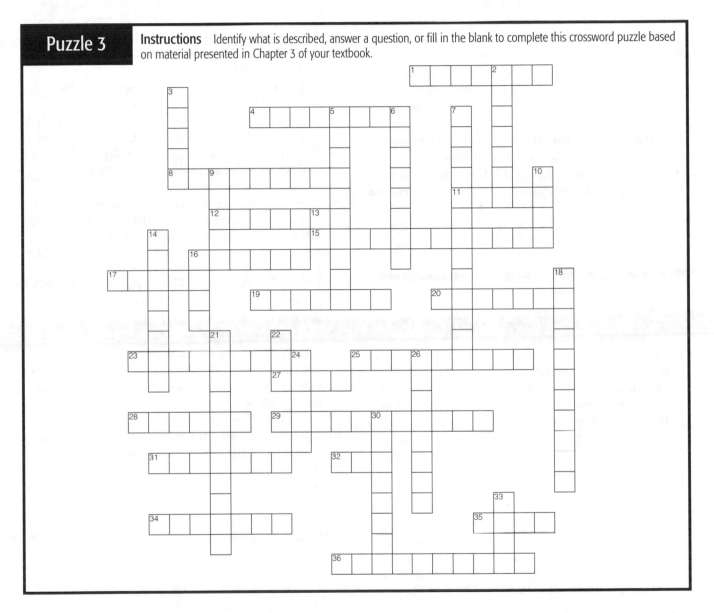

Across

1. A tabular summary of test scores in which the test scores are grouped by intervals, also referred to as class intervals. It's a(n) _____ frequency distribution.

4. An indication of the nature and extent to which symmetry is absent in a distribution.

8. A graph with vertical lines drawn at the true limits of each test score (or class interval), forming a series of contiguous rectangles.

11. A descriptive statistic of variability derived by calculating the difference between the highest and lowest scores in a distribution.

12. It's a system of measurement in which all things measured can be rank-ordered, where the rank-ordering implies nothing about exactly how much greater one ranking is than another, and there is no absolute zero point on the scale. Like most scales in psychology and education, this describes a(n) _____ scale.

15. In a psychometric context, a set of test scores arrayed for recording or study.

16. A measure of central tendency derived by identifying the middlemost score in a distribution.

17. It's a system of measurement in which all things measured can be rank-ordered. The rank-ordering does imply something about exactly how much greater one ranking is than another. Equal intervals exist between each number on the scale. And all mathematical operations can be performed meaningfully because a true or absolute zero point exists. It's a(n) _____ scale.

19. An adjective describing the central tendency of a distribution of scores in which two scores occur an equal number of times and both scores tie for the designation as the most frequently occurring score in the distribution.

20. A standard score derived from a scale with a mean of 5 and a standard deviation of approximately 2.

23. A measure of variability equal to the arithmetic mean of the squares of the differences between the scores in a distribution and their mean. Write it in its plural form.

25. It's a tabular listing of scores along with the number of times each score occurred. It's a(n) _____ distribution.

27. According to the Motion Picture Association of America, PG-13 is a rating in which parents are strongly cautioned that some material in a movie may be inappropriate for children under 13 years of age. Like PG-13, this rating is made on a scale much like that described in 31-Across. It is used to signify that no one under 17 will be admitted. *Note:* You will have to answer this based on general knowledge, as this was not mentioned in the chapter. Also, remove the hyphen to make it fit in 4 spaces.

28. It's a bell-shaped, smooth, mathematically defined curve highest at the center and then gradually tapering on both sides, approaching but never actually touching the horizontal axis. It's a(n) _____ curve.

29. A description of the kurtosis of a distribution where the distribution is relatively flat in its center.

31. It's a system of measurement in which all things measured are classified or categorized based on one or more distinguishing characteristics and placed into mutually exclusive and exhaustive categories. It's a(n) _____ scale.

32. A graphic illustration of data wherein numbers indicative of frequency are set on the vertical axis, categories are set on the horizontal axis, and the rectangular bars that describe the data are typically noncontiguous. This type of graph is called a(n) _____ graph.

34. In general, it's a statistic indicative of the average or middlemost score between the extreme scores in a distribution. Could be the mean, the median, or the mode. It's a measure of _____ tendency.

35. A z score has a mean set at _____ and a standard deviation set at one.

36. A description of the kurtosis of a distribution where the distribution is not extremely peaked or flat in its center.

Down

2. It's a graphic illustration of data wherein numbers indicative of frequency are set on the vertical axis, test scores or categories are set on the horizontal axis, and the data are described by a continuous line connecting the points where the test scores or categories meet frequencies. It's a frequency _____ .

3. A diagram or chart composed of lines, points, bars, or other symbols that describe and illustrate data.

5. It's a variety of standard score scale that conceptually results from the "stretching" of a skewed distribution into the shape of a normal curve, usually through a process of nonlinear transformation. It's called a(n) _____ standard score scale.

6. It's a measure of variability that is equal to the square root of the averaged squared deviations about the mean. Stated another way, it's a measure of variability that is equal to the square root of the variance. What we mean to say is that it's a(n) _____ deviation.

7. It's an ordinal statistic of variability equal to the difference between the third and the first quartile points in a distribution that has been divided into quartiles. It's the _____ range.

9. It's a raw score that has been converted from one scale into another scale, the latter scale (1) having some arbitrarily set mean and standard deviation, and (2) being more widely used and readily interpretable. It is commonly referred to as a standard _____ .

10. A measure of central tendency derived by calculating an average of all scores in a distribution.

13. An abbreviation for average deviation.

14. A system of measurement in which all things measured can be rank-ordered, where the rank-ordering contains equal intervals between them, each unit on the scale is equal to each other unit on the scale, and there is no absolute zero point. It's a(n) _____ scale.

16. A measure of central tendency derived by identifying the most frequently occurring score in a distribution.

18. A description of the kurtosis of a distribution where the distribution is relatively peaked in its center.

21. An indication of how scores in a distribution are scattered or dispersed.

22. Named for Thorndike, a *T*-score is standard score calculated using a scale with a mean set at 50 and a standard deviation set at _____ .

24. A set of numbers or other symbols whose properties model empirical properties of the objects or traits to which numbers or other symbols are assigned.

26. One of three dividing points between the four quarters of a distribution, each typically labeled as Q_1, Q_2, and Q_3.

30. An indication of the nature of the steepness (peaked versus flat) of the center of a distribution.

33. A measure of variability that is equal to the interquartile range divided by two. It is the _____-interquartile range.

EXERCISE 3-1
MOVIES AND MEASUREMENT

Men in an Upper Percentile

OBJECTIVE

To learn about the extremes of the normal curve through independent study

BACKGROUND

Assessment is employed in a variety of settings for diverse reasons. Employers, for example, use tools of assessment to screen and select applicants who have a high probability of performing well at their jobs. Tommy Lee Jones and Will Smith met the seemingly rigorous criteria for employment as *Men in Black* in the film of the same title. At least according to that film, the abilities of these men were found to be superior and at the extremely high end of the normal curve.

YOUR TASK

Engage in independent study to learn more about the normal curve, particularly the characteristics of it at the high and the low extreme. Write a brief essay entitled "Going to the Extremes of the Normal Curve" in which you discuss characteristics of scores that fall at the extremely high end as well as the extremely low end of the normal curve.

EXERCISE 3-2
SCALES OF MEASUREMENT IN EVERYDAY LIFE

OBJECTIVE

To gain greater familiarity with various scales of measurement by generating some original examples

BACKGROUND

In your textbook, scales of measurement are discussed in the context of psychological testing and assessment. However, examples of nominal, ordinal, interval, and ratio scales can be found in everyday life. Here are some examples:

Nominal scales. Perhaps the most common example of nominal measurement is the number printed on a football jersey. The number is there for the purpose of identifying the player. It cannot meaningfully be added to, subtracted from, or multiplied or divided by any other number.

Ordinal scales. Have you ever been to a wine tasting and been asked to rank-order various wines from least favored to most favored? If so, you have had firsthand experience with ordinal measurement. Although rank-ordering is permitted with ordinal measurement, remember that no implication is made regarding how much greater one ranking is than another. It would be statistically incorrect to say that a wine ranked first was twice as good as the wine ranked second, three times as good as the wine ranked third, and so on. There is no absolute zero point in an ordinal scale; without individual units of measurement, zero is without meaning. All of the wines being ranked have some taste, and no wine has absolutely no taste.

Interval scales. As with ordinal scales, interval scales contain no absolute zero point. As an illustration, consider the measurement of temperature. Zero degrees Fahrenheit is not indicative of the complete absence of temperature. Because there is no absolute zero point on the Fahrenheit scale, it would not be meaningful to make statements in terms of ratios. While we can say that the difference between 20 and 40 degrees Fahrenheit is the same as the number of degrees difference between 75 and 95 degrees Fahrenheit, we cannot accurately say that 40 degrees is twice as hot as 20 degrees.

Ratio scales. A ratio scale for measuring temperature is the Kelvin scale. Unlike the Fahrenheit or centigrade scales, the Kelvin scale has a true zero point. On the Kelvin scale, 0 degrees is the temperature at which molecular activity ceases. One can legitimately state that 20 degrees Kelvin is twice as warm (or half as cold) as 10 degrees Kelvin, because equal intervals exist between the numbers on the scale, and the scale has a true zero point.

YOUR TASK

Provide additional examples of nominal, ordinal, interval, and ratio measurement from everyday life. Explain why each of your examples qualifies as that type of measurement. If you cannot think of an everyday example for any particular scale of measurement, make up your own scale.

EXERCISE 3-3

REVIEWING DESCRIPTIVE STATISTICS

OBJECTIVE

To obtain firsthand experience in describing a distribution of data using descriptive statistics

BACKGROUND

Like other exercises in this book, this one contains step-by-step illustrations designed to explain the calculation of selected statistics typically used in the fields of psychological and educational measurement. In general, a model of calculations is provided, and it is then up to you to calculate those same statistics in the same way, using similar data.

In Table 3-1 you will find raw scores on a hypothetical, 100-item, multiple-choice test where one point was awarded for each correct answer and all scores could range from 0 (none correct) to 100 (all correct). The scores for the 25 students in the class are also illustrated in the form of a frequency distribution (Table 3-2), a grouped frequency distribution (Table 3-3), a frequency polygon (Figure 3-1), a histogram (Figure 3-2), and a bar graph (Figure 3-3)—one in which it has been assumed for the purpose of illustration that a raw score of 65 or higher had been arbitrarily set in advance to be a passing grade.

MEASURES OF CENTRAL TENDENCY

Let's now calculate the arithmetic mean, the median, and the mode—the *measures of central tendency*—for this distribution of test scores.

The Mean

The *mean*, denoted by the symbol $\overline{X}$ (and pronounced "X bar"), is equal to the sum of the observations (or test scores in this case) divided by the number of observations. Symbol-

TABLE 3-1   Data from Your Measurement Course Test

Student	Score (number correct)
Judy	78
Joe	67
David	69
Miriam	63
Valerie	85
Diane	72
Henry	92
Gertrude	67
Paula	94
Martha	62
Bill	61
Homer	44
Robert	66
Michael	87
Brandon	76
Mary	83
"Mousey"	42
Barbara	82
John	84
Donna	51
Uriah	69
Leroy	61
Ronald	96
Vinnie	73
Patty	79

TABLE 3-2   Frequency Distribution of Scores from Your Test

Score	f (Frequency)
96	1
94	1
92	1
87	1
85	1
84	1
83	1
82	1
79	1
78	1
76	1
73	1
72	1
69	2
67	2
66	1
63	1
62	1
61	2
51	1
44	1
42	1

TABLE 3-3 *A Grouped Frequency Distribution*

Class Interval	Frequency
96–100	1
91–95	2
86–90	1
81–85	4
76–80	3
71–75	2
66–70	5
61–65	4
56–60	0
51–55	1
46–50	0
41–45	2

FIGURE 3-2 *Data from Your Measurement Course in a Histogram*

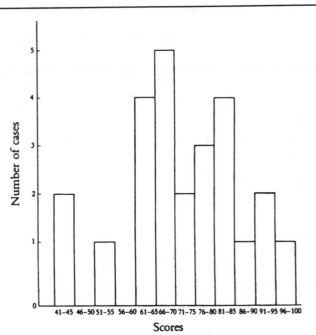

FIGURE 3-1 *Data from Your Measurement Course in a Frequency Polygon*

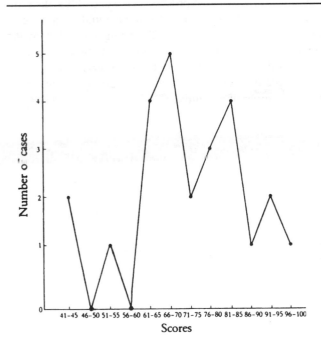

FIGURE 3-3 *Data from Your Measurement Course in a Bar Graph*

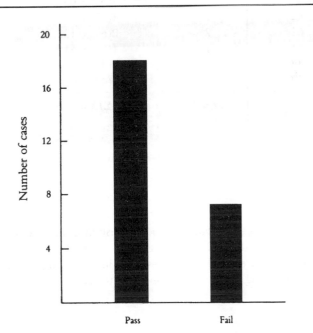

ically written, the formula for the mean is: $\bar{X} = \Sigma X/n$ where the Greek uppercase sigma (Σ) represents "summation," X is a test score, and n is equal to the number of observations or test scores. An arithmetic mean can also be calculated from a frequency distribution. The formula for calculating the mean from grouped data is as follows:

$$\bar{X} = \frac{\Sigma fX}{n}$$

where f is the corresponding frequency of the occurrence of a score. The step-by-step process is as follows:

Step 1
   List each of the observations—each test score, or X in this case—in the first column.

Step 2
   List the corresponding frequency of each score in an adjacent column, thus creating a frequency distribution.

Step 3
   Multiply each score by its corresponding frequency.

Step 4
   Add the products obtained in Step 3 above—that is, add all of the fXs.

Step 5

Divide the number (*n*) of measurements or scores—the total of the frequencies.

Inserting the test score data into the computation procedures listed for each of the steps listed above and the computation of the mean for the grouped data would look like this:

X	f	fX
96	1	1(96) = 96
94	1	1(94) = 94
92	1	1(92) = 92
87	1	1(87) = 87
85	1	1(85) = 85
84	1	1(84) = 84
83	1	1(83) = 83
82	1	1(82) = 82
79	1	1(79) = 79
78	1	1(78) = 78
76	1	1(76) = 76
73	1	1(73) = 73
72	1	1(72) = 72
69	2	2(69) = 138
67	2	2(67) = 134
66	1	1(66) = 66
63	1	1(63) = 63
62	1	1(62) = 62
61	2	2(61) = 122
51	1	1(51) = 51
44	1	1(44) = 44
42	1	1(42) = 42
$\Sigma f = 25$		$\Sigma fX = 1803$

$$\overline{X} = \frac{1803}{25} = 72.12$$

The Median

The *median* is the middle score in a distribution, and the simplest way of determining its value in a distribution of 25 scores would entail listing the scores in ascending (or descending) magnitude and then locating the center:

96
94
92
87
85
84
83
82
79
78
76
73
72
69
69
67
67
66
63
62
61
61
51
44
42

The *median* is the middle score in a distribution, and it is determined by a two-step process: (1) listing all the data (including repeating scores) in order of magnitude—in increasing or decreasing order, and (2) finding the value of the middle observation. For an odd number of observations, the median is the value of the $[(n + 1)/2]^{\text{th}}$ observation.

In the present example, let's begin by arranging the data in increasing order of magnitude:

42
44
51
61
61
62
63
66
67
67
69
69
72
73
76
78
79
82
83
84
85
87
92
94
96

Having done that, we can now solve for the median, referred to in some statistical writings as $\tilde{X}$ ("X tilde," pronounced like the "tilda" in "Matilda").

The expression above tells us that the median is equal to the value of $[(n + 1)/2]^{\text{th}}$ observation or the value of the 13th observation. Counting the 13th observation in the distribution of scores we've been working with, we find 72. Therefore, we can say that the median of this distribution is 72, or put another way, $\tilde{X} = 72$.

Suppose that, instead of an odd number of observations, our task was to calculate the median from an even number of observations. For the purposes of illustration, let's add 97 to the list of observations, thereby raising n in this case to 26. For an even number of observations, the median is equal to the arithmetic mean of the $(n/2)^{\text{th}}$ and the $[(n/2) + 1]^{\text{th}}$ observations. The data listed in increasing order of magnitude are as follows:

42
44
51
61
61
62
63
66
67
67
69
69
72
73
76
78
79
82
83
84
85
87
92
94
96
97

The value of the $(n/2)^{\text{th}}$ observation is the value of the $(26/2)^{\text{th}}$ or 13th observation. The 13th observation is equal to 72.

The value of the $[(n/2) + 1]^{\text{th}}$ observation is the value of the $[(26/2) + 1]^{\text{th}}$ or 14th observation. Here, the 14th observation is equal to 73.

We can now solve for the value of the median as follows:

$$\tilde{X} = \frac{72 + 73}{2} = 72.5$$

Just before moving on from our discussion of the median to a discussion of another measure of central tendency, the mode, let's take note of the case where there are repeated scores at the median. For example, suppose the 14th observation in the data above was not 73 but 72. The $(n/2)^{\text{th}}$ or 13th observation would still be 72. However, the $[(n/2) + 1]^{\text{th}}$ or 14th observation is now also 72 (instead of 73). The solution for the median in this instance would be as follows:

$$\tilde{X} = \frac{72 + 72}{2} = 72$$

The Mode

The *mode* is the most frequently occurring score in a distribution of scores. In the distribution of measurement test scores we've been using, there is no *one* score that is *the* most frequently occurring score. Three scores (69, 67, and 61) are "the most frequently occurring." In this instance then, we would say that the distribution is *trimodal;* it has three modes.

MEASURES OF VARIABILITY

Variability is an indication of how scores in a distribution are scattered or dispersed. Statistics that describe the amount of variation include the range, the interquartile range, the semi-interquartile range, the standard deviation, and the variance.

The Range

The *range* of a distribution is equal to the difference between the highest and lowest scores. In the present example, it is equal to the difference between the highest (96) and lowest (42) scores, or 96–42. Performing the subtraction, we find the difference to be 54; we therefore say that the test scores in this distribution have a range of 54.

The Interquartile and Semi-Interquartile Ranges

Conceptually, the calculation of an interquartile range (Table 3-4) entails the division of a distribution of observations—in the present example test scores—into four quarters so that 25% of the test scores fall into each of the quarters (Figure 3-4); the interquartile range (IR) is equal to the difference between the score at the third quartile (Q_3) and the score at the first quartile (Q_1). The *semi*-interquartile range is simply the IR divided by 2.

Some calculation is necessary to determine the value of Q_1 and Q_3 so that IR can be determined. To calculate Q_3 we may use the following formula:

$$Q_3 = U_{ri} - \left[\left(\frac{C_{ri} - .75n}{f_{ri}} \right) (W_{ri}) \right]$$

U_{ri} is the upper real limit of the relevant interval.
C_{ri} is the cumulative frequency of the relevant interval.
f_{ri} is the frequency of the relevant interval.
W_{ri} is the width of the relevant interval.

Note that in this formula for the computation of the third quartile, .75 is a constant; this is because we are computing the point at or below which 75% of the scores fall. The "relevant interval" is the first class interval where the cumulative frequency is greater than or equal to .75n—or in this case, greater than or equal to (.75)(25), or 18.75.

The calculation of Q_1 is similar to the calculation of Q_3 except that the constant in the expression np is .25 and not .75. This is because we are calculating the point at or below which 25% of the scores fall:

TABLE 3-4 *Calculating an Interquartile Range (IR)*

	Score	Frequency	Cumulative Frequency	
	96	1	24 + 1 = 25	
	94	1	23 + 1 = 24	
	92	1	22 + 1 = 23	
	87	1	21 + 1 = 22	
	85	1	20 + 1 = 21	
	84	1	19 + 1 = 20	
Q_3	81	1	18 + 1 = 19	Q_3
	82	1	17 + 1 = 18	
	79	1	16 + 1 = 17	
	78	1	15 + 1 = 16	
	76	1	14 + 1 = 15	
	73	1	13 + 1 = 14	
Q_2	72	1	12 + 1 = 13	Q_2
	69	2	10 + 2 = 12	
	67	2	8 + 2 = 10	
	66	1	7 + 1 = 8	
Q_1	63	1	6 + 1 = 7	Q_1
	62	1	5 + 1 = 6	
	61	2	3 + 2 = 5	
	51	1	2 + 1 = 3	
	44	1	1 + 1 = 2	
	42	1	1 + 0 = 1	

For Q_3 the relevant interval is the first class interval where the cumulative frequency is greater than or equal to .75n. In this example, the relevant interval is the first class interval where the cumulative frequency is greater than or equal to:

(.75)(25), or 18.75

Thus, the relevant interval is 83, when the cumulative frequency is 19.

For Q_1, the relevant interval is the first class interval where the cumulative frequency is greater than or equal to .25n. In this example, the relevant interval is the first class interval where the cumulative frequency is greater than or equal to:

(.25)(25), or 6.25

Thus, the relevant interval is 63 when the cumulative frequency is 7.

The calculations for Q_3 and Q_1 are shown below:

$$Q_3 = 83.5 - \left[\left(\frac{19 - 18.75}{1} \right)(1) \right]$$

$$= 83.5 - \left[(.25)(1) \right]$$

$$Q_3 = 83.5 - .25 = 83.25$$

$$Q_1 = 63.5 - \left[\left(\frac{7 - 6.25}{1} \right)(1) \right]$$

$$= 63.5 - \left[(.75)(1) \right]$$

$$Q_1 = 63.5 - .75 = 62.75$$

Note: For Q_2, otherwise known as the median, the relevant interval is the first class interval where the cumulative frequency is greater than or equal to:

(.50)(25), or 12.5

Thus, the relevant interval is 72 where the cumulative frequency is 13:

$$Q_2 = 72.5 - \left[\left(\frac{13 - 12.5}{1} \right)(1) \right]$$

$$= 72.5 - \left[(.5)(1) \right]$$

$$Q_2 = 72.5 - .5 = 72$$

Knowing the value of Q_3 and Q_1, we can now solve for the value of IR in the present example:

$$IR = Q_3 - Q_1$$
$$IR = 83.25 - 62.75$$
$$IR = 20.5$$

What if we had used the distribution of test scores as they appear in Table 3-3 (instead of as they appear in Table 3-2)? Do you think Q_1, Q_2, and Q_3 would come out to be exactly the same? Now do the calculations; the answer may surprise you.

In essence, the interquartile range is a measure of variability that conveys information about the middle part of a distribution of scores—the scores between the 25th and 75th percentiles. In many test manuals, you may come across a reporting of the variability of scores not in terms of the interquartile range but rather in terms of the semi-interquartile range (one-half the interquartile range). The reporting of one-half the interquartile range is done to convey information about how far, on average, the 25th percentile lies from the median of the distribution, and how far, on average, the 75th percentile lies from the median of the distribution. The semi-interquartile range is perhaps used most frequently when data in the distribution of test scores are highly skewed.

FIGURE 3-4   *A Quartered Distribution*

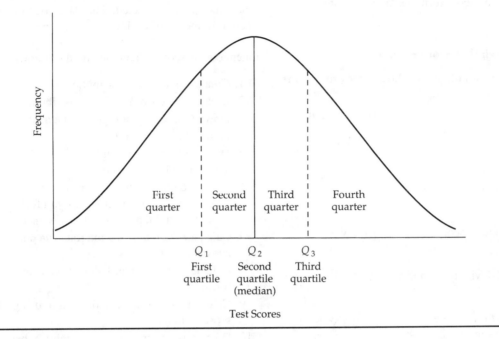

The Average Deviation

The *average deviation* (AD) is equal to the sum of the deviation scores divided by the total number of scores. The formula for the AD is as follows:

$$AD = \frac{\Sigma |X - \overline{X}|}{n} = \frac{\Sigma |x|}{n}$$

where the lowercase italicized "x" signifies a score's deviation from the mean (obtained by subtracting the mean from the score). The bars on each side of the *x* indicate that the number should be read as its absolute value—devoid of a positive or a negative sign (though positive for practical purposes). All of the deviation scores are then summed and divided by the total number of scores. In Table 3-5 we calculate the AD for the distribution of test scores we've been working with.

While the AD is used relatively rarely as a measure of variation, the computation of an AD provides a good conceptual introduction to a much more widely used measure of variability, the last one we will discuss in this chapter.

The Standard Deviation

The *standard deviation* (SD) is a measure of variability that is equal to the square root of the average squared deviations about the mean. Stated another way, the SD is equal to the square root of the variance. The *variance* is equal to the arithmetic mean of the squares of the differences between the scores in a distribution and their mean.

Step-by-step general instructions for calculating the variance and an SD are followed by a step-by-step illustration of the calculation of the variance and the SD for the data in the

TABLE 3-5   *Calculating an Average Deviation*

X	$X - \overline{X}$	$|X - \overline{X}|$ or $|x|$
96	96 − 72.12 = 23.88	23.88
94	94 − 72.12 = 21.88	21.88
92	92 − 72.12 = 19.88	19.88
87	87 − 72.12 = 14.88	14.88
85	85 − 72.12 = 12.88	12.88
84	84 − 72.12 = 11.88	11.88
83	83 − 72.12 = 10.88	10.88
82	82 − 72.12 = 9.88	9.88
79	79 − 72.12 = 6.88	6.88
78	78 − 72.12 = 5.88	5.88
76	76 − 72.12 = 3.88	3.88
73	73 − 72.12 = .88	.88
72	72 − 72.12 = .12	.12
69	69 − 72.12 = − 3.12	3.12
69	69 − 72.12 = − 3.12	3.12
67	67 − 72.12 = − 5.12	5.12
67	67 − 72.12 = − 5.12	5.12
66	66 − 72.12 = − 6.12	6.12
63	63 − 72.12 = − 9.12	9.12
62	62 − 72.12 = −10.12	10.12
61	61 − 72.12 = −11.12	11.12
61	61 − 72.12 = −11.12	11.12
51	51 − 72.12 = −21.12	21.12
44	44 − 72.12 = −28.12	28.12
42	42 − 72.12 = −30.12	30.12

$$\Sigma = 287.12 \quad AD = \frac{287.12}{25}$$
$$= 11.4848$$

distribution of the test scores we've been working with in this chapter. Two methods, referred to as "the deviation score formula" and the "raw score formula," are presented.

Step-by-Step Calculation of the Variance and Standard Deviation: The Deviation Score Formula

The deviation score formula is as follows. This formula requires these six steps:

THE FORMULA

Step 1

Calculate the mean.

$$\overline{X} = \frac{\Sigma X}{n}$$

Step 2

Calculate each deviation score.

$$(X - \overline{X})$$

Step 3

Square each deviation score.

$$(X - \overline{X})^2$$

Step 4

Sum the squared deviation scores.

$$\Sigma(X - \overline{X})^2$$

Step 5

Divide the sum of the squared deviations by the sample size. This measure, s^2, is the variance.

$$\frac{\Sigma(X - \overline{X})^2}{n}$$

Step 6

Calculate the square root of the variance; the square root of s^2 is s, the standard deviation.

$$\sqrt{\frac{\Sigma(X - \overline{X})^2}{n}}$$

Step-by-Step Calculation of the Variance and Standard Deviation: The Raw Score Formula

The raw score formula is as follows. This formula requires these five steps:

THE FORMULA

Step 1

Square each raw score and sum them.

$$\Sigma X^2$$

Step 2

Divide the summed raw scores by the number of raw scores.

$$\frac{\Sigma X^2}{n}$$

Step 3

Calculate the mean of the raw scores and square it.

$$\left(\frac{\Sigma X}{n}\right)^2 = \overline{X}^2$$

Step 4

Subtract the squared mean from the quotient obtained in Step 2; this yields the variance.

$$\frac{\Sigma X^2}{n} - \overline{X}^2$$

Step 5

The square root of the variance is the standard deviation.

Refer to Table 3-6 on page 33 for the actual calculations.

YOUR TASK

Collect data, and then use descriptive statistics to describe the data you've collected. The data you collect will be the height in inches of each of your classmates. List the names and heights—much as we listed the hypothetical measurement course scores—and then do the following:

1. Create a frequency distribution.
2. Create a grouped frequency distribution.
3. Draw a frequency polygon of the data.
4. Draw a histogram of the data.
5. Draw a two-bar bar graph labeled "65 Inches and Over" and "64 Inches and Under."
6. Calculate the arithmetic mean, the median, and the mode, and comment on which you feel is the best measure of central tendency in this instance.
7. Calculate the range, the interquartile range, and the average deviation.
8. Calculate the standard deviation using the raw score formula.
9. Calculate the standard deviation using the deviation score formula.
10. Discuss which measure of variability best describes the variability in the distribution and why.

EXERCISE 3-4
ACCUMULATING DATA ON A MOCK PERSONALITY INVENTORY

OBJECTIVE

To obtain firsthand experience in administering a (mock) personality test while accumulating test data (that will be manipulated in exercises to come)

BACKGROUND

Have you ever administered a personality test to anyone? The chances are good that at this stage in your career you probably have not—that is, until now. In Appendix A you will find a mock personality test—the Midtown Manhattan Practice Personality Inventory (MMPPI). As part of this exercise, your task is to take on the role of test administrator. After you have administered it, file the test protocol (answer sheet) in a safe place; you will need to refer to it in future exercises.

YOUR TASK

Within the next week, "at your leisure," take a few minutes to administer the MMPPI to someone of college age. As a

TABLE 3-6 *Calculating the Standard Deviation Using Both the Raw Score and Deviation Score Formulas*

X	X^2	$X - \overline{X}$	$(X - \overline{X})^2$	Calculations	
				Deviation Score Formula	Raw Score Formula
96	9216	23.88	570.2544	$\overline{X} - 72.12$	$\overline{X} - 72.12$
94	8836	21.88	478.7344	$\Sigma(X - \overline{X})^2 = 4972.64$	$\overline{X}^2 = (72.12)^2 = 5201.29$
92	8464	19.88	395.2144		
87	7569	14.88	221.4144		
85	7225	12.88	165.8944	$\dfrac{\Sigma(X - \overline{X})^2}{n} = \dfrac{4972.64}{25}$	$\dfrac{\Sigma X^2}{n} = \dfrac{135005}{25} = 5400.2$
84	7056	11.88	141.1344		
83	6889	10.88	118.3744	$= 198.91$	
82	6724	9.88	97.6144		
79	6241	6.88	47.3344		
78	6084	5.88	34.5744	$\sqrt{198.91} = 14.10$	$\dfrac{\Sigma X^2}{n} - \overline{X}^2 = 5400.2 - 5201.29$
76	5776	3.88	15.0544		
73	5329	.88	.7744		$= 198.91$
72	5184	−.12	.0144		$\sqrt{198.91} = 14.1$
69	4761	−3.12	9.7344		
69	4761	−3.12	9.7344		
67	4489	−5.12	26.2144		
67	4489	−5.12	26.2144		
66	4356	−6.12	37.4544		
63	3969	−9.12	83.1744		
62	3844	−10.12	102.4144		
61	3721	−11.12	123.6544		
61	3721	−11.12	123.6544		
51	2601	−21.12	446.0544		
44	1936	−28.12	790.7344		
42	1764	−30.12	907.2144		

class, decide on a way to achieve an approximately even balance between male and female testtakers; as you will see, the same number of testtakers in each group will be desirable for one fact of the upcoming data analysis.

The MMPPI is a *mock* personality test—one that bears only some cosmetic resemblance at best to a real personality inventory. Still, in your capacity as test administrator (and student of psychological measurement), there are three things that you must keep firmly in mind:

1. *Be professional.* Because the test isn't a real test and because responses to it do not really tell anything about the respondent one way or another, the temptation may exist to treat the exercise casually; *refrain from that temptation!* You will defeat the purpose of the exercise if you are joking or otherwise unprofessional in your approach. Remember that while testing and research data collection need not always be a solemn task—it can even be an enjoyable experience—it must never be treated as a joke.

2. *Obtain informed consent prior to testing.* In the present instance, "informed consent" simply means that a disclosure to the testtaker has been made with respect to the nature and purpose of the test as well as the use to which the findings will be put. Note that as part of the sample form for an informed consent to take the MMPPI, it is also noted that the data will be neither confidential nor privileged.

3. *Fully debrief the testtaker at the time the testtaker is given feedback on the testing.* A full debriefing entails a

complete description of the study, a full explanation of any deception that was part of the study, and an honest, straightforward response to any questions the testtaker has regarding the study. The bottom line here is that, at the end of the study, the testtaker should not only feel good about having participated but also might feel that he or she has learned something about the way students learn about testing.

Materials Needed for Administering the MMPPI

The materials you will need for administering the MMPPI are as follows:

1 copy of the test
1 test protocol
2 number 2 pencils

Administration Instructions

The examiner places two number 2 pencils alongside face-up copies of the MMPPI and the MMPPI answer sheet and then says the following:

> Please read the following instructions along with me as they appear on your answer form while I read them aloud. The

MMPPI consists of 100 items, each item to be answered either "True" or "False." While there is no formal time limit, do not take too long thinking about any one item; answer each item quickly with your first response—your first response is your best response. Answer all of the items without skipping any. Remember that there are no right or wrong answers to any of the questions, so please feel free to give your first and uncensored response to each of the questions. Please use a number 2 pencil to blacken each of the answer grids, and make sure that your responses are blackened fully and that erasures are fully erased.

The MMPPI is a test devised for the sole purpose of teaching students about the process of psychological testing. The test has not been shown to reliably or validly indicate anything about anyone's personality. Your responses to this test are neither confidential nor privileged; data from this as well as other tests will be used as part of a class exercise. We would, however, like you to use a code name for the purpose of taking this test; please enter that code name in the appropriate space below.

After testtakers have completed the last item, they are informed that you will be getting back to them sometime before the end of the term with feedback regarding the test. Indeed, you will be getting back to them, but what you tell them . . . well, that's the subject of a future exercise.

THE MIDTOWN MANHATTAN PRACTICE PERSONALITY INVENTORY (MMPPI)

Directions:

The MMPPI consists of 100 items, each item to be answered either "True" or "False." While there is no formal time limit, do not take too long thinking about any one item; answer each item quickly with your first response—your first response is your best response. Answer all of the items without skipping any. Remember that there are no right or wrong answers to any of these questions, so please feel free to give your first and uncensored response to each of the questions. Please use a number 2 pencil to blacken each of the answer grids, and make sure that your responses are blackened fully and that erasures are fully erased.

The MMPPI is a test devised for the sole purpose of teaching students about the process of psychological testing. The test has not been shown to reliably or validly indicate anything about anyone's personality. Your responses to this test are neither confidential nor privileged; data from this as well as other tests will be used as part of a class exercise. We would, however, like you to use a code name for the purpose of taking this test; please enter that code name now:

CODE NAME _____

(continued)

THE MIDTOWN MANHATTAN PRACTICE PERSONALITY INVENTORY (MMPPI) *(continued)*

Directions:

Answer each question either "True" or "False" by blackening the appropriate grid with a number 2 pencil.

1. T | | F | | 26. T | | F | | 51. T | | F | | 76. T | | F | |
2. T | | F | | 27. T | | F | | 52. T | | F | | 77. T | | F | |
3. T | | F | | 28. T | | F | | 53. T | | F | | 78. T | | F | |
4. T | | F | | 29. T | | F | | 54. T | | F | | 79. T | | F | |
5. T | | F | | 30. T | | F | | 55. T | | F | | 80. T | | F | |
6. T | | F | | 31. T | | F | | 56. T | | F | | 81. T | | F | |
7. T | | F | | 32. T | | F | | 57. T | | F | | 82. T | | F | |
8. T | | F | | 33. T | | F | | 58. T | | F | | 83. T | | F | |
9. T | | F | | 34. T | | F | | 59. T | | F | | 84. T | | F | |
10. T | | F | | 35. T | | F | | 60. T | | F | | 85. T | | F | |
11. T | | F | | 36. T | | F | | 61. T | | F | | 86. T | | F | |
12. T | | F | | 37. T | | F | | 62. T | | F | | 87. T | | F | |
13. T | | F | | 38. T | | F | | 63. T | | F | | 88. T | | F | |
14. T | | F | | 39. T | | F | | 64. T | | F | | 89. T | | F | |
15. T | | F | | 40. T | | F | | 65. T | | F | | 90. T | | F | |
16. T | | F | | 41. T | | F | | 66. T | | F | | 91. T | | F | |
17. T | | F | | 42. T | | F | | 67. T | | F | | 92. T | | F | |
18. T | | F | | 43. T | | F | | 68. T | | F | | 93. T | | F | |
19. T | | F | | 44. T | | F | | 69. T | | F | | 94. T | | F | |
20. T | | F | | 45. T | | F | | 70. T | | F | | 95. T | | F | |
21. T | | F | | 46. T | | F | | 71. T | | F | | 96. T | | F | |
22. T | | F | | 47. T | | F | | 72. T | | F | | 97. T | | F | |
23. T | | F | | 48. T | | F | | 73. T | | F | | 98. T | | F | |
24. T | | F | | 49. T | | F | | 74. T | | F | | 99. T | | F | |
25. T | | F | | 50. T | | F | | 75. T | | F | | 100. T | | F | |

(continued)

THE MIDTOWN MANHATTAN PRACTICE PERSONALITY INVENTORY (MMPPI) *(continued)*

Directions:

Answer each question either "True" or "False" by blackening the appropriate grid with a number 2 pencil.

1. T | | F | |	26. T | | F | |	51. T | | F | |	76. T | | F | |
2. T | | F | |	27. T | | F | |	52. T | | F | |	77. T | | F | |
3. T | | F | |	28. T | | F | |	53. T | | F | |	78. T | | F | |
4. T | | F | |	29. T | | F | |	54. T | | F | |	79. T | | F | |
5. T | | F | |	30. T | | F | |	55. T | | F | |	80. T | | F | |
6. T | | F | |	31. T | | F | |	56. T | | F | |	81. T | | F | |
7. T | | F | |	32. T | | F | |	57. T | | F | |	82. T | | F | |
8. T | | F | |	33. T | | F | |	58. T | | F | |	83. T | | F | |
9. T | | F | |	34. T | | F | |	59. T | | F | |	84. T | | F | |
10. T | | F | |	35. T | | F | |	60. T | | F | |	85. T | | F | |
11. T | | F | |	36. T | | F | |	61. T | | F | |	86. T | | F | |
12. T | | F | |	37. T | | F | |	62. T | | F | |	87. T | | F | |
13. T | | F | |	38. T | | F | |	63. T | | F | |	88. T | | F | |
14. T | | F | |	39. T | | F | |	64. T | | F | |	89. T | | F | |
15. T | | F | |	40. T | | F | |	65. T | | F | |	90. T | | F | |
16. T | | F | |	41. T | | F | |	66. T | | F | |	91. T | | F | |
17. T | | F | |	42. T | | F | |	67. T | | F | |	92. T | | F | |
18. T | | F | |	43. T | | F | |	68. T | | F | |	93. T | | F | |
19. T | | F | |	44. T | | F | |	69. T | | F | |	94. T | | F | |
20. T | | F | |	45. T | | F | |	70. T | | F | |	95. T | | F | |
21. T | | F | |	46. T | | F | |	71. T | | F | |	96. T | | F | |
22. T | | F | |	47. T | | F | |	72. T | | F | |	97. T | | F | |
23. T | | F | |	48. T | | F | |	73. T | | F | |	98. T | | F | |
24. T | | F | |	49. T | | F | |	74. T | | F | |	99. T | | F | |
25. T | | F | |	50. T | | F | |	75. T | | F | |	100. T | | F | |

EXERCISE 3-5
FIGURE THIS

OBJECTIVE

Obtain firsthand computational experience figuring out problems related to material presented in the chapter.

BACKGROUND

Use your knowledge of material presented in Chapter 3 in your textbook to tackle *Your Task* in what follows.

YOUR TASK

1. Professor Filtch administered the final exam to his class of 20 students. Their scores are as follows: 89, 76, 90, 91, 82, 68, 95, 88, 90, 77, 80, 85, 80, 84, 80, 55, 50, 59, 69, 70. For these exam scores find the following:
   a. Mean
   b. Median
   c. Mode
   d. Range
   e. Standard deviation
   f. Variance
2. For Professor Filtch's class scores, construct a grouped frequency distribution with 10 point intervals.
3. Convert the first 5 students' exam scores into z scores.
4. Convert the last 5 students' exam scores into T scores.
5. Professor Filtch's exam includes 20 questions, each worth 1 point. What type of measurement scale is represented? Explain.
6. Identify the quartile scores for final exam scores for the professor's class.

THE 4-QUESTION CHALLENGE

1. Measurement using continuous scales
   a. always involves error.
   b. is always ordinal in nature.
   c. is always normally distributed.
   d. all of the above

2. The term *class intervals* is best associated with
   a. socioeconomic status of a sample of testtakers.
   b. a frequency distribution of testtaker scores.
   c. a grouped frequency distribution of testtakers' scores.
   d. measures of central tendency and variability.

3. Equal to the square root of the averaged squared deviations about the mean, this statistic is called
   a. the range.
   b. the standard deviation.
   c. the average deviation.
   d. the semi-interquartile range.

4. The normal curve
   a. is bell-shaped.
   b. has no skewness.
   c. has a median and mode of the same value.
   d. all of the above

CHAPTER 4

Of Tests and Testing

Instructions Identify what is described, answer a question, or fill in the blank to complete this crossword puzzle based on material presented in Chapter 4 of your textbook.

Across

1. The analysis of relationships among variables for the purpose of understanding how one variable may predict another.

4. We speak of descriptive statistics based on a group of testtakers in a given period of time rather than norms obtained by formal sampling methods. In other words, we speak of _____ norms.

7. In regression, it's an estimate of the magnitude of error. It's the standard error of the _____ .

8. Norms specifically designed for use as a reference in the context of the age of the testtaker who achieved a particular score are known, logically enough, as _____ norms.

11. Normative information with regard to some limited population frequently of specific interest to the test user is referred to as _____ norms.

13. Equivalency tables for scores on nationally standardized tests designed to measure the same thing are referred to as national _____ norms.

16. An expression of the percentage of people whose score on a test or measure falls below a particular raw score. It also may be defined as a converted score that refers to a percentage of testtakers.

19. An expression of the degree and direction of correspondence between two things when each thing is continuous in nature.

22. In contrast to the process described in 19-Down, _____-referenced testing and assessment is a method of evaluation and a way of deriving meaning from test scores by evaluating an individual testtaker's score and comparing it to scores of a group of testtakers. In other words, test scores are understood relative to other test scores on the same test.

25. It's the process of arbitrarily selecting some people to be part of a sample because these people are readily available and not necessarily because they are most representative of the population being studied. Here we speak of _____ sampling.

26. In contrast to the process described in the previous item (25-Across), this is a process of selecting some people to be part of a sample because it is believed those people are representative of the population being studied. Now we are speaking of _____ sampling.

27. It's a system of scoring wherein the distribution of scores obtained on the test from one group of testtakers is used as the basis for the calculation of test scores for future administrations. The SAT and the GRE are examples of tests that are scored by means of a(n) _____ reference group scoring system.

28. The analysis of relationships between more than one independent variable and one dependent variable for the purpose of understanding how each independent variable may predict the dependent variable is a process called _____ regression.

29. Descriptive statistics based on a group of testtakers in a given period of time rather than on norms obtained by formal sampling methods are known as _____ norms. By the way, this term is different from but synonymous with the term described in 4-Across.

30. The process of developing a sample based on specific subgroups of a population is referred to as _____ sampling.

Down

1. Developed by Spearman, it goes by various names, including the rank-order correlation coefficient and the rank-difference correlation coefficient. This index of correlation may be the statistic of choice when the sample size is small and both sets of measurements are ordinal in nature.

2. A group of people presumed to be representative of the total population or universe of people being studied or tested.

3. Norms derived from a standardization sample that was nationally representative of the population may be referred to as _____ norms.

4. The last name that modified the oft-used product-moment correlation measure.

5. A straightforward, unmodified accounting of performance, usually numerical in nature and typically used for evaluative or diagnostic purposes, may be referred to as a(n) _____ score.

6. It's both a research tool and the name of the result of combined statistical information across various studies. It's called a(n) _____-analysis.

9. Norms specifically designed for use as a reference in the context of the grade of the testtaker who achieved a particular score are called _____ norms.

10. The analysis of the relationship between one independent variable and one dependent variable is referred to as _____ regression.

12. An extremely atypical plot point in a scatterplot, much like an extremely atypical finding in research.

14. _____ is the process of test development whereby a test is administered to a representative sample of testtakers under clearly specified conditions, and the data are scored and interpreted so that a context for future test administrations with other testtakers is established.

15. _____ is the process of deriving or creating norms.

17. A(n) _____ score may be thought of as a reference point, usually numerical, derived as a result of judgment, that is used to divide a set of data into two or more classifications, with some action to be taken or some inference to be made on the basis of these classifications.

18. Norms for any defined group within a larger group may be referred to as _____ norms.

19. _____-referenced testing and assessment is a method of evaluation and a way of deriving meaning from test scores by evaluating an individual's score with reference to a set standard (or criterion).

20. A(n) _____ sample is an arbitrarily selected group of people who serve as a sample in a research study primarily because they are readily available, not necessarily because they are most representative of the population being studied.

21. A value indicative of how much variance is shared by two variables being calculated is called a coefficient of _____ .

22. Also referred to as a *norm group,* it's a group of people presumed to be representative of the universe of people who may take a test, whose performance data on a test may be used as a reference source or context for evaluating individual scores. In other words, it's a(n) _____ sample.

23. The controversial practice of norming on the basis of race or ethnic background is known as _____-norming.

24. A graphic description of correlation achieved by graphing the coordinate points of the two variables.

EXERCISE 4-1
MOVIES AND MEASUREMENT

Will this man become a wolf when the moon is full?

OBJECTIVE

To learn more about the concept of correlation, especially as it relates to the full moon and "lunatic" behavior

BACKGROUND

In *Wolf,* Jack Nicholson transforms into a werewolf when the moon is full. In fact, many published studies have noted an association between a full lunar presence and strange, if not "lunatic," behavior.

YOUR TASK

Write a brief essay entitled, "The Correlation Between the Presence of the Full Moon and So-Called Lunatic Behavior." The essay should be based on your own independent research regarding myths and legends (such as the legend of the werewolf) as well as published scientific studies on the topic (such as the work of Rotton and Kelley, 1985). Conclude your essay by stating your opinion as to whether a correlation really exists between the presence of the full moon and lunatic behavior.

EXERCISE 4-2
TRANSFORMED SCORES: PERCENTILES

OBJECTIVE

To enhance understanding of and provide firsthand experience with transformed scores and, in particular, percentile scores

BACKGROUND

Harold Seashore's brief article, "Methods of Expressing Test Scores," provides a succinct review and elaboration of some of the material contained in your textbook. It will be helpful to read it before proceeding to the material on percentile scores that follows.

METHODS OF EXPRESSING TEST SCORES

Harold G. Seashore

An individual's test score acquires meaning when it can be compared with the scores of well-identified groups of people. Manuals for tests provide tables of norms to make it easy to compare individuals and groups. Several systems for deriving more meaningful "standard scores" from raw scores have been widely adopted. All of them reveal the relative status of individuals within a group.

The fundamental equivalence of the most popular standard score systems is illustrated in the chart on the next page. We hope the chart and the accompanying description will be useful to counselors, personnel officers, clinical diagnosticians, and others in helping them to show the uninitiated the essential simplicity of standard score systems, percentile equivalents, and their relation to the ideal normal distribution.

Sooner or later, every textbook discussion of test scores introduces the bell-shaped normal curve. The student of testing soon learns that many of the methods of deriving meaningful scores are anchored to the dimensions and characteristics of this curve. And he or she learns by observation of actual test score distributions that the ideal mathematical curve is a reasonably good approximation of many practical cases. He or she learns to use the standardized properties of the ideal curve as a model.

Let us look first at the curve itself. Notice that there are no raw scores printed along the baseline. The graph is generalized; it describes an idealized distribution of scores of any group on any test. We are free to use any numerical scale we like. For any particular set of scores, we can be arbitrary and call the average score zero. In technical terms we "equate" the mean raw score to zero. Similarly we can choose any convenient number, say 1.00, to represent the scale distance of one standard deviation.[1] Thus, if a distribution of scores on a particular test has a mean of 36 and a standard deviation of 4, the zero point on the baseline of our curve would be equivalent to a raw score of 36; one unit to the right, $+1\sigma$, would be equivalent to 40, $(36 + 4)$; and one unit to the left, -1σ, would be equivalent to 32, $(36 - 4)$.

---

[1]The mathematical symbol for the standard deviation is the lowercase Greek letter sigma, or σ. These terms are used interchangeably in this article.

The Normal Curve, Percentiles, and Selected Standard Scores

Percent of cases under portions of the normal curve: 0.13% | 2.14% | 13.59% | 34.13% | 34.13% | 13.59% | 2.14% | 0.13%

| Standard Deviations | -4σ | -3σ | -2σ | -1σ | 0 | $+1\sigma$ | $+2\sigma$ | $+3\sigma$ | $+4\sigma$ |

Cumulative percentages rounded: 0.1% | 2.3% (2%) | 15.9% (16%) | 50.0% (50%) | 84.1% (84%) | 97.7% (98%) | 99.9%

Percentile Equivalents: 1 | 5 | 10 | 20 30 40 50 60 70 80 | 90 | 95 | 99
Q₁ | Md | Q₃

z-scores	−4.0	−3.0	−2.0	−1.0	0	+1.0	+2.0	+3.0	+4.0
T-scores		20	30	40	50	60	70	80	
CEEB Scores		200	300	400	500	600	700	800	
NCE Scores		1	10	20 30	40	50	60	70	80	90	99

Stanines: 1 | 2 | 3 | 4 | 5 | 6 | 7 | 8 | 9
Percent in stanine: 4% | 7% | 12% | 17% | 20% | 17% | 12% | 7% | 4%

Wechsler Scales Subtests		1	4	7	10	13	16	19	
Deviation IQ σ 15		55	70	85	100	115	130	145	
Otis-Lennon σ 16		52	68	84	100	116	132	148	

The total area under the curve represents the total number of scores in the distribution. Vertical lines have been drawn through the score scale (the baseline) at zero and at 1, 2, 3, and 4 sigma units to the right and left. These lines mark off subareas of the total area under the curve. The numbers printed in these subareas are percents—*percentages of the total number of people.* Thus, 34.13 percent of all cases in a normal distribution have scores falling between 0 and −1σ. For practical purposes we rarely need to deal with standard deviation units below −3 or above +3; the percentage of cases with scores beyond ±3σ is negligible.

The fact that 68.26 percent fall between ±1σ gives rise to the common statement that in a normal distribution roughly two-thirds of all cases lie between plus and minus one sigma. This is a rule of thumb every test user should keep in mind. It is very near to the theoretical value and is a useful approximation.

Below the row of deviations expressed in sigma units is a row of percents; these show *cumulatively* the percentage of people that is included *to the left* of each of the sigma points. Thus, starting from the left, when we reach the line erected above −2σ, we have included the lowest 2.3 percent of cases. These percentages have been rounded in the next row.

Note some other relationships: The area between the ±1σ points includes the scores that lie above the 16th percentile (−1σ) and below the 84th percentile (+1σ)—two major reference points all test users should know. When we find that an individual has a score 1σ above the mean, we conclude that his score ranks at the 84th percentile in the group of persons on whom the test was normed. (This conclusion is good provided we also add this clause, at least subvocally: *if this particular group reasonably approximates the ideal normal model.*)

The simplest facts to memorize about the normal distribution and the relation of the *percentile* system to deviations from the average in sigma units are seen in the chart. They are:

Deviation from the mean	−2σ	−1σ	0	+1σ	+2σ
Percentile equivalent	2	16	50	84	98

To avoid cluttering, the graph reference lines have not been drawn, but we could mark off ten-percent sections of area under the normal curve by drawing lines vertically from the indicated decile points (10, 20, . . . , 80, 90) up through the graph. The reader might do this lightly with a colored pencil.

We can readily see that ten percent of the area (people) at the middle of the distribution embraces a smaller *distance* on the baseline of the curve than ten percent of the area (people) at the ends of the range of scores, for the simple reason that the curve is much higher at the middle. A person who is at the 95th percentile is farther away from a person at the 85th percentile in units of *test score* than a person at the 55th percentile is from one at the 45th percentile.

The remainder of the chart, that is, the several scoring scales drawn parallel to the baseline, illustrates variations of the *deviation score* principle. As a class these are called *standard scores.*

First, there are the *z scores.* These are the same *numbers* as shown on the baseline of the graph; the only difference is that the expression σ has been omitted. These scores run, in practical terms, from −3.0 to +3.0. One can compute them to more decimal places if one wishes, although computing to a single decimal place is usually sufficient. One can compute z scores by equating the mean to 0.00 and the standard deviation to 1.00 for a distribution of any shape, but the relationships shown in this figure between the z score equivalents of raw scores and percentile equivalents of raw scores are correct only for normal distributions. The interpretation of standard score systems derives from the idea of using the normal curve as a model.

As can be seen, *T* scores are directly related to z scores. The mean of the raw scores is equated to 50, and the standard deviation of the raw scores is equated to 10. Thus a z score of +1.5 means the same as a *T* score of 65. *T* scores are usually expressed in whole numbers from about 20 to 80. The *T* score plan eliminates negative numbers and thus facilitates many computations.

The College Entrance Examination Board uses a plan in which both decimals and negative numbers are avoided by setting the arbitrary mean at 500 points and the arbitrary sigma at another convenient unit, namely, 100 points. The experienced tester or counselor who hears of a College Board SAT-V score of 550 at once thinks, "Half a sigma (50 points) above average (500 points) on the CEEB basic norms." And when he hears of a score of 725 on SAT-N, he can interpret, "Plus 2¼σ. Therefore, better than the 98th percentile."

Yet another standard score is the recently developed Normal Curve Equivalent, or NCE. This score, used primarily for reporting in federally funded programs such as Title I, has a mean of 50 and a standard deviation of 21.06. Note that this choice of mean and standard deviation will yield a range of scores from about 1 to 99. Note also that the *T* scores, percentile ranks, and NCEs all have 50 as the mean reference point, a possible source of confusion to those who do not insist on careful labeling of data and of scores of individuals in their records.

Another derivative of the general standard score system is the *stanine* plan, developed by psychologists in the Air Force during the war. The plan divides the norm population into nine groups, hence "standard nines." Except for stanine 9, the top, and stanine 1, the bottom, these groups are spaced in half-sigma units. Thus, stanine 5 is defined as including the people who are within ±0.25σ of the mean. Stanine 6 is the group defined by the half-sigma distance on the baseline between +0.25σ and +0.75σ. Stanines 1 and 9 include all persons who are below −1.75σ and above +1.75σ, respectively. The result is a distribution in which the mean is 5.0 and the standard deviation is 2.0.

Just below the line showing the demarcation of the nine groups in the stanine system, there is a row of percentages that indicates the percent of the total population in each of the stanines. Thus 7 percent of the population will be in stanine 2 and 20 percent in the middle group, stanine 5.

Interpretation of the Wechsler scales depends on a knowledge of standard scores. A subject's raw score *on each of the subtests* in these scales is converted, by appropriate norms tables, to a standard score, based on a mean of 10 and a standard deviation of 3. The sums of standard scores on the Verbal Scale, the Performance Scale, and the Full Scale are then converted into IQs. These IQs are based on a standard score mean of 100, the conventional number for representing the IQ of the average person in a given age group. The standard deviation of the IQs is set at 15 points. In practical terms, then, roughly two-thirds of the IQs are between 85 and 115, that is, ±1σ. IQs of the type used in the Wechsler scales have come to be known as *deviation IQs,* as contrasted with the IQ developed from scales in which a derived mental age is divided by chronological age.

Users of the Wechsler scales should establish clearly in their minds the relationship of subtest scaled scores and the deviation IQs to the other standard score systems, to the ordinary percentile rank interpretation, and to the deviation units on the baseline of the normal curve. For example, every Wechsler examiner should recognize that an IQ of 130 is a score equivalent to a deviation of $+2\sigma$, and that this IQ score delimits approximately the upper two percent of the population. If a clinician wants to evaluate a Wechsler IQ of 85 along with percentile ranks on several other tests given in school, he can mentally convert the IQ of 85 to a percentile rank of about 16, this being the percentile equal to a deviation from the mean of -1σ. Of course he should also consider the appropriateness and comparability of norms. It should also be noted here that many ability tests, especially group-administered paper-and-pencil tests such as the *Otis-Lennon School Ability Test* use a standard deviation of 16, rather than 15, in computing their standard score indices.

Efficiency in interpreting test scores in counseling, in clinical diagnosis, and in personnel selection depends, in part, on facility in thinking in terms of the major interrelated plans by which meaningful scores are derived from raw scores. It is hoped that this graphic presentation will be helpful to all who in their daily work must help others understand the information conveyed by numerical test scores.

While Seashore's article provides a brief overview of transformed scores in general, in this as well as succeeding exercises we will be focusing on specific transformed scores—beginning here with *percentiles.* As typically employed in the field of psychological testing, a percentile may be defined as a raw score that has been converted into an expression of the percentage of testtakers whose score falls below a particular raw score. Percentile scores are widely used in the manuals of—as well as other literature on—commercially published standardized tests. It is therefore incumbent upon the student of psychological testing to understand how they are used (as well as how they are *not* used).

Raw scores may be converted to percentiles through the use of the following formula:

$$P = n_L/N \times 100$$

where P = percentile, n_L = the number of scores lower than the score being converted to a percentile, and N = the total number of scores.

For practice with this formula, let's refer back to the distribution of the measurement class test scores that appeared in Table 3-1 (page 26) and focus on Valerie's raw score of 85. The conversion of that raw score to a percentile would proceed as follows:

Step 1

Insert the value of n_L into the equation.

$$P = \frac{20}{N} \times 100$$

The value of n_L is found by simply counting the number of scores that were lower than Valerie's. In this case, $n_L = 20$.

Step 2

Insert the value of N into the equation.

$$P = \frac{20}{25} \times 100$$

In this example, N is equal to 25 because there were a total of 25 scores.

Step 3

Solve for P.

$$P = 0.80 \times 100 = 80$$

The numerator (20) divided by the denominator (25) is equal to 0.80. The product of 0.80 multiplied by 100 is 80. We now know that Valerie's score falls at the 80th percentile.

YOUR TASK

1. Select any five other students from the distribution of test scores in Table 3-1 and convert their raw scores to percentiles.

2. Test your ability to make proper interpretations from percentile scores by circling either T for True or F for False for each of the 10 statements on pages 44 and 45. Because this test is provided as a learning experience for you—and not as an aid to your instructor's evaluation of you—make it a learning experience by jotting down any questions or comments that arise as you think about which answer is correct. Be sure to raise your questions or comments in class.

EXERCISE 4-3

STANDARD, STANDARDIZED, AND NORMALIZED STANDARD SCORES

OBJECTIVE

To enhance understanding of, as well as provide firsthand experience with, standard scores

BACKGROUND

As generally used in the field of psychological testing, the term *standard score* refers to a raw score that has been converted from one scale into another scale—the latter typically being one that is more widely used and interpretable—that has some arbitrarily set mean and standard deviation. A *z*

THE INTERPRETING PERCENTILE SCORES TEST[2]

ANSWER	ITEM	QUESTIONS/COMMENTS
T F	1. Tim is a sixth-grader. He obtains a percentile score of 70 in reading on a published standardized test. This means that Tim got 70 percent of the items correct.	
T F	2. Mary gets a raw score (not a percentile score) of 70 correct on reading. She is in Tim's sixth-grade class. This score and Tim's percentile score of 70 indicate that Mary and Tim both are good readers.	
T F	3. Susie, a third-grade student, scores at the 30th percentile in arithmetic at the end of the school year. Scores this low are regarded as failing, and therefore Susie should be retained for another year in arithmetic instruction so that she will not be handicapped in the future.	
T F	4. Bill receives a percentile score of 90 at the beginning of the year and moves up to a percentile score of 99 by the end of the year. Jim, similarly, moves from the 50th percentile to the 59th. They make about equal progress.	
T F	5. There is little difference between Sally's score of the 98th percentile and Jeanne's score of the 99.9th percentile, but there is a large difference between Rebecca's 84th percentile and Sally's 98th percentile.	
T F	6. Mrs. Henderson is the new principal at Hartford Elementary. She sets as her goal getting every pupil up to the 50th percentile within four years of her arrival at Hartford Elementary. With diligent effort and full cooperation from the staff and administration, this is a reasonable goal for most modern schools.	
T F	7. Mrs. Henderson wants to evaluate the standing of each grade in Hartford Elementary by comparing Hartford students' achievement with the average achievement in a representative sample of elementary schools in the nation. She obtains the percentile scores for each second-grade pupil in reading and averages them. The average of these percentiles is the percentile rank for her school's second-graders.	

[2]John R. Hills, "Interpreting Percentile Scores," From *Hills' Handy Hints*. Reprinted by permission of the publisher, National Council on Measurement in Education, Washington, D.C.

ANSWER		ITEM	QUESTIONS/COMMENTS
T	F	8. Mr. Brown learns that Mrs. Henderson wants to compare the performance of each grade in Hartford with other schools. He is correct in claiming that unless the test publisher provides norms on school means, comparisons of Hartford means with the mean performances in other schools cannot be made.	
T	F	9. Rebecca scores at the 84th percentile on the reading test, while Helmut scores only at the 75th percentile. Clearly Rebecca is a better reader than Helmut.	
T	F	10. Miss Spolano is the school counselor at Hartford. She claims that scores on the reading test should not be reported as percentiles but as percentile bands. However, the percentile bands are so wide for Gretchen, from the 37th percentile to the 58th percentile, that only by getting the percentile score itself do you have an accurate measure of how well Gretchen reads.	

score, for example, is a raw score that has been transformed to a scale that has a mean set at 0 and a standard deviation set at 1. To illustrate this, consider the following example. Todd, a senior at a prestigious university, earned a score of 90 on a test of Greek literature, a score of 62 on a test in chemical engineering, and a score of 50 on a test of floral arrangement. With that information—the raw scores—alone, what can you say about Todd's performance on these tests? The answer here is that you can't say very much. Oh, you might suspect that Todd was a Renaissance man with quite varied academic and artistic interests—either that or someone who is vocationally unfocused and in need of counseling. But without knowing more information about where these raw scores place Todd's performance within the total distribution of raw scores for each of these tests, it would be impossible to draw any meaningful conclusions regarding his relative performance in each of these areas.

Suppose that the scores for all three of the tests were approximately normally distributed and that (1) the distribution of the Greek literature scores had a mean of 100 and a standard deviation of 10, (2) the distribution of chemical engineering test scores had a mean of 50 and a standard deviation of 12, and (3) the distribution of floral arrangement test scores had a mean of 50 and a standard deviation of 15. Now, what statements can be made regarding Todd's relative performance on each of these three tests?

Todd did best on the chemical engineering test; his raw score of 62 falls at a point one standard deviation above the mean. Todd's next best score was on the floral arrangement test; his raw score of 50 falls exactly at the mean of the distribution of scores. And finally there is Todd's performance

on the Greek literature test; his raw score of 90 falls at a point one standard deviation below the mean. Converting Todd's raw scores to a scale that has a mean of 0 and a standard deviation of 1—that is, converting Todd's raw scores to z scores—we can say that Todd achieved a z score of +1 on the chemical engineering test, a z score of 0 on the floral arrangement test, and a z score of −1 on the Greek literature test. The general formula used to transform raw scores into z scores entails subtracting the mean from the raw score and dividing by the standard deviation. The general formula is as follows:

$$z = \frac{X - \overline{X}}{s}$$

where z is the value of the obtained standard score,
X is the value of the raw score to be transformed,
$\overline{X}$ is the value of the mean of the distribution of raw scores, and
s is the value of the raw score distribution standard deviation.

Now let's use this formula to convert Todd's raw score of 62 on the chemical engineering test to a z score (just to make sure that a raw score that lies exactly one standard deviation above the mean does indeed transform to a z score of +1):

$$z = \frac{X - \overline{X}}{s} = \frac{62 - 50}{12} = 1$$

Standard scores may be used to compare performance of different testtakers on different tests. Suppose we wanted to know if Todd's score on his Greek literature test was better than Mousey's score on his measurement examination.

You will recall that Mousey earned a raw score of 42 on the test, and that the mean and standard deviation of the test were respectively 72.12 and 14.10. Using the general formula (above) and presuming for the purpose of this illustration that the scores on this test were distributed normally, let's now convert Mousey's raw score of 42 to a standard score:

$$z = \frac{X - \overline{X}}{s} = \frac{42 - 72.12}{14.10} = -2.136$$

Having calculated a value of z that is greater than -2, it can be seen that Mousey's score on the examination fell more than two standard deviations below the mean. We can therefore say Todd's performance on his Greek literature test was superior to that of Mousey on the measurement examination.

While z scores are relatively simple to use, they are not without computational disadvantages. Because a z score can be equal to 0 or can be negative, certain types of data manipulations with them become awkward. It is also a fact of life that many testtakers (as well as parents of testtakers) bristle at hearing their test scores reported as negative numbers. How would you feel if you were told that your score on your last measurement examination was -2.136? For these reasons (as well as others), alternative standard score systems have been developed to linearly transform z scores (as well as raw scores) to a scale that does not contain negative numbers. Such systems are all "standard" to the extent that both the mean and the standard deviation of the new scale have been arbitrarily set. The general formula for linearly converting a z score to a new standardized score (NSS) may be expressed as follows:

$$NSS = ASD(z) + AM$$

where NSS is the new standardized score,
ASD is the value of the arbitrarily set standard deviation,
z is the value of the standard score to be transformed, and
AM is the value of the arbitrarily set mean.

As an example, let's convert a z score of 1 to a "new" score on a "new" scale. Let's set the new scale to have a mean of 50 and a standard deviation of 10. And let's christen all scores derived on this scale as T scores—this out of respect and esteem for psychologist E. L. Thorndike. Using the formula presented above, the "New Standardized Score" (NSS) or "T" score equivalent of a z score of 1 could be calculated as follows:

$$NSS = ASD(z) + ASM$$
$$T = 10(1) + 50$$
$$T = 60$$

By the way, W. A. McCall beat us to the development of T scores by 70 or so years—right down to naming the scale after Professor Thorndike. But take heart; there are many new scales just waiting to be created. Use the formula above to convert a z score of 1 to a new scale—call this new scale

any name you wish—that has a mean set of 1,000 and a standard deviation set at 300. What is the value of a z score of 1 on this scale? the value of a z score of -1? the value of a z score of -2.136? What is the z score equivalent of a score of 1600 on this new scale?

The general formula used to linearly convert a raw score to a new standardized score may be expressed as follows:

$$NSS = ASD\left(\frac{X - \overline{X}}{SD_x}\right) + ASM$$

where NSS is the value of the new standardized score,
ASD is the value of the arbitrarily set standard deviation,
X is the value of the raw score to be converted,
$\overline{X}$ is the value of the mean of the raw scores,
SD_x is the value of the standard deviation of the raw scores, and
ASM is the arbitrarily set mean.

Suppose we wanted to convert Mousey's raw score of 42 (from the class examination data distribution that had a mean of 72.12 and a standard deviation of 14.10) to a new standardized score that had a mean of 1,000 and a standard deviation of 300. Using the formula above, and presuming again that the class examination data were approximately normal in their distribution, the calculation of the new standard score would proceed as follows:

$$NSS = ASD\left(\frac{X - \overline{X}}{SD_x}\right) + ASM$$
$$NSS = 300\left(\frac{42 - 72.12}{14.10}\right) + 1,000$$
$$NSS = 300\left(\frac{-30.12}{14.10}\right) + 1,000$$
$$NSS = 300(-2.136) + 1,000$$
$$NSS = -640.851 + 1,000$$
$$NSS = 359.149$$

Mousey's raw score of 42 converted to the new standardized score is 359.149.

Some of the terms used by clinicians, researchers, test manual and book authors have not been entirely consistent—or standard—with respect to systems of standard scoring. Thus, for example, some test manuals and books reserve the term *standard score* only for use with reference to z scores; raw scores (as well as z scores) linearly transformed to any other type of "standard" scoring systems—that is, transformed to a scale with an arbitrarily set mean and standard deviation—are differentiated from z scores by the term *standardized*. Thus, while a z score would be referred to as a "standard score," a T score would be referred to as a "standardized score." Another point of terminology (and potential source of confusion) that you should be aware of concerns the term *normalized standard score* (also sometimes referred to simply as a "normalized score"). An explanation follows with reference to Figure 4-1.

FIGURE 4-1 *The Normal Curve and Some Transformed Score Equivalents*

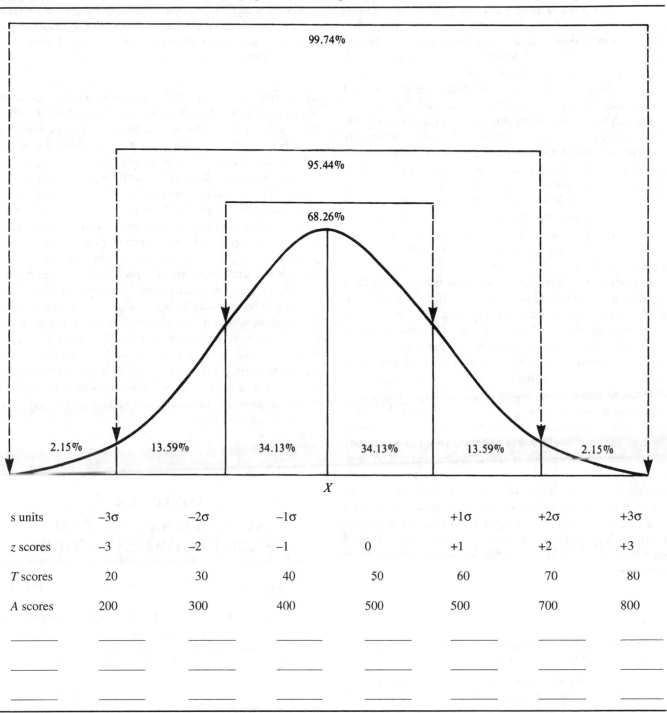

s units	-3σ	-2σ	-1σ		$+1\sigma$	$+2\sigma$	$+3\sigma$
z scores	-3	-2	-1	0	$+1$	$+2$	$+3$
T scores	20	30	40	50	60	70	80
A scores	200	300	400	500	500	700	800

The normal curve is, for all intents and purposes, a theoretical abstraction; although it exists in theory, one would be hard put to find "real-world" test (or any other) data that were distributed in a perfectly normal fashion. Although many such "real-world" distributions of data—particularly those containing very large numbers of observations—may come close to being normally distributed, none is a truly normal frequency distribution; one requirement in this regard would be that the tails of the curve never touch the baseline but only approach it as they trail off into infinity in either direction. When data are said to be normally distributed, what is really meant, in most (if not all) cases, is that the data are *approximately* normally distributed. The concept of a normal curve, even if it is only a theoretical abstraction, is very useful; the normal frequency distribution is a well-known entity from which data can be easily interpreted, compared, and manipulated. And if test users have data that are not distributed normally, it may well be to their advantage to use statistical procedures to transform the data into a normal form—to "normalize" the data.

Assume for the moment that a test user has a distribution of test scores (on a variable we'll call V) that is not distributed normally. And assume further that the test user has good reason to believe that V is actually normally distributed in the population and that the present (non-normal) distribution was only an artifact of something such as poor sampling or a poor instrument of measurement. Provided some other technical assumptions are met, the test user may wish to use statistical procedures to "normalize" the distribution of data. Conceptually, such normalization may involve the stretching and pulling of a skewed curve to approximate the shape of a normal curve. A *normalized standard score scale* is a scale of standard scores that corresponds to a distribution of observations that has been "molded" to approximate the normal curve. If this scale has a mean arbitrarily set at 50 and a standard deviation arbitrarily set at 10, a given score on this scale might be referred to as a T score.

In practice, test manual and book authors as well as others have been somewhat casual in their labeling of various standard scoring systems. The best way for a test user to determine, for example, if a T score referenced in a test manual is a normalized standard score or simply a standardized score, is to look for reference to this point in the manual itself (or, if such references are lacking, contact the test publisher).

One last point about "stretching," "pulling," and "molding" data to approximate a normal distribution. You may know from personal experience that when you've had to stretch, pull, or in other ways attempt to mold your body into a garment, say a pair of jeans, the jeans didn't fit, feel, or wear the same as when you didn't have to go to such heroics to get into them. There's an analogy there somewhere with respect to test data; technical problems may arise as a function of your fashioning of a normal distribution. For example, highly skewed data "forced" into a normal shape may yield distorted images of the distances between certain raw scores.

YOUR TASK

1. Approximately what percentage of the test scores were higher than Mousey's? Lower?

2. Approximately what score would Mousey's raw score be equal to as a T score? As an A score?

3. Select five other scores from the class examination data, convert them to z scores, indicate where they fall on the graph (by drawing them in similar to the way we've drawn in Mousey's score on Figure 4-1), and answer Questions 1 and 2 above with respect to each of these five scores.

4. Explain the differences between each of the following three terms as they have been used in the measurement literature:
   a. standard score
   b. standardized score
   c. normalized standard score

5. Devise and give a name to three new standardized scoring systems and fill in the blank spaces in Figure 4-1 for each of them. Next, determine what Mousey's measurement examination test score would be in terms of these new standardized scores.

Frequency distributions of data may vary widely; some, for example, give a lopsided appearance, with the majority of cases piled up to the left or right of center. Other distributions of data vary in appearance, from being as peaked as a triangle to being as flat as a rectangle. But amidst the peaks, valleys, and plateaus of the graphs of other frequency distributions stands the bell-shaped normal frequency distribution or normal curve—a distribution that can be defined precisely mathematically (Hays, 1973) and a standard by which to compare other frequency distributions. The measurement of many human physical and psychological characteristics yields frequency distributions that approximate the normal frequency distribution; this is especially true when highly reliable and valid measuring tools are employed with large samples. When test data do not yield a normal frequency distribution, the test user may attempt—provided certain technical assumptions permit—to statistically transform the data to fit the normal curve. Because so much is known about the normal frequency distribution, data in this form tend to be easier to interpret. In Figure 4-1 there are some standard and standardized score equivalents for various points along the normal curve (the blank spaces are there for you to insert values for your own standardized scoring systems).

EXERCISE 4-4
STANINES, SAT/ACT, AND GRADE-EQUIVALENT SCORES

OBJECTIVE

To enhance understanding of and sharpen interpretation skills with respect to converted scores such as stanines and SAT/ACT scores as well as scores expressed as grade-equivalents

BACKGROUND

Researchers during World War II developed a standardized score with a mean of five and a standard deviation of approximately two. Divided into nine units, this "standard nine" scale was referred to as a *stanine*. Today, stanines are employed, among other settings, in many school systems for recording data into students' permanent records. And while we're on the subject of data in student records, data from standardized educational tests are often recorded in converted scores called grade-equivalents, and data from college entrance examinations such as those administered by American College Testing (ACT) and Educational Testing Service—including the Scholastic Aptitude Test (SAT)—are recorded in standardized scores called *A* scores.

Following is a brief article prepared by The Psychological Corporation explaining what stanines are and how they are used and including a ten-item true/false test on stanines.

STANINES AND THEIR COMPUTATION FOR LOCAL USE

The interpretation of test results for purposes of comparison and evaluation is an important feature of the educative process. In order that this may be effectively done, it is necessary to transform the raw scores obtained through testing into some kind of derived scores. There are various methods of doing this, of which the three most commonly used are conversions to percentile ranks, grade equivalents, and stanines. This latter method was first used extensively by the military during World War II as a system for transforming masses of test data into one simple and workable form. The stanine scale (short for STAndard-NINE scale) transforms data into values ranging from 1 to 9, and thus makes possible the translation of various kinds of information into one-digit scores, comparable in form and easily added to develop composite scores.

The advantages of this simple nine-point scale are equally valid in the field of education, and stanines have now come into widespread use as a means of interpreting individual raw scores on many types of tests. Stanine groupings are coarse enough to prevent overinterpretation of small differences, yet they differentiate sufficiently for most practical purposes.

The Nature of the Stanine Scale

Like other commonly used statistical means of expressing scores, the stanine scale is dependent on the assumption that the measured trait is distributed normally in the general population, so that a graphic representation of that distribution would closely approximate the so-called bell-shaped curve. In a normal raw-score distribution, the greatest number of cases are concentrated near the middle while the remaining cases are distributed symmetrically on either side, decreasing as the distance from the center becomes greater. It follows that, within the limits imposed by a particular raw-score distribution, transformed stanine scores can be expected to conform to the proportions of this normal curve with a fixed percent of cases (rounded) falling within each of the nine stanine classifications. This is illustrated in Figure 1.

In this scale, raw scores are converted to scores ranging from 1 (low) to 9 (high) with a mean of 5 and a standard deviation (S.D.) of 2.[3] Each stanine (except 1 and 9) is ½ S.D.

Figure 1 Stanines and the Normal Curve

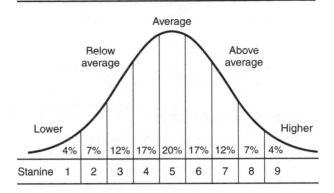

in width, the middle stanine of 5 extending from ¼ S.D. below to ¼ S.D. above the mean. As may be noted in Figure 1, the normal (bell-shaped) curve never quite touches the baseline, since extreme scores in stanines 1 and 9 extend considerably beyond ½ S.D. The top of stanine 8, in terms of distance from the mean, is +1¾ S.D. and marks off approximately 46 percent of the 50 percent of cases above the mean. Stanine 9, then, includes all the remaining cases (roughly the top 4 percent) no matter how far from the mean they may extend. Similarly, stanine 1 extends downward indefinitely from 1¾ S.D. below the mean.

Stanines can be described quantitatively as follows:

9 Very superior
8 Superior
7 Considerably above average
6 Slightly above average
5 Just average
4 Slightly below average
3 Considerably below average
2 Poor
1 Very poor

Occasionally it is desirable to use larger groupings. For this purpose, stanines 1, 2, and 3 are generally considered low; stanines 4, 5, and 6, average; and stanines 7, 8, and 9, high.

Unlike grade equivalents or percentile ranks, stanines 2 through 8 are equally spaced steps in the scale—that is, a stanine 8 is as much better than a stanine 6 as a stanine 5 is better than a 3. Because of this characteristic, the scale is particularly appropriate for making comparisons among scores or for profiling scores of individuals. The scale is also well adapted to use by the teacher in grouping students for instruction and has the advantage of de-emphasizing insignificant differences among pupils' scores.

It must be remembered, however, that whenever gross groupings are made from more finely expressed measures, there are bound to be sharp divisions *between* steps. This drawback is inherent to the stanine system. For example, assume that raw scores 10 to 15 are included within stanine 8, and 16 to 19 within stanine 9; a raw-score difference of just one point could change the stanine classification. Thus, a raw score of 15 would place a student at the upper end of

---

[3]The mean of a group of scores, or numbers, is the arithmetic average. The standard deviation is a statistical unit indicating the degree to which the scores tend to spread out or vary.

stanine 8, whereas one additional raw-score point would have placed the same student in stanine 9, at its lower end. Since there is an inescapable error of measurement in any test score, such a small difference as one raw-score point could be due entirely to chance. Therefore, in comparing several *stanine* scores for an individual, differences of only one stanine should *not* be regarded as significant.

Appropriate Uses of Stanines

Wherever it is possible to arrange data in rank order—from highest (or best) down to lowest (or poorest), stanines may be used. Consequently, they are not only useful in expressing test scores but in tabulating teachers' rankings, performance ratings, and similar data. Stanines obtained from the distribution of any such scores may be compared with those obtained from any other set, provided, of course, the data are derived from the *same group of individuals.* For example, arithmetic stanines may be compared with reading stanines; mental ability stanines may be compared with achievement stanines. From these data, bivariate (two-way) charts, graphically depicting the relationship between two measures, can easily be constructed. These charts may be used either for visual identification of atypical cases or as the first step in computing a correlation coefficient. Figure 2 is an example of such a chart.

Figure 2 Bivariate Chart Showing the Relationship Between ALP Mathematics Composite Prognostic Stanines and Metropolitan Mathematics Problem-Solving Stanines for the Eighth Grade in One Community

Metropolitan Achievement Tests: Problem Solving LEVEL Adv. FORM F

Mental Ability Test: ALP Math Comp. Prog. Score LEVEL Adv I FORM A

STANINE	1	2	3	4	5	6	7	8	9	TOTAL	
9									2	2	ABOVE AVERAGE
8		L				2	1		1	4	
7						1	2	1		4	13%
6			1	1	2 E	6	2			12	AVERAGE
5			1	1	5	3	3			13	
4			5	5	8	1	2			21	57%
3	1	1	6	2	2		1			13	BELOW AVERAGE
2	1	3	4	1				N		9	
1		1	1							2	30%
TOTAL	2	5	18	10	17	13	11	1	3	80	
	BELOW AVERAGE 31%			AVERAGE 50%			ABOVE AVERAGE 19%				

ALP MCPS	Mean = 4.5	S. D. = 1.8
MAT P. S.	Mean = 4.8	S. D. = 1.8

Because stanine scales always have the same mean and variability (standard deviation), stanines obtained from the same group on various measures may be combined into composite scores for use in prediction. For instance, stanines from a prognostic test may be combined with those derived from previous grades and teachers' ratings to form a composite predictor of success in a foreign language.

An individual profile of a pupil's scores on several measures may easily be constructed. Such a profile will almost automatically indicate the pupil's standing within the total group in each area measured. That same profile may also be used to portray the pupil's relative strengths and weaknesses from one area to another. It should be noted again, however, that in interpreting stanine scores, *only differences of two or more stanines should be regarded as significant.* National stanine norms provided by a test publisher can, of course, be used in profiling scores from the various subtest areas *in a single test battery,* but the test user should remember that only when stanines are based on the *same* population will comparisons between them be valid. On the other hand, *locally* developed stanines, if available, may be used to profile scores from tests whose standardization populations were *not* the same and whose *national* stanines are therefore not directly comparable.

Reporting pupil progress to parents can be easily and effectively done through the use of stanines. In fulfilling this important responsibility, it is critically important that reports be presented in a comprehensible form that will help home and school work together effectively toward the education of each child. Stanines can be more readily understood by parents than other types of transformed scores. They are less liable to serious misinterpretation than are grade equivalents, for example, and, because there are only nine levels, the stanines do not give the impression that measurement is more precise than it really is, as is the case with percentile ranks of 100 differentiated scores.

Counseling and guidance of pupils in educational and vocational decision-making may be greatly enhanced by the use of graphic representations of the pupil's performance on a wide variety of measures. The stanine system is admirably adapted to this type of profiling.

Establishing Local Norms in Terms of Stanines

The use of *local* score distributions or norms has long been advocated by professional test publishers as a useful adjunct to national norms. The techniques for establishing some types of local norms are quite complex. The stanine system, however, simplifies the process, and local distributions of scores expressed as stanines offer distinct advantages. The use of local stanines makes it possible to compare individual performance across all of the locally administered standardized tests. When the local stanines are based on a comparatively large group, such as all pupils in a given grade within the system, subgroups of the total may also be compared in terms of these local stanines. Two or more measures given to the same group—measures on which the scores have been translated into local stanines—may be plotted on bivariate (two-way) charts. Finally, local stanine norms may be established for distributions of scores on measures for which no national normative data are available, such as locally constructed tests and teachers' ratings.

The basic decision to be made before any computation can be done concerns the selection of an appropriate group on which to base the stanine scale. This is critical, since the stanine system assumes that the raw-score distribution approximates normality. If a small group, such as a classroom, were chosen, it would be highly unlikely that it would reflect a normal distribution of the trait being measured. At what point, then, is a group large enough to make reasonable an assumption of normal distribution? This is difficult to answer, but it is significant that the scoring service of The Psychological Corporation cautions against the development of local norms for groups of fewer than 100 pupils per grade level.

Even with a group of 100 or more, it is important to look at the distribution of raw scores to see whether there is a severe restriction in their range, or whether scores pile up at the top or bottom rather than in the middle. If the score distribution departs significantly from normality in either of these respects, great caution must be exercised both in the computation of stanines and in their interpretation.

In computing local stanines, it is always preferable to work with raw scores rather than any type of transformed scores so that none of the precision of the original data will be lost in translation. The first step is to determine the theoretical number of cases that should be assigned to each stanine level. This is done by multiplying successively the total number of cases in the distribution by the theoretical percent of cases at each stanine level.

In the example given in Figure 3, the total number of cases has been arbitrarily set at 325. The theoretical percents for each stanine have been transferred from Figure 1, where they are shown just above the line at the base of the curve. Theoretical frequencies are shown in the third column: for stanine 9, $.04 \times 325 = 13$; for stanine 8, $.07 \times 325 = 22.75$ (23), etc. Note that the theoretical percent desired at each stanine has been rounded to a whole percent and that rounding is also necessary in determining the theoretical frequencies. If, due to rounding, the theoretical frequencies do not add to the actual number of cases in the distribution, an adjustment must be made.

It rarely happens that a distribution of raw scores can be divided *exactly* according to the theoretical percents. (Only if the scores constitute a precisely normal distribution would this be true.) Therefore, the assignment of scores to stanine levels is unlikely to be precisely in accordance with the theoretical values. Above all, it must be remembered that *everyone having the same raw score must be assigned the same stanine.*

Figure 3 Frequency Desired at Each Stanine Level for a Group of 325 Scores

STANINE	Theoretical Percent	Theoretical Frequency
9	4	13
8	7	23
7	12	39
6	17	55
5	20	65
4	17	55
3	12	39
2	7	23
1	4	13
Total	100%	325

A Computational Example

Assigning stanine values to a given set of raw scores becomes a relatively simple procedure. Figure 4 shows an example of a completed worksheet for computing the reading stanines for a single grade level within a single community. The total number of cases is again 325. The directions below list the steps involved in preparing this worksheet.

Step 1

Arrange test papers or answer sheets in rank order from high to low. Note the highest and the lowest obtained scores, and on the worksheet, set up the scale of the Raw Score column to cover this range.

Step 2

In the adjacent column of frequencies (f), opposite each raw score, write the number of individuals who, by actual count, obtained that score.

Step 3

Add the frequencies in the f column and write the total at the bottom of the column. This is shown to be 325.

Step 4

Starting at the bottom of the f column, count off the scores in Stanine 1; in this case, it is possible to include just 13 scores, the exact theoretical frequency for this group. Draw a line to mark off these scores tentatively as Stanine 1, and enter the number 13 in the Actual Frequency column.

Figure 4   Sample Worksheet for Assigning Actual Stanine Values to a Group of 325 Scores

XYZ Reading Test Intermediate Battery Form Q in Grade 5			
Raw Score	**f**	**Actual Frequency**	**STANINE**
42	1		
41	1		
40	2	17	9
39	6		
38	7		
37	4		
36	9	27	8
35	4		
34	10		
33	7		
32	13	39	7
31	19		
30	11		
29	14	53	6
28	16		
27	12		
26	13		
25	11	64	5
24	18		
23	22		
22	16		
21	11	53	4
20	14		
19	12		
18	13		
17	14	35	3
16	8		
15	9		
14	6	24	2
13	3		
12	6		
11	2		
10	3		
9	2		
8	2	13	1
7	2		
6	1		
5	0		
4	0		
3	0		
2	1		
Total	**325**	**325**	

(A) → points to raw score 25

Step 5

For Stanine 2, the theoretical frequency is 23. A choice must be made here between 6 + 3 + 6 = 15 (too few) or 6 + 3 + 6 + 9 = 24, only one too many. Since the latter choice is preferable, scores of 12 through 15 are included, and a line is drawn between 15 and 16 to mark off Stanine 2.

Step 6

Work upward, marking off Stanines 3 and 4. Notice that in this example, the tentative actual frequencies are 35 and 53. In marking off Stanine 3, 35 cases have been included, although ideally there should be 39. However, to include the next score (19), another 12 cases would have to be added, making 47, and the original 35 is closer to the desired 39 than is 47. To this point, Stanines 1 through 4, 125 cases have been included where 130 were desired.

Step 7

Now mark off Stanine 5. In the example, 64 cases have been included rather than the theoretical 65, but adding either 12 or 16 would spoil the shape of the curve. Check the midpoint in Stanine 5 (between 24 and 25 at A). The actual number of cases assigned to this point is 165, closely approximating half of 325, or 162.5.

Step 8

Now continue counting off the frequencies for Stanines 6, 7, 8, and 9. After having made a tentative assignment, make any adjustments necessary to bring the actual frequencies at each level into the closest possible agreement with the theoretical frequencies.

Step 9

Check the symmetry of the stanine assignment; there should be about the same number of cases in Stanines 1 and 9, 2 and 8, 3 and 7, 4 and 6. In the example, the greatest discrepancy is between the 17 and 13 of Stanines 9 and 1, respectively. A possible adjustment would be to shift the 7 cases at score 38 from Stanine 9 to Stanine 8. This would leave 10 cases in Stanine 9, slightly closer to the 13 in Stanine 1, but Stanine 8 would now include 34 cases. Shifting the 10 at score 34 would leave the desired 24, but neither Stanine 7 nor 6 could absorb these ten extra cases. The logical conclusion is to leave the allocations as first set up.

It can easily be seen that the smaller the group and the less precisely normal the distribution of their scores, the more difficult is the task of assigning stanines and the more subjective is the judgment involved. However, it is important to note that a discrepancy between actual and theoretical frequencies is of less consequence at the extremes than it is in the middle range of the table, since the stanine assignment of fewer pupils is affected.

YOUR TASK

Test your understanding of stanines as well as SAT/ACT scores and grade-equivalent scores by taking the three ten-item tests that follow.[4] Circle either Y for Yes or N for No for each of the questions in the Yes/No tests and either T for True or F for False for each of the statements in the True/False test.

Because these tests are provided as a learning experience for you—and not as an aid to your instructor's evaluation of you—make it a learning experience by jotting down any questions or comments that arise as you think about which answer is correct. Be sure to raise your questions or comments in class.

THE STANINE SCORES INTERPRETATION TEST

ANSWER	ITEM	QUESTIONS/COMMENTS
Y N	1. Mary is a sixth-grader. She receives a stanine score of 0 on her standardized test in mathematics. This means that Mary's score is very low compared with other sixth-graders. Is that correct?	
Y N	2. Bill receives a stanine score of 5 on the same standardized mathematics test that Mary took. He is also in the sixth grade. The score of 5 means that Bill is doing average work in mathematics, and he would be at the 50th percentile for sixth-graders. Is that correct?	
Y N	3. Pedro receives a stanine score of 6.5 on the mathematics test. This score should be interpreted as being midway between the sixth and seventh stanines.	
Y N	4. Cindy is in the same class as Bill, Mary, and Pedro. On the mathematics test, she receives a stanine score of 9. Her mother wants to know just how high that score is—what percent of pupils perform less well than Cindy. Ms. Billingsley tells Cindy's mother that 96 percent of students in Cindy's grade performed less well than Cindy. Is this an accurate statement of Cindy's percentile rank?	
Y N	5. Alfonso's stanine score is 7. Mr. Rivera is more familiar with standard scores than stanines. He asks Ms. Billingsley how many standard deviations above the mean a stanine score of 7 is. Ms. Billingsley immediately responds, "One." Does Ms. Billingsley have a trick for remembering such things so well?	
Y N	6. Mr. Rivera decides that Ms. Billingsley really knows her stanines. So he pushes his luck and asks her what percent of students	

(continued)

[4]"Interpreting Stanine Scores," "Interpreting SAT & ACT Scores," and "Interpreting Grade-Equivalent Scores," all by John R. Hills from *Hills' Handy Hints,* published by and reprinted with the permission of the National Council on Measurement in Education, Washington, D.C.

THE STANINE SCORES INTERPRETATION TEST (continued)

ANSWER	ITEM	QUESTIONS/COMMENTS
	got stanine scores of 7, Ms. Billingsley thinks for a moment. Then she replies, "In a normal distribution, 12 percent of the scores will be in the seventh stanine." Taken aback by the speed of her response, Mr. Rivera asks whether another trick was involved. Is there?	
Y N	7. Mr. Tatnall overhears the conversation between Ms. Billingsley and Mr. Rivera and decides to contribute another guide. He suggests that stanines are the same as deciles. So, he says, the first stanine would be the same as the first decile, the second stanine and the second decile would be equivalent, and so on. Is Mr. Tatnall correct?	
Y N	8. Mr. Rivera decides to ask one more question. He has found that most of his students receive the same stanine scores in the fifth grade that they got in the fourth grade or even the third grade. He concludes that they are not making much progress in school. Is that correct?	
Y N	9. Mr. Tatnall asks what he should do about Patricia, who went down from the fifth stanine last year to the fourth stanine this year in reading comprehension. Should Mr. Tatnall be worried about this?	
Y N	10. Mr. Rivera then asks about his student Elena, whose stanine score in reading comprehension went up from the fourth stanine to the sixth stanine. Is that big a difference important?	

THE SAT/ACT INTERPRETATION TEST

ANSWER	ITEM	QUESTIONS/COMMENTS
Y N	1. Donald tells Mr. Henkin, the counselor at Burnside High School, that he has just received his Scholastic Aptitude Test (SAT) scores and that his Verbal (V) and Mathematical (M) scores are both about 400. He is disappointed because those scores are well below average. Is the average SAT score 500?	
Y N	2. Mary tells her best friend, Susie, that her SAT score is 900. Susie is impressed, because her scores are only V of 450 and M of 450. Did Mary perform better than Susie?	

THE SAT/ACT INTERPRETATION TEST *(continued)*

ANSWER		ITEM	QUESTIONS/COMMENTS

Y   N   3. Jeremy receives his SAT scores and his ACT scores in the mail. His ACT scores were much lower than his SAT scores. He has two SAT scores (495 and 515), but his ACT report has five scores, with numbers such as 17 and 18. Adding all five ACT scores together won't produce a total as high as one of the SAT scores. Did he perform less satisfactorily on the ACT?

Y   N   4. Susie adds together her V and M scores on the SAT and gets a total of 1225. She looks at her ACT scores of 22, 23, 21, and 23 and expects them to add up to 89, but her ACT composite score is only 22. Has her ACT composite been calculated incorrectly?

Y   N   5. Harold took both the SAT and the ACT. He estimates that for college-going students the SAT score mean is about 450 and the ACT score mean is about 17. However, he gets ACT scores with an average near 20, but his SAT scores are only around 400. Is something wrong because he is above the mean on one test but below the mean on the other?

Y   N   6. Tulawney, the star student of Burnside High School, took both the SAT and the ACT in the fall of her senior year. She scored near 700 on each of the SAT scores and near 25 on each of the ACT scores. She had so much fun taking these tests and did so well that at the next opportunity she took them both again. To her dismay, her scores on both the SAT and the ACT are lower on the second testing. She goes to Mr. Henkin to find out what is wrong, and he tells her not to worry. She should have expected her scores to be lower on the second testing. Is Mr. Henkin correct?

Y   N   7. Willie took the SAT one year and got a Verbal score of 450. He was not satisfied, so he studied vocabulary diligently for a year and then took the test again. His Verbal score went up to 500. He recommended to everyone that they study vocabulary the way he did because his score improved so much after only one year. Is Willie's vocabulary study responsible for his improved SAT Verbal score?

Y   N   8. Sue Ellen wants to go to college very much, but her ACT composite score in her

(continued)

THE SAT/ACT INTERPRETATION TEST (continued)

ANSWER	ITEM	QUESTIONS/COMMENTS

junior year was only 11. In order to raise that score, she studied diligently during the next year. She wants to raise her achievement in natural science, social science, and mathematics because ACT tests include questions based on high school courses in those areas. When she takes the ACT again, her composite goes up to 14. The school principal, on hearing this, asks at a faculty meeting whether this kind of diligent study should be prescribed for all students who have low ACT scores. Mr. Henkin says that Sue Ellen's experience does not justify such a conclusion. Her improvement might readily have occurred without the extra study. Is that true?

Y   N   9. Elijah took the Preliminary Scholastic Aptitude Test (PSAT) in his junior year and received a V score of 65 and an M score of 63. He asks Donald to help him decide what these scores mean. Donald says that they are very low. Donald is disappointed in his SAT scores, which are about 400, but that is much higher than scores of only 65 and 63. Then Elijah goes to Sue Ellen for advice. She has been thrilled to get her ACT score composite up to 14 after a year of hard work. She says that scores in the sixties are very high. Elijah has been influenced by a statistician, so he concludes that if one person says his scores are low and the other says they were high, the scores must be about average. Is that correct?

Y   N   10. Mr. Livingston, the Commissioner of Education, is working hard to improve education in his state. He looks at the mean SAT scores for students in his state this year and finds them little different from last year. Have his efforts been fruitless because the mean SAT scores has not increased?

THE GRADE-EQUIVALENT SCORES INTERPRETATION TEST

ANSWER	ITEM	QUESTIONS/COMMENTS

T   F   1. Tim is a sixth-grader. He obtains a GE score of 9.2 in reading. This means that Tim scored well above average sixth-graders on reading.

T   F   2. A GE score for Tim of 9.2 means that he can read as well as ninth-graders in the second month of the school year.

THE GRADE-EQUIVALENT SCORES INTERPRETATION TEST (*continued*)

ANSWER		ITEM	QUESTIONS/COMMENTS
T	F	3. Tim's GE score of 9.2 on reading means that, when a group of ninth-graders in their second month were tested on ninth-grade reading material, they received scores equivalent to Tim's score.	
T	F	4. Tim's GE score of 9.2 on reading means that Tim could well be put in a class of ninth-graders for material in which reading skills are important.	
T	F	5. Tim's 9.2 GE in reading means that, in a flexible school in which children work on materials at their own level, Tim should be put into a ninth-grade class for instruction in reading.	
T	F	6. Tim obtains a GE score of 7.3 in arithmetic on the same test battery from which his reading GE score was 9.2. This means that in reading Tim is nearly two years ahead of his performance in arithmetic.	
T	F	7. GE scores of 9.2 in reading and 7.3 in arithmetic indicate that Tim is further ahead of his own class in reading than in arithmetic.	
T	F	8. Tim's GE of 9.2 in reading was from fall testing in the sixth grade. Tested in the spring, he receives a GE score of 8.0. That indicates that his reading skills have declined during the school year. Some effort should be expended to find out why and whether such losses can be expected to continue.	
T	F	9. When tested in September, 30 percent of the students in Mr. Brown's fifth-grade class get GE scores below 5.1. Something needs to be done to help his students reach grade level. Also, the third- and fourth-grade teachers should improve the instruction given to students before they reach Mr. Brown.	
T	F	10. Jones Elementary School is an inner-city school. The Jones school mean GE score in reading in first grade is .6. The mean increases each year until by the sixth grade it is up to 3.2. Thus, the Jones mean is .4 year behind at the first grade and nearly 3 years behind by the sixth grade. Because the Jones students are falling further behind the national average each year, the reading program, the teachers, and the administration are inadequate to meet the learning needs of the Jones school students.	

EXERCISE 4-5
NORMS

OBJECTIVE

To enhance understanding of and provide firsthand experience with norms

BACKGROUND

Given the many varied ways that tests can be constructed, knowledge of a raw score on a given test seldom provides enough information to make a meaningful interpretation of performance on the test. Raw scores that have been converted to z, T, A, C, sten, stanine, or other such scores tend to be more readily interpretable.[5] However, given the fact that there exists for the purpose of reporting test scores such a wide variety of derived scales, it is imperative that test developers and writers of test manuals provide the users of such materials with information sufficient to understand the particular scale employed. *Norms* describe the performance on a test of a representative group of testtakers (the *normative* sample) and provide a context for interpreting testtakers' scores. Ideally, and in accordance with guidelines set forth in the *Standards* (1985), the description of a published, standardized test's norms should include, at a minimum, all of the following:

- a description of the scales used in reporting the scores of testtakers in the normative sample, as well as (1) the rationale for using the scales selected, and (2) a description of how the scaled scores were derived from the raw scores;
- a rationale for why raw scores and not scaled scores are being employed, if indeed that is the case;
- a description of the normative study including the year(s) in which the normative data were gathered. The description of the methodology should be in detail sufficient to permit evaluation of its appropriateness. Specifically, a presentation of the sampling design, the normative sample, and descriptive statistics as well as response rates should be included; and
- the normative sample should consist of people similar in many respects to the people on whom a test user might wish to compare test performance.

In addition, the section on norms in a published test manual might encourage users of the test to develop their own local norms.

YOUR TASK

Picture yourself as a professor in the measurement class at a hypothetical institution we'll call Western Hootsville University. And remember that data from Table 3-1 (how can you forget it?)? That's the data from the course in tests and measurement that *you* teach.

Your counterparts in the state university system, that is, the professors who teach the same course at Eastern Hootsville University, Northern Hootsville University, and Southern Hootsville University, all think that the test from which the data from Table 3-1 were derived is the greatest thing since sliced bread. You have letters on your desk from each of these three instructors asking not only for a copy of your precious exam but the norms to go with it—this so each of the professors can see how their respective students stack up against those at Western. Being the magnanimous person that you are, you write back that you will send them not only the exam but also an exemplary set of norms to go with it.

And by this point you have no doubt gleaned that your assignment in this task is to create an exemplary set of norms for your class's test data. While you will have to employ your creative imagination in writing about such aspects of the norms as your description of the "normative sample," you can be quite concrete about other matters such as the descriptive statistics. To the best of your ability, make the description of the norms you create look and "feel" similar to the section on norms that you might find in the manual of a well-standardized published test. If you have no idea what such a section might look like, consult the manuals of some standardized tests.

EXERCISE 4-6
THE PEARSON *r*

OBJECTIVE

To enhance understanding of and provide firsthand experience with the calculation and interpretation of a coefficient of correlation—specifically, the Pearson *r*

BACKGROUND

Correlation is an expression of the degree of correspondence between two things. A coefficient of correlation (*r*) expresses a linear relationship between two variables. More technically, it reflects the degree of concomitant variation between a single independent variable (an *X* variable) and a single dependent variable (a *Y* variable). The *coefficient of correlation* is the numerical index that expresses this relationship; it tells us the extent to which *X* and *Y* are "co-related." The most commonly used coefficient of correlation is a statistic devel-

---

[5]The *C* scale (see Guilford & Fruchter, 1978) is an 11-unit scale with a standard deviation of 2. A modified version of the *C* scale is the "standard ten" or *sten* scale (Canfield, 1951), a 10-unit *C* scale that has been used in tests such as the 16 PF.

oped by Karl Pearson referred to alternatively as the Pearson r, r, or the Pearson product-moment correlation coefficient.

A sound understanding of the concept of correlation is essential to the study of psychological testing and assessment. As we will see in the following chapter on the subject of reliability, a correlation coefficient is the statistical tool used to describe the relationship between one's score on a test and one's score on a re-test with the same instrument. And then again in the chapter on the subject of validity, we will see how, for example, a correlation coefficient is used to describe the relationship between an observed score on a test and the "true score."

YOUR TASK

1. Create a scatterplot.

Regardless of the primary text you are using in this course, you will no doubt find coverage of the use of a *scatterplot* or *scatter diagram*—a graph—to describe the correlation that exists between two variables. Refer to that material in order to create a scatterplot of the data described below.

Student	Number of Hours Spent Preparing	Final Exam Score
Malcolm	23.0	98
Heywood	16.0	92
Mervin	0.5	45
Zeke	12.0	80
Sam	9.0	76
Macy	10.0	57
Elvis II	1.0	61
Jed	14.0	88
Jeb	8.5	70
Lcroy	15.0	90

The final examination data for the second graduating class—a total of ten students—enrolled in a new trade school called the "Home Study School of Elvis Presley Impersonators" is provided. Adjacent to the final examination score (which no doubt was a take-home test) is the actual number of hours each student spent studying and otherwise preparing for the exam. What is the direction and magnitude of the correlation between time spent in preparation and score on the final examination? Use your scatterplot to estimate an answer to this question.

2. Calculate and interpret a Pearson r.

How strong is the relationship between number of hours spent in preparation for the final examination and raw score on that examination? What is the nature of the direction of that relationship—positive or negative? The Pearson r is the most widely used of several alternative measures of correlation. It is the statistical tool of choice

when the relationship between the variables is linear and when the two variables being correlated are continuous (that is, they can theoretically assume any value). What follows are two formulas used to calculate a Pearson r, one to be used with deviation scores, the other to be used with raw scores. Each formula is explained in step-by-step fashion; all you have to do is the setting up and the calculations.

The Deviation Score Formula

The deviation score formula for calculating the Pearson r is as follows:

$$r = \frac{\Sigma(X - \overline{X})(Y - \overline{Y})}{\sqrt{\Sigma(X - \overline{X})^2 \Sigma(Y - \overline{Y})^2}}$$

Applying the formula above to the study of time/final examination data and letting X equal the number of hours studied and Y equal the score on the final examination, a Pearson r can be calculated using the step-by-step procedure described below.

THE DEVIATION SCORE FORMULA FOR CALCULATING THE PEARSON r

Step 1

Set up a table with the following seven headings, one next to the other, across the top:

$$X, Y, x, y, xy, x^2, \text{ and } y^2$$

Step 2

List the values for X next to the corresponding values for Y in the table.

Step 3

Calculate the mean for $X(\overline{X})$ and the mean for $Y(\overline{Y})$ and then use this information to calculate deviation scores (x and y) for each value of X and Y. Recall that a deviation score is found by subtracting from each value the mean of its respective distribution ($X - \overline{X}$ and $Y - \overline{Y}$).

Step 4

Multiply each x by its corresponding y and sum all of the products.

$$\Sigma[(x)(y)] = 949.2$$

Step 5

Square each x and then sum all of the squares. Do the same for the corresponding values of y—square each of them and then sum all of the squares.

$$\Sigma x^2 = 416.4$$

$$\Sigma y^2 = 2678.1$$

A Scatterplot of Study Time and Final Examination Scores

Step 6

Multiply one sum of the squared deviation scores by the other sum of the squared deviation scores and find the square root of their product.

$$\sqrt{(\Sigma x^2)(\Sigma y^2)} = 1056.0118$$

Step 7

Substitute the values you have calculated for the appropriate terms in the formula and solve for the Pearson *r*.

$$r = \frac{949.2}{\sqrt{(416.4)(2678.10)}} = \frac{949.2}{1056.0118} = .899$$

Now that you are an expert in the use of the deviation score formula, why not broaden your horizons by calculating the Pearson *r* using the raw score formula.

THE RAW SCORE FORMULA FOR CALCULATING THE PEARSON *r*

The raw score formula for calculating the Pearson *r* is as follows:

$$r = \frac{N\Sigma XY - (\Sigma X)(\Sigma Y)}{\sqrt{[N\Sigma X^2 - (\Sigma X)^2][N\Sigma Y^2 - (\Sigma Y)^2]}}$$

Applying the formula above to the study time/final examination data and letting *X* equal the number of hours studied and *Y* equal the score on the final examination, a Pearson *r* can be calculated in the following way.

Step 1

Set up a table with the following five headings, one next to the other, across the top:

$$X, Y, XY, X^2, \text{ and } Y^2$$

Step 2

List the values for *X* next to the corresponding values for *Y* in the table. Sum all of the values for *X* and note that sum at the bottom of the *X* column. Sum all of the values for *Y* and note that sum at the bottom of the *Y* column.

$$\Sigma X = 109 \quad \Sigma Y = 757$$

Step 3

Multiply each value of *X* by its corresponding value of *Y* and fill in the product in the corresponding place in the *XY* column. Sum all of these products to obtain ΣXY and note that sum at the bottom of the *XY* column.

$$\Sigma XY = 9200.5$$

Step 4

Square all of the values of *X* and then sum all of these values, noting the sum at the bottom of the X^2 column.

Square all of the values of *Y* and then sum all of these values, noting the sum at the bottom of the Y^2 column.

$$\Sigma X^2 = 1604.5 \quad \Sigma Y^2 = 59983$$

Step 5

Insert the appropriate numbers into the formula and solve for *r*.

$$r = \frac{10(9200.5) - (109)(757)}{\sqrt{[10(1604.5) - (109)^2][10(59983) - (757)^2]}}$$

$$r = \frac{9492}{\sqrt{[4164][26781]}} = \frac{9462}{10560.118} = .899$$

Regardless of whether the deviation or the raw score formula is employed, you probably—we hope—calculated the value of *r* to be .899. What does the calculated Pearson *r* of .899 mean? Is this number statistically significant given the size and nature of the sample? Could this result have occurred by chance? Explain with reference to a table of critical values of Pearson *r* in your statistics textbook.

EXERCISE 4-7
"HELLO" TO RHO

OBJECTIVE

To introduce, explain, and provide a computational example of rho

BACKGROUND

Rho is a correlation coefficient used when one or both of the variables to be correlated is ordinarily scaled—that is, when one or both of the variables to be correlated is in the form of rank-order data. Note that while we refer to this statistic simply as rho for the sake of brevity, it has been referred to in numerous other ways in the psychometric literature, including "Spearman's rho," "the Spearman rho," the "rank-order coefficient of correlation," and "the rank-difference correlation coefficient." The formula for rho is as follows:

$$\text{rho or } r_s = 1 - \frac{6\Sigma d^2}{n^3 - n}$$

Here *d* is equal to the algebraic difference in ranks for each object or persons in two distributions of ranks, and *n* is the sample size (or the number of pairs of ranks). Note that rho is often symbolized with the usual symbol for a correlation coefficient (*r*) along with an italicized *s* subscript, the *s* standing for Spearman.

While the formula for rho is of course different from the formula for the Pearson *r*, you should understand, as

Nunnally (1978, p. 134) pointed out, that rho is "only a short-cut version" of the Pearson r, and "the results obtained by applying rho are exactly the same as those obtained by applying . . . [the Pearson r] to two sets of ranks." By the way, it is also true that two other indices of correlation, the phi coefficient and the point-biserial coefficient (both to be discussed subsequently), are also special cases of the product-moment correlation; thus, r, rho, phi, and the point-biserial coefficients of correlation are identical in the mathematical sense.

An example of the type of situation in which rho would be employed in the correlational analysis is the case where two trained behavioral observers rank each of 25 children in a classroom on the variable "hyperactivity." Rho would be used to determine how much agreement there was between the raters. Two personnel managers might rank-order 20 job applicants with respect to suitability for employment; again, rho would be used to obtain an index of the level of agreement. Nunnally (1978, pp. 134–135) reviewed other types of data analysis situations where rho might be employed.

What better way is there to illustrate what's involved in calculating rho than some "hands-on" data analysis? Imagine that ten would-be beauty school attendees take a beauty school's qualifying examination in order to determine whether they will be accepted for training. Some of the ten applicants are male, some are female; some eventually take jobs in the world of cosmetology, while others explore ways to become licensed travel agents or dental hygienists. Understand that, although some of this information—such as entry or nonentry into the field of beauty—may seem irrelevant at the moment, we will shortly be using it to further illustrate correlational concepts.

The beauty school accepts all ten applicants contingent on their ability to finance (or have the government finance) their tuition, and once everyone's all paid up, six weeks of rigorous and intensive training begins. At the conclusion of training, and with a plethora of courses such as Advanced Hair Streaking, Blow Drying 101, and Independent Study in Pedicure, a final examination is administered. Included in the table below is demographic information and career disposition information, as well as raw score (number of items

Student	Sex	Entered into a Career in Beauty?	"A" Score	"B" Score
1. Randy	Male	NO	86	84
2. Shelly	Female	YES	91	93
3. Terry	Male	YES	75	77
4. Robin	Female	NO	64	61
5. Sandy	Female	NO	73	75
6. Leslie	Male	YES	82	80
7. Chris	Female	NO	79	81
8. Kim	Male	YES	79	76
9. Francis	Male	NO	88	85
10. Freddy	Female	YES	80	89

correct) on the beauty school's pre-admission qualifying test (Test A) and post-training final examination (Test B). For the record, both tests are of the 100-item, short-answer variety with one point awarded for each correct answer.

YOUR TASK

Is there a relationship between the pre-admission score on the qualifying examination and the comprehensive end-of-course examination? If so, how would you describe it? Ordinarily, a Pearson r would be calculated to determine the answer to this question—given that we have interval-level data to work with (the test scores) and not merely rankings. However, for the purpose of obtaining computational experience with rho, we (i.e., you) will convert these data into ranks; and that's Step 1.

Step 1

To solve for r_s, begin by placing the data into ranked form if they are not already in ranked form.

You are going to get a little—not much, just a little—help in getting started. Fill in the blank spaces below for the beauty school data.

Student	"A" Score	"B" Score	Rank Order of "A" Score	Rank Order of "B" Score
1. Randy	86	84	3	4
2. Shelly	91	93	—	—
3. Terry	75	77	—	—
4. Robin	64	61	—	—
5. Sandy	73	75	—	—
6. Leslie	82	80	—	—
7. Chris	79	81	—	—
8. Kim	79	76	—	—
9. Francis	88	85	—	—
10. Freddy	80	89	—	—

Step 2

Believe it or not, the worst is over and it's all downhill from here. All you need do is subtract each "B" ranking from its corresponding "A" ranking to obtain a d score. Once you've obtained the d score, square it. Now sum the squares.

Step 3

Solve for rho.

Having calculated rho, what can you say about the relationship between scores on the beauty school's pre-instruction and post-instruction tests?

For more practice with rho, respond to the following two questions.

1. Professors Go and Nogo team-teach a seminar in ethics to ten students. The students in this ethics seminar recently

took a midterm examination that consisted of one essay question. As an initial step in evaluating their students' work, the two professors have each rank-ordered the papers, assigning the number 1 to the best paper and the number 10 to the worst. Using Spearman's rho, calculate a coefficient of correlation between the two professors' rankings. What does rho tell us about the respective judgments of Go and Nogo?

Student	Professor Go	Professor Nogo
Tiffany	5	3
Levelor	1	2
Harley	4	4
Macy	9	7
Dreyfus	8	8
Scotch	2	1
Andersen	10	9
Visine	7	10
Hershey	3	6
Chrysler	6	5

2. Seven students complete the hypothetical "Reading Rank-Order Test" (RROT) twice, with the second test administration conducted two weeks after the first. The RROT does not provide a score for each student. Rather, the tests produce a rank-ordering of the students in terms of the reading ability evidenced on the test. On the first administration of the test, Kimba did best, followed by Julep, Steve, Edie, Nodu, Ike, and Tina. On the second administration, Julep did best, followed by Steve, Kimba, Tina, Ike, Edie, and Nodu. After completing the values for the table that follows, calculate Spearman's rho. What can you conclude from these data?

Student	Test	Retest
Kimba		
Julep		
Nodu		
Steve		
Edie		
Tina		
Ike		

EXERCISE 4-8

OTHER COEFFICIENTS OF CORRELATION

OBJECTIVE

To introduce and gain some firsthand experience with other coefficients of correlation

BACKGROUND

In addition to r and rho, there are times when, because of the nature of the data or the sample, other correlation coefficients may be employed. These other coefficients include the biserial r, the point-biserial r, the tetrachoric r, and the phi coefficient.

Denoted by the symbol r_b, the biserial r is appropriate when the two variables to be correlated are continuous in nature but one of the two has been arbitrarily dichotomized. Inherent in the formula for the calculation of the biserial r is a correction for the arbitrary dichotimization of the dichotomized variable; the result is an estimate of the Pearson r that would have been obtained had the data not been dichotomized.

Referring back to the beauty school example, let's suppose we arbitrarily classify all scores of 65 or over on the final examination as "Pass" and all scores of 64 or under as "Fail." And now let's further suppose that we wished to correlate score on test "A" (see Exercise 4-6) with pass/fail status on test "B." The appropriate coefficient of correlation to calculate would be r_b. As another example of the way in which biserial correlation may be used, consider the case of a teacher or researcher interested in performance on one item of a test—was the item passed or failed?—in relation to score on the entire test; a right-wrong test item may be viewed as an artificially dichotomized measure of whatever is being assessed by the test as a whole. Biserial correlation coefficients are frequently calculated (or approximated) by means of tables designed for that purpose; should you have occasion to calculate it by means of its formula, that formula (complete with an explanation on how to calculate it) can be found in advanced statistics texts (such as Lord & Novick, 1968).

Denoted by the symbol r_{pb}, the point-biserial r is a correlation coefficient appropriate for use with a variable that is continuous in nature (such as score on the entry-level test for the beauty school) and another variable that is a true—not an arbitrary—dichotomy (such as sex of student). In the process of developing a test of ability, for example, we might use r_{pb} to examine the nature of the relationship between an individual item on a test (whether it was answered correctly or incorrectly) and the raw score (number scored as correct) on the entire test. To learn about the nature of the relationship between entry-level test score and gender in the beauty school data, we would calculate r_{pb} as follows:

$$r_{pb} = \sqrt{\frac{n_1 n_0}{N}} \left(\frac{\bar{X}_1 - \bar{X}_0}{\sqrt{\Sigma \left(X - \bar{X} \right)^2}} \right)$$

Let's preface our explanation of the terms in the expression above by noting that whether an examinee is male or female will have to be denoted by some quantitative code for "male" and "female." The simplest code we can think of for use here is 0 = male and 1 = female. Having said that, we explain that in the expression above X represents the continuous variable (score on the entry-level test), $\overline{X}$ is equal to the mean of all of the scores on the entry-level test, and X_0 and X_1 are respectively representative of scores for male and female testtakers, while n_0 and n_1 are respectively representative of the number of male and female testtakers. N is equal to the total number of testtakers. Knowing all of that, your task is to solve for r_{pb} and then interpret your findings.

The tetrachoric r, denoted by the symbol r_t, is appropriate for use when the two variables to be correlated have been arbitrarily reduced to a dichotomy. The end product of the calculation of r_t approximates what the Pearson r would have been if the data had been continuous and the assumptions inherent in the use of the Pearson r had been met. Referring back to the beauty school example, suppose a score of 65 or over on each of the two tests was arbitrarily designated as a passing grade, while a score of 64 or under was arbitrarily designated as a failing grade. The tetrachoric r would be the appropriate statistic to determine the nature of the relationship that exists between passing or failing the entry-level test and passing or failing the final examination. However, even the dean of the beauty school might shy away from calculating r_t once he or she found out how complicated a process it is (see Lord & Novick, 1968).

The phi coefficient, denoted by the Greek letter *phi* (ϕ) is a coefficient of correlation designed for use with true dichotomies. Referring one more time to the beauty school example, if you were interested in calculating the relationship between entry into the field of beauty and sex, the phi coefficient would be the correlation coefficient of choice. In test development, the phi coefficient is frequently employed to examine the nature of the relationship between correct/incorrect response on a particular item and some truly dichotomous variable (such as graduate/dropout). In the following equation, let's assume that both of the dichotomous variables being correlated can be coded using the same type of 0/1 coding system we presented in our description of the point-biserial r. Now the phi coefficient of correlation for variables X and Y could be calculated using the following formula:

$$\phi_{XY} = \frac{p_{(XY)1} - (p_{X1})(p_{Y1})}{\sqrt{(p_{X1})(1 - p_{X1})(1 - p_{Y1})}}$$

Here, $p_{(XY)1}$ represents the proportion of testtakers scoring "1" on both X and Y, p_{X1} represents the proportion of testtakers scoring "1" on X, and p_{Y1} represents the proportion of testtakers scoring "1" on Y. Applying the code system of 0 = male, 1 = female, 0 = did not enter field of beauty, and 1 = did enter field of beauty, and using X to denote the occupational disposition variable while using Y to denote the sex variable, we could set up the coding table used to calculate phi as follows:

Student	(Y) Sex	Sex Code	(X) Entered Field	Field Code
Randy	Male	0	NO	0
Shelly	Female	1	YES	1
Terry	Male	0	YES	1
Robin	Female	1	NO	0
Sandy	Female	1	NO	0
Leslie	Male	0	YES	1
Chris	Female	1	NO	0
Kim	Male	0	YES	1
Francis	Male	0	NO	0
Freddy	Female	1	YES	1

YOUR TASK

1. What is the nature of the relationship between entry-level test score and sex? What was the value of the point-biserial r you calculated?

2. What is the nature of the relationship between gender and entry into the beauty field in this study? What was the value of the phi coefficient you calculated?

EXERCISE 4-9

AN EXERCISE IN REGRESSION

OBJECTIVE

To enhance understanding of and provide firsthand experience with the concept of regression

BACKGROUND

In the language of statistics, the definition of *regression* parallels that of its more usual definition of "reversion to some previous state"; in statistics, the reversion referred to is a reversion to the mean. In your text, you probably read about how a regression line is the line of best fit with respect to raw data expressed in the form of a scatterplot. Here we will try to approach the concept of regression from another perspective, focusing on what is actually meant by the concept of *reversion to the mean*. Consider now this hypothetical example:

This year, 100,000 people, each of whom is very much like John and Mary (in terms of variables such as age, socio-economic status, and so forth), have taken a test called the "National Extraversion Test" (NET). The mean score (or "extraversion quotient"—EQ) for all those people was 100, and the standard deviation was 5. John's EQ according to the test was 110 and Mary's was 90.

Given that there is error inherent in the measurement of EQ scores, take a guess about the nature of the "true score" of John and Mary on the NET. Specifically, if you had to guess, would you say that John's "true score" is probably higher or lower than 110? And what about Mary's "true score"? Would you guess that it was higher or lower than 90?

If you are like most people, you would guess that, since the average score on the test is 100, John's "true score" is probably lower than 110. And using the same logic, you would probably guess that Mary's "true score" is higher than 90. If you in fact made such inferences, you have illustrated for yourself the concept of "regression to the mean."

Knowing no other information than an individual's raw score on a test (we'll refer to it as X), the group's mean score (we'll refer to it as $\overline{X}$), and a reliability estimate of the test (we'll refer to it as r_{xx}), we can obtain an estimate of the individual's true score ($\hat{T}$, read "T hat") on the test by using the following formula:

$$\hat{T} = r_{xx}\left(X - \overline{X}\right) + \overline{X}$$

Suppose then that the reliability estimate (r_{xx}) of the NET was .5; what would you estimate John's EQ score to be? How about Mary's? The predicted true score for John is 105, and the calculations follow below. You're on your own if you're curious about Mary's true EQ.

The predicted true score for John would be calculated as follows:

$$\hat{T} = .5(110 - 100) + 100$$

$$= .5(10) + 100$$

$$= 5 + 100$$

$$= 105$$

In testing and assessment, the situation sometimes arises wherein we have knowledge of a score on one test (or one particular form of a test) and from that information we would like to predict to some criterion (such as a score on another test, a score on another form of the same test, or a grade-point average). Consider in this context some data for scores found to be equivalent on the hypothetical "Helping Out Others Test" (HOOT) and another (hypothetical) test distributed by a European publisher, the "Rome Altruism Test" (RAT). Simply for the sake of convenience, let's label the HOOT scores as X and the RAT scores as Y:

HOOT (X)	RAT (Y)
10	10
30	20
50	30
60	40
70	50
80	60

Knowing that the scores on the two tests are related as indicated above, and knowing what a testtaker scored on one of these two tests, we would be able to calculate—and thus

predict with some accuracy—the testtaker's score on the other test. Exactly how accurate our prediction will be will depend on the nature of the correlation between the variables in question; the higher the correlation between the two variables—that is, the stronger the absolute (positive or negative) magnitude of the relationship between the variables—the more accurate our prediction.

The formula used to calculate the regression equation is the same as the equation for a straight line:[6]

$$\hat{Y} = a + bX$$

In the equation for the straight line, a is the Y intercept, and b is the slope of the line (otherwise expressed as the change in Y divided by the change in X, or $\Delta Y/\Delta X$). In the regression equation, $\hat{Y}$ (the predicted value for Y—read as "Y hat") is substituted for Y, and a and b are referred to as *regression coefficients*. In the regression equation,

$$a = \overline{Y} - b\overline{X}$$

and

$$b = \frac{n\Sigma XY - (\Sigma X)(\Sigma Y)}{n\Sigma X^2 - (\Sigma X)^2}$$

Suppose you knew that Hector's score on the HOOT was 78; what would you predict Hector's score on the RAT to be? To answer this question, you might proceed as follows.

Step 1

Set up a table that lists the values of X, the values of Y, and the values of XY and X^2. You will also need to determine the values of the expressions below:

ΣY

ΣX

ΣX^2

$(\Sigma X)^2$

We'll get you started by setting up the table and inserting the values X and Y.

X	Y	XY	X	X²	Y²
10	10				
30	20				
50	30				
60	40				
70	50				
80	60				

---

[6]Elsewhere you may have seen this same formula expressed in an alternate form: $Y = mx + b$.

Step 2

Calculate *b*, using the following formula:

$$b = \frac{n\Sigma XY - (\Sigma X)(\Sigma Y)}{n\Sigma X^2 \ (\Sigma X)^2}$$

Step 3

Solve for *a*, using the following formula along with the values you obtained in the prior two steps:

$$a = \bar{Y} - b\bar{X}$$

Step 4

Write the resulting regression equation. Thus to predict Hector's score on the RAT, given Hector's score on the HOOT (*X* = 78), we would solve for $\hat{Y}$ as follows:

$$\hat{Y} = a + bX$$

where *b* and *a* were the calculated values found in Steps 2 and 3, respectively, and *X* = 78.

Suppose now a revised form of the HOOT was published (the HOOT-Revised), and you could more accurately predict RAT scores by using a combination of HOOT and HOOT-Revised scores; because more than one score would be used to predict a criterion score, a *multiple regression* equation would be necessary. And you will no doubt breathe a sigh of relief when we tell you that multiple regression is beyond the scope of this book.

YOUR TASK

1. Draw a scatterplot (on the facing page) of the HOOT and RAT data presented above. Then draw in—without any calculations or reference to any formulas—what looks to you like the best "line of best fit" for the data.
2. If you knew that Hector's score on the HOOT was 78, what would you estimate his score on the RAT to be?

EXERCISE 4-10

FIGURE THIS

OBJECTIVE

Obtain firsthand computational experience figuring out problems related to material presented in the chapter

BACKGROUND

Use your knowledge of material presented in Chapter 4 in your textbook to tackle *Your Task* in what follows.

YOUR TASK

A psychologist in New Mexico is asked to test two children who were involved in a tragic fire that resulted from a faulty furnace installation. Results of the testing will be used as part of the information in an emotional damages lawsuit. Rosa is 8 and Benito is 13. They speak Spanish at home with their family and attend a school where instruction is in English. The psychologist administers the Short Personality Inventory and Trauma Upset Profile (SPITUP). The SPITUP has two samples from which norms were developed. In a sample of typically developing children (Typical), groups of twenty-five boys and twenty-five girls were included in each of the following age groups: 9, 10, 11, 12, and 13. Within the typically developing norm group, ten percent of the children in each age group were African American and the rest of the children in the sample were Caucasian. The second (Clinical) sample also included groups of twenty-five boys and twenty-five girls in each of the age groups from age 9 to age 13. The clinical group included children who presented for psychiatric services at Mental Health Centers and hospitals and other treatment facilities. Forty percent of the children in the sample were African American, one percent in each age group were Hispanic children, and the rest were Caucasian. All of the children in both norm samples live in Iowa. The psychologist uses the Clinical sample in her interpretation of the test results.

1. With which group are Rosa and Benito being compared? How many children are Benito and Rosa being compared with?
2. What assumptions are made by this comparison?
3. Based on your understanding of standardization and appropriate norm samples, describe the problems the psychologist will have when explaining her use of the SPITUP when cross-examined by the opposing attorney.

REFERENCES

Canfield, A. A. (1951). The "sten" scale—A modified C-scale. *Educational and Psychological Measurement, 11,* 295–297.

Guilford, J. P., & Fruchter, B. (1978). *Fundamental statistics in psychology and education* (6th ed.). New York: McGraw-Hill.

Hays, W. L. (1973). *Statistics for the social sciences* (2nd ed.). New York: Holt, Rinehart & Winston.

Lord, F. M., & Novick, M. R. (1968). *Statistical theories of mental test scores.* Menlo Park, CA: Addison-Wesley.

Nunnally, J. C. (1978). *Psychometric theory* (2nd ed.). New York: McGraw-Hill.

Rotton, J., & Kelley, I. W. (1985). Much ado about the full moon: A meta-analysis of lunar-lunacy research. *Psychological Bulletin, 97,* 286–306.

Standards for educational and psychological testing. (1985). Washington, DC: American Psychological Association.

Scatterplot of HOOT and RAT Data

THE 4-QUESTION CHALLENGE

1. With regard to the "do's" and "don'ts" of cultural sensitivity in assessment and test use, which of the following list of "do's" is actually a "do not"?
   a. assume that a test that has been translated into another language is automatically equivalent in every way to the original.
   b. strive to incorporate assessment methods that complement the worldview and lifestyle of assessees who come from a specific cultural and linguistic population.
   c. consideration of cultural hypotheses as possible explanations for findings.
   d. be aware of the cultural assumptions on which a test is based.

2. Which is a criterion-referenced test?
   a. the final competition on *American Idol*
   b. an examination for entry into the electricians union
   c. a teacher-made midterm examination scored on a curve
   d. none of the above

3. Which of the following assumptions about psychological assessment is *most controversial*?
   a. psychological traits and states can be quantified and measured.
   b. test-related behavior predicts non-test-related behavior.
   c. testing and assessment can be conducted in a fair and unbiased manner.
   d. various sources of error are part of the assessment process.

4. *Meta-analysis* is a term used to describe
   a. a tendency of scores to fan out from the mean.
   b. a graphic technique for representing regression.
   c. a variant of psychoanalysis developed by Carl Jung.
   d. a method for combining information across studies.

CHAPTER 5

Reliability

Puzzle 5

Instructions Identify what is described, answer a question, or fill in the blank to complete this crossword puzzle based on material presented in Chapter 5 of your textbook. Answers presented to clues in capital letters should be considered as "free spaces" in the puzzle.

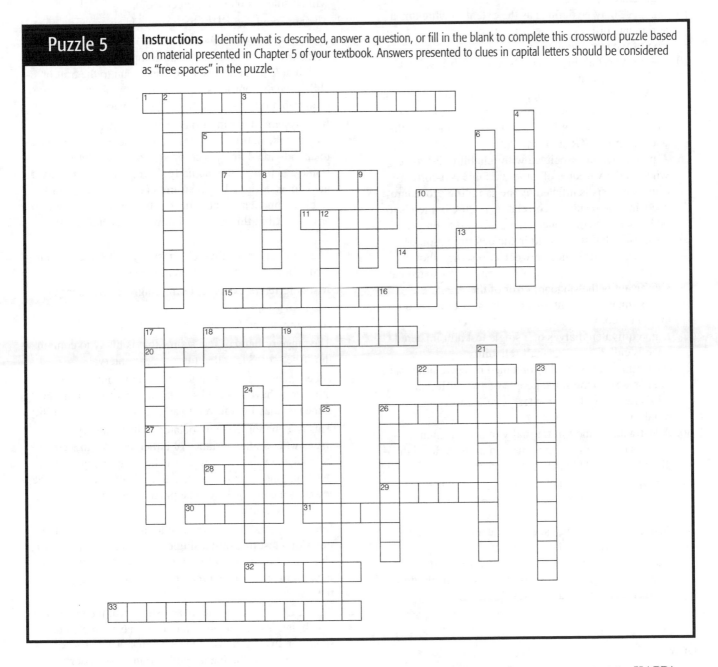

Across

1. In generalizability theory, an index of the influence that particular facets have on a test score is called a coefficient of _____ .

5. A measure of inter-scorer reliability originally designed for use in instances in which scorers make ratings using nominal scales of measurement is called the KAPPA statistic.

7. A measure of variability equal to the arithmetic mean of the squares of the differences between the scores in a distribution and their mean.

10. In the true score model, the component of variance attributable to true differences in the ability or trait being

measured inherent in an observed score or distribution of scores is referred to as _____ variance.

11. Another name for the standard error of measurement is standard error of a(n) _____ .

14. It's the subject matter of the test items.

15. The extent to which individual test items of a test measure a single construct is referred to as test _____ .

18. _____ may be defined as the extent to which measurements differ from occasion to occasion as a function of measurement error.

20. Even-odd reliability or ODD-even reliability, it's all the same. Or is it?

22. M. W. Richardson worked with G. Fredric _____ to develop their own measures for estimating reliability. In fact, M. W. is the _R,_ and G. Fredric is the _K_ in the widely known KR-20 formula.

26. A phenomenon associated with reliability estimates, wherein the variance of either variable is a correlational analysis is inflated by the sampling procedure used and the resulting correlation coefficient tends to be higher as a consequence, is _____ of range.

27. A statistic designed to aid in the determination of how large a difference between two scores should be before the difference should be considered statistically significant is the standard error of the _____ .

28. An estimate of the internal consistency of a test obtained by correlating two pairs of scores obtained from equivalent halves of a single test administered once is called _____-half reliability.

29. An estimate of reliability obtained by correlating pairs of scores from the same people on two different administrations of the same test is called test-_____ reliability.

30. A test with a time limit, usually of achievement or ability and usually with items of a uniform level of difficulty, is called a(n) _____ test.

31. He, Spearman, and their "prophecy" have been immortalized in texts dealing with statistics and measurement.

32. Also known by names such as "raters" or "observers," they typically enter data, not rulings.

33. The extent to which individual items of a test do not measure a single construct but instead measure different factors is referred to as test _____ .

Down

2. An estimate of parallel-forms reliability or alternate-forms reliability is called a coefficient of _____ .

3. A statistic widely employed in test construction and used to assist in deriving an estimate of reliability, it is equal to the mean of all split-half reliabilities. It is coefficient _____ .

4. An estimate of test-retest reliability obtained during time intervals of six months or longer is called a coefficient of _____ .

6. A(n) _____ test is usually one of achievement or ability with (1) either no time limit, or a time limit that is so long that all testtakers will be able to attempt all items, and (2) some items that are so difficult that no testtaker will be able to obtain a perfect score.

8. The now outdated RULON formula is an equation once used to estimate internal consistency reliability.

9. In the true score model, it's the component of variance attributable to random sources irrelevant to the trait or ability the test purports to measure in an observed score or distribution of scores. It's _____ variance.

10. It's a system of assumptions about measurement that includes the notion that a test score, and even a response to an individual item, is composed of (1) a relatively stable component that actually is what the test or individual item is designed to measure, and (2) relatively unstable components that collectively can be accounted for as error. All of this is better known as generalizability _____ .

12. The standard against which a test or a test score is evaluated; it may take many different forms.

13. Also referred to as content sampling, we refer here to _____ sampling.

16. An abbreviation for item response theory.

17. The range or band of test scores that is likely to contain the "true score" is called the _____ interval.

19. An estimate of the extent to which item sampling and other error have affected scores on two versions of the same test may be referred to as _____ forms reliability.

21. This is a phenomenon associated with reliability estimates wherein the variance of either variable in a correlational analysis is restricted by the sampling procedure used, and the resulting correlation coefficient tends to be lower as a consequence. The phenomenon is called _____ of range.

23. Internal _____ is a reference to how consistently the items of a test measure a single construct obtained from a single administration of a single form of the test and the measurement of the degree of correlation among all of the test items.

24. _____ forms reliability is an estimate of the extent to which item sampling and other error have affected test scores on two versions of the same test when, for each form of the test, the means and variances of observed test scores are equal.

25. Also referred to as the standard error of a score, it is the standard error of _____ .

26. A general term to refer to an estimate of the stability of individual items in a test is _____ consistency reliability.

EXERCISE 5-1
MOVIES AND MEASUREMENT

A perfect "10"?

OBJECTIVE

To think about the concept of the reliability of evaluations in an everyday context

BACKGROUND

Dudley Moore (right) rates Bo Derek as a "perfect 10" in the classic film, *10*. This rating is presumably based on subjective criteria related to beauty and related factors. Such ratings can provide a convenient point of departure for discussing psychometric issues such as reliability.

YOUR TASK

Write a brief essay entitled "The Reliability of Interpersonal Ratings" in which you make reference to Dudley Moore and Bo Derek in the film *10*. Discuss how the "test-retest reliability" of such ratings might change over time as a function of various events.

EXERCISE 5-2
THE CONCEPT OF RELIABILITY

OBJECTIVE

To enhance understanding of the concepts of *reliability* and *error variance*

BACKGROUND

Broadly speaking, the concept of *reliability* as used in the context of psychological testing refers to the attribute of consistency in measurement. According to what is referred to as the *true score* model or theory, a score on a test reflects not only the "true" amount of whatever it is that is being measured (such as the true amount of an ability or the true amount of a particular personality trait) but also other factors including chance and other influences (such as noise, a troublesome pen—virtually any random, irrelevant influence on the testtaker's performance). A *reliability coefficient* is an index of reliability—one that expresses the ratio between the "true" score on a test and the total variance. We place the word "true" in quotes because, as Stanley (1971, p. 361) so aptly put it, a true score "is not the ultimate fact in the book of the recording angel." Rather, a *true score* on a test is thought of as the (hypothetical) average of all the observed test scores that would be obtained were an individual to take the test over and over again an infinite number of times. More technically, a true score is presumed to be the remaining part of the observed score once the observed score is stripped of the contribution of random error. Recall that

$$X = T + E$$

where X represents an observed score, T represents a true score, and E represents an error score (a score due to random, irrelevant influences on the test). Now let's focus on the squared standard deviations—or variances (symbolized by lowercase sigmas)—of observed scores, true scores, and error scores. The formula that follows,

$$\sigma^2 = \sigma_{tr}^2 + \sigma_e^2$$

indicates that the total variance (σ^2) in an observed score (or a distribution of observed scores) is equal to the sum of the true variance (σ_{tr}^2) and the error (σ_e^2) variance.

The reliability of a test—denoted below by the symbol r_{xx} to indicate that the same ability or trait (x) is being measured twice—is an expression of the ratio of true to observed variance:

$$r_{xx} = \frac{\sigma_{tr}^2}{\sigma^2}$$

If all of the observed scores in a distribution were entirely free of error—and in essence equal to true scores—the calculated value of r_{xx} would be 1. If all of the observed scores in a distribution contained equal parts error and "true" ability (or traits, or whatever), the calculated value of r_{xx} would be .5. The lower range of a reliability coefficient is .00, and a coefficient of .00 would be indicative of a total lack of reliability; stated another way, such a quotient would be indicative of total error variance (and a total absence of any variance due to whatever it was that the test was supposed to have been measuring).

How is a reliability coefficient calculated? While the ratio of true to observed variance serves us well in theory, it tends not to be very useful in everyday practice. For most data, we will never know what the "true" variance is, and so calculating a reliability coefficient is more complicated than the simple construction of the ratio. The reliability of a test is typically estimated using the appropriate method from any of a number of existing methods. Before getting to specifics, however, let's go back to the expression indicating that the observed variance is equal to the true variance plus the error variance,

$$\sigma^2 = \sigma_{tr}^2 + \sigma_e^2$$

and rewrite that expression as follows,

$$\sigma_{tr}^2 = \sigma^2 - \sigma_e^2$$

and then substitute the resulting terms into the expression of the ratio of true to observed variances:

$$r_{xx} = \frac{\sigma^2 - \sigma_e^2}{\sigma^2}$$

Solving for r_{xx}, we derive the following expression of test reliability:

$$r_{xx} = 1 - \frac{\sigma_e^2}{\sigma^2}$$

In practice, an estimate of reliability as reflected in a reliability coefficient is calculated by means of a coefficient of correlation such as the Pearson r or Spearman's rho—whichever is the appropriate statistic for the data. For example, if the reliability coefficient to be calculated is of the test-retest variety, you may wish to label scores from one administration of the test as the X variable and scores from the second administration of the test as the Y variable; the Pearson r would then be used (provided all of the assumptions inherent in its use were met) to calculate the correlation coefficient—then more appropriately referred to as a "coefficient of reliability." Similarly, if the reliability coefficient to be calculated is a measure of interscorer reliability, you may wish to label Judge 1's scores as the X variable and Judge 2's scores as the Y variable and then employ either the formula for the Pearson r or the Spearman rho (the latter being the more appropriate statistic for ranked data). An exception to this general rule is the case where a measure of internal consistency is required; here, alternative statistics to r (such as coefficient alpha) may be more appropriate.

YOUR TASK

Answer these three questions in detail:

1. Is it possible to develop a test that will be totally free of error variance? Explain why or why not.
2. As an academic exercise, what if you wished to develop an ability-type test that in no way reflected the testtaker's ability? In other words, contrary to the question above, in which you asked whether it would be possible to develop a totally error-free test, here you are being asked if it is possible to develop a test that would reflect nothing but error.
3. Describe the role the concept of *correlation* plays in the concept of *reliability*.

EXERCISE 5-3

TEST-RETEST AND INTERSCORER RELIABILITY

OBJECTIVE

To enhance understanding of and provide practical experience with the computation of test-retest reliability and interscorer reliability

BACKGROUND

As part of Exercise 4-5, you were made privy to final examination score data for a class from a new home-study trade school of impersonation. Let's now suppose that one morning the chancellor of that school wakes up with a severe headache, terrible cramps, and a sudden interest in the area of psychometrics. Given this newfound interest, the chancellor insists that all of the school's ten students must re-take the same (take-home) examination—this so that a coefficient of test-retest reliability can be calculated. Let's further suppose that only a week or so has elapsed since each of the students first took the (not so) final examination. All of the students comply, and the data for the first administration of the final examination as well as its re-administration are presented below:

Student	Final Exam Score	Retest Score
Malcolm	98	84
Heywood	92	97
Mervin	45	63
Zeke	80	91
Sam	76	87
Macy	57	92
Elvis II	61	98
Jed	88	69
Jeb	70	70
Leroy	90	75

YOUR TASK

If you liked the exercise in Chapter 4 in which you calculated what in essence was an alternate forms reliability coefficient, you should also like your task here: calculating a test-retest coefficient of correlation.

1. a. Create a scatterplot of these data. Simply by "eye-balling" the obtained scatterplot, what would you say about the test-retest reliability of the final examination the school is using?
   b. For the purpose of this illustration, let's assume that all of the assumptions inherent in the use of a Pearson r are applicable. Now use r to calculate a test-retest reliability coefficient. What percentage of the observed variance is attributable to "true" differences in ability on the part of the testtakers, and what percentage of the observed variance is error variance? What are the possible sources of error variance?
2. Let's say that instead of final examination score and re-test data, the scores listed represented the ratings of two former *Star Search* judges with respect to criteria like "general ability to impersonate Elvis Presley," "accent," and "nonoriginality." Relabeling the data for the final examination as "Judge 1's Ratings," and relabeling the data for the retest as "Judge 2's Ratings," rank-order the data and calculate a coefficient of interscorer reliability using Spearman's rho. To help get you started, a table you can use to convert the judge's ratings to rankings follows. After you've computed the Spearman rho, answer these questions: What is the calculated coefficient of interscorer reliability coefficient, and what does it mean?

Student	Judge 1 Rating	Judge 1 Ranking	Judge 2 Rating	Judge 2 Ranking
Malcolm	98	___	84	___
Heywood	92	___	97	___
Mervin	45	___	63	___
Zeke	80	___	91	___
Sam	76	___	87	___
Macy	57	___	92	___
Elvis II	61	___	98	___
Jed	88	___	69	___
Jeb	70	___	70	___
Leroy	90	___	75	___

EXERCISE 5-4
USING THE SPEARMAN-BROWN FORMULA

OBJECTIVE

To enhance understanding of and provide firsthand experience with the Spearman-Brown formula

BACKGROUND

"What is the nature of the correlation between one half of a test and the other?" "What will be the estimated reliability of the test if I shorten the test by a given number of items?" "What will be the estimated reliability of the test if I lengthen the test by a given number of items?" In answer to these and related types of questions, the appropriate tool is the Spearman-Brown formula.

Reduction in test size for the purpose of reducing test administration time is a common practice in situations where the test administrator may have only a limited amount of time with the testtaker. In the version of the Spearman-Brown formula used to estimate the effect of reducing the length of a test, r_{sb} is the Spearman-Brown formula, n represents the fraction by which the test length is being reduced, and r_{xy} represents the reliability coefficient that exists prior to the abbreviation of the test:

$$r_{sb} = \frac{nr_{xy}}{1+(n-1)r_{xy}}$$

Let's assume that a test user (or developer) wishes to reduce a test from 150 to 100 items; in this case, n would be equal to the number of items in the revised version (100 items) divided by the number of items in the original version (150):

$$n = \frac{100}{150} = .67$$

YOUR TASK

1. Assuming the original 150-item test had a measured reliability (r_{xy}) of .89, use the Spearman-Brown formula to determine the reliability of the shortened test.
2. Now, how about some firsthand experience in using the Spearman-Brown formula to determine the number of items that would be needed in order to attain a desired level of reliability? Assume for the purpose of this example that the reliability coefficient (r_{xx}) of an existing test is .60 and that the desired reliability coefficient (r_{xx}) is .80. In the expression of the Spearman-Brown formula below, n is equal to the factor that the number of items in the test would have to be multiplied by in order to increase the total number of items in the test to the total number needed for a reliability coefficient at the desired level, r' is the desired reliability, and r_{xx} is the reliability of the existing test:

$$n = \frac{r'(1-r_{xx})}{r_{xx}(1-r')}$$

Thus, for example, if n were calculated to be 3, a 50-item test would have to be increased by a factor of 3 (for a total of 150 items) in order for the desired level of reliability to have been reached. Try one example on your own. Assume now,

A Scatterplot of Test and Retest Scores

A Scatterplot of the Ratings of Judge 1 and Judge 2

for the purpose of example, that a 100-item test has an $r_{xx} = $ .60. In order to increase the reliability of this test to .80, how many items would be necessary?

UNDERSTANDING INTERNAL CONSISTENCY RELIABILITY

OBJECTIVE

To enhance understanding of the psychometric concept of internal consistency reliability as well as methods used to estimate it

BACKGROUND

This exercise is designed to stimulate thought about the meaning of an estimate of internal consistency reliability. Your instructor may assign one, all, or only some of the parts of this exercise.

YOUR TASK

1. In your own words, write a brief (about a paragraph or two) essay entitled "The Psychometric Concept of Internal Consistency Reliability."
2. Using your school library, locate and read three primary sources having to do with methods of obtaining an estimate of internal consistency. On the basis of what you have learned from these articles, rewrite the essay you wrote in Part 1, incorporating the new information. Your new essay should be no more than two pages.
3. A number of different methods may be used to obtain an estimate of internal consistency reliability. In a sentence or two, describe when each of the following would be appropriate:
   a. the Spearman-Brown formula
   b. coefficient alpha
   c. KR-20
4. Each of the following statements is true. In one or two sentences, explain why this is so.
   a. An internal consistency reliability estimate is typically achieved through only one test session.
   b. An estimate of internal consistency reliability is inappropriate for heterogeneous tests.
   c. An estimate of internal consistency reliability is inappropriate for speeded tests.
   d. When estimating internal consistency reliability, the size of the obtained reliability coefficient depends not only on the internal consistency of the test but also on the number of test items.

FIGURE THIS

OBJECTIVE

Obtain firsthand computational experience figuring out problems related to material presented in the chapter

BACKGROUND

Use your knowledge of material presented in Chapter 3 in your textbook to tackle *Your Task* in what follows.

YOUR TASK

1. The school psychologist administered an IQ test with a mean of 100 and a standard deviation of 15 to six children. Their scores were as follows: Sam 85, Jean 100, Byron 126, LaKeisha 115, Hector 68, Hai 145. The reliability coefficient is .85 for this test. Calculate the following:
   a. Standard error of measurement for the test
   b. 68% confidence interval for Sam and Jean
   c. 95% confidence interval for Byron and LaKeisha
   d. 99% confidence interval for Hector and Hai
2. Dexter took an IQ test and obtained a score of 105. He also took a math teacher achievement test and obtained a score of 140. Both tests have a mean of 100 and standard deviation of 15. The reliability coefficient for the IQ test is .82 and for the math teacher achievement test is .91. Calculate the standard error of difference for Dexter's two test scores.
3. LaRonta also took the math teacher achievement test and obtained a score of 145. Calculate the standard error of difference and compare LaRonta and Dexter's performance. Who would you want to teach you statistics and why?

REFERENCE

Stanley, J. C. (1971). Reliability. In R. L. Thorndike (Ed.), *Educational measurement* (2nd ed.). Washington, D.C.: American Council on Education.

THE 4-QUESTION CHALLENGE

1. A coefficient of reliability is
   a. a proportion that indicates the ratio between true score variance on a test and the total variance.
   b. a proportion that indicates the ratio between a partial universe score and the total universe.

c. equal to the ratio between the variance and the standard deviation in a normal distribution.

d. equal to the standard error of the difference between parallel forms of two criterion-referenced tests.

2. Test construction, test administration, and test scoring and interpretation are
   a. sources of error variance.
   b. the sole responsibility of a test publisher.
   c. "facets" according to true score theory.
   d. variables affected by inflation of range.

3. A measure of a test's internal consistency reliability could be obtained through the use of
   a. Kuder-Richardson formula 20.
   b. Cronbach's coefficient alpha.
   c. the Spearman-Brown formula.
   d. all of the above

4. In contrast to a power test, a speed test
   a. has a time limit designed to be long enough to allow all testtakers to attempt all items.
   b. can yield a split-half reliability estimate based on only one administration of the test.
   c. tends to yield score differences among testtakers that are based on performance speed.
   d. tends to yield spuriously inflated estimates of alternate forms reliability.

CHAPTER 6

Validity

Puzzle 6 **Instructions** Identify what is described, answer a question, or fill in the blank to complete this crossword puzzle based on material presented in Chapter 6 of your textbook.

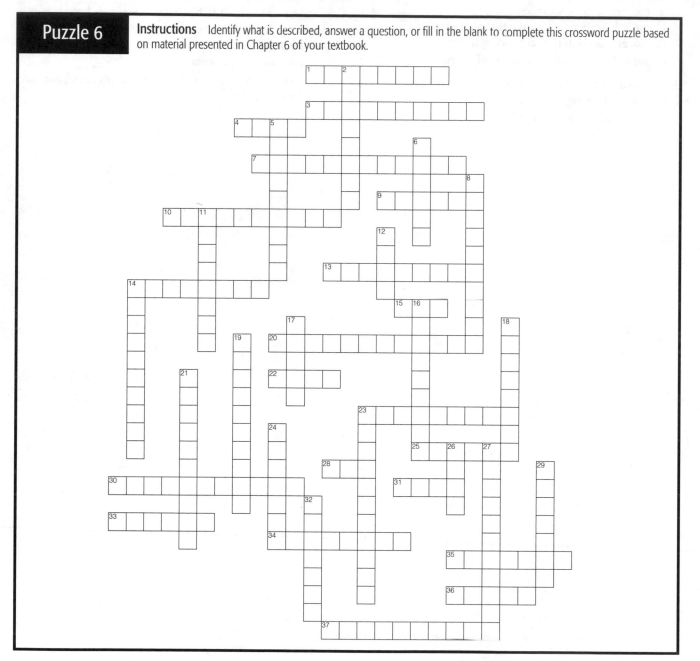

Across

1. A less-than-accurate rating in an evaluation by a rater whose general tendency is to be overly critical in making ratings is referred to as a(n) _____ error.

3. Research that entails gathering evidence relevant to how well a test measures what it purports to measure for the purpose of evaluating the validity of a test or other measurement tool is called a(n) _____ study.

4. A judgment regarding how well a test or other tool of measurement measures what it purports to measure based solely on "appearances," such as the content of a test's items. This is what is meant by _____ validity.

7. With reference to construct validity, data from a test or other measurement instrument showing little relationship between test scores or other variables with which the scores on the test being construct-validated should

not theoretically be correlated are referred to as
_____ evidence.

9. The name of an American film that may have served as the inspiration for the creation of *Crouching Tiger, Hidden Dragon;* but more related to psychometrics, and specifically to Chapter 6 of Cohen & Swerdlik, a correlational technique mentioned in the chapter called the multitrait-multimethod _____ .

10. _____ validity may be defined as a form of criterion-related validity that is an index of the degree to which a test score is related to some criterion measure obtained at the same time.

13. It's an informed, scientific idea that was developed to describe or explain behavior. Some examples include "intelligence," "personality," "anxiety," and "job satisfaction."

14. A false _____ may be defined as an inaccurate prediction or classification indicating that a testtaker did possess a trait or other attribute being measured, when in reality the testtaker did not.

15. The proportion of people a test accurately identifies as possessing or exhibiting a particular trait, behavior, characteristic, or attribute is commonly referred to as its _____ rate.

20. _____ factor analysis is a class of mathematical procedures employed when a factor structure has been explicitly hypothesized and is tested for its fit with regard to observed relationships.

22. A set of circumstances resulting in a tendency on the part of a rater to be positively disposed and insufficiently critical in ratings is referred to as a(n) _____ effect.

23. A logical result or deduction in a reasoning process.

25. They provide an estimate of the extent to which inclusion of a particular test in a selection system will actually improve selection. They are Taylor-Russell _____ .

28. Abbreviation for content validity ratio.

30. Synonymous with internal consistency, _____ of test items may be interpreted as one type of evidence for the test's construct validity.

31. A factor inherent in a test that systematically prevents accurate, impartial measurement.

33. A numerical or verbal judgment that places a person or an attribute along a continuum identified by a scale of numerical or word descriptors is called a(n) _____ scale.

34. It occurs as the result of a rater's tendency to be too forgiving and insufficiently critical in assigning ratings, and it is referred to as a _____ error.

35. With reference to factor analysis, this is a metaphor suggesting that a test (or an individual test item) carries with it a certain amount of one or more abilities which, in turn, has a determining influence on the test score (or on the response to the individual test item). Here, we speak of a factor _____ .

36. When the slope of a regression line is different between groups, a test or measurement procedure may systematically yield different validity coefficients for members of different groups. What exists here is _____ bias.

37. It's a type of error that occurs when less-than-accurate ratings or evaluations are made by a rater due to that rater's tendency to be too forgiving or insufficiently critical. It is called by various names, one of which was the correct answer to 34 Across. It is also referred to as the _____ error.

Down

2. It's a correlation coefficient that provides a measure of the relationship between test scores and scores on a criterion measure. It is otherwise known as a(n) _____ coefficient.

5. The standard against which a test or a test score is evaluated. It may take any of several different forms.

6. It's a class of mathematical procedures, frequently employed as data reduction methods. It is, of course, _____ analysis.

8. A(n) _____ table may be defined as information presented in tabular form designed to illustrate the likelihood that an individual testtaker will score within some interval of scores on a criterion measure.

11. An inaccurate prediction or classification indicating that a testtaker did not possess a trait or other attribute being measured, when in reality the testtaker did. This is referred to as a false _____ .

12. The proportion of people a test or other measurement procedure fails to identify accurately with respect to the possession or exhibition of a particular trait, behavior, characteristic, or attribute is commonly referred to as the _____ rate.

14. A form of criterion-related validity that is an index of the degree to which a test score predicts some criterion measure is _____ validity.

16. When a test or measurement procedure systematically underpredicts or overpredicts the performance of members of a particular group, a situation that is technically referred to as _____ bias exists.

17. A(n) _____ validation study may be defined as the process of gathering evidence relevant to how well a test measures what it purports to measure for the purpose of evaluating the validity of the test. It is typically undertaken in conjunction with a population that is different from the population for whom the test was originally validated.

18. The extent to which a test or other tool of assessment is used in an impartial, just, and equitable way.

19. The method of _____ groups is a procedure for gathering construct validity evidence that entails demonstrating that scores on a test vary in a predictable way as a function of group membership.

21. This is a term typically used with reference to the construct-validation of a test. When other instruments designed to measure the same or a similar construct all point to the same judgment or conclusion with regard to a test, these data may be referred to as _____ evidence regarding the construct validity of the test being evaluated.

23. Used in the context of predictive validity, _____ validity refers to the explanatory power of additional predictors over and above the predictors that are already in use.

24. This is a type of rating error wherein the rater exhibits a general and extreme reluctance to issue ratings at either the positive or negative extreme, and so all or most ratings cluster in the middle of the rating continuum. This is called a(n) _____ tendency error.

26. The _____ rate is an index, usually expressed as a proportion, of the extent to which a particular trait, behavior, characteristic, or attribute exists in a population.

27. _____ factor analysis is a class of mathematical procedures employed to estimate factors, extract factors, or decide how many factors to retain.

29. A procedure that requires the ordinal ordering of persons, scores, or variables into relative positions or degrees of value.

32. _____ validity refers to a judgment regarding how adequately a test or other tool of measurement samples behavior representative of the universe of behavior that it was designed to sample.

EXERCISE 6-1
MOVIES AND MEASUREMENT

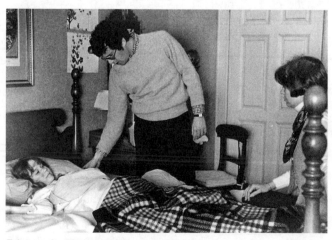

Diagnosis: Possession?

OBJECTIVE

To think about the concept of the validity of evaluations

BACKGROUND

The photo on this page was taken on the set of the classic horror film *The Exorcist*. The two females portray mother (Ellen Burstyn) and daughter (Linda Blair), and the male is the film's director, William Friedkin. The film was the subject of great controversy when it was first released over a quarter-century ago, owing to its haunting depiction of a little girl who was said to be possessed. For students of psychological assessment, the film raised some intriguing questions regarding diagnosis.

YOUR TASK

Demonstrate your knowledge of validity in its various forms in a brief essay entitled, "Validating a Test for Possession." In it, discuss the problems and issues faced by one seeking to validate any instrument or assessment methodology that purports to be useful in diagnosing possession.

EXERCISE 6-2
THE CONCEPT OF VALIDITY

OBJECTIVE

To enhance understanding of and provide firsthand experience with the concept of validity

BACKGROUND

The word *validity* as applied to a test refers to a judgment concerning how well a test does, in fact, measure what it purports to measure; more specifically, it is a judgment based on evidence about the appropriateness of inferences drawn from test scores. One way of conceptualizing validity has been with respect to the following three-category taxonomy:

    content validity
    criterion-related validity
    construct validity

Within the context of the three-category taxonomy, the validity of a test may be evaluated by (1) scrutinizing its content, (2) relating scores obtained on the test to other test scores or other measures, and (3) executing a comprehensive analysis of not only how scores on the test relate to other test scores and measures but also how they can be understood within some theoretical framework for understanding the construct the test was designed to measure. These three approaches to validity assessment are not mutually exclusive; each should be thought of as one type of evidence that, with others, contributes to a judgment concerning the validity of the test. However, although all three types of validity evidence contribute to a unified picture of a test's validity, a test user may not need to know about all three types of validity evidence; depending upon the use to which a test is being put, one or another of these three types of validity evidence may not be as relevant as the next.

YOUR TASK

1. Select any psychological trait such as introversion, aggressiveness, independence—any one will do. Suppose now that someone has created a new test to measure whatever psychological trait you identified above. The new test appropriately enough is called "The Test of *[fill in the blank with the name of the trait]*."

   Because you are keenly interested in this particular psychological trait and want to know if indeed this new test is measuring what it purports to measure, you begin writing a proposal for a grant to conduct a test validation study. *Validation* is the process of gathering and evaluating validity evidence; one speaks, for example, of content validation strategies, criterion-related validation strategies, and construct validation strategies. Briefly outline what you plan to do in order to obtain content-, criterion-, and construct-related validity evidence.

   Oh, and there is one other thing . . .

2. The concept of *face validity* refers more to what a test appears to measure than to what the test actually measures; it in essence relates to a judgment concerning how relevant the items appear to be to the subject matter of the test. If a test definitely appears to measure what it purports to measure "on the face of it," it could be said to be high in face validity. Face validity is not an acceptable basis for interpretive inferences from test scores. Still, face validity is important to the extent that it exerts an influence on the way the testtaker approaches the testing situation. Include in your description of content-, criterion-, and construct-related validation strategies how you might attempt to determine whether the new test was high or low in face validity.

EXERCISE 6-3

THE QUANTIFICATION OF CONTENT VALIDITY

OBJECTIVE

To enhance understanding of and provide firsthand experience with the concept of content validity

BACKGROUND

Content validity refers to a judgment concerning how adequately a test samples behavior representative of the universe of behavior the test was designed to sample. In many instances the determination of whether or not a test is content valid depends upon the opinion of a panel of experts or judges. Thus, for example, a panel of experts in the area of shyness might be called upon to determine if a test of shyness adequately samples the universe of shy/not shy–type behaviors.

Lawshe (1975) developed what he called a *content validity ratio (CVR)* to be used in conjunction with ratings made by a panel of experts. For example, suppose a panel of experts were called upon to decide whether skill in (or knowledge of) a particular area, as measured by a test item, was essential to the performance of a job. And let's say the panelists could rate the behavior tapped by the test item as either essential, useful but not essential, or not necessary. The more panelists who perceived the item as essential, the greater the degree of content validity. The formula for the *CVR* is as follows:

$$CVR = \frac{n_e - N/2}{N/2}$$

Here, n_e is equal to the number of panelists indicating "essential," and N is the total number of panelists. When fewer than half the total number of panelists indicate "essential," the *CVR* will be negative. If exactly half of the panelists indicate "essential," the *CVR* will be 0. And when more than half but not all the panelists indicate "essential," the *CVR* will range between .00 and .99.

In content-validating a test, the content validity ratio is calculated for each item. The items for which agreement could have occurred by chance are eliminated. Table 6-1 from Lawshe (1975) provides the minimum *CVR* values needed for significance at the .05 level. In the case where

TABLE 6-1 *Minimum Values of the Content Validity Ratio for Significance at p = .05 (one-tailed test)*

Number of Panelists	Minimum Value
5	.99
6	.99
7	.99
8	.75
9	.78
10	.62
11	.59
12	.56
13	.54
14	.51
15	.49
20	.42
25	.37
30	.33
35	.31
40	.29

there are ten panelists, an item would need a minimum *CVR* of .62 for significance at the .05 level.

YOUR TASK

In order to provide you with some firsthand experience with the calculation of a *CVR,* imagine the following scenario. An experimental psychologist by the name of Nussbaum has devoted her research life to addressing questions such as (1) why so many Ph.D.'s seem to have problems correctly spelling and punctuating "Ph.D." and (2) the associations people have to various smells. In the latter context, she has been developing a new test to measure associations conjured by different scents and has called upon a panel of 20 experts (all of whom are Ph.D.'s with a well-documented ability to spell and punctuate their degree appropriately) to assist in the project. The test, christened the Nussbaum Olfactory Schedule (NOS), contains 50 items—each of which entails the administration of a stimulus smell (such as a rose, pine, and lemon-scented dishwashing liquid). Each item is rated by each expert as imparting either a "unique smell," "an odor with some potential," or "a totally not unique smell." The idea here is to assemble items with unique smells. The ratings for the first five items appear below. Using the symbol n_u to indicate the number of panelists judging a particular item or stimulus to be unique, and calculating the *CVR* for each item, determine whether you would include each of these items in the NOS and explain why.

Item 1: 9 of the judges rated it unique.
Item 2: 10 of the judges rated it unique.
Item 3: 12 of the judges rated it unique.
Item 4: 14 of the judges rated it unique.
Item 5: 17 of the judges rated it unique.

EXERCISE 6-4

PREDICTING A CRITERION SCORE

OBJECTIVE

To enhance familiarity and provide firsthand experience with the process of predicting a criterion score

BACKGROUND

One important application of the validity coefficient is its use in predicting a criterion score. Suppose, for example, that on the basis of a college entrance examination, a college admissions officer seeks to predict what an applicant's grades might look like at the end of the first semester of college.

You will recall that, in general, as r_{xy} approaches 1.00, prediction accuracy increases; as r_{xy} approaches 0.0, prediction accuracy decreases. In order to be able to predict individual criterion scores, the test user or test developer needs validation data from a representative sample of a defined

population—predictor test scores (which we will refer to as *X* scores) as well as criterion scores (which we will refer to as *Y* scores). One procedure for calculating an estimated criterion score (referred to as *Y′* and pronounced "Y prime") entails the following:

- computation of the respective means and standard deviations of *X* and *Y;*
- substitution of the appropriate values into a formula for the linear regression equation; and
- solving the equation to determine the value of *Y′*.

If the relationship between the two variables (the test score and the criterion score) is linear, a linear regression for prediction of the criterion such as outlined below may be employed.

Step 1

Determine the specific regression equation from the general formula based on the data by substituting the respective means and standard deviations of *X* and *Y* into the general formula. The general formula for predicting a criterion score is

$$Y' = \left[(r_{xy}) \left(\frac{s_y}{s_x} \right) (X - \bar{X}) \right] + \bar{Y}$$

where Y' = the estimated criterion score
r_{xy} = the Pearson *r*
s_y = the standard deviation of the criterion scores
s_x = the standard deviation of the predictor scores
X = an individual predictor score
$\bar{X}$ = mean of the predictor scores
$\bar{Y}$ = mean of the criterion scores

After the means and standard deviations are substituted into the general formula, the equation reduces to $Y' = aX + b$ in which *a* and *b* are, as we noted in Chapter 4, regression coefficients. Also as we noted in Chapter 4, the reduced equation is recognizable as the equation for a straight line.

Step 2

Choose one individual test score. Substitute the score for *X* and solve for *Y′*.

To predict any criterion score from any test score, repeat Step 2. Mathematically, one can also predict the test score (*X*) from a knowledge of the criterion score (*Y*).

As an example, let's assume a high school guidance counselor has conducted a validation study of a hypothetical test we will call the "Freshman Grade Predictor" (FGP). The counselor has before him the last year's class of students' FGP scores obtained while the students were still seniors in high school. The counselor also has before him the students' grade-point indices for their first year of college (for those students who attended college). If the test scores on the FGP are indeed valid for predicting freshman grades, then the test will be a boon to the counselor with respect to the counseling of future classes of students, as well as the advising of school officials on sundry matters (such as those regarding the placement of students in accelerated, average, or remedial classes).

Letting X stand for a score and Y stand for a "score" on the predictor (actually grade-point average), let's assume that the counselor observed the following:

$r_{xy} = .89$ This is an expression of a correlation coefficient, though in the present context it would more appropriately be referred to as a *validity coefficient*. It expresses the coefficient of correlation that exists between the predictor and criterion variables.

$s_y = .6$ The standard deviation of grade-point averages for the first year of college-level work is .6.

$s_x = 10$ The standard deviation of FGP test scores is 10.

$\overline{X} = 50$ The mean of FGP test scores is 50.

$\overline{Y} = 2.0$ The mean grade-point average for the first year of college work is 2.0.

The general formula for the regression equation and the appropriate substitutions are as follows:

$$Y' = \left[(r_{xy}) \left(\frac{s_y}{s_x} \right) (X - \overline{X}) \right] + \overline{Y}$$

$$Y' = \left[(.89) \left(\frac{0.6}{10.0} \right) (X - 50) \right] + 2.0$$

$$Y' = \left[(.89)(.06)(X - 50) \right] + 2.0$$

$$Y' = \left[(.05)(X - 50) \right] + 2.0$$

$$Y' = \left[0.5X - 2.5 \right] + 2.0$$

$$Y' = .05X - .5 \qquad \text{(a)}$$

The reduced equation (a) is the regression equation with which we can now predict freshman grade-point average with knowledge of only a single test score.

Assume now that this is a new school year. The counselor needs all the help he can get to answer this question: Should Paul be placed in an accelerated class? The overall grade-point average of students in the accelerated class is 3.0. Paul's score on the FGP was 80. Knowing Paul's test score, the counselor can estimate Paul's freshman grade-point average; this may be one—and only one—bit of information used to decide if Paul should indeed be placed in an accelerated class. The validation study had indicated that the validity coefficient between FGP test scores and freshman grade-point average is .89. Substituting Paul's test score into the regression equation obtained from the validation study, we obtain the following:

$$Y' = .05X - .5$$

$$Y' = .05(80) - .5$$

$$Y' = 3.5$$

The counselor estimates Paul's freshman grade-point average to be about 3.5. The next question the counselor needs answered is "How accurate is this estimate?" The standard error of estimate (s_{est}) comes into play here.[1] This statistic allows one to determine how much of the score is attributable to error in the statistical sense (recall that "error" is the difference between the observed score and the predicted score), and its formula is as follows:

$$s_{est} = s_y \sqrt{1 - r_{xy}^2}$$

where s_{est} = standard error of estimate,
  s_y = standard deviation of the criterion score, and
  r_{xy} = the correlation (validity) coefficient.

Using the data from the example above:

$$s_y = .6$$

$$r_{xy} = .89$$

$$s_{est} = .6 \sqrt{\left(1 - .89^2\right)}$$

$$= .6 \sqrt{(1 - .792)}$$

$$= .6 \sqrt{(.208)}$$

$$= .6(.456)$$

$$= .27$$

What is the meaning of the .27 we obtained? To interpret this result, recall that with respect to units of the standard error of measurement:

± 1 = approximately 68% of the area under the normal curve

± 2 = approximately 95% of the area under the normal curve

± 3 = approximately 99.7% of the area under the normal curve

Similarly, with regard to a predicted score and the standard error of estimate, the approximate probabilities are as follows:

68% that the predicted score will occur within $\pm 1\ s_{est}$

95% that the predicted score will occur within $\pm 2\ s_{est}$

99.7% that the predicted score will occur within $\pm 3\ s_{est}$

If Paul's predicted grade-point average (Y') were 3.5 with $s_{est} = .27$, the probability is 95% that his actual grade-point average would fall within $\pm 2\ s_{est}$ of his predicted grade-point average, or $3.5 \pm .54$ (or between 2.96 and 4.04). If the correlation were higher, the standard error of estimate would be smaller, and the interval within which a predicted score would be most likely to occur would be narrower. The guidance counselor will have to look to other sources, such as teacher recommendations, in drawing his conclusion about placement in the accelerated class.

---

[1] Sometimes expressed as $S_{y \cdot x}$ and read "the standard deviation of Y for a given value of X."

For the sake of example, let's consider the case wherein the FGP correlates almost perfectly with freshman grade-point average—where r_{xy} equals .99. The regression equation, assuming the means and standard deviations for X and Y stayed the same as above, would be

$$Y' = \left[(r_{xy}) \left(\frac{s_y}{s_x} \right) (X - \bar{X}) \right] + \bar{Y}$$

$$Y' = \left[(.99) \left(\frac{.6}{10} \right) (X - 50) \right] + 2.0$$

$$Y' = [.0594X - 2.97] + 2$$

$$Y' = .0594X - .97$$

Paul's estimated criterion score based on a test score of 80 would be

$$Y' = .0594(80) - .9 = 3.782$$

and the standard error of estimate would be

$$s_{est} = s_y \sqrt{1 - r^2}$$

$$= .6 \sqrt{(1 - .99^2)}$$

$$= .6 \sqrt{(1 - .9801)}$$

$$= .6 \sqrt{.0199}$$

$$= .6(.14)$$

$$= .08$$

We can see that with a correlation (validity) coefficient of .99, the counselor could be 95% confident that Paul's grade-point average would occur within $\pm 2s_{est}$, which is 3.77 $\pm$ .16—between 3.61 and 3.93. Notice the prediction interval is narrower than the one computed with the lower correlation coefficient of .89.

Now let's suppose the FGP did not correlate at all with high school grade-point average. With $r_x = 0.0$, the regression equation reduces to $Y' = \bar{Y}$:

$$s_{est} = s_y \sqrt{1 - r^2}$$

$$= .6 \sqrt{1 - 0.0^2}$$

$$= .6 \sqrt{1}$$

$$= .6(1)$$

$$= .6$$

With reference to these data, one could say with 95% confidence that Paul's high school grade-point average would occur within $\pm 2(.6)$ (or between 0.8 and 3.2).

The three examples cited to illustrate the relationships between the correlation (validity) coefficient and the standard error of estimate may be summarized as follows:

r_{xy}	s_{est}	Predicted Criterion Range at 95% Confidence Level
.89	.27	2.8 to 3.8
.99	.08	3.6 to 3.9
.00	.60	0.8 to 3.2

Note that as r_{xy} approaches 1.00, the standard error of estimate shrinks, and the interval within which the criterion score is likely to occur also shrinks. Stated another way, as r_{xy} approaches 1.00, the more precisely we can predict the range within which a criterion score is likely to occur.

To use s_{est} meaningfully as a measure of error in predicting criterion scores, the XY relationship should not only be linear, but the variances of the respective X and Y distributions should not be significantly different from one another. One easy though imprecise way to assess linearity is by drawing a scatterplot of the data. If the cloud of dots appears to bend (and you aren't suffering from visual defects or hallucinations, and haven't been drinking or otherwise had your state of consciousness altered), suspect nonlinearity of the data. The scatterplot may also reveal unequal variances, a condition known as *heteroscedasticity* (*hetero* means "different"; *scedastic* means "scatter"). Heteroscedasticity occurs when there is wider variability in criterion performance among, for example, the high-scoring testtakers as compared with the low-scoring testtakers. The resulting scatterplot is wider toward one end of the bivariate distribution. Figure 6-1 provides an example of heteroscedastic data. Chronological age is the X variable; mental age as determined by performance on the hypothetical "National Intelligence Test" (NIT) is the Y variable. The wider variability at the upper end suggests there is wider variation in mental age among the (chronologically) older testtakers.

In this exercise we have examined and illustrated statistical considerations with respect to the relationship between two variables (correlation) and the prediction of one variable from another (regression). As you are—or should be—aware, corresponding statistical techniques exist for use with more than one predictor variable; these corresponding techniques are multiple correlation and multiple regression. If, for example, we were trying to predict married subjects' criterion performance on a "life satisfaction test" (LST), we might administer a number of different (predictor) tests—perhaps the following three: a marital satisfaction test, a job satisfaction test, and a self-satisfaction test. After administering these three tests as well as the criterion LST to a sample of respondents, the results from a multiple correlation might indicate that the self-satisfaction test is more highly correlated with the criterion than the other two tests and should therefore be "weighted" more heavily in the multiple regression equation. Of course, it's a lot more complicated than that, and the interested reader is referred to any of the many current statistics texts that discuss in detail the techniques of multiple correlation and multiple regression.

FIGURE 6-1 *Heteroscedastic Scatterplot Showing the Relationship Between Chronological Age and Mental Age as Measured by the NIT*

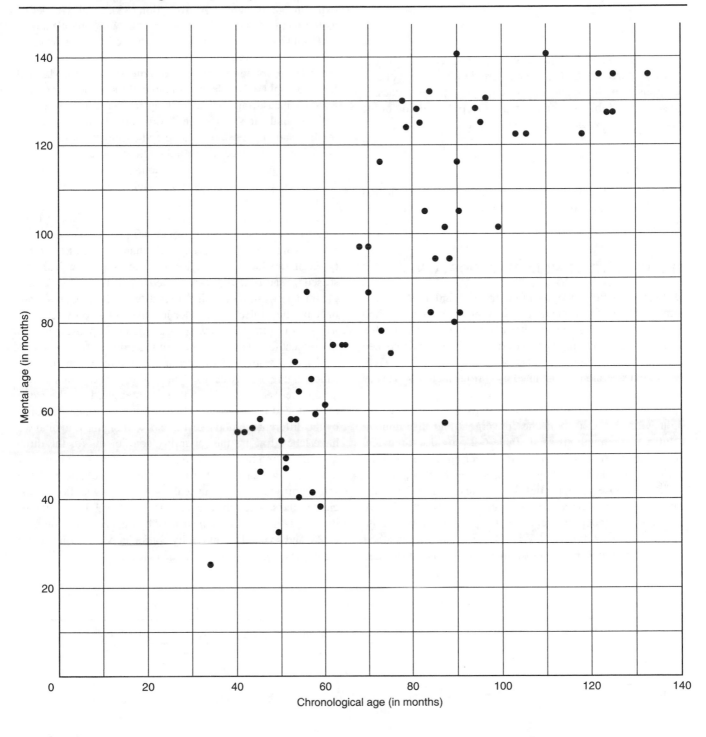

YOUR TASK

Walk in the shoes of the guidance counselor described earlier and decide whether another candidate for accelerated class placement, Karla, should or should not be placed in the accelerated class. Karla's score on the FGP was 86, r_{xy} was equal to .75, and s_y was equal to .87. After you give your answer, provide a word or two about how sure you are.

THE MULTITRAIT-MULTIMETHOD MATRIX

OBJECTIVE

To enhance understanding of how a multitrait-multimethod matrix (Campbell & Fiske, 1959) can function to provide insights regarding the convergent and discriminant validity of the methods used

BACKGROUND

In the example that follows, values for three traits as obtained by three methods will be inserted into a matrix of correlations. The template for insertion of these values is presented in Table 6-2, and a step-by-step description of the insertion of the values is presented in Tables 6-3 through 6-8.

YOUR TASK

After reading the description of the multitrait-multimethod that follows, respond to questions 1 and 2 at the end of this exercise.

THE MULTITRAIT-MULTIMETHOD MATRIX

Multitrait means "two or more traits," and *multimethod* means "two or more methods." The multitrait-multimethod matrix (Campbell & Fiske, 1959) is the matrix or table that results from correlating variables (traits) within and between methods. Values for any number of traits (such as aggressiveness or extraversion) as obtained by various methods (such as behavioral observation or a projective test) are inserted into the table, and the resulting matrix of correlations provides insight with respect to both the convergent and discriminant validity of the methods used. Table 6-2 provides a preview of the basic structure of the matrix when measures of three traits have been obtained by the use of three methods.

Let's suppose you have developed a test you wish to validate that purports to measure the trait "job satisfaction" (JS). Your test is a paper-and-pencil, self-report measure of satisfaction in the workplace. Using the multitrait-multimethod design, you would need to examine at least one other vari-

able. You select marital satisfaction (MS) as a second trait to examine. "For good measure," you add a third trait to the experimental design: self-satisfaction (SS), a trait you define as the comfort and satisfaction one has with oneself alone, including personal comfort and satisfaction with level of academic, financial, and social achievement. If strong correlations were found to exist between measures of JS, MS, and SS, you might conclude that all three of these measures were actually measuring the same thing, a construct you might call "general life satisfaction." Alternatively, moderate correlations among these traits assessed by the instruments you are using would suggest that although all three may be components of general satisfaction, each also contributes something unique; each represents a viable trait separate and distinct from the others.

As illustrated in Table 6-3, the three methods you have elected to use are (1) a self-report rating scale, (2) a spouse rating scale, and (3) a peer questionnaire; each of the three types of satisfaction traits we are interested in will be assessed by each one of these methods. This means, for example, that a measure of "self-satisfaction" will be obtained not only by the subject himself or herself, but also by the subject's spouse (that is, how self-satisfied the spouse believes the subject to be) and by a peer of the subject.

The data required for insertion into the matrix include the following: reliability coefficients, validity coefficients, correlations between the different traits measured by the same method, and correlations between different traits measured by the different methods. In Table 6-4, along the diagonal we have labeled **a,** are the reliability coefficients for the three traits measured by the same method. Focusing on this part of the matrix we can see that the reliability coefficient of the self-report job satisfaction scale is .98, the reliability coefficient of the self-report marital satisfaction is .94, the reliability of self-satisfaction as measured by the peer questionnaire is .88, and so on. The reliability coefficients will typically be the highest values reported in the matrix.

TABLE 6-2   *Basic Structure of a Multitrait-Multimethod Matrix for Three Traits Assessed by Three Methods*

	Method 1			Method 2			Method 3		
	Trait 1	Trait 2	Trait 3	Trait 1	Trait 2	Trait 3	Trait 1	Trait 2	Trait 3
Method 1									
Trait 1	.								
Trait 2	.	.							
Trait 3	.	.	.						
Method 2									
Trait 1	.	.	.	.					
Trait 2	.	.	.	.	.				
Trait 3	.	.	.	.	.	.			
Method 3									
Trait 1	.	.	.	.	.	.	.		
Trait 2	.	.	.	.	.	.	.	.	
Trait 3	.	.	.	.	.	.	.	.	.

TABLE 6-3 *A Multitrait-Multimethod Matrix for Three Measures of Satisfaction Assessed by Three Different Methods*

	Self-Report			Spouse Rating Scale			Peer Questionnaire		
	JS	MS	SS	JS	MS	SS	JS	MS	SS
Self-report									
JS	.								
MS	.	.							
SS	.	.	.						
Spouse rating scale									
JS	.	.	.	.					
MS	.	.	.	.	.				
SS	.	.	.	.	.	.			
Peer questionnaire									
JS	.	.	.	.	.	.	.		
MS	.	.	.	.	.	.	.	.	
SS	.	.	.	.	.	.	.	.	.

TABLE 6-4 *Multitrait-Multimethod Matrix With Reliability Coefficients Inserted*

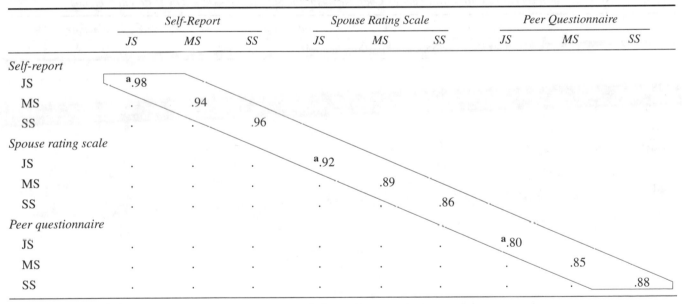

	Self-Report			Spouse Rating Scale			Peer Questionnaire		
	JS	MS	SS	JS	MS	SS	JS	MS	SS
Self-report									
JS	[a].98								
MS	.	.94							
SS	.	.	.96						
Spouse rating scale									
JS	.	.	.	[a].92					
MS	.	.	.	.	.89				
SS	.	.	.	.	.	.86			
Peer questionnaire									
JS	.	.	.	.	.	.	[a].80		
MS	.	.	.	.	.	.	.	.85	
SS	.	.	.	.	.	.	.	.	.88

Another part of the matrix contains correlations between different traits using the same method; it is highlighted in Table 6-5 in the solid triangles labeled **b.** If tests are actually measuring different constructs, these correlations should be relatively low. Self-report measures of marital satisfaction and job satisfaction correlate .50—a fact that suggests that while they are measuring something in common, they are also both contributing unique information as well. Much the same could be said about the self-satisfaction measures, which also seem to fall in the .40 to .60 range.

A third part of the matrix contains the validity coefficients—designated in Table 6-6 along the **c** diagonals. Here we see the correlations between the same trait using different methods. For example, the validity coefficient between job satisfaction by self-report and job satisfaction by spouse rating is .65; the validity coefficient between marital satisfaction by spouse rating and marital satisfaction by peer questionnaire is .72.

As illustrated in Table 6-7, a fourth component of the matrix contains correlations between different traits using different methods (**d** triangles). The value of these correlation coefficients will be among the lowest in the matrix if evidence of construct validity is deemed to be present.

The complete multitrait-multimethod matrix is presented in Table 6-8. For satisfactory evidence of construct validity, the validity coefficients (representing correlations between

TABLE 6-5   *Multitrait-Multimethod Matrix, with Correlations Between Different Traits Using the Same Methods Highlighted*

	Self-Report			Spouse Rating Scale			Peer Questionnaire		
	JS	MS	SS	JS	MS	SS	JS	MS	SS
Self-report									
JS	.								
MS	b.50	.							
SS	.42	.59	.						
Spouse rating scale									
JS	.	.	.	.					
MS	.	.	.	b.40	.				
SS	.	.	.	.60	.52	.			
Peer questionnaire									
JS	.	.	.	.	.	.	.		
MS	.	.	.	.	.	.	b.10	.	
SS	.	.	.	.	.	.	.50	.46	.

TABLE 6-6   *Multitrait-Multimethod Matrix with Validity Coefficients for the Same Trait Assessed by Different Methods*

	Self-Report			Spouse Rating Scale			Peer Questionnaire		
	JS	MS	SS	JS	MS	SS	JS	MS	SS
Self-report									
JS	.								
MS	.	.							
SS	.	.	.						
Spouse rating scale									
JS	c.65	.	.	.					
MS	.	.61	.	.	.				
SS	.	.	.66	.	.	.			
Peer questionnaire									
JS	c.59	.	.	c.69	.	.	.		
MS	.	.55	.	.	.72	.	.	.	
SS	.	.	.58	.	.	.68	.	.	.

the same traits using different methods) in the **c** diagonal should be higher than correlations between different traits, same methods (**b** triangles); they should also be higher than correlations between different traits, different methods (**d** triangles). If job satisfaction correlated with marital satisfaction using different methods (validity coefficients), it should be higher than job satisfaction correlated with marital satisfaction by the same method. If the correlation between self-report job and marital satisfaction were higher than job satisfaction by self-report correlated with job satisfaction by peer questionnaire, one could assume that the scores on self-report were affected substantially by some other factor common to the method (such as desire to respond in a socially desirable way).

1. A sports psychologist conducted a study dealing with the relationship between anxiety-before-the-game and athletic skill in high school football players. In the study, all varsity football players at Warren G. Harding High School rated themselves on two variables: anxiety-before-the-game and athletic skill. The Harding High football coaching staff rated all of the varsity football players on the same two variables. Surveying the multitrait-multimethod matrix that resulted, what might you conclude?

TABLE 6-7 *Multitrait-Multimethod Matrix with Correlations for Different Traits Assessed by Different Methods*

	Self-Report			Spouse Rating Scale			Peer Questionnaire		
	JS	MS	SS	JS	MS	SS	JS	MS	SS
Self-report									
JS	.								
MS		.							
SS			.						
Spouse rating scale									
JS	.	d.10	.15	.					
MS	d.02	.	.18		.				
SS	.04	.10	.			.			
Peer questionnaire									
JS	.	d.08	.11	.	d.00	.04	.		
MS	d.01	.	.09	d.00	.	.02		.	
SS	.06	.11	.	.02	.05	.			.

TABLE 6-8 *A Sample Multitrait-Multimethod Matrix*

	Self-Report			Spouse Rating Scale			Peer Questionnaire		
	JS	MS	SS	JS	MS	SS	JS	MS	SS
Self-report									
JS	a.98								
MS	b.50	.94							
SS	.42	.59	.96						
Spouse rating scale									
JS	c.65	d.10	.15	a.92					
MS	d.02	.61	.18	b.40	.89				
SS	.04	.10	.66	.60	.52	.86			
Peer questionnaire									
JS	c.59	d.08	.11	c.69	d.00	.04	a.80		
MS	d.01	.55	.09	d.00	.72	.02	b.10	.85	
SS	.06	.11	.58	.02	.05	.68	.50	.46	.88

	Self-Evaluation		Coaches' Evaluation of Student	
	Anxiety	Skill	Anxiety	Skill
Self-evaluation				
Anxiety	.95	—	—	—
Skill	.40	.80	—	—
Coaches' evaluation of student				
Anxiety	.77	.15	.86	—
Skill	.10	.15	.20	.71

2. A hypothetical study examined the relationship among SAT Verbal and Math scores, final grade in high school courses in math and English, and final grade in college courses in freshman math and English. The resulting multitrait-multimethod matrix follows. A colleague in the English department has called on you to share your expertise in psychometrics. Explain to your colleague the meaning of each of the coefficients in the matrix. Impart your thoughts on the reliability and validity of each of the scales based on the matrix. Conclude with a summary statement regarding the nature of the relationship among SAT Verbal and Math scores, final grade in high school courses in math and English, and final grade in college courses in freshman math and English.

	SAT		High School		College	
	Math	Verbal	Math	Verbal	Math	Verbal
SAT						
Math	.95	—	—	—	—	—
Verbal	.56	.96	—	—	—	—
High school						
Math	.77	.20	.80	—	—	—
Verbal	.18	.69	.55	.77	—	—
College						
Math	.73	.10	.78	.66	.40	—
Verbal	.17	.30	.80	.75	.80	.46

EXERCISE 6-6

FACTOR ANALYSIS I: AN OVERVIEW

OBJECTIVE

To impart an understanding in general terms of what is meant by "factor analysis"

BACKGROUND

Factor analytic techniques are increasingly employed in the development of psychological tests as well as in research on tests. This exercise seeks to impart a basic overview of factor analysis.

YOUR TASK

Read the essay on factor analysis that follows. Then, make a list of at least three questions regarding what factor analysis is, how it is conducted, and what is done with it. At the discretion of your instructor, you may be asked to submit the questions for class discussion.

FACTOR ANALYSIS: WHAT IT IS, HOW IT'S DONE, AND WHAT TO DO WITH IT[2]

All scientists attempt to identify the basic underlying dimensions that can be used to account for the phenomena they study. For example, physicists refer to inferred dimensions or constructs such as "force" or "energy" in their attempt to identify and account for a large number of physical phenomena that occur in the universe. Behavioral scientists speak of other dimensions, constructs, or factors in their own attempt to identify, label, and understand behavioral phenomena.

Consider the case of a psychologist involved in personality research who has accumulated data on hundreds of testtakers who each sat for a dozen personality tests—personality tests that are supposed to measure about six dozen personality dimensions (also called "traits"). After analyzing the data, the psychologist may come to the conclusion that only three or four dimensions of personality are being measured by all those tests. Or, how about a hypothetical instrument we'll call the "Test of Executive Potential" (TEP)—a test that claims to provide scores on 21 dimensions or factors related to managerial success. After extensive research and experience with the TEP, an industrial/organizational psychologist might conclude that the TEP actually measures only ten dimensions or factors related to managerial success. In each of these cases, the behavioral scientist began with measurements on several variables, analyzed the data, and concluded as a result of data analyses that some basic dimensions or factors could more efficiently account for the observed data. Several different, related procedures may be used to analyze data for the purpose of identifying basic dimensions or factors. Collectively, these techniques are known as *factor analysis*.[3]

What Is Factor Analysis?

We will define *factor analysis* as "a set of mathematical techniques used to identify dimensions underlying a set of empirical measurements." To examine the process, let's do an informal kind of factor analysis. Imagine that you are a clinical psychologist and a new patient, a 45-year-old woman whom you refer to as "Annette O.," has just entered your office for her first consultation. Days before, when she had made the appointment, this woman would not explain over the phone why she sought therapy. In fact, she wouldn't even tell you her last name! After a brief exchange of pleasantries you say, "How may I be of help to you?" And then it all comes out.

Annette tells you how unhappy and miserable she is; a long-term relationship ended abruptly three months before this consultation when the man she was seeing suddenly decided that he wanted to go to school full-time to become a court reporter. Since that day she's been experiencing headaches, stomach pains, poor appetite, an inability to get a good night's sleep (or even feel very calm anytime during the day), a reluctance to get out of bed in the morning, a general and overwhelming feeling of dread, and an outbreak of acne—the likes of which she hadn't seen since adolescence.

During the course of this initial session with Annette, you are not only an "active listener" but an "active watcher" as well. You pay close attention not only to her verbal behavior but also to her nonverbal behavior. You note the generally sad expression on her face, the nonstop

---

[2]Prepared by Louis H. Primavera and Bernard S. Gorman.

[3]Keep in mind, however, that although for our purposes we speak of "factor analysis" in the singular sense—as if it were one technique, like "simple addition"—there are many different ways of factor-analyzing data, and some may yield results that differ from others.

hand-wringing behavior, the plaintive cry in her voice, and the fact that you're almost completely out of tissues.

As your clock signals the end of the session, two words—neither one of them uttered among the hundreds of words spoken during the course of the session—seem to summarize much of the information you obtained in this first session with Annette: "depression" and "anxiety."

Turning the pages in your calendar with one hand while you try gracefully to fumble for your pen (which during the course of the session fell between the cracks of your leather chair) with the other, your mind races to thoughts of alternative therapy plans. You are too preoccupied to reflect on the elements of the process that has just transpired. One way of looking at that process is to think of it as data reduction. You have mentally reduced mounds of data to a more manageable and workable amount. More specifically, there were five steps in that process. Step 1 involved your observation of the person's behavior during the therapy session. In Step 2, you tried to understand how the themes that you observed went together—that is, what observations were similar to one another. Step 3 involved decisions regarding what everything you saw and heard had in common—that is, what the processes or underlying dimensions were. Step 4 involved a decision on your part regarding the relative weights or importance of each of the dimensions; depression and anxiety were the dimensions that struck you as most prominent. Step 5 involved your formulation of a plan of therapeutic intervention—a plan for using the data in a way that you deem will best help Annette.

As we shall soon see, the five-step process described above in many ways parallels the five-step description of factor analysis that follows. A major difference, of course, is that factor analysis, as it is typically used in psychology, is based on the administration of a number of measures to a scientifically selected sample of people—not one person's subjective observations and judgments about another person. Also, before moving on from the question "What is factor analysis?" we might make note of what factor analysis is *not*. The process of factor analysis is sometimes confused with the process of *cluster analysis*—a set of methods for grouping similar measures without necessarily searching for underlying, quantifiable dimensions.

How Is Factor Analysis Done?

Our goal here is to convey a general understanding of the process of factor analysis, as used in psychological measurement, not a "nuts-and-bolts" primer on how to do it. The mathematical procedures used in factor analysis are very complex. The reader who is interested in a more mathematically detailed, how-to-do-it presentation is referred to other sources, such as Gorsuch (1983).

Step 1

The first step in doing a factor analysis involves choosing a set of tests or measures. These measures or variables could be items on one test or two or more complete tests. For the purpose of this discussion, we will refer to these variables—either test items or whole tests—simply as "measures." Once you choose the measures that you wish to use, you administer them to a sample of testtakers. This sample is selected—as in all good empirical research—to represent the population to which you wish to generalize your results. This first step is similar to the initial step in the therapy session described above: careful observation of the patient's behavior.

Step 2

The second step in factor analysis is to compute all correlations among the set of measures that you have chosen to represent the construct or constructs. Recall that in Step 2 in Annette's initial therapy session, you decided, through some subjective process, which of the patient's behaviors were similar to each other. The second step in a factor analysis may also be thought of as a process of distilling relationships, though here the method is not so subjective. Instead, mathematically computed coefficients of correlation are used.

Correlation coefficients provide a gauge of the degree of similarity that exists between measures. Correlations quantify the degree to which two variables have something in common. The squared value of the correlation coefficient, called the *coefficient of determination,* is interpreted as the proportion of variance shared by two variables. It provides a quantitative index of how much two measures have in common. For example, if we found that a test of anxiety correlated .60 with a test of neuroticism, then we could conclude that they had .36, or 36 percent, shared variance; that is, 36 percent of what was being measured by the anxiety test was also measured by the neuroticism test. The correlations are arranged into a matrix of intercorrelations, and this matrix is used in the next step of the process.

Step 3

The third step in a factor analysis is to factor the matrix of intercorrelations among a set of measures. This step is similar to the third step in the therapy session; there decisions were made regarding what the major underlying dimensions of the patient's behaviors were. The matrix of intercorrelation is factored using one or more mathematical procedures.

Factoring is a term that you may already have some familiarity with. You probably remember hearing a grade-school teacher use the term to describe a method in algebra by which a large, unwieldy expression was made more manageable by division of common factors. In modern factor-analysis methods, computer programs analyze the matrix of intercorrelations into a smaller matrix of a few common factors.

Most of the factoring procedures used in factor analysis produce a set of independent, uncorrelated factors. Most of them also can produce as many factors as there are variables. Some of these factors are thought to be *common factors,* and others are thought to be *specific factors* and *error factors.* Common factors represent the dimensions that all the measures have in common. They are the underlying, basic dimensions that scientists seek to identify—the basic taxonomies of fields of scientific endeavor. Specific factors are simply those factors that are related to some specific aspect of the measuring procedure but are not common to any of the other measures in the analysis. Error factors refer to error of measurement or unreliability, which is always a part of any measuring process.

It is up to the researcher to decide which of the factors produced by the factor analysis are the common factors, since that is usually the purpose for doing factor analysis. The problem of identifying which of the factors are the common factors has occupied a great deal of the factor analysis literature and will not be covered here. Most factor analysts agree that this identification process is complex and difficult. A great deal of converging evidence is needed to make the decision as to which factors are the common factors. However, as we shall see shortly, common factors usually "stand out" in an understandable pattern.

Now, let's see how the first three steps of a factor analysis might work.

An Example of Steps 1–3 in Practice

Suppose that an educational psychologist wants to study both mathematics and verbal ability. She researches the literature and comes up with a test plan from which she constructs the five items that she believes will measure both these abilities. It's a good bet that, in practice, many more than five items would be needed to adequately represent the two factors of interest, but for now, five items provide a manageable example. Item 1 is a vocabulary item, and Item 3 is a word analogy problem. Item 2 tests a basic algebra concept, and Item 4 tests a basic geometry concept. Item 5 is an algebra word problem.

The researcher uses a standard factor-analysis computer program, which first computes the matrix of intercorrelations among the measures. The matrix of intercorrelations for the five items is presented in Table 1. Each entry in the matrix is a correlation coefficient between two of the items. Note in Table 1 that the correlation between the vocabulary item and the algebra concept item is .22 and that the correlation between the geometry item and the algebra word problem is .47. Now, examine the rest of this matrix of intercorrelations. Is any particular pattern present?

The vocabulary and the word analogy items have a high correlation, but each has low correlations with the algebra concept and geometry concept items. The algebra concept and geometry items have a high correlation, but each has a low correlation with the vocabulary and word analogy items. The algebra word problem has a moderate correlation with the other four items. These results suggest that there are two factors underlying these five items, with the vocabulary and word analogy items being most associated

Table 1 The Matrix of Intercorrelations Among the Five Items

		Item			
	1	*2*	*3*	*4*	*5*
1 Vocabulary	1.00	.22	.77	.20	.50
2 Algebra	.22	1.00	.21	.65	.48
3 Analogy	.77	.21	1.00	.19	.52
4 Geometry	.20	.65	.19	1.00	.47
5 Algebra-Word	.50	.48	.52	.47	1.00

with one factor and the algebra and geometry concept items being associated with the second factor. It also seems that the algebra word problem may be associated with both factors.

In the present example, it's relatively easy to see that the patterns of correlations suggest what the two underlying factors might be for this set of five items. However, finding common factors would be an overwhelming task if you had a large number of items (for example, 100 or more). For this reason, you would probably need a method that would find these underlying dimensions in an objective way. Mathematical factoring is just such a method.

After the computer program computes the matrix of intercorrelations among all the measures, it next factors that matrix. Using the results from the computer program and several converging criteria that include some mathematical indices as well as interpretability, the educational researcher decides that there are two common factors underlying these five items.[4]

The entries in Table 2 are called "factor loadings" and can be treated like correlations between the measure and the underlying factors. Item 1, a vocabulary item, "loads" or correlates very highly with Factor I and very low with Factor II. Item 2, an algebra problem, correlates very low with Factor I and very highly with Factor II. In interpreting this factor matrix, it is necessary to decide what size or magnitude a factor loading should have before we can consider it to have a meaningful or important contribution to a factor. There is no agreed-upon significance test for factor loadings, and therefore it is necessary to specify some value that indicates that a factor loading is meaningful or important. Cattell (1978) proposed a concept he called *salience*—a concept analogous to another concept that is no doubt more familiar to you, that of *significance.* Cattell proposed that, as a rule, a factor loading might be considered salient if it is greater than either .30 or .40. The choice

---

[4]To make the factors most interpretable, it is often necessary to use another mathematical procedure called *rotation.* Rotation is a mathematical procedure that adjusts the results of factor analysis so that it will be more interpretable without distorting the relationship of the factors to the original data. The interested reader is again directed to Gorsuch (1983) for a more detailed explanation.

Table 2 The Results of the Factor Analysis of the Five Items

	Factors		
	I	II	Communality
Vocabulary	.917	.101	.851
Algebra	.113	.885	.796
Analogy	.925	.094	.864
Geometry	.086	.891	.801
Algebra-Word	.594	.573	.681
Eigenvalue	2.700	1.30	
Percent of total variance	54.000	26.000	

of the value for salience is dependent on the size of the sample of subjects. If the sample is small (say, less than 100), factor loadings of .40 or greater may be thought to be salient. If the sample is large, a value of .30 or greater may be used as the cutoff for salience. For the present example, we chose a value of .30 as the cutoff because we know—because we made up the example—that the educational psychologist used a very large sample of subjects for her study.

The salient factor loadings have been underlined in Table 2. Using this criterion for salience or meaningfulness, you can see that the vocabulary and word analogy items load saliently on Factor I and that the algebra concept and geometry concept items load saliently on Factor II. These items are called *factorially simple* items because they load saliently on only one factor. It can be seen that these factorially simple items reflect only one dimension or factor. The algebra word problem loads saliently on both Factors I and II. A variable that loads saliently on more than one factor is called *factorially complex* because it reflects more than one dimension.

Nowhere in the statistical procedure of factor analysis is it written, or even suggested, how the names for common factors should be derived. That is a task left to the factor analyst, and sometimes there is a great deal of subjectivity when naming them. Common factors may be named anything from "Factor I" to "Introversion" to "Belief in an Afterlife" to . . . whatever seems reasonable on the basis of the data at hand. With respect to factorially simple measures, the investigator typically makes some decision on the name of the factor based on the dimension the factors seem to have in common. The factorially complex items are, it is hoped, interpretable and understandable through the names given the factors. Before reading on, what names would *you* give the factors in Table 2?

We named Factor I "Verbal Ability" because we judged verbal ability to be a primary dimension or ability for completing vocabulary and analogy problems. We named Factor II "Mathematical Ability" because we judged this ability to be the primary dimension or ability used for solv-ing algebra and geometry problems. Through the names that we gave to the two factors, the algebra word problem can be interpreted as a measure of *both* mathematical and verbal abilities.

You may have chosen different names for the factors from the names we chose. Similar problems—those related to different names for observations—often arise in factor-analytic research and may even be responsible for theoretical debates about what the underlying dimensions for a given set of behaviors really are. For one example, the interested reader is referred to the debate over how many factors there *really* are in the factor analytically derived 16PF (Personality Factors) test (see Cattell & Krug, 1986; Comrey & Duffy, 1968; Eysenck, 1972; Guilford, 1975; and Howarth & Browne, 1971).

Step 4

Getting back to Annette O.'s therapy session and, more specifically, the fourth step in the model presented above, recall that the psychologist decided that Annette's behavior was symptomatic of depression and, secondarily, of anxiety. In making that judgment, the psychologist assigned relative importance to each of the factors or dimensions. Similarly, the results of a factor analysis provide a numerical index called an *eigenvalue,* or characteristic root. An eigenvalue is a number that indicates the relative strength or importance of each of the factors. Eigenvalues from most factor analyses will vary from a value of 0.0 to that equal to the number of measures that are being factored. Divide the eigenvalue by the number of variables in the analysis and multiply the result by 100, and you will obtain the percent of total variance accounted for by a given factor. The eigenvalues and the total percent of variance associated with each of the two factors for the five items are given at the bottom of Table 2. Note that for these five items, the Verbal Ability Factor (54%) is more than twice as strong as the Mathematical Ability Factor (26%). The results of a factor analysis will allow us to estimate not only how many factors or dimensions there are for a set of measures but also the relative importance or strength of each of these factors.

Step 5

The final step in the therapy session scenario described above entailed your planning of a therapeutic intervention, perhaps with regard to your judgment concerning the relative importance of the observed symptomatology. Analogously, once factor analysts decide on the number of factors in a factor analysis, they can compute an index called *communality*. Communality assesses how well each measure is explained by the common factors. You will recall that the square of a correlation can be interpreted as the proportion of variance that two measures have in common. The square of a factor loading provides an indication of how much a factor and a measure have in common. Square each factor loading for a measure and then add the sum of the squares; the sum will be equal to the total proportion of variance of all of the common factors that is accounted for by that measure. The communality for the algebra concept item was computed by squaring its factor loadings, .113 and .885, and adding them together. Since communalities can vary between 0.0 and 1.0, we can see that all the measures in this analysis have a moderate to strong communality. Try computing the communalities for the other four items yourself.

What Does One Do with a Factor Analysis?

Over the last 20 years, a great increase in the use of factor analysis in many areas of psychological research has occurred. This increase is due partially to the availability of high-speed computers and relatively easy-to-use computer programs. Factor analysis is used in numerous ways, such as:

- finding underlying factors of ability tests
- identifying personality dimensions
- identifying clinical syndromes
- finding dimensions of worker satisfaction
- finding the dimensions that people use when judging social behaviors

One way that factor analysis should *never* be used is as a haphazard method to attempt to make order from chaos; *it is totally inappropriate to factor-analyze just any set of measures with the hope of finding meaningful common factors.* A factor analysis should be planned as a tool that will be used at some appropriate point in a study. Do I understand the problem thoroughly? Do I understand the phenomena for which I am attempting to identify common factors? Are the measures I've chosen the best available ones with respect to the phenomena I'm investigating? These are only some of the questions that must be raised (and satisfactorily answered) before the execution of a factor analysis.

Suppose you were interested in identifying the dimensions of the construct "anxiety." Ideally, you would need to choose the test(s) or test items that most clearly represented what is known about anxiety. To accomplish this, you would read as much of the psychological literature about anxiety as possible and choose the measure(s) that you thought best represented the domain of anxiety. Again, the measuring tool you ultimately select must ideally be one about which a good deal is known—one with demonstrated reliability and validity. To do otherwise would be to impair your ability to identify—and jeopardize the likelihood of identifying—meaningful factors. Further, poor "up-front" homework will lessen the likelihood that your work will be replicable; the factors you identify will probably not be found in subsequent studies by other researchers. In this context, a modern saying springs to mind: "Garbage in, garbage out."

There are many technical issues in conducting a factor analysis that are beyond the scope of this introductory presentation. Our main goal was to introduce you to some of the basics. More in-depth approaches to this very important technique of data analysis are as far away as your campus library!

EXERCISE 6-7

FACTOR ANALYSIS II: THE CORRELATION MATRIX

OBJECTIVE

To enhance understanding of the role of the correlation matrix in the process of factor analysis

BACKGROUND

A brief elaboration on the presentation of factor analysis in your text follows. Read it carefully before attempting to respond to the question that follows.

FACTOR ANALYSIS AND THE CORRELATION MATRIX

A table of intercorrelations called a *correlation matrix* is a key element of a factor analysis. A matrix of correlations contains correlational information regarding two or more variables. The advent of high-speed data processing equipment makes possible the creation and analysis of a correlation matrix with hundreds of variables or more. In our model below (Table 6-9), there are only five variables (*A, B, C, D,* and *E*). As we will explain, these five variables could represent individual test items, tests, or test batteries. An assumption inherent in the application of a factor analysis is that the test items (tests or test batteries) are reliable and valid. The correlation between a variable and itself as represented in the matrix (for example, variable *A* in a row and variable *A* in a column) is always 1.

The five variables in our sample correlation matrix could represent five items on the same test. Alternatively, the five variables could represent a total of five items from different tests. The correlations between any two of the items imparts information regarding how the items are related. For example, a high positive correlation (.9) exists between variable *A*

TABLE 6-9   *A Sample Correlation Matrix for Variables* **A, B, C, D,** *and* **E**

	A	B	C	D	E
A	1.00	.18	.32	.09	.90
B	——	1.00	.27	.04	.95
C	——	——	1.00	.28	.03
D	——	——	——	1.00	.02
E	——	——	——	——	1.00

and variable *E*. Let's suppose that variables *A* and *E* both represent true/false items on a personality test. Variable *A* represents an item that reads, "I enjoy meeting new people," and variable *B* represents an item that reads, "Under the right circumstances, I can be the life of the party." The high correlation between the items tells us that in responding to these two items, testtakers tend to respond in the same way. Thus people who report that they enjoy meeting new people also report a potential of being the life of a party. People who report that they do not enjoy meeting new people also tend not to be the life of a party.

The five variables in our sample correlation matrix could represent composite scores on five different tests. In another example, the five variables might represent composite scores as a result of the administration of five different groups of tests. The correlations between any two of the variables would then impart information regarding how the tests (or test groups) are related. For example, a low correlation (.04) exists between variable *B* and variable *D*. Let's suppose that variables *B* and *D* both represent composite scores on two different personality test batteries. Variable *B* represents a composite score on a test battery called the Overall Assertiveness Tests (OATs), and variable *D* represents a composite score on a test battery called the Remarkable Creativity Tests (RCTs). The low correlation between the two test batteries tells us that there is no discernable relation between assertiveness and creativity. A highly assertive individual may or may not be creative, just as a highly creative person may or may not be assertive.

As its name implies, factor analysis entails "factoring" the correlations in the matrix. Factoring may be a familiar concept from algebra, where it involves a method of making a large, unwieldy algebraic expression more manageable by breaking it down into factors. Likewise, the correlation matrix in factor analysis is made more manageable by factoring. The objective is to wind up with a smaller number of factors than variables. In the example above wherein variables *A* and *E* were representative of true/false personality test items, a factor analyst might conclude that the two items tap a single factor labeled "introversion/extraversion." A "true" response on both of the items might earn the testtaker points toward a designation of "extraverted personality." A "false" response on both of the items might earn the testtaker points toward a designation of "introverted personality."

The actual process of factor analysis may take place in many different ways. Numerous methods exist for determining which correlations in the matrix yield common factors (such as introversion/extraversion in the example above), specific factors (not common to many of the variables), or factors that reflect error or unreliability in measurement (Comrey, 1992). In one approach, the factor analyst evaluates what is called the *scree criterion,* or what is perceived as a natural dividing point in the relative importance of the factors. You have probably engaged in a similar exercise if you have ever been involved in assigning grades based on a curve of test scores. As an example, let's say that the following scores represented the top ten scores in a particular class: 92, 92, 91, 90, 90, 89, 82, 81, 80, and 80. In deciding the number of *A*s to assign, one might look for clusters of scores, separated by gaps in the distribution. Here, depending on other factors, the grade of *A* might be assigned to the first six students, even if 89 and 90 are not usually considered to be in the *A* range. The grades from 89 to 92 seem to form a natural cluster, clearly separated from the next highest grades, which are in the low 80s. In a way, this is similar to what happens when the scree criterion is applied; clusters of factors that logically seem to go together are identified.

Another approach to determining which of many possible factors are common factors—an approach that is typically used along with the scree criterion—entails analysis of the *eigenvalues* (pronounced I-gen-values), or the numerical indices of the relative strength or importance of each factor. When the scores on two tests tend to vary together, the measures are said to "share variance." Factors that share a large amount of variance with the many measured variables have high eigenvalues and are likely to be viewed as common factors. Low eigenvalues indicate that the factor may be a specific factor or an error factor.

A detailed discussion of factor analytic procedures is beyond the scope of this book. Our modest objective here has been to provide but a first step in understanding the conceptual basis of this widely used but technically complex statistical tool.

YOUR TASK

What follows is a correlation matrix for four items (here labeled *W, X, Y,* and *Z*) on a true/false test of introversion/extraversion. Based on the data you observe, write four items on this test represented by *W, X, Y,* and *Z* and a brief explanation of why you wrote the items that you did.

Correlation Matrix for Variables **W, X, Y,** *and* **Z**

	W	*X*	*Y*	*Z*
W	1.00	.98	.97	.09
X	—	1.00	.99	.03
Y	—	—	1.00	.07
Z	—	—	—	1.00

EXERCISE 6-8

FACTOR ANALYSIS III: ANALYZING A PUBLISHED ARTICLE

OBJECTIVE

To read and analyze a journal article that illustrates how factor analysis can be used to shed light on the construct validity of a test

BACKGROUND

Factor analysis is widely used in the development of psychological tests as well as in research on tests. In this exercise, you will be asked to locate and read an article in which factor analysis was used to shed light on the construct validity of a test.

YOUR TASK

Impulsivity is widely believed to be highly correlated with juvenile delinquency; juvenile delinquents tend to act on impulse rather than with a great deal of forethought. Consistent with this view, one might predict that a test designed to measure impulsivity, if it is indeed a valid measure of impulsivity, would correlate highly with a measure of juvenile delinquency. But what if a measure of impulsivity did not correlate highly with delinquency? Would that measure automatically not be a valid measure of impulsivity? Before you answer, keep in mind that there may be different kinds of impulsivity. Some tests of impulsivity may be measuring cognitive impulsivity, and other tests may be measuring behavioral impulsivity. In fact, this is exactly what White, Moffitt, Caspi, Bartusch, Needles, & Stouthamer-Loeber (1994) found in their study of the construct validity of eleven measures of impulsivity.

Read the White et al. (1994) study with an eye toward learning about the use of factor validity in exploring the construct validity of tests. Then answer the following questions.

1. What criteria did White et al. use in selecting the tests of impulsivity they would use in their study?

2. What criteria did White et al. use in selecting subjects in their study?

3. After having collected their data, White et al. calculated correlations between the measures they used and organized their information in a correlation matrix. What kinds of correlations would you have expected between the measures if all of the measures had defined impulsivity in the same way and were all valid measures of it?

4. What kind of correlations did White et al. calculate, and how did they explain this finding?

5. After factoring the correlation matrix, White et al. determined that four variables loaded on one factor they called "behavioral impulsivity." What were the four variables that loaded on that factor?

6. Continuing to factor, White et al. determined that six variables loaded on a second factor they called "cognitive impulsivity." What were these six variables?

7. White et al. noted that the two factors they derived may have more to do with the way impulsivity is measured than anything else. Behavioral impulsivity is a factor associated with impulsivity when impulsivity is measured by rating scales administered to observers (such as parents and teachers of impulsive subjects). Cognitive impulsivity is a factor more associated with tasks completed by the subjects themselves. Future factor analytic research could help to clarify the actual nature of the factors if (1) tasks can be identified that reflect behavioral impulsivity (and thus load on behavioral impulsivity), or (2) ratings can be made that reflect cognitive impulsivity (and thus load on cognitive impulsivity). Write a simple research outline to follow up on the White et al. study.

8. White et al. found that their measure of delinquency was significantly correlated with both of the impulsivity factors derived from the factor analysis. The correlation was stronger with the Behavioral Impulsivity factor ($r = .44$) as compared to the Cognitive Impulsivity factor ($r = .16$). This suggests that studies that use measures that reflect the Behavioral Impulsivity factor are more likely to find that delinquency is related to impulsivity than are studies using measures that primarily reflect the Cognitive Impulsivity factor. In general, what do these findings tell us about the construct validity of the measures used in the White et al. study?

EXERCISE 6-9
"FAIRNESS" AND "BIAS"

OBJECTIVE

To enhance understanding of the terms *fairness* and *bias* as those terms are used in the field of psychological testing

BACKGROUND

If an individual does not perform satisfactorily on a test and as a consequence is deprived of something he or she wants, it would not be unheard of for the individual to claim—almost reflexively—that the test was unfair. While some tests may indeed be unfair or "biased" in the psychometric sense (and other tests may be inherently fair and unbiased but used in an unfair way), responsible test developers, publishers, and users strive to serve the general good by promoting fair, unbiased tests.

YOUR TASK

Drawing on your own background and experience, your textbook, and The Psychological Corporation article that follows, answer the following three questions:

1. Describe in your own words a "fair test."
2. Describe in your own words a "biased test."
3. What can be done to eliminate unfair and biased tests?

FAIRNESS AND THE MATTER OF BIAS

Lois E. Burrill and Ruth Wilson

Potential bias in standardized tests is a topic of great concern to test users. This concern can probably be traced back into the early twenties, but during the decade of the sixties, as the nation became acutely aware of racial discrimination and the denial of basic civil rights in many quarters, new issues were raised. Charges were made concerning the "fairness" of commercially developed ability and achievement tests for many of the students in our schools.

The claim was made that the tests were designed for white, middle-class children growing up in suburban communities. Thus, it was charged, the tests were inherently inappropriate, invalid, or unfair to pupils who are black, poor, or living in the inner core of our old urban centers. More recently, charges of "sex bias" have been added to the others. It has been claimed that tests support and reinforce the stereotypes of sex roles dominant in the middle-class culture and thus penalize children who do not respond as required by these cultural patterns.

Unfortunately, there is at the present time no consensus in regard to what bias is or how to eliminate it. The word "bias" comes up in most of the discussions about fairness. However, this term is rarely defined in any precise or operational way. Like "creativity," bias seems to be a term that people believe they understand intuitively; yet they cannot easily formulate a definition. Faced with this dilemma, publishers such as The Psychological Corporation have attempted to deal with the concept of fairness—in all its complexity—in three different areas: first, fairness in relation to the normative information published for the test; second, fairness in the content of the actual test questions; and third, fairness in the way test results are used for decision making.

Fairness and the Quality of Norms

Most publishers, including The Psychological Corporation, have taken great pains to ensure that national norms are truly representative of the nation as a whole. In order to do this, children of all ethnic groups, socioeconomic levels, and geographical regions are represented in their norms samples in the proportions in which they exist in the national population. Moreover, boys and girls from urban, suburban, and rural communities, large schools, and small, public, parochial, and independent schools are included on the same proportional basis.

Precision has recently been added to this selective process through the use of census data based on school system boundaries rather than on political units. Thus, the charge that the norms for most tests are based entirely on the performance of middle-class whites simply is not true.

Although particular school systems may differ in composition from the total population, national norms have meaning and importance for all school systems. They describe one reality: the typical performance of the nation's school children. By so doing, they form an important frame of reference; they are a point of departure for decision making. It should be understood, however, that by virtue of their being a representative sampling of all the wide variations found in the United States, national norms present a composite picture of national performance, and there are few communities in the entire nation matching that composite picture across all comparisons. In many communities, the discrepancies between local characteristics and those represented as typical (by the norm) are, in fact, great.

Test publishers recognize this fact, and, today, test manuals report normative data carefully for all test users to examine. The care with which these data are collected is evidence of the usefulness of the norms that accompany the test and should be evaluated thoughtfully by the potential test user.

The danger here is in using only one frame of reference. National norms provide one important yardstick; others are also available, and each one adds a different dimension to the picture. Some test publishers collect and publish information concerning the performance of specific groups. Many provide scoring services designed to enable school systems to interpret their test scores in terms of local norms. Item analysis, matching test questions with specific instructional objectives, provides criterion-referenced interpretation. Test users are encouraged to use as many frames of reference as possible in interpreting test results.

Fairness and the Content of the Test

One of the essential characteristics of a good test is *validity*, a technical testing term usually defined as "the degree to which a test measures what it is intended to measure." In nontechnical language, fairness and validity are roughly synonymous, so it is probably not coincidental that bias is often perceived in terms of test validity. Test validity is frequently broken down further into several categories: face validity—the appearance of measuring what is intended; predictive validity—the ability of the test to accurately predict a future performance or other criterion; and content validity—the adequacy of the sample of questions to assess the area being measured. For each of these types of validity or fairness, there are various ways of identifying invalidity or unfairness due to bias.

Face Validity—Facial Bias

The term *facial bias* has been coined recently to describe situations where particular words, pictures, item formats, or other characteristics of the test *appear* to disfavor some group, regardless of whether any statistical evidence can be collected to show that they actually affect scores on a test. In respect to facial bias, the following points need to be considered: (1) Is the question or its presentation offensive to some group? (2) Does the question "turn off" some children, either psychologically or emotionally? (3) Is the context of the question so alien to the child's experiential background that he or she is unable to answer a question that should not depend on that background?

These questions concern the "cultural fairness" of a test. It must be recognized that attempts to build tests that are "culture-free" have been unsuccessful. There are no differences among individuals in their responses to test questions that cannot be attributed, to some extent, to differences in culture; "Each of us lives in a somewhat different culture. Not only Eskimos and Africans but also Vermonters and Virginians, farmers and townspeople, boys and girls, even first-born and next born in the same family live in somewhat different 'cultures.' The differences are not equally great in all these instances, but they exist as differences in all cases, and they can be used to support the charge that any item that discriminates is unfair."[5] Since test scores that do not differentiate among individuals would be meaningless, the issue is not one of trying to eliminate all distinctions but rather of establishing controls for relevant cultural parameters.

Publishers are aware of possible sources of unintentional bias. For example, some items may appear to be more relevant to one geographic region than another; others may appear to favor males over females. These and many other aspects must be considered in item selection in order to produce an instrument that is sufficiently balanced to be appropriate for general use. The format of the test may influence the performance of children who are unfamiliar with the testing process; where several different types of items are included on one page, without being introduced by practice items, an unreasonable burden is placed on these children.

In meeting this responsibility, test publishers have given renewed and intensified attention to certain aspects of the traditional test-development enterprise. Until fairly recently, most standardized tests were constructed by white middle-class people, who sometimes clumsily violated the feelings of the testtakers without even knowing it. One could say that they were not so much culture biased as "culture blind." More recently, however, much has been done to modify test-development procedures in order to ensure the appropriateness of the final instruments for all the uses to which they may be put.

The Psychological Corporation has, for example, instituted staff training programs. Such matters as sensitivity to prejudice, stereotypes, and material offensive to particular groups; over- or underemphasis on the worth, capabilities, or importance of particular racial, religious, or ethnic segments of the national population; inclusion of minority as well as majority examples of worthy Americans in all areas of life and culture; and the delineation of life in con-

temporary urban environments, as well as rural, have become part of the criteria for judging the validity of test items. Artwork has been revised to eliminate the "mom, dad, two kids plus dog" stereotype of family composition. Adult figures include uncle, grandfather, or some other model as well as "Father." Urban scenes are depicted in the artwork, and children and adults who are clearly minority group members are pictured.

Vocabulary is another area of concern. For example, in some proposed items, reviewers have found the term "black" used in ways that might be considered derogatory. Thus a story about a crow (described as a big, black bird) who stole shiny dimes was rewritten to eliminate the possible connection of "black" with "theft."

Staff members have been made aware of possible "sex bias." Steps have been taken to avoid the over- or underrepresentation of either sex group in test items and artwork or the portrayal of either sex in restricted or stereotypic roles. Recent test publications represent males and females with approximately equal frequency, exhibit a full range of activities and personality traits for both, and show mixed-sex activities. All types of work are presented positively, and both males and females are shown participating in a wide range of vocations and household situations.

Vocabulary places a limitation here, particularly at the primary grades. Curricular materials are "sex biased" in terms of presenting male nouns and pronouns at a generally earlier level than the corresponding female words. It is equally difficult to replace the gender-specific items with sexually neutral words at these lower levels. For example, curricular materials introduce the words "man," "policeman," "fireman," etc. in the primary grades, while alternate titles such as "human," "adult," "police officer," "firefighter," etc., are not introduced before the fourth grade. Since test publishers adhere to the principle of using grade-controlled vocabulary, the problem of eliminating all "sex-biased" items is a complicated one.

In recent years, test publishers have included on their professional staff, both in full-time and consultant roles, persons who can advise in matters of "culture blindness." Materials in tests under development are reviewed by black people, Spanish-speaking Americans, and others who are familiar with the needs and styles of pupils from a variety of minority backgrounds, soliciting their reactions to any content that might be, unintentionally, inappropriate or offensive for some children.

Such consultants have a constructive role to play in each of the five major steps in test development. During the blueprinting stage, they review the outline or scheme of the tests and identify content of special pertinence or irrelevance to minority students. During content development, they make suggestions as to potential item bias, insensitive content, and unclear or potentially biased artwork. They also review plans for the statistical analysis of potential bias during item analysis and standardization stages. Finally, they review the final draft and suggest special needs of minority children as concerns test reporting.

[5]Ebel, Robert L., *Essentials of Educational Measurement.* Englewood Cliffs, NJ: Prentice-Hall, 1972, p. 505.

Despite the continuing efforts made in this regard, no publishers can make an *a priori* statement that a given test is "not discriminatory." Matters of face validity or facial bias, whether ethnic, sexist, geographic, or socioeconomic, are essentially judgmental, rarely subject to psychometric or statistical proof. Although publisher and authors exert every possible effort to ensure that the content of the test itself, the questions asked, the language in which they are asked, the artwork, format, and time limits are unbiased and free from prejudice, each agency selecting a test must make its own final judgmental decisions concerning its appropriateness for the particular group involved.

Predictive Validity—Bias of Selection/Prediction

Predictive validity refers to the accuracy with which scores on certain types of tests indicate future success in some area of learning or endeavor. Unfairness, prejudice, or discrimination in these test scores is known as bias of selection/prediction. A number of statistical procedures have been developed to identify this type of bias in tests that are being used for prediction or selection. The entire spring 1976 issue of *Journal of Educational Measurement* was devoted to this important area of concern. Although these procedures will not be described in detail here, it is important to note that each procedure is based on somewhat different assumptions about the definition of what is fair or unbiased prediction. Further, they are contradictory in their results.

In this situation, it is not the statisticians or the researchers who must decide what is fair. There is a larger issue involved that must be decided by society as a whole. Then, appropriate statistical analysis can be used or new methods developed to assess whether or not a test is biased by *that* definition.

Content Validity—Item Bias

Until the mid-seventies, efforts to deal with facial bias and with bias in prediction received far greater attention than issues concerning item bias. This was probably due to the assumption that achievement test items—questions assessing what was taught in school—were unlikely to exhibit bias other than facial bias. However, for years, researchers have been struggling with the question of how to identify this kind of bias.

Item bias may occur when, for reasons not readily apparent even to trained editors or expert judges, a test question is shown to function for different groups in some systematically different way. Some critics of tests have claimed that for a test to be unbiased, each subgroup of interest (ethnic groups, the two sexes, etc.) must perform alike in regard to the mean score on each item of the test. This definition, of course, assumes that the groups are actually alike with respect to whatever is being measured by the test question, and that observed differences in scores are, therefore, the results of an unfair item. Others anticipate that the groups may perform somewhat differently on individual questions but insist that such differences should

balance out over the test as a whole. Again, the groups are presumed to be equal in ability on the skill domain being tested by the set of items.

This assumption of equality is difficult to support, however, when it comes to achievement of ethnic minority groups. Even when the inherent ability or potential of the groups is assumed to be equal, one certainly cannot assume the groups have had equal opportunity to acquire the knowledges and skills in question. Indeed, to do so, and to eliminate items that show differences, might well have the effect of destroying the empirical evidence of the lack of equal educational opportunity or the need for improved instructional programs to right the balance.

The statistical or psychometric problem, then, has been to find ways of identifying which differences in performance are real (and need to be acknowledged) and which are the result of bias in the way the question is asked (and need to be corrected by changing or eliminating the question). A number of procedures have been proposed by researchers—each beginning with an attempt to define the kind of bias the method is intended to isolate.

One of the earliest of these approaches, and perhaps the most widely recognized, is that based on the psychometric notion of "interaction" between group membership and item performance. In this definition, it is assumed that a consistent difference in performance may not be due to bias, but that questions that have a far greater- or lesser-than-average difference between groups may be biased. Among the procedures using this approach, perhaps the best known is Angoff's delta plot procedure, described in Anastasi's measurement text.[6]

Another way of trying to identify item bias is based on the relationship of performance on each test question to performance on the test as a whole. When this statistic, known as item-test correlation, shows a significantly greater- or lesser-than-average difference between two groups, the item may be considered biased, according to this approach.

One of the most promising procedures explored during the seventies was developed by Janice Scheuneman at The Psychological Corporation. This technique, known as modified chi-square analysis, defines lack of bias as follows: For population groups with the same total score on the test in which the item appears, the proportion of each group who respond correctly to an item will be the same. If this is not true, bias is suspected. Using this definition and standard statistical techniques, it is possible to determine the probability that a given item is unbiased. Where the probability is low, the item may need to be discarded.

The 1976 edition of the Metropolitan Readiness Tests was analyzed for ethnic bias, using this procedure, and all items suspected of bias were eliminated from the final forms. The procedure was also used in the development of

---

[6]Anastasi, Anne, *Psychological Testing.* Fourth Edition. New York: Macmillan, 1976, pp. 222–224.

the Otis-Lennon School Ability Test. These procedures, reported in the research literature, constitute one of the most comprehensive attempts on the part of any test publisher to reduce ethnic bias in their tests.

The procedures described above all rely on techniques and statistics developed from classical test theory. Recently a new approach to test construction and scaling has been explored by many publishers, including The Psychological Corporation. Known as latent-trait theory, this methodology also holds much promise for the identification of item bias. The psychometric characteristics of any test question may be portrayed graphically in the form of a curve, called the item-characteristic curve. Bias may be defined by this method as differences in the shape of that curve for various ethnic groups.

To utilize any of these statistical procedures for identifying item bias, the test constructor must be able to identify the group membership of the individuals involved in the item analysis. Of course, from a publisher's point of view, this identification is not an invasion of privacy, since scores are never assembled with the demographic data. In fact, ethnic, sex, and other demographic data are only used to generate the p-values, item-test correlations, and other data used to test for item bias. In the past, this requirement has caused considerable difficulty. Although schools and communities are anxious for evidence or proof that tests are not biased, they are very reluctant to permit collection of the data necessary to conduct the research. Thus, many tests are still not being examined for item bias, even though the publisher is anxious to do so and the necessary techniques are available.

Fairness in Use of Tests for Decision Making

The validity of test results can be influenced adversely by the way in which the test is administered. Members of some minority groups often approach the testing situation with negative feelings about their chances of success. The teacher's own attitude when administering the test may produce tension, anxiety, or even hostility in some students. On the other hand, the teacher can encourage students to do their best by establishing an atmosphere of mutual trust and by emphasizing the fact that the purpose of testing is not merely to assign grades and check mastery but to help the students to profit by their own strengths and overcome their weaknesses.

Unfortunately, there have been flagrant examples of misuse of test information. Test publishers do not consider that their responsibility ends with the development of appropriate instruments. Rather, they are extending their efforts to provide the necessary guidelines for appropriate interpretation and use. In test manuals and accessory materials, comprehensive treatment is given to such matters as the nature of the particular tests, proper (and improper) inferences that may be drawn from test results, and cautions and limitations regarding the interpretation. In particular, information is given about how test results can be used in a number of concrete situations in urban centers, in specially funded projects, and the like. Issues of bias in interpretation and use have been addressed not only in the test manuals but also in service publications, professional papers, conferences, journal articles, etc.

In particular, it must be said clearly and frequently that achievement test scores are indicative information that must be used in conjunction with everything else a school knows about an individual. Test results must not be used to make inferences about the worth of individuals or, especially in the case of students who have suffered educational disadvantage, about their potential for learning. Test scores should be seen as formative, rather than summative, as warning signals rather than stop signs.

Summary

In their efforts to eliminate bias from published tests, the makers of these instruments seek the cooperation of parents, community groups, and school boards, as well as school administrators and teachers. Although much has been done to define, analyze, and eliminate bias in test instruments, much remains to be done. Perhaps the greatest single achievement in this regard is the recognition of the problem and the realization that the common goal can only be gained through the combined efforts of test publishers and test users.

EXERCISE 6-10
FIGURE THIS

OBJECTIVE

Obtain firsthand computational experience figuring out problems related to material presented in the chapter

BACKGROUND

Use your knowledge of material presented in Chapter 6 in your textbook to tackle *Your Task* in what follows.

YOUR TASK

Professor Lactose is an educational psychologist who is constructing a new test to measure children's motor coordination. He decided to give children ice cream cones with two scoops of ice cream as a method to measure coordination. His indicator of motor coordination is amount of time between the ice cream cone being placed in the child's hand and the ice cream falling to the ground (drop-plop ratio). While norming his test, he is alarmed to discover that children in the sample all across the southern United States are far clumsier than all the children in the sample from the northern United States.

1. Professor Lactose, who lives in Wisconsin, is arguing for the face validity of the test, while his colleague at a University in Florida is arguing against the face validity of the test. Choose one of the positions and present the argument for (or against) the test's face validity.
2. Explain how Professor Lactose failed to consider the concept of validity when he constructed his motor coordination test.
3. How could Professor Lactose increase the validity of his test?

REFERENCES

Campbell, D. T., & Fiske, D. W. (1959). Convergent and discriminant validation by the multitrait-multimethod matrix. *Psychological Bulletin, 56,* 81–105.

Cattell, R. B., & Krug, S. E. (1986). The number of factors in the 16 PF: A review of the evidence with special emphasis on methodological problems. *Educational and Psychological Measurement, 46,* 509–522.

Comrey, A. L. (1992). *A first course in factor analysis.* Hillsdale, NJ: Erlbaum.

Comrey, A. L., & Duffy, K. E. (1968). Cattell and Eysenck factor scores related to Comrey personality factors. *Multivariate Behavioral Research, 4,* 379–392.

Eysenck, H. J. (1972). Primary or second-order factors: A critical consideration of Cattell's 16PF battery. *British Journal of Social and Clinical Psychology, 11,* 265–269.

Gorsuch, R. L. (1983). *Factor analysis* (2nd ed.). Hillsdale, NJ: Erlbaum.

Guilford, J. P. (1975). Factors and factors of personality. *Psychological Bulletin, 82,* 802–814.

Howarth, E., & Browne, J. A. (1971). An item factor analysis of the 16-PF. *Personality, 2,* 117–139.

Lawshe, C. H. (1975). A quantitative approach to content validity. *Personnel Psychology, 28,* 563–575.

White, J. L., Moffitt, T. E., Caspi, A., Bartusch, D. J., Needles, D. J., & Stouthamer-Loeber, M. (1994). Measuring impulsivity and examining its relationship to delinquency. *Journal of Abnormal Psychology, 103,* 192–205.

THE 4-QUESTION CHALLENGE

1. A "valid test" is most typically a test that has been shown to be valid
   a. for a particular use with a particular population.
   b. for general use with people from all cultures.
   c. only for use with members of the norming group.
   d. only for use with members of the local validation study.

2. It's the degree to which an additional predictor explains something about the criterion measure not explained by predictors already in use. It is
   a. construct validity.
   b. content validity.
   c. incremental validity.
   d. concurrent validity.

3. Which term does not belong?
   a. halo effect
   b. severity error
   c. central tendency error
   d. random error

4. Which would *not* be an effective tool for an affirmative action program?
   a. a sliding band
   b. within-group norming
   c. differential cutoffs
   d. elimination of eigenvalues

CHAPTER 7

Test Development

Puzzle 7   **Instructions**   Identify what is described, answer a question, or fill in the blank to complete this crossword puzzle based on material presented in Chapter 7 of your textbook.

Across

1. _____ item analysis encompasses various nonquantitative procedures designed to explore how individual test items work, both as compared to other items in the test and in the context of the whole test.

3. The process by which a measuring device is designed and calibrated, and the way numbers (or other indices which are scale values) are assigned to different amounts of the trait, attribute, or characteristic being measured.

4. The process of test validation may involve viewing the test performance of a group of testtakers in the light of how well the test predicts a criterion. Sometimes revalidation of a test is conducted using a sample of testtakers other than the group on which the test was originally validated. The latter process is referred to by this hyphenated term.

7. Sometimes, the test validation process is conducted on two or more tests using the same sample of testtakers. When used to create norms or in the revision of existing norms, this process may also be referred to as *co-norming* or this other hyphenated term.

9. It is the extent to which an individual test item is used in a just, equitable, and nondiscriminatory way. One way of defining it is in terms of item characteristic curves (ICCs). Here, item _____ is evaluated by analyzing the ICCs for the different groups of people taking the test and whether or not those ICCs are significantly different.

12. It's a general term to describe various procedures, usually statistical in nature, that are designed to explore how individual test items work, both as compared to other items in the test and in the context of the whole test. We are speaking here of item _____ .

15. It's the reservoir or well from which items on the final version of a test will be drawn (or discarded). It's the item _____ .

17. A method of evaluation in which test responses earn credit toward placement in a particular class or category with other testtakers. In some instances, testtakers must meet a set number of responses corresponding to a particular criterion in order to be placed into a specific category or class. It is referred to as _____ scoring.

18. To test or not to test, that is one of the questions. Other questions will have to be addressed in this initial stage of test development called test _____ .

19. It's kind of like an audition, but for test items. Test developers call it a test _____ .

21. In the context of personality assessment and other contexts in which the nature of the test is such that responses are not keyed correct or incorrect, the item _____ index indicates how many testtakers responded in a particular direction to an item. This index may range in theory from zero (no testtaker responded with such an answer) to *x* (where *x* is the total number of items on the test). In the context of achievement tests, where there exists responses that are keyed correct, this same statistic is referred to as an *item-difficulty index*.

22. A revealing curve. Hint: Reread 9-Across.

23. An instrument containing a system of ordering numerical or verbal descriptors on which judgments concerning the presence/absence of magnitude of a particular trait, attitude, emotion, or other variable are indicated. The instrument referred to here is more commonly known as a(n) _____ scale.

26. It's a form of test item that requires the testtaker to select a response, as opposed to creating a response. True/false, multiple-choice, and matching-type items are some examples of test items written in a(n) _____ -response format.

27. In test development, it's a method of developing ordinal scales by a sorting task that entails judgment of a stimulus in comparison with every other stimulus that may be used on the test. It's called _____ scaling.

28. This is a statistic designed to provide an indication of how internally consistent a test is. The higher this index is, the greater the test's internal consistency. We are speaking of an item _____ index.

29. It's a statistic designed to indicate how adequately an item separates or discriminates between high scorers and low scorers on a test, and it's called an item _____ index.

Down

2. Like it or not, this variety of summative scale, named for its creator, typically lists five alternative responses on a continuum. And the name of that creator would be . . . ?

3. Validity _____ refers to the decrease in item validities that inevitably occur after cross-validation.

5. It's a form of test item that requires testtakers to create a response, as opposed to selecting a response. An essay test and a short-answer test both feature this _____ -response format.

6. Item _____ is a general reference to the form, plan, structure, arrangement, or layout of individual test items, as well as the type of response required of the testtaker.

8. In the context of achievement or ability testing and other contexts in which there exists a response that is keyed correct, this is a statistic that indicates how many testtakers responded correctly to an item. This index, which may range in theory from zero (no testtaker responded with the answer keyed correct) to *x* (where *x* is the total number of items on the test), is called an item _____ index.

10. Time waits for no person. Time does not even wait for tests. At some point in the life cycle of a test, it is time for test _____ .

11. It's a statistic designed to provide an indication of the degree to which a test is measuring what it purports to measure; the higher the item-_____ index, the greater the test's criterion-related validity.

13. Responding to a test question by means of intuition the process of elimination, or just taking a chance on a particular response.

14. A _____ review consists of a study of test items, usually during the test development process, in which the items are examined for fairness to all prospective testtakers and for the presence of offensive language, stereotypes, or situations.

15. The preliminary research surrounding the creation of a test, with the general objective typically being the discovery of how best to measure, gauge, assess, or evaluate the targeted construct(s). It's all referred to as _____ work or research.

16. The _____-trait model is a system of assumptions about measurement and the extent to which each test item measures a trait.

17. _____ scaling is a system of scaling in which stimuli are placed into one or two or more alternative categories that differ quantitatively with respect to some continuum.

18. _____ scoring is a method of scoring whereby points or scores accumulated on individual items or subsets are tallied and the higher the total sum, the higher the individual is presumed to be on the ability (trait or other characteristic) being measured.

20. It's an index derived from the summing of selected scores on a test or subtest, and it's called a(n) _____ scale.

21. In an effort to root out any possible sources of bias in a test being developed, a method of qualitative item analysis involving _____ panels may be employed.

24. Named for its developer, _____ , a system of scaling wherein items range sequentially from weaker to stronger expressions of the attitude or belief being measured.

25. One might characterize it as the "hard hat" stage of test development; it's test _____ .

EXERCISE 7-1
MOVIES AND MEASUREMENT

OBJECTIVE

To apply general principles of test development

BACKGROUND

Steve Martin portrays a famed but slightly deranged neurosurgeon in *The Man with Two Brains*. Let's now imagine the (highly unlikely, probably impossible) scenario that a would-

Steve Martin and friends in **The Man with Two Brains**

be test developer was inspired by this movie to develop a new instrument, the Martin Measure of Multiple Personality (MMMP), a test designed to diagnose the presence of multiple personality.

YOUR TASK

Demonstrate your knowledge of the test development process by serving as an advisor to the would-be developer of the MMMP. Write a brief memo to the developer entitled "Developing the MMMP" in which you outline each of the stages in the development process that the MMMP would have to go through. End your memo with a list of problems or issues that you anticipate would have to be resolved if the MMMP were ever to become a widely accepted measure of multiple personality.

EXERCISE 7-2
THE TEST DEVELOPMENT PROCESS: PART 1

OBJECTIVE

To enhance understanding, stimulate thought, and provide firsthand experience with respect to the process of developing a psychological test

BACKGROUND

Stated in general terms, the process of developing a test may be thought of as occurring in five stages:

1. test conceptualization
2. test construction
3. test tryout
4. analysis
5. revision

One can learn about the "nuts and bolts" of the test development process not only from descriptions in textbooks but from real-world accounts of the process in sources such as professional journals. In the reprinted article that follows, Abadzi and Florez (1981) describe not only the procedures used in developing their test but the trials and tribulations as well.

YOUR TASK

Read the following article and then answer these questions with reference to it:

1. If the process of test development is conceptualized as occurring in five steps (test conceptualization, test construction, test tryout, item analysis, and test revision), identify each of these steps with reference to the Puerto Rico Self-Concept Scale.

2. With reference to each of the five steps in the test development process cited above, what questions do *you* have regarding the process of developing the Puerto Rico Self-Concept Scale; in other words, what would you like to know more about?

3. With reference to each of the five steps in the test development process cited above, what suggestions for future direction do you have to offer the authors of this test?

CONSTRUCTING THE PUERTO RICO SELF-CONCEPT SCALE: PROBLEMS AND PROCEDURES[1]

The Puerto Rico Self-Concept Scale was developed for the purpose of assessing the relationship of self-concept with academic achievement and other school-related variables in Puerto Rico. An 88-item scale that can measure self-concept in the 4th, 7th, and 10th grades was constructed. Empirical criterion keying was used for the development

---

[1]By Helen Abadzi and Sonia Florez and reprinted with permission from *Applied Psychological Measurement*.

of items that were also adapted to the phraseology used by local students. After small-group testing, the 264-item bank was administered to 2,445 students. Item analyses focused on item discrimination. Scores showed a low but significant correlation with previous year's grade-point average. Overall scale reliability was .93. A 34-item short form had overall reliability of .84. Preliminary norms were prepared from existing data.

The educational community in the United States is becoming increasingly interested in the identification of personal variables that affect student performance. The self-concept of a student is considered an important variable related to academic achievement. Significant though mostly moderate correlations have been demonstrated by several researchers between measurements of self-concept and student grades (Bloom, 1976; Brookover, Patterson, & Thomas, 1962; Campbell, 1967; Fink, 1962; Gill, 1969; Gordon, 1966; Purkey, 1970).

Coppersmith (1967) considers the self-concept to be an individual's self-evaluation. More than 200 scales have been constructed that attempt to elicit this self-evaluation through various methods. Factor analyses carried out on some of the instruments indicate the presence of such factors as physical appearance, peer relations, school performance, leadership, and opinions about oneself (Muller & Leonetti, 1972; Richmond & White, 1971; Stanwyck & Felker, 1971).

There seems to be a continuous interaction between the self and academic achievement, each directly influencing the other (Purkey, 1970). In evidence of this intricate relationship, the Commonwealth of Puerto Rico, Department of Education, developed a project whose purpose was to measure the self-concept of Puerto Rican students and to study its interactions with academic achievement. Accordingly, specifications for a self-concept scale were set.

The scale to be constructed should (1) make possible the assessment of the relationship between student self-concept and academic performance; (2) identify students with low self-concept at the 4th, 7th, and 10th grade level; and [sic] (4) measure changes from one grade level to the other. These specifications made it necessary to consider the development of a single form that could be used with 4th, 7th, and 10th grade boys and girls and that would discriminate between students having high and low self-concepts. The construction of the scale consequently reflected what Cronbach (1970) calls the "bandwidth-fidelity dilemma": A test to be used with many grades and purposes might be less effective in measuring specific self-concept areas, or it might be less reliable and valid for one of the grades. On the other hand, a separate test for each grade would not measure between-grade changes without elaborate equating procedures. Balancing time and costs against benefits, it was decided to develop the scale according to specifications and to study the results.

Methodology of Scale Construction

Items for this scale were constructed using homogenous methods of scale construction. As a first step toward the construction of this scale, approximately 200 pieces of research were reviewed. Test items were constructed to reflect the results of those studies whose findings differentiated between persons with low and high self-concept. For example, a negative correlation between self-concept and anxiety has been found (Thompson, 1972). Accordingly, some test items measuring anxiety were constructed, such as the following: "Me preocupo mucho por los problemas que puedan surgir" (I worry a lot about problems that may come up). In addition, approximately 30 available self-concept instruments were reviewed. Their methods of approach to the problem and their item analysis results were studied. Items with high indices of discrimination or items that loaded highly on one of the self-concept–related factors were considered for adoption. As a result, 290 test items were constructed in a draft form in Spanish. A dichotomous response format was used, with students indicating whether the item was or was not true most of the time. The Likert-type scale was not used because it had been previously employed in a fourth-grade scale with little success (Whitmore, 1975). Instead, it was decided to use dichotomous items and to include in the final scale a larger number of items than would have otherwise been employed.

A problem of major importance in the construction of this or any other scale in Puerto Rico is the attention that must be paid to the local culture and language. Self-concept, an individual's self-evaluation, has been defined in research according to Anglo standards of achievement and has been used with little change in instrument construction for Chicano children (Muller & Leonetti, 1972). On the other hand, there are no research findings to support the view that it may be defined differently in Puerto Rico, an island that has been under United States control for the past 80 years. A study by Hernández (1964) lists Puerto Rican adolescent problems and needs very similar to those in the mainland United States. It was therefore hypothesized that self-concept on this island could basically be measured in the same way as on the mainland. Evidence to support this hypothesis was offered in that many items developed on the basis of mainland United States correlates of self-concept had considerable discriminating power (see Table 7-3). The authors, however, recommend tentative use and careful investigation of items whose content has been validated in a culture other than that of intended use.

It was considered important to construct a scale whose language reflected the Spanish spoken by Puerto Rican children. Colloquial Spanish varies from country to country. The authors found a few scales in Spanish, mostly constructed for Mexican American (Chicano) children, but the language in itself was not always usable because constructions frequent among Chicanos are not used by Puerto Ricans. Also, test items could not be directly translated from English because of word frequency problems; the style of many items in scales that were directly translated was disappointing. The language problem was accompanied by the fact that neither author is Puerto Rican. One is a Peruvian who has lived in Puerto Rico for ten years, and the other is a Greek, very fluent in Spanish, who lived on the island for six months. It was decided to enlist the aid of the school districts. Six school personnel members formed a committee that met with the authors several times. The committee reviewed all the items that had been developed and rephrased them, using the expressions Puerto Rican children use. Care was taken not to alter the meaning. With the committee's valuable help, 264 items were developed. The vocabulary used was such that fourth-grade students could understand it. Though local expressions were used, no common grammatical errors were included. No item was longer than one and a half lines. Half of the items had negative syntactical constructions.

The 264 items were randomly separated into three forms of 88 in each. Then, the committee members took copies and administered them to small groups of students in their districts, noting the time it took fast and slow readers of various grades to complete the forms, the words students did not know, expressions that were not clear, and reactions to the scale. As a result of the small-group administration, several changes were made. It was found that younger students did not respond correctly to the items that contained negative constructions. Therefore, all negative constructions were changed into positive while the negative meaning was kept. The scoring key for the items was prepared according to the findings of the previously conducted literature search. Each item was to be given a score of "1" if answered in the direction that indicated high self-concept. The scale score was to be an unweighted total of items answered in the desirable direction.

Method of Data Collection

Classes containing a total of 3,134 4th, 7th, and 10th graders in equal numbers were selected at random following a sampling procedure routinely used by the Department of Education, whose main purpose is to include a proportionate number of rural and city students. Only public schools were sampled. The 264 items separated in three forms were administered to the students, who marked their answers on computer-scored sheets. Precise test instructions were prepared and sent to the teachers, who administered the forms to their classes.

The three forms were administered to the students, one each day during three consecutive days. This way each student took all three subsets of the item bank. Answer sheets were collected, and data were analyzed by the Department of Education computer center. When data were processed, 690 answer sheets had to be eliminated as a result of incorrect or missing student numbers. Therefore, a total of 2,445 returns were used for data analysis.

Item Analysis Results

The main purpose of item analysis was to identify items that discriminated between students who scored high and low on the self-concept scale. The analysis was performed on the 264 items and gave difficulty and discrimination indices. The latter were phi coefficients computed for each item between numbers of "right" and "wrong" responses according to the scoring key and number of students whose total score was in the upper and lower 27%. The distribution that resulted was negatively skewed and very leptokurtic. Split-half and Kuder-Richardson reliability coefficients computed for each scale ranged from .83 to .89. The items that had phi coefficients of .4 or higher were selected for each grade separately, and selections for the three grades were compared.

Generally, there was agreement across grades. Thirty-four items had phi coefficients of .4 and above in all three grade levels. Fifty others showed phi coefficients of .4 to .6 for two grades, while in the third, coefficients ranged from .3 to .39. These 84 items were selected for a second analysis. Since the 10th grade was found to share slightly fewer items with phi coefficients of .4 with the other grades, nine more items were added that had coefficients of .3 to .39 at the other levels.

In the second analysis, which included 93 items, the score distribution approached normality much more, and the reliability coefficients rose. They ranged from .89 to .94 (see Table 7-1). Phi coefficients also increased; most items showed phi's of .4 and above in all three grades. The five least discriminating items were eliminated, leaving a scale with a total of 88 items. The 34 best discriminating items in all grade levels were analyzed separately, and it was found that they could provide a short form of the scale (Table 7-3). Kuder-Richardson and split-half reliability coefficients for the short form ranged from .83 and .87 (see Table 7-1).

The 88 selected items were classified on the basis of their content in four categories: (1) school and work (27 items); (2) peer relationships (23 items); (3) self-description (29 items); and (4) parent-student relationships (8 items). Preliminary norms in percentile form were developed for each grade level from existing data.

The scores obtained on the 88 selected items by the 2,445 students were correlated with the students' grade-point average (GPA) of the previous year. A Pearson correlation of .28 was obtained, which is significant at the .0001 level for this sample size. This is lower than the average of .5 reported by Bloom (1976), possibly because the GPA did not reflect current performance and possibly because GPA in Puerto Rico public schools reflects only Spanish, English, and math. . . .

Discussion

The scale that was developed seems to have high internal consistency reliability in all three grade levels. Its reliability was highest at the 7th grade level because this grade shared many highly discriminating items with the other two (see Table 7-1).

The method of homogenous scale construction used for item construction provides a basis for the construct validity of the scale. The content of the items is in many respects similar to that of other school-age self-concept scales. The correlation with previous year's grade-point average served as an indicator of criterion-related validity.

Mean self-concept scores increased from one grade to the next (see Table 7-2). This is consistent with previous findings (Thompson, 1972). At each grade level the score distribution also became more negatively skewed (−.45, −.71, and −1.07, respectively). Small percentages of students received nearly "perfect" scores (1%, 4%, and 4% in each grade level), but there were no scores approaching zero. This indicates that the scale can successfully be used for the identification of students in all three grade levels who have a low self-concept.

A strong effort was made to balance the numbers of positive and negative items. The most discriminating items, however, tended to be negative. As a result, the 88-item scale contains only 33% positive items. It seems that it is the lack of a negative quality rather than the existence of a positive quality that characterizes students with high self-concepts in the public schools of Puerto Rico.

The short form of the scale could be used for data collection from groups, particularly if time is very limited,

Table 7-1   Reliability Coefficients for the Self-Concept Scale

| | Grade | | | |
Form and Coefficient	4th	7th	10th	Overall
Long form (88 items)				
K-R 20	.92	.94	.94	.93
Split-half	.92	.93	.93	.93
Short form (34 items)				
K-R 20	.85	.86	.86	.86
Split-half	.83	.87	.85	.85

Table 7-2   Scale Statistics

| Central Tendency and | Grade | | | |
Dispersion Measures	4th	7th	10th	Overall
Long form (88 items)				
Mean	67.90	69.83	72.44	67.66
Standard deviation	13.15	14.15	13.45	10.01
Skewness	−0.45	−0.71	−1.07	−0.75
Kurtosis	2.41	3.00	4.29	3.71
Short form (34 items)				
Mean	24.39	25.02	26.04	25.08
Standard deviation	6.19	6.36	5.85	6.17
Skewness	−0.47	−0.70	−1.04	−0.75
Kurtosis	2.31	2.84	3.78	3.14

Table 7-3 The Ten Most Discriminating Items and Overall Phi Coefficients

Item	Phi
7. Generalmente estoy atrasado (a) en mi trabajo. (I am generally behind with my work.)	.57
16. Soy más lento (a) que mis compañeros para hacer los trabajos de la clase. (I am slower than my classmates in doing homework.)	.54
24. Muchas veces me siento completamente inútil. (Many times I feel completely useless.)	.53
26. Muchas veces dejo las cosas sin terminar. (Many times I leave things unfinished.)	.62
33. Generalmente, los maestros me hacen preguntas difíciles de contestar. (Teachers generally ask me difficult questions.)	.53
44. Se me olvida fácilmente lo que aprendo. (I easily forget what I learn.)	.58
53. A menudo me da coraje. (I often get angry.)	.54
55. Si la maestra hace una pregunta tengo miedo de contestar. (I am afraid to answer if the teacher asks a question.)	.59
60. Mis maestros me ponen a hacer cosas tan difíciles, que no puedo hacerlas. (Teachers make me do things that are too difficult for me.)	.57
62. Quisiera ser otra persona. (I would like to be someone else.)	.53

Escala de Autoconcepto, 1980

since only a few minutes are necessary for its administration. The 88-item scale can be administered within a 50-minute class period to 4th graders and in much less time (20 to 30 minutes) to upper grades. It is reliable and broad enough in content to permit self-concept assessment of individual students in the Puerto Rico public schools who have third-grade reading skills (see a sample of items in Table 7-3). More statistical work on the scale can produce a set of subscores that will focus on relations with school, peers, and descriptions of self.

Further research is necessary. The divergent validity of the scale regarding reading skills and comprehension must be measured. Test-retest reliability should be established, as well as a correlation with an external criterion of self-concept. If administratively possible, the scores should be correlated with current grade-point averages that include all subjects taken. Norms based on the final format of the scale should be established and supplemented with private school data if private schools in Puerto Rico are to use this instrument. It might also be possible to use this scale to assess the self-concept of Puerto Rican children in the continental United States if it is established that they have adequate reading and language skills in Spanish to respond to it.

THE TEST DEVELOPMENT PROCESS: PART 2

OBJECTIVE

To further enhance understanding, stimulate thought, and provide firsthand experience with respect to the process of developing a psychological test

BACKGROUND

Different test developers approach the process of test development in different ways. In an article entitled "A Sequential System for Personality Scale Development," psychologist/test author Douglas N. Jackson (1970) afforded readers an inside look at the process of developing the Personality Research Form (PRF). What follows below is an abbreviated form of that article.

YOUR TASK

Read about the development of the PRF while keeping in mind the general procedures involved in test development described in Chapter 7 of your textbook. If you were also assigned Exercise 7-2, contrast Jackson's approach to that of Abadzi and Florez. Additionally, what recommendations do you have for making the PRF a better test? For example, if the test developer were to update validation research on the PRF, what type of validation study would you recommend? Would you recommend co-validation with another test of personality? What other recommendations might you make to this test developer?

ANATOMY OF THE DEVELOPMENT OF A TEST: THE PERSONALITY RESEARCH FORM (PRF)

According to Douglas Jackson (1970), the PRF was developed in the hope that "by a careful application of modern conceptions of personality and of psychometric theory and computer technology more rigorous and more valid assessment of important personality characteristics would result" (p. 62). More specifically, Jackson viewed four interrelated principles as essential to the development of the PRF (as well as other tests of personality). He described them as follows:

1. The importance of psychological theory (see Cronbach & Meehl, 1955; Loevinger, 1957)
2. The necessity for suppressing response style (for example, suppressing the tendency to respond in socially desirable ways or the tendency to respond nonpurposively or randomly) (see Jackson & Messick, 1958)
3. The importance of scale homogeneity and scale generalizability
4. The importance of fostering convergent and discriminant validity

Jackson (1970) labeled four major stages in the development of the PRF as follows:

I. The substantive definition of personality scale content
II. A sequential strategy in scale construction
III. The appraisal of the structural component of validity
IV. Evaluation of the external component of validity

In abbreviated, simplified fashion, each stage is described here.

I: The Substantive Definition of Personality Scale Content

A. The Choice of Appropriate Constructs

Jackson (1970) advised that "the first step in constructing a personality test is to decide what to measure" (p. 66). If, for example, a test or a scale within a test is to measure "aggressiveness," a clear definition of this construct must be arrived at. Do we mean physical aggression? verbal aggression? overt aggression? covert aggression? all of these? The answers to these and related questions will depend on variables such as the objectives of the test and the length of the test (Cronbach & Gleser, 1965). An additional consideration in selecting a construct for measurement concerns how much is already known about it: "It is easier to prepare large numbers of items for dimensions whose correlates are well established" (Jackson, 1970, p. 67).

The PRF was based on personality variables conceptualized and defined by Henry Murray and his colleagues (1938). To help lay the foundation for items to be written that would be high in validity, mutually exclusive definitions of each personality variable had to be derived if they did not already exist. For example, *exhibitionism* had to be clearly distinguished from *need for social recognition*.

B. The Development of Substantively Defined Item Sets

Jackson (1970, p. 67) described this step as "the most difficult of all—the creation and editing of the item pool of some three thousand items, comprising the set from which PRF scales were finally developed." He went on to describe the evaluation and editing of each item with respect to the following criteria:

- their conformity to the definition of the scale for which they were written
- the adequacy of the negative instances of the trait
- their clarity and freedom from ambiguity
- their judged freedom from extreme levels of desirability bias
- their judged discriminating power and popularity levels when administered to appropriate populations
- their judged freedom from various forms of content bias and their representativeness as a set
- the degree to which they conformed to the definition of the scale for which they were written as well as their "fortuitous convergence with irrelevant constructs, particularly those which were to be included in the PRF" (p. 68).

C. A Multidimensional Scaling Evaluation of Substantive Item Selection

The empirical value of rational judgment methods used in item selection was demonstrated by means of a technique called "multidimensional successive intervals scaling" (Torgerson, 1958). Through the use of judges' ratings of descriptions of hypothetical people, information was obtained with respect to (1) the number of dimensions along which items were perceived to differ and (2) the scale value of each stimulus on each of the dimensions.

D. Empirical Evaluation of Homogeneity of Postulated Item Content

An empirical evaluation of the structured properties of the set of theoretically defined items was undertaken by means of the administration of provisional scales to an approximately equal number of male and female university students. Estimates of item reliability were obtained through the use of the KR-20 formula. The median reliability was found to be .925 with the highest reliability estimate being .94 for six of the scales: Aggression, Endurance, Exhibition, Harm Avoidance, Order, and Social Recognition. Interestingly, the lowest reliability estimate (.80) was obtained for the scale called "Defendence." Of this finding, Jackson (1970, pp. 71–72) wrote, "This is not at all surprising, since defensive people might be less willing to admit defensiveness consistently."

II. A Sequential Strategy in Scale Construction

Responses to each of the items on the provisional PRF underwent a computerized item analysis to determine if the item would be retained or rejected. Some of the criteria employed at this stage of the test development process follow:

- Infrequently endorsed items—or items that almost everyone would endorse—were to be eliminated, because they reveal little about respondents. Stated more technically, they will fail to appreciably add to the reliability and validity of the test because of their small variances. Further, such items have been found to elicit stylistic tendencies

Figure 1 Comparison of Parallel Forms (Source: Jackson, 1970)

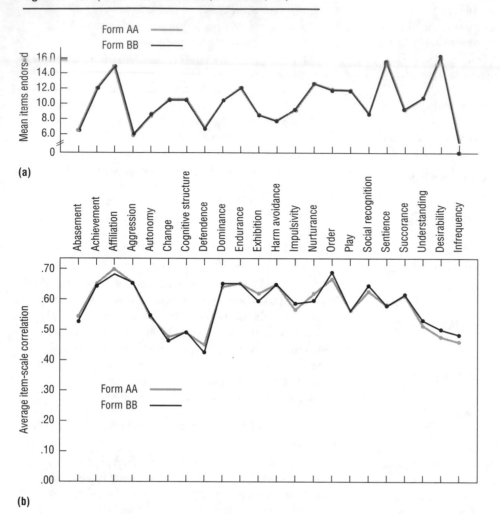

(a)

(b)

to respond deviantly or nonpurposively. For these reasons, items with a *p* value of either below .05 or above .95 were eliminated. An obvious exception to this rule would be items deliberately selected for use in the *Infrequency scale,* a scale designed to detect nonpurposive or random responding and related response styles. A sample item on this scale might be one like "I have visited the Republic of Samoa during the past year."

- If an item correlated higher with any content-scale total score other than the one it was written for, the item was eliminated. This helped to ensure convergent and discriminant validity.
- An evaluation was made as to the degree to which the item elicited tendencies to respond desirably. This was accomplished, at least in part, by evaluating each item's correlation with a desirability scale.
- An evaluation was made of the item's saturation as indicated by the magnitude of its correlation with the total scale.
- An evaluation was made of the item's content saturation in relation to its desirability bias as

indicated by a specially devised Differential Reliability Index.

- Items were assigned to parallel forms of the test on the basis of item and scale statistical properties. The rigor with which this process was executed can be seen graphically in Figure 1.
- Each item was subjected to a final substantive review designed to evaluate its generalizability and its representativeness with respect to scale content.

III. The Appraisal of the Structural Component of Validity

Steps were taken to ensure that optimal levels of homogeneity existed. Ideally, homogeneity would be attributable to the test's content as opposed to response style or other variables.

IV. Evaluation of the External Component of Validity

Paid volunteers who lived in Stanford University housing and who were all "well acquainted with one another" served as the sample for the validity study. Jackson (1970, p. 88) noted that each subject sat for a four-hour assessment battery including two forms of the PRF, a set of behavior ratings of 20 variables relevant to the 20 PRF content scales, and 600 adjectives measuring the same 20 traits relevant to each of the 20 scales. Subjects responded true or false to each of the 600 adjectives as self-descriptive, and later judged the desirability of each of them in other people. This latter task was included to appraise the hypothesis that a person's point of view about the desirability of a trait would tell us something valid about that person's own personality (Jackson, 1964; Stricker et al., 1968).

An examination of correlations between PRF scales and appropriate criterion measures revealed that there was substantial convergent and discriminant validity associated with PRF scales.

EXERCISE 7-4
SCALING THE BOUNDS OF CONSCIOUSNESS

OBJECTIVE

To provide firsthand experience in the scaling of a test

BACKGROUND

Testtakers are presumed to range in the degree to which they exhibit or possess a characteristic measured by a valid test. In general, the higher or lower the score on the test, the more or less of the characteristic the testtaker is presumed to possess. But how are numbers assigned to responses so that a test score can be calculated?

YOUR TASK

Read the following description of the scaling of the hypothetical "Depth of Hypnosis Scale" (DHS). After you have read it, and with reference to your textbook, write a brief essay on alternative ways the scaling of the DHS could have been approached.

DEPTH OF HYPNOSIS SCALE

Suppose you wish to develop a "Depth of Hypnosis Scale" (DHS) whereby the higher a subject scores on the test, the deeper the subject is presumed to be in a hypnotic trance. You make an arbitrary decision that two of the requirements for this test are that it be brief and easily administered. In the interest of simplicity you make a preliminary decision that there will be ten items on this test and that possible scores on this test will range from 0 to 10. A score of 0 shall indicate a nonhypnotized state and a score of 10 shall indicate the deepest hypnotic state.

The next step is to assemble an item pool, consisting perhaps of twenty or so possible items from which you will ultimately select the ten items that you feel measure the construct. One way to assemble this item pool is to enlist the aid of a number of expert hypnotists and instruct each to compose a list of ten behaviors that, from their experience, represent ten indicators of depth of hypnosis in ascending order. By examining where there is a consensus among the experts and by resolving discrepancies between the judgments of the experts (by methods such as interviewing the experts or researching the literature), a scale will begin to emerge. You might find that some items on that scale, each scores Yes or No (with one point assigned for each Yes answer), are as follows (in ascending Guttman, as given by the experts):

1. Subject does not obey any commands at all.
2. Subject obeys simple command that his or her eyelids are "stuck together" and, in fact, is unable to open eyes.
5. Subject responds to suggestion of positive hallucination (such as "there is a white elephant in the room").
6. Subject responds to suggestion of negative hallucination (such as "there is no one else in the room but you and me"—when the room is actually filled with people).
10. Suggestion of analgesia (inability to experience pain) is strong enough to sustain patient through major surgery without administration of anesthesia.

Some points about the DHS and the method used to derive it are useful in shedding light on scales and scaling methods in general. The DHS is an ordinal scale because the different "depths" are more than merely named, they are ranked. Yet the interval level of measurement is not reached by the DHS, because it is not necessarily the case that equal intervals exist between points on the scale. Ordinal scales such as the DHS can be derived by numerous methods, such as through the use of *sorting techniques* whereby the people doing the ranking (usually referred to as the "judges" or "raters") sort a pile of cards with respect to the degree to which they believe a particular trait is reflected.

Sorting techniques can also be used to derive nominal scales. For this purpose, subjects would be instructed to sort the cards (or objects or whatever) into mutually exclusive categories, each category then being assigned a number and/or a name. Sorting tasks may even be used to obtain interval scales—or scales that are at least presumed to be equal (Thurstone, 1927; Thurstone & Chave, 1929).

EXERCISE 7-5
GUTTMAN SCALING

OBJECTIVE

To provide firsthand experience in the creation of a Guttman scale

BACKGROUND

A Guttman scale lists items that range sequentially from weaker to stronger expressions of the attitude, belief, or feeling being measured. A feature of Guttman scales is that they are designed so that all respondents who agree with the stronger statements of the attitude will also agree with milder statements. Here is a sample:

Directions: Circle the letter of the statement with which you agree.

Item 1

A. If the woman in a mature, responsible, financially secure, loving, married couple is infertile, then the couple should have the right to contract with a surrogate mother to bear the father's child.

B. If a mature, responsible, financially secure, loving, married couple is infertile, then they have a right to adopt a child.

C. If a mature, responsible, financially secure, loving, married couple is having difficulty conceiving a child, then they have the right to seek medical intervention.

D. All mature, responsible, financially secure, loving, married couples have a right to have children.

If this were a perfect Guttman scale, all respondents who agree with item *A* (the most extreme position) should also agree with items *B, C,* and *D,* which appear to represent progressively less extreme positions. All respondents who do not agree with *A* but who do agree with *B* should also agree with *C* and *D,* and so forth.

YOUR TASK

Using Guttman scaling, write one test item on any topic you wish.

EXERCISE 7-6
ITEM ANALYSIS:
QUANTITATIVE METHODS

OBJECTIVE

To enhance understanding of and provide firsthand experience with various methods of quantitative item analysis

BACKGROUND

Which items within a pool of possible items represent the best items? Which items need to be modified or eliminated in order to make the test a better test? These are typical questions asked by many test developers (as well as test users),
and the process of answering them typically entails item analysis. *Item analysis* refers to a test item evaluation process involving quantitative and/or qualitative methods. In this exercise we focus on *quantitative* methods designed to yield information regarding characteristics of test items such as level of difficulty and power of discrimination. In Exercise 7-6 we focus on *qualitative* methods of item analysis designed to yield information regarding characteristics of test items such as ambiguity and social desirability.

Exactly which of the many available quantitative item analytic techniques will be employed will vary as a function of variables related to (a) the nature of the test and (b) the item analyzer's definition of "best items." For example, while computation of indices of both item difficulty and item discrimination would be appropriate when analyzing an achievement test (or any test where there are right or wrong answers), only the computation of one of these indices—the index of item discrimination—would be appropriate with respect to a personality test (or any test where there are no right or wrong answers). In cases where the correlation of items with some external criterion (such as a personality trait or some other factor) is deemed essential, other quantitative techniques such as factor analysis may be an integral component of the item analysis process. Factor analysis may also be used to learn about the internal consistency of a test, as might other methods designed to yield indices of item reliability. An item-validity index (a measure of the validity of individual items) is yet another measure that may be derived quantitatively to answer the question "Which items are the best?"

YOUR TASK

In Part 1 of this exercise, your task is to calculate and interpret an item-difficulty index and an item-discrimination index. Part 2 is comprised of a series of short-answer problems related to item analysis.

In preparation for Part 1, your *instructor's* task is to make up a list of ten words to be administered in the form of an impromptu spelling test. The list should contain a mix of words estimated to be of low, middle, and high level of difficulty for college-age testtakers. The instructor reads each of the ten words aloud as each student writes it out. At the conclusion of the test, students find a partner to exchange papers with and all papers are scored. Still holding on to their partner's test paper, all students will individually report the performance of the testtaker of the paper they are holding as the instructor tallies the information at the board. The objective here will be to work together as a class to obtain an item-difficulty index and an item-discrimination index for each of the ten items (words) on the test.

Part 1

1. *Calculating and interpreting an item-difficulty index.* What proportion of the examinees got the item right? An

index of item difficulty provides the answer to this question, and it can be found by using the following formula:

$$p_1 = \frac{\text{number of examinees who got the item correct}}{\text{number of people who attempted to answer the item}}$$

where p_1 stands for "item-difficulty index for item 1."

In the process of calculating an item-difficulty index for each of the ten items on the test, you will discover firsthand the paradoxical meaning of the term *item-difficulty index*. More specifically, you will find that the *higher* the index of item difficulty, the *easier* the item. You will also find the reverse to be true: the lower the index of item difficulty, the more difficult the item.

Items on tests where the objective is maximum discrimination across the entire range should contain an assortment of items ranging in difficulty level from about .40 to about .70. However, occasions do arise—particularly in very selective screening situations—where the test user might find a test containing items with an average difficulty of .1. But for the test we've been working with in this exercise, the .40 to .70 range will do just fine; now, which items on the spelling test would you recommend for elimination (or modification)? Which items would you recommend for inclusion in a revised form of the test (assuming a revised form of the test was planned)?

2. *Calculating and interpreting an item-discrimination index.* "Are testtakers who are thought to be higher in the ability measured by the test more likely to get the item right than testtakers who are thought to be lower in the ability measured by the test?" "Are testtakers who are thought to possess more of a personality trait measured by a specific personality test more likely than other testtakers to respond to a personality test item in a predicted direction?" These are the kinds of questions on which a discrimination index is designed to shed light.

Symbolized by d, an *item-discrimination index* is a measure of the difference between the proportion of high scorers answering an item correctly and the proportion of low scorers answering the item correctly; the higher the value of d, the greater the number of high scorers answering the item correctly.[2] The group of high and low scorers may be comprised of testtakers who respectively achieved the top and bottom 25% to 33% of the scores. A negative value of d is indicative of a situation where low-scoring examinees are more likely to answer the item correctly than high-scoring examinees—a situation that calls for action such as revision or elimination of the item.

While there exist many methods of measuring item discrimination, the one you will be using to obtain d for each item in your spelling test is simple and straightforward. Here are the steps you'll be following as a class:

Step 1
Sort all of the test papers into one of three groups on the basis of the test score. The three groups that papers will be sorted into will be the high scorers (Group H), the medium scorers (Group M), and the low scorers (Group L). Based on the number of papers in the class, use the most convenient figure between 25% and 33% as the cutoff point. For example, if there are twelve students in the class, you may wish to use the 33% figure as a cutoff point—this so there will be four papers in each of the three groups.

Step 2
Focusing solely on the papers in Group H, ask "How many members of this group got the item correct?" for each item.[3] For each item, express the answer to this question as a proportion with N (the total number of testtakers in Group H) as the denominator.

Step 3
Focusing solely on the papers in Group L, ask "How many members of this group got the item correct?" for each item. For each item, express the answer to this question as a proportion with N (the total number of testtakers in Group L) as the denominator.

Step 4
For each item, solve for d by subtracting the proportion you obtained for L from the proportion you obtained for H.

Three questions that may come up as you calculate and then attempt to interpret item-discrimination indices for each of the ten items in the spelling test are as follows:

- What value of d is an acceptable cutoff? At what point can I be assured I have an item good enough to be included in my revised test?
- Why was the data from Group M not used in the calculation of d?
- How should one proceed if the test results are not amenable to a clear separation of high-, middle-, and low-scoring papers?

There are no hard-and-fast rules regarding what constitutes an acceptable cutoff point for an index of

---

[2]"Translating" this explanation with reference to personality testing and the measurement of a specific personality trait, d is a measure of the difference between the proportion of testtakers who scored high on the particular personality trait being measured and the proportion of testtakers who scored low on the particular personality trait being measured.

[3]"Translating" to the language of testing where there are no right or wrong answers—such as in personality testing—this question might be rephrased, "How many members of this group responded to this particular item in the way that indicated that they did possess the trait in question?" More specifically, on a test of introversion where Group H was composed of people whose overall score on the test was high, the relevant question would be "How many members of Group H responded to this particular item in the way that we would expect introverts to respond?"

discrimination. There are many ways to calculate such an index, and each of these may yield different values. In practice, the setting of an acceptable level of item discrimination—like the setting of an appropriate level of item difficulty—will depend on the nature of the test and the use of the test data. As a rule of thumb for the purposes of this exercise, let's arbitrarily set .40 as an acceptable level of item discrimination; any item with a d value of .40 or better (higher) will be eligible for inclusion in the revised form of the test.

The data from the middle range of scores on the test, Group M, were not used in order to clearly separate respondents in terms of ability—in the present instance, spelling ability. The presumption is that the high scorers on this test are more able spellers than are the low scorers on the test. But what can be said about the examinees who scored in the middle range? These respondents could be either good spellers who, due to error in the psychometric sense, did not exhibit their "true" ability on the test or, alternatively, relatively poor spellers who, due to error in the psychometric sense, did much better on this particular test than might have been expected based on their "true" ability. You may then ask, "Why not more precisely discriminate between the extreme (upper/lower) groups by using only the top and bottom 5% or 10% of scorers?" The answer here is that if the sample is large enough, such a practice would be feasible. In most applications, however, employing only the top and bottom 5% of respondents would yield too few cases with which to work.[4]

In attempting to calculate d with respect to your instructor's spelling test items (or with any other application), you may find that your data are not amenable to clear separation into high-, medium-, and low-scoring groups. You would like to keep the number of cases in Group H and Group L equal, and to do so may mean that Group M contains a different number of cases (or precious few cases or no cases at all). Sometimes in this effort to balance the two extreme groups (H and L), an excess of scores of one or another value occurs in one or the other groups. The operative term in eliminating these excess scores is *do it randomly*. One simple way for eliminating data is to use a coin; flip it, saying, "Heads you stay, tails you go." Up one notch in sophistication from that technique is reference to a table of random numbers (found in most introductory statistics texts); with all test papers coded by number, simply eliminate those test papers with a code number that corresponds to the number(s) in the random numbers table that appear(s) first.

Part 2

If Part 1 of this exercise has left you craving for more experience with the concept and practice of item analysis, assume now that you are the author of a 100-item (draft) test for a ninth-grade-level American history test (AHT) and that your objective is to have this test distributed by a commercial test publisher. You envision the final version of the AHT as containing only 50 items and plan to use item analysis as a tool in helping you to eliminate 50 items while retaining the "best" remaining items. You recently administered the test to 100 ninth-graders, and those data are waiting to be analyzed.

1. Using your textbook as well as any other relevant books as a resource, briefly describe how you would (or would not) use the following indices in your efforts to narrow the field of 100 AHT items to the best 50 items:

   - item-difficulty index
   - item-validity index
   - item-reliability index
   - item-discrimination index

2. What follows are two sample items from your AHT:

   AHT ITEM #1

   Who was Vice President of the United States under President Jimmy Carter?
   a. Gerald Ford
   b. George Bush
   c. Walter Mondale
   d. Bob Dole

   AHT ITEM #2

   What was the name of the first communication satellite launched by the United States?
   a. *Sputnik*
   b. *Telstar*
   c. *Comtrex*
   d. *Orbitron*

   Like the items above, each AHT item contains four possible answers. What is the probability of guessing correctly on this (or any single item) on the basis of chance alone?

3. What is the optimal level of item difficulty for any AHT item?

4. If 60 of the 100 examinees were correct in their response to Item 47, what is the item-difficulty index for Item 47?

5. If 69 of the 100 examinees were correct in their response to Item 93, what is the item-difficulty index for Item 93?

---

[4]We note in passing that some computerized item-discrimination programs are sophisticated and elegant enough to incorporate the middle range of scores in the computation of an item-discrimination index. For our pencil-and-paper purposes, however, use of the extreme (upper/lower) groups will suit us just fine.

6. Which item was the more difficult, Item 93 or Item 47?

7. Calculate the item-score standard deviation of Item 93 and Item 47.

8. Item 16 has an item-score standard deviation of .40. The point-biserial correlation between the item score and the total test score is .75. What is the item-reliability index of Item 16?

9. From all of the test papers for the 100 students who took the AHT you form two groups—Group *H,* which consists of the upper-scoring 27% of the papers, and Group *L,* which consists of the lower-scoring 27% of the papers. You put aside for the moment all of the test papers that fall into the middle range (46% of the papers). There are a total of 27 papers in Group *H* and a total of 27 papers in Group *L.* The table below illustrates the number of test-takers in each group who responded correctly to each of the two items listed below:

Item	H	L
1	25	8
2	9	14

Determine the item-discrimination index (d_i) for each of these items. Which item is the better of two? Why?

10. After looking at the data for Item 2 (below), decide whether or not you believe this item to be a good item. Provide a brief rationale for your opinion based on (a) the overall contrast in performance with respect to the *H* and *L* groups and (b) the performance of the distractor choices. How might you go about revising this item if indeed you find it to be in need of revision?

Item 2

	Alternatives			
Group	a	b*	c	d
H	15	9	2	1
L	3	14	4	6

*answer keyed as correct

11. Now look at the data for response to Item 1. What can you conclude from it?

Item 1

	Alternatives			
Group	a	b	c*	d
H	2	0	25	0
L	18	0	8	0

*answer keyed as correct

ITEM ANALYSIS: QUALITATIVE METHODS

OBJECTIVE

To enhance understanding of and provide firsthand experience with various methods of qualitative item analysis

BACKGROUND

In addition to methods of item analysis that utilize numbers, statistics, graphs, formulas, and the like—quantitative methods—there exists another class of methods that may be used to analyze and evaluate test items. This latter group of techniques, referred to as *qualitative* in nature, relies instead on techniques such as one-on-one interviews and group discussion. In what we will refer to as the Think Aloud method, an examinee verbalizes thoughts as they come to mind in the process of having the test individually administered. Another method, the Small Group Discussion method of qualitative item analysis, is just that—a group discussion of reactions to each of the items on the test as each item is administered.

YOUR TASK

As a class, you will conduct a qualitative item analysis using a combination of the Think Aloud, and Small Group Discussion techniques. The stimulus for this analysis will be the MMPPI (see Appendix A).

The instructor (or student) interviewer/moderator will read each item aloud, and class members—each playing the role of a testtaker—will respond with some of their impressions regarding various aspects of the time. In order to better understand each item and the process by which testtakers might mentally arrive at an answer to each, the moderator should encourage testtakers to think aloud as they arrive at an answer. Additionally, information regarding the perceived ambiguity, offensiveness, inappropriateness, or foolishness of each item will be important when conducting a qualitative item analysis. And if the test being analyzed were a veritable personality test—as opposed to a mock personality test—other variables to watch for in the analysis would include the extent to which an item is perceived as an invasion of privacy, the *transparency* of an item, and the *social desirability* of an item.

Transparency refers to the extent to which examinees can "see right through" an item, and unless there is some specific reason to the contrary, the less transparent an item is, the better. Consider, for example, a test examining the personality variable of locus of control. An item such as "I usually wear seatbelts in a car" is better—at least with respect to transparency—than an item such as "I feel that I have little control over my life." While both items tap perceived locus of control—the extent to which people feel that they are the masters of their own fate—the seatbelt item does it in a subtler (and more preferable) way.

Social desirability is another factor that may bias a test-taker's response to an item on a personality test; the term refers to a tendency to respond to personality test items in a way that will place the respondent in the most favorable light (regardless of what the true response to the item might be). Look at the two personality test items that follow and ask yourself which answer, True or False, is the socially desirable response:

	True	False
1. I hope to be able to take care of my parents in their old age.	| |	| |
	True	False
2. I tend to betray my friends.	| |	| |

For Item 1, the socially desirable response is True, and for Item 2 the socially desirable response is False. For obvious reasons many testtakers—especially those taking a personality test as part of a hiring, promotion, or some other selection process—may strive to make all of their responses fall in the socially desirable range. Personality test developers have attempted to counter this tendency in a number of ways such as (1) motivating testtakers to respond candidly by persuading them that it is in their best interest to do so; (2) building faking detection scales (such as the MMPI Lie Scale) into the test; and (3) structuring the test so that the testtaker must respond to one or more alternatives that are equally undesirable. The latter technique entails writing what are called *forced-choice* types of items such as the following:

Which is true (or more true than the other)—*a* or *b*?

(a) I tend to betray my friends.
(b) I tend to double-deal my business associates.

While you may not find transparency or social desirability response bias to be major factors influencing responses to the MPPI, in practice these (as well as related) factors may be quite problematic to test developers and test users.

EXERCISE 7-8
WRITING NORM-REFERENCED TEST ITEMS

OBJECTIVE

To enhance understanding of and obtain firsthand experience with test-item writing

BACKGROUND

"What range of content should my test items cover?" "Which of the many different types of item formats should be employed?" These are but two of the many questions that must be answered by the creator of a test—be it a test to be nationally standardized or a test to be used for a one-time classroom administration.

YOUR TASK

1. Develop a five-item test on the following subject: "American History from 1940 to 1980." All five of the items should be of the same item format. (For the sake of this test construction exercise, let's limit the choice of item formats to the following three: multiple-choice, true/false, or essay.)
2. Provide a brief rationale for (a) the range of content your test covers and (b) your choice of item format.
3. Checking against the discussion of the criteria for "good" items found in your textbook, "troubleshoot" the items you've written; are they indeed "good" items? Why or why not?
4. Now rewrite all five items into a different one of the three item formats (multiple-choice, true/false, or essay); are the rewritten items also "good" items (according to the criteria set forth in your text)? Why or why not?
5. Discuss some of the feelings and/or questions you had in completing the four tasks above. What did you feel good or confident about? What did you lack confidence about or feel you wished to know more about? What do you think it takes to be a good item writer and test developer?

EXERCISE 7-9
WRITING CRITERION-REFERENCED TEST ITEMS

OBJECTIVE

To obtain firsthand experience in creating items for a criterion-oriented test

BACKGROUND

Some tests are designed so that an individual's test score is compared to the scores of other testtakers. You know from your own experience that many of the tests you have taken in school were graded by the instructor "on a curve," that is, with reference to the performance of your classmates. Other tests are designed so that they evaluate mastery of a particular area; an adequate or "passing" score on the latter type of test requires meeting some established criterion. Physicians, attorneys, psychologists, airline pilots, and other professionals must all meet some minimal criteria before being licensed to practice their professions; standing among other testtakers may not count for much in this context, especially since the ability of fellow testtakers may vary widely.

YOUR TASK

All states have a written examination as well as a road test for licensure as a driver. Write three true/false items that you believe should be included on the written examination for a driver's license in every state. Then write a paragraph or two explaining why these items are (or should be) criterion-referenced as opposed to norm-referenced. Finally, write another paragraph or two recounting the similarities and differences entailed in writing norm-referenced test items (such as in the previous exercise) and criterion-referenced items.

EXERCISE 7-10
CONTRASTING THE VIEWS OF TWO TEST DEVELOPERS

OBJECTIVE

To appreciate the differences in various approaches to test development by reading accounts of the process written by test developers

BACKGROUND

The companion Web site for Cohen & Swerdlik (2005) may be found at *www.mhhe.com.* This site contains numerous resources, including a number of "Test Developer Profiles" that describe the approach to test development of many test developers.

YOUR TASK

Write a brief essay in which you contrast the views of two test developers (as stated in their Test Developer Profiles) about developing a psychological test.

EXERCISE 7-11
FIGURE THIS

OBJECTIVE

Obtain firsthand computational experience figuring out problems related to material presented in the chapter

BACKGROUND

Use your knowledge of material presented in Chapter 7 in your textbook to tackle *Your Task* in what follows.

YOUR TASK

A teacher constructs a test to measure the mastery of concepts she has taught this week. Ten students take the test, which consists of five items. Eight students correctly answer item one; one student has the correct answer for item two; two students get item three correct; two correctly answer item four; and nine get item five correct.

1. Calculate the item difficulty index for each item.
2. Explain to the teacher what the item difficulty data means about her test.
3. Explain when you might choose to create a norm-referenced test. Provide at least three examples of when norm-referenced tests would be appropriate.
4. Explain when you might choose to create a criterion-referenced test. Provide at least three examples of when criterion-referenced tests would be appropriate.

REFERENCES

Abadzi, H., & Florez, S. (1981). Constructing the Puerto Rico Self-Concept Scale. *Applied Psychological Measurement, 5,* 237–243.

Bloom, B. (1976). *Human characteristics and school learning.* New York: McGraw-Hill.

Brookover, W. B., Patterson, A., & Thomas, S. (1962). *Self-concept of ability and school achievement.* East Lansing, MI: U.S. Office of Education, Cooperative Research Project No. 845, East Lansing Office of Research & Publications, Michigan State University.

Campbell, P. B. (1967). School and self-concept. *Educational Leadership, 24,* 510–515.

Coppersmith, S. (1967). *The antecedents of self-esteem.* San Francisco: W. H. Freeman.

Cronbach, L. (1970). *Essentials of psychological testing* (3rd ed.). New York: Harper & Row.

Fink, M. B. (1962). Self-concept as it relates to academic achievement. *California Journal of Education Research, 13,* 57–62.

Gill, M. P. (1969, April). *Patterns of achievement as related to the perceived self.* Paper presented at the annual meeting of the American Educational Research Association, Los Angeles, CA.

Gordon, I. J. (1966). *Studying the child in the school.* New York: Wiley.

Hernández, M. (1964). *Necesidades y problemas de los estudiantes adolescentes de escuela superior en Puerto Rico.* Hato Rey, Puerto Rico: Departamento de Instrucción Pública, Oficina de Evaluación.

Jackson, D. N. (1970). A sequential system for personality scale development. In C. D. Spielberger (Ed.), *Current topics in clinical and community psychology.* Vol 2. New York: Academic Press.

Muller, D. G., & Leonetti, R. (1972). *Primary Self-Concept Scale: Test Manual.* Ft. Worth, TX: National Council for Bilingual Education. (ERIC Document Reproduction Service, No. ED 062847)

Puerto Rico Departamento de Instrucción Pública, Centro de Evaluación. (1980). *Escala de autoconcepto.* Hato Rey, Puerto Rico: Author.

Purkey, W. W. (1970). *Self-concept and school achievement.* Englewood Cliffs, NJ: Prentice-Hall.

Richmond, B. O., & White, D. F. (1971). Sociometric predictors of the self-concept among fifth- and sixth-grade children. *Journal of Educational Research, 64,* 425–429.

Stanwyck, D. J., & Felker, D. W. (1971, April). *Measuring the self-concept: A factor analytic study.* Paper presented at the annual meeting of the National Council of Measurement in Education, New York. (ERIC Document Reproduction Service, No. ED 053161)

Thompson, W. (1972). *Correlates of the self concept* (Monograph No. 6). Nashville, TN: Dede Wallace Center.

Thurstone, L. L. (1927). A law of comparative judgment. *Psychological Review, 34,* 273–286.

Thurstone, L. L. (1959). *The measurement of values.* Chicago: University of Chicago Press.

Thurstone, L. L., & Chave, E. J. (1929). *The measurement of attitude.* Chicago: University of Chicago Press.

Whitmore, J. R. (1975). *Thinking about my school, TAMS: The development of an inventory to measure pupil perception of the elementary school environment* (R & D Memorandum No. 125). Palo Alto, CA: Stanford University, Stanford Center for Research and Development in Testing. (ERIC Document Reproduction Service, No. ED 100998)

THE 4-QUESTION CHALLENGE

1. Scaling may be defined as
   a. the assignment of numbers according to rules.
   b. the process of setting rules for assigning numbers in measurement.
   c. a method for estimating the strength of a particular trait in testtakers.
   d. the shrinkage of item validities that occurs after cross-validation.

2. Guttman scales yield this level of measurement:
   a. nominal
   b. ordinal
   c. interval
   d. ratio

3. An index of an item's difficulty is obtained by calculating the proportion of
   a. the total number of testtakers who got the item right.
   b. the total number of testtakers who reported the item to be difficult.
   c. the total number of testtakers who got the item right compared to a matched sample of testtakers.
   d. none of the above

4. An item characteristic curve is a graphic representation of
   a. testtaker responses to correct versus distractor alternatives.
   b. characteristics of performance on orally administered versus paper-and-pencil tests.
   c. characteristics of performance on written versus computer-administered tests.
   d. testtaker ability plotted by probability of correct response.

CHAPTER 8

Intelligence and Its Measurement

Puzzle 8

Instructions Identify what is described, answer a question, or fill in the blank to complete this crossword puzzle based on material presented in Chapter 8 of your textbook.

Across

1. In Gardner's theory of multiple intelligences, _____ intelligence is equated with a capacity to form accurate self-perceptions, to discriminate accurately between emotions, and to be able to draw upon one's emotions as an effective guide.

5. Based on Luria's writings, _____ processing is a type of information processing whereby information is processed in a sequential, bit-by-bit fashion and arranged and rearranged until it is logical.

7. A term that may be used in place of the one in 5-Across.

9. _____ loading is an index of the degree to which a test incorporates the vocabulary, concepts, traditions, knowledge, and feelings associated with a particular culture.

10. The belief that heredity and environment interact to influence the development of one's mental capacity and abilities is embodied in _____ .

14. Whether there is one general form of intelligence or an intellect made up of many independent abilities has been debated by proponents of different _____ theories of intelligence. (Hint: This term is hyphenated.)

16. In Piagetian theory, a(n) _____ is an action or mental structure that, when applied to the world, leads to knowing or understanding.

19. In Cattell's two-factor theory of intelligence, _____ intelligence refers to acquired skills and knowledge that are very much dependent on formal and informal education.

20. The humorous name given to the gifted children who participated in study of intelligence initiated in 1916 by Lewis M. Terman.

23. The first two letters in this acronym for an information processing model developed by Luria stand for planning and attention.

25. The _____ technique is a method of peer appraisal in which members of a class, team, work unit, or other type of group are asked to select or vote for people in response to a question or statement.

26. _____ intelligence is a popularization of aspects of Gardner's theory of multiple intelligences, with emphasis on the notions of interpersonal and intrapersonal intelligence.

28. John B. Carroll's conception of mental abilities and processing, with g at the broadest level, followed by eight abilities or processes at the second level, and a number of more narrowly defined abilities and processes at the third level. This describes Carroll's _____ theory of cognitive abilities. (Hint: It's a hyphenated term.)

32. In the Horn-Cattell model of intelligence, _____ abilities are cognitive abilities that decline with age and tend not to return to pre-injury levels after brain damage.

34. Measured intelligence using a normed instrument rises each year subsequent to the year the test is normed, and this usually occurs in the absence of any academic divi-

dend. This phenomenon of "intelligence inflation" has come to be known as the _____ effect.

35. The distinguishing manner of an infant or child's observable actions and reactions; when they get older, the term "personality" is more appropriate.

36. An attribute associated with performance that is consistently remarkable in any positively valued area.

37. The doctrine of _____ holds that all living organisms are preformed at birth and that intelligence, much like other preformed "structures," cannot be improved upon by environmental intervention.

Down

1. In Gardner's theory of multiple intelligences, _____ intelligence refers to the ability to understand other people, what motivates them, how they work, and how to work cooperatively with them.

2. The *I* in the abbreviation SOI stands for _____ .

3. The _____ level is a stage in a test achieved by a testtaker as a result of that testtaker meeting some preset criteria to discontinue testing in a test or subtest.

4. An italicized, lower case g stands for _____ intellectual ability.

6. The _____ theory of intelligence is an approach that focuses on the mechanisms by which information is processed; that is, how information is processed rather than what is processed. (hyphenated term)

8. In Cattell's two-factor theory of intelligence, _____ intelligence comprises nonverbal abilities, which are less dependent on culture and formal instruction than the alternative intelligence.

11. The primary elements of Spearman's _____ theory of intelligence are g, s, and e. (hyphenated term)

12. In Piagetian theory, the plural of *schema*.

13. _____ is the doctrine that holds that one's abilities are predetermined by genetic inheritance and that no amount of learning or other intervention can enhance what is genetically encoded to unfold.

15. The _____ response is evidence of an infant's capacity for responsiveness, and it consists of the eyes brightening and widening in response to the presentation of a stimulus.

17. _____ processing is a type of information processing whereby information is integrated and synthesized all at once and as a whole.

18. The _____ response is indicative of an infant's capacity for responsiveness and is evidenced by the action of turning in the direction of a stimulus.

21. In the Horn-Cattell model of intelligence, _____ abilities are cognitive abilities that do not decline with age and that return to pre-injury levels after brain damage.

22. Mental _____ , now seldom used, is an index that refers to the chronological age equivalent of one's performance on a test or a subtest.

24. In Piagetian theory, one of two basic mental operations through which humans learn; this one involves the

active organization of new information into what is already perceived, known, or thought.

27. The term _____ *model* is usually applied to a theoretical model organized into two or more layers, where each succeeding layer is subsumed or incorporated by the preceding layer.

29. In Piagetian theory, one of two basic mental operations through which humans learn; this one involves change from what is already known, perceived, or thought to fit with new information.

30. In psychometrics, the term _____ may be applied to a test that is purportedly devoid of the influence of any particular culture and therefore does not favor people from any culture. In reality, this concept is more an ideal than an attainable reality, as all tests reflect culture to greater or lesser degrees. (Hint: It's a hyphenated term.)

31. One definition of it is: "a multifaceted capacity that manifests itself in different ways across the lifespan but in general includes the abilities and capacities to acquire and apply knowledge, to reason logically, to plan effectively, to infer perceptively, to exhibit sound judgment and problem-solving ability, to grasp and visualize concepts, to be mentally alert and intuitive, to be able to find the right words and thoughts with facility, and to be able to cope, adjust, and make the most of new situations."

33. _____ processing is a type of information processing whereby information is integrated and synthesized all at once and as a whole.

EXERCISE 8-1
MOVIES AND MEASUREMENT

OBJECTIVE

To enhance understanding of and provide firsthand experience with the development of a definition of intelligence

BACKGROUND

In the now classic film *Saturday Night Fever,* paint store clerk/disco dancer Tony Manero (John Travolta) attempts to win over Stephanie (Karen Lynn Gorney), a fellow resident of Bay Ridge, Brooklyn, who aspires to the life of a sophisticated Manhattanite. In a scene shortly after the two rehearse for an upcoming disco dance contest, Tony—perhaps feeling inadequate—asks Stephanie if she thinks that he is intelligent. Stephanie responds with a laugh and some indecision but ultimately concludes, "Yeah, maybe. Maybe intelligent." Among other things, the scene is a lesson in the relativity of the attribution of intelligence and the importance of keeping in mind not only the object of the assessment but also the frame of reference of the assessor. In fact, widely differing views as to the meaning of "intelligence" exist among psychologists, educators, and lay people. Studies conducted by Robert Sternberg (1982) with lay people, for example, have

On the Nature of "Intelligence"

yielded definitions as diverse as "displays common sense" to "reads with high comprehension." Among professionals, the views that intelligence is a kind of evolving biological adaptation to the outside world and that "intelligence is whatever intelligence tests measure" are only some of the many beliefs that have been expressed regarding the concept of intelligence.

YOUR TASK

This is a two-part task that entails (1) developing your own conception of intelligence, and (2) comparing it to some of the existing definitions. Let's do it in stepwise fashion:

Step 1

List ten things—they could be single words or terms—that you believe are characteristic of "adult intelligence."

1. _____
2. _____
3. _____
4. _____
5. _____
6. _____
7. _____
8. _____
9. _____
10. _____

Step 2

List ten things that you believe to be characteristic of the construct "unintelligence" (again confining your observations to the adult age range).

1. _____

2. _____

3. _____

4. _____

5. _____

6. _____

7. _____

8. _____

9. _____

10. _____

Step 3

On the basis of the characteristics you cited above, write a paragraph or two setting forth what you conceive intelligence in adults to be.

Step 4

Compare and contrast the definition of intelligence you derived with "intelligence" as it has been conceived of and defined by each of the following:

a. Francis Galton

b. Alfred Binet

c. David Wechsler

d. Charles Spearman

e. E. G. Boring

INTERPRETING IQ SCORES

OBJECTIVE

To enhance understanding of the types of interpretation that can legitimately be made—as well as the types of interpretation that *cannot* legitimately be made—on the basis of intelligence test data

BACKGROUND

IQ data are used in school systems as well as in other settings for the purpose of making determinations of students' level of learning ability and academic performance. Learning difficulties may be diagnosed on the basis of an intelligence test, and such data may serve as a guide to an assignment of special educational opportunities. Yet as Professor John R. Hills of Florida State University has asked, ". . . can IQ scores do all these things for us?"

YOUR TASK

To help better understand the information that IQ scores can and cannot provide, Hills provides the following ten questions. Mark each item True or False while noting any questions or comments to be raised in class.

THE INTERPRETING IQ SCORES TEST[1]

Tests that provide IQ scores are widely used in schools. A score that tells how "bright" a student is, or how readily he or she will learn in school, would be a handy bit of information, and it might be essential as a trustworthy and reliable guide for diagnosing learning difficulties, for providing students with special educational opportunities, or for predicting future educational performance. But can IQ scores do all these things for us? Try the following questions about scores from intelligence tests. Indicate whether the stated interpretation of the IQ score is sound. Circle either T or F for each question. Mark a response for each question; there is no penalty for guessing. This is an untimed test.

ANSWER		ITEM	QUESTIONS/COMMENTS
T	F	1. Manny got an IQ score of 115. This score means that Manny's innate ability to do things that require brains or intelligence is about one standard deviation above the mean or at about the 84th percentile.	
T	F	2. Manny's IQ score came from a recent revision of a widely used intelligence test	

---

[1]By John R. Hills, "Interpreting IQ Scores." From *Hills' Handy Hints,* reprinted by permission of the publisher, the National Council on Measurement in Education, Washington, D.C.

THE INTERPRETING IQ SCORES TEST *(continued)*

ANSWER	ITEM	QUESTIONS/COMMENTS

with a long and honored history. One can be confident that the score was derived by finding Manny's Mental Age on the basis of his answers to the test questions, dividing that by his Chronological Age, and multiplying by 100, as in (MA/CA) $\times$ 100 = IQ.

T   F   3. If Manny had been given a different IQ test, one that was used as widely and with an equally long and illustrious history, the resulting IQ score would be about the same level (within 2 or 3 points either way).

T   F   4. If Manny received the IQ score of 115 when he was in the sixth grade, we know that he was old enough that the score will remain stable, neither increasing nor decreasing appreciably for many years.

T   F   5. Manny happens to be black. Knowing this, we can estimate that Manny's score is lower than it should be because IQ tests are biased against minority groups.

T   F   6. The test that Manny took had two scores, one for Verbal skills and one for Performance or Nonverbal skills. The difference between the Verbal and Nonverbal IQs was 15 points. A skilled clinician can use that information by itself to make a useful diagnosis of emotional disturbance or organic brain injury.

T   F   7. Manny's brother, Sherman, took the same IQ test and got a score of 102. Because Sherman's score is below 110, there is little chance that he could be admitted to a college.

T   F   8. The IQ test that Manny and Sherman took was an established and highly respected test, but the publisher still may not have checked to see whether the IQ scores are useful for predicting performance in school and may not have published relevant results in the test manual.

T   F   9. Although Manny's teacher needs to know Manny's score, and it should be posted in the school records, Manny should not be allowed to know what his IQ score is.

T   F   10. If someone had taken Manny aside and showed him how to do some of the kinds of items on the IQ test and let him practice on those kinds of items a bit, his score might have been noticeably higher.

EXERCISE 8-3
"MENTAL AGE"

OBJECTIVE

To impart a historical and conceptual understanding of the now seldom-used concept of "mental age"

BACKGROUND

For many years after intelligence tests were first introduced, the concept of a mental age played a critical role in the computation of an intelligence quotient (IQ).

YOUR TASK

After reading the essay that follows, answer these questions:

1. Describe how mental age was once used in the calculation of an IQ.
2. Describe the intuitive appeal of the mental age concept.
3. Describe the drawbacks of using the mental age concept when describing test results.

"MENTAL AGE" AND IQ

Have you ever found yourself telling someone something like, "You're acting like a two-year-old?" Such statements reflect the great intuitive appeal the concept of "mental age" holds—the idea that someone can behave in a way that is more typical of a person who is either younger or older. Perhaps the first reference to "mental age" in the scholarly literature was made by Esquirol (1838), who observed that an idiot—one diagnostic classification of mental retardation of the day—was incapable of learning at the same rate as other people of the same age. Duncan and Millard (1866) and Down (1887) were referring to mental age when they suggested that, to increase one's understanding of mentally retarded children, it would be helpful to compare their behavior and abilities to younger children—a practice that has continued long after such a recommendation was first made (Goodman, 1978). Another early reference to the concept of mental age came when a psychiatrist, Hall (1848), testified during a murder trial that it was his professional opinion that the defendant in the trial had the knowledge of a 3-year-old.

The first use of the mental-age concept in a test was in 1877 when S. E. Chaille published an infant test in the *New Orleans Medical and Surgical Journal*. This infant test included items arranged according to age level. The assignment of particular age levels was made by determining the levels at which the tests were commonly passed. It was Alfred Binet, however, who refined the mental-age concept—first referring to it as "mental level"—made it

more concrete in definition, and popularized it. Terman and Merrill (1960, p. 5) remind us that "One of Binet's basic assumptions of the original scale was that a person is thought of as normal if he can do the things persons of his age normally do, retarded if his test performance corresponds to the performance of persons younger than himself, and accelerated if his performance exceeds that of persons his own age." The mental-age concept brought to Binet's test a readily comprehensible "yardstick" by which the examinee's intellectual functioning could be gauged, a yardstick that no doubt also served to stir professional—as well as popular—interest in the test.

Similar to the infant tests that had been developed by Chaille, the placement of items in the 1916 revision of the Binet-Simon scale (Terman) at various age levels had been determined by calculating the age level at which the majority of normal children in the standardization sample passed the particular item. The first step in the calculation of an individual's mental age entailed finding the sum of the total number of mental-age credits assigned to test items passed (including all items that were below the established basal age but presumed to be passed). The "mental age" for a testtaker was the "ceiling" (or highest) age level passed by the examinee. A conversion table in the manual indicated what a mental age was equivalent to in terms of an intelligence quotient (IQ). But what is an "IQ"?

Soon after Binet's death in 1911, Stern (1914) introduced the notion of a "mental quotient," suggesting that the index of intellectual functioning derived from the Binet-Simon test could be expressed as the ratio of the testtaker's mental age to his or her chronological age—and then multiplied by 100 for the sake of convenience and to eliminate decimals:

$$\text{mental quotient} = \frac{\text{mental age}}{\text{chronological age}} \times 100$$

Thus, if a child earned a mental-age equivalent exactly equal to his or her chronological age, his or her mental quotient would be equal to 100.

The concepts of mental age and ratio IQ were not without their critics. For example, L. L. Thurstone (1926) attacked the mental-age concept as ambiguous, and he urged test users as well as test developers to abandon its usage. In place of the concept of mental age, Thurstone advocated percentile scores or standard scores based on the mean and standard deviation of raw scores of the normative group within each level.

David Wechsler was among those psychometrists who agreed with Thurstone. In the intelligence tests that Wechsler developed, the concept of mental age was completely abandoned. Wechsler argued that the intelligence level of, say, an 18-year-old retarded adult with a calculated mental age of 9 was qualitatively quite different from that of a 7-year-old with a calculated mental age of 9—yet both would be described in mental-age terminology as "9 years." Wechsler also pointed to conceptual difficulties inherent in the ratio IQ concept. For example, a 5-year-old with a mental age of 6 and a 10-year-old with a mental age of 12 would both have an IQ calculated to be 120, yet one child would be two years advanced in mental age, whereas the other would only be one year advanced in mental age. Wechsler further observed that the concept of mental age has little utility in describing adult functioning, as "mental age" ceases to be very meaningful beyond certain ages; is a 28-year-old apt to have more intellectual ability than a 29-year-old, for example? A test developer would be hard put to develop an intelligence test where mean scores on the test would increase with age at the ages, for example, of 20, 25, 30, 35, and 40. Because growth in intellectual abilities is disproportionately rapid in the first few years of life and through early childhood, it would appear to be a mistake to equate the 16-year-old with a calculated mental age of 14 to the 4-year-old with a calculated mental age of 2; although both individuals' calculated mental ages are exactly two years behind their chronological ages, the degree of overall impairment is probably much greater in the 4-year-old.

As an alternative to the ratio IQ, Wechsler proposed what he called a "deviation IQ"—a measure to describe how much an individual's intellectual ability deviates from the average performance of others of approximately the same chronological age. Initially devising a test to measure adult intelligence, Wechsler (1939) culled the standardization sample's data and constructed tables so that the person who scored just at the average level for his or her age group (for example, 20 to 24 years of age) would receive an IQ of 100. The standard deviation was set at 15 points, meaning, for example, that IQs ranging from 85 to 115 would also be considered to be within the normal range of Wechsler tests. With the development of Wechsler's tests for children, IQs were obtained by comparing the child's performance to the average performance of those of his or her age.

In contrast to previous editions of the Stanford-Binet, the third (1960) edition of this test no longer expressed testtakers' performance in terms of a ratio IQ but, like the Wechsler scales, expressed performance in terms of a deviation IQ. Terman and Merrill (1960) noted that the deviation IQs avoided the inadequacies of the ratio IQs in that

> (a) a given IQ now indicates the same relative ability at different ages, (b) a subject's IQ score, ignoring errors of measurement, remains the same from one age to another unless there is a change in ability level, and (c) a given change in IQ indicates the same amount of change in relative standing regardless of the ability level of the subject. (pp. 27–28)

Although the 1960 revision of the Stanford-Binet yielded a deviation IQ, it remained an age scale with the "guiding principle . . . [having been] to secure an arrangement of tests that makes the average mental age that the scale gives agree closely with chronological age" (Terman & Merrill, 1960, p. 25). By 1986 and the publication of the fourth edition of the Stanford-Binet, the concept of mental age had essentially become a term of historic interest rather than practical value.

EXERCISE 8-4
SUCCESSIVE AND SIMULTANEOUS PROCESSING

OBJECTIVE

To enhance understanding of two types of information processing: successive and simultaneous

BACKGROUND

Successive and simultaneous processing are two different, sometimes complementary, styles of information processing. In successive processing, also referred to as sequential processing, each bit of information is individually processed in a logical, sequential fashion. By contrast, in simultaneous processing, also referred to as parallel processing, information is integrated and synthesized at once and as a whole.

Examples of stimuli likely to be processed in successive and simultaneous fashion are presented in Figure 8-1 (page 126). Contrast course outline "A" (likely to be processed in simultaneous fashion) with course outline "B" (likely to be processed in successive fashion).

YOUR TASK

Create two forms of some other stimulus, and explain why one is more likely to be processed in successive fashion while the other is more likely to be processed in simultaneous fashion.

EXERCISE 8-5
RATING THE GIFTED

OBJECTIVE

To provide firsthand experience in the development of a rating scale

BACKGROUND

How are gifted people identified? Intelligence tests are widely used for this purpose, although, as you might expect from what you have read so far in this chapter, the definition of "gifted" may change as a function of the particular test used. Models of intelligence range from the unidimensional, as in Spearman's (1927) *g*, to the multidimensional—3 dimensions according to Sternberg's (1985) triarchic theory and 120 according to Guilford (1967; Comrey et al., 1988). Tests in the Wechsler series of tests (as well as other intelligence tests) yield two primary factors: a verbal factor and a performance factor. The verbal and performance

FIGURE 8-1 *Successive and Simultaneous Processing.*

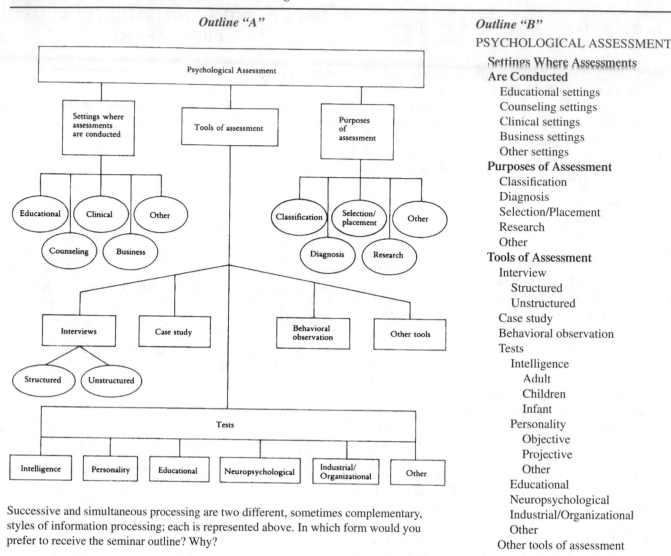

Outline "A"

Outline "B"
PSYCHOLOGICAL ASSESSMENT

Settings Where Assessments Are Conducted
   Educational settings
   Counseling settings
   Clinical settings
   Business settings
   Other settings
Purposes of Assessment
   Classification
   Diagnosis
   Selection/Placement
   Research
   Other
Tools of Assessment
   Interview
      Structured
      Unstructured
   Case study
   Behavioral observation
   Tests
      Intelligence
         Adult
         Children
         Infant
      Personality
         Objective
         Projective
         Other
      Educational
      Neuropsychological
      Industrial/Organizational
      Other
   Other tools of assessment

Successive and simultaneous processing are two different, sometimes complementary, styles of information processing; each is represented above. In which form would you prefer to receive the seminar outline? Why?

scores taken together yield what is known as a full scale score—interpreted by professionals to reflect *g* and colloquially referred to as "IQ." In some programs designed to identify gifted children, a cutoff point for a (high) IQ on a Wechsler test is established for the criterion used to define giftedness. This practice is questionable because it obscures (1) superior performance on individual subtests if the record as a whole is not superior, (2) a significant discrepancy, if one exists between the verbal and performance scores, and (3) the fact that each of the subtests administered does not contribute equally to *g;* stating this third point in the language of factor analysis, the various subtests "load" differentially on *g*. In one study that employed gifted students as subjects, Malone et al. (1991) cautioned that their findings might be colored by what is called a "ceiling effect." Some of the subtests apparently had too low a ceiling to accurately gauge the gifted student's ability, and a greater range of items at the high end of the difficulty continuum would have been preferable. One practical implication of Malone et al.'s (1991) findings was that "the use of the overall IQ score to classify students as gifted, or as a criterion for acceptance into special advanced programs, may contribute to the lack of recognition of the ability of some students" (p. 26).

Identification of the gifted should ideally be made not simply on the basis of an intelligence test but also on the basis of the goals of the program for which the test for giftedness is being conducted. Thus, for example, if an assessment program is undertaken to identify gifted writers, common sense indicates that a component of that assessment program should be a writing sample taken from the examinee and evaluated by an authority in the area. It is true, however, that the most effective—and most frequently used—instrument for identifying gifted children is an intelligence test. School systems screening for candidates for gifted programs might employ a group test for the sake of economy. A group test frequently employed for this purpose is the Otis-Lennon School Ability Test. To screen for social abilities or aptitudes, tests such as the Differential Aptitude Test or Guilford et al.'s (1974) Structure of Intellect (SOI) test may be administered. Creativity might be assessed through the use of the SOI, through personality and biographical inventories (Davis, 1989), or through other measures of creative thinking.

Numerous other assessment tools may be pressed into use to identify gifted people. Nominating techniques may be employed whereby people such as parents, teachers, and peers answer questions such as "Who has the most leadership ability?" "Who has the most original ideas?" and "Who would you most like to help you with this project?" Although teacher nomination is a widely used method of identifying gifted children, it is not necessarily the most reliable one (Jacobs, 1970; Tuttle & Becker, 1980). The gifted child may be a misbehaving child in the classroom, and this misbehavior may be due to boredom with the low level of the material being presented. The gifted child may ask questions of or make comments to the teacher that the teacher either doesn't understand or misconstrues as smart aleck in nature. Clark (1988) outlines specific behaviors that gifted children may display in the classroom. Parents are probably better judges than are teachers; however, there is some evidence suggesting that parents tend to be quite conservative when assessing their children's abilities (Mandell & Fiscus, 1981).

Behavior rating scales such as Clark's (1979) Rating Scale for the Identification of Gifted Children may provide a useful adjunct to instruments used in identifying gifted children (Figure 8-2). Some behavior rating scales designed for use with children who have emotional difficulties may also have application in the evaluation of giftedness (Landrum & Ward, 1993). The case-study method, in which information from home, school, and other sources is collected and integrated, provides an excellent basis on which to make a determination of giftedness. Included in the case study are not only formal psychological test data but also the results of sociometric techniques (such as nominating techniques), if available, and any autobiographical material that is available—statements of interests and aspirations that have been recorded. A complete assessment of the gifted child will contain not only adequate documentation of the giftedness but also a report on any islets of difficulty that may exist with respect to physical, psychological, social, or academic functioning.

YOUR TASK

Using the above-referenced emotional criteria as a model, develop a half-dozen items of your own to measure *social* development. To answer this question, you will have to think about all possible factors that contribute to people becoming social in nature.

FIGURE 8-2 *Excerpt from a Rating Scale for the Identification of Gifted Students. Teachers using this rating scale (cited in Clark, 1979) would be asked to evaluate individual children on the items shown.*

Emotional Development

Check the column that best describes this child's emotional development. Please note that a high score may not be desirable on all of the items that follow.

	Little		Moderate		Much
	1	2	3	4	5
42. *Emotional Stability.* Is able to cope with normal frustrations of living; adjusts to change with minimum of difficulty.					
43. *Emotional Control.* Expresses and displays emotions appropriately; emotional outbursts rarely occur.					
44. *Openness to Experience.* Appears to be receptive to new tasks or experiences; seems able to take reasonable risks; can respond naturally to unusual or unexpected stimuli.					
45. *Enthusiasm.* Enters into most activities with eagerness and whole-hearted participation; maintains enthusiasm for duration of activity.					
46. *Self-Acceptance.* Seems to understand and accept self; able to view self in terms of both limitations and abilities.					
47. *Independence.* Behavior usually is dictated by his or her own set of values; is concerned with the freedom to express ideas and feelings.					

EXERCISE 8-6
GRAPPLING WITH SOME MEASUREMENT ISSUES

OBJECTIVE

To enhance understanding of and obtain firsthand experience with some of the issues attendant to the measurement of intelligence

BACKGROUND

Ever since people have attempted to define and measure intelligence, numerous differences and issues have arisen regarding the nature of such definitions and measurements. Is intelligence "encoded," and does it merely "unfold" with age? Alternatively, is an individual born with a mind like a *tabula rasa* (blank slate), and does it remain for environmental influences to entirely influence the course of its development? As people and groups of people differ systematically in terms of physical characteristics, so do they differ in terms of intellectual (as well as personality-related) characteristics? These are some of the many questions that have been raised regarding the nature and measurement of intelligence.

YOUR TASK

Expand on the definition of intelligence you developed by imagining that a test based on your conception of intelligence (YCI) has been developed.

1. How is intelligence as you have defined it acquired? Is it solely the product of heredity? Of learning? Of an interaction between the two? Explain.
2. How might factors such as personality and gender influence measure intelligence?
3. According to your definition and test of intelligence, would you expect to find systematic differences between groups of people with respect to observed performance on it? Explain with reference to different groups of people such as people of different cultural or racial groups.
4. According to your definition and test of intelligence, how stable would you predict measurements of intelligence to be over time?
5. Is your test "culture-loaded"? How might you decrease such culture-loading? What if you wished to *increase* the culture-loading of the test; what might you do?
6. A critic of both your conception of intelligence and your test charges that you have improperly defined intelligence and that your test is limited to measuring intelligence only as you have defined it. Explain how you would respond to this critic noting where you would agree or not with the view expressed.
7. An organization called GEPDEF (Green-Eyed People's Defense Emergency Fund) files a lawsuit claiming that

your test unfairly discriminates against green-eyed people; on the basis of preliminary research by GEPDEF, it's been found that people with green eyes tend to score lower on your test than people with any other eye color. Your attorney has asked you to draft a brief response indicating (a) why the charge of bias is unfounded, and (b) how the preliminary research by GEPDEF may have been experimentally flawed. What might you say?

EXERCISE 8-7
MORE ISSUES, MORE GRAPPLING

OBJECTIVE

To grapple with some more of the issues and questions inherent in the definition and measurement of intelligence

YOUR TASK

Answer each of the following five questions in detail sufficient to provide evidence of your own thoughts on each of the topics:

1. Shockley (1971, p. 375) has argued that "nature has color coded groups of individuals so that statistically reliable predictions of their adaptability to intellectually rewarding and effective lives can easily be made and profitably used by the pragmatic man-in-the-street." Do you agree with Shockley? Why or why not? What are your own thoughts regarding Shockley's statement?
2. Arthur Jensen (1980, pp. 737–738) has written that differences in measured intelligence between the races,

   should not be permitted to influence the treatment accorded to *individuals* of any race—in education, employment, legal justice, and political and civil rights. . . . Those who would accord any treatment to *individuals* solely by virtue of their race will find no rational support in any of the scientific findings from psychological testing or present day theories of differential psychology.

   Do you agree? Why or why not? What are your own thoughts regarding this statement by Jensen?
3. In "Thinking about Human Abilities," Horn (1988, p. 645) raises a thought-provoking question:

   When one looks for a studied moment at the myriad of abilities that humans display, it's as if one were to look into the heavens on a clear night and become stirred by the ceaseless drift of the clouds of the Milky Way. On such a night one might be dimly aware that there is order and system in the celestial white. But where among the drifting haze might one draw dimensions to represent this order? At first there is no answer to this question, only befuddlement. The same is true for human abilities. They appear as freefloating swarms emerging from spaces of unknown many dimensions. Is there genuine order in this throng, or can one at least impose an order that will not do great injustice to the complexity and still enable one to organize thinking and talking about it?

What is *your* answer to this question? By the way, in thinking about your answer, you may wish to consult Horn's (1988) article or some of his other writing on the subject (for example, Horn 1986a, 1986b, 1985).

4. Eric Heiden's ability in speed skating earned him an unprecedented five gold medals in the XIIIth Winter Olympics, with Olympic records shattered in each of the competitions. Would Heiden have accomplished this feat had he been born in the Bronx? Appalachia? Cairo? Had he been born in 1935? Had he been born to royalty? Do you think that the place, time, and other such circumstances enter into the extent to which innate ability is or is not cultivated?

5. "Tests of intelligence should be culture-specific." Make an argument for this statement.

6. "Tests of intelligence should be culture-free." Make an argument for this statement.

EXERCISE 8-8

YET MORE GRAPPLING: *THE BELL CURVE* CONTROVERSY

OBJECTIVE

To think critically about issues raised in the book *The Bell Curve*

BACKGROUND

In 1994, a book entitled *The Bell Curve: Intelligence and Class Structure in American Life* by Richard Herrnstein and Charles Murray became a stimulus for widespread public debate on the nature of intelligence as well as the implications of group differences in measured intelligence (Neisser et al., 1996; Rushton, 1997; Weidman, 1997; Zenderland, 1997). Although the book was given extraordinary attention in the print and electronic media, many people, aware of a similar spectacle in the late 1960s, had a sense of *déjà vu* about it all. To place discussion of *The Bell Curve* in proper historical perspective, then, let's begin with a brief look backward.

In a *Harvard Educational Review* article entitled "How Much Can We Boost IQ and Scholastic Achievement?" Arthur R. Jensen (1969) presented evidence that Blacks score lower on average than Whites on standardized intelligence tests. Jensen argued that this difference was due primarily to genetic rather than environmental influences. His analysis of the available data suggested to him that the frequency of genes carrying higher intelligence is lower in the Black population as a whole than in the White population. He estimated that the variability in measured intelligence was about 20% due to heredity. The article touched off a storm of public controversy about intelligence tests. Few people seemed to be without a strong opinion about the value of intelligence tests, what group differences in intelligence really meant, and what the government should or should not do as a result of such differences.

Citing many of the same studies and data that Jensen (1969) had used to make his case, Herrnstein and Murray (1994) also noted racial and ethnic differences in intelligence, which they presumed to be partly the result of genetics. Herrnstein and Murray went further, however, speculating on the meaning such group differences might have for the future of the United States. These authors envisioned a future wherein differences in measured intelligence divide society into a cognitive elite, fiercely defensive of its material possessions, and a cognitive underclass, more disposed to making ends meet through crime or dependency on social programs. To slow society's march to the apocalypse they envisioned, Herrnstein and Murray made a number of recommendations, including (1) the cessation of affirmative action programs (such programs are viewed as having a negative effect on race relations because the unqualified are unfairly promoted); (2) the cessation of remedial education programs (the effects of such efforts have been questionable, and the dollars could be better spent on further developing talent in the talented); and (3) the cessation of welfare and other such programs, which, according to Herrnstein and Murray, encourage young, unwed mothers—usually with low intelligence—to reproduce. The message of *The Bell Curve* was that society should stop trying to eradicate differences between groups. Because differences between groups cannot be changed by any known means, society would do better to try to find ways for people with different intellectual levels to live together with dignity for all.

From this account of *The Bell Curve* and from what you might know of the book from other sources, what do you think of its thesis? Commit your thoughts to writing before reading our comments, which follow.

Some Thoughts on *The Bell Curve*

- Because of complex methodological difficulties in conducting such research, it is difficult to estimate with any real accuracy the respective contributions of heredity and environment to measured intelligence.

- Because of complex methodological difficulties in conducting research on social programs, it is difficult to estimate the true impact of such environmental interventions. For example, most studies show that the beneficial effects of Head Start programs erode over time. Critics of such studies argue that such erosion is due not to genes but to the return of children to environments where the learning that has taken place will not be reinforced.

- Even Richard Herrnstein (1982) acknowledged that measured intelligence could be raised, although he wrote that "raising it much is hard, given existing methods of teaching and measurement" (p. 74).

- Many of Herrnstein and Murray's conclusions and recommendations have more to do with political opinion than scientific findings. For example, political opinion about the role of government in providing aid to the poor—irrespective of measured IQ—varies considerably.
- Although group differences in measured intelligence do exist, no such thing as group intelligence exists. Thus, intelligence is ultimately an individual, one-by-one matter. Further, the personal and social value of measured intelligence is tempered by a number of other factors, such as one's values and motivation.
- Herrnstein and Murray's forecast of a dysgenic trend in intelligence due to overbreeding by people with low intelligence is not reality, according to Williams and Ceci (1997, p. 1234): "In general, the gap does not seem to have increased or decreased reliably since the late 1980s. Thus, one could be heartened that the racial gap is not increasing, or one could be saddened that the closing of the gap has not continued. But regardless of one's reaction to these most recent data, they do not support the suspicion that dysgenesis is taking place but rather that it is too recent to be detected."
- According to Herbert (1994), Catholics have a legacy of discrimination in Northern Ireland, where they tend to test 15 points lower than Protestants on intelligence tests. Because both groups are White, Herbert (1994) construes such evidence as having a lesson for Herrnstein and Murray with regard to the influence of heredity as opposed to environment in measured intelligence.
- As Sternberg (1986) has argued, there are alternatives to intelligence as measured by intelligence tests, such as a streetwise type of intelligence that Sternberg calls "practical intelligence." Because ways of measuring practical intelligence have not been established, it is impossible to tell what, if any, differences among groups exist with respect to this form of intelligence and what the implications of such differences might be.
- Arthur Jensen, whose research called attention to differences in measured intelligence among groups, is among those who have advocated equal education opportunities for all. Further, Jensen (1980, pp. 737–738) has argued that differences in measured intelligence between the races "should not be permitted to influence the treatment accorded to *individuals* of any race—in education, employment, legal justice, and political and civil rights. The well-established finding of a wide range of individual differences in IQ and other abilities within all major-racial populations and the great amount of overlap of their frequency distributions absolutely contradicts the racist philosophy that persons of different races should be treated differently, one and all, only by reasons of their racial origins. Those who would accord any treatment to individuals solely by virtue of their race will find no rational support in any of the scientific findings from psychological testing or present day theories of differential psychology."

YOUR TASK

Research the scholarly literature for more published views on *The Bell Curve*. Then, on the basis of everything you and your classmates have read about this book, conduct a group discussion in which the book's pros and cons are touched on.

REFERENCES

Clark, B. (1979). *Growing up gifted.* (3rd ed.). Columbus, OH: Merrill.

Comrey, A. L., Michael, W. B., & Fruchter, B. (1988). J. P. Guilford (1897–1987). *American Psychologist, 43,* 1086–1087.

Davis, G. A. (1989). Testing for creative potential. *Contemporary Educational Psychology, 14,* 257–274.

Down, J. L. (1887). *On some of the mental afflictions of childhood and youth.* London: J. & A. Churchill.

Duncan, P. M., & Millard, W. (1866). *A manual for the classification, training, and education of the feeble-minded, imbecile, and idiotic.* London: Longmans, Green.

Esquirol, J. E. D. (1838). *Des malades mentales considerees sous les rapports medical, hygienique et medicolegal.* Paris: Balliere.

Goodman, J. F. (1978). Wanted: Restoration of the mental age in the 1972 revised Stanford-Binet. *Journal of Special Education, 12,* 45–49.

Guilford, J. P. (1967). *The nature of human intelligence.* New York: McGraw-Hill.

Guilford, J. P., et al. (1974). *Structure-of-Intellect Abilities.* Orange, CA: Sheridan Psychological Services.

Hall, B. F. (1848). The trial of William Freeman. *American Journal of Insanity, 5*(2), 34–60.

Herbert, B. (1994, October 26). Throwing a curve (editorial). *New York Times,* p. A27.

Herrnstein, R. J. (1982, August). IQ testing and the media. *Atlantic Monthly,* 68–74.

Herrnstein, R., & Murray, C. (1994). *The bell curve.* New York: Free Press.

Horn, J. L. (1985). Remodeling old models of intelligence: Gf-Gc theory. In B. B. Wolman (Ed.), *Handbook of intelligence.* New York: Wiley.

Horn, J. L. (1986a). Intellectual ability concepts. In R. J. Sternberg (Ed.), *Advances in the psychology of human intelligence.* Hillsdale, NJ: Erlbaum.

Horn, J. L. (1986b). Some thoughts about intelligence. In R. J. Sternberg & D. K. Detterman (Eds.), *What is intelligence? Contemporary viewpoints on its nature and definition.* Norwood, NJ: Ablex.

Horn, J. L. (1988). Thinking about human abilities. In J. R. Nesselroade & R. B. Cattell (Eds.), *Handbook of multivariate psychology.* New York: Plenum.

Jacobs, J. (1970). Are we being misled by fifty years of research on our gifted children? *Gifted Child Quarterly, 14,* 120–123.

Jensen, A. R. (1969). How much can we boost IQ and scholastic achievement? *Harvard Educational Review, 39,* 1–123.

Jensen, A. R. (1980). *Bias in mental testing.* New York: Free Press.

Landrum, M. S., & Ward, S. B. (1993). Behavioral assessment of gifted learners. *Journal of Behavioral Education, 3,* 211–215.

Malone, P. S., Brounstein, P. J., van Brock, A., & Shaywitz, S. S. (1991). Components of IQ scores across levels of measured ability. *Journal of Applied Social Psychology, 21,* 15–28.

Mandell, C. J., & Fiscus, E. (1981). *Understanding exceptional people.* St. Paul, MN: West.

Neisser, U., Boodoo, G., Bouchard, Jr., T. J. et al. (1996). Intelligence: Knowns and unknowns. *American Psychologist, 51,* 77–101.

Rushton, J. P. (1997). Race, IQ, and the APA report on *The Bell Curve. American Psychologist, 52,* 69–70.

Shockley, W. (1971). Models, mathematics, and the moral obligation to diagnose the origin of Negro IQ deficits. *Review of Educational Research, 41,* 369–377.

Spearman, C. (1927). *The abilities of man: Their nature and measurement.* New York: Macmillan.

Stern, W. (1914). *The psychological method of testing intelligence.* Baltimore: Warwick & York.

Sternberg, R. J. (1982, April). Who's intelligent? *Psychology Today,* 30–33, 38–39.

Sternberg, R. J. (1985). *Beyond IQ: A triarchic theory of human intelligence.* Cambridge: Cambridge University Press.

Sternberg, R. J. (1986). Intelligence is mental self-government. In R. J. Sternberg & D. K. Detterman (Eds.), *What is intelligence?* (pp. 141–148). Norwood, NJ: Ablex.

Terman, L. M. (1916). *The measurement of intelligence.* Boston: Houghton Mifflin.

Terman, L. M., & Merrill, M. A. (1960). *Stanford-Binet Intelligence Scale Manual for the Third Revision: Form L-M.* Boston: Houghton Mifflin.

Thurstone, L. L. (1926). The mental age concept. *Psychological Review, 33,* 268–278.

Tuttle, F. B., & Becker, A. (1980). *Characteristics and identification of gifted and talented students.* Washington, DC: National Education Association.

Wechsler, D. (1939). *The measurement of adult intelligence.* Baltimore, MD: Williams & Wilkins.

Weidman, N. (1997). Heredity, intelligence and neuropsychology; or why *The Bell Curve* is good science. *Journal of the History of the Behavioral Sciences, 33,* 141–144.

Williams, W. M., & Ceci, S. J. (1997). Are Americans becoming more or less alike? Trends in race, class, and ability differences in intelligence. *American Psychologist, 52,* 1226–1235.

Zenderland, L. (1997). *The Bell Curve* and the shape of history. *Journal of the History of the Behavioral Sciences, 33,* 135–139.

THE 4-QUESTION CHALLENGE

1. Which is true regarding the 1921 Symposium on Intelligence?
   a. No two psychologists agreed on a definition.
   b. Edwin Boring's definition won widespread acceptance.
   c. Ways of measuring intelligence were standardized.
   d. Carl Spearman's definition won widespread acceptance.

2. A major theme running through the theories of intelligence of Binet, Wechsler, and Piaget is
   a. assimilation.
   b. accommodation.
   c. interactionism.
   d. pluralism.

3. According to Cattell's two-factor theory of intelligence, the factor that is being tapped by a memory-for-digits test item is
   a. successive processing.
   b. simultaneous processing.
   c. crystallized intelligence.
   d. fluid intelligence.

4. Henry Goddard's research on Martin Kallikak was discredited for many reasons including the fact that
   a. it was based on the idea that feeblemindedness was a recessive gene
   b. Goddard placed excessive emphasis on the role of environment in upbringing
   c. data analysis had actually been conducted by Goddard's assistant, Abraham Myerson
   d. it had been gathered when Kallikak happened to be under severe stress

Tests of Intelligence

Puzzle 9 **Instructions** Identify what is described, answer a question, or fill in the blank to complete this crossword puzzle based on material presented in Chapter 9 of your textbook.

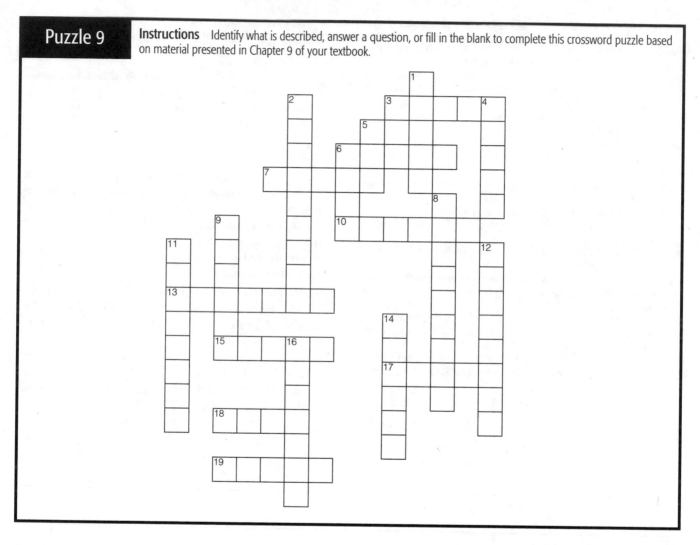

Across

3. In response to the need for personnel screening during World War I, the U.S. Army developed the Army _____ test, a test of intelligence that was primarily verbal in nature.

6. The _____ level is a stage in a test achieved by a testtaker as a result of that testtaker meeting some pre-set criteria to continue being posed test items on a test or subtest. For example, having responses to two consecutive items scored as correct on an ability test that contains increasingly difficult items may establish a "base" from which to continue testing.

7. His test was adapted for use in the United States by Lewis Terman at Stanford University, and it became known as the Stanford-_____ .

10. A test answer sheet developed by a test publisher for the purpose of checking the accuracy of examiners' scoring is called a(n) _____ protocol.

13. The _____ level is a stage in a test achieved by a testtaker as a result of that testtaker meeting some pre-set criteria to discontinue testing in a test or subtest.

15. A(n) _____ form is a version of test that has been abbreviated in length, typically to reduce the time needed for test administration, scoring, and interpretation.

17. It's an index of intelligence derived from the ratio of the testtaker's mental age as calculated from a test, divided by his or her chronological age and multiplied by 100 to eliminate decimals. It is called a(n) _____ IQ.

18. The abbreviation for a subtest of the ASVAB made up of 100 items designed to measure general ability and used in the selection of military recruits.

19. In contrast to an age scale, which has items grouped by expectations with regard to age and performance, a _____ scale is a test with items organized into subtests by category of item.

Down

1. The acronym for a test designed to measure school ability in students in kindergarten through grade 13.
2. The _____ IQ is a variety of standard score used to report "intelligence quotients" (IQs) with a mean set at 100 and a standard deviation set at 15. On the Stanford-Binet, it is also referred to as a test composite, and it represents an index of intelligence derived from a comparison between the performance of an individual test-taker on a test and the performance of other testtakers of the same age in the test's standardization sample.
4. The abbreviation for a test administered to prospective new recruits in the armed services and "the most widely used multiple aptitude test in the United States," according to its publisher.
5. An abbreviation for a test of creativity. A not-so-remote association to this abbreviation is actor James Cagney in one of those *film noire* crime movies saying the line, "You dirty _____ !"
6. In response to the need for personnel screening during World War I, the U.S. Army developed the Army _____ test, a test of intelligence that was primarily nonverbal in nature.
8. A test score or index derived from the combination and/or mathematical transformation of one or more test scores is referred to as a test _____ .
9. In ability testing, a procedure that entails the continued administration of test items beyond that level at which the test manual dictates discontinuance is referred to as testing the _____ .
11. Long before there was a WB television network, there were tests called the W-B I and W-B II. The W in each of these tests stands for _____ .
12. Maude Merrill taught here.
14. His middle name was Madison.
16. A subtest used to direct the testtaker to a suitable level of items is called a _____ test.

EXERCISE 9-1

MOVIES AND MEASUREMENT

OBJECTIVE

To apply generative thinking in devising a task to measure intelligence

BACKGROUND

In a scene from the classic film entitled *Charly*, which was based on the book *Flowers for Algernon*, Cliff Robertson

Getting It Together

attempts to put the pieces together on a Wechsler object assembly task. In fact, many different types of tasks have been employed in efforts to measure that elusive construct, "intelligence."

YOUR TASK

Think of some task that you believe should be used on a measure of intelligence. It could be a task that is as routine as tying a shoelace, or something wholly unique that you must describe in detail. Discuss this task in a brief essay entitled, "A Proposed New Task to Measure Intelligence." Include in your essay some mention of the aspects of intelligence that you believe are tapped by this task.

EXERCISE 9-2

TELEVISION AND MEASUREMENT

OBJECTIVE

Identify the cognitive abilities tapped by an intellectually challenging situation; in this case, a television game show.

BACKGROUND

Prospective contestants for the television game show variously called *Who Wants to Be a Millionaire?* and *Who Wants to be a Super Millionaire?* (Figure 9-1) have been selected in various ways. In one version of the selection process, applicants are prescreened by means of a telephone quiz in which general knowledge and speed are key factors. From the pool of people who are successful in the telephone screening, ten are selected (by lottery) for

FIGURE 9-1   *Who Wants to Name the Cognitive Abilities Being Tapped?*

appearance on stage. These contestants are posed a time-limited, "fastest finger question" in which they must put four alternative responses in the correct order by means of keypad entry. The contestant who successfully does this fastest, advances to the "hot seat."

Once in the hot seat, the contestant will be asked a series of multiple-choice questions deemed to be successively more difficult in nature. There is no time limit to respond to these questions. However, one wrong answer and it's curtains for the contestant. The contestant has three "life-lines" or aids to help answer the questions, each of which may be used only once. The "50/50" lifeline reduces the alternative responses from four to two. The "Ask the Audience" lifeline polls the studio audience for their opinion as to the correct answer. And the "Phone a Friend" lifeline allows the contestant to speak to one friend for 30 seconds (from a list of ten friends given to the show staff in advance of the taping).

YOUR TASK

Let's assume the creators of this television program based their concept for it on the belief that the more intelligent the contestant, the further up the ladder to the top prize the contestant would go. From the description above, as well as your own knowledge, if any, of this television program, how would you describe the way its creators might envision "in-

telligence"? In your answer, make sure to consider all of the myriad abilities related to the screening task, the fastest-finger task, and each of the lifelines.

EXERCISE 9-3

TESTS OF INTELLIGENCE

OBJECTIVE

To enhance understanding of and obtain firsthand experience with tests of intelligence

BACKGROUND

Binet's test of intelligence was the forerunner of generations of intelligence tests to come. The Wechsler tests were devised to assess an individual's "overall capacity to understand and cope with the world around him" (Wechsler, 1974, p. 5). Because the tests share a common theoretical foundation, they are also similar in structure. The Ordinal Scales of Psychological Development and The Concept Assessment Kit-Conservation are based on "intelligence" as conceived by the Swiss psychologist Jean Piaget. These two tests were designed to shed light on aspects of the developmental stage the testtaker is in with reference to Piaget's theory of cognitive development. Of course, many other tests exist to measure special intellectual abilities and talents that are not typically subsumed under the heading "intelligence."

YOUR TASK

In the previous chapter you were asked to develop your own definition of intelligence and to imagine that a test based on that definition (the YCT test) had been developed. Now it is time to develop that test. Using everything you know about the different types of tasks used to measure intelligence and related abilities, outline a plan for a test of intelligence that is consistent with your own conceptualization. To add some, but not a lot of, structure and uniformity to this task, we will again limit our focus to adult intelligence. Let's also say that the total number of subtests included in your test of intelligence will be ten. Now, briefly answer each of the following ten questions:

1. Name and describe each of the ten subtests.
2. Provide a rationale for including each of these ten subtests.
3. Does your test contain both verbal and nonverbal (performance) subtests? Why or why not?
4. How would you develop the actual items to be used in each of these subtests?
5. Describe the process by which your test would be normed.
6. Describe the process by which you would establish the psychometric soundness of your test.
7. Describe how each of the subtests should be administered; if, for example, your test contains both verbal and nonverbal subtests, will such tests be administered in alternating fashion? Why?
8. Briefly describe the scoring and interpretation of each of the subtests.
9. Will the scoring on each of the subtests in some way contribute to some global measure of intelligence (such as an IQ)? Why or why not?
10. For what purposes would you recommend that your test be used? In what circumstances or under what conditions would you advise against its use?

EXERCISE 9-4

TAILORING WITHOUT NEEDLES OR THREAD

OBJECTIVE

To impart firsthand experience in the creation of items to be used in an adaptive testing format

BACKGROUND

Adaptive testing refers to testing that is individually tailored to the testtaker. Other terms used to refer to adaptive testing include tailored testing, sequential testing, branched testing, and response-contingent testing. As typically employed in tests of ability, adaptive testing might pose to a testtaker a question in the middle range of difficulty. If the testtaker responds correctly to the item, an item of greater difficulty is posed next. If the testtaker responds incorrectly to the item, an item of lesser difficulty is posed.

YOUR TASK

Create three test items, each of a different level of difficulty, to tap a student's knowledge of the material in Chapter 9 of Cohen & Swerdlik (2005). The items should be suitable for placement in an adaptive testing format. Item 1 should be designed to be of an intermediate difficulty level. If the testtaker failed to respond correctly to Item 1, the testtaker would be administered Item 2, an item that is less difficult than Item 1. If the testtaker responded to Item 1 correctly, the testtaker would be administered Item 3, an item that is more difficult than Item 1.

EXERCISE 9-5

INFORMAL "FACTOR ANALYSIS" AND TESTS OF INTELLIGENCE

OBJECTIVE

To enhance understanding of how factor analysis can be used in the development of intelligence tests and in the measurement of the construct validity of an intelligence test

BACKGROUND

As discussed in Chapters 8 and 9 of Cohen and Swerdlik (2005), different intelligence tests define intelligence in different ways. Accordingly, we would expect factor analysis of test items for various construct-valid intelligence tests to vary in predictable ways.

YOUR TASK

Conduct an "eyeball" analysis of Figure 9-2, which shows sample items from the Otis-Lennon School Ability Test (OLSAT). Based on this sample of items, what factors would you say this test appears to be measuring? Why? From the theories of intelligence you are aware of, which one do you think is closest to the theory that guided the development of the OLSAT? How do the factors measured by the OLSAT compare to those measured by another major intelligence test such as the SB5 or the WISC-IV?

FIGURE 9-2 *Sample OLSAT Items*

● <u>Verbal Analogy</u> items assess the ability to infer the relationship between a pair of words and to select a word that bears the same relationship to a given stimulus word.

   Bird is to nest as bee is to

   f   hive   g   flower   h   buzz   j   sting   k   wasp

● <u>Verbal Classification</u> items assess the ability to determine which word in a set does not belong, according to some principle operative within the set.

   Which word does *not* go with the other four?

   a   tall   b   big   c   small   d   short   e   loud

● <u>Sentence Completion</u> items assess the ability to determine logical relationships among words in a sentence in order to supply a missing word.

   Choose the word that *best* completes this sentence:

   We will not begin the meeting _____ everybody is here.

   a   because   b   until   c   if   d   when   e   after

● <u>Sentence Arrangement</u> items assess the ability to integrate a group of words into a meaningful sentence.

   If the words below were arranged to make the *best* sentence, with which letter would the <u>last</u> word of the sentence <u>begin</u>?

streets	the	caused	to	rain	heavy	flood

   a   s   b   f   c   h   d   r   e   c

● <u>Numeric Inference</u> items assess the ability to evaluate the relationship among pairs or trios of numbers and to select a number that is related to a stimulus number in the same way.

   The numbers in each box go together by following the *same* rule. Decide what the rule is, and then find the number that goes where you see the question mark (?) in the last box.

   10, 5   6, 3   16, ?   a   2   b   4   c   8   d   11   e   13

● <u>Quantitative Reasoning</u> is dependent on the ability to evaluate groups of numbers in order to infer relationships among them and to infer and apply computational rules.

● <u>Figural Analogy</u> items assess the ability to infer the relationship between a pair of geometric shapes and to apply that relationship in selecting a shape that is related to a stimulus shape in the same way.

● <u>Series Completion</u> items assess the ability to predict the next step in a geometric series in which each element changes according to a given rule.

   The drawings in the first part of the row go together to form a series. In the next part of the row, find the drawing that goes where you see the question mark (?) in the series.

EXERCISE 9-6
MUCH ADO ABOUT MENSA

OBJECTIVE

To encourage independent thought about the nature of intelligence and, in particular, some social implications of this concept

BACKGROUND

Mensa is a club in which the key requirement for membership is being in the top 2 percent of measured intelligence. The notion of such a club smacks of elitism to some people, although it is quite appealing to others.

YOUR TASK

Read the following material on Mensa, then write an essay expressing your own thoughts on the organization and the test items employed to screen for membership.

MENSA

You may belong to a social, professional, or religious fraternity or sorority in which you engage in a wide variety of activities such as athletics, discussion groups, museum trips, speaker presentations, and parties. There is one social organization that is like these groups in all respects except that the requirement for membership is proof of high intelligence. That organization is called Mensa, and it has more than 70,000 members worldwide, with chapters not only throughout the United States but also in Europe, South America, Australia, India, Israel, and Japan. Members include cab drivers, physicians, homemakers—in short, a wide variety of people in a wide variety of occupations.

Mensa was founded in England by two attorneys as a kind of round-table discussion club for a group of intellectual equals; in fact, the word *Mensa* is derived from the Latin word for "table." The group was founded shortly after World War II, its primary agenda then to discuss and arrive at ways of preserving world peace. Today, the objectives of the organization would not appear quite so ambitious; the group is a social club that also fosters scientific pursuits through an educational and research foundation and through a research journal. The group also awards scholarships to postsecondary students to encourage them to fulfill their intellectual potential; some chapters have a group to aid in the rehabilitation of high-IQ prison inmates. Special-interest groups existing within Mensa cover different kinds of activities ranging from astronomy to motorcycles to Zen.

According to Mensa, each year about 30,000 people attempt to qualify for membership; but since only people whose measured IQs fall within the top 2 percent in intelligence qualify, only about 2 of every 50 people who apply are admitted. Are you interested in joining Mensa? If so, contact the local chapter and request a membership application. They will send you a list of intelligence tests that you may have taken at one time or another in your life; and if you can document that your score on any of the tests meets the club's cutoff point, you pay your dues and you're in. If you are unable to document your IQ to the club's satisfaction, it's going to take a bit more effort on your part. For a nominal fee, the club will send you a take-home IQ test with questions similar to those in Table 9-1 (page 138). If you pass the take-home test, you then will be invited to take, for a nominal fee, a proctored test. If you then score high enough to pass Mensa muster on the proctored test, you're invited to join. Needless to say, there are some people—many of whom might qualify for membership—who do not view such an organization in positive terms but who instead see it as elitist and snobbish.

EXERCISE 9-7
CREATE AN ALTERNATIVE MEASURE: THE MUSIC APPRECIATION TEST (MAT)

OBJECTIVE

To enhance understanding of and obtain firsthand experience with alternative measures of intelligence

BACKGROUND

Professionals who study intelligence appreciate that traditional tests of intelligence provide only a sample of an individual's intellectual ability. Intellectual skills and abilities such as critical thinking and artistic talent, for example, may not be tapped in traditional measures of intelligence.

YOUR TASK

Using any popular song—and let's define "popular" as a song that is among the top twenty in sales as listed in the current issue of *Billboard Magazine*—develop a "Music Appreciation Test" (MAT). The administration instructions for the MAT will be as follows:

I am going to play a tape of a song. After you hear the song, you are going to be asked some questions about it. Please listen

Table 9-1 *Try These Typical IQ-Test Questions*

1. What word means the same as (p-a-y) in one sense and the same as (b-o-t-t-o-m) in another sense?

2. Which of the following sentences best describes the meaning of the old bromide "The used key is always bright"?
    a. Keep on the scene in order to stay with it.
    b. If you use a test key, you will appear bright.
    c. New devices often don't work well.
    d. Old ideas are the best.

3. Which one of the following games does not belong in the group?
    a. Chess
    b. Bridge
    c. Go
    d. Mah-jongg
    e. Backgammon

4. The word *procure* is the opposite of which of the following words?
    a. retain
    b. abscond
    c. forfeit
    d. appropriate
    e. purchase

5. Complete the following analogy: Green is to yellow as orange is to _____ .
    a. blue
    b. purple
    c. brown
    d. yellow
    e. white

6. The word *aggravate* means the same as which of the following words?
    a. burden
    b. enrage
    c. infect
    d. intensify
    e. complain

7. Which of the following words are most opposite in meaning?
    a. intense
    b. extensive
    c. majority
    d. extreme
    e. diffuse

8. Which one of the following words does not belong in the group?
    a. stone
    b. brick
    c. canoe
    d. pontoon
    e. oar

9. Which two of the following words have the most similar meanings?
    a. divulge
    b. divert
    c. reveal
    d. revert

10. Complete the following analogy: Mountain is to land as whirlpool is to _____ .
    a. fluid
    b. wet
    c. sea
    d. sky
    e. shower

11. The old saying "Don't trade horses when crossing a stream" most nearly means which of the following?
    a. You might fall off and get wet.
    b. Don't attempt something until you are fully prepared.
    c. Decide what you are going to do before you do it.
    d. Don't change plans when something is half completed.

12. If a house is 36 feet long and 27 feet wide, how wide would a house of the same proportions be if it were 72 feet long?

13. Which number, when multiplied by 4, is equal to ¾ of 112?

14. What word means the same as (h-i-r-e) in one sense and the same as (b-e-t-r-o-t-h) in another sense?

15. Which word does not belong in the following group?
    a. car
    b. moon
    c. fish
    d. happy
    e. belief

16. If seven belly dancers can lose 20 pounds altogether in eight hours of dancing, how many additional belly dancers would be needed to lose that same 20 pounds in only four hours of dancing, providing the new dancers shed weight only half as fast as the original seven dancers?
    a. 7
    b. 21
    c. 27
    d. 14
    e. 12

17. Which two of the following words are the most similar in meaning?
    a. autonomy
    b. autocracy
    c. oligarchy
    d. dictatorship

18. What number comes next in the following series? 2, 3, 5, 9, 17 _____

19. Some Mensa members are geniuses. All geniuses have some human virtue as redeeming qualities. Using these two facts, which of the following conclusions is most correct?
    a. Mensa members all have some virtues.
    b. All geniuses are quality Mensa members.
    c. Some Mensa members have redeeming qualities.

20. The old saying "The good is the enemy of the best" most nearly means which of the following?
    a. If you are good, you will best your enemy.
    b. Be good to your best enemy.
    c. Don't accept less than your best.
    d. The good struggle against the best.

Mensa Quiz Answers

1. (Foot). 2. (a). 3. (b). 4. (c). 5. (d). 6. (d). 7. (a & e). 8. (a). 9. (a & c). 10. (c). 11. (d). 12. (54 feet). 13. (21). 14. (engage). 15. (d). 16. (d). 17. (b & d). 18. (33). 19. (c). 20. (c).

Scoring Scale

Give yourself one point for each correct answer. You receive an additional four points if you completed the test in less than 10 minutes; three points if you completed it in less than 15 minutes; two points if you completed it in less than 20 minutes; and one point if you completed it in less than 25 minutes.

Source: Grosswirth (1980)

The authors of this text note that the original article contained a score interpretation guide indicating that a score of 20–24 qualified you as a "perfect candidate" for Mensa; 15–19 and you were still a candidate; 10–14 and "you might want to try the Mensa test"; and fewer than 10—"forget about joining." Of course, how much faith you place in a test interpretation guide should at least in part be a function of your evaluation of the psychometric soundness of the test. With no evidence as to reliability or validity of this test, we would advise that regardless of your test score, should you desire to join—go for it!

---

to the song carefully so that you will be prepared to answer the questions. I will play the song only once. Ready?

Using a portable cassette recorder (or whatever equipment is available in the setting where the test is being conducted), the examiner then plays the song. After the song has been played in its entirety, the examiner hands the respondent a sheet with the MAT test questions—questions that you have prepared about the song. The questions may be in any format—true/false, short answer, essay, or whatever. Along with the questions, devise a corresponding answer key. Once having devised this test, answer each of the following:

1. Describe the process of norming this test.
2. How would the psychometric soundness of this test be established?
3. What problems do you foresee in administering, scoring, and interpreting this test? How might these problems be dealt with?

4. Describe why you think your test taps some aspect of intelligence not tapped by traditional measures of intelligence.
5. How might your test be used in everyday practice?
6. How might cultural factors influence scores on your test?
7. How might you make this test less culture-bound?

EXERCISE 9-8

ADMINISTERING THE MAT

OBJECTIVE

To obtain firsthand experience in administering a would-be alternative measure of intelligence

BACKGROUND

In the previous exercise, you developed the Music Appreciation Test (MAT). In this exercise, you administer the MAT to a friend or neighbor and obtain their reaction.

YOUR TASK

Ask a friend or neighbor to serve as a subject to take the MAT. Explain to that person that the MAT is not a real psychological test but one made up by you as part of an exercise in developing alternative measures of intellectual ability. After the testtaker has taken it, discuss with him or her how the test would be scored and interpreted. Obtain and record feedback about the test administration, scoring, and interpretation process from the point of view of the subject. What are the subject's thoughts about the test? Does he or she believe it to be, on its face, a valid alternative measure of intelligence? What "bugs" need to be worked out on the basis of this pilot administration, scoring, and interpretation of your test? How might you revise the test and these procedures before administering it again?

EXERCISE 9-9
PICK A TEST OF INTELLIGENCE

OBJECTIVE

To learn more about individual and group tests of intelligence not reviewed in the textbook

BACKGROUND

The approach in your textbook is to highlight only a few of the many tests that exist in any given area. For every test covered in your textbook there may well be dozens of other tests designed to measure the same attribute(s). The Pick a Test exercise represents an opportunity to learn more about a particular test not covered in your textbook.

YOUR TASK

Using *Tests in Print,* the Internet, or any other resource you choose, discover a test of intelligence that was not mentioned in your textbook. Then answer the following:

1. Describe what the test measures.
2. Who would be most apt to use this test? Why? Include in your answer sample questions the test user might hope to answer through the use of this test.

3. Who would be most apt to take this test? Why?
4. Describe the full range of people to whom it would be appropriate to administer this test, and include comments about who would not be appropriate. If the test may be group-administered, describe how this test lends itself to group administration.
5. Describe what is known about the test's reliability.
6. Describe what is known about the test's validity.
7. Imagining that you are a measurement consultant, would you recommend this test to clients who are test users? Why or why not?

REFERENCES

Grosswirth, M. (1980). Mensa: It's a state of mind—but a mind finely tuned. *Science Digest, 87,* 74–79.

Wechsler, D. (1974). *Manual for the Wechsler Intelligence Scale for Children-Revised.* New York: Psychological Corporation.

THE 4-QUESTION CHALLENGE

1. A primary use of group tests of ability or intelligence is
   a. screening large numbers of people.
   b. measuring reading ability.
   c. gauging applicants' ability by means of a power test.
   d. all of the above
2. Which statement is true?
   a. Validity sets a limit on a test's reliability.
   b. Validity sets a limit only on a test's inter-rater reliability.
   c. The validity of a test is limited only by the test's inter-rater reliability.
   d. The validity of a test is limited by its reliability.
3. Which test is used by the United States Department of Defense as a means of screening candidates and determining the most suitable job positions?
   a. WAIS-IV
   b. ASVAB
   c. OLSAT
   d. SB5
4. Which statement is true about the Army Alpha test?
   a. its correlation with the Stanford-Binet was unacceptable
   b. its correlation with officer ratings were unacceptable
   c. it was designed for use with illiterate recruits
   d. it was developed for use in a matter of weeks

CHAPTER 10

Preschool and Educational Assessment

Puzzle 10 — **Instructions** Identify what is described, answer a question, or fill in the blank to complete this crossword puzzle based on material presented in Chapter 10 of your textbook.

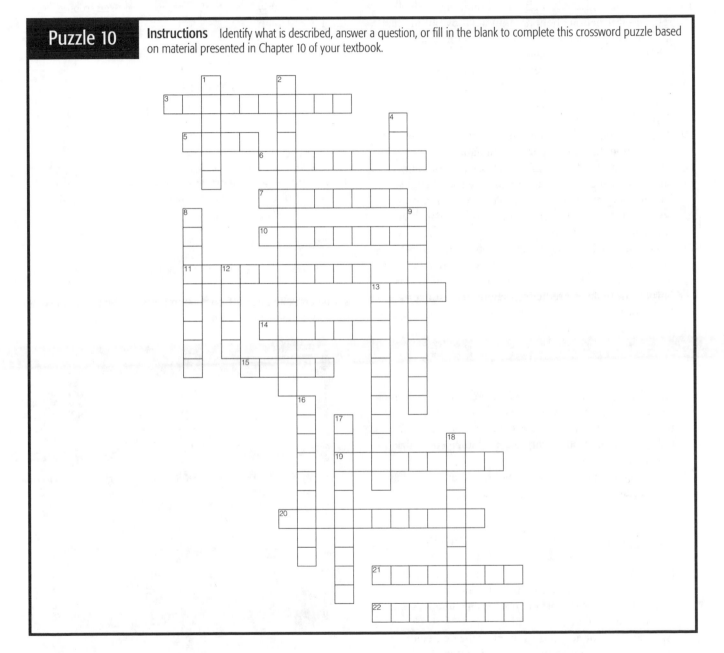

Across

3. As used in educational contexts, _____ information is test or other data used to pinpoint a student's difficulties for the purpose of remediating those difficulties.

5. As used in educational contexts, *at* _____ may be defined in different ways by different school districts. In general, however, it is a reference to functioning that is deficient and in possible need of intervention.

6. A questionnaire arranged in such a form so as to allow the person completing it to place marks next to each item indicative of information, such as the presence or absence of a specified behavior, thought, event, or circumstance.

7. A(n) _____ disability is a disorder in which there exists a discrepancy between ability and achievement.

10. Also known as performance-based assessment, _____ assessment may be defined as an evaluation

with regard to relevant, meaningful tasks that may be conducted to examine learning of academic subject matter but that also demonstrate the student's transfer of that study to real-world activities.

11. _____ information may be defined as test or other data that are used to make judgments such as class placement, pass/fail, and admit/reject decisions.

13. _____ appraisal is a method of obtaining evaluation-related information about an individual by polling that individual's friends, classmates, work colleagues or other peers.

14. A(n) _____ test is a pretest or routing test, usually for the purpose of determining the level of the actual test that will be most appropriate for administration.

15. A psychoeducational test battery with a hyphen.

19. A graphic representation of peer appraisal data or other information that is interpersonal in nature.

20. Curriculum-based _____ is a type of curriculum-based assessment characterized by the use of standardized measurement procedures to derive local norms to be used in the evaluation of student performance on curriculum-based tasks.

21. It's a test which usually focuses more on informal as opposed to formal learning experiences and is designed to measure both learning and inborn potential for the purpose of making predictions about the testtaker's future performance. It's called a(n) _____ test.

22. The author of a psychoeducational battery.

Down

1. A(n) _____ scale is a system of ordered numerical or verbal descriptors on which judgments concerning the presence/absence or magnitude of a particular trait, attitude, emotion, or other variable are indicated by the person making the ratings.

2. A packaged kit that contains tests that measure both abilities and educational achievement is called a _____ test battery.

4. The abbreviation for a test which was originally called the British Intelligence Test, then called the British Ability Scales, and now . . . this.

8. In preschool assessment, a _____ tool is an instrument or procedure used as a first step in identifying a child who is "at risk" or functioning in some way that may not be within normal limits.

9. An evaluation of accomplishment or the degree of learning that has taken place, usually with regard to an academic area, is called a(n) _____ test.

12. This rating scale was developed by an obstetrical anesthesiologist who saw a need for a simple, rapid method of evaluating newborn infants and determining what action, if any, was necessary.

13. An evaluation of performance tasks according to criteria developed by experts from the domain of study tapped by those tasks is called a(n) _____ assessment.

16. It's a tool of assessment designed to evaluate whether an individual has acquired the requisites to begin a particular program or perform some task. It's a(n) _____ test.

17. A school-based evaluation that clearly and faithfully reflects what is being taught is referred to as curriculum-based _____ .

18. Quite simply, it's a tool of assessment used to predict. It's called a(n) _____ test.

EXERCISE 10-1
MOVIES AND MEASUREMENT

OBJECTIVE

To obtain firsthand experience in assessing aspects of a preschooler's physical, cognitive, and social development

BACKGROUND

Among other things, the preschool period is a time for increasing socialization experiences, enhancement of language skills, and shedding of confusion between fantasy and reality. Arnold Schwarzenegger attempted to help matters along

Governor Arnold charming future voters in **Kindergarten Cop.**

in *Kindergarten Cop.* In this three-part exercise, it will be you and your classmates who will learn firsthand about the world of preschoolers. Part A entails assessment of physical development, Part B entails assessment of cognitive development, and Part C entails assessment of language and social skills.

You and your classmates have been selected to make a presentation at the "Annual Conference on the Experience of Being a Preschool Child." The exact date—and length—of this annual conference will be determined by your instructor, and the location will be your classroom. Each participant must come prepared with fascinating observations about the experience of being a preschooler—observations gleaned from firsthand assessment of a preschooler. If all three parts of this exercise are assigned, it is suggested that they be executed over the course of separate sessions. Make certain to note the child's age (including date of birth for reference) on all assessment reports.

YOUR TASK

For all three parts of this exercise, you are going to need access to a preschool child (age 4, give or take a year or so) and the consent of the child's parent (or guardian) to conduct the exercises. If you do not have your own child to work with, a child that belongs to a friend, a neighbor, a relative—even a complete stranger in married student housing—will do. Explain to the parent the purpose of the assessment—that it is a requirement for a course designed to help provide experience with testing preschoolers. Describe in advance all of the "tests" that will be administered. Additionally, inform the adult(s) who grants permission that while you will be pleased to share your "findings," (1) you are using training materials and not any valid psychological test; (2) for the purposes of this exercise you are making your best judgments regarding your observations, but you are not a trained or expert observer; and (3) no norms exist for these tests, and it is therefore impossible for you to gauge how typical or "normal" the child's performance is. It is suggested that the parent be not only present during the assessment but an active participant in it as well, acting as the examiner; you will then be free to devote your complete energy and attention to the task of observation and evaluation.

Part A: Physical Tests

The only material needed for this first exercise is a ball that is more or less baseball size and as weightless (such as the plastic versions that are available) as possible.

1. **The Walking Test**
   The child is instructed by the parent to walk from one end of a room to the other. Any difficulties noted?

2. **The Skipping Test**
   The child is now instructed to skip from one end of a room to the other. Any difficulties noted?

3. **The Hopping Test**
   The child is instructed to hop on his or her right foot from one end of the room to the other. Afterward, the child is instructed to return hopping on her or his left foot. Any difficulties noted?

4. **The Circle Walk/Skip/Hop Test**
   As a means of further assessing gross motor development, repeat Tests 1, 2, and 3, this time by having the child walk, skip, and hop around a circle (3-foot diameter or so) that has been defined in this room by an imaginary line. Any difficulties noted?

5. **The Shoe-and-Sock Test**
   As a means of helping you to assess fine motor coordination, the parent asks the child to remove his or her shoes and socks and then put them back on. Any difficulties noted?

6. **The Ball-Catch Test**
   The child's task here is to catch a ball that is (1) rolled on the floor to him or her, (2) lobbed directly to him or her, and (3) thrown up in the air so that it must be caught like a fly ball. Your task is to observe and report on the child's performance with respect to such factors as ability to visually track the ball and to coordinate muscular movements in order to successfully catch the ball. The parent repeats each mode of presenting the ball to the child three times before moving on to the next.

Part B: Tests of Cognitive Development

It is during the preschool years that the child develops the ability to mentally represent objects and events—in Piagetian terms, there is a shift from the sensorimotor to a preoperational level of development. The exercises in this section are based in part on the work of Piaget (1969; see also Ginsburg & Opper, 1988) as well as others (Gelman & Gallistel, 1986). For each of these, the only materials needed are a clean table and a dozen or so napkins of each of two colors. It does not matter what the two different colors of the napkins are, but they must be distinctly different in color. For the purposes of this example, let's say that one stack is white and the other is red.

With the parent acting as examiner and you as the observer, the following three tests are administered to the child.

1. **The Dinner Guest Test**
   Seated at the kitchen or dining room table, the parent is instructed to hold up a stack of napkins (one color only) and say to the child: "There will be four people having dinner here tonight, and each person will get their own napkin. Would you count out four napkins and place them on the table?"

   If the child does this correctly, the parent praises his or her performance and says, "Good. Now there are four napkins on the table." Make sure the napkins are spread out as if for four place settings before going to the second test in this series.

If the child does not do this correctly, he or she is given the opportunity to correct the number of napkins placed with a prompt from the parent such as, "No, that's not right; I said four people are coming, and each one will get their own napkin. So place four napkins on the table." Napkins placed on the table are replaced in the stack and handed to the child. If the child does not place the correct number of napkins this time, the parent places four napkins on the table, spread out as if for four place settings and says, "Now there are four napkins on the table."

2. The Conservation Test

With only the four napkins on the table, and with the child watching, the parent now stacks the four napkins into one pile and asks the child, "Are there still four napkins on the table now?" The answer to this question will depend, at least in part, on whether or not the child demonstrates the Piagetian concept of conservation—that is, an understanding that the rearrangement of objects or of a mass still contains the same amount of that object or mass. Again, the child is praised for a correct answer. If the child gives an incorrect answer, she or he is given an explanation, complete with a demonstration, that there are indeed four napkins on the table. At the end of the exercise, all of the napkins are collected and replaced in the stack of napkins of the same color.

3. The Classification Test

3a. The parent now places the original stack of napkins, along with an approximately equal-size stack of napkins of a different color, at about the center of the table. Handing one of the red napkins to the child, the parent says, "This is a red napkin. Place it with the other red napkins." The child is praised for a correct response and given a second chance if the response is incorrect. The child is shown the correct response if the second response is also incorrect.

3b. Now, handing one of the white napkins to the child, the parent says, "This is a white napkin. Place it with the other white napkins." Again, the child is praised for a correct response and given a second chance if the response is incorrect. The child is shown the correct response if the second response is also incorrect. If the child "fails" both 3a and 3b of this test, discontinue the Classification Test. If the child responds correctly to at least one part of this test, continue with 3c.

3c. The parent says, "We're going to set the table for four people, and each person is going to get his or her own napkin. There will be two boys coming, and the two boys will get red napkins. There will be two girls coming, and the two girls will get white napkins. So now, set the table for the two boys with two red napkins, and for the two girls with two white napkins."

3c may prove difficult for many preschoolers, especially those at the younger end of the preschool age range.

Still, the task may prove informative to the observant examiner in terms of how the child deals with the task and questions asked. The child who does not respond correctly at first is given another explanation and one additional chance to put out two red and two white napkins before the test is terminated. So that the "test session" ends on a successful note, it is suggested that, if the child fails this last task, the parent ask an additional question that the child is sure to succeed on (such as "Let me hear you count to five").

Part C: Language and Social Development

Unlike the short and incomplete sentences of the toddler, the language of the preschooler sounds very much like English—that is, after you discount the fabricated words. Development of social skills is also proceeding; however, as with language skills, such skills have not reached the level of the school-age child. For example, the preschooler is able to have fun playing with friends while not being able to take cognitively their point of view; this type of situation may result in pain or injury to an unsuspecting playmate who is perceived as an obstacle to enjoyment or pleasure.

For Part C, observe the child interacting with other children and make a report of your findings. Make an appointment with the parent and child to observe the child for a two-hour period. A morning, afternoon, or early evening time period will do, but it must be some period of time wherein the child can be observed interacting with other children. As you observe the child, listen to the language that is used; how many new words have the preschoolers coined during your period of observation? How would you characterize the quality of the communication between the youngsters? What can you say about the level of socialization you observe? What kinds of efforts are made, if any, by one child to help another? When does adult assistance seem to be required to maintain smooth social interaction?

EXERCISE 10-2
ASSESSMENT IN THE SCHOOLS

OBJECTIVE

To enhance understanding of the process of psychological assessment in the schools

BACKGROUND

Tests of intelligence, achievement (both general and specific), and aptitude (both general and specific) are but a few of the types of tests regularly administered in educational settings—you know that not only from your reading but also from your own personal experience. The three brief articles that follow should expand on that knowledge base. And after you've read each of them, incorporate what you've learned into your written response to the scenario that follows.

YOUR TASK

You are the principal of a new, private elementary school called the "Progressive and Enlightened School" (PES)—a school that caters to a bright, enlightened, and upwardly mobile clientele of parents. You are writing a letter to the parents of the 100 or so pupils enrolled in the school to explain to them the role psychological tests will play in their child's education. Write a draft of your letter, beginning with "Dear Parent," and proceed to discuss the following:

- why tests of school ability (as well as related abilities) are (or are not) necessary in a school setting
- the role tests will (and will not) play at PES
- how any tests used at PES will be selected
- how parents will be informed of findings with respect to readiness, achievement, and ability

In writing this letter you may wish to draw on your textbook, your own knowledge and experience, and any of the four articles reprinted below as sources.

ASSESSING SCHOOL ABILITY

Ruth Wilson

The principal task of the school is to facilitate cognitive learning in children. There are, of course, many other goals: to contribute to self-understanding and character development, to foster and encourage artistic abilities and manual skills, and to develop social qualities and physical health, to name a few. Yet, important as they may be, other goals can never be viewed as alternatives to cognitive learning.

Different children show different degrees of the ability to learn in school, and in order to achieve equality of educational opportunity, such variations must be taken into account. To bring a child to maximum functioning level, it is necessary to start where he or she is at the time. Each child's strengths and weaknesses must be assessed so that educational plans may be realistic and effective.

Every teacher realizes that it is unreasonable to expect the same level and speed of attainment, or the same quality of understanding and learning, from all pupils. For the teacher to meet responsibly his or her duties, instruction must be tempered to the needs and qualifications of each learner insofar as this is possible. Decisions concerning what instructional methods and materials to use will necessarily involve prediction.

The process of making predictions goes on constantly. Explicitly or implicitly, judgments are made about how well each pupil is going to perform. Observation is essential to decision making; but in the absence of reliable test scores, such important functions as the assigning or placing of pupils, adapting instruction to their needs, discovering their talents, and evaluating their progress become

more difficult and less objective. A school ability test is designed to give important, objective evidence concerning the general ability that underlies each pupil's performance in all areas of academic learning. It is an efficient and dependable means of obtaining *some* of the information necessary for sound decision making and for predicting future scholastic attainment.

Purpose and Content of a School Ability Test

What skills and abilities are necessary for learning new things in school? Children must be able to perceive accurately, to recognize and recall what has been perceived, to think logically, to perceive relationships, to abstract from a set of particulars, and to apply a generalization or abstraction to a new and different context.

These mental operations lend themselves to objective measurements through performance on such tasks as detecting likenesses and differences, recalling words and numbers, recognizing absurdities, defining words, following directions, classifying, establishing sequence, and solving arithmetic and analogy problems. Tasks of this type (associative and relatively abstract in character) are less subject to the effect of previous in-school learning than is the material found on achievement test batteries or tests covering one specific curricular area. Yet they are clearly school-related and indicative of potential for future school success.

Tests of general school ability, which assess current status by measuring performance on tasks such as the above, have as one of their chief purposes the prediction of rate of learning in school. Although such tests are quite comprehensive, they make no attempt to assess the totality of the pupil's intellectual functioning, nor do they constitute an indexing of the whole of an individual's intellectual ability. For this reason, the term "school ability" is a more accurate and precise description of that which is measured than the more general terms "intelligence" and "mental ability."

Scores on any test of this nature are the result of complex and interacting influences, including environmental and experiential elements. They should never be taken in a deterministic sense, but should be perceived as descriptive of the *pupil at a given time*. However, numerous studies testify to the fact that, as predictors of future scholastic attainment, they are very useful.

Uses of Test Results

How can the results of a school ability test be helpful to teachers and administrators? Knowledge of each pupil's general ability, since it underlies performance in all domains of learning, provides valuable insights into the following areas of concern.

1. How does this pupil's present capacity for scholastic work compare with what he or she is actually achieving in each area? In what areas is he or she doing less

well than might be expected in view of overall learning ability?

2. Are the goals that have been set challenging enough in view of this pupil's ability to learn? Does this test's score support observations of the pupil's performance made in the classroom? What chance does this pupil have for succeeding in accelerated or enriched programs?

3. Are the instructional goals that have been set too high for this pupil? In what curricular areas does this pupil need further diagnostic evaluation and perhaps remediation? In view of all available evidence, should the pupil be referred to the school counselor or psychologist for further evaluation?

Teachers and administrators faced with these concerns must make decisions using whatever information is available to them. By yielding an objective measure of potential for learning, the school ability test is a valuable complement to teacher judgment and informal appraisal. Properly used and interpreted, results from this type of test become a positive factor in ensuring that all pupils—from all backgrounds—are assisted in gaining as much as possible from their educational experience.

Three general uses of the school ability test are implicit in the questions posed above. These are:

a. Identification of the Gifted and Talented

One of the notable things about ability tests is that they unearth talent that might be and frequently is overlooked in the absence of such tests. Classroom instruction is most often geared to the needs and interests of pupils of average ability, while the needs of low-ability pupils are so obvious that they demand the teacher's special attention. Consequently, the gifted children are the most often neglected; many of them "languish in idleness." Contrary to widespread belief, these children frequently cannot grow toward their potential without special assistance. Placed in unchallenging educational environments, which sometimes are even hostile to their behavior, they tend to conceal their extraordinary abilities and even bury them in underachievement. In fact, in the absence of test scores, gifted children are frequently identified as behavior problems. "Prevented from moving ahead by the rigidity of normal school procedures, . . . the gifted youngster typically takes one of three tacks: (1) he drifts into a state of lethargy and complete apathy; (2) he conceals his ability, anxious not to embarrass others or draw their ridicule by superior performance; or (3) not understanding his frustration, he becomes a discipline problem."[1]

Talent is available in all quarters, on all levels, but it is the culturally different child who poses the most difficult identification problem. In the absence of a good testing program, minority children and children from a low socioeconomic level often stand little chance of being correctly identified as gifted and given an appropriate education.

Historically, standardized ability tests first opened up many of the top colleges in America to bright youths from lower-class backgrounds who had previously been passed over by traditional methods of selection.[2] With the passage of the Gifted and Talented Children's Educational Assistance Act in 1974 (ESEA Title IV Amendment), the United States government has mandated that special educational opportunities be afforded to all school children evidencing outstanding ability. Here again, the school ability test has a critical role to play.

b. Preliminary Screening of Pupils Requiring Special Educational Treatment

Where ability scores indicate that the instructional goals of a particular classroom exceed the capacity of some of the pupils, it is incumbent upon teachers and administrators to make the necessary adjustments so that these pupils, also, can get the most from their educational experiences. Teachers, unfortunately, sometimes use low ability scores to explain why some pupils do not learn rather than to help all pupils learn more. Too little attention is paid to the fact that, whatever the level of ability, the range of potential achievement associated with it is large. By providing an appropriate environment for learning, pacing instruction to the varied learning rates of pupils, and adapting instructional strategies to respond to their needs, teachers can foster the achievement of the so-called "slow learner."

The data obtained from school ability testing should be supplemented by other information before any important decisions are made concerning these low-scoring pupils. Group tests provide little opportunity for direct observation of the pupil's behavior or for identifying the cause of poor performance; rather, they indicate the need for further testing and careful screening so that appropriate instructional intervention may be planned. Public Law 94-142, the Education for All Handicapped Children Act, establishes sound guidelines for use in such cases. It requires that, in making placement decisions, a school district draw upon information from a variety of sources, including aptitude tests, but it prohibits placement in programs solely on the basis of test scores or on psychometric input viewed in isolation (PL 94-142, Sections 121a.531, 121a.533). The regulations ensure that the identification and placement process is a multidisciplinary activity, with decisions based on a variety of sources of information which, taken together, give a comprehensive view of the "total child."

In this regard, special attention should be given to children of minority groups. School ability tests are measures of learned or developed abilities in the broadest sense, and implicit in any comparison of scores is the assumption that all examinees have had an equal opportunity to learn the

---

[1]Excerpted by special permission from "The Other Minority," by Harold C. Lyon, Jr., *Learning: The Magazine for Creative Teaching,* Vol. 2, No. 5 (January 1974), p. 65, © by Education Today Co., Inc.

[2]*Report of the Commission on Tests: I. Righting the Balance* (New York: College Entrance Examination Board, 1970), pp. 11–32.

types of things included in the tests. Studies show that middle- and upper-class children are generally encouraged by their parents to develop verbal and reasoning abilities, while such home training is less common among other groups. Background factors can contribute to the creation of handicaps to learning, and test scores may indicate the need for special instructional programs and strategies to overcome this disadvantage.

It is important to remember that *predictive validity* of the test as regards the pupil's ability to cope with school-related material is not called into question for low scorers. It is the *use* made of the information that calls for a special degree of discernment and sensitivity.

c. Comparison of School Ability with Actual Achievement

For the majority of pupils, the most important use of a school ability test is to provide a basis for comparison between their potential for learning and their actual performance. For this group, comparison with others is relatively unimportant; the concern of teachers and administrators is to evaluate the relationship between each pupil's measured achievement and what could reasonably be expected, based on his or her school ability score.

Data of this kind are best obtained through comparing scores attained on a school ability test with those derived from a standardized achievement test. The significance of such a comparison rests in the distinction between *what is tested* on these two types of tests.

Achievement tests assess highly specific types of behaviors that are taught in school, behaviors that represent important outcomes of instructional programs. In order to obtain dependable information concerning instructional outcomes, separate tests are given for each of the instructional domains, such as reading, mathematics, science, social studies, etc. Typically, achievement tests also yield a total battery score, but this score is not the basis of potential/achievement comparisons. Pupils do not learn "in general" as a result of instruction in school; they learn to spell, to read, to compute, to use language correctly, and to function in other specific ways. The purpose of these comparisons is to determine whether pupils read as well as their ability indicates they are able, or whether they compute as well, etc.

School ability tests, on the other hand, are not constructed in accordance with curricular objectives or goals of instruction. They are made up of tasks designed to measure generalized cognitive traits and abilities. Many of these tasks involve verbal and numerical symbols, yet the content is usually quite different from that in a reading or mathematics test. Most general ability tests administered to pupils in grade 3 and below require no reading at all by the pupils, while tests at the upper levels are so constructed that reading ability itself is not a major source of variance in test scores. For example, the readability level of a school ability test administered to fifth-grade pupils might be substantially lower than that of fifth-grade reading ma-

terials. Likewise, with the test items requiring arithmetic skills, the difficulty of the item is centered on the conceptual process or problem analysis, not on arithmetic or computational abilities.

Performance on a school ability test reflects the cumulative influence of a great many experiences encountered both in and out of school. In contrast, achievement tests measure the effect of the school's instructional program. By comparing scores received on these two types of tests, a teacher can judge the effectiveness of classroom instruction as regards each individual pupil and can establish appropriate educational goals, methods, and paces for each pupil to make optimal progress.

Testing the Culturally Different Child

School ability tests are designed to predict the performance of pupils in the present school system; their norms supply useful information concerning the probability that a particular child will succeed, *as a pupil,* in the traditional American school. Typically, public education has functioned to blur cultural distinctions. Most instruction is in English, and the curricular content focuses on Anglo-American institutions, history, and literature. The values that the schools strive to cultivate are themselves culturally saturated.

For children and adults alike, cultural differences may become cultural handicaps when individuals move out of the culture in which they have been reared and endeavor to function, compete, or succeed within another culture. In planning instructional programs, it is essential to consider the extent to which a child's background affects his or her ability to learn.

The skills and knowledge measured in ability tests are precisely those required for success in school. Though they may be culturally influenced, these are the criteria for assessing a pupil's likelihood of succeeding in learning what is being taught in school. In fact, no device captures those consequences of cultural differences that are *important to schooling* as efficiently as the general ability test.

The attempt to estimate *general mental ability* from such a test, however, is based on the assumption that all pupils have had substantially equal opportunity to learn the types of things included in the test and that all pupils are equally motivated to do their best on the test. Although absolute equality in these regards is impossible, the majority of schoolchildren meet these qualifications, and for these children, a school ability test may yield an appropriate assessment of general ability; however, for some minority groups within the general population, these assumptions cannot be made.

The common characteristic of these minority groups is membership in a culture other than the dominant one in American society. Racial and ethnic backgrounds are factors, as is economic status.

For many pupils within these minority groups, the assumption that they have had the opportunity to learn the types of things included on ability tests is open to question. For such pupils, the significance of ability test scores should be limited to the prediction of success in school—to measuring *school ability*. Any interpretation of scores as being indicative of *general mental ability* must be tempered by considerations of the cultural background of the examinees.

The classroom teacher involved in the education of culturally different children should recognize that the educational difficulties displayed by these pupils may represent a difference in background, rather than a special kind of intellectual difficulty, and should concentrate on getting the children to transfer skills they already possess to the tasks they encounter in the classroom.

The assumption of equal motivation to do well on a test is also brought into question with this group of children. Among the relevant conditions differing from culture to culture are interest in the test content, the desire to surpass others or to do well on a test, rapport with the examiner, and past habits of solving problems individually or cooperatively.

A teacher must be extremely careful when testing children of races and cultures other than his or her own and should be alert to any nuances in their behavior that suggest their test performance might be invalid. Cultural differences can create communication problems that affect not only the rapport but the child's ability to understand and respond to the test questions. Every attempt should be made to elicit the child's best performance, without, in the process, compromising standard procedures.

By far the most important consideration in the testing of culturally diverse groups pertains to the use made of the scores. In using tests to evaluate minority children's performance, special efforts must be made to study and learn about their cultural patterns. Care must be taken that no inferences are drawn about some presumed inherited, immutable capacity. The task of a conscientious teacher is to ponder what lies behind the test scores and use them to the educational advantage of the children.

To the evaluation of the teacher, which will always be subjective and may also be unduly influenced by personal biases and prejudices, school ability tests add an objective standard of learning potential, which, properly understood, works to the advantage of minority children. Such objectivity is necessary if programs are to be evaluated accurately, decisions on curriculum are to be based on evidence, and educational opportunities are not to be denied due to bias and discrimination.

Conclusion

For all groups and at all levels within the educational system, the need exists for the identification of talent, for better diagnosis and understanding of the nature of learning disabilities, for setting realistic instructional goals and establishing appropriate paces. These needs must be met if all pupils are to profit from their educational experience. No single piece of information is adequate to the task, but when considered in conjunction with other available data, scores on a school ability test make a unique contribution.

Properly used and interpreted, this type of test can be a useful tool in channeling individual aptitudes and talents into those avenues of endeavor that will be most rewarding to the individual.

SELECTION AND PROVISION OF TESTING MATERIAL

Roger T. Lennon, **Test Department**

The educational historian who comes to write the story of American education during the 1950s and since can hardly fail to note, as one of its distinctive features, the pervasive use of the standardized test, at every level and for a variety of purposes. The best available estimate indicates that some 200,000,000 standardized tests are administered annually in the schools of this country—and the trend, which has been steadily in the direction of greater use of such tests, shows no sign of abating.

The majority of the standardized tests used—perhaps two-thirds of them—are so-called "achievement" tests, seeking to measure attainment of specified instructional goals. The second largest category is general or special ability—aptitude—tests, seeking to measure learner characteristics, for improved guidance or educational diagnosis. The sheer volume of standardized testing, to say nothing of the profound impact such testing has on so many phases of the educational enterprise, calls for the most thoughtful attention to selection and provision of the best testing materials.

Standardized Tests and the Instructional Process

Standardized tests are indeed essential "instructional" materials. Let us consider for a moment some of the functions that standardized tests most commonly serve, the better to appreciate how inextricably bound up they are with the instructional process.

1. *Tests provide measures of status* in particular skills or content areas for a pupil, a class, or a school. They reveal where the learner or group is at a given time and thus provide a clue to the level at which instruction must be pitched. If we are to adapt instruction to the particular needs of individual pupils, it follows that we need dependable information as to precisely how they differ in their attainment or mastery—and such information is most easily come by through the use of standardized tests.

2. *Tests provide measures of growth, development, or progress* toward desirable educational goals. Measurement of growth presupposes repeated administrations of tests; from these repeated measurements we may infer the extent to which the learner is in fact making progress toward instructional goals and whether his rate of progress compares favorably with what is typi-

cal for his peers or with what may reasonably be expected of him in light of his ability.

3. *Tests provide measures of differential status,* revealing areas of relative strength and weakness that are of significance for guidance purposes.
4. *Tests provide analytical or diagnostic information,* which permits sharper definition of learning difficulties and enables instruction to be brought to bear more forcefully on points where it is most needed.
5. *Tests provide inventories of skills,* which serve both as checks on progress and as guides to further instruction.
6. *Tests are one source of data essential for continuing evaluation* of the adequacy of the total instructional program.

It is axiomatic that evaluation is an integral part of the instructional process. Education without evaluation, as someone has put it, is target practice in the dark; without knowledge of the efficacy of our efforts, improvement is impossible. Standardized tests are by no means the whole of evaluation, but they are a rich source of the kind of data on which sound evaluation must depend.

In a word, tests are fact-finding devices; they do nothing but develop in an economical, reliable manner information that helps the teacher, the supervisor, and the administrator to discharge more effectively their instructional responsibilities. Standardized tests are means, not ends; they are a necessary first step in understanding the learner, in keying instruction to his needs, and in evaluation. The prominence that they have come to enjoy in American education is perhaps the best witness to their status as true instructional aids.

In the light of what has been said about the role of tests as instructional materials, let us turn to the proper selection and provision of tests. Perhaps the most fruitful way to approach this topic is to place it in the larger context of planning a testing program, for testing is most effective when carried on as part of a comprehensive, continuous program rather than on a sporadic, *ad hoc* basis to meet particular or transient needs. I should like to consider briefly several aspects of planning a testing program: the "who," the "what," the "when," and the "how" of such planning.

The Testing Program: Whose Responsibility?

Almost every member of a school's staff who is charged in any way with responsibility for the instructional program is vitally concerned with test data. Rare is the supervisor, the administrator, the counselor, the psychologist, or the director of research who feels no need of such data as a basis for carrying on his work. Since each has a stake in the application and interpretation of test results, the planning of testing and selection of tests will be done best if it takes account of their respective needs for test data. Their interests are sometimes common, sometimes diverse.

The device that many school systems have found effective in giving voice to these varied elements is the testing committee, a standing committee with membership representative of the several elements, charged with responsibility for planning the system's testing program and keeping it under continuing review. The chairman of this committee may be a director of testing or research, a director of instruction, a psychologist, the superintendent, or some other staff member, according to local organizational practice; the important thing is to insure a broadly based concept of testing throughout the entire system.

A testing committee, like any committee, will be successful only to the extent to which it perceives its mission with clarity. As a first duty, the committee needs to formulate an explicit statement of the purposes to be served by testing—a definition of the particular goals sought by the testing program—in effect, a policy statement on testing for the system. The committee needs, moreover, to bring to its task, or develop as it goes, certain special knowledges and skills that will enable it to make proper choices among available tests and sound judgments as to the conduct of a program, use of results, etc. Not every member of a testing committee need be a test expert, nor would this ordinarily be either feasible or desirable. Every member, however, ought to realize or be informed about the importance of such features as reliability, adequacy of standardization, equivalence of forms, and the like, so that all can appreciate the need for giving some weight to those factors in making their choices.

At the same time, test selection should not be made altogether on purely statistical considerations. In the selection of achievement tests, particularly, major weight should be given to what we term the "content validity" of the test— the extent to which the skills or knowledge measured by the test are in accord with, and sample reasonably from, the body of skills and knowledge established as the goals of instruction in the local program. And it may be noted in passing that appraisal of this type of validity is not always best made by the psychologist or test expert, but by the teacher or the supervisor, who is closer to the curriculum and the content of instruction.

Responsibility for testing, therefore, is shared by many in the school system. The various persons or groups contribute to the selection of instruments on the basis of their special knowledges or interests. A testing committee will best discharge its planning and selection responsibilities when it is systematically trained for this task, informed about the criteria that should prevail in the selection of tests, and alert to the varied uses to which test data will be put.

The Testing Program: Its Scope

If we accept the essential relation between instruction and evaluation, then it follows that the scope, or "what," of an evaluation program is as broad as the range of instructional goals. A testing committee—perhaps better an "evaluation" committee—should concern itself with evidence as to the attainment of *all* the instructional goals of the system. Many of them, to be sure, will not lend themselves to assessment through standardized tests, but in planning a comprehensive testing program, the committee should at least canvass the possibilities of finding and using suitable test instruments for all outcomes.

To speak of a testing "program" implies comprehensiveness, continuity, regularity, and medium- or long-range planning of testing activities, with corollary implications for the scope of the testing committee's work. The committee should be aware of the advantages inherent in the use of a single battery of tests that covers a wide range of grades; only through such a battery can comparisons across subjects and over the range of grades be made most dependably. There are merits in continued use of a given test or battery over a period of years, if meaningful longitudinal studies of pupils are to be made. At the same time, achievement tests, like textbooks, do become obsolete and should be replaced by more current editions or by newer testing instruments. Weighing the pros and cons of changing tests is a good example of the type of judgment the committee needs to exercise.

The testing committee will need to consider the frequency with which tests should be administered, the establishment of priorities among testing needs, the choice of appropriate grades in which to administer various types of tests, the time of year at which the various tests should be administered, arrangements for scoring, types of reporting systems, and the dissemination of test results in the most expeditious manner to all those having need of them. It has, of course, the crucial task of selecting, or at least of recommending the selection of, the tests to be used.

The Testing Program: When to Plan

A testing committee's work should be viewed as continuous, and its deliberations should look to the future as well as to planning for more or less immediate testing needs. A testing program should be planned between six months and a year in advance of the time when it is actually to take place, depending somewhat on whether it is a spring or a fall program, on local budgeting practices, on the size of the system and consequent communications and training problems, and similar factors. When a major program is being contemplated, one that covers many subjects at many grade levels with a single battery, it will ordinarily be desirable to think in terms of establishing a program that will be maintained for several years. In giving thought to this type of program, it is well to have in mind such matters as the availability of alternate forms and the possibility that revised editions of the test in question will be appearing over the period of the proposed program.

The "How" of Test Selection

Let us assume that a school system, through its testing committee, has defined its testing needs; has planned a program to the extent of knowing what kinds of tests are to be given, at what grade levels, at what time of year; and is now ready to choose the tests most appropriate for the purposes. How does it go about making a selection from among the many available tests?

The first requisite, of course, is that the committee know what tests are available. Just as with textbooks, it finds this out from study of the catalogs of the various test publishers. There are about ten publishers of tests for school use, whose publications probably account for more than 90 percent of all standardized tests used in schools. The catalogs of these publishers describe their respective offerings in various areas, and the committee can readily determine which tests it ought to consider or examine in given fields. Tests should never be selected on the basis of titles alone or catalog descriptions; there is no substitute for actual examination of a test prior to selection. Publishers will be glad to send examination copies of their tests to committees considering test selection.

In making a selection, there should, most importantly, be an assessment of content validity, in the case of achievement tests, of "predictive" validity, for aptitude tests. There should be evaluation of the technical attributes of the test—reliability, adequacy of norms, appropriateness of difficulty level, etc. There should be consideration of the mechanics of the instrument—its ease of administration, its scoring, etc. And, increasingly, consideration is being given to the availability of services: can arrangement be made for outside scoring, analysis, preparation of pupil reports, etc.?

There are resources available to the committee to help with the task of test evaluation. Among these should be mentioned the *Standards for Educational and Psychological Tests and Manuals* developed by a joint committee of the American Psychological Association, the American Educational Research Association, and the National Council on Measurement in Education. These *Standards*[3] describe desirable practices in the reporting of information about tests and serve in effect as a guide or checklist for appraising tests. *Mental Measurements Yearbook,*[4] a compilation of critical reviews of published tests issued periodically, is a rich source of helpful information.

Provision of Test Materials

Since we are concerned not only with the selection but with the *provision* of tests, it is appropriate to say a few words about the ordering of test materials and about provision for them in the budget. As with any supplies, you are likely to get what you want if you order well in advance and if you are careful, in placing the order, to give complete information. An astonishing number of test orders cannot be filled without correspondence because schools

---

[3] Available in pamphlet form from the American Psychological Association, 1200 Seventeenth St., N.W., Washington, D.C. 20036.

[4] O. K. Buros, Editor, The Gryphon Press, Highland Park, N.J.

fail to indicate such essential information as level, form, or edition. You will get better service from test publishers if you will familiarize yourself with the information on ordering that is a part of practically every test catalog. Moreover, because testing is seasonal and so many school systems want tests at about the same time, it is helpful to place orders well in advance so that they will not be subject to the delays that are incidental to peak seasons.

It is important, too, to give thought to budgetary provision for test materials. While the amounts required for even a very comprehensive program of standardized tests are negligible in relation to the total outlay per pupil for instructional services, they should, nevertheless, be definitely and specifically provided for in a budget for such materials. At the elementary level an expenditure of approximately 50¢ per pupil per year will, on the average, provide adequate test materials to cover the major subject-matter areas; at the secondary level an expenditure of $1.25 per student per year will provide not only achievement test materials but also mental ability and special aptitude tests for a comprehensive guidance program. Increasingly, schools are seeking to have scoring and other services accomplished for them on a service basis, and these additional services, if desired, should also be provided for in the budget. Costs for scoring an achievement battery begin at about 30¢ per pupil and range upward to as much as $1.25 or even more, depending upon the complexity of the test battery involved, the amount of statistical analysis called for, the variety and scope of reports, etc.

Summary

Selection and provision of adequate standardized test material may be viewed as a continuing responsibility of several different elements in the school system—teachers, supervisors, guidance counselors, psychologists, administrators—whose varying needs and views on testing should be given voice through a permanent committee on testing. Like selection of textbooks, selection of tests calls for sophistication and understanding as to the characteristics that differentiate one instrument from another, as to the appropriateness of given materials in a given school system, and as to the ease with which given materials may be handled by the personnel in a given school system.

Selection of tests should be based primarily on the suitability of the chosen instruments for the purposes to which they are to be put: Where the primary emphasis is on the improvement of instruction, then the greatest weight in test selection ought to be given to the content validity of the materials.

There should be specific provision in the budget for standardized test materials. Planning should be sufficiently in advance of the intended use of the materials to permit ordering and local distribution of the materials in ample time for testing. As with any instructional materials, the ultimate criterion is the extent to which the information provided by standardized tests makes a genuine contribution to improved instruction of pupils.

SOME THINGS PARENTS SHOULD KNOW ABOUT TESTING

A Series of Questions and Answers

Q. Why do the schools test our children?

A. It is no news to parents that children differ. Even within a single family, some children learn to walk or to talk sooner than others. One child may be a good reader; another may excel in sports. When children come into school, the teacher needs to know as much as possible about how they differ in order to be able to match the classroom teaching to the specific needs of the children. The school administration also needs to be able to plan for the long-term education of the pupils.

Q. Why do teachers need to use published tests?

A. Commercially published tests give the teacher much important information about the pupils, information that the teacher cannot obtain. Of course, teachers get a great deal of information about their pupils by observing their day-to-day work in class and by testing their progress with teacher-made tests. Commercially published tests are written by people who are experts in writing test questions. These people are also curriculum specialists who know what is being taught in schools all across the country. Most commercially published tests cover a wide range of skills in one test, whereas teacher-made tests usually cover only a single unit of work. But perhaps the most important reason for using commercially published tests is that the school can use the results obtained from them to compare a pupil's school progress with the school progress of other children throughout the country. These comparisons can be made because the tests are *norm-referenced* and *standardized* on a *national population.*

Q. What do you mean by *norm-referenced*?

A. Knowing that a pupil got 40 questions right on a test doesn't give you enough information by itself. How many questions were there? Were they easy or hard? Is 40 a "good," "average," or "poor" score? Often, what we really want to know is how this score compares with the scores of other pupils of the same age or in the same grade. Is it high, medium, or low *in relation to* the scores of pupils in some large group? This way of describing performance is called *norm-referenced,* and the numbers that are used to give meaning to a pupil's performance are called *norms* or *norm-referenced scores.*

Q. What does *standardized* mean?

A. The test publisher develops the *norms* or norm-referenced scores by a process called *standardization*. In order to find out what scores are high, medium, or low, the publisher must give the test to a large number of school-children across the country. The pupils who will be in this *national population sample* will be carefully chosen. They cannot all live in one area; they cannot all go to big schools; they cannot all be of one race or socioeconomic group. The publisher will use government census data and his own experience and knowledge to select a group of several thousand pupils so that their scores on the test will represent the scores that would have been obtained if all the millions of children in the country had been tested.

Once the test has been written and the standardization group has been selected, the test publisher must make sure that the test's directions are so clear and so specific that the test can always be presented in the same way to all pupils. This is done so that all children have the same chance to know what they are supposed to do on the test. A test that has been written in this way and given to a carefully se-lected group of pupils in a controlled manner is said to be a *standardized test*.

Q. How do you get norms from standardization?

A. The norms are a way of summarizing how the pupils in the standardization group did on the test. In this sense, the pupils make the norms, not the test-maker. After the test has been given, the test publisher has something that looks like this:

> 120 third-graders correctly answered 29 questions
> 180 third-graders correctly answered 28 questions
> 215 third-graders correctly answered 27 questions

and so on for each grade and each possible score. In order to make this information easier to understand, the test pub-lisher summarizes it. One way of doing this is by report-ing, for each test, the average score in each grade. These are called *grade-equivalent norms*. Another way is to re-port what percentage of the pupils in a grade scored at or below a certain score. These are called *percentile rank norms*. A third type of norm describes how far a pupil's performance is above or below the average performance for that grade. These are called *standard scores*. (The most common standard score is a stanine.) All of these methods of expressing a score are simply ways of indicating where a particular score fits into the *pattern* of all the scores earned by the pupils in the norm group.

Q. What do you mean by the *pattern* of scores?

A. For practically any characteristic you can name, there are differences among individuals. There is an average (or medium, or typical) weight, or height, or shoe size, or reading test score. But there is also wide variation in both directions from that average. The weights, heights, or read-ing scores of most people tend to bunch up close to an av-erage weight, or height, or reading ability. And there are fewer people at the extremes; i.e., there are fewer adults who are six inches taller or shorter than the average than there are those who are only one inch taller or shorter than the average. The average and the pattern of scores for any characteristic can be determined, and one individual's score can always be described in terms of the whole pat-tern. For most characteristics measured by educational tests, the pattern of scores looks something like this:

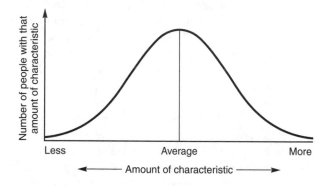

Q. You say norms can be expressed in several ways. What is a *percentile rank*?

A. A percentile rank tells you what percent of the pupils in the norm group got the same score or a lower score on the test. For example, if a score of 25 correct answers on a cer-tain test for fourth-graders has a percentile rank of 52, it means that 52 percent of the pupils in the norm group scored 25 or lower on the test. Since the norm group was representative of all fourth-graders in the nation, it is esti-mated that a pupil scoring 25 on the test is performing at a level equal to or above 52 percent of all the fourth-graders in the nation. For most standardized achievement tests, percentile ranks are developed separately for each grade and for a particular time of the year. A score of 25, for example, may have a percentile rank of 52 for a fourth-grader in the fall of fourth grade and a percentile rank of 47 in the spring of fourth grade. A percentile rank is not in any sense a "percent correct." It is *not* the percent of ques-tions the pupil answered correctly, but rather the percent of pupils in the norm group who scored at or below that score.

Q. What is a *stanine*?

A. A stanine is a score on a nine-unit scale from 1 to 9, where a score of 5 describes average performance. The highest stanine is 9; the lowest is 1. Stanines are based on the pattern of scores described earlier. Except for 1 and 9, they divide the baseline into equal amounts of the charac-teristic being measured. Stanine 8 is as far above average (5) as stanine 2 is below average. As is shown in the figure below, most pupils score in the middle three stanines; 54 percent will score in stanines 4, 5, and 6. On the other hand, very few (4 percent) will score a stanine of 1 or a stanine of 9. The relationship of stanines and percentile ranks can also be seen in this figure.

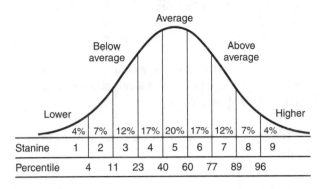

Teachers may use stanines to describe a pupil's performance to the parents during a parent-teacher conference. The stanines may also be used to group pupils for special instruction. Since there are only nine stanines, students, parents, and teachers are not likely to give too much weight to small differences among scores. Sometimes stanines are combined into more general classifications with verbal descriptions. Stanine 9 describes higher performance; stanines 7 and 8, above average; stanines 4, 5, and 6, average; stanines 2 and 3, below average; and stanine 1 describes lower performance, *in relation to the norm group's performance*. Remember, stanines, like all other norms, describe comparative, not absolute, performance.

Q. But we usually hear about *grade equivalents.* What are they?

A. A grade equivalent indicates the grade level, in years and months, for which a given score was the average or middle score in the standardization sample. For example, a score of 25 with the grade equivalent of 4.6 means that, in the norm group, 25 was the average score of pupils in the sixth month of the fourth grade. If, after the test has been standardized, another pupil in the sixth month of the fourth grade were to take the same fourth-grade test and score 25 correct, his performance would be "at grade level" or average for his grade placement. If he were to get 30 right or a grade equivalent of 5.3, he would have done as well as the typical fifth-grader in the third month *on that test.* This does not mean that the fourth-grader can do all fifth-grade work. There are many things a fifth-grader has learned that are not measured on a fourth-grade test. Similarly, a 3.3 grade equivalent for a fourth-grader would mean that he is performing, on the fourth-grade test, the way the average pupil in the third month of third grade would perform on that same test. It does *not* suggest that he has learned only third-grade material.

Although grade equivalents may sound like a simple idea, they can be easily misunderstood. For this reason, schools are increasingly coming to rely on percentile ranks and stanines as more useful ways to interpret scores in relation to a norm group. In fact, some publishers recommend that grade equivalents *not* be used to report to teachers, parents, pupils, or the general public.

Q. Newspapers sometimes write about "scoring at or above the norm." What does scoring *at the norm* mean?

A. Whereas the word *norms* is used to describe the full range of scores the norm group obtained, the term *the norm* refers only to the midpoint in that range. People sometimes refer to *the norm* as the acceptable or desirable score. This is inaccurate. On a norm-referenced test, *the norm* is the average score obtained by the pupils who took the test during its standardization. *The norm* only indicates what is average; it does *not* describe how good that performance is in absolute terms. Suppose a reading test were given to a large, representative, national norm group and the average score for the group was 25. *The norm* for that group, then, is 25. It must be remembered, however, that of all the pupils in the national norm group, *half scored above 25 and half scored at or below 25!*

When the norm is expressed as a grade equivalent, it is still describing the middle score in the norm group. If the norm group was tested in the sixth month of grade 4, the average score for the group would convert to the grade equivalent of 4.6. But note that even in that norm group, fully half of all pupils actually in the sixth month of the fourth grade scored at or below that norm or "grade level." If the same test is then given to another group, it would not be surprising to find many pupils scoring "below the norm." Remember, half of the norm group itself scored at or below the norm; that's the meaning of the word.

Q. But if a child's reading is "below the norm," that means the child is a poor reader, doesn't it?

A. Not necessarily. It probably means he is not reading as well as the *average* American child in his grade, assuming that the test was well standardized. But it doesn't tell you how well the average child reads. If most of the children in the norm group read "well," *the norm* or average represents good reading. If most children read poorly, *the norm* would represent "poor" reading. Whether the norm group reads well or poorly is a judgment the test cannot make. Such decisions must be made by schools and parents.

Q. But wouldn't it be worthwhile to try to teach all children to read at or above the norm?

A. Suppose that, to score *at the norm* on a fourth-grade test, a pupil must answer 25 questions out of 40 correctly. Then, suppose we improve the teaching of reading so that all fourth-grade children in the nation score at least 25 and many score much higher than 25. Now all children are reading "at or above the norm," right? Wrong! As the scores have changed, so has their average—*the norm.* If you were to standardize the test again, you might find that the middle or average score for the national norm group is now 31 out of 40. So, *the norm* now is 31, not 25, and half the pupils are still reading at or below the norm and half are reading above the norm. In other words, if everybody is above average, it's not the *average* anymore! This is the reason that *the norm* is not an absolute goal for everyone to attain. It is simply a statement of fact about the *average* of a group. If they all read better, then the norm moves higher. You've done something worthwhile, indeed, but it didn't bring everyone "up to the norm"! (The norm for a test that was standardized in the 1950s is no longer *the norm,* since more than half the pupils now read better than that. This is one of the reasons new tests must be standardized by the publishers every few years.)

Q. Some parents and teachers claim that most published standardized tests are unfair to minority group and inner-city children. Is that true?

A. There are really two questions involved here. The first has to do with the knowledge area being measured. Is it "fair," for example, to test a pupil's knowledge of addition? If this skill is considered important and is part of the school's curriculum, then it is "fair" to test a child's mastery of this skill. It is important that parents and the school know how well each child performs on each skill. Of course, very few people would consider that mastery of addition was *not* a necessary skill. Test publishers try to concentrate on areas that most people consider important. However, if a test measures many areas that a community does *not* consider important, then the test should not be used in that community.

Assuming that it *is* important to measure particular areas, a second question must still be answered. Does the test measure the areas "fairly"? Have some test questions been stated in a way that will give certain children an "unfair" advantage? Will some questions "turn off" some children so that they will not do their best? Test publishers have been giving increasing attention to the question of the fairness of their tests. Many writers and editors from different backgrounds are involved in test-making. Questions are reviewed by members of several ethnic groups to correct for unintentional, built-in biases. In addition, the topics in most reading tests are chosen to be unfamiliar to almost all students. This helps to ensure that scores are based on reading skill and not on familiarity with the subject matter of the particular passage.

Q. Are national norms valid for all children?

A. Yes, national norms *do* have meaning and significance for all school systems. National norms represent one reality—they represent the pattern of performance of *all the nation's schoolchildren.* All kinds of schools in all parts of the country are represented in that total pattern. The pattern of scores in any *one* area, even in a large city, is not likely to match the total pattern exactly. Differences are to be expected and should be explained to parents and the general public.

However, our children are growing up in a rapidly changing, competitive, and highly mobile society. After attending school in one community, they may, in later years, have to compete in the job market with others from all over the country. Thus, it is valuable for parents and school personnel to be able to evaluate local school performance in relation to the nation as a whole.

Q. But aren't there other useful comparisons to be made?

A. Of course! And there are other kinds of norm groups besides the national norm group. The group chosen for comparison should depend on what information the school needs. It is quite possible and often advisable to compare individual pupils with pupils in a district or city, with other pupils in similar communities nearby, with all pupils in the state, and so on. These regional or local norms are developed in a way similar to that for national norms. However, they describe the pattern of performance for some more narrowly defined group.

Q. Why don't you have tests that tell you whether or not a pupil has learned a skill, regardless of what other pupils know?

A. Such tests do exist; they are called *objective-referenced* or *criterion-referenced tests.* In fact, the tests teachers use in their own classrooms are more like this kind of test than they are like norm-referenced tests. Suppose a teacher has given the class ten words to learn how to spell. At the end of the week, a teacher-made spelling test is given to see whether or not each pupil has learned to spell those ten words. The teacher is not interested in what percent of pupils nationally can spell those words; the question is, rather, "Can John spell these words or not?" An objective-referenced or criterion-referenced test is, then, a test that is used to determine whether or not an individual pupil has met an objective or a criterion of performance. An objective may be stated something like this: "The pupil can add two two-digit numbers requiring regrouping." Important questions arise, however, when you begin to plan an objective-referenced test. How many correct answers are needed to show that the pupil has achieved the objective? At what grade level should we expect a pupil to meet the objective? Should every pupil be expected to meet every objective? These are not easy questions to answer. Who will make the decisions? Other questions arise when a child does achieve the objective. Is it typical for a fourth-grader to achieve this objective? Do most fourth-graders know how to perform this task? Answering these questions brings us back to a comparison among individuals—or to a norm-referenced interpretation of test scores.

Of course, it is not necessary to choose between these two kinds of tests or ways of interpreting test results. Each way of looking at a pupil's performance provides useful information about what the schools are teaching and about what pupils are learning. In the future, more tests will probably be designed to offer both kinds of interpretation.

Q. Where can I get more information about testing?

A. You might first contact the testing coordinator or guidance director in your local school system. If there is a college or university nearby, you might seek information from the professor who teaches courses in tests and measurements. The testing of children is an important responsibility. We feel it is also part of our responsibility, as test publishers, to help you understand why and how testing is done. The staff of the Test Department at Harcourt Brace Jovanovich, Inc., will be glad to be of service. Write to one of our offices if you would like more help from us.

ON TELLING PARENTS ABOUT TEST RESULTS

In recent years and in various parts of the country, concerned parents have brought lawsuits against the schools, charging them with negligence for failure to supply adequate information about the progress of their children. Regardless of the legal merits of such cases, it is easy to understand and sympathize with the irate parents who, in some cases, have discovered only after their children have graduated from high school that they have some serious learning problem. A ruling by the courts is not necessary in order that a judgment may be made; the lack of adequate communication between the school and the parents can and often does pose a serious problem.

Two interdependent principles provide a sound basis for communicating with parents. First, parents have the right to know whatever the school knows about the abilities, the performance, and the problems of their children; and, second, the school has the obligation to communicate understandable and usable knowledge.

The parent's right to know is indisputable. But to know what? What type of communication is required of the schools in order that they may meet their obligation to supply understandable and usable information? The school grades that are periodically sent home on the children's report cards are sometimes misinterpreted by the parents. This is particularly true where homogeneous grouping is practiced in the school with grading based on performance within the group. A slow learner placed in a low section may stand well in that group and thus earn good grades while still performing below level for the grade as a whole. Testing across the entire grade level is necessary to reveal these discrepancies. In fact, it is difficult to get a complete and accurate idea of a child's performance without comparing it with the performance of other children of the same age and educational background. Such a comparison is best made through the use of a standardized test. Results obtained from standardized tests are by no means the only element needed to evaluate the child's progress, but they are a major element, contributing information important to both the school and the parent.

However, the same statistical data that make standardized tests useful to administrators and teachers can be the source of confusion and misunderstanding to parents unless they are put in the proper context. Before interpreting individual results for parents, it is important that they understand what standardized tests are like and what can and cannot be expected of them. Many schools adopt the policy of sending home a brief introductory statement on testing in general as a preparation for teacher conferences with individual parents.[5]

At the elementary level, the most advantageous way of telling parents about their children's standing in school is the parent-teacher conference. Ideally, both parents should be present, although in many cases, a discussion with one parent or a brief conference during a parents' day or night might suffice. Written communications mailed to the home or comments included with report cards are not desirable substitutes for a face-to-face discussion.

It is both reasonable and practical for the teacher to assume the responsibility of talking with the parents. The teacher is in contact with the child each school day and is most intimately aware of his or her behavior. It is the teacher who is identified in the minds of the parents as the person who is guiding and directing their child and is in all other ways responsible for the child's school learning. Moreover, the teacher is often in the best position to judge how much and what kinds of information should be communicated to individual parents.

No single reporting procedure can be appropriate for every kind of parent. To well-adjusted or well-educated parents, a numerical report of test scores may enhance their understanding of their child's status and of what the school has to give. To somewhat insecure and less knowledgeable parents, the identical information may result in misunderstanding that will be damaging to the child. Whenever test scores are given to parents, it is important to point out both their value and their weaknesses. The teacher should be prepared to explain why a particular test was chosen, the relevancy of its norms to the immediate situation, and the uses that are to be made of the test results. Since norms are expressed in numbers, parents may assume that they are infallible measures. In fact, they represent a range of values, not an absolute value. Also, they are subject to variation, part of which is due to the test itself while a larger part is due to the constantly changing conditions of the child.

---

[5]*Test Service Notebook No. 34,* "Some Things Parents Should Know About Testing," could serve this purpose. Copies are available from The Psychological Corporation.

Most parents will be best able to use and understand test scores when they are reported qualitatively, that is, when they are carefully explained in terms of what the child can and cannot do in the various subject areas. Added to the parents' wholesome desire to know how their child compares with other children is the desire to be of assistance in the improvement of the child's achievement. The parent-teacher conference gives the opportunity for exploring this possibility in practical and concrete terms.

Reporting on Readiness

Test results should never be reported to parents in a way that might give the erroneous impression that the child's educational future can be determined by the scores. This is particularly true in reporting on readiness. Readiness tests, which assess the skills and abilities that must be present before instruction in such fundamentals as reading and mathematics can be effective, are generally the first standardized tests given to the child. Tests in basic concepts determine whether the child has the necessary foundation for organizing his or her own experience, understanding the teacher, and communicating with others. Other types of readiness tests measure performance in those language, listening, and numerical skills that are important for early school success. They supply teachers and parents with valuable information concerning the *present* status of the child.

At this level, numerical scores can be particularly misleading. Children who are just beginning school are in a critical stage of development. Natural growth processes, planned activities, and normal experiences at home and at school can lead to rapid changes in the child's responses. Test results are best reported to parents in non-numerical, descriptive terms. A performance rating of *high, average,* or *low* is sufficient for all practical purposes; this should be accompanied by concrete examples of those specific skills and abilities in which the child needs help.

Many parents are in a position to give this help, and a good parent-teacher conference will include a description of activities that can easily be carried out at home. *The Metropolitan Readiness Test,* for example, offers a four-page Parent-Teacher Conference Report. This, in addition to describing the test and reporting the child's rating, gives a list of ways in which parents can help in skill development. The teacher is encouraged to use the report as the basis of discussion with the parents, but it is *not* recommended that it be mailed to the home. It is intended to facilitate joint teacher-parent planning for meeting the child's instructional needs.

However, test results and their applications are not the only components of a good report. It is the total child, with all the complexities and uniqueness of an individual personality, that is the concern of the parents. Social adjustment, behavioral patterns, emotional response, and general health are but a few of the other factors that contribute to an understanding of growth and development. When this type of information is coupled with an analysis of test results, the parents are in a better position to understand and benefit from the teacher's communication.

As an example of the type of information that might be given as the result of readiness testing, the following sample report might be helpful: "Your child, Alice, has good auditory and visual skills but is below average in language skills and lacks some of the basic concepts necessary to understand directions and communicate with others. Here are some of the things you can do to help her.

1. Read and look at books with her. Ask her to tell you about the pictures and stories.
2. Make up stories and ask her to end them.
3. Play word games in which you say a word and Alice says a word that means the opposite. Use words like 'above-below'; 'over-under'; 'inside-outside'; 'near-far.' Help her to understand these concepts by simple demonstrations.
4. Ask your child to sort objects according to size, type and use. Get her to explain what she has done.

Alice shows an eagerness to learn, but it is obvious that her lack of language skills makes communication difficult. She enters willingly into those activities that don't require speech but is shy and withdrawn during discussions or storytelling activities. She is receiving special help in class, but you can make learning easier for her by the help you give at home."

Another possible report on readiness, and one that unfortunately is often overlooked by teachers, might contain the following considerations: "Your child, Stephen, is ready to learn to read. Children with his skills have nothing to gain from our kindergarten readiness program and are likely to become bored with school if they are not allowed to progress at their own rate. It is when Stephen is not interested in what the class is doing that he becomes restless and disruptive. Let's discuss the advantages of having him join a reading group in Ms. X's class where the children are just at his level."

All information should be presented in a positive manner that will result in maximum benefit for the individual child, but the backbone of the report must be a truthful analysis of the pupil's present status.

Perhaps the most difficult report to make to parents is the type that must include the following considerations: "The results of Eric's posttest in readiness confirm the conclusions I have already reached regarding his progress. As you know, his initial scores were very low. I feel that, over the past months, you and I have worked as a well-integrated team in our efforts to help him. However, he has continued to fall farther and farther behind the children in his group. It is painful to watch, since he is very sensitive and well aware of his own difficulties. I would like to refer him to our school psychologist for further testing. There is a great deal that can be done through specialized instruction once the child's particular learning difficulty is identified."

Reporting on Achievement

Children's achievement in school can be reported to parents in two ways: by comparison with their peers and by comparison with their own past performance. The first type of report answers the question, "Is my child doing as well as other children of the same age and grade?" The second addresses the question, "How is my child progressing? Do the test scores indicate normal growth and development?" Both types of information can be readily obtained through analysis of the results of a standardized achievement test.

National and local norms provide the basis for comparisons across grade levels. National norms are based on a carefully selected sample representative of the nation's entire school population. They represent one important reality about the child's performance, but since no local community corresponds completely with a national cross section, norms based on the school system or district can also contribute to an accurate assessment.

Through the use of norms, the raw scores obtained by a pupil are converted into several different types of derived scores, each of which has usefulness to teachers and administrators. However, they are not all equally appropriate for reporting to parents. In this respect, the different kinds of scores vary considerably in the problems they pose.

Grade equivalents and *standard scores* of various kinds may substitute the illusion of precise, scientific communication for real communication. Standard scores have no more meaning for parents than raw scores, unless there is an opportunity for extensive explanation. Grade equivalents *seem* simple and straightforward, but serious misunderstandings may result from their use. For example, on a test given in the sixth month of the fifth year, the pupil with a grade equivalent of 5.6 would be performing "at grade level." A classmate with a grade equivalent of 7.3 would have done as well as the typical seventh-grader in the third month *on that fifth-grade test.* However, this does not mean that the fifth-grader can do seventh-grade work, since there are many things a seventh-grader has learned that are not measured on a fifth-grade test. In the same way, a 3.3 grade equivalent for a fifth-grader does *not* suggest that only third-grade material has been learned but that performance on the fifth-grade test was what might be expected of the average student in the third month of the third grade, given a fifth-grade test. Because they can so easily be misunderstood, grade equivalents are not recommended for reporting to parents.

If *percentile ranks* are to be used as part of the content of a report, their two essential characteristics must be made clear: (1) that they refer not to the percent of questions answered correctly but to the percent of children whose performance the pupil has equalled or surpassed, and (2) who, specifically, are the children with whom the pupil is being compared. The second point, a definite description of the comparison or norm group, is especially important in making the meaning of test results clear. Percentile ranks are specific to the particular group on which they are based and are not comparable from one subject to another. Parents may be misled if they learn of the standing of their child in one group and assume that this can be directly compared with the standing in another group.

Probably the best statistical data to give to parents are those produced through *stanine* groupings. Although they differentiate sufficiently for most reporting purposes, these broad categories prevent overinterpretation of small differences. Stanines may be based on the national standardization sample or on local community and school system distributions. They have the advantages of being comparable from one level to another up and down the scale. This simple nine-point scale is an easy concept to explain and illustrate and supplies sufficient information to tell parents where their child stands in relation to the peer group, both nationally and locally.

Stanines are defined descriptively as follows:

9 Very superior
8 Superior
7 Considerably above average
6 Slightly above average
5 Average
4 Slightly below average
3 Considerably below average
2 Poor
1 Very poor

Using these designations as a basis, the teacher can prepare reports that are qualitatively descriptive and that give an overall picture of the pupil's adjustment, not merely an isolated piece of information concerning how he or she scored on a particular test.

For example, users of the *Stanford Achievement Test* might use stanines to construct reports on three individual pupils as follows:

	Stanine		
Stanford Test	Pupil TM Gr 4	Pupil HD Gr 5	Pupil NH Gr 6
Vocabulary	6	6	5
Reading Comp.	3	8	6
Word Study Skills	3	3	7
Math. Conc.	6	5	9
Math. Comp.	6	4	7
Math. Appl.	7	5	5
Spelling	4	4	7
Language	3	5	6
Social Science	5	7	6
Science	3	7	7
Listening Comp.	6	9	5
OLMAT	5	6	5

Combining these data with work in the classroom and the teacher's own observations, a report to the parents for each of these pupils might contain the following remarks:

Pupil TM: "Tommy's best work is in mathematics, in which his achievement is above average. His Vocabulary and Listening Comprehension scores are also above average. These require no reading. Tommy's greatest need is to improve in reading. He is being given special instructions in phonics and is being encouraged to read more. If you will get easy, interesting books for him to read at home, the practice should be beneficial."

Pupil HD: "Helen is above average in Comprehension, both Reading and Listening. This ability is also reflected in her scores in Science and Social Studies. She has contributed a great deal to our class by developing and caring for our science table. She seems particularly interested in biology and has reported on some very interesting things. Her Word Study Skills are below average, and this could account for her Spelling scores, which are also slightly below average. I would also like to see her improve in Math. I will be sending home worksheets in Computation and Word Parts; you can help her by seeing that she does this homework and by giving her any assistance she needs."

Pupil NH: "Nancy's work is at or above average in all her subjects. She is a hard worker and seems to need approval. I hope you will be satisfied, as I am, with the quality of her work and will not try to push her to excel. She is a nervous child who seems to have difficulty making friends. I would like to see her entering into our games and play activities with the same enthusiasm she brings to her school work."

Stanine scores may also be used to supply the parents with information concerning the ongoing progress of their child. A cumulative pupil profile, including test scores for several years, can express in graphic form the consistencies and inconsistencies of both strengths and weaknesses. If a pupil has been losing ground in some subject area or is not performing at the level indicated by his or her achievement in previous years, a comparison of stanines on a graph or chart will afford a rapid, visual appraisal. Parents easily grasp the concepts involved in such profiling and welcome a frank explanation of accumulated test information.

The example that follows is for the *Metropolitan Achievement Tests* and shows the pupil's accumulated scores during the period from first to fourth grade. Each subtest has been plotted each year on the graph, and the record has been transmitted from one teacher to the next as the child advanced through school.

In discussing Louis' record with his parents, the fourth-grade teacher might note the following:

"There have been no unusual changes in Louis' progress from year to year. His reading skills are very good and have remained higher than his mathematics skills. Although a difference of one stanine is not usually considered significant, it appears that Louis is losing ground in mathematics. Failure to master very basic skills in the first

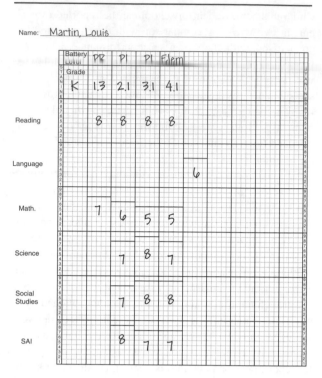

Metropolitan Achievement Tests Cumulative Record

Name: Martin, Louis

or second grade may have put him at a disadvantage. Even though his current achievement is at an average level, I felt diagnostic testing was needed. Our test showed that Louis' skills in subtraction are poor. Since he is able to finish reading assignments before the rest of the class, I am using this time to help him with his math."

Most achievement tests furnish the teacher with detailed information that would help to support the conclusions reached regarding Louis' progress in mathematics. A cluster analysis will show the number right out of the number possible for all the mathematics objectives covered by the test. In the example, Louis' low scores in problem solving and operations are indicative of the nature of his difficulty. This type of analysis by instructional objective is a useful method of reporting in detail on a child's particular strengths and weaknesses.

Reporting on Ability

The use of stanines also makes possible the construction of expectancy charts containing usable and readily understood information. These charts enable a teacher to interpret a pupil's obtained score on an achievement test by comparison with the score that would be expected for children of the same grade and level of scholastic aptitude. Of course, these "expectancies" must be based upon actual data obtained through the administration of specific achievement and school ability tests to the *same student population*. The resulting bivariate charts afford a general classification as follows: (1) low achiever—low achieve-

Cluster Analysis

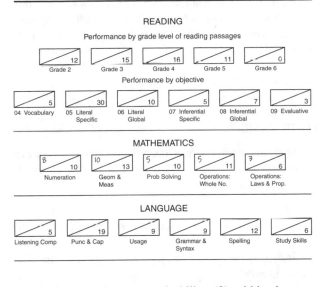

READING

Performance by grade level of reading passages

12	15	16	11	0
Grade 2	Grade 3	Grade 4	Grade 5	Grade 6

Performance by objective

5	30	10	5	7	3
04 Vocabulary	05 Literal Specific	06 Literal Global	07 Inferential Specific	08 Inferential Global	09 Evaluative

MATHEMATICS

8 10	10 13	5 10	5 11	3 6
Numeration	Geom & Meas	Prob Solving	Operations: Whole No.	Operations: Laws & Prop.

LANGUAGE

5	19	9	9	12	6
Listening Comp	Punc & Cap	Usage	Grammar & Syntax	Spelling	Study Skills

ment in relation to measured ability, (2) within the expected range—school ability and achievement well related, and (3) high achiever—high achievement in relation to measured ability.

The following chart shows the relationship between a school ability test and an achievement test in mathematics computation for a fourth-grade class of 25 pupils:

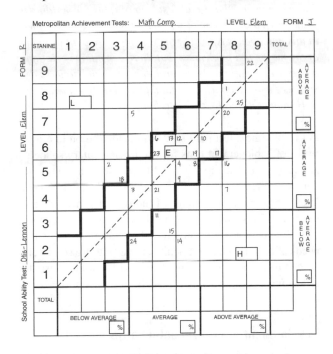

Where norms for a school ability test and an achievement battery have been based on the same population, it is possible to establish the predicted achievement range for each pupil in each of the learning areas covered by the achievement battery. Based on standardization data, each score obtained on the ability test is equated to a limited range of scores in the domains of reading, mathematics, science, etc. By comparing these established ranges with

the actual score achieved by each pupil in these domains, it is possible to determine whether individual achievement is comparable with what can reasonably be expected.

For example, when the fifth edition of the *Metropolitan Achievement Tests* is given in combination with the *Otis-Lennon School Ability Test,* achievement and ability can be compared by means of the Individual Report shown below.

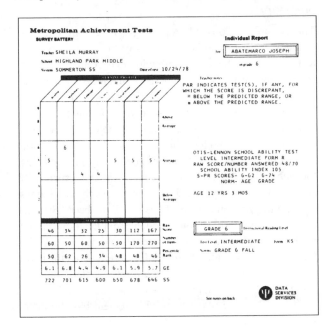

Although Joseph's achievement scores are average, his School Ability Index indicates that he is not performing as well as might be expected. This is particularly true in Language and Science, where he falls well below the predicted range. A report to his parents might include the following observations: "Joseph is much more interested in sports than he is in classroom activities. Although he has no difficulty keeping up with his lessons, his scores are somewhat disappointing. He is often disruptive in class, distracting the other children and neglecting his work. He says he wants to be a physician, and probably he has the necessary ability. I hope you can help me convince him that the study habits he forms now will help him later on and that our classroom work in science is a good preparation for more advanced studies. Frankly, his low score in Language surprises me. I feel he was just being careless when taking the test."

This type of comparison, between the pupil's own ability and present achievement, is the most important use of a school ability test for the vast majority of pupils. Other uses exist, such as screening for learning disabilities and identifying the gifted. However, no constructive purpose can be served by reporting the results of an ability test, *in isolation,* to parents. Although these tests give useful and reliable information regarding the pupil's likelihood of success in school-related subjects, the results obtained are subject to serious misunderstanding by those who do not recognize their limitations and their focus. Too often, school ability scores are regarded as measuring a fixed characteristic of the child tested and are used as a basis for a final conclusion rather than as a piece of information useful in further planning. Teachers should be aware of the potential danger of indiscriminately reporting these test scores to parents.

Summary

The examples of possible reports given here are intended to increase the teacher's awareness of the many ways that test scores can be combined with classroom work and teacher observations to give parents an understandable and usable assessment of their child's status and progress. Without the firm statistical basis made possible by the administration of a standardized test, an objective standard, essential to a true understanding of a child's school work, is missing. Parent-teacher conferences may fail by being too subjective, by stressing behavior at the expense of achievement, or by the inclusion of such ambiguous (though true) statements as "he is doing his best." Statistical data presented without adequate explanation can be misleading and useless. Test scores should be evaluated by the teacher in the light of other information about the pupil such as performance in class, attitude, motivation, etc. Mere numbers, no matter how accurate or comprehensive, can never take the place of good judgment based on personal experience.

Reports to parents may have far-reaching effects. Parental hopes and plans for their child's future will be largely based on the information they receive from the school. If these plans are unrealistically high, they have the right to know, even though the knowledge may be disappointing. On the other hand, parents should be alerted to the exceptional talents of their children in time to make long-term plans for an adequate educational future. Test scores form a basis upon which cooperation between parents and the school can be built toward the common goal of achieving the best possible education for our children.

EXERCISE 10-3
STANDARDIZED ACHIEVEMENT TESTS

OBJECTIVE

To enhance understanding of and provide firsthand experience with standardized achievement tests

BACKGROUND

Achievement tests measure accomplishment and may be classified along any of several dimensions such as standard-ized/unstandardized, general/specific, and evaluative/diagnostic.[6] But how is a standardized achievement test developed? And how should the results of an administration of a standardized achievement be reported to the community? After you've read the two articles that follow, you'll be better prepared to answer these questions and those that follow below.

YOUR TASK

You wish to create a standardized achievement test to evaluate mastery of the material in the chapter on educational assessment in your textbook.

1. In broad terms, state how you might go about developing such a standardized achievement test. Include a half-dozen or so sample items.
2. Discuss your plan for reporting the results to the community.

HOW A STANDARDIZED ACHIEVEMENT TEST IS BUILT

Lois E. Burrill, Test Department

There is no one, "hard-and-fast" set of rules for building a standardized achievement test series. Each step described in this notebook is typical of the way tests are built by many of the major test publishers, but there are many variations possible in technique. In general, the text which follows describes the development of standardized achievement tests at Harcourt Brace Jovanovich, Inc.

Let us assume a test publisher has decided to build a new series of achievement tests for use in elementary schools. Achievement tests are designed to measure the extent to which pupils have "achieved" or mastered the skills and knowledge that are the goals of the school's instructional program. The school should then be able to use the test results in planning an instructional program to meet the needs of each pupil. Since achievement tests are so closely related to curriculum, the publisher will build his tests to reflect what is typically being taught in classrooms around the country.

Development of Experimental Forms

An essential prelude, then, to determining what the content of the test will be is the identification of what is being taught country-wide: in other words, an analysis of the curriculum. Curricular analysis for a major achievement series

---

[6]This dimension refers to the ultimate use of the achievement test data: Will the data be used primarily to make an overall evaluation of mastery or to uncover diagnostic information about the examinee's strengths and weaknesses with respect to the subject matter?

Figure 1 Part of a Topical Analysis of Fifth-Grade Mathematics Texts. A, B, C, etc., refer to various well-known textbook series. The number entries are the percent of total pages devoted to the topic. Taken from Curricular Analysis for *Metropolitan Achievement Tests*, 1970 Edition.

Topic/Text	A	B	C	D	E
Fractions	23.4	29.0	26.4	23.4	19.4
Geometry	11.5	19.0	10.3	11.5	5.9
Rates & Ratios	13.2	2.0	2.6	12.3	2.5
Decimals	5.8	1.3	3.9	5.8	8.4
Graphs & Scale Drawings	2.7	4.0	4.8	2.7	4.4
Place Value	1.5	—	2.3	1.5	3.4
Measures	1.2	—	2.6	1.2	1.6
Other Number Bases	—	—	1.3	—	2.8

is a long and arduous task. It requires the detailed summarizing of published textbook series, syllabi, outlines of objectives, and other current curricular material from across the country. (See Figure 1.) In addition to analyses of current texts and course outlines, curriculum experts in each of the skills and subject matter areas to be tested are consulted for suggestions as to what trends the curriculum might be taking in the future. Since curricular analysis and prepublication research typically extend over a period of several years, it is essential for the test publisher to make an evaluation of future curriculum trends. (The transition from "traditional" to "modern" mathematics during the sixties is an example of the type of curricular change the test developer must anticipate in his determination of what content should be included.)

The end result of this process is a set of content outlines specifying behavioral objectives in each subject and skill area. The relative emphasis given to each objective is also analyzed so as to provide an indication of the percent of the test questions that should be developed to measure each one. The test developer will use this information as a blueprint in planning the building of the test. Often, these blueprints will be sent to curriculum experts for their review and comment.

The next step in the process is the actual writing of the test questions or items. Questions may be written by test authors, by teachers whom they employ to write questions, and/or by members of the publisher's staff. Item writing is not a simple process. The question, or stem, must state clearly what is being asked; the correct answer must be clear and unambiguous, and the incorrect choices (distractors) must be both attractive (to the examinee who *does not* know the answer) and clearly incorrect (to the examinee who *does* know the answer). Before ever being tried out, each test question may go through several cycles of editing, rewriting, and review by different experts. Curriculum specialists will study the questions to check that they measure objectives being taught in the classroom. Test construction experts will review them to be sure questions conform to rules of good item-writing. Other experts will

review questions to determine that the context of the question does not bias its validity for any particular subgroup of the population and to make sure they will not psychologically or emotionally "turn off" a youngster. Any drawings to be used in test questions must be planned, executed, and (particularly at the lower grade levels) carefully edited and reviewed right along with the test questions to be certain that all the objectives of the question are being met.

All questions in a standardized test will be "tried out" before being included in the final version of the test. Test publishers know from past experience that, no matter how thorough the reviewing process, a number of proposed questions will have to be discarded at that time for any of a number of reasons, which will be discussed below. At HBJ, editors also want to have a surplus of usable questions so that they can choose the best ones from among them. The total number of questions written, therefore, may be as many as three to four times the number of questions needed for the final versions of the test.

Many other details are discussed at this time. For example, decisions are made concerning the directions to the teacher and to the pupil. Sample questions will be written to acquaint the pupil with the task he will be asked to perform. Methods of indicating responses, types of answer documents, size of type, format of booklets, and such topics will be discussed.

After the many questions have been written and edited, they are assembled into experimental test forms for "tryout" and subsequent analysis. Typically, each of these experimental forms looks like a final test form and meets the specifications set up for the test in the blueprint. Often, however, each form has more items per objective than the final form is planned to have, and some or all forms may include sets of questions experimenting with a new "item type" or a new set of directions. In page size, layout, typography, directions for administration, etc., these forms will, however, be virtually identical with those planned for the final edition, since all these aspects of the test must also be "tried out" along with the items before final decisions are made.

Tryout: National Item Analysis Program

Tryout administration of these experimental forms is called an "item analysis" program. A publisher such as HBJ plans a research program in order to get a variety of information about the questions that have been developed for the test:

1. the difficulty level of each question—that is, what percent of the pupils in the total tryout group answer the question correctly.

2. the discrimination of each question—that is, how well the answering of this question correctly distinguishes between students who score high (within the top 27% of the sample) on the total test and those who score low (within the bottom 27% of the sample).

3. the grade progression in difficulty—that is, if a question is used in tests for several successive grades, does a progressively greater percent of pupils answer the question correctly at successively higher grades?

In addition to the statistical characteristics of individual questions, other types of information are obtained during the course of a good item analysis program. For example, teachers administering the experimental forms are requested to complete questionnaires asking their judgment concerning the appropriateness of content for their own classroom, the clarity of directions and questions, and other pertinent matters regarding the test.

The schools participating in an item analysis program are carefully chosen to be representative of the population for whom the test is designed. The communities are typically selected on the basis of such factors as size, geographical location, and socioeconomic level (as indicated by adult level of income and education, previous test results for pupils, etc.). A test of scholastic aptitude or mental ability is often administered as part of this achievement test tryout program in order to check on the ability levels represented by the participating schools and to provide a basis for matching the groups taking the various experimental forms.

Wherever possible, classroom teachers themselves administer the tests so that the administration situation will correspond as closely as possible with that in which the final published tests will be used. However, in a tryout administration, the tests are typically administered without time limits so as to give each pupil ample opportunity to attempt all items on the experimental form. Teachers record the time required for their classes so that final time limits can be determined in such a way as to make certain that every pupil will be able to finish the test in the allotted time. Experimental forms are also often administered in the grade just above and the one just below those for which the questions are ultimately intended, in order to secure further data on the questions.

Development of Final Forms

The selection of test items for the final forms of the tests is begun only after the results of the item analysis program have been carefully studied and interpreted by the team of authors and editors. (See Figure 2.) The final selection of these questions depends jointly on content specifications and statistical requirements. A number of general statistical guidelines for selection are usually set up for use in all tests in the series. The following set of guidelines was used for a recently published achievement series:

1. average difficulty level—the median difficulty level for the questions in the final test should be .55 for the target grade level (an average of 55 percent of pupils answering an item correctly).

Figure 2   Item Card Showing Data from the Item Analysis Research Program. 63.1 percent of the pupils in grade 3 answered this question correctly. Of the top 27 percent group, 90.1 percent got the correct answer; 25.6 percent of the bottom group also answered correctly. 9.3 percent of the total group marked "Don't Know," and 5 percent omitted the item. (Note the total percent correct for each grade 2–5, the grade progression of these percents correct, and the discrimination values for each grade. This is a pretty good item.)

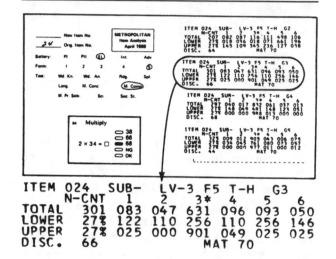

ITEM 024	SUB–		LV–3	F5 T–H		G3
N–CNT	1	2	3 ✱	4	5	6
TOTAL	301	083	047	631	096	093	050
LOWER	27%	122	110	256	110	256	146
UPPER	27%	025	000	901	049	025	025
DISC.	66			MAT 70		

2. range of difficulty values—the various questions in the final form should range in difficulty from .90 to .20 for the pupils in the grade for which the test is intended.
3. item discrimination—except for very easy or very difficult questions, the items in the final form must distinguish clearly between high- and low-scoring pupils.
4. grade progression—the difficulty level of each question for each grade in which it was tested should indicate an increasingly larger percent correct, grade by grade.

The questions that have survived the tryout administration phase are again reviewed by outside experts who are familiar with the needs and styles of pupils from a variety of minority backgrounds in an attempt to make sure that no questions are inappropriate or offensive to such children. Then the selected items are divided into the various final forms in such a way as to make each form match both the content and statistical specifications previously agreed upon. Both careful development of content specifications and tryout of all proposed questions are vital to the building of a test that will be worth standardizing.

The procedure described above could be applied, with some modifications, to many test-building tasks, whether or not norms were to be developed for the instrument. However, in order to complete the development of a *standardized* test, several further steps must be taken. Part of a typical definition of a standardized test would read something like ". . . and interpreted in reference to certain normative information." The development of those norm data is the next step in the building of a standardized test.

Norming: The National Standardization Program

Norms provide the means for comparing the performance of one pupil or group of pupils with that of some particular reference group. There are many types of reference groups which might be used. Norms may be developed by age or sex, for particular geographical areas, for private schools, for suburban areas, or for other distinct groups. To develop a norm, however, the norm group must be carefully defined.

Let us suppose that our hypothetical test publisher has determined that the group for which his test is being developed is the total elementary school population. Therefore, the most important norm data he must collect is for that reference group. He has already collected preliminary data from one sample of the national school population in his item analysis. Now, by a process called standardization, he will develop national normative information for the final forms of the test. This research program will yield data on the performance of a sample of pupils selected to represent the total population of pupils. When the sample has been well chosen, one can assert with reasonable confidence that the norms developed from these data truly reflect the performance of the national school population in all its variety. The quality of the job the test developer does in selecting this sample population and in describing it to the user will, therefore, have tremendous long-range effects on the confidence with which test users can apply the norms.

Many variables are used to select these "reference group" samples and later to describe them. They include characteristics of pupils themselves (chronological age, sex, mental ability scores, etc.), characteristics of school systems (public-private, teachers' salaries, time spent teaching various subjects and skills, etc.), and characteristics of the communities which the schools serve (geographical area, size of city, level of adult schooling and income, etc.). Clearly, the characteristics that are used as criteria in sampling should be those which have been shown to be related to test performance and on which information is reasonably accessible both to test developer and to test user. For example, Harcourt Brace Jovanovich, Inc., in selecting school systems for its standardization samples, uses the following community variables:

1. size of community
2. geographic region
3. socioeconomic index (the community's median family income and median years of schooling for persons over 24 years, combined and classified in some manner)

Using national census data for each of these variables, the test developer will draw up a model to indicate how many sample cases from communities of various types should be included in the total so as to reflect the makeup of the total national school population. School systems, chosen randomly from a list of all schools, are classified with respect to each of these variables and assigned to a cell. Certain school systems then are invited to participate in the standardization. These systems are selected in such a way as to produce a representative sample of all school systems in the nation. Other similarly classified school systems are selected as alternates to fill needed slots whenever a chosen system is unable or unwilling to participate. Schools agreeing to inclusion in the sample will be asked to provide many other pieces of information that will be useful in describing the sample population. Included in such questionnaires may be items regarding teachers' salaries and experience, promotion and grouping policies, length of school year, entrance age, availability of kindergarten experience, textbooks in use, tests used in the system, etc.

The test developer may also set up criteria for his norm group in terms of individual pupil characteristics—usually chronological age and mental ability as measured by some standardized instrument. Although he cannot get more than a rough indication of these attributes before his actual testing begins, he will adjust his sample afterwards, as is illustrated in the following example. Frequently, a criterion for the norm group is that the mental ability of the pupils match the mental ability of the national population both in average ability and the spread above and below average. This is usually checked by administering, along with the achievement test being standardized, an already-standardized mental ability test. The data thus collected will be analyzed to determine the median mental ability as well as the variability of ability scores for the sample. Some adjustments may have to be made, either by eliminating cases or by weighting the results of various school systems, in order to correct any errors in the original selection of the sample and to make sure that the total national school population is in fact accurately represented in this standardization sample. If the original design was well planned, little adjustment will be necessary.

The development of the norms themselves is one of the most important aspects of standardized test construction. From the scores of the pupils in the norm sample, distributions of raw scores on each level or "battery" of the tests are made. To give meaning to these scores and to provide national benchmarks, various kinds of national norms may be developed. For elementary achievement tests, the types most often developed include grade equivalents (GEs), percentile ranks (PRs), and stanines (Ss). The Harcourt Brace Jovanovich Test Department usually provides all three types of national norms for its new tests. The following sections briefly describe each type of norm and the way in which it is developed.

The development of grade-equivalent norms is quite complicated, and several steps are required. First, in order to be able to translate raw scores from several different batteries or levels of the test into a single scale of grade equivalents, the raw scores on each level of the test must be related to the raw scores on the other levels. To accomplish this, pairs of tests are given to special, experimental groups, and the equivalent raw scores from one test to the next are determined. In this way, raw scores on all levels can be translated into a single set of numbers. These numbers are then marked along the vertical axis of a graph, with the school years marked along the horizontal axis in months (1.0–9.9). Next, the median (middle) scores from each grade level of the standardization sample are plotted on the graph, and the straight lines connecting each pair of points are smoothed out into a curved line. (See Figure 3.) From this norm line, then, the grade-equivalent scores for each possible test score can be read and tabled. It must be remembered, however, that the only grade equivalents that are actually derived from the standardization testing are those for the one time of year at which the test was standardized: i.e., 3.2, 4.2, 5.2, etc. The other grade equivalents are estimates taken from the smoothed curve between the obtained grade equivalents. This "interpolation" of the in-between grade equivalents involves the assumption that growth is evenly spread throughout the school year.

This explanation of how the grade-equivalent norms are developed may also help explain the meaning of the grade equivalent. It is a way of expressing how the raw score of a pupil taking one test compares with the scores obtained by the *average pupils at each grade level* in the standardization administration of all levels of the test. If a pupil achieves a raw score equal to a grade equivalent of 5.8, that means his *score* was similar to that of the average fifth-grader in the eighth month of the fifth grade. From the explanation given above, however, it also can be seen that a third-grader, taking the test designed for the third grade, may have answered a quite different set of questions from the set answered by the fifth-grader taking a fifth-grade set of questions, although both achieve the same grade-equivalent score.

Percentile rank norms provide quite a different interpretation of test scores. Instead of comparing a pupil with average pupils over a whole range of grade levels, his score is compared only with those of others at his own approximate grade placement. A percentile rank for a given raw score indicates the percent of pupils at a particular grade placement in the norm group who received scores equal to or lower than the given raw score. Developing percentile rank norms for the time of year the test was standardized is a relatively simple matter. The distribution of raw scores for the grade is plotted on a normal percentile chart, a smooth curve is fitted to the points, and the PR for each raw score is read off. (See Figure 4.) Our test developer could let it go at that and provide percentile rank norms only for the time of year the test was standardized. However, he will probably want to provide at least two, perhaps three, sets of norms for various times of the school year (beginning, middle, and end of year, for example). Unless he standardizes his test at all of these times and with very carefully matched groups, he will have to "interpolate" norms for times of the year other than those at which he actually standardized. This is not complicated, but it involves again the assumption that growth proceeds at a constant rate throughout the school year. (See Figure 5.)

Stanine norms make use of a nine-point scale of standard scores, with a mean of 5 and a standard deviation of 2. For a normal distribution of scores such as those obtained in a national standardization, the correspondence between percentile ranks and stanines is fixed. For such distributions, the development of stanines is automatic, once percentile ranks are available. For example, the range of percentile ranks 40 through 59 becomes stanine 5. (See Figure 6.)

National norms, as described above, have meaning for all school systems, regardless of the ways in which a system's pupils may be different from the national population as a whole. This is true because national norms describe one reality, i.e., the typical performance of the nation's schoolchildren. In this respect they are an important frame

Figure 4   Schematic Illustration of Percentile Rank Norm Lines for One Subtest, Grades 5.1 and 6.1

R.S.	Percentile		1	5 10 20 30 50 70 80 90 95	99
	5th	6th			
30-31		100			
28-29	100	98			
26-27	99.7	95			
24-25	99	89			
22-23	98	82			
20-21	95	73			
18-19	91	64			
16-17	84	53			
14-15	75	43			
12-13	63	33			
10-11	50	24			
8-9	35	15			
6-7	20	8.3			
4-5	8.3	3.2			
2-3	2.1	.7			
0-1	.2	.1			

1   5 10 20 30 50 70 80 90 95   99
Percentile Scale

Figure 3   Schematic Illustration of Grade-Equivalent Norm Line for One Subtest, Grades 2.2–9.2

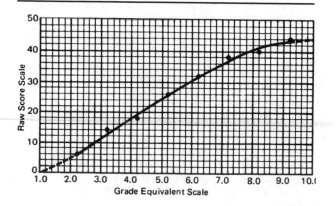

Figure 5 Schematic Illustration of Percentile Rank Norm Lines for Beginning, Middle, and End of Year

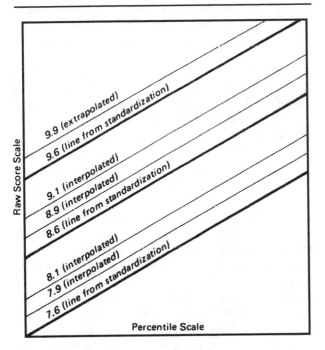

Figure 6 Schematic Illustration of a Normal Distribution of Scores, Showing the Relationship Between Percentile Ranks and Stanines

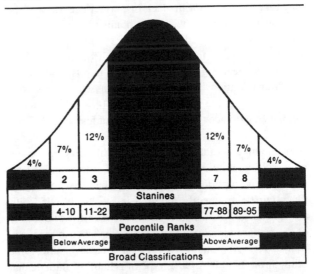

of reference. However, our test publisher may choose to provide other sets of norms for certain subgroups of the population. Thus, he may develop distributions of raw scores for pupils in large cities or for suburban areas, for geographical regions or for types of schools (Catholic school norms, for example). From these distributions, the publisher may develop percentile rank or stanine norms. It should be noted, however, that grade-equivalent norms are never developed for any norm group other than the national school population.

The Manual: Information for the Test User

In selecting a standardized test series to fill his own testing needs, the prospective test user should look for assurances that the test is appropriate for his system and that, in fact, the norm sample population is "representative" of the total national school population. The test developer, in his manual for the test, will usually take care to describe the way in which the norm or standardization group was chosen and, as well, to describe that sample in terms of other criteria related to school performance. The test user should, moreover, look for evidence that the test itself is good of the purposes for which he intends to use it, since even "beautiful norms" are worthless if they are for a test with no value in his specific situation. The test publisher will probably collect the pertinent information and data into a manual for the test. Much of what the test user needs to evaluate the true worth of the test itself will typically be presented in sections labeled *validity* and *reliability*.

Validity may be described as the degree to which a test serves the purpose for which it is used; that is, how close it

comes to doing what you want it to do. Since validity is specific to the purposes of the test, different kinds of validity evidence are appropriate to different kinds of tests. Most survey achievement tests are intended to assess current status in the subject areas being tested. They are in this sense, then, a sample set of items which are representative of a universe of information. The type of validity information most needed by the user is the blueprint or set of specifications on which the test was built and which has been described earlier. Test publishers will typically include some such content outline information in the manual. The user himself will then make his own determination of *content validity:* that is, the degree to which the test's specifications match his school's own objectives and curriculum. Included in the manual as well may be a discussion of the way in which the blueprint was developed, by whom, and other pertinent data.

The test developer cannot present statistical data to support a claim of content validity, since such validity must be specific to each school. Publishers may, however, present correlations of test scores with some other criterion (perhaps another well-known achievement test) as evidence of the validity or usefulness of the new test.

One of the most fundamental requirements of any measurement is that it be reliable; in other words, the obtained scores should be dependable. Test *reliability* may be described as the extent to which a test is consistent or stable in its measurement of whatever it is measuring. As with other measuring instruments, however, no test is perfectly accurate. The degree of accuracy possible depends in part on the fineness of the distinctions the test is expected to make. The greater the spread of scores the pupils have obtained, the more reliably the test will be able to distinguish among them. Since there is no one reliability figure for a test, the figures the test publisher presents are estimates of the test's reliability under typical circumstances. The publisher will also present, along with the reliability estimates, estimates of the "measurement error." In this way, the user may take into account the lack of perfect accuracy of the test when he interprets the scores obtained.

We noted, in the section describing the item analysis, the attention given to the degree to which questions distinguished between high- and low-scoring pupils. The total of the discrimination indices for questions chosen for final forms gives a crude indication of reliability and thus a preliminary assurance that the standardized test will be fairly reliable.

At the time of standardization, several statistical procedures will be employed in analyzing the data, and the results will be reported as evidence of the test's reliability. One statistic frequently reported is the "split-half" reliability coefficient, which is obtained when the two halves of the test are correlated to provide an answer to the question, "How consistently is the test measuring the same thing throughout?" Another type of reliability statistic that may be presented is the "test-retest" or "alternate-form" reliability coefficient, which is an indication of the correspondence between results on alternate forms and thus a measure of their reliability.

Since no test score is ever completely reliable, the test's developer may include data in his manual estimating the possible magnitude of error in the obtained scores of individuals. These data are called standard errors of measurement and are usually given for each test at each grade. He may also present data concerning the heterogeneity of his norm sample by giving the standard deviations of test scores of his norm groups as well as their mean and median scores. When more than one form of a test is published, the test developer may provide evidence in the test manual that the alternate forms are comparable. As we have seen, the final forms are built to be as alike as possible in terms of item analysis data. However, the standardization program will probably either standardize each form directly or include a supplementary experimental program in which alternate forms will be administered to matched groups in order to relate scores on other forms to scores on the standardized form.

The test developer may include data concerning the intercorrelations among subtest scores in his achievement battery, the correlation of the achievement test scores with mental ability test scores, data concerning sex differences in test scores, and so on. Finally, the test publisher will usually give the test user suggestions for the interpretation and use of test scores by teachers, curriculum specialists, guidance counselors, and administrative personnel. These should be considered "must" reading for any test user who wishes to get the greatest possible benefit from his use of the test.

When all of these procedures have been completed and the results analyzed and interpreted and written up in a way the test user will find meaningful, the new standardized achievement test is ready for publication.

The paragraphs above have described only the building of a standardized achievement test. Of course, many other types of test instruments may be built and standardized by a test publisher, including tests of general mental ability or school learning potential, prognostic and diagnostic tests of various types, tests of specific aptitudes, interest and personality measures, etc. Many of the steps in developing these other types of tests are similar to those described above; in other ways, however, they may be quite different. In choosing the questions for a standardized scholastic aptitude test, for instance, emphasis would be placed not on the content of the curriculum but rather on skills or tasks which are found to be predictive of success in academic programs. In such cases, too, the type of validity sought is predictive rather than content validity, and the estimates of reliability will be concerned more with stability over time than are those used in estimating the reliability of achievement measures.

Standardized tests are an important tool for evaluation of the educational process, but they are not the only type of test that publishers build. The essence of a standardized test is in the use of a norm-reference: that is, that scores on the test are described in terms of a comparison with the scores others have made on the same test. The other major category of test instruments is those that use a criterion-reference rather than a norm-reference. Scores on criterion-referenced tests are described not in terms of a comparison with what others have done but in terms of the degree of attainment of some specific criterion or standard of achievement.

Because criterion-referenced and norm-referenced tests are built for different purposes and used in different ways, the techniques used to build them are also somewhat different. The present publication deals only with norm-referenced tests. A later publication will take up the question of how a criterion-referenced test is built.

The development of a good test instrument, of whatever type, is a time-consuming and demanding task. At Harcourt Brace Jovanovich, Inc., several years of research and development go into the publication of a major standardized test series. The painstaking care with which a published test has been developed, however, will help to assure that the resulting instrument will be of value to all those involved in the educational process.

REPORTING STANDARDIZED ACHIEVEMENT TEST RESULTS TO THE COMMUNITY

Lois E. Burrill

A recent development in the field of education has been the emergence of the notion of "accountability." There has been growing public concern about the quality of our educational system and about the effectiveness of the money being spent for education both locally and at the federal level. There is nothing especially new in the concept of educational responsibility. Implicit in local supervision of the educational process is the requirement that school personnel keep the public informed concerning educational matters. However, the demand for "hard data," for facts and figures, for scientific quantification of the educational process has been growing steadily.

In the past, many school administrators have been extremely reluctant to publicize test results, because they recognized the possibility of misunderstanding and the dangers of misinterpretation. A disgruntled school board member has been quoted as saying, "The school officials seem to assume that the public cannot understand (the meaning of test scores) if results are announced."

How can these opposing viewpoints be reconciled? There are two principles that we believe should govern decisions regarding the reporting of test score information to the community. They are:

1) Specific score units, such as grade equivalents, percentile ranks, stanines, and standard scores, are not self-interpreting. Consequently, they may become sources of error and confusion within the school system itself as well as in the public press. Most measurement specialists are aware that test scores by themselves represent incomplete information about school achievement. Certainly, the non-specialist cannot be expected to interpret isolated test scores correctly.

2) On the other hand, in our tradition of tax-supported, community-controlled public education, the public *has* the "right to know." In fact, if an educational system is to operate at all, the public should be in possession of *all* the pertinent information upon which educational decisions are to be made. Since testing is a legitimate educational activity, part and parcel of the total instructional program, parents, school board members, and the entire tax-paying public must be fully informed about this aspect of the school's instructional program.

These two principles, taken together, indicate that the school must be ready to report test results (as well as all other kinds of information about the functioning of the school) to its constituency as a matter of course. To communicate effectively, schools must report enough information and in such a way as to make it meaningful and useful to the general public. The key phrase is *effective communication*. The highly technical statistical summaries prepared by testing professionals should be avoided.

The community to which this discussion refers is more inclusive than that of the system's pupils and their parents; it extends to all residents of the community. In a broad sense, of course, effective communication is necessary with several "communities," i.e., the pupils themselves, their parents, and the school staff. Further discussion regarding the reporting of individual or group test results to these communities is, however, beyond the scope of this discussion. We have also chosen to limit the discussion to the reporting of results on standardized achievement tests.

This should not be taken to mean that effective communication does not include the reporting of information concerning other parts of the testing program—far from it. But while many school systems have differing policies with regard to both the administration and the reporting of aptitude, mental ability, interest and/or personality tests, the majority of school systems do have survey achievement testing programs. Furthermore, the public is probably most interested in knowing about students' achievement in the skills and knowledges that are the goals of the instructional program.

Planning a Program of Effective Communication

Although the focus of this presentation is on the reporting of test results to the public, the test results are really only one aspect of the total testing program of the school. The whole program may be considered to have three major phases: (a) designing and planning the program, (b) administration of the tests, and (c) interpreting and using the results. Effective communication between school and community should be planned for and included in each of these phases.

Effective Communication Before Testing Begins

The first steps toward reporting test information should be taken well in advance of the actual testing dates for the current year. There are a number of topics that may be presented to the community at the time the testing program is planned. Effective communication at this time will help to prepare the way for better understanding of both the uses and the limitations of standardized test data. The following paragraphs include examples of this type of reporting.

1. The nature of the testing program

a. Why are you testing? School personnel may recognize the role of measurement in the teaching-learning process, but it is helpful to develop a clear statement for the public. Every effort should be made to clarify the rationale behind survey achievement testing and to help the public become aware of the usefulness of test results in the ongoing planning of the school. At the same time, it must be made quite clear that survey tests do not answer all the questions that need to be asked and that the total evaluation process of the school includes many additional techniques.

b. What are you testing? The public should be informed about what testing is being done; that is, what tests are being used, at what grades, and in what skills or content subject matter areas. The school's report might well include the publisher's description of what each test or subtest is designed to measure. A time schedule for testing might also be included here.

c. What real use will be made of the results? This question is part of the larger one involving the school's reasons for testing in the first place, but some specific information is in order here. Will results be used in decisions regarding remedial reading staffing? In the evaluation of a new math program? In a longitudinal study of some aspect of the instructional program? The public should be informed of these special uses of test results in decision making as well as about the ongoing evaluation of strengths and weaknesses in the instructional program.

d. What is a standardized test, anyway? What is a grade equivalent? What are norms? Test publishers and users are so accustomed to their own jargon that it is sometimes difficult to remember that it is not well understood by others. There are a number of concepts that are important for the public to understand. It would be well to describe how a standardized test differs from a teacher-made classroom test, how national norms are derived and what they mean, and so on. Descriptive definitions of testing terms may prove useful to the school staff charged with writing releases concerning the school's testing program and may also serve as a quick reference for news media personnel. A publication containing a narrative description of such terms is available upon request from Information and Advisory Services, The Psychological Corporation.

II. The uses and limitations of standard achievement tests

It is advisable to emphasize, *before testing begins,* that standardized test scores, valuable as they may be, are only part of the school's total evaluation program. They cannot "tell all." Many goals of the school's program cannot be measured by a paper-and-pencil test. Attitudes, interests, and many other areas must be evaluated in other ways. The public should also be cautioned that scores from even the best available tests lack precision. When information is expressed in numbers, we are all prone to assume a degree of exactness that test scores do not merit. It is important to point out that our instruments for measuring a child's height or weight or eyesight are more precise than those we have for measuring his reading comprehension or his potential to master a foreign language. The public should be cautioned that test results are estimates based on observations and that, as with all observations, there are inherent limitations to their use. These comments need to be made *before* testing begins, although they bear repeating when test results are reported. Waiting until after the results are in to point out the shortcomings of testing may appear to the public as an avoidance of responsibility. On the other hand, mention of the limitations of standardized tests should not be allowed to overshadow the fact that test scores are usable and useful; that they can be, in fact, tremendously valuable as part of the total evaluation process.

III. Nonschool factors related to achievement

It is a common misconception that the average achievement test scores can be interpreted by themselves as a di-

rect index of the effectiveness of school instruction. Too often, tests are taken to be an accurate yardstick for measuring the quality of teaching—even of education in general. If the scores surpass the national norms, there is a strong temptation to consider them as "proof" of the superiority of a school's teachers, methods, and/or materials. If the scores are lower than norm, there is a tendency to blame the school and even individual teachers or administrators.

It is all too easy to forget that many other factors are involved in the determination of a group's average performance. Characteristics of the pupil population, their parents, and the community as a whole may influence the relative achievement of the pupils to a considerable degree. Every pupil's achievement pattern is the result of a highly complex combination of factors that have been interacting for many years, both prior to and during school attendance. The quality of the instruction received is, naturally, vitally important, but it is far from being the only factor influencing achievement. Some of the factors considered to be most crucial are discussed briefly in the following paragraphs. The list is by no means complete, but the characteristics discussed may be those the school will wish to include in pretesting releases.

It should be noted that several variables known to correlate with school achievement are *not* mentioned in these paragraphs, among them the racial mix of the school population, socioeconomic status of parents, and educational level of parents. The omission is intentional. Although it is known that these factors are statistically related to achievement at the present time, the nature of the relationship is by no means clear. And it is likely that the reason these variables *seem* to predict achievement is that they form a rough index to the more general characteristics described below, especially those relating to the nature of the community. While it is far easier to quantify "years of education of adults" than it is to quantify "value placed on education," the more critical variable is almost certainly the latter. We would urge, therefore, that any discussion of the nonschool factors related to achievement stress these affective characteristics rather than the census-type data.

Discussion of the factors influencing achievement is difficult at best, and unless it is well done, the resulting story may appear to "whitewash" the school of any responsibility for student achievement, when in fact the instructional program should attempt to compensate for any influences that may handicap learning.

A. Characteristics of the individual pupil

Potential for academic learning. In school-learning aptitude, as with most other human characteristics, there is a wide range of individual differences. Pupils differ greatly in their ability to demonstrate mastery of the skills and knowledges that are the goals of our instructional system.

Personal characteristics. Although it is difficult to assess the extent of their influence, it is inevitable that a pupil's health, personality traits, social adjustment, and interests affect, to some extent, both a pupil's achievement and the ability to demonstrate that achievement on a standardized achievement test. Desire to learn, interest in school, and willingness to put forth maximum effort are also contributing factors.

Activities outside of school. The way in which a child spends his or her time outside of school hours may either stimulate or tend to retard progress in school.

Previous attendance and achievement pattern. Pupils who move frequently from school to school, or who are absent from school a considerable proportion of the time, may be handicapped in their ability to profit from classroom instruction. School learning is a sequential process, with each day's achievement and each year's performance building on competencies already developed. Pupils who have not mastered the basic skills will experience increasing difficulty over the years not only in those skills but also in other content areas that utilize those skills, e.g., reading skills in social studies, mathematics skills in physics. Previous experiences of "success" and "failure" in school, as perceived by the pupil, may also affect confidence and the motivation to do well.

B. Characteristics of pupils' homes and of the community at large

The value placed on education. A pupil's perception of school, its importance, and its value is influenced most strongly by family attitudes. But to a considerable extent, the community as a whole also plays a role in providing an atmosphere where formal learning is either valued and sought after or considered as something from which to escape.

The degree of school-home and school-community cooperation. In many instances, the effectiveness with which the school communicates both with parents and with the total community has a marked influence on the attitude and performance of pupils within the school. In like manner, the degree to which parents and community are involved in the school's goals and activities may profoundly affect the pupil performance level in the school.

The opportunities provided by home and community for augmenting school learning. The average pupil is under the direct influence of a teacher about thirty hours a week during the nine or ten months of the school "year." It is, therefore, likely that some of the learning measured in an achievement test takes place *outside* the classroom. The degree to which *outside* learning experiences reinforce and enrich classroom instruction may have considerable influence on measured achievement.

IV. School-related factors influencing achievement

If the school wishes to do so, some of these factors may also be discussed in releases made prior to testing. Factors that may be mentioned include per-pupil expenditure, classroom size, special staff available, teacher experience and training, and staff mobility or turnover. We would also include here the school's preparedness to instruct pupils whose native language is not English. In other words, the factor critically affecting the achievement of non-English-speaking children is not their native language, but the ability of the school to plan an appropriate instructional program for them.

Effective Communication at the Time of Testing

The school's survey testing program itself typically extends over a period of several weeks. During this period, the communication emphasis is directed primarily toward teachers, parents, and pupils rather than toward the community at large. To get the most from the testing program, school administrators should make every effort to ensure that the entire school staff supports the program; that they understand why the testing is being done, how the results are to be used, and the role each of them plays in the program's success. Truly effective communication with teachers and other school personnel would include pretest workshops, used to demonstrate techniques of test administration and to explain how the information obtained will be useful to them in their daily classroom work.

In turn, teachers and other school staff need to be able to communicate effectively with pupils and their parents. The anticipation as well as the actual experience of taking a test is sometimes an upsetting experience for children. The notion of testing may be anxiety-producing for parents as well. We talk about testing as being fundamentally for the good of the pupils, but how well is this fact communicated to them and to their parents? If teachers themselves are persuaded of the value of the testing, they may be able to talk with their pupils, explaining why the test is being given and how a better understanding of their own strengths and weaknesses can be helpful to them. Most importantly, pupils and their parents need to be reassured that the testing is being done *for* them, not *to* them, and that its purpose is not to label or judge individuals but to enable the school to plan for their continued learning. To create this climate for a successful testing program is not easy, but the degree to which it is achieved will have real significance for the value of the test results.

Effective Communication After Testing Is Completed

Reporting test results is the most difficult phase of effective communication between school and community. The task of making numerical data meaningful to the school staff and especially to the general public is critical to the success of the entire testing venture. Since the ways in which these data are reported and interpreted are extremely important, appropriate personnel within the system must give careful thought to two questions: *What* should be reported to *whom*? And *how* should the information be presented? No data should be released to the news media or any other group until they have been carefully analyzed and put into a format that will make them comprehensible to the audience to whom they are being reported. It is important, however, that this process be completed as soon as possible after the test results are available. A "leak" that leads to the publication of the data out of its appropriate context and without meaningful interpretation can be painfully counterproductive.

The following steps, taken prior to the release of test data to the news media or the general public, have proved helpful in a number of communities. First, the appropriate school administrators should be informed regarding test results for the system in general and for their individual districts or buildings in particular. Giving them this information before it is released to the public is not merely a courtesy. These administrators at the local district or building level will carry much of the burden of later explanation and interpretation of results, and it is critical that they be prepared to answer any questions that may arise. In a number of large school districts principals and other administrative personnel are called together and presented with the test results along with explanations of their import. They are given an opportunity to comment on or question the data and the interpretation placed on these data. In some school districts, administrators are also given a kit of materials containing a suggested agenda for a local-level meeting, capsule information on the testing program of the school system, good, down-to-earth layman's definitions of test terms, and information regarding types of test scores and what they mean. Some of these materials could be made into visual aids to be used in reporting to parents and other concerned citizens.

In many school systems, posttest workshops are held for teachers and other school staff to inform them of the results for their own classrooms, buildings, and districts both in relation to local or national normative data and in relation to results of past years' testing programs. Appropriate subjects for these workshops are: reporting test information to pupils and parents, the teachers' use of the test score information in improving and individualizing instruction, and the implications of test results for restructuring the curriculum.

A third procedure that has been found helpful in many areas is a carefully planned presentation of test results to the local school board. Such a presentation might parallel that described above for the school's administrative personnel. It is most important that lay school board members be given an adequate interpretation of what the results mean (and what *cannot* be inferred as well). Often this information is presented to the board in a formal report incorporating charts, graphs, and other descriptive information.

Once a formal report has been made to the school board, the document becomes public information. In the past, many school districts have been content to let the report "speak for itself." However, many school districts find it advisable to hold a press "briefing" or background session for representatives of the local press, radio, and television. At such a session, conducted by appropriate school personnel, information regarding the how and why of the testing program may be added to data in the written report. Explanations of the nature of standardized tests, types of scores, the meaning of "norms," and factors that influence achievement might also be included in such a session. The news coverage of the testing program is more likely to contain accurate interpretations of the test data if reporters have had an opportunity to become informed about tests and testing in general as well as about the specific results. Reporters must also be given ample opportunity to ask questions and to challenge the school staff's interpretation of the data. The school's representative must be prepared to answer difficult questions.

One further comment should be made. Distortion in the reporting of test results is sometimes an inevitable result of political or factional controversy within the community. More often, however, misrepresentation of the test results is not deliberate but is due to a lack of understanding on the part of the writer, reporter, or graphic artist who attempts to interpret a table of figures provided by the school system. Some common misunderstandings will be discussed below, but, in general, the more complete the information supplied by the school system, the more likely it is that the published accounts will accurately report the results of the testing program.

Guidelines for Preparing Reports of Achievement Test Results

Determining what achievement test results should be reported to the community is, in the final analysis, an administrative policy decision that must be made at the local level. It should be understood, therefore, that the following discussion includes suggestions that we believe merit thoughtful consideration.

1. Do not use grade equivalents in reporting test results to the community.

Grade equivalents *seem* simple and straightforward, but serious misunderstandings may result from their use. For example, a score of 5.2 on a third-grade test does not mean that the pupil is capable of doing fifth-grade work; it simply means that the third-grader did as well *on that third-grade test* as the average fifth-grader would be expected to do on the same test. Likewise, a score of 1.2 would not mean that the third-grader could do only first-grade work. It would mean that, on that test, the average first-grader would probably achieve the same score.

2. In reporting average scores for groups of pupils, do not use mean scores unless your test provides norms for group averages. Do not use individual pupil norms to interpret mean group performance.

Most recently published standardized achievement batteries (including the Metropolitan and Stanford) provide group norms as well as individual pupil norms. Group norms describe the distribution of group averages within the standardization; the more familiar individual norms describe the distribution of individual pupils' scores. It is not hard to see that individuals vary much more than do groups; therefore, to use the wrong benchmark may be very misleading to the public.

For example, let's suppose that a particular score on a fifth-grade reading test converted to a percentile rank of 54 and a stanine of 5 for an individual pupil. However, to have a group—say all fifth-graders in a system—have that same score as an *average* (mean) would place that group much higher in the distribution of group averages—perhaps as high as stanine 7 or 8.

3. If the test you are using does not provide norms for group averages, then report the score corresponding to the local median or 50th percentile point rather than the mean.

The median of a group of scores describes the achievement level of the typical pupil and may be more appropriately interpreted in terms of individual norms than may a mean. The mean is influenced by any extreme scores at either the high or low end of the score scale. For example, in a group of five scores—7, 6, 5, 5, 4—the median score is 5; the mean is 5.4. If, however, the highest score was 10, instead of 7, the median would remain 5, but the mean (arithmetic average) would be 6, in spite of the fact that only one score was *above* 6. For such a group of scores (10, 6, 5, 5, 4), the median of 5 is more descriptive of "average" or "typical" performance than is the mean of 6.

If only a single score is reported for a group, it becomes particularly important to point out that, in any large group, there is a *range* or spread of scores. Even where the middle score is low, there *are* many individuals performing at higher levels. To demonstrate again, in the set of scores 10, 6, 5, 5, 4, although median performance is 5, one score in the set is far above the median score.

In presenting this kind of material in a report of scores, the school administrator might wish to point out that the "national norm" is, in fact, the *median* for the national standardization group and to emphasize that where a score is identified as the "national norm," fully one-half of the national sample were in fact scoring at or below that "norm," while half were scoring above the norm. It should be pointed out that a "norm" in this sense is simply a description of median or typical performance as it has been measured by the test instrument and is not in any way to be construed as a standard of excellence.

Some communities insist on having test results reported in terms of the "percent of pupils scoring below the norm." If the report shows that 60 percent of its fourth-graders are reading "below the norm," it should clearly state that, in the national population, *50* percent of the pupils are reading "below the norm." It is also wise to point out that 40 percent of the local group are, in fact, performing above the norm.

4. If possible, report scores representing several points in the total score distribution.

A single reported score may give some useful information about the typical performance of a group of pupils, but it cannot be expected to give the full picture of that group's performance. It is useful to know how far above the median the top pupils are and how far below the typical pupil the poorer pupils are. School administrators may choose to report the extremes of the score range (the highest and lowest scores obtained by the group), or they may prefer to report scores in terms of stanine ranges. The most widely used method, however, is to report the scores corresponding to the midpoints of the upper and lower halves of the score distribution. These two points represent the 75th and 25th percentiles, respectively. Together with the median, they divide the full range of scores into quarters at quartile points Q_3, Q_2, and Q_1.

Compare two groups with the *same* median, or typical score of 50, on a test with scores from 1 to 100.

Points in the Score Range	Scores for Group A	Scores for Group B
75th percentile (Q_3)	90	60
50th percentile (median)	50	50
25th percentile (Q_1)	40	20

For each group, we have reported the three scores that divide the group into four subgroups, each including one-fourth of the pupils of the group. Although both groups have the same median, more of the pupils in Group A are obtaining very high scores than in Group B, and fewer are obtaining extremely low scores. These additional pieces of information indicating the spread of achievement *within the group* have considerable implication for the instructional decision maker, and such data, when added to the median results, make the scores far more meaningful.

The reporting of scores for other points of the distribution can be carried further. Scores may be reported for the 10th and 90th percentile points in addition to those for the 25th, 50th, and 75th, but as a rule, beyond a certain point, reporting on more numbers increases the chance of public confusion.

5. Wherever appropriate, report test results in terms of more than one norm group or frame of reference.

For most standardized tests, national norm data are available as a benchmark or reference point to use in evaluating local test performance. By using national norms as a basis of comparison, the local school system can describe the performance of its pupils in terms of a group representative of pupils in the entire United States. National norms, since they are a representative sample of all the wide variations found in the United States, present a composite picture of national performance. However, there are very few individual communities in the entire nation that match that composite picture across all comparisons. In some communities, the discrepancies between local characteristics and those represented as the typical (by the national norm) are so great that the comparison may seem worthless, irrelevant, or even dangerous. Nevertheless, national norms do have meaning and importance for all school systems, regardless of the ways in which individual systems may differ from "norm," since they do describe the typical performance of the nation's schoolchildren. They form one frame of reference, a point of departure for decision making. In interpreting a school district's test results in relation to the national norm, school administrators may wish to point out the differences between their communities and the national norm group by making reference to the factors influencing achievement, mentioned above.

The meaningfulness of local test results may be enhanced by comparison of the system's scores with those of appropriate reference groups other than the national norm group. For example, state or regional norms may be used, if such are available; large-city, independent-school, and/or suburban "norms" have been developed by a few test publishers. Many other such "norms" have been or could be developed by school districts cooperating among themselves, or by county or state agencies.

The example below illustrates the possibilities of multiple comparisons.

Third-Grade Reading Comprehension
(Standard Scores for March Testing)

Percentile Point	District	State	Nation
75th	52	61	54
50th	32	37	36
25th	11	15	12

From this table, it is easily understood that the typical (median) score for the city's pupils is 32, whereas that of the state is 37 and that of the nation (national norm) is 36. Statements about the 75th and 25th percentile points—25 percent of the city's pupils were above 52, but one-fourth of the state's were above 61—are also easy to grasp. This table records test performance at three points in the total distribution for each of three different groups. Of course, when several sets of norms are reported, care must be taken to ensure that they all represent performance on the same measure and at the same time in the school year.

One of the most effective comparisons to be made is that of the school's current performance with its own past performance. A table showing 75th, 50th, and 25th percentile points for this year's score distribution as compared with last year's, or as compared with a local "norm" established using several years' results, can be used very effectively to demonstrate changes in the pattern of local achievement.[7]

6. Whatever reference or norm groups are used in the report should be carefully defined and described for the reader.

In the last analysis, a "norm" is not simply a table of numbers but rather a description of the performance of real people at a certain time in their lives. The reader of the report should be informed about who that group of real people were. He must be able to judge how important, relevant, or useful he feels it is for the district's children to be compared with that norm group of children.

We have made previous mention of many intangible factors that seem related to the achievement of schoolchildren. There are, however, other characteristics of school districts and of the communities they serve that have also been shown to have a strong relationship to achievement levels and that *can* be measured and quantified. In selecting a national norm sample, publishers consider a number of such characteristics, many of which are reported in manuals or technical reports. Among the factors considered, perhaps the most commonly reported community statistics are the median family income and the median number of years of schooling completed by adults in the community. School characteristics reported include average class size, pupil-teacher ratio, teachers' training and experience, absentee rate, and pupil mobility.

To add further meaning to the test results, some of these variables should be considered in reporting local data. Such information requires careful explanation. The lay public may find it surprising to learn that adult income level, for example, is related to school achievement level. Some further clarification is needed, pointing out that it is not income per se but the nature of the community that is important. Much of what a community can offer to its children is related to its socioeconomic level, and measures of income (and educational background) are simply indices of more general characteristics. Moreover, it would be erroneous to claim that differences between the local community and the national norm group are the *direct cause* of corresponding differences in obtained test scores. Although researchers have found definite relationships between test results and some of the variables mentioned above, it is not at all certain that they are related in a cause-and-effect pattern. Since many of these factors are closely interrelated, it is often impossible to determine which factors are operating in a given situation. Furthermore, there are other intangible factors at work, influencing relationships one way or another, including those factors listed above. Finally, the report must make every effort to discourage the public from concluding that, because a relationship is found to exist, it is inevitable and unchangeable. It would be altogether false to permit the public to conclude from such data, "Since our community income level is well below the national average, we cannot hope ever to find our average fourth-graders reading at or above the national norm." Communities well below the norm in many characteristics may still have schools whose typical pupils perform at or above the norm.

---

[7]Test Service Notebook 133 on the measurement of growth describes how such figures are to be interpreted.

On the other hand, when a number of community and/or school characteristics are radically different from those of the national norm population, it would not be surprising to find that other characteristics, such as reading achievement scores, are also different. And while these community characteristics cannot be held accountable for the total achievement picture in a school system, they are important. Further, many of these characteristics are beyond the ability of the school to change or control. Important and difficult decisions must be made at the local level concerning which factors of this type should be reported and what explanations of them should be made in the accompanying text.

7. Wherever possible, avoid presenting tabular data showing within-community comparisons.

While it is helpful to compare the performance of individuals (or groups) with that of several reference groups of which they are a part, it is not particularly useful to compare any performance with that of some group of which one is *not* a member. In the same way, formal comparisons of one school with another, one area of the district with another, one racial, ethnic, or socioeconomic subgroup with another rarely serve any useful purposes and, indeed, might have many undesirable consequences. It is almost inevitable that the public will tend to "rate" the groups by their test results, since each is likely to vary in its level of median performance, regardless of the fact that the spread of scores among pupils within each subgroup will be even greater than the spread of group medians within the district.

If a school district is obliged to release test information on a school-by-school basis, every effort should be made to give the reader of the report adequate information for drawing appropriate conclusions from the data. Information about each school's characteristics in comparison with those of the district as a whole might be included in a fashion similar to that suggested above for the city and the national norm group.

8. Where possible, report information concerning performance on specific behavioral objectives.

Currently, much attention is being focused on the development, at the local level, of specific curriculum objectives and their expression in terms of observed behavior, and the demand for information about local pupil performance in terms of these objectives is growing. Each item included in a norm-referenced survey achievement test *does* measure a specific curriculum objective that could be stated in behavioral terms. Some test publishers issue reports tying the item to the objective. In other cases, an item analysis option is part of the scoring service for the test. In reporting to the community, information concerning performance by specific behavioral objectives should be included if possible. Parents and other interested adults in the community can easily understand this type of reporting because it describes definite tasks to which they can relate their own experience. Thus, a school district may report that

> By April of grade 4, we expect that 60 percent of all pupils should be able to compute correctly the difference between two four-digit numbers, when the problem is set in the horizontal form. In the standardized test recently administered, 50 percent of our fourth-graders responded correctly to an item measuring this objective.

Many objectives may not be clearly understood without an example of the required behavior. Thus, in the above report the following sentence might be added: "An example of such a problem might be $9863 - 5429 = ?$" However, it should be clearly understood that actual items from the test must *not* be used in such a report, and readers should be told that examples used are not from the test itself.

If local item analysis data comes from a testing date roughly equivalent to the time of year at which national normative data were collected, the district may wish to report, along with its local "percent correct" for an item or group of items, the parallel information for the norm group. Thus to the statement above could be added,

> In the national norm group for the test, however, 65 percent of fourth-graders were able to respond correctly to this item.

Of course, the district report must not stop with simply reporting these figures. The action to be taken as a result of these findings should also be included in the report. Were the expectations unrealistic? Should the curriculum be changed? The question "What are you going to do about it?" must be approached in the report.

9. Interpret test results in terms of their curricular implications.

Skills such as phonics and mathematics computation, which are fairly closely defined and which are hierarchical in their development, lend themselves best to this type of interpretation. For example, the school might report,

> This year, we have revised and expanded our phonics program in grade 1 as part of our restructuring of the elementary reading curriculum. From analysis of tests given in previous years, we had determined that our pupils were having more difficulty than the national school population with the matter of reversals, i.e., reading *pin* for *nip*, *dab* for *bad*, etc. We therefore tried to strengthen our instructional program in this area.
>
> On the test recently administered to our first-graders, there were four items measuring this skill at various levels of difficulty. Below are the data on the percent of pupils answering each item correctly on the national norm population and in our own system.

Percent Answering Correctly

	National	Local
(a).	70	80
(b).	75	85
(c).	65	75
(d).	50	60

Districtwide Reading and Math Third-Grade Scores

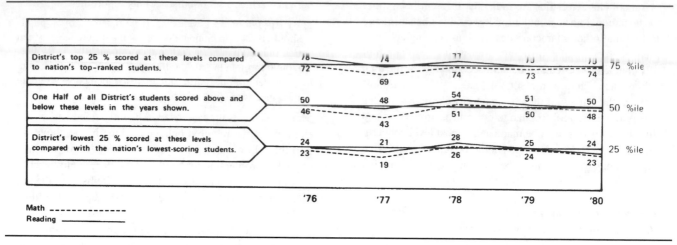

Math - - - - - - - - - - - - -
Reading _____

Districtwide Stanford Reading and Math Median Scores

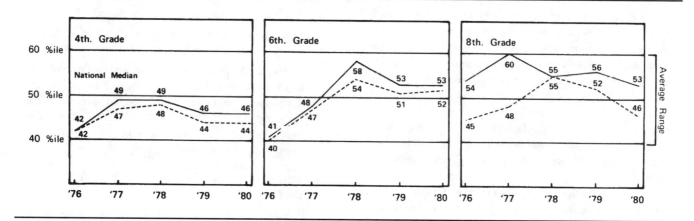

From this information, our reading supervisors are encouraged to feel that difficulty with reversals has been overcome by the revised instructional program. In fact, our pupils are now performing at a level somewhat above the national norm in this particular area. They will, of course, continue to check this periodically.

Of course, due to space limitations, data from only a few items or groups of items can be reported in this way. Yet, a few examples should be given to demonstrate that analysis of achievement test performance on specific content is a valuable tool for instructional planning.

10. Supplement tables with charts, profiles, and diagrams.

Effective communication is difficult to achieve with the exclusive use of statistical tables. In order to help parents and the community at large to understand the import and significance of the numbers, materials should be presented graphically as well. Charts, profiles, diagrams, and the like

are effective ways of underlining the important summary information, which may otherwise stay buried within the tables of numbers. See examples above.

Conclusion

Effective communication requires that the school's report to the community be well planned and well executed. The report must be simple, direct, and easy to understand. Although charts and visuals may help to explain, the most important aspect of the report is the clarity of its textual message. Perhaps most importantly, the school's message about the implications of the test results—what they mean and what actions are to be taken—must be carefully thought out and presented in a straightforward manner that will be clear to all readers: parents, teachers, and the concerned public. After all, test results are only resources for the decision-making process. In order to be useful, they must be well used.

EXERCISE 10-4
FIRSTHAND PORTFOLIO ASSESSMENT

OBJECTIVE

To impart memorable firsthand experience in the construction of portfolios and the practice of portfolio assessment

BACKGROUND

Portfolio is synonymous with work sample, and *portfolio assessment* refers to the evaluation of one's work samples. In this definition, "work sample" is defined quite broadly and may refer to anything from a drawing of a tree by a third-grader to the audiotape of a new jingle created by an advertising copywriter. Portfolio assessment in some occupations, such as those related to art, architecture, journalism, and music, has a very long history. Job applicants in such fields have traditionally been evaluated to a large degree not on the basis of test scores but rather on the basis of past accomplishments as evidenced by a portfolio.

YOUR TASK

Create a portfolio to illustrate all that you have learned about psychological testing and assessment to date. The portfolio should be used to convince your instructor that, regardless of grades you have received on any examinations to date, you really should be running an "A" in this course at this time. Submit the portfolio to your instructor. Await feedback.

EXERCISE 10-5
AUTHENTIC ASSESSMENT . . . REALLY!

OBJECTIVE

To enhance understanding of authentic assessment in an educational context

BACKGROUND

Authentic assessment in educational contexts has been viewed as a tool to gauge performance on meaningful tasks, including tasks that are transferable to nonacademic settings. Authentic assessment of students' writing skills would therefore be based on writing samples rather than on responses to multiple-choice tests. Authentic assessment of students' reading would be based on tasks that have to do with reading—preferably "authentic" reading such as an article in a local newspaper as opposed to a piece contrived especially for the purposes of assessment. Students in a college-level psychopathology course might be asked to identify patients' psychiatric diagnoses on the basis of videotaped interviews with the patients.

YOUR TASK

Create a way to assess "authentically" a student's knowledge of Chapter 10 of Cohen & Swerdlik (2005).

EXERCISE 10-6
PICK A PRESCHOOL TEST

OBJECTIVE

To learn more about preschool and educational tests not reviewed in the textbook

BACKGROUND

The approach in your textbook is to highlight only a few of the many tests that exist in any given area. For every test covered in your textbook there may well be dozens of other tests designed to measure the same attribute(s).

YOUR TASK

Using *Tests in Print,* the Internet, or any other resource you choose, discover a preschool test that was not mentioned in your textbook. It may be an individual test, or it may be a group test. It may be a test of achievement or a test of aptitude. It may be any kind of test at all, so long as it is designed for use with preschoolers. Then, use all of the resources at your disposal to answer the following:

1. Describe what the test measures.
2. Who would be most apt to use this test? Why? Include in your answer sample questions the test user might hope to answer through the use of this test.
3. Who would be most apt to take this test? Why?
4. Describe the full range of people to whom it would be appropriate to administer this test, including comments about who would be inappropriate.
5. Describe what is known about the test's reliability.
6. Describe what is known about the test's validity.
7. Imagining that you are a measurement consultant, would you recommend this test to clients who are test users? Why or why not?

REFERENCES

Gelman, R., & Gallistel, C. R. (1986). *The child's understanding of number.* Cambridge, MA: Harvard University Press.

Ginsburg, H. P., & Opper, S. (1988). *Piaget's theory of intellectual development* (3rd ed.). Englewood Cliffs, NJ: Prentice-Hall.

Piaget, J. (1969). *The child's conception of the world* (J. Tomlinson & A. Tomlinson, Trans.). Totowa, NJ: Littlefield, Adams.

THE 4-QUESTION CHALLENGE

1. According to the section of Chapter 10 that dealt with professional school admission tests, which does not belong?
   a. PCAT
   b. ATAT
   c. APAT
   d. AHPAT

2. In the years since the SAT was standardized in 1941, SAT scores have tended to
   a. rise.
   b. fall.
   c. stay the same.
   d. alternately rise and fall.

3. Which statement is true about sequential learners?
   a. They solve problems best by synthesizing many parallel pieces of information.
   b. If they are weak in simultaneous processing, they may have difficulty using maps.
   c. They tend to have problems with tasks such as memorization of a list of spelling words.
   d. They may have difficulty following oral instructions and understanding rules of games.

4. Which television program might employ a sociogram to help organize key data?
   a. *The Price is Right*
   b. *Survivor*
   c. *Fear Factor*
   d. *Who Wants to Be a Super Millionnaire?*

CHAPTER 11

Personality Assessment: An Overview

Puzzle 11   **Instructions**   Identify what is described, answer a question, or fill in the blank to complete this crossword puzzle based on material presented in Chapter 11 of your textbook.

Across

3. The _____ approach to test scoring and interpretation is one in which the presumed strength of a measured trait is interpreted relative to the measured strength of other traits for that same testtaker.

6. A narrative description, graph, table, or other representation of the extent to which a person has demonstrated certain targeted characteristics on a test.

7. The _____ approach to assessment is characterized by efforts to learn how a limited number of personality traits can be applied to all people.

9. Initials that abbreviate what is probably the most widely used and widely researched personality test.

11. In a _____ interview, questions are posed from a guide, and the interviewer has little if any leeway to deviate from that guide.

14. _____ management may be defined as an attempt to manipulate others' opinions and impressions through the selective exposure of some information, including false information, usually coupled with the suppression of other information.

15. It's a set of cognitive and behavioral characteristics by which individuals define themselves as members of a particular group; one's sense of self.

16. Culturally _____ psychological assessment is an approach to evaluation that is keenly perceptive and responsive to issues of acculturation, values, identity, worldview, language, and other culture-related variables as they may impact the evaluation process and the interpretation of data.

17. It's a reference group of testtakers who share specific characteristics and whose responses to test items serve as a standard by which items will be included or discarded from the final version of a scale. Hint: It is two words. For the purposes of this puzzle only, we have separated these two words with a hyphen.

19. This hyphenated term refers to a type of item format sometimes used in personality tests where each of two or more answers is roughly equivalent to social desirability.

24. An individual's unique constellation of psychological traits and states, including aspects of values, interests, attitudes, worldview, acculturation, sense of personal identity, sense of humor, cognitive and behavioral style and related characteristics.

27. The phrase to _____ with refers to thinking, feeling, or behavior on the part of one individual that resonates in some familiar way with the experiences of another individual.

28. The _____ effect refers to a type of rating error wherein the rater views the object of the rating with extreme favor and evidences a tendency to bestow ratings that are inflated in a positive direction.

29. The concept of _____ of control has to do with one's perceptions regarding the source of things that happen to one.

31. A personality _____ is a constellation of traits and states that is similar in pattern to one identified category of personality within a taxonomy of personalities.

34. The unique way people interpret and make sense of their perceptions in light of their learning experiences, cultural background, and related variables. Hint: It's two words that have been combined into one.

36. _____ criterion keying refers to the process of using criterion groups to develop test items wherein the scoring or keying of items has been demonstrated empirically to differentiate among groups of testtakers.

37. This personality type as described by Friedman and Rosenman is characterized by competitiveness, haste, restlessness, impatience, feelings of being time-pressured, and strong needs for achievement and dominance. Hint: In this puzzle, there is no space between the two terms.

38. This tool of assessment is a technique in which the assessee's task is to sort a group of statements, usually in perceived rank order ranging from "most descriptive" to "least descriptive." The statements, traditionally presented on index cards, may be sorted in ways designed to reflect various perceptions such as how respondents see themselves or how they would like to see themselves. Hint: It's hyphenated.

39. A test response style characterized by agreement with whatever is presented.

Down

1. Another name for this type of rating error is *leniency error*.

2. The process by which an individual's thoughts, behaviors, values, identity, and worldview develop in relation to the general thinking, behavior, customs, and values of a particular cultural group.

4. Less-than-accurate rating or error in evaluation by a rater due to that rater's general tendency to be overly critical in making ratings. This describes a _____ error.

5. It may be defined as any distinguishable, relatively enduring way in which one individual varies from another.

8. A process by which an individual assumes a pattern of behavior that is characteristic of another person or group of people.

10. The _____ approach is one characterized by efforts to learn about each individual's unique constellation of personality traits, with no attempt to characterize each person according to any particular set of traits.

12. This personality type, in marked contrast to the one described by the same researchers in 36-Across, is much more mellow and laid back. Hint: In this puzzle, there is no space between the two terms.

13. The semantic _____ technique is an item format characterized by bipolar adjectives separated by a 7-point rating scale on which respondents select one point to indicate their response.

16. The transitory exhibition of a trait, indicative of a relatively temporary predisposition to behave in a particular way.

18. The standard against which a test or a test score is evaluated.

20. The error of _____ tendency is characterized by less-than-accurate ratings or evaluations by a rater as a result of that rater's general tendency to make ratings at or near the midpoint of the scale.

21. One's attitudes, beliefs, opinions, and related thoughts about oneself. (A hyphenated term.)

22. Socially _____ responding is characterized by responses that are in conformity with widely accepted norms and expectations.

23. According to Rokeach, _____ values are guiding principles to help someone attain some objective. Examples are honesty and ambition.

25. According to Rokeach, _____ values are guiding principles and modes of behavior that are end-point objectives. Examples are "a comfortable life" and "an exciting life."

26. The standardization sample for the original MMPI consisted of approximately 1,500 people. They were referred to as the "normal _____ group," and their test results were contrasted with members of criterion groups drawn from a population of people diagnosed in some way.

30. It's a general term to describe the process wherein an assessee supplies information about himself or herself in any of several forms, such as responses to questions, keeping a diary, or reporting on self-monitoring thoughts and/or behaviors. This hyphenated term is _____ .

32. A response _____ may be defined as a tendency to respond to a test item or interview question in some characteristic manner, regardless of the content of the item or question.

33. Taken at face value, it means "new or recent form"; but don't take it at face value. We refer here to the first part of an acronym in the name of the five-factor personality inventory developed by Costa and McCrae.

34. A shorthand summary of a testtaker's scores on the MMPI clinical and validity scales is a _____ . Hint: A term containing two words, always separated by a space, that have been run together with no space only for the purposes of this puzzle.

35. That which an individual prizes; ideals believed in.

EXERCISE 11-1
MOVIES AND MEASUREMENT

OBJECTIVE

To enhance understanding of and provide firsthand experience with the concept of "personality" and its assessment

"Which personality shall we assess today?"

BACKGROUND

Most of us have only one of them, but in *The Three Faces of Eve,* Eve (Joanne Woodward) had three or more of them. This still from that film shows Eve with her husband (David Wayne) consulting with her psychiatrist (Lee J. Cobb) for the problem of multiple personality. It may be used as a point of departure for discussion of issues regarding the nature of personality (in the singular form) as well as multiple personality.

Just as a number of different theories regarding the nature of intelligence have been set forth, so different personality theorists have set forth a variety of definitions of "personality." Many such definitions make reference to constructs such as traits, states, and type. A *trait* has been defined in many ways, but for our purposes we may define it, after Guilford (1959, p. 6), as "any distinguishable, relatively enduring way in which one individual varies from another." *State* refers to the transitory exhibition of a personality trait. *Personality* may be defined as a unique constellation of traits and states, and *personality type* may be defined as a constellation of traits and states that is similar in pattern to one identified category of personality within a taxonomy of personalities.

YOUR TASK

1. Using terms such as "traits," "states," and "personality type," develop your own definition of the word *personality;* what does "personality" mean *to you*?

2. Outline a plan for measuring personality based on the definition you developed. In your outline, be sure to address each of the following questions:
   - What is the purpose of the personality test you've developed? What is it designed to do?
   - Is it to be used to measure traits, types, states, or some combination thereof?
   - Is it to be used to distinguish people on the basis of the healthiness of their personalities? Is it to be used to distinguish people on the basis of the suitability of their personalities for a particular kind of work? Is it to be used in general research on personality?
   - What kinds of items will your test contain? How will you decide on the content and wording of these items? Would you, for example, rely on a particular theory of personality in devising these items? Or would you rely on no particular theory but rather on your own life experiences?
   - In writing your test items, did you use a true/false format or some other format? Will the items of your test be grouped in any particular order?
   - How might you convincingly demonstrate that your test measures what it purports to measure?
3. Which tools of test construction do you think you would employ, and why?
   a. logic and reason
   b. theory
   c. data reduction methods such as factor analysis
   d. criterion groups

EXERCISE 11-2
TYPE CASTING

OBJECTIVE

To enhance understanding of the concept of "personality type"

BACKGROUND

Hypotheses and notions about various types of people have appeared in the literature through the ages. Perhaps the most primitive personality typology was the humoral theory of Hippocrates. Centuries later, the personality theorist Alfred Adler (1927/1965, 1933/1964) would differentiate personality types in a way that was somewhat reminiscent of Hippocrates (Table 11-1). Note that Adler's description of personality types emphasized variables such as social interest and the vigor with which one attacked life's problems.

YOUR TASK

Identify a well-known actor, actress, politician, celebrity, or historical personage that you believe might be aptly described by one Adlerian personality type description. Explain why you believe this person fits Adler's conception of people who are of this personality type.

EXERCISE 11-3
CULTURALLY INFORMED ASSESSMENT

OBJECTIVE

To obtain firsthand experience in the practice of culturally sensitive assessment

BACKGROUND

Cohen and Swerdlik (2005) defined *culturally informed assessment* as an approach to evaluation that is keenly perceptive about and responsive to issues of acculturation, values, identity, worldview, language, and other culture-related variables that may adversely impact the evaluation process and/or the interpretation of the resulting data. Cohen and

TABLE 11-1   *Two Typologies: Adler and Hippocrates*

Adlerian Type	Corresponding Type of Hippocrates
Ruling type: This type of person exhibits high activity but in an asocial way; typical of "bossy" people and, in the extreme, homicidal people.	Choleric type
Getting type: This type of person has low social interest and a moderate activity level; typical of people who are constantly depending on others for support.	Phlegmatic or sluggish type
Avoiding type: This type of person has very low social interest combined with a very low activity level; method of coping is primarily avoidance.	Melancholic type
Good Man type: This type of person has high social interest combined with a high activity level; she or he lives life to the fullest and is very much concerned with the well-being of her or his fellow human beings.	Sanguine type

Source: Adler (1927/1965)

Swerdlik went on to suggest that when planning an assessment in which there is some question regarding the projected impact of culture, language, or some related variable on the validity of the assessment, the assessor might prepare by reading existing case history data with an eye toward pre-evaluating the assessee's level of acculturation. The assessor might also contact family, friends, clergy people, professionals, and others who know the assessee to obtain additional culture-related information prior to the assessment (assuming the assessor is authorized to do so and has the assessee's written permission). Prior to the formal assessment, the assessor may consider a screening interview with the assessee, in which various culture-related issues are discussed. Some of the questions that may be raised during such an interview are:

- Describe yourself.
- Describe your family. Who lives at home?
- Describe roles in your family, such as the role of mother, the role of father, the role of grandmother, the role of child, and so forth.
- What traditions, rituals, and/or customs were passed down to you by family members?
- What traditions, rituals, and/or customs do you think it is important to pass to the next generation?
- With regard to your family situation, what obligations do you see yourself as having? What obligations does your family have to you?
- What role does your family play in everyday life?
- How do the roles of males and females differ from your own cultural perspective?
- What kind of music do you like?
- What kinds of foods do you eat most routinely?
- What do you consider fun things to do? When do you do these things?
- Describe yourself in the way that you think most other people would describe you. How would you say your own self-description would differ from that description?
- How might you respond to the question, "Who are you?" with reference to your own sense of personal identity?
- With which cultural group or groups do you identify most? Why?
- What aspect of the history of the group with which you most identify is most significant to you? Why?
- Who are some of the people who have influenced you most?
- What are some things that have happened to you in the past that have influenced you most?
- What sources of satisfaction are associated with being you?
- What sources of dissatisfaction or conflict are associated with being you?
- What do you call yourself when asked about your ethnicity?
- What are your feelings regarding your racial and ethnic identity?

- Describe your most pleasant memory as a child.
- Describe your least pleasant memory as a child.
- Describe the ways in which you typically learn new things. In what ways might cultural factors have influenced this learning style?
- Describe the ways you typically resolve conflicts with other people. What influence might cultural factors have in this way of resolving conflicts?
- How would you describe your general view of the world?
- How would you characterize human nature in general?
- How much control do you believe you have over the things that happen to you? Why?
- How much control do you believe you have over your health? Your mental health?
- What are your thoughts regarding the role of work in daily life? Has your cultural identity influenced your views about work in any way? If so, how?
- How would you characterize the role of doctors in the world around you?
- How would you characterize the role of lawyers in the world around you?
- How would you characterize the role of politicians in the world around you?
- How would you characterize the role of spirituality in your daily life?
- What are your feelings about the use of illegal drugs?
- What is the role of play in daily life?
- How would you characterize the ideal relationship between human beings and Nature?
- What defines a person who has power?
- What happens when one dies?
- Do you tend to live your life more in the past, the present, or the future? What influences on you do you think helped shape this way of living?
- How would you characterize your attitudes and feelings about the older people in your family? Older people in society in general?
- Describe your thinking about the local police and the criminal justice system.
- How do you see yourself ten years from now?

YOUR TASK

Identify a person who is a member of a cultural group that is in the minority in your area, and ask for that person's assistance in this interviewing exercise. If such a person is not available, another student may play the role of the interviewee. Role-play a pre-assessment interview with the interviewee, the purpose of which is to obtain a sense of the interviewee's level of acculturation. Use the interview questions presented above as a guide, but keep in mind that not every question must be asked, the order of questions may vary, and the wording of the questions may be changed to facilitate communication. Also, remember the critical importance of rapport when conducting an interview. Be sensitive to cultural differences in readiness to engage in self-disclosure about family or other matters that may be perceived as too personal to discuss with a stranger—especially in a practice interview.

EXERCISE 11-4
THE NEO-PI-R

OBJECTIVE

To enhance understanding of the NEO-PI-R by reading and commenting on an account of its creation written by its authors

BACKGROUND

In a relatively short period of time since its creation, the NEO-PI-R has become a very widely used general measure of personality. In this exercise, the test's authors present a brief description of this test.

YOUR TASK

After reading the material on the NEO-PI-R that follows, write down three questions you have about this test. Your instructor may then allot some class time in which the class discusses some or all of the questions raised.

THE REVISED NEO PERSONALITY INVENTORY (NEO-PI-R)

Paul T. Costa, Jr., and Robert R. McCrae

In some respects, the Revised NEO Personality Inventory (NEO-PI-R; Costa & McCrae, 1992) is a new instrument. Our research on Neuroticism, Extraversion, and Openness to Experience began in the mid-1970s; we did not begin to measure Agreeableness and Conscientiousness until 1983. Research has continued since publication of the NEO-PI in 1985, resulting in a manual supplement issued in 1989 and a major revision introducing facet scales for Agreeableness and Conscientiousness in 1992. Further, more modest developments are planned (Costa & McCrae, 1997). We hope and believe the NEO-PI-R incorporates the latest advances in personality structure and assessment; the "neo" in the title is an intended pun.

In other respects, the NEO-PI-R is profoundly conservative, deeply rooted in the research of generations of personality psychologists. Most of the traits it measures have long been familiar, and scale labels have been chosen to emphasize continuity with past conceptualizations. The psychometric strategies for item selection and scale validation benefited from the insight and experience of many previous researchers and theorists. Even the data we used to formulate our model and validate our instrument were in many cases collected years ago by colleagues in longitudinal studies. We are therefore particularly pleased and honored to appear in a volume alongside some of the great contributors to personality assessment. We hope to carry on their traditions.

The Evolution of the NEO-PI-R

The 1970s were not the most auspicious time to undertake the development of a new personality inventory. Personality psychology was in crisis, rocked by critiques from Mischel (1968), Fiske (1974), and Shweder (1975). If the field had a future, it seemed to be in interactionism (Magnusson & Endler, 1977) rather than in trait psychology. And if one insisted on using conventional personality measures, why add another instrument to the already crowded field? What did we hope to accomplish by introducing the NEO-PI?

Our decision was based on two beliefs. First, we were committed to the basic correctness of trait psychology: We believed that there were consistent and enduring individual differences in ways of thinking, feeling, and acting; that individuals were capable of describing themselves with reasonable accuracy if asked appropriate questions; and that psychometric tools (such as factor analysis) and principles (such as construct validation) could be used to develop useful measures of traits (cf. Briggs, 1985). These tenets would not have been controversial in the 1930s or the 1950s and can hardly be considered inflammatory today, but they were not widely shared at that time. The development and use of personality measures in the past two decades have contributed substantially to the reinstatement of these basic principles.

Second, we felt that existing instruments were less than optimal. Quite aside from the many scales of dubious validity that contributed so much to what Block (1977) called the "litter-ature" of personality, we found that even the best instruments were lacking in some respect. Eysenck and Eysenck's (1975) Extraversion and Neuroticism scales, for example, were reliable and valid measures of two fundamental dimensions of personality, but they could hardly encompass the full range of individual differences, and they did not allow any differentiation among the more specific traits that each dimension subsumed. Cattell, Eber, and Tatsuoka's (1970) Sixteen Personality Factor Questionnaire (16 PF) offered more scope and specificity, but its scales had been widely criticized for lack of a replicable factor structure (see Howarth, 1976).

A Three-Factor Model

Our research began with analyses of the 16 PF in the Veterans Administration's Normative Aging Study (Costa & McCrae, 1976). At first we were interested in the question of structural changes with age: Were the relations among traits, summarized as higher-order factors or clusters, different for old versus young or middle-aged men? It is impossible to answer this question until one knows what the structure is at each age, and thus we were faced with the perennial problem of determining the "correct" number of factors and their appropriate rotation. Our later research (Costa & McCrae, 1980b) showed that there are no age differences in structure, but by that time we had become interested in the problem of structure for its own sake. We ultimately decided on a fairly parsimonious solution: a three-factor model that included Neuroticism (N), Extraversion (E), and Openness (O). The first two factors were common in analyses of the 16 PF (as Anxiety and Exvia) and, in addition, clearly corresponded to the major dimensions of Eysenck's system. The third dimension allowed us to go a step beyond Eysenck's work, identifying a new fundamental dimension (Costa & McCrae, 1986).

We quickly became convinced of the importance of this new dimension of Openness to Experience (McCrae & Costa, 1985b, 1997a), seen first in the 16 PF Bright, Tender-minded, Imaginative, and Liberal-thinking scales. Although it had not often been viewed as a basic trait dimension, related concepts had often been proposed: Rogers's (1961) openness to feelings and the low pole of Rokeach's (1960) dogmatism were clearly related, and Fitzgerald (1966) and Coan (1974) had not only developed the idea but had also created scales and showed that such facets as openness to aesthetics and ideas covaried in a single dimension. It was from them that we took the term *Openness*. We were subsequently delighted to find that Tellegen and Atkinson (1974) had also identified this as a third major dimension, which they called *Absorption*.

Richard Coan's Experience Inventory became the basis for our own scales to measure Openness (Costa & McCrae, 1978), and our success in measuring facets of this dimension led us to create scales to measure aspects of N and E. The EASI-III scales of Buss and Plomin (1975) were an important influence both in form and content. We admired the simple, straightforward wording Buss and Plomin used as well as some of the distinctions they drew. For example, we included Anxiety and Hostility as facets of N, just as they had included Fear and Anger in their General Emotionality domain.

Rather than adopt the factor-analytic language of first-order and second-order factors, we began to speak of N, E, and O as broad *domains* of traits and more specific traits as their *facets* (Costa & McCrae, 1995). Our approach was to measure each domain by summing scores on a half-dozen facet scales. The user would thus have highly reliable measures of three global domains, as well as more specific information on traits within each domain. (Mershon and Gorsuch, 1988, gave an empirical demonstration of the predictive value of measuring specific traits as well as broad factors, confirming the utility of the domain-and-facet approach.)

We called the resulting questionnaire the NEO Inventory and brought it to Baltimore when we joined the National Institute on Aging (Costa & McCrae, 1980b). Research with that instrument showed the utility of the three-dimensional model in understanding such phenomena as somatic complaints (Costa & McCrae, 1980a), psychological well-being (Costa & McCrae, 1984), ego development (McCrae & Costa, 1980), and vocational interests (Costa et al., 1984). The validity of the scales themselves was demonstrated by convergence with other instruments and with spouse ratings on a third-person form of the NEO Inventory (McCrae, 1982). The three domains of N, E, and O were clearly central variables in personality psychology, but they were just as clearly incapable of addressing the full range of individual differences. What about trust and altruism? What about self-control and need for achievement?

Rediscovery of the Five-Factor Model

Although we were aware of its limitations, we—like most personality psychologists—had come to accept them as inevitable. Surely, every personality test would have omissions; how could we hope to measure all traits? How many traits *should* an inventory measure? At about this time, Goldberg (1981, 1983) revived a line of research that claimed a solution to this problem (John et al., 1988). His analyses were based on the assumption that individual differences in personality are so important for social interaction that every culture must have evolved words to express them; over the centuries, all important traits would have been encoded in the natural language. The scope of personality traits is thus given by the scope of trait names; if we can determine the structure of the traits listed in the dictionary, we can determine the structure of personality (Norman, 1963). Although this rationale was not accepted by many psychologists (e.g., Block, 1995), who doubted the ability of laypersons to perceive the full range of psychological characteristics, the approach was strengthened by the fact that different researchers in this field consistently identified similar dimensions, called by Norman Extraversion or Surgency, Agreeableness, Conscientiousness, Emotional Stability, and Culture. This five-factor model appeared to provide a robust and comprehensive description of the natural language of traits, if not traits themselves.

It was clear to us that Norman's Extraversion strongly resembled ours, and that his Emotional Stability was the polar opposite of our N. There was some suggestion that Culture was a variant of O. An empirical test (McCrae & Costa, 1985c) confirmed these hypotheses and also pointed to the importance of Agreeableness (A) and Conscientiousness (C), domains unrepresented in the NEO Inventory. We therefore constructed questionnaire scales to measure these two domains (McCrae & Costa, 1987) and published the final instrument as the NEO Personality Inventory (Costa & McCrae, 1985). A series of subsequent analyses has shown that the five-factor model operationalized by the NEO-PI was in fact extraordinarily comprehensive: It encompassed

Table 1 *Domains and Facets of the Revised NEO Personality Inventory*

Domain/Facet	Domain/Facet
Neuroticism	**Agreeableness**
Anxiety	Trust
Angry Hostility	Straightforwardness
Depression	Altruism
Self-Consciousness	Compliance
Impulsiveness	Modesty
Vulnerability	Tender-Mindedness
Extraversion	**Conscientiousness**
Warmth	Competence
Gregariousness	Order
Assertiveness	Dutifulness
Activity	Achievement Striving
Excitement Seeking	Self-Discipline
Positive Emotions	Deliberation
Openness	
Fantasy	
Aesthetics	
Feelings	
Actions	
Ideas	
Values	

Source: Costa, P. T., Jr., & McCrae, R. R. (1998). The Revised NEO Personality Inventory (NEO-PI-R). In S. R. Briggs, J. M. Cheek, & E. M. Donahue (Eds.). *Handbook of adult personality inventories*. New York: Plenum.

dimensions in Murray's needs (Costa & McCrae, 1988), the interpersonal circumplex (McCrae & Costa, 1989b), Jungian typologies (McCrae & Costa, 1989a), and the items of Block's (1961) California Q-Set (McCrae et al., 1986).

The major limitation of the NEO-PI was the lack of facet scales for A and C. We were confident that important facets of these domains could be identified and measured, but we did not want to delay publication of the instrument while we conducted the necessary research. Item selection and facet validation studies were conducted in several samples (Costa et al., 1991), and the Revised NEO Personality Inventory (NEO-PI-R) was published in 1992. In addition to adding facet scales for A and C, the revision replaced 10 of the original 144 N, E, and O items. The current version has 240 items, new and more representative norms, a hand-scoring answer sheet that incorporates the scoring template, and enhanced computer scoring and interpretation. Table 1 lists the domains and facets measured by the instrument.

References

Block, J. (1961). *The Q-sort method in personality assessment and psychiatric research*. Springfield, IL: Charles C Thomas.

Block, J. (1977). Advancing the psychology of personality: Paradigmatic shift or improving the quality of research? In D. Magnusson & N. S. Endler (Eds.), *Personality at the crossroads: Current issues in interactional psychology* (pp. 37–64). Hillsdale, NJ: Erlbaum.

Block, J. (1995). A contrarian view of the five-factor approach to personality description. *Psychological Bulletin, 117,* 187–215.

Briggs, S. R. (1985). A trait account of shyness. In P. Shaver (Ed.), *Review of Personality and Social Psychology* (pp. 35–64). Beverly Hills: Sage.

Buss, A. H., & Plomin, R. (1975). *A temperament theory of personality development.* New York: Wiley.

Cattell, R. B., Eber, H. W., & Tatsuoka, M. M. (1970). *The handbook for the Sixteen Personality Factor Questionnaire.* Champaign, IL: Institute for Personality and Ability Testing.

Coan, R. W. (1974). *The optimal personality.* New York: Columbia University.

Costa, P. T., Jr., & McCrae, R. R. (1976). Age differences in personality structure: A cluster analytic approach. *Journal of Gerontology, 31,* 564–570.

Costa, P. T., Jr., & McCrae, R. R. (1978). Objective personality assessment. In M. Storandt, I. C. Siegler, & M. F. Elias (Eds.), *The clinical psychology of aging* (pp. 119–143). New York: Plenum.

Costa, P. T., Jr., & McCrae, R. R. (1980a). Somatic complaints in males as a function of age and neuroticism: A longitudinal analysis. *Journal of Behavioral Medicine, 3,* 245–257.

Costa, P. T., Jr., & McCrae, R. R. (1980b). Still stable after all these years: Personality as a key to some issues in adulthood and old age. In P. B. Baltes & O. G. Brim, Jr. (Eds.), *Life span development and behavior* (Vol. 3; pp. 65–102). New York: Academic Press.

Costa, P. T., Jr., & McCrae, R. R. (1984). Personality as a lifelong determinant of well-being. In C. Malatesta & C. Izard (Eds.), *Affective processes in adult development and aging* (pp. 141–157). Beverly Hills: Sage.

Costa, P. T., Jr., & McCrae, R. R. (1985). *The NEO Personality Inventory Manual.* Odessa, FL: Psychological Assessment Resources.

Costa, P. T., Jr., & McCrae, R. R. (1986). Major contributions to personality psychology. In S. Modgil & C. Modgil (Eds.), *Hans Eysenck: Consensus and controversy* (pp. 63–72, 86, 87). Barcombe Lewes Sussex, England: Falmer.

Costa, P. T., Jr., & McCrae, R. R. (1988). From catalog to classification: Murray's needs and the five-factor model. *Journal of Personality and Social Psychology, 55,* 258–265.

Costa, P. T., Jr., & McCrae, R. R. (1992). *Revised NEO Personality Inventory (NEO-PI-R) and NEO Five-Factor Inventory (NEO-FFI) Professional Manual.* Odessa, FL: Psychological Assessment Resources.

Costa, P. T., Jr., & McCrae, R. R. (1995). Domains and facets: Hierarchical personality assessment using the Revised NEO Personality Inventory. *Journal of Personality Assessment, 64,* 21–50.

Costa, P. T., Jr., & McCrae, R. R. (1997). Stability and change in personality assessment: The Revised NEO Personality Inventory in the year 2000. *Journal of Personality Assessment, 68,* 86–94.

Costa, P. T., Jr., McCrae, R. R., & Dye, D. A. (1991). Facet scales for agreeableness and conscientiousness: A revision of the NEO Personality Inventory. *Personality and Individual Differences, 12,* 887–898.

Costa, P. T., Jr., McCrae, R. R., & Holland, J. L. (1984). Personality and vocational interests in an adult sample. *Journal of Applied Psychology, 69,* 390–400.

Eysenck, H. J., & Eysenck, S. B. G. (1975). *Manual of the Eysenck Personality Questionnaire.* San Diego: EdITS.

Fiske, D. W. (1974). The limits for the conventional science of personality. *Journal of Personality, 42,* 1–11.

Fitzgerald, E. T. (1966). Measurement of openness to experience: A study of regression in the service of the ego. *Journal of Personality and Social Psychology, 4,* 655–663.

Goldberg, L. R. (1981). Language and individual differences: The search for universals in personality lexicons. In L. Wheeler (Ed.), *Review of personality and social psychology* (Vol. 2; pp. 141–165). Beverly Hills: Sage.

Goldberg, L. R. (1983, June). *The magical number five, plus or minus two: Some considerations on the dimensionality of personality descriptors.* Paper presented at a Research Seminar, Gerontology Research Center, Baltimore.

Howarth, E. (1976). Were Cattell's "personality sphere" factors correctly identified in the first instance? *British Journal of Psychology, 67,* 213–236.

John, O. P., Angleitner, A., & Ostendorf, F. (1988). The lexical approach to personality: A historical review of trait taxonomic research. *European Journal of Personality, 2,* 171–203.

Magnusson, D., & Endler, N. S. (1977). *Personality at the crossroads: Current issues in interactional psychology.* Hillsdale, NJ: Erlbaum.

McCrae, R. R. (1982). Consensual validation of personality traits: Evidence from self-reports and ratings. *Journal of Personality and Social Psychology, 43,* 293–303.

McCrae, R. R., & Costa, P. T., Jr. (1980). Openness to experience and ego level in Loevinger's sentence completion test: Dispositional contributions to developmental models of personality. *Journal of Personality and Social Psychology, 39,* 1179–1190.

McCrae, R. R., & Costa, P. T., Jr. (1983). Social desirability and scales: More substance than style. *Journal of Consulting and Clinical Psychology, 51,* 882–888.

McCrae, R. R., & Costa, P. T., Jr. (1985b). Openness to experience. In R. Hogan & W. H. Jones (Eds.), *Perspectives in personality* (Vol. 1; pp. 145–172). Greenwich, CT: JAI Press.

McCrae, R. R., & Costa, P. T., Jr. (1985c). Updating Norman's "adequate taxonomy": Intelligence and personality dimensions in natural language and in questionnaires. *Journal of Personality and Social Psychology, 49,* 710–721.

McCrae, R. R., & Costa, P. T., Jr. (1986). Personality, coping, and coping effectiveness in an adult sample. *Journal of Personality, 54,* 385–405.

McCrae, R. R., & Costa, P. T., Jr. (1987). Validation of the five-factor model across instruments and observers. *Journal of Personality and Social Psychology, 52,* 81–90.

McCrae, R. R., & Costa, P. T., Jr. (1989a). Reinterpreting the Myers-Briggs Type Indicator from the perspective of the five-factor model of personality. *Journal of Personality Assessment, 57,* 16–40.

McCrae, R. R., & Costa, P. T., Jr. (1989b). The structure of interpersonal traits: Wiggins's circumplex and the five-factor model. *Journal of Personality and Social Psychology, 56,* 586–659.

McCrae, R. R., & Costa, P. T., Jr. (1997a). Conceptions and correlates of Openness to Experience. In R. Hogan, J. A. Johnson, & S. R. Briggs (Eds.), *Handbook of personality psychology* (pp. 269–290). Orlando: Academic Press.

McCrae, R. R., Costa, P. T., Jr., & Busch, C. M. (1986). Evaluating comprehensiveness in personality systems: The California Q-Set and the five-factor model. *Journal of Personality, 54,* 430–446.

Mershon, B., & Gorsuch, R. L. (1988). Number of factors in the personality sphere: Does increase in factors increase predictability of real-life criteria? *Journal of Personality and Social Psychology, 55,* 675–680.

Mischel, W. (1968). *Personality and assessment.* New York: Wiley.

Norman, W. T. (1963). Toward an adequate taxonomy of personality attributes: Replicated factors structure in peer nomination personality ratings. *Journal of Abnormal and Social Psychology, 66,* 574–583.

Rogers, C. R. (1961). *On becoming a person: A therapist's view of psychotherapy.* Boston: Houghton Mifflin.

Rokeach, M. (1960). *The open and closed mind.* New York: Basic.

Shweder, R. A. (1975). How relevant is an individual difference theory of personality? *Journal of Personality, 43,* 455–484.

Tellegen, A., & Atkinson, G. (1974). Openness to absorbing and self-altering experiences ("absorption"), a trait related to hypnotic susceptibility. *Journal of Abnormal Psychology, 83,* 268–277.

EXERCISE 11-5

GEORGE WASHINGTON'S 16 PF

OBJECTIVE

To impart firsthand experience with a computerized, narrative report of personality based on a widely used personality test

BACKGROUND

Figure 11-1 is a computerized, narrative report for the scoring and reporting of the 16 PF of George Washington (as in "father of our country") at age 44. No, the publishers of the 16 PF were not distributing the test as early as 1776. Rather, several psychologists familiar with the test were asked to study biographical information on Washington and then derive a profile showing how they think he would have scored.

YOUR TASK

Read and comment in writing on George Washington's 16 PF. Knowing George Washington's place in American history, what if anything about this report surprises you? What if anything about this report are you not surprised by?

Now pretend you are a vocational counselor at a large and prestigious vocational counseling firm. Going through the file of a 44-year-old client named George Washington, you find this 16 PF report. Just on the basis of this report, what type of career would you advise Mr. Washington to pursue? Why? Make sure to discuss the role of cultural factors in your decision.

FIGURE 11-1   *George Washington's 16 PF*

"Now, where am I supposed to get a number 2 pencil?"

```
        N A R R A T I V E    S C O R I N G    R E P O R T
      for The Sixteen Personality Factor Questionnaire — 16 PF


     This report is intended to be used in conjunction with professional
  judgment. The statements it contains should be viewed as hypotheses
  to be validated against other sources of data.   All information in
  this report should be treated confidentially and responsibly.

  NAME-George Washington                            July 4, 1776
                                                    AGE-44; SEX-M

  * * * * * * * * * * * *  VALIDITY SCALES  * * * * * * * * * * * * * *
  *                                                                  *
  *   Validity indicators are within acceptable ranges.             *
  *      Faking good/MD (sten) score is very low (2).               *
  *      Faking bad (sten) score is extremely low (1).              *
  * * * * * * * * * * * * * * * * * * * * * * * * * * * * * * * * * * *
```

FIGURE 11-1 *(continued)*

```
        SCORES                           16 PF    PROFILE
     Raw  Sten        LEFT MEANING   1 2 3 4 5 6 7 8 9 10  RIGHT MEANING      %
          U  C                                 average

      7   4  4   A    Cool, Reserved      !<---     !    Warm, Easygoing     23
     12  10 10   B    Concrete Thinking   !   --------->  Abstract Thinking  99
     23   9  9   C    Easily Upset        !   ------->    Calm, Stable       96
     15   7  7   E    Not Assertive       !   --->!       Dominant           77
     10   4  4   F    Sober, Serious      !<---     !     Enthusiastic       23
     17   8  8   G    Expedient           !   ----->      Conscientious      89
     23   9  9   H    Shy, Timid          !   ------->    Venturesome        96
      4   3  3   I    Tough-Minded     <------     !       Sensitive          11
      6   5  5   L    Trusting            !  <-     !      Suspicious         40
     10   4  4   M    Practical           !<---     !      Imaginative        23
      9   6  6   N    Forthright          !   ->    !      Shrewd             60
      6   4  4   O    Self-Assured        !<---     !      Self-Doubting      23
      8   5  5   Q1   Conservative        !  <-     !      Experimenting      40
     16   9  9   Q2   Group-Oriented      !   ------->    Self-Sufficient    96
     19   9  9   Q3   Undisciplined       !   ------->    Self-Disciplined   96
      9   5  5   Q4   Relaxed             !  <-     !      Tense, Driven      40
```

Note: "U" indicates uncorrected sten scores. "C" indicates sten scores corrected for distortion (if appropriate). The interpretation will proceed on the basis of corrected scores. This report was processed using
male adult (GP) norms for Form A.

SECOND-ORDER FACTORS   COMPOSITE SCORES

Extraversion..average (4.5)   Neuroticism...below average (3.6)
Anxiety.......low (2.9)   Leadership....very high (9.4)
Tough Poise...high (7.8)   Creativity....very high (8.7)
Independence..high (7.5)
Control.......very high (8.9)   Profile Pattern Code = 2133

PERSONAL COUNSELING OBSERVATIONS

    Adequacy of adjustment is above average (7.4).
    Rigidity of behavior controls is very high (8.9).

PRIMARY PERSONALITY CHARACTERISTICS OF SPECIAL INTEREST

    Capacity for abstract skills is extremely high.
    Problems are approached with calm emotional stability and
realism.
    Regard for strict moral standards, duty, and conscientious
perseverance is high.
    He is venturesome, socially bold and spontaneous, and not
easily inhibited. This tendency is very high.
    As a person, he is realistic, tough-minded, and unsentimental.
    Being self-sufficient, he prefers tackling things
resourcefully, alone.
    He has a definite self-concept and sets out to control himself
to fit what he feels his social reputation requires.

(continued)

FIGURE 11-1 *(continued)*

BROAD INFLUENCE PATTERNS

His attention is directed about equally toward the outer environment and toward inner thoughts and feelings. Extraversion is average (4.5).

At the present time, he sees himself as less anxious than most people. His anxiety score is low (2.9).

Tasks and problems are approached with emphasis upon rationality and getting things done. Less attention is paid to emotional relationships. This tendency is high (7.8).

His life style is independent and self-directed leading to active attempts to achieve control of the environment. In this respect, he is high (7.5).

He tends to conform to generally accepted standards of conduct and has probably internalized societal standards as his own. He feels strongly obligated to meet his responsibilities. This tendency is very high (8.9).

VOCATIONAL OBSERVATIONS

At client's own level of abilities, potential for creative functioning is very high (8.7).

Potential for benefit from formal academic training, at client's own level of abilities, is very high (9.4).

In a group of peers, potential for leadership is very high (9.4).

Potential for success in jobs that reward interpersonal, sales, and persuasive skills is very high (8.5).

Potential for success in job areas that reward precision and dependability is high (7.8).

Potential for growth to meet increasing job demands is extremely high (10.0).

The extent to which the client is accident prone is very low (2.1).

OCCUPATIONAL FITNESS PROJECTIONS

In this segment of the report his 16 PF results are compared with various occupational profiles. All projections should be considered with respect to other information about him, particularly his interests and abilities.

1. ARTISTIC PROFESSIONS

   Artist.........................extremely high (10.0)
   Musician......................high (8.1)
   Writer........................extremely high (10.0)

2. COMMUNITY AND SOCIAL SERVICE

   Employment Counselor..........high (8.2)
   Firefighter...................extremely high (10.0)
   Nurse.........................very high (8.6)
   Physician.....................average (6.2)
   Police Officer................high (8.0)
   Priest (R.C.).................average (5.3)
   Service Station Dealer........average (5.9)
   Social Worker.................below average (4.4)

FIGURE 11-1 *(continued)*

3. SCIENTIFIC PROFESSIONS

```
      Biologist......................extremely high (10.0)
      Chemist........................extremely high (10.0)
      Engineer.......................very high (9.4)
      Geologist......................very high (9.4)
      Physicist......................extremely high (10.0)
      Psychologist...................extremely high (9.7)
```

4. TECHNICAL PERSONNEL

```
      Accountant.....................extremely high (10.0)
      Airline Flight Attendant.......average (6.1)
      Airline Pilot..................very high (9.1)
      Computer Programmer............extremely high (10.0)
      Editorial Worker...............extremely high (10.0)
      Electrician....................extremely high (10.0)
      Mechanic.......................extremely high (10.0)
      Psychiatric Technician.........extremely high (10.0)
      Time/Motion Study Analyst......high (8.0)
```

5. INDUSTRIAL/CLERICAL PERSONNEL

```
      Janitor........................very high (8.5)
      Kitchen Worker.................average (5.7)
      Machine Operator...............high (8.1)
      Secretary-Clerk................high (7.8)
      Truck Driver...................above average (7.4)
```

6. SALES PERSONNEL

```
      Real Estate Agent..............high (7.9)
      Retail Counter Clerk...........above average (6.9)
```

7. ADMINISTRATIVE AND SUPERVISORY PERSONNEL

```
      Bank Manager...................very high (8.5)
      Business Executive.............extremely high (9.0)
      Credit Union Manager...........high (8.4)
      Middle Level Manager...........very high (9.3)
      Personnel Manager..............high (7.6)
      Production Manager.............very high (8.8)
      Plant Foreman..................high (8.2)
      Sales Supervisor...............very high (8.5)
      Store Manager..................below average (4.4)
```

8. ACADEMIC PROFESSIONS

```
      Teacher-Elementary Level.......above average (6.5)
      Teacher-Junior High Level......below average (3.5)
      Teacher-Senior High Level......below average (3.7)
      University Professor...........high (7.5)
      School Counselor...............above average (7.3)
      School Superintendent..........very high (9.3)
      University Administrator.......extremely high (10.0)
```

Item Summary

Item responses have not been provided.

EXERCISE 11-6

EMPIRICAL CRITERION KEYING— CALIFORNIA STYLE

OBJECTIVE

To introduce the California Psychological Inventory (CPI), a personality test that was developed by the method of empirical criterion keying

BACKGROUND

The CPI has been described as the "kissing cousin" of the MMPI because it was developed by so similar a method. The reading that follows contains more detailed information on the CPI.

YOUR TASK

Read the description of the CPI that follows, and then respond in writing to the following two tasks:

1. Describe similarities and differences between the CPI and the MMPI-2.
2. Describe in detail a situation in which you think a counselor might wish to use the CPI with a client and what the objective of the testing would be.

CALIFORNIA PSYCHOLOGICAL INVENTORY

In contrast to the MMPI, which was developed to assess maladjustment, the CPI was designed for use with normal populations aged 13 and older, and its scales emphasize more positive and socially desirable aspects of personality than do the scales of the MMPI.

The CPI was originally published in 1956 and revised in 1987 and 1996. The original edition of the test contained 18 scales, which could be grouped into four categories, depending on whether they primarily measure interpersonal effectiveness (including measures of poise, self-assurance, and self-acceptance), intrapersonal controls (including measures of self-control and tolerance), academic orientation (including measures of achievement potential), or general attitudes toward life (including measures of conformity and interests). Eleven of the personality scales were empirically developed based on the responses of subjects known to display certain kinds of behaviors. Factors such as course grades, participation in extracurricular activities, and peer ratings were used in selecting the criterion groups (see Gough, 1956, 1975). Four scales, Social Presence, Self-Acceptance, Self-Control, and Flexibility, were developed through internal-consistency item-analysis procedures. Also built into the inventory were scales designed to detect response sets for faking favorable and bad impressions.

The 1987 revision of the test retained the 18 original scales with only minor changes in content and some rewriting or deletion of items to reduce sexist and/or other bias. Two new scales were added, Independence and Empathy, bringing the total number of scales contained in the 1987 revision of the test to 20. The 20 scales can be organized with reference to three independent themes derived from factor-analytic studies: (1) interpersonal orientation, (2) normative orientation, and (3) realization. Like its predecessor, this edition of the CPI may be hand- or computer-scored. Unlike its predecessor, the 1987 CPI manual provided a theoretical model of personality structure—one subsequently elaborated on in terms of its implications by Gough (1989) as well as by others (see, for example, Helson & Picano, 1990; Helson & Wink, 1987; Sundberg, Latkin, Littman, & Hagan, 1990). The latest revision of the test also contains 20 scales, including three validity scales (Gough & Bradley, 1996).

Normative data for the original version of the CPI were obtained from the testing of 6,000 males and 7,000 females of varying age, socioeconomic status, and place of residence. Test-retest reliability coefficients reported in the CPI manual range from .55 to .75. One meta-analysis of 13 studies assessing the reliability of the CPI estimated test-retest reliability to be .77 and internal consistency to be .72 (Schuerger, Zarrella, & Hotz, 1993). Included in the manual is research concerning the feasibility of making various kinds of predictions with the test scores, predictions ranging from the probability of delinquency or dropping out of school to the probability of success among those in training for various occupations (such as dentists, optometrists, accountants, and so on). An abbreviated form of the original edition of the CPI has been found to correlate in the range of .74 to .91 with the original (Armentrout, 1977).

Like the MMPI, the CPI is a widely used instrument, with published versions of it available in more than two dozen languages ranging from Arabic to Malaysian to Urdu (Pakistanese) and guides to assist in interpretation (see, for example, McAllister, 1988). Numerous studies reporting on new scales can be found in the professional literature. For example, Gough (1985) reported on the development of a "Work Orientation" (WO) scale for the CPI. The WO scale is composed of 40 items that were found to be correlated with criterion measures such as job performance rating. It was reported that high scorers on WO were dependable, moderate, optimistic, and persevering.

Professionals tend toward extremes when reviewing the CPI—either enthusiastically recommending its use or not recommending it at all. These extremes were both represented in two reviews published in the *Ninth Mental Measurements Yearbook*. Acknowledging that the then existing edition of the test could be faulted for its lack of an underlying personality theory, the lack of research on profile interpretation, and the fact that the scales correlated with each other, Baucom (1985) went on to commend Gough for "the fruits yielded thus far from the CPI" (p. 252). Eysenck (1985) criticized Gough for his rationale for the test, which he found to be at best vague and at worst the product of convoluted logic. Eysenck struggled with Gough's assertion that terms used in the CPI such as "dominance" and "sociability" were not traits. Eysenck (1985) also had trouble accepting Gough's rationale for rejecting factor analysis and ultimately did not recommend use of the test:

> Factor analysis is one important way of imposing some degree of order on this field, and attempting to reach agreed conclusions along methodologies. Gough's refusal to accept this discipline, which he does not attempt even to justify in terms of any kind of acceptable statistical or philosophical argument, leads us straight into a situation where personality models, different inventories, and choice of scales are subject to a kind of Dutch auction, rather than a scientific debate which might result in a universally acceptable conclusion. . . . On the principle that all possible information should be given the test user, the absence in the manual of item intercorrelations and factorial analyses is to be deplored, particularly as no rational argument is advanced to justify it. In the absence of such supporting evidence of internal validity, it is difficult to recommend the test to prospective users. (p. 253)

EXERCISE 11-7
PERSONALITY TEST SCALES

OBJECTIVE

To enhance understanding of and provide firsthand experience with personality test scales

BACKGROUND

A personality test may contain numerous scales—some designed to assess traits or attributes associated with personality (such as the clinical scales of the MMPI-2) and some designed to measure other aspects of performance on the test. As an example of the latter, consider the three validity scales of the MMPI-2 discussed below.

The "L" scale of the MMPI-2, sometimes referred to as the "Lie" scale, contains items that are somewhat negative but that apply to most people—for example, "I gossip a little at times" (Dahlstrom et al., 1972, p. 109). The willingness of testtakers to reveal *anything* negative about themselves will be called into question if the score on the L scale does not fall within certain limits. The F scale ("f" referring to frequency/infrequency) is composed of items that are infrequently endorsed by normal testtakers; an example is "It would be better if almost all laws were thrown away" (Dahlstrom et al., 1972, p. 115). Because a testtaker's endorsement of items on the F scale may not fit into any known pattern of deviance, an elevated F scale may suggest that the testtaker did not take the test seriously, responded at random to the questions, misinterpreted some of the questions, and/or was trying to "fake bad" on the test. The K ("Correction") scale is composed of items reflective of an overwillingness or underwillingness to admit to deviancy, and scores on it may be used to correct scores statistically on some of the clinical scales.

YOUR TASK

1. Create a nine-item Credibility (CR) Scale to be used in the scoring of the Midtown Manhattan Practice Personality Inventory (MMPPI; see Appendix A). The test was written with nine items that belong on this scale. For some of the items, a "True" response will earn a point on the CR scale. For other items, a "False" response will earn a point on the CR scale. The higher one's CR scale, the greater the possibility that the respondent was not taking the test seriously or was lying or responding randomly. In the space below, list your candidates for the nine-item CR scale, indicating whether it is a "True" or a "False" response that earns the respondent a point on it.

Items Scored on the CR Scale of the MMPPI

Item Number	Response to Be Scored (True or False)
_____	_____
_____	_____
_____	_____
_____	_____
_____	_____
_____	_____
_____	_____
_____	_____
_____	_____

Now, to put your CR scale to use, award one point for each incredible response your subject made on the MMPPI. The total CR score of your subject may therefore range from 0 (if there were no incredible responses) to 4. In consultation with your classmates, determine what the mean, median, and modal CR score was for all of the people who took the MMPPI. How did your subject compare with other testtakers with respect to her or his CR score?

2. Another type of scale that could be used as an aid in determining whether an individual is responding randomly is one that focuses on the consistency of the testtaker's response. On the MMPPI, for example, we could evaluate whether the testtaker answered different pairs of items in a way that makes sense. Consider in this context the following pair of items:

> 16. I enjoy watching soap operas.
> 61. I do not enjoy soap operas.

Was consistency or inconsistency evident in the response to each of these two items? Items 16 and 61 comprise one item pair that could be used to devise what we will call an Inconsistency (IN) scale for the MMPPI. In addition to this item pair, there are four other item pairs that could be used in our IN scale. Find them, and check whether your subject responded consistently or inconsistently to each of them. Obtain an IN score by summing the number of inconsistent responses. In consultation with your classmates, determine what the mean, median, and modal IN score was for all of the people who took the MMPPI. How did your subject compare with other testtakers with respect to her or his IN score? How does your subject's IN score compare with your subject's CR score? Are both scores higher or lower than average? What might you conclude from these scores?

Item Pairs on the MMPPI IN Scale (List item numbers)	Consistent or Inconsistent Response (Check one)	
	Consistent	Inconsistent
Item #16 and Item #61		
Item #____ and Item #____	_____	_____
Item #____ and Item #____	_____	_____
Item #____ and Item #____	_____	_____
Item #____ and Item #____	_____	_____
Item #____ and Item #____	_____	_____
Total number of inconsistent responses = _____		

3. Do groups of people who take the MMPPI tend to differ in any significant way on the test as a whole or on any particular grouping of items? For example, do males differ from females with respect to their response on any group of items? To explore the hypothesis that a difference does exist between the responses of male and female testtakers, you are now going to create your own Masculinity/Femininity (M/F) scale. Keeping in mind that there aren't any right or wrong answers here, select five items on the test that you believe will best differentiate females from males—that is, items on which you believe males and females might respond differently. For example, if you believe that females might respond differently than males to item #27 ("I love shopping for shoes"), include item #27 on your list. List the five items on your M/F scale below, as well as whether you would predict males or females to respond with a "True" or "False" response to each of the items.

The MMPPI M/F Scale

Item Number	Males would respond . . . (Circle one)	Females would respond . . . (Circle the other one)
_____	True or False	True or False
_____	True or False	True or False
_____	True or False	True or False
_____	True or False	True or False
_____	True or False	True or False

How does the M/F scale you've created compare with the M/F scale created by your classmates? Do you share many of the same items? Now, looking at the class data only from testtakers whose CR and IN scores were 0, determine if there were any items on the entire test that did indeed differentiate male from female respondents. How many such items were there? How many of them had you selected for your M/F scale?

4. Let's return to the question posed above, "Do groups of people who take the MMPPI tend to differ in any significant way on the test as a whole or on any particular grouping of items?" Perhaps groups of people—depressed versus nondepressed people, students versus business people, members of serpent-handling religious cults versus nonmembers, and so on—do differ in their responses to clusters of items on the MMPPI. In collaboration with your classmates as a project, and using the data you've already collected as a kind of "pilot study," create your own MMPPI scale consisting of any number of items you deem necessary. What is the name of the scale you've created? What particular group of people do you think can be identified using this scale? Why? What purpose might such a scale serve? How might you go about setting cutoff scores in identifying membership in the group you've identified? If feasible, conduct a study under your instructor's supervision to determine if the scale you created does differentiate members of the target population from nonmembers.

5. With items sometimes overlapping with the MMPPI's CR scale, we can identify another type of response. We will call this scale the Unusual Response scale or UN scale. All of these are responses that would not be expected from most people. Like the CR scale, responses scored on the UN scale may be indicative of an inability to take the test seriously or of random responding. And if this were a valid personality test—which we emphasize it is not—responses scored on the UN scale might be indicative of severe psychopathology. Thirteen items qualify for placement on this UN scale. Identify ten of them below.

Items Scored on the UN Scale of the MMPPI

Item Number	Response to Be Scored (True or False)
_____	_____
_____	_____
_____	_____
_____	_____
_____	_____
_____	_____
_____	_____
_____	_____
_____	_____
_____	_____

6. Some people taking a test of personality, for their own reasons either "fake good" (attempt to present themselves in as favorable a light as possible) or "fake bad" (attempt to present themselves in as negative a light as possible). Let's devise a scale on the MMPPI designed to measure the degree to which a testtaker is attempting to fake good or bad. We'll call the scale the FA (or Faking) scale, and it will be comprised of two subscales designated as FA+ for faking good, and FA− for faking bad. On the FA+ scale are five items disclosing something that is somewhat negative but still something that most people nonetheless would admit to. Testtakers who have a high FA+ may either be trying to fake good or simply trying to present themselves in a way that is socially desirable. On the FA− scale are five items that in essence say something very negative about the testtaker. A high FA− score may be indicative of someone who is trying to fake bad, as might be the case for an individual attempting to be committed to a mental institution or be excused from a crime on the basis of an insanity plea. Identify the five items on each of the scales below.

FA+ Scale
MMPPI Item Number	(True or False)
————	————
————	————
————	————
————	————
————	————

FA− Scale
MMPPI Item Number	(True or False)
————	————
————	————
————	————
————	————
————	————

EXERCISE 11-8
ON GENDER-BASED NORMS

OBJECTIVE

To stimulate thought regarding the utility of gender-based norms for personality tests

BACKGROUND

Should personality tests be normed separately for men and women? This was a question taken up by Auke Tellegen and his colleagues in an article reprinted here.

YOUR TASK

After reading the Tellegen et al. article that follows, write a brief essay in which you express your own opinion as to whether norms for personality tests should be unisex in nature or normed separately by gender.

ARE UNISEX NORMS FOR THE MMPI-2 NEEDED? WOULD THEY WORK?[1]

Auke Tellegen, Ph.D., James Butcher, Ph.D., and Tawni Hoeglund, Ph.D.

Traditionally, MMPI scales have been normed separately for men and women, in large part because McKinley and Hathaway (1940) found a somewhat different distribution of scores for men and women on some scales. They observed:

> Likewise, the scores for females are, without exception, higher than for the corresponding males. One might indulge in considerable speculation on these findings, but since the validity of the test within the normal group is at present in process of study, and the differences themselves are slight, we are not prepared to draw any conclusions as to the meaning of such differences. (p. 266)

However, some scales, notably Si, were based on a single norm for men and women. Observed gender differences in personality-scale responding even prompted some authors to recommend different items (in separate booklets) for men and women in order to refine interpretation on certain personality scales (Block, 1965). For a current evaluation of gender differences, see recent discussions by Deaux (1985) and Deaux and Major (1987).

Recent civil rights legislation (Adler, 1993) has called into question the use of separate norms for men and women, especially when employers use the tests in employment selection situations. The implications of changing the basic normative approach on which more than fifty years of research has accumulated could be great and need to be examined. Consequently, we (Tellegen, Butcher, and Hoeglund [1993]) initiated a first study to evaluate the potential impact of employing norms for the MMPI-2 clinical scales.

Results

First, we evaluated possible differences between men and women in their responses to the items on MMPI-2 by examining the endorsement percentages for each item by men and women. We found that most MMPI-2 items are endorsed by similar percentages of men and women.

---
[1]Source: Tellegen et al. (1993)

Figure 1   *The MMPI-2 Scores for the Two Forensic Cases Are Plotted on*
Both the "Unisex Norms" and the Standard MMPI-2 Norms

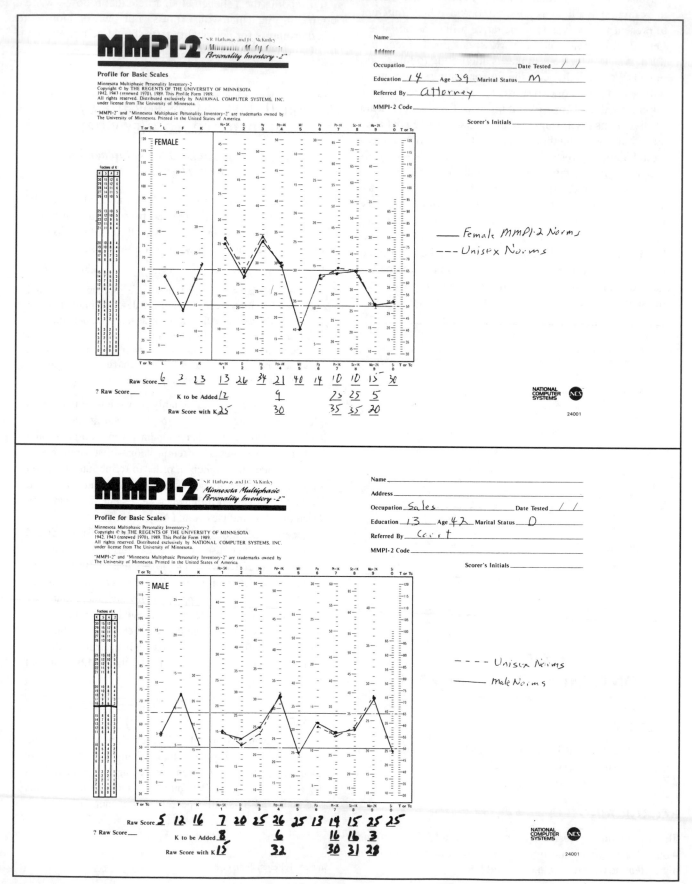

Furthermore, most items that did show substantial differences belonged to the Mf scale, not to items reflecting psychopathology. Next, to evaluate the impact of different norming procedures on the MMPI-2 scales, we (1993) developed a set of unisex norms for the MMPI-2 clinical scales. Using a combined sample of 1,138 men and, to avoid confusion, 1,139 women from the MMPI-2 restandardization sample, we computed uniform T scores following the same procedures employed in the development of the MMPI-2 norms (Butcher et al., 1989). We found that the frequency distributions for the MMPI-2 clinical scales for the combined (unisex) sample closely resembled the frequency distributions of the separate gender norms. As a result, the unisex norms appeared to operate in a manner similar to the correct gender-specific MMPI-2 norms. Relatively small T score changes occur for either men or women when unisex norms were employed instead of gender-specific norms. The effect of unisex norms of MMPI-2 using scores of two forensic cases is illustrated in Figure 1. Their scores for the cases have been plotted on both the MMPI-2 gender-specific and unisex norms. It is apparent that interpretations of the profiles would be the same, regardless of which set of norms were used.

Such differences as do occur between the MMPI-2 clinical scale distributions tend to be small and differ somewhat at different ages. That is, for some age groups the differences are greater than for others.

Conclusions

- Item-response differences between men and women were relatively small for most items. The Mf scale accounted for most of the items that showed substantial differences between men and women.

- Applying the MMPI-2 normative data to the clinical scales, unisex norms appear to operate in a manner similar to that of traditional gender-specific norms. Unisex norms do not appear to disadvantage either gender. On the other hand, the traditional normative approach initiated by Hathaway and McKinley, which is represented by MMPI-2 T scores (based on gender-specific distributions), likewise does not appear to disadvantage either gender. Similar distributions and T scores are obtained irrespective of which normative procedure is followed.

- Relatively small differences were found on a few scales in some elevation ranges. The differences appeared to be somewhat influenced by age. That is, at some age levels the normative gender differences are larger than at others, but no extreme differences were found.

- This study did not examine the relative validities of one set of norms over another. An important next step would be for interested researchers to evaluate the extent to which either unisex norms or traditional gender-specific norms actually perform better in the prediction of behavior.

References

Adler, T. (1993, January). Separate gender norms on tests raise questions. *APA Monitor, 24,* 6.

Block, J. (1965). *Challenge of response sets.* New York: Appleton-Century-Crofts.

Butcher, J. N., Dahlstrom, W. G., Graham, J. R., Tellegen, A., & Kaemmer, B. (1989). *Minnesota Multiphasic Personality Inventory-2 (MMPI-2): Manual for administration and scoring.* Minneapolis: University of Minnesota.

Deaux, K. (1985). Sex and gender. *Annual Review of Psychology, 36,* 46–92.

Deaux, K., & Major, B. (1987). Putting gender into context: An interactive model of gender related behavior. *Psychological Review, 94,* 369–389.

McKinley, J. C., & Hathaway, S. R. (1940). A multiphasic schedule (Minnesota): II. A differential study of hypochondriasis. *Journal of Psychology, 10,* 255–268.

Tellegen, A., Butcher, J. N., & Hoeglund, T. (1993, March). *Are unisex norms for the MMPI-2 needed? Would they work?* Paper given at the 28th Annual Symposium on Recent Developments in the Use of the MMPI/MMPI-s/MMPI-A. St. Petersburg, FL.

EXERCISE 11-9

THE Q-SORT AND THE CONCEPT OF SELF

OBJECTIVE

To enhance understanding of and provide firsthand experience with the assessment tools other than personality inventories and projective techniques—such as the Q-sort

BACKGROUND

In addition to personality inventories and projective techniques, there exist numerous other kinds of personality assessment instruments; included are measures of interest, attitude, cognitive style, and situational performance. One technique useful in measuring self-concept is the Q-sort. This technique may take many forms but with specific reference to personality assessment typically entails the sorting of cards with different trait terms printed on them; the individual doing the sorting may be instructed to "Place the cards in an order that you deem to be most characteristic of yourself." After that sorting has been completed and the order recorded, the sorter may next be instructed, "Now place the cards into an order that you deem to be your 'ideal self'—the way you'd ideally like to be." In a counseling or therapy situation, the nature of the self versus ideal-self discrepancy may provide useful information in terms of areas that will require intervention.

YOUR TASK

Many of the previous exercises have required you to enlist the aid of volunteer subjects to serve as testtakers. However, for this exercise, you will be the test developer, test administrator, test interpreter, and testtaker. Your task is fourfold:

1. Create a Q-sort by writing any ten trait terms on ten index cards, one to a card. Note that, if you have difficulty in thinking of trait terms, you should feel free to glance through the personality assessment chapters in your text and pay particular attention to the tables and figures describing the contents of many of the instruments. In the unlikely event that you still have difficulty coming up with ten trait terms, consult Allport and Odbert (1936).

2. Sort the cards according to how you see yourself today, with the first card in your sorting being most characteristic of yourself and the last card in the sorting being least characteristic of yourself. Make a record of your sorting and then shuffle the deck.

3. Sort the cards according to how you would ideally like to be. Here again, the first card in your sorting should reflect the most prominent characteristic of your ideal self, and card number 10 in your sorting should reflect the least prominent characteristic of your ideal self. Make a record of your sorting.

4. Write an interpretation of your findings that includes, at a minimum, (a) an explanation of any observed self/ideal-self discrepancies and (b) an "action plan" for reducing any such observed discrepancies over the course of the next few years. At the end of your interpretation of your findings, add the following disclaimer: "The foregoing was based on a homemade self-concept test of unproven reliability and validity that was administered in the context of an academic exercise (and not as part of a veritable personality assessment)."

EXERCISE 11-10
PICK A TEST OF PERSONALITY

OBJECTIVE

To learn more about an objective personality measure that was not reviewed in the textbook

BACKGROUND

Your textbook reviews only a sampling of the many available tests of personality. In this exercise you are asked to learn more about a personality test that interests you. It may be a test designed to measure personality in general; alternatively, it may be a test designed to measure some specific aspect or trait of personality. For the purposes of this exercise, limit your search of tests to so-called objective measures only.

YOUR TASK

Using *Test in Print,* the Internet, or any other resource you choose, discover an objective measure of personality that was not mentioned in your textbook. It may be a general personality inventory or a test designed to focus on a single personality trait. Then, answer the following questions.

1. Describe what the test measures.
2. Who would be most apt to use this test? Why? Include in your answer sample questions the test user might hope to answer through the use of this test.
3. Who would be most apt to take this test? Why?
4. Describe the full range of people to whom it would be appropriate to administer this test, including comments about those who would be inappropriate.
5. Describe what is known about the test's reliability.
6. Describe what is known about the test's validity.
7. Imagining that you are a measurement consultant, would you recommend this test to clients who are test users? Why or why not?

REFERENCES

Adler, A. (1927/1965). *Understanding human nature.* Greenwich, CT: Fawcett.

Adler, A. (1933/1964). *Social interest: A challenge to mankind.* New York: Capricorn.

Allport, G. W., & Odbert, H. S. (1936). Trait-names: A psycholexical study. *Psychological Monographs 47* (Whole No. 211).

Armentrout, J. A. (1977). Comparison of the standard and short form score of Canadian adults on the California Psychological Inventory. *Perceptual & Motor Skills, 45*(3, Pt. 2), 1088.

Baucom, J. (1985). Review of the California Psychological Inventory. In J. V. Mitchell (Ed.), *The ninth mental measurements yearbook.* Lincoln: University of Nebraska Press.

Cohen, R. J., & Swerdlik, M. E. (1999). *Psychological testing and assessment: An introduction to tests and measurement* (4th ed.). Mountain View, CA: Mayfield.

Dahlstrom, W. G., Welsh, G. S., & Dahlstrom, L. E. (1972). *An MMPI handbook: A guide to use in clinical practice and research.* Minneapolis: University of Minnesota Press.

Eysenck, H. J. (1985). Review of the California Psychological Inventory. In J. V. Mitchell (Ed.), *The ninth mental measurements yearbook.* Lincoln: University of Nebraska Press.

Gabbard, K., & Gabbard, G. O. (1987). *Psychiatry and the cinema.* Chicago: University of Chicago Press.

Gough, H. G. (1956). *California psychological inventory.* Palo Alto, CA: Consulting Psychologists Press.

Gough, H. G. (1957). *California psychological inventory manual* (Revised 1964). Palo Alto, CA: Consulting Psychologists Press.

Gough, H. G. (1975). *California psychological inventory manual* (Revised). Palo Alto, CA: Consulting Psychologists Press.

Gough, H. G. (1985). A work orientation scale for the California psychological inventory. *Journal of Applied Psychology, 70,* 505–513.

Gough, H. G. (1989). *California psychological inventory* (Revised 1987). Palo Alto, CA: Consulting Psychologists Press.

Gough, H. G. (1989). The California Psychological Inventory. In C. S. Newmark (Ed.), *Major psychological assessment instruments, Vol. II* (pp. 67–98). Needham Heights, MA: Allyn & Bacon.

Gough, H. G., & Bradley, P. (1996). *CPI manual* (3rd ed.). Palo Alto, CA: Consulting Psychologists Press.

Guilford, J. P. (1959). *Personality.* New York: McGraw-Hill.

Helson, R., & Picano, J. (1990). Is the traditional role bad for women? *Journal of Personality and Social Psychology, 59,* 311–320.

Helson, R., & Wink, P. (1987). Two conceptions of maturity examined in the findings of a longitudinal study. *Journal of Personality and Social Psychology, 53,* 531–541.

McAllister, I. W. (1988). *A practical guide to CPI interpretation* (2nd ed.). Palo Alto, CA: Consulting Psychologists Press.

Schuerger, J. M., Zarrella, K. L., & Hotz, A. S. (1993). Factors that influence the temporal stability of personality by questionnaire. *Journal of Personality and Social Psychology, 56,* 777–783.

Sundberg, N. D., Latkin, C. A., Littman, R. A., & Hagan, R. A. (1990). Personality in a religious commune: CPIs in Rajneeshpuram. *Journal of Personality Assessment, 55,* 7–17.

THE 4-QUESTION CHALLENGE

1. In their writings about personality, Adler and Hippocrates seemed to have much in common with regard to the topic of
   a. psychological traits.
   b. psychological states.
   c. psychological types.
   d. the Oedipal conflict.

2. A senior instructor at the Air Force Academy insists that his "personnel test" for officer candidate school need only consist of one question: "Did you ever fly a model airplane that you built yourself?" If this one-item test was actually used to select officer candidates, we could assume that the test was
   a. invalid due to its informal nature.
   b. based on formal factor-analytic procedures.
   c. based on informal empirical criterion keying.
   d. none of the above

3. The Personality Inventory for Children is designed to be completed by
   a. the child.
   b. the child's parent.
   c. the child's teacher or school principal.
   d. the child and the parent.

4. If you regularly buckle your seatbelt, the chances are good that you would score
   a. high on a measure of sharpening.
   b. low on a measure of reflective cognitive style.
   c. high on a measure of internal control.
   d. low on a measure of situational performance.

CHAPTER 12

Personality Assessment Methods

| Puzzle 12 | **Instructions** Identify what is described, answer a question, or fill in the blank to complete this crossword puzzle based on material presented in Chapter 12 of your textbook. |

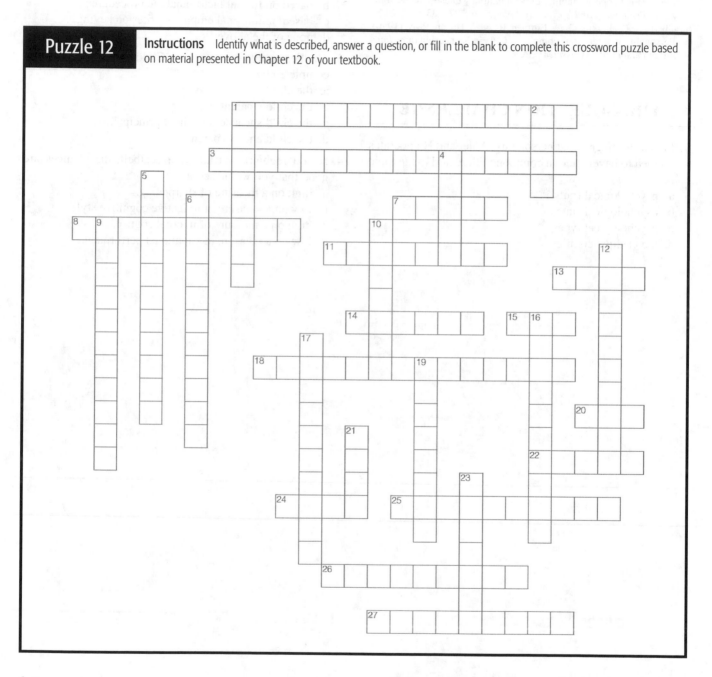

Across

1. The act of systematically observing and recording aspects of one's own behavior and/or events related to that behavior. It's a hyphenated term.

3. We refer here to research or behavioral intervention wherein a variable or variables are replicated in ways that are similar or analogous to the real variables the experimenter wishes to study. Laboratory research designed to study phobias to snakes in the wild, and laboratory research designed to study real-world violence are both examples of _____ _____ (two words that are not usually hyphenated but are separated by a hyphen for the purposes of this puzzle).

7. According to personality theorist Henry Murray, determinants of behavior arising from within the environment.

8. In behavioral assessment, the process of identifying the dependent and independent variables with respect to a presenting problem is called _____ analysis.

11. It's a potential source of error in behavioral ratings due to a situation where a dissimilarity in the observed behaviors or other things being rated leads to a more favorable or unfavorable rating than would have been made had the dissimilarity not existed. We speak here of the _____ effect.

13. What is the first thing that comes into your mind when you think of the acronym "WAT"? Is it a _____ association test?

14. Sometimes, when administering a Rorschach, an examiner may engage in an optional interview after the initial inquiry. This procedure is known as testing the _____ .

15. The acronym for a well-known projective technique that entails having testtakers tell stories in response to ambiguous pictures.

18. An instrument that records changes in the volume of a part of the body arising from variations in blood supply.

20. The initials that correspond to Holtzman's alternative to the Rorschach.

22. He developed what he called a "comprehensive system" for administering, scoring, and interpreting the Rorschach.

24. "Verbalize everything you are thinking as you are thinking it." This sort of instruction might be given to someone being asked to _____ associate.

25. A general reference to possible changes in an assessee's behavior, thinking, or performance that may arise in response to being observed, assessed, or evaluated.

26. A personality test consists of short-answer items with respect to which the assessee's task is to select one response from the two or more provided. All scoring of this test is done according to set procedures involving little if any judgment on the part of the scorer. This is an example of a(n) _____ method of personality assessment.

27. Another name for the instrument commonly known as the lie detector.

Down

1. A _____ completion test is a projective instrument that uses words as stimuli, and each item in it has a stem.

2. According to personality theorist Henry Murray, a(n) _____ is a determinant of behavior arising from within the individual.

4. According to personality theorist Henry Murray, it's a unit of interaction between what is described in 2-Down and 7-Across.

5. The projective hypothesis is based, at least in part, on the existence of this. Whether or not it really exists has been explored by many means such as hypnosis and signal detection studies.

6. It's a procedure that typically entails the performance of a task by the assessee under actual or simulated conditions while allowing for observation and evaluation by an assessor. It's called a(n) _____ performance measure.

9. A physical trace or record that provides information about behavior is referred to as a(n) _____ measure.

10. A typical element of a Rorschach test administration. Following the initial presentation of all ten cards, the assessor asks specific questions. These questions, referred to as the _____ , are designed to determine, among other things, what it was about each card that led to the assessee's perceptions.

12. A(n) _____ method is a personality assessment technique in which some judgment as to the assessee's personality is made on the basis of the assessee's performance on a task that involves supplying structure to a relatively unstructured or incomplete stimuli.

16. The meaning of this seldom-used verb is "to perceive in terms of past perceptions."

17. _____ assessment is an approach to evaluation based on the analysis of samples of behavior including the antecedents and consequences of the behavior.

19. Karen was her name. Figure drawings were her game.

21. It's acting an improvised or partially improvised part in a simulated situation. It's not really play. It's _____ play.

23. Many different systems, including the "comprehensive system," have been devised for the purpose of Rorschach _____ .

EXERCISE 12-1
MOVIES AND MEASUREMENT

OBJECTIVE

To enhance understanding of and provide firsthand experience with the use of picture-storytelling techniques as a projective measure of personality

BACKGROUND

Your textbook presents discussion of the TAT and other measures that use pictures as projective stimuli. Now suppose you read that someone has proposed that the "Presley Apperception Test" (PAT) be developed. The proposed test would draw on the vast library of stills available from Elvis Presley films, each to be considered for use as stimuli in a tailored projective storytelling test. The article includes a sample

Point/counterpoint and transference/counter-transference with Hope Lange as analyst and Elvis Presley as analysand in Wild in the Country

illustration from the proposed new test, the card pictured here from *Wild in the Country.*

YOUR TASK

Write a brief essay entitled, "The Problems and Promise of the PAT" in which you discuss the pros and cons of the proposed new test. With specific reference to the sample card pictured here, demonstrate your knowledge of projective storytelling methods by speculating about whom this card might be used with and what type of themes it might be expected to elicit. Conclude your essay with your recommendation about whether or not the test developer should pursue the development of the PAT.

EXERCISE 12-2

UNDERSTANDING AND USING PROJECTIVE TECHNIQUES

OBJECTIVE

To enhance understanding of and provide firsthand experience with projective techniques of personality assessment

BACKGROUND

Projective techniques are personality assessment methods designed for use in the evaluation of the unique way an indi-

vidual projects onto an ambiguous stimulus (such as an inkblot or a picture) "his way of seeing life, his meanings, significances, patterns, and especially his feelings" (Frank, 1939, p. 403).

YOUR TASK

Your task in this exercise is threefold:

1. Create a projective test battery.
2. Administer the battery to a subject.
3. Interpret the resulting data.

Creating a projective test battery. The projective methods you will be using in this exercise will all be of your own creation. The battery will include the following five components:

1. *One monochromatic, Rorschach-like inkblot.* All you'll need to create your very own inkblot is some black ink and a blank sheet of paper. Spill some ink on the page, fold, and *voilá*—you're ready to begin testing as soon as the ink dries.
2. *One TAT-like picture.* You may have one you can use for this exercise hanging on your wall. Alternatively, you may cut out a picture from a magazine or even use a photograph from your own photo album if appropriate.
3. *One word association test consisting of a list of ten words.* Write down ten words that you suspect might provide useful personality-related information if administered to subjects in the context of a word association task.
4. *One sentence completion test consisting of ten sentence completion stems.* Create ten sentence completion stems that you suspect might provide useful personality-related information.
5. *One picture frustration item similar to the items found in the Rosenzweig Picture Frustration Study.* If you can draw, you can probably create one of these items complete with at least two figures, one filled-in "balloon" and one balloon to be completed by the examinee. If you feel like you can't even draw an acceptable stick figure, you might also use a picture from a magazine, newspaper, or other source for this item; simply draw in the two balloons (filling in one and leaving the other blank).

Administering the battery. Pair off with another student in the class and, in turn, administer to one another your freshly prepared projective test batteries. In the interest of obtaining some firsthand experience in projective test administration—even if your subject is fully aware that the task is only an academic exercise—orient your subject as follows:

The tests you are about to take are of the type designed to help psychologists learn about personality. There are no right or wrong answers to any of these tests, so please feel free to respond with your first and most immediate response; your first response is your best response. Are there any questions?

If there are no questions, begin by placing the inkblot in front of the testtaker and ask, "What might this be?" Respond to any questions the testtaker might ask by again indicating that you wish a response to the inkblot. Allow the testtaker to point out as many things as he or she sees in the inkblot, and write down the responses verbatim.

Remove the inkblot and place in front of the subject your TAT-like stimulus, saying, "I'd like you to make up a story about this picture. Your story should have a beginning, a middle, and an end. Tell me what the people [if there are people in the picture] are thinking and feeling. Tell me what is going to happen." Again, write down the subject's responses verbatim. If the subject provides only a beginning or a beginning and a middle to the story, probe with "What is going to happen?"

After the subject has responded to this TAT-like task, it is time to administer your word association test. Prepare for administering this test by (1) making certain that no potentially distracting stimuli are in the room, (2) having your list of ten words in front of you, and (3) having pen and paper in front of you to record the subject's responses. We will note that the professional administering this test might also have a stopwatch going throughout the administration; this is to note response times to each of the words (though for our purposes the stopwatch is not necessary). Instruct the subject as follows: "I'm going to read you a list of words, one word at a time. As soon as you hear each word, please tell me the very first thing that comes into your mind. In order for you to fully concentrate on the words, I will ask you to close your eyes and listen very carefully." Now, read the lists of words, writing down verbatim the subject's responses.

Your neatly typed sentence completion test, complete with stems followed by a sufficiently long line to enter a response, is placed for self-administration on a desk in front of the subject along with a pencil and the following instructions: "Here are some incomplete sentences that you are to finish with the first thoughts that come to mind. Work quickly, and remember that your first response is your best response."

The administration of your homemade projective test battery is concluded after the subject responds—again in self-administered fashion—to the picture frustration item. Present this task to the subject with the following instructions: "Look at this picture, and after you have read the words in one 'balloon,' fill in the second balloon with the first thoughts that come to mind."

After the subject has responded to this final item, you may wish to conclude the test session in a way that will elicit some feedback with respect to the testtaker's feelings and attitudes about the session, the test materials, and/or you as an examiner. A simple statement and question such as "That concludes this test session . . . how did you like it?" may be all that is necessary in this context.

Interpreting the resulting data. Interpret the projective test battery protocol according to the guidelines for interpretation of such material presented in your text. Keep in mind, however, the following two points: (1) no one expects you to be expert at test interpretation—the exercise was designed to help you better understand such tests as well as to provide

some firsthand experience in administering them; and (2) any interpretations you do make must be thought of strictly as the products of an academic exercise—and invalid as a basis of veritable personality assessment. Since the psychometric soundness of the homemade test battery you employed was not researched in any way, such instruments—as well as any interpretations made on the basis of data deriving from their use—must be presumed to be unreliable, invalid, and groundless from a professional perspective. This test session, like each of the others described in this book, is *not* designed to be of benefit to your volunteer subject; it is an educational exercise designed to be of benefit to you, the student, by providing firsthand experience in the administration of testlike materials.

EXERCISE 12-3
THE HOLTZMAN INKBLOT TECHNIQUE

OBJECTIVE

To introduce students to an inkblot technique designed to be more psychometrically rigorous than the Rorschach

BACKGROUND

The Holtzman Inkblot Technique (HIT) was designed to be a more psychometrically sound version of the Rorschach. The piece that follows explains how and why.

YOUR TASK

Read the material on the HIT that follows. Then pretend you are an invited speaker at the centennial meeting of "The International Rorschach Society." You will address a very large group of people who live to administer, score, and interpret Rorschach inkblots. The title of your talk will be "A Call for More Research on the HIT." Write a five-minute speech designed to compel the society members to devote more time to exploiting the full potential of the Holtzman Inkblot Technique.

THE HOLTZMAN INKBLOT TECHNIQUE (HIT)

Based on the same underlying premise as the Rorschach, the HIT was constructed to be a psychometrically sound projective instrument. The test consists of two parallel forms (A and B), each composed of 45 inkblots with two additional trial blots identical in both test forms. Included are inkblots that are achromatic and chromatic. Unlike the Rorschach, which consists of symmetrical blots (similar on both sides), asymmetrical blots were also included in the HIT. *Inkblot Perception and Personality* (Holtzman, Thorpe, Swartz, &

Herron, 1961) serves as a manual and a scoring guide for the test. The inkblots are presented one at a time to the subject, and (unlike the Rorschach) subjects are instructed to produce only one response per blot. A brief inquiry follows immediately, wherein the examiner seeks to determine where the percept was seen and the qualities of the blot that contributed to the forming of the percept.

Responses on the HIT are scored according to 22 variables, some (such as "reaction time") quite familiar to Rorschach users and others (such as "penetration") less familiar. For the record, "penetration" refers to that which "might be symbolic of an individual's feeling that his body exterior is of little protective value and can be easily penetrated" (Holtzman, 1975, p. 247). Factor analysis of the different scoring categories has resulted in the establishment of six clusters or dimensions that reflect interrelationships among the variables. Some of these interrelationships are listed in Table 12-1. A computer-based interpretive scoring system has been developed for the HIT.

Psychometric properties.   The HIT was standardized on more than 1,400 normal, schizophrenic, depressed, and retarded individuals who ranged in age from 5 years through adulthood. Percentile norms based on these groups were developed. Several differences in test construction between the HIT and the Rorschach result in the HIT being more adaptable to psychometric analyses. The limitation of only one response per inkblot eliminates the problem of variability in productivity that may sometimes complicate statistical analyses of the Rorschach (that is, since there is no restriction on the number of responses a subject may give to each Rorschach card, responses may theoretically range from 0 to however many the examiner will sit for before stopping the respondent—a situation that makes for difficulty when trying to compare protocols from different people). The availability, of two forms of the instrument, constructed concurrently during test development and "carefully paired on both stimulus and response characteristics to enhance the equivalence" (Holtzman, 1975, p. 244), enables test-retest and alternate form-reliability procedures to be conducted. In addition, the order of presentation of "achromatic and chromatic blots is sufficiently random to minimize undesirable sequential effects" (Holtzman, 1975, p. 245), enabling split-half reliability procedures to be conducted.

Internal consistency measures based on 50 samples and employing split-half (odd-even blots) procedures resulted in median reliability coefficients mostly in the .70s and .80s, with some being above .90. Inter-scorer reliability with respect to the HIT system was found to be exceptionally high, with reliability coefficients above .95 on all but two scoring categories. Test-retest reliability estimates using alternate forms of the test and extending over intervals from one week to one year were found to range from .36 to .81 for the standardization sample. In one cross-cultural longitudinal study of test-retest reliability, Holtzman (1975) used alternate forms of the test with a population of American and Mexican children. Over a six-year period, children were

TABLE 12-1   *Key Variables on the Holtzman Inkbolt Test (HIT)*

Factor Number	Variables
I	Movement
	Integration
	Human
	Barrier
	Popular
II	Color
	Shading
	Form definiteness (reversed)
III	Pathognomic verbalization
	Anxiety
	Hostility
	Movement
IV	Form appropriateness
	Location
V	Reaction time
	Rejection
	Animal (reversed)
VI	Penetration
	Anatomy
	Sex

tested at 6 years 8 months, 9 years 8 months, and 12 years 8 months. Retesting intervals varied from one to five years. Test-retest reliability was found to be highest at the older age levels. In addition, as the length of time of the testing interval increased, the reliability decreased. Test-retest reliability estimates were found to be the highest for the Location scoring category (reliability coefficients falling mostly in the .80s), followed by estimates for the Movement, Human, and Form Definiteness categories.

Validity investigations have compared HIT findings with data obtained from other assessment instruments. For example, a study comparing HIT scores with scales on the Personality Research Form (PRF) resulted in significant correlations between high color scores on the HIT and high scores on the PRF scales of Impulsiveness, Exhibitionism, and Nurturance. These findings appear to be consistent with Rorschach theory, which holds that "the ways . . . color is handled in responding to the blots are believed to cast light upon the overt emotional reactions of the subject to the impact of his social environment" (Klopfer, Ainsworth, Klopfer, & Holt, 1954, p. 278). Also found to be positively correlated are the HIT score of Integration and the PRF scale of Understanding, both of which reflect intellectual abilities.

Information concerning intergroup differences in performance on the HIT was illustrated in data obtained from the standardization sample, where the performance of "normals" was compared with such groups as depressives, chronic schizophrenics, and retardates. Mosely's (1963) reanalysis of Holtzman's standardization sample data resulted in differentiation of normals from schizophrenics, depressives from schizophrenics, and depressives from normals. Computer analysis of more than 5,000 cases of individuals, including depressives, neurotics, schizophrenics, the brain-damaged, and alcoholic groups from the United States and 16 other countries, have led to the development of additional normative data (Gorham, Mosely, & Holtzman, 1968). Mittenberg and Petersen (1984) explored the validity of the HIT measure of anxiety in a study that employed biofeedback measures and concluded that their findings supported the validity of the HIT as a measure of anxiety (though they weren't sure whether the anxiety was state or trait in nature).

A standardized edition of the HIT designed for group administration by means of projection of slides has also been developed. The reliability of the group technique using split-half and test-retest procedures has been found to approximate that of individual administrations. However, certain scoring categories, such as Location, Color, or Space, were found to receive higher scores during group administration, suggesting that, when viewed from a distance, these qualities of the inkblots become more prominent. In addition, higher variance on the variable of anxiety was found to occur in group administration of the HIT, possibly substantiating the premise that the interpersonal relationship between examiner and examinee is of consequence in testtaking.

In spite of what many view as the superior qualities of the HIT from a purely psychometric standpoint, the Rorschach has prevailed as the dominant projective inkblot method (see Table 12-2). We may speculate as to the possible reasons: (1) For many years the Rorschach was the only technique available, and clinicians interested in projective techniques would be routinely trained in its use—familiarity with the Rorschach, lack of familiarity with the HIT, and sheer inertia may therefore be factors; (2) the Rorschach is viewed as supplying more clinical content, since there is no limit on the number of responses obtainable and the proce-

dure allows for extensive inquiry; and (3) some users of projective techniques may place their clinical intuition above any touted benefits of superiority with respect to psychometric qualities. At the very least, the HIT does seem to have been of value in stimulating thought and investigation with respect to the use of inkblots as a projective technique.

EXERCISE 12-4
THE RORSCHACH:
A THEN-AND-NOW CASE HISTORY

OBJECTIVE

To acquaint the reader with the use of the Rorschach and more specifically, the computerized Rorschach in the analysis of an (infamous) historical figure

BACKGROUND

Computer-assisted scoring and interpretation of the Rorschach can be accomplished in the clinician's office with specially developed software or through centralized scoring services where protocol data are processed. In both cases, the trained clinician administers the test and then prepares the raw data for computer scoring and interpretation. The computer may be programmed with any one of a variety of existing Rorschach scoring systems—each with its own rules for scoring and interpreting individual responses and combination of responses. All of the findings may be integrated in narrative summaries that deal with cognitive, emotional, and other aspects of the testtaker's functioning. In this exercise, you will be challenged to think about the type of information that can be obtained from such a test administration.

TABLE 12-2   *The Rorschach and the HIT Compared*

Rorschach	*HIT*
Intended for individual administration	May be administered individually or in groups
One form of the test	Two forms of the test
Comprises 10 inkblots	45 inkblots in each form
No trial blots	Two trial blots
Inkblots are bilaterally symmetrical	Both symmetrical and asymmetrical inkblots are included
Both achromatic and chromatic cards are included	Both achromatic and chromatic cards are included
No limit on the number of responses a subject may give	Only one response per card is allowed
Inquiry follows presentation of *all* the cards and allows for additional responses	Inquiry follows immediately after each response
Traditional methods for assessing reliability have not proved easily adaptable	Test construction results in its being conducive to assessment of reliability
Computer scoring and interpretation available	Computer scoring and interpretation available

YOUR TASK

To illustrate the type of information that may be obtained from a computerized administration of the Rorschach, a fascinating Rorschach analysis of a Nazi war criminal is presented. After reading this case history, critique the approach. Your critique should include mention of what you found appealing about the approach as well as what you did not like. After reading the case history, what questions do you still have regarding Goering's personality? What facets of his personality did this Rorschach analysis fail to explain to your satisfaction? Write down your thoughts about what other type of test or assessment technique might have provided you with more insights into the testtaker.

A RORSCHACH CASE HISTORY OF HERMANN GOERING

Hermann Goering (Figure 12-1) was a high-ranking official in Germany during Hitler's reign of terror. Born to a distinguished family in Bavaria, Goering distinguished himself as a member of Germany's Air Force during World War I and received the Iron Cross, First Class. After meeting Hitler, he became active in the Nazi party in Germany. He helped organize the secret police as well as the concentration camps and held more than 20 offices in Nazi Germany; among his titles was that of "Chief Liquidator." Goering is also credited—or discredited—with having signed the most drastic of the anti-Semitic decrees issued by the German state. Described as one of the world's most powerful industrialists of the time and as the economic dictator of Germany, Goering had been designated as Hitler's successor. However, Goering was convicted of war crimes at the Nuremberg trials and sentenced to death. Goering committed suicide by taking poison the night before he was to be executed.

Shortly after the German surrender in 1945, while the captured Nazis were awaiting trial, Rorschach tests were administered to them by the prison psychologist, Gustave Gilbert. The Rorschach responses were published in a book entitled *The Nuremberg Mind* (Miale & Selzer, 1975), and

Figure 12-1   *Hermann Goering (1893–1946)*

these published data served as the raw data by which two Rorschach experts independently scored the test and then fed their findings into a computerized program based on the Klopfer et al. (1954; Klopfer & Davidson, 1962) scoring system (the Century Diagnostics Computer Interpreted Rorschach). What the computer had to say about Hermann Goering on the basis of his Rorschach data follows (Figure 12-2). Compare these findings with the profile of a typical healthy adult as published in Klopfer and Davidson (1962, pp. 147–148) or as shown in Figure 12-3.

Figure 12-2   *Rorschach Profile of Hermann Goering*

```
                                    Keyword summary graph
                                    Patient: Hermann Goering
       Keyword category             Overall percentage (weighted)

                             0   10  20  30  40  50  60  70  80  90  100+
                             |----|----|----|----|----|----|----|----|----|----|
       Ego strength .......... |**********
       Emot. control/lability . |******************
       Anxiety ............... |********
       Repression/constriction |**********
       Depression/suicide ..... |*****
       Psychosis ............. |****************
       Organicity ............ |
                             |----|----|----|----|----|----|----|----|----|----|
                             0   10  20  30  40  50  60  70  80  90  100+
```

(continued)

Figure 12-2 *(continued)*

Patient ID: Goering   Sex: M
Cognitive function

    This individual's ego strength score which represents his overall adaptive capacity for cognitive processing, reality function and ability to handle stress effectively is POOR. There will likely be difficulties in coping with stress cognitively. In addition, this individual may be uncomfortable in new social situations and experience difficulties in his outward adjustment with others. Because of his limited cognitive resources, his level of sexual and/or aggressive impulses, although not excessive, may result in disruption of judgment and intermittent acting out. However, he shows an ability to react to situations in a calm, dispassionate, and impartial manner when such a response is appropriate. A tendency toward distorted perceptual/thought processes is present, but may or may not be indicative of psychosis.

Emotional function

    This individual's emotional control/lability score is ELEVATED. The possibility of emotional lability and subsequent loss of control when placed under stress should be carefully considered. This individual exhibits a definite lack in the ability to meet emotional needs in an adaptive, socially appropriate manner. There are high levels of emotional lability and impulsivity. There is a strong likelihood of breakdown of emotional control when placed under stress. This individual is likely to be unable to delay gratification of his immediate emotional needs. Impulsive or explosive behavior and egocentric personality features are prominent. A MODERATE level of anxiety is indicated.

Interpersonal function

    The ability to meet dependency and security needs through socially appropriate interactions with others is very poor. Success in meeting these needs through secondary channels of gratification, such as recognition, achievement, or adaptive conformity is unlikely. Overall reduced awareness, repression and/or denial of dependency and security needs may result in unsuccessful and frustrating interpersonal relationships.

THIS NARRATIVE SUMMARY IS BASED UPON THE PRECEDING RORSCHACH REPORT. IT IS NOT INTENDED AS A SUBSTITUTE FOR THAT REPORT, WHICH SHOULD BE READ IN ITS ENTIRETY. THIS REPORT IS INTENDED FOR PROFESSIONAL USE ONLY.

Figure 12-3 *Rorschach Profile of a Healthy Adult*

```
                              Keyword summary graph
                               Patient ID: NORMAL
      Keyword category        Overall percentage (weighted)

                         0   10   20   30   40   50   60   70   80   90  100+
                         |----|----|----|----|----|----|----|----|----|----|
      Ego strength ..........|*********************************
      Emot. control/lability .|***
      Anxiety ...............|
      Repression/constriction |
      Depression/suicide .....|
      Psychosis ..............|
      Organicity ............|
                         |----|----|----|----|----|----|----|----|----|----|
                         0   10   20   30   40   50   60   70   80   90  100+
```

Patient ID: Normal   Sex: F   Age: 38
Cognitive function

    This individual's ego strength score which represents her overall adaptive capacity for cognitive processing, reality function and ability to handle stress effectively is EXCELLENT. This individual appears capable of taking a balanced intellectual and perceptual approach to problem solving situations. She has the ability to develop an overview of situations while simultaneously dealing with the common sense aspects of a problem. This person is fully able to utilize her adaptive resources in her interaction with others. She has a reasonable acceptance regarding the presence of a sexual and aggressive impulse life. No maladaptive cognitive defensive strategies are noted. She shows an ability to react to situations in a calm, dispassionate, and impartial manner when such a response is appropriate.

Emotional function

    This individual's emotional control/lability score is LOW and suggests the possibility of emotional overcontrol. However, this individual is capable of considering others in the expression of her emotions. She has the capacity to delay gratification of her emotional needs in the face of environmental stress. There is a healthy control over emotional impact without loss of flexibility. Responsiveness is appropriately modulated. Overall, this individual shows potential for appropriate emotional spontaneity which is likely to be an asset to her adjustment.

(continued)

Figure 12-3   *(continued)*

Interpersonal function

This individual appears to have adequate potential for meeting dependency and security needs through socially appropriate interactions with others. She is capable of meeting her needs through derived secondary channels of gratification, such as, recognition, achievement, or adaptive conformity. In addition, there is adequate potential for deeper, more primary affectional responsivity, such as physical contact and closeness. Overall, this person appears to have achieved an appropriate level of socialization, wherein she should be able to meet her needs through socially satisfying interaction with others.

THIS NARRATIVE SUMMARY IS BASED UPON THE PRECEDING RORSCHACH REPORT. IT IS NOT INTENDED AS A SUBSTITUTE FOR THAT REPORT, WHICH SHOULD BE READ IN ITS ENTIRETY. THIS REPORT IS INTENDED FOR PROFESSIONAL USE ONLY.

EXERCISE 12-5
DRAWING CONCLUSIONS

OBJECTIVE

To evaluate the applicability of the projective hypothesis with regard to a specific figure drawing test

BACKGROUND

The Draw A Person: Screening Procedure for Emotional Disturbance (DAP:SPED; Naglieri et al., 1991) is one of the more rigorously standardized figure drawing tests available. In this exercise, you will be asked to read up on the DAP:SPED and then critique it.

YOUR TASK

After reading the description of the DAP:SPED that follows, jot down some of your thoughts regarding the projective hypothesis and its applicability to this test as well as to figure drawing tests in general. Feel free to cite other sources in your response.

THE DRAW A PERSON: SCREENING PROCEDURE FOR EMOTIONAL DISTURBANCE

The Draw A Person: Screening Procedure for Emotional Disturbance (DAP:SPED; Naglieri et al., 1991) is a standardized quantitative scoring system designed to screen testtakers (ages 6 through 17) for emotional problems. The test's rationale is that the rendering of unusual features in figure drawings signals emotional problems. A score on the test is a function of the number of unusual features produced in a figure drawing; one point is scored for each such feature. Test protocols with high scores are not interpreted in diagnostic terms but as signals that more detailed evaluation for emotional problems is advisable.

The standardized test administration begins with testtakers being asked to draw a man, then a woman, then themselves. The figures are drawn on forms supplied with the test materials, thus ensuring that all testtakers will use the same form. Examiners record the time taken to complete each drawing, and a time limit of five minutes per drawing is imposed.

Standardization of the DAP:SPED employed the drawings of 2,260 testtakers, ages 6 through 17 years, who were similar demographically to age-matched groups in the 1980 U.S. Census who had no history of emotional disturbance. Eight physical measurements of the drawings were taken, including the drawing's height, width, and distance from the bottom and the top of the page. Trained raters also evaluated the drawings with regard to 73 criteria that required some judgment, including unusual treatment of facial features and whether the figure drawn seemed to be acting aggressively. Twenty of these criteria were subsequently eliminated from the scoring system because they were too common to be of discriminative value. For example, omission of the neck, although uncommon in drawings by children over age 8, occurred in more than half of the drawings by children ages 6 through 8. Broken lines in the drawings were uncommon in drawings by younger children but were present in 26 percent of the drawings by 13- to 17-year-olds. Six other criteria were eliminated because they had low or negative item–total correlations and thus reduced the internal consistency of the scoring system. In the end, 47 criteria were selected for use, along with the eight measurements of the drawing. Raw scores on the test are obtained by scoring one point for each unusual feature, including unusual aspects of the drawing's measurements. As a result, the highest possible raw score for a single drawing is 55.

For each age group, a certain number of unusual features is considered to be within normal limits. For example, across all three drawings (man, woman, self), the average 9- to 12-year-old boy produces 11 unusual features. To facilitate score interpretation, the total number of unusual features in the three drawings is converted into a *T* score based on the performance of the standardization sample. Different *T*-score conversion tables are presented in the test manual for males and females in each of three age groups.

Adequate levels of reliability are reported for the DAP: SPED. Recall that special attention was given to internal-consistency reliability in the selection of scoring criteria. This produced good results in the final scoring system: internal-consistency reliability of the DAP:SPED as measured by coefficient alpha ranged from .67 to .78 with a median value of .74. Other indices of reliability are also at acceptable levels. Total test scores obtained by two raters correlated .84. Test-retest reliability over a one-week interval was .67.

Four validity studies are also reported in the test manual. The focus in each of these studies was on the test's ability to function as a screening device. Specifically, the test's ability to identify emotionally disturbed individuals as such without identifying nonemotionally disturbed individuals as being emotionally disturbed was assessed. The initial validity study involved 162 subjects with an average age of 10.6. Of these, 81 had been identified as emotionally disturbed within the school system. The other 81 were members of the standardization sample matched to the emotionally disturbed group on relevant demographic variables, serving as "normal" controls. As a group, the 81 emotionally disturbed children scored higher (T score = 55.3) than the normal controls (T score = 49.5). Using these data, the test developers established the criterion of a T score of 55 or higher as an indicator of possible emotional disturbance.

The remaining three validity studies reported in the test manual used a similar procedure. The test records of groups of emotionally disturbed children or adolescents were compared with those of demographically similar children without emotional disturbance from the standardization sample. The results of these studies are summarized in the table. Based on these data, the test's authors suggested that the DAP:SPED is a valid predictor of emotional disturbance, although they acknowledged the need for additional research.

Motta et al. (1993a, 1993b) evaluated Naglieri et al.'s (1991) validity data and concluded that the DAP:SPED lacked criterion-related validity. Motta et al. did not dispute that testtakers who are emotionally disturbed earn higher scores on the test than normal controls. Rather, they expressed concern that the test might misidentify emotionally disturbed children as normal (called a "false negative" error) and misidentify normal children as emotionally disturbed (called a "false positive" error). To understand why, consider that Naglieri et al. did not present criterion-related validity coefficients but chose instead to present this information in terms of mean T scores and standard deviations. The DAP:SPED manual does contain sufficient information to compute correlations, which function as validity coefficients. The correlation coefficients for the four validity studies are approximately .31, .45, .22, and .27, respectively. By presenting the validity data in this familiar metric, you can quickly see that the validity of the test is not strong. At most, 20 percent of the variability in classifications of children as emotionally disturbed or not is associated with DAP:SPED test scores.

There is a second way of translating the results of the validity studies into a form that allows us to examine the test's utility as a screening measure. This involves determining how many misclassifications would be made if scores 55 and higher, as suggested by Naglieri and colleagues, are used to identify students as likely to have emotional disturbance. As noted previously, two types of classification errors can occur: People without emotional disturbance may have scores 55 or larger ("false positives"), and people with emotional disturbance may have scores under 55 ("false negatives"). The two types of errors are associated with distinct costs. If people without emotional disturbance score 55 or over, additional evaluation will be done, which should indicate that these individuals are not emotionally disturbed. The cost here is the evaluator's time to do the additional testing and the possibility of anxiety or unwarranted concern on the part of the child's family. If people with emotional disturbance score under 55, they will not be evaluated; their need for special services may be overlooked, leading to a personal cost if they could have benefited from special services.

False-positive and false-negative rates from the first validity study in the manual are presented by McNeish and Naglieri (1993). When a T score of 55 is used to classify children, a false-negative rate of 51 percent is found: 41 of the 81 emotionally disturbed children, or 51 percent, are misclassified as not emotionally disturbed. The false-positive rate is 32 percent: 26 of the 81 controls are misclassified as emotionally disturbed. Overall, 59 percent of the students are correctly identified, and 41 percent are misclassified. If we consider that simply classifying the children using some random method, such as flipping a coin, would have resulted in the correct classification of approximately 50 percent of the children, we can see that the test is improving on chance classifications by only a small amount.

From these considerations, the conclusion drawn by Motta and colleagues seems justified: The DAP:SPED has adequate reliability but questionable criterion validity. This is not surprising, as the authors focused on reliability

Mean T Scores (and Standard Deviations) on DAP:SPED

Study (from DAP:SPED Manual)	Emotionally Disturbed Children	"Normal" children from the Standardization Sample
Validity Study 1	55.3 (10.6)	49.5 (8.6)
Validity Study 2	57.0 (6.4)	49.1 (8.1)
Validity Study 3	54.8 (9.2)	49.7 (9.0)
Validity Study 4	56.6 (10.3)	49.9 (9.0)

in test development by dropping unreliable items but did not address item validity. Validity could be addressed with an empirical criterion-keying approach. For instance, the existing DAP:SPED items could be applied to the drawings of emotionally disturbed and "normal" children; those items that distinguished between groups could be retained. If such a scale demonstrated good validity on a different sample of children (cross-validation), the scale might function well as a screening device. However, in its current state, the DAP:SPED does seem to lack the validity necessary for a screening device.

EXERCISE 12-6

DEVELOPING NORMS FOR A PROJECTIVE TEST

OBJECTIVE

To enhance understanding of the issues surrounding norm development for projective tests

BACKGROUND

A trend in the development of new projective instruments is toward more norm-referenced as opposed to purely clinical and intuitive interpretation of data. One such norm-based projective instrument is the Roberts Apperception Test for Children (RATC).

YOUR TASK

Read the description of norm development for the RATC that follows. Then, write a brief commentary on what you read, including any questions you would like to ask the test author.

DEVELOPING NORMS FOR A PROJECTIVE TEST

Glen Roberts, Ph.D.

The norming process was especially interesting because of the unexpected responses of the well-adjusted children in contrast to those of the clinic population. Practically all of the prior testing with the cards had been undertaken with clinic children, so we had no idea what to expect from the well-adjusted children. In the attempt to develop an objective scoring system, we had defined scales that accounted for most of the story content. These scales were termed *clinical* because they measured such content as anxiety, aggression, depression, rejection, dependency, conflict, and punishment and had been identified as occurring in the

stories of the clinic children. Furthermore, we had little or no idea that age was such a significant factor in the production of stories by the well-adjusted children, because the developmental age factor had not been apparent with the clinic population.

It was a pleasant surprise to experience that well-adjusted 6- and 7-year-olds tended to give complete stories with positive outcomes and supportive interactions among the figures. The positive outcomes for the 6- and 7-year-olds tended to be easy closures to the stories. In testing the 8- and 9-year-olds, the children not only ended the stories with a positive ending but included some process in how the outcome was attained. It became obvious that there were two levels of resolution. Starting at age 13, the adolescents resolved the stories with positive outcomes, included a more detailed or elaborated process, and often added a learning principle or generalization for solving future situations. The elaboration of the process and the frequent learning principle for situations in the future required a third level of resolution.

The clinic population, because of the wide variety of presenting problems and disorders, tended to give a wide range of responses concerning the outcomes of their stories. One of the significant methods of differentiating between the well-adjusted population and the clinical population is the examination of the ability to resolve the stories with a positive outcome appropriate to the developmental age norms. The clinic children, in general, tend to leave their stories unresolved regardless of age. If they include a resolution, it usually is Resolution 1, which identifies the tendency to not understand how to include process in handling a feeling or solving a problem. Only infrequently will a clinic child achieve a Resolution 3. Clinic adolescents may end their story with a Maladaptive Outcome, which identifies acting out behavior, physical aggression or destruction, manipulation of others, or death of a main character. Maladaptive Outcome is scored when the situation or feeling is made worse by the subsequent action in the ending.

Using Card 3 with versions for boys (3-B) and girls (3-G), the following sample stories will illustrate different types of story resolution at different ages and the consequential need for norms for different age groups.

Resolution I

Well-adjusted 6-year-old boy

He's doing his homework. He's sad because he doesn't want to do it. He gets it done and goes outside and plays.

Story ends with positive outcome but is closure with no process of how he achieved being done.

Resolution II

Well-adjusted 11-year-old boy

The kid looked like he's stuck on a problem in school, and he's trying to figure it out, and finally he looks it up and tries harder and finds the answer.

Story ends with positive outcome, and some process is included by trying harder and looking it up.

Resolution III

Well-adjusted 15-year-old girl

She's probably taking a test at school, and she didn't really study the night before, and now she's regretting that she didn't do it, because she doesn't know how she's going to do on it. She'll probably do OK because she read the book and took notes in class, and she'll learn from the experience to study harder the next time.

Story ends with positive outcome, process is elaborated by the reading of the book and taking notes, and the principle learned for the future is described by she'll "learn and study harder next time."

Unresolved

Well-adjusted 7-year-old girl

The girl doesn't know how to do her homework because it's hard, and she's getting mad.

The situation and feeling are left hanging in the present.

Unresolved

Clinic case, 12-year-old boy

This kid has just had to go to school for the first day and he's angry, Oh, man, where did the summer go? Fiddling with his pencil and stuff, and he's playing around and the teacher is telling him, "Hey, get to work," but he just doesn't feel in the mood. This is probably the story of my life.

The situation and feelings are not dealt with, and we don't know what happens next as an ending.

Note: Preadolescents and adolescents may end their stories with outcomes that contribute further to the problem and are scored as Maladaptive Outcome.

Maladaptive Outcome

Clinic case, 12-year-old girl

Looks aggravated trying to do her homework or a test or something. She doesn't understand it. She probably doesn't feel like raising her hand for help, feels boring to her. Just really doesn't want to do it, acting stubborn. Tired and bored. Gets a bad grade and doesn't care.

Identifies the feelings and situation but doesn't solve it, and the story ends in a negative outcome.

Maladaptive Outcome

Clinic case, 14-year-old girl

She just got back from school. She's been absent for a week, and she's got a lot of homework. She's got a report and three papers to do, and she's mad, and she's going to rip it up.

Identifies the situation and feeling but ends the story by aggressive resistance.

A challenge in constructing any thematic projective test is to develop an objective and clinically relevant scoring system. The development of such a system demands coordination of clinical experience and knowledge of theory in a research program.

EXERCISE 12-7

THE PSYCHOMETRIC SOUNDNESS OF PROJECTIVES

OBJECTIVE

To enhance understanding of and provide firsthand experience with the process of establishing the reliability and validity of a projective instrument

BACKGROUND

A hypothetical psychologist by the name of Williams has developed a hypothetical projective instrument called the Williams Inkblot Projective Method (WIPM). Williams believes that the test (which consists of ten monochromatic inkblots administered in much the same fashion as the Rorschach) can be of great value in identifying sadists. Williams calls upon you as an expert consultant in the area of tests and measurement—which immediately tells you something about Williams's judgment—to advise him how he might design a study to research the reliability and validity of the test.

YOUR TASK

Write a letter to Williams asking any questions you might have while explaining (a) the problems inherent in conducting such research with a Rorschach-like test, and (b) how he might proceed.

EXERCISE 12-8
PICK A PROJECTIVE TEST OF PERSONALITY

OBJECTIVE

To learn more about a projective test not reviewed in the textbook

BACKGROUND

Your textbook reviews only a sampling of the many available projective tests of personality. In this exercise, you are asked to learn more about a projective test that interests you.

YOUR TASK

Using *Tests in Print,* the Internet, or any other resource you choose, discover a projective test of personality or other projective method that was not mentioned in your textbook. Then, answer the following questions:

1. Describe what the test measures.
2. Who would be most apt to use this test? Why? Include in your answer sample questions the test user might hope to answer through the use of this test.
3. Who would be most apt to take this test? Why?
4. Describe the full range of people to whom it would be appropriate to administer this test, including comments about who would be inappropriate.
5. Describe what is known about the test's reliability.
6. Describe what is known about the test's validity.
7. Imagining that you are a measurement consultant, would you recommend this test to clients who are test users? Why or why not?

EXERCISE 12-9
SELF-OBSERVATION

OBJECTIVE

To obtain firsthand experience in behavioral self-observation

BACKGROUND

One widely used tool in behavioral assessment is self-observation. In this exercise, you will be asked to first read about an instrument that employs self-observation in one of its forms and then conduct a brief self-observation.

YOUR TASK

Read the description of the Social Skills Rating System (SSRS) that follows. Then create your own rating system and one original item for each of the five SSRS scales (Cooperation, Assertion, Responsibility, Empathy, and Self-Control). Complete each of the five items, rating yourself with regard to today's behavior. Finally, write a paragraph or two recounting the ease or difficulty you experienced in writing the items, and then responding to them.

THE SOCIAL SKILLS RATING SYSTEM

The Social Skills Rating System (SSRS; Gresham & Elliott, 1990) was designed to measure social skills in individuals from preschool through high school (ages 3 to 18 years) using teacher and parent forms and a student self-report form (grades 3 through 12). The Social Skills Scale assesses positive social behaviors in five areas (Cooperation, Assertion, Responsibility, Empathy, and Self-Control), and the Problem Behavior Scales measure behavior in three areas referred to as "externalizing" problems (including behaviors with observable impact and consequences, such as delinquent-type behaviors), "internalizing" problems (including problems such as fearfulness and inhibitions), and hyperactivity. Items on the Social Skills Scales are rated on the basis of frequency (never, sometimes, or very often) and their importance (not important, important, critical), whereas the Problem Behavior Scales are rated on frequency (never, sometimes, or very often). Sample items from the Social Skills Scales and Problem Behavior Scales are presented in Table 12-3.

The SSRS was standardized on a national sample of 4,170 children during the spring of 1988. An attempt was made to approximate the 1990 U.S. Census estimates for the variables of race or ethnicity, geographic region, and community size. Overall, the standardization sample was 73 percent White and 27 percent minority. Southern and North Central states as well as central city, suburban, and small-town communities were somewhat overrepresented in the standardization sample, whereas Western and Northeastern areas along with rural communities were underrepresented. The number of disabled students in the standardization sample was greater than in the United States population (17.3 percent versus 11.0 percent). Median internal consistency (coefficient alpha) reliabilities were .90 for the Social Skills Scale and .84 for the Problem Behavior Scale across all forms and levels. Test-retest reliability was assessed, with samples of teachers, parents, and students rating the same students four weeks after the original ratings. Test-retest correlations for Social Skills ranged from .68 (students) to .85 (teachers) to .87 (par-

Table 12-3 Sample Items from the Social Skills Rating System—Elementary Level

Social Skills Subscales	Teacher Form	Parent Form	Student (Self-Rating) Form
Cooperation	Finishes class assignments within time limits.	Completes household tasks within a reasonable time.	I finish classwork on time.
Assertion	Initiates conversations with peers.	Starts conversations rather than waiting for others to talk first.	I start talks with class members.
Responsibility	(Not in this form)	Reports accidents to appropriate persons.	(Not in this form)
Empathy	(Not in this form)	(Not in this form)	I feel sorry for others when bad things happen to them.
Self-Control	Controls temper in conflict situations with peers.	Controls temper when arguing with other children.	I control my temper when people are angry at me.

Problem Behaviors Subscales	Teacher Form	Parent Form	Student (Self-Rating) Form
Externalizing Problems	Gets angry easily.	Gets angry easily.	(Not rated by students)
Internalizing Problems	Appears lonely.	Appears lonely.	(Not rated by students)
Hyperactivity	Is easily distracted.	Is easily distracted.	(Not rated by students)

Adapted from Gresham and Elliott (1990).

ents) and for Problem Behaviors from .65 (parents) to .84 (teachers). Initial validity studies compared the SSRS with similar instruments, including the Child Behavior Checklist, and produced moderate to high correlations. Correlations between the SSRS and the social and communication skills subtests on a measure of adaptive behavior would provide evidence of scale validity. In a sample of primary-grade children with disabilities, these correlations ranged from .38 to .64 (median = .50; Merrell & Popinga, 1994). Evidence of the criterion-related validity comes from research that shows that the SSRS can distinguish between children who do and do not have disabilities or behavioral problems (Bramlett et al., 1994; Stinnett et al., 1989).

EXERCISE 12-10

SITUATIONAL PERFORMANCE ROLE PLAY

OBJECTIVE

To enhance understanding of and provide firsthand experience with situational performance measures

BACKGROUND

A *situational performance measure* is a procedure that allows for observation and evaluation of an individual under a standard set of circumstances; it typically involves performance of some specific task under actual or simulated conditions.

YOUR TASK

In this exercise, you and your classmates role-play participants at a town meeting of the town where your school is located. All of you are town council members except for four of you who have volunteered—or "been volunteered"—to play the role of one of the following town commissioners:

- the Police Commissioner
- the Fire Commissioner
- the Sanitation Commissioner
- the Commissioner of Education

The scenario for this situational performance measure is as follows: The town mayor (role-played by none other than your instructor) informs all assembled of the necessity for a 20 percent budget cut in the upcoming year. The 20 percent budget cut could be taken entirely from the police, fire, sanitation, or education budget, or it could be divided in any way between each of these town agencies.

The four commissioners are each asked to make a case against any budget-cutting of their respective departments in an impromptu speech lasting no longer than five minutes; each speech, made before the entire town council, should make as strong a case as possible for exemption from any budget cuts. Town council members, all keen listeners and behavioral observers, take notes on points made by each of the commissioners and prepare to make recommendations to the mayor as to the apportionment of the budget cuts. After all four commissioners have been given the opportunity to plead their case, the mayor calls upon each town council member for an opinion as to how the upcoming budget cuts should be apportioned (and why).

After the last town council member has "voted" regarding apportionment of the budget cuts, and after the mayor has properly thanked the commissioners for their efforts, all town council members (as well as all commissioners and the mayor) resume their more mundane roles in the classroom and list and discuss the skills and abilities that a "town meeting"–type situational performance measure can potentially tap. How might the personnel manager of a large corporation employ this type of task to screen and/or select applicants for executive positions? Are there any other types of applications for which you could envision the use of a measure such as this?

REFERENCES

Allport, G. W., & Odbert, H. S. (1936). Trait-names; A psycholexical study. *Psychological Monographs, 47* (Whole No. 211).

Bramlett, R. K., Smith, B. L., & Edmonds, J. (1994). A comparison of nonreferred, learning disabled, and mildly retarded students utilizing the Social Skills Rating System. *Psychology in the Schools, 31,* 13–19.

Deri, S. (1949a). *Introduction to the Szondi Test.* New York: Grune & Stratton.

Deri, S. K. (1949b). The Szondi Test. *The American Journal of Orthopsychiatry, 19,* 447–454.

Frank, L. K. (1939). Projective methods for the study of personality. *Journal of Psychology, 8,* 389–413.

Gordon, L. V. (1953). A factor analysis of the 48 Szondi pictures. *Journal of Psychology, 36,* 387–392.

Gorham, D. R., Mosely, E. C., & Holtzman, W. H. (1968). Norms for the computer scored Holtzman Inkblot Technique. *Perceptual & Motor Skills Monograph Supplement, 26,* 1279–1305.

Gresham, F. M., & Elliott, S. M. (1990). *Social Skills Rating System.* Circle Pines, MN: American Guidance Service.

Guertin, W. H. (1951). A factor analysis of some Szondi pictures. *Journal of Clinical Psychology, 7,* 232–235.

Holtzman, W. H. (1975). New development in Holtzman Inkblot Technique. In P. McReynolds (Ed.), *Advances in psychological assessment* (Vol. 3).

Holtzman, W. H., Thorpe, J. S., Swartz, J. D., & Herron, E. W. (1961). *Inkblot perception and personality: Holtzman Inkblot Technique.* Austin, TX: University of Texas Press.

Klopfer, B., Ainsworth, M., Klopfer, W., & Holt, R. R. (1954). *Developments in the Rorschach technique: Vol. 1. Technique and theory.* Yonkers-on-Hudson, NY: World.

Klopfer, B., & Davidson, H. (1962). *The Rorschach technique: An introductory manual.* New York: Harcourt.

Lubin, A., & Malby, M. (1951). An empirical test of some assumptions underlying the Szondi Test. *Journal of Abnormal and Social Psychology, 46,* 480–484.

McNeish, T. J., & Naglieri, J. A. (1993). Identification of individuals with serious emotional disturbance using the Draw a Person: Screening Procedure for Emotional Disturbance. *Journal of Special Education, 27,* 115–121.

Merrell, K. W., & Popinga, M. R. (1994). An alliance of adaptive behavior and social competence: An examination of relationships between the Scales of Independent Behavior and the Social Skills Rating System. *Research in Developmental Disabilities, 15,* 39–47.

Miale, F. R., & Selzer, M. (1975). *The Nuremberg mind.* New York: Quadrangle Books.

Mittenberg, W., & Petersen, J. D. (1984). Validation of the Holtzman Anxiety Scale by vasomotor biofeedback. *Journal of Personality Assessment, 48,* 360–364.

Mosely, E. C. (1963). Psychodiagnosis on the basis of the Holtzman Inkblot Technique. *Journal of Projective Techniques and Personality Assessment, 27,* 86–91.

Motta, R. W., Little, S. G., & Tobin, M. I. (1993a). The use and abuse of human figure drawings. *School Psychology Quarterly, 8,* 162–169.

Motta, R. W., Little, S. G., & Tobin, M. I. (1993b). A picture is worth less than a thousand words: Response to reviewers. *School Psychology Quarterly, 8,* 197–199.

Mussen, P. H., & Krauss, S. R. (1952). An investigation of the diagnostic value of the Szondi Test. *Journal of Abnormal and Social Psychology, 47,* 399–405.

Naglieri, J. A., McNeish, T. J., & Bardos, A. N. (1991). *Draw a Person: Screening Procedure for Emotional Disturbance—Examiner's manual.* Austin, TX: Pro-Ed.

Prelinger, E. (1950). On the reliability of the Szondi Test. *Psychological Service Center Journal* (Brooklyn College), *3,* 227–330.

Prelinger E. (1952). Kleine studie uber die verlasslichkeit des Szonditests (A note on the validity of the Szondi Test). *Psychological Abstracts, 26,* No. 5625.

Stinnett, T. A., Oehler-Stinnett, J., & Stout, L. J. (1989). Ability of the *Social Skills Rating System-Teacher* version to discriminate behavior disordered, emotionally disturbed, and nonhandicapped students. *School Psychology Review, 18,* 526–535.

Szondi, L. (1947). *Experimentelle triebdiagnostik.* Bern: Hans Huber.

Szondi, L. (1948). *Schicksalanalyse.* Basel: Bruno Schwabe.

Webb, M. W. (1987). Lipot Szondi (1893–1986). *American Psychologist, 42,* 600.

Wiegersma, S. (1950). Een onderzoek naar de gelddigheid van de Szonditest voor de psycholgische praktijk. [Investigation of the validity of the Szondi Test for psychological practice]. *Psychological Abstracts, 25,* No. 372.

THE 4-QUESTION CHALLENGE

1. A Rorschach assessment may entail a "testing the limits" procedure if the assessor would like to know more about the assessee's
   a. ability to respond to a whole card versus details of the card.
   b. understanding of the task and what is required.
   c. ability to respond to vague versus more structured instructions.
   d. all of the above

2. In traditional interpretations of figure drawings, the rendering of large eyes has been associated with
   a. compensatory tendencies.
   b. suspiciousness.
   c. fear of nearsightedness.
   d. dependency.

3. The behavioral approach to assessment, in contrast to more traditional approaches, tends to treat personality constructs as
   a. summaries of specific behavior patterns.
   b. reflections of enduring, underlying traits or states.
   c. behaviors that may be targeted for change.
   d. all of the above

4. With regard to behavioral assessment, controversy exists regarding the extent to which
   a. traditional psychometric assumptions apply.
   b. functional analyses are sufficiently thorough.
   c. unobtrusive measures are truly unobtrusive.
   d. self-monitoring play can be employed in analogue research.

CHAPTER 13

Clinical and Counseling Assessment

Puzzle 13 **Instructions** Identify what is described, answer a question, or fill in the blank to complete this crossword puzzle based on material presented in Chapter 13 of your textbook.

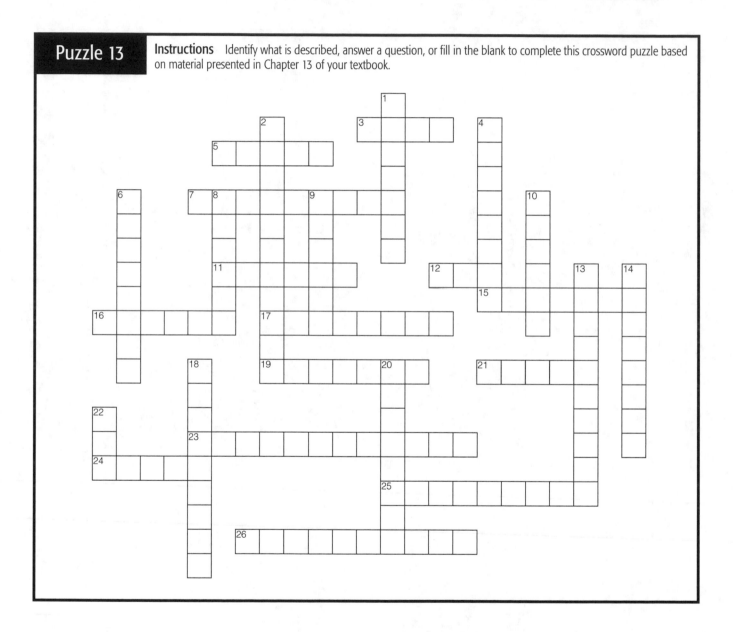

Across

3. The *Tarasoff* case established the duty of mental health professionals to _____ endangered parties of their peril.

5. The expression "oriented-times-_____" is a quick way to convey that a person is oriented to person, place, and time.

7. This misspelling of "addressing" forms an acronym that may be used to help recall various sources of cultural influence when assessing clients—but for this puzzle, put an "s" back in.

11. _____ psychology is a specialty area of psychology that focuses on understanding the role of psychological variables in the onset, course, treatment, and prevention of illness, disease, and disability.

12. A person is not responsible for criminal conduct if, at the time of such conduct, as a result of a mental disorder or defect, the individual lacked substantial capacity either to appreciate the criminality of the conduct or to

conform to the requirements of the law. This is known as the _____ standard.

15. Psychological assessment of child and parents are both parts of a typical _____ evaluation.

16. Sometimes referred to as the "Aunt Fanny" effect, it is the consequence of one's belief that a vague personality description truly describes oneself. In reality, that same personality description may be applicable to most anyone. What is being referred to here is known as the _____ effect.

17. _____ is a legal term indicative of an inability to tell right from wrong, a lack of control, or a state of other mental incompetence or disorder sufficient to prevent that person from standing trial, being judged guilty, or entering into a contract or other legal relationship.

19. Child _____ may be defined as the failure on the part of an adult responsible for a child to exercise a minimum degree of care in providing the child with food, clothing, shelter, education, medical care, and supervision.

21. Child _____ may be defined as the nonaccidental infliction or creation of conditions that result in the child's physical injury or emotional impairment, or a sexual offense committed against a child.

23. The view that a disorder is conceived as a harmful failure or dysfunction of internal mechanisms to perform their naturally selected functions has been termed the _____ view of mental disorder.

24. An MMPI-2 scale, called the MacAndrew Alcoholism Scale, referred to simply as the _____ , was originally constructed to aid in differentiating alcoholic from nonalcoholic psychiatric patients. (Note: It's a hyphenated term.)

25. It was designed to retain the best features of a hypnotic interview but without the hypnotic induction. During the _____ interview, the interviewee is encouraged to use imagery and focused retrieval to recall information.

26. Similar in many respects to the field of clinical psychology is the field of _____ psychology.

Down

1. _____ care is a health care system wherein the products and services provided to patients by a participating network of health care providers are mediated by an administrative agency of the insurer that works to keep costs down by fixing schedules of reimbursement to the providers.

2. _____ is a three-part element of the mental status examination with respect to self, place, and time— whether the interviewee knows who he or she is, where the interview is taking place, and the date of the interview.

4. The theory and application of psychological evaluation in a legal context is referred to as _____ psychological assessment.

6. The term _____ battery may be used to refer to a group of at least three different types of tests for the purpose of evaluating three different spheres of functioning: intelligence, personality, and neuropsychological functioning.

8. The _____ standard is a standard of legal insanity that holds that defendants are not held culpable for their criminal actions if their actions were the product of a mental disease or defect.

9. The mental _____ examination is a specialized interview used to screen for intellectual, emotional, and neurological deficits by incorporating areas such as the interviewee's appearance, behavior, memory, affect, mood, judgment, personality, thought content, thought processes, and state of consciousness.

10. An interview purposely designed to pressure the interviewee in some way in order to gauge reaction to that pressure is referred to as a(n) _____ interview.

13. _____ to stand trial is one of the many competencies that may be evaluated by psychological tests. This competency has to do with understanding the charges against one and being able to assist in one's own defense.

14. An interview conducted after a hypnotic state has been induced in the interviewee is called a(n) _____ interview.

18. The _____ is a tool of assessment by which information is gathered through reciprocal communication.

20. _____ psychology is that branch of psychology that has as its primary focus the prevention, diagnosis, and treatment of abnormal behavior.

22. If you want facts related to the diagnosis of any mental disorder, you may wish to consult one or another version of this.

EXERCISE 13-1

MOVIES AND MEASUREMENT

OBJECTIVE

To research available measures for gauging the quality of a relationship in therapy

BACKGROUND

In the film _Halloween_, psychiatrist Dr. Loomis (Donald Pleasance) attempts to rectify a therapeutic failure using rather unorthodox techniques. One question that might arise from a viewing of the film concerns the instruments available for gauging the quality of the relationship between therapists and their clients.

A psychiatrist attempts to terminate therapy with a most difficult patient in Halloween.

YOUR TASK

Conduct research to identify an instrument designed to measure the quality of a relationship between therapists and clients. Write a brief review of one such instrument.

EXERCISE 13-2

THE INTERVIEW AS A TOOL OF ASSESSMENT

OBJECTIVE

To enhance understanding of and provide firsthand experience with selected tools of clinical and counseling assessment

BACKGROUND

Clinical psychology is that branch of psychology that has as its primary focus the prevention, diagnosis, and treatment of abnormal behavior. Like clinical psychology, *counseling psychology* is a branch of psychology that is also concerned with the prevention, diagnosis, and treatment of abnormal behavior, but its province tends to be the less severe behavior disorders and the "everyday problems in living" (such as marital and family communication problems, career decisions, and difficulties with school study habits). Three tools of assessment commonly employed by both clinical and counseling psychologists (as well as other psychologists) are the interview, the case study, behavioral observation, and tests. Here we focus on the clinical interview.

One special type of interview is a *mental status examination*—the parallel of the general physical examination conducted by a physician. A mental status examination is used to screen for intellectual, emotional, and neurological deficits.

YOUR TASK

One student will play the role of "depressed oil heir/heiress," while another student will play the role of clinician/interviewer. The rest of the class is the attentive, note-taking audience. The scene is that the last family-owned oil well has just run dry, and the imminent fear is that he or she may actually have to go out and work for a living. Other problems—which the role-player can invent—add to the depressed state of mind. The clinician will conduct an entire mental status interview as outlined by Cohen and Swerdlik (2005). Included will be questioning or observation with respect to each of the areas listed in Table 13-1.

The action begins with the depressed patient knocking on the door outside of the room where the interview will be conducted. The interviewer (as well as the audience of vicarious interviewers) should be aware that the mental status examination begins from the first moment the interviewee enters the room; the examiner takes note of the examinee's appearance, gait, and so forth.

In clinically interviewing patients with different presenting problems, there are unique considerations that the trained clinician/interviewer is—or should be—aware of. For example, in interviewing a severely depressed individual, it is advisable for the interviewer to cover topics such as:

- *Changes in eating behavior.* Depression may bring with it disturbances in eating—either an increase in or a diminution of food intake.
- *Changes in sleeping habits.* Depression typically brings with it a desire to sleep more than usual and a reluctance to get out of bed in the morning. If the depression is accompanied by severe anxiety, sleep patterns may be disrupted by a shortening of the amount of restful sleep the patient is able to obtain.
- *Changes in sexual behavior and desire.* Depression may bring with it disturbances in sexual behavior or a decrease in usual sexual desire. Alternatively, an increase in interest in sexual activity may be the consequence of the use of such activity as a kind of "antidepressant."
- *Leisure pursuits and hobbies.* Decreased interest in hobbies and previously favored pastimes may be an accompaniment of depression. The decreased interest in such activities may be symptomatic of decreased interest in life in general.
- *Depersonalization.* In very severe cases of depression, aspects of the patient's identity that should readily be familiar to the patient seem alien to him or her. Has the patient lost sight of his greatest personal assets? Does the patient experience an emptiness where there once was a sense of fulfillment? These may be signs of depersonalization.
- *Preoccupation with the past.* Is there an overabundance of thought content that is tied to sorrowful past events? This

TABLE 13-1 *Areas Covered by a Mental Status Examination*

- *Appearance.* Is the patient's dress and general appearance appropriate?

- *Behavior.* Is anything remarkably strange about the patient's speech or general behavior during the interview? Does the patient exhibit facial tics, involuntary movements, difficulties in coordination or gait?

- *Orientation.* Is the patient oriented to person; that is, does he know who he is? Is the patient oriented to place; that is, does she know where she is? Is the patient oriented to time; does he or she know the year, the month, and the day?

- *Memory.* How is the patient's memory for recent and long-past events?

- *Sensorium.* Are there any problems related to the five senses?

- *Psychomotor activity.* Does there appear to be any abnormal retardation or quickening of motor activity?

- *State of consciousness.* Does consciousness appear to be clear, or is the patient bewildered, confused, or stuporous?

- *Affect.* Is the patient's emotional expression appropriate? For example, does the patient (inappropriately) laugh while discussing the death of an immediate family member?

- *Mood.* Throughout the interview, has the patient generally been angry? depressed? anxious? apprehensive? What?

- *Personality.* In what terms can the patient best be described? Sensitive? Stubborn? Apprehensive? What?

- *Thought content.* Is the patient hallucinating—seeing, hearing, or otherwise experiencing things that aren't really there? Is the patient delusional—expressing untrue, unfounded beliefs (such as the delusion that someone follows him or her everywhere)? Does the patient appear to be obsessive—does the patient appear to think the same thoughts over and over again?

- *Thought processes.* Is there under- or overproductivity of ideas? Do ideas seem to come to the patient abnormally slow or fast? Is there evidence of loosening of associations? Are the patient's verbal productions rambling or disconnected?

- *Intellectual resources.* What is the estimated intelligence of the interviewee?

- *Insight.* Does the patient realistically appreciate his or her situation and the necessity for professional assistance if such assistance is necessary?

- *Judgment.* How appropriate has the patient's decision making been with regard to past events and future plans?

Source: Cohen & Swerdlik, 2002.

- *Physical complaints.* In assessing the depressed individual, it is important to also probe for physical complaints such as aches and pains, gastrointestinal disorders such as diarrhea, and dryness or unpleasant taste in the mouth.

- *Social withdrawal.* Although in the early stages of depression social contacts might be sought, as the depression deepens social withdrawal becomes more the rule. Sometimes this withdrawal is accompanied by the conception of oneself as a burden to others.

- *Sense of loss.* Sometimes a precipitating factor in an acute—as opposed to a chronic—depression is a sense of loss. The loss may have been of virtually anything ranging from a love object (such as a family member or friend) to an element of one's own self-concept (such as a loss of power, position, and/or self-esteem).

- *Suicidal ideation.* It is incumbent upon the assessor of a severely depressed individual to be attuned to communications both overt and symbolic, and both verbal and non-verbal, that may be indicative of suicidal ideation. Is the option of suicide perceived as a viable one to regain control over one's fate? Is the option of suicide perceived as the only way to control extreme anger toward someone else (and a desire to commit homicide)? Is the option of suicide seen as "the only way out" of a situation that is perceived as dreadful? Does the depressed individual have a realistic plan for how the suicide would actually be committed? Is there a history of suicidal gestures? These are but a few of the relevant questions to be asked of the depressed patient in this context.

The *manner* in which the depressed individual is interviewed is also important. On an initial interview especially, it is very important that the interviewer be serious yet sympathetic and inquisitive regarding many of the patient's complaints; patients must perceive that a safe environment exists for discussing their feelings and that the interviewer is "with them." Humor on the part of the interviewer or even a misplaced smile during the initial interviews may be perceived as a sign that the interviewer does not understand, refuses to accept, or will not tolerate the severity of the situation as the patient sees it.[1]

Just prior to terminating the mental status interview, the student conducting the interview should ask for questions directed to the patient from the floor. Audience members will then have the opportunity to direct any questions they wish to the patient. All such questions should be designed to

---

is yet another area to explore with the severely depressed patient.

- *Slowness in body movements.* The vim, vigor, and pep of the spirited cheerleader is the antithesis of the stereotypical, very slow-moving, depressed individual. It is an effort for the depressed patient to do simple things such as stand up from a seated position, and it may take a depressed person several minutes to perform a simple task such as buttoning a shirt.

---

[1]Humor may well have a place in an interview with a depressed patient with whom the interviewer/therapist has developed a good rapport over the course of several months or years. In this context the author recalls a therapy patient of long standing (who had not originally sought treatment for depression) becoming acutely depressed over a career-related setback. In one session, the patient tearfully confided that she had seriously thought of throwing herself in the path of an oncoming subway train. My response: "Then I think we should think about clearing up your bill." The patient laughed heartily—the first time she had done so in weeks. This comment, made to this particular patient under those conditions, was therapeutic.

either (1) cover territory in a mental status examination that was not covered during the interview proper, or (2) clarify an answer to a question that was not quite clarified during the interview.

After all questions have been entertained by the patient, it's time to write up the findings. Each class member (including the student who played the patient) will write his or her report describing the mental status of the depressed patient character.

P. T. BARNUM AND THE MMPPI

OBJECTIVE

To enhance understanding of and provide firsthand experience with the "Barnum effect"

BACKGROUND

Remember that individual to whom you administered the MMPPI? It's now time to provide that individual with some feedback . . . well, feedback of a sort.

You may already be aware of a phenomenon referred to in the psychological literature as the "Barnum effect"—the fact that people tend to accept vague and general personality descriptions as uniquely applicable to themselves without realizing that the same description could be applied to just about anyone. But does this effect really work?

YOUR TASK

Contact the person(s) who sat for the MMPPI and/or your projective test battery and request that they read and evaluate a personality description that was derived from those tests; the evaluation is made on the separate form that follows the personality description on the next page. All evaluation forms are brought back to class for discussion. All subjects receive the same "feedback" as to their performance on the MMPPI; the feedback is the following general personality description that has been used in a number of studies researching the Barnum effect.

After your subject has read and evaluated the personality description on the next page, it's time for a thorough debriefing. Explain to the subject exactly what the Barnum effect is. In this context it may be useful, for explanatory purposes, to make reference to horoscopes as an analogy. Explain also the value to you in learning about the Barnum effect—the value in avoiding what Meehl (1956) termed "pseudosuccessful clinical procedures in which personality descriptions from tests are made to fit the patient largely or wholly by virtue of their triviality."

Debriefing should also take place with respect to the MMPPI itself, despite the fact that you initially presented it

to your subject as an academic exercise and not as a meaningful test. Your explanation of the exercise might briefly make reference to the psychometric concepts of *reliability* and *validity* and how such terms are applied to "real" psychological tests. Explain further that, because the test you administered was unresearched and therefore considered to be unreliable and invalid, any results could not be construed to be meaningful in any way. Thank the subject for helping to provide you with firsthand experience in learning about the structure and administration of tests, and ask whether you could answer any questions they might have about the MMPPI or about testing in general.

THE MULTITRAIT-MULTIMETHOD MATRIX REVISITED

OBJECTIVE

To review the multitrait-multimethod matrix using an example from the literature in clinical assessment

BACKGROUND

As you may recall from Chapter 6, a multitrait-multimethod matrix can be used to organize information related to the construct validity of tests. McCann (1990) used this psychometric tool to evaluate the construct validity of the MMPI and the MCMI-II. The multiple traits evaluated were anxiety, depression, psychotic thought, and substance dependence (including alcoholism and drug dependence). The multiple methods were the two tests themselves (the MCMI-II and the MMPI). Table 13-2 (page 221) lists the four traits studied, along with the specific scales of the two instruments used to measure those traits.

McCann (1990) studied the scores of 85 psychiatric inpatients who had completed both the MCMI-II and the MMPI. The scales of interest from the two tests were correlated and entered into a multitrait-multimethod matrix. A portion of the resulting matrix is in Table 13-3 (page 221). The same variables listed in Table 13-2 are listed across the top and down the side of the matrix in Table 13-3.

YOUR TASK

1. What in the matrix provides you with information about the convergent validity of the two tests?
2. How would you characterize the convergent validity of the two tests?
3. What in the matrix provides you with information about the discriminant validity of the two tests?
4. How would you characterize the discriminant validity of the two tests?

PERSONALITY DESCRIPTION

You have a strong need for other people to like and admire you. You have a tendency to be critical of yourself. You have a great deal of unused capacity that you have not turned to your advantage. While you have some personality weaknesses, you are generally able to compensate for them. Your sexual adjustment has presented some problems for you. Disciplined and controlled on the outside, you tend to be worrisome and insecure inside. At times you have serious doubts about whether you have made the right decision or done the right thing. You prefer a certain amount of change and variety and become dissatisfied when hemmed in by restrictions and limitations. You pride yourself on being an independent thinker and do not accept others' opinions without satisfactory proof. You have found it unwise to be too frank in revealing yourself to others. At times you are extraverted, affable, and sociable, whereas at other times you are introverted, wary, and reserved. Some of your aspirations tend to be pretty unrealistic.

EVALUATION OF PERSONALITY ASSESSMENT INTERPRETATION

Please check one.

I feel that the interpretation was:

_____ Excellent

_____ Good

_____ Average

_____ Poor

_____ Very Poor

TABLE 13-2 *Four Traits Evaluated by Means of the MMPI and MCMI-II*

General Construct	MCMI-II Scale	MMPI Scale
Anxiety (Anx)	A: Anxiety	Manifest Anxiety S
Depression (Dep)	D/CC: Dysthymia and Major Depression	Scale 2
Substance Dependence (Sub)	B/T: Alcohol and Drug Dependence	MacAndrew (MAC) Sc
Psychotic Thought (Psy)	SS: Thought Disorder	Scale 9

TABLE 13-3 *Multitrait-Multimethod Matrix of MCMI-II and MMPI Scales[2]*

	MCMI-II Scales				MMPI Scales		
	Anx	Dep	Sub	Psy	Anx	Dep	Sub
MCMI-II Scale							
Anxiety	—	—	—	—	—	—	—
Depression	.94	—	—	—	—	—	—
Substance Dependence	.53	.56	—	—	—	—	—
Psychotic Thought	.75	.77	.62	—	—	—	—
MMPI Scale							
Anxiety	.84	.86	.51	.78	—	—	—
Depression	.51	.58	.08	.41	.65	—	—
Substance Dependence	−.05	−.05	.40	.13	−.02	−.27	—
Psychotic Thought	.00	.00	.47	.19	.04	−.34	.57

[2]Note that McCann did not report the reliability of the scales, so dashes appear on the main diagonal in place of reliability coefficients.

EXERCISE 13-5
PICK A CLINICAL TEST

OBJECTIVE

To learn more about clinical measures not reviewed in the textbook

BACKGROUND

The approach in your textbook is to highlight only a few of the many tests that exist in any given area. For every test covered in your textbook, there may well be dozens of other tests designed to measure the same attribute(s).

YOUR TASK

A list of clinical measures along with a brief description of each follows in Table 13-4 (page 222). From this list, select one test that you think you would like to know more about. Then answer the following:

1. Describe what the test measures.
2. Who would be most apt to use this test? Why? Include in your answer sample questions the test user might hope to answer through the use of this test.
3. Who would be most apt to take this test? Why?

4. Describe the full range of people to whom it would be appropriate to administer this test, including comments about who would be inappropriate.
5. Describe what is known about the test's reliability.
6. Describe what is known about the test's validity.
7. Imagining that you are a measurement consultant, would you recommend this test to clients who are test users? Why or why not?

EXERCISE 13-6
PICK A DEVELOPER
OF A CLINICAL TEST

OBJECTIVE

To stimulate generative thinking regarding the process of developing a clinical test

BACKGROUND

The companion Web site for Cohen & Swerdlik (2005) may be found at *www.mhhe.com/psychtesting6*. This site contains numerous resources, including a number of Test Developer Profiles that describe the approach to test development of many test developers.

TABLE 13-4 *Some Clinical Measures*

Test	Description
The Childhood Autism Rating Scale	For ages 2 and up, this observer rating scale is designed to assist in the identification of children with autism and rule out the autism syndrome in children who are otherwise developmentally disabled.
Family Relations Test: Children's Version	For ages 3 to 15, this card sorting test is designed to measure relative importance of different family members and explore emotional relations.
Mental Status Checklist for Children	For ages 5 to 12, this measure employs interview, case study, and behavioral observation methods for the purpose of evaluation and treatment.
North American Depression Inventories for Children and Adults	For ages 7 and up, this self-report measure is designed to evaluate various aspects of depression.
Mental Status Checklist for Adolescents	For ages 13 to 17, this measure employs interview, case study, and behavioral observation methods for the purpose of evaluation and treatment.
Suicidal Ideation Questionnaire	For ages 13 to 18, this is a self-report measure of suicidal ideation.
Beck Hopelessness Scale	For ages 13 to 80, this is a self-report measure that assesses expectations about the future and evaluates risk of suicide.
Whitaker Index of Schizophrenic Thinking	For ages 16 and older, this multiple-choice test gauges the degree to which evidence of schizophrenic thought processes are present.
Student Adaptation to College Questionnaire	For first-year college students, this is a self-report measure of adjustment to college life.
Couples' Pre-Counseling Inventory (Revised Edition)	For adults, this measure entails self-report on variables related to a couple's strengths and weaknesses by both members of the couple.
Dyadic Adjustment Scale	For adults, this test is designed to measure adjustment in a cohabiting or marital relationship.
The Custody Quotient	For parents in a custody dispute, this interview followed by an interviewer-completed rating scale is designed to be a measure of parenting skills and other variables relevant to a custody decision.
Personal History Checklist for Adults	Designed to provide a systematic self-report method for history-taking.
Psychiatric Diagnostic Interview (Revised)	For adults, this structured interview is designed to determine the current or past existence of a psychiatric disorder.
S-D Proneness Checklist	For adults, this interviewer-completed checklist is designed to help evaluate suicide proneness and depressive tendencies.

YOUR TASK

From all of the Test Developer Profiles on the Web site, identify one developer of a clinical test that most interests you. After reading the Test Developer Profile, write a brief essay entitled "Some Advice to Future Developers of Clinical Tests." In this essay, when giving that advice, incorporate material from the experience of the test developer in the Test Developer Profile you read. Note: Do not pick either of the same two test developers you picked in completing Exercise 7-9.

EXERCISE 13-7

CRITIQUE A SCALE

OBJECTIVE

Exercise critical thinking with regard to a published attitude scale

BACKGROUND

Many tests useful in health psychology research may also be useful in clinical and counseling contexts. In an effort to learn more about the attitudes of adolescents toward condoms, Janet St. Lawrence and her colleagues (1994) modified an existing scale (Sacco et al., 1991) to create the Condom Attitude Scale—Adolescent Version (Table 13-5). This instrument yields data that may be valuable not only in research applications but in individual and group counseling.

YOUR TASK

Write a written evaluation of the Condom Attitude Scale—Adolescent Version, as if you were a reviewer for a clinical journal. You may wish to suggest ways the scale could be improved, or new applications for it. Note that scale items marked (R) are reverse scored. That is, the respondent *loses* a point for agreeing with the statement.

TABLE 13-5 *Condom Attitude Scale—Adolescent Version*

1. Using a condom takes the "wonder" out of sex. (R)

2. I am concerned about catching AIDS or some other sexually transmitted disease.

3. A condom is not necessary when you and your partner agree not to have sex with anyone else. (R)

4. Condoms are messy. (R)

5. A condom is not necessary if you know your partner. (R)

6. Using condoms shows my partner I care about him/her.

7. A condom is not necessary if you're pretty sure the other person doesn't have a sexually transmitted disease. (R)

8. If I'm not careful, I could catch a sexually transmitted disease.

9. I wouldn't use a condom if my partner refused. (R)

10. People who carry condoms would have sex with anyone. (R)

11. I wouldn't mind if my partner brought up the idea of using a condom.

12. Condoms create a sense of safety.

13. People who use condoms sleep around a lot. (R)

14. If I'm not careful, I could catch AIDS.

15. Condoms take away the pleasure of sex. (R)

16. If my partner suggested using a condom, I would respect him or her.

17. Other people should respect my desire to use a condom.

18. I worry that I could catch a sexually transmitted disease.

19. If my partner suggested using a condom, I would feel relieved.

20. People who carry condoms are just looking for sex. (R)

21. A condom is not necessary when you are with the same partner for a long time. (R)

22. If my partner suggested using a condom, I would think he/she was only being cautious.

23. Condoms protect against sexually transmitted diseases.

REFERENCES

McCann, J. T. (1990). A multitrait-multimethod analysis of the MCMI-II clinical syndrome scales. *Journal of Personality Assessment, 55,* 465–476.

Meehl, P. E. (1956). Wanted: A good cookbook. *American Psychologist, 11,* 263–272.

Sacco, W. P., Levine, B., Reed, D. L., & Thompson, K. (1991). Attitudes about condom use as an AIDS-relevant behavior: Their factor structure and relation to condom use. *Psychological Assessment, 3,* 311–326.

St. Lawrence, J. S., Reitman, D., Jefferson, K. W., et al. (1994). Factor structure and validation of an adolescent version of the Condom Attitude Scale: An instrument for measuring adolescents' attitudes toward condoms. *Psychological Assessment, 6,* 352–359.

THE 4-QUESTION CHALLENGE

1. When an interviewer nods his or her head or vocalizes "um-hmmm" during the course of an interview, the interviewer
   a. may inadvertently reinforce interviewee verbalizations.
   b. is most typically conducting a mental status examination.
   c. is testing the limits of the interviewee's mood and affect.
   d. none of the above

2. In a mental status examination, the abbreviation "Oriented × 3" is used to convey the information that patients
   a. can stand up, sit down, and lie down without assistance.
   b. can accurately point in three directions by a compass.
   c. know their own name, where they are, and the date.
   d. none of the above

3. In the jargon of psychological testing and assessment, a *battery* refers to
   a. a response to a TAT card that keeps going and going.
   b. an assaultive gesture on the part of the testtaker.
   c. a testtaker state of heightened achievement motivation.
   d. none of the above

4. The model presented for teaching culturally informed psychological assessment contains three major components of the curriculum. Which of the following is *not* one of those major components:
   a. supervised training and experience in culturally informed assessment
   b. mentoring and guidance by community elders and role models
   c. sound foundation in general principles of assessment
   d. sound foundation in general issues of culture as they relate to assessment

CHAPTER 14

Neuropsychological Assessment

Puzzle 14

Instructions Identify what is described, answer a question, or fill in the blank to complete this crossword puzzle based on material presented in Chapter 14 of your textbook.

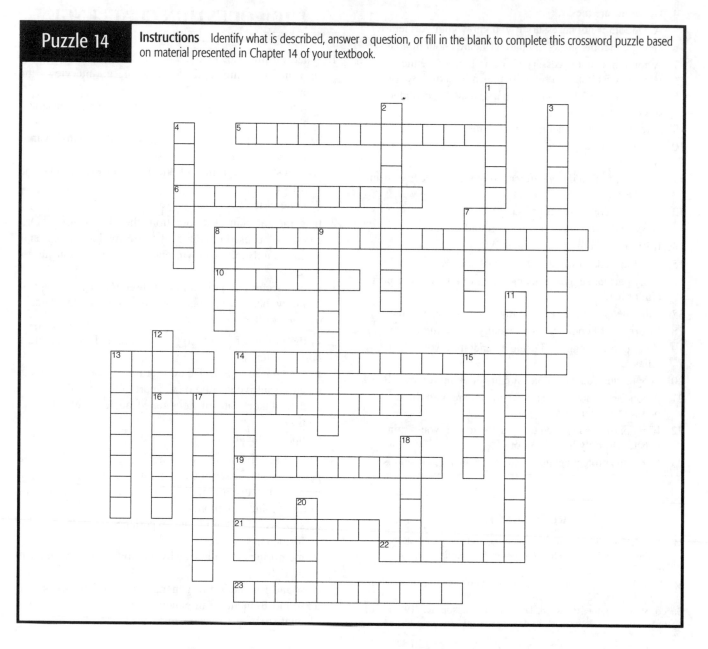

Across

5. A pattern of subtest scores on a Wechsler test that Wechsler himself viewed as suggestive of neurological deficit is called a _____ index or quotient. Hint: Like Dairy Queen, it may be abbreviated "DQ."

6. It's a type of item that taps visual-conceptual, visual-motor, planning, and other cognitive abilities by means of a task in which the testtaker must connect the circles

in a logical fashion. It is called a _____-_____ item.

8. A type of assessment that focuses on the relationship between brain functioning and behavior is _____ assessment.

10. Study of the pattern of test scores on a Wechsler (or other) test for the purpose of identifying a configuration known to be associated with a particular diagnosis is called _____ analysis.

13. A prepackaged test battery containing a number of standardized tests to be administered in a prescribed fashion is referred to as a _____ battery.
14. The Bender is an example of a test that is designed to measure _____ _____ ability. (Hint: It's a hyphenated word.)
16. It's a task that entails identifying a pictured stimulus in a neuropsychological context, for example, in response to items in the Boston Naming Test. This task is referred to as _____ naming.
19. Memory for how to do certain things or perform certain functions like riding a bicycle or making entries on a keyboard is referred to as _____ memory.
21. A loss of ability to express oneself or to understand spoken or written language due to neurological deficit. Hint: Not to be confused with a condition in which the desire to eat is lost or diminished.
22. It's composed of various kinds of neurons or nerve cells. The part that consists of the brain and the spinal cord is referred to as the _____ nervous system.
23. It's a procedure for evaluation or treatment that does not involve intrusion (by surgical procedure, x-ray, or any other manner) into the client's body. Observation of a client walking or skipping is an example of such a _____ procedure.

Down

1. Draw on your knowledge of well-known neuropsychological screening instruments to come up with a gestalt for a famous name that is synonymous with this test.
2. It's both a reference (now seldom used) to organic brain damage and a type of functional consequence that attends such damage.
3. Memory of factual material is referred to as _____ memory.
4. Any past complaints a client has regarding sensory or motor problems, disturbances in balance, memory, speech, body temperature control, and the like will all be noted as part of a neuropsychological _____ .
7. The Bruininks-Oseretsky tests not only one's ability to pronounce it but gross and fine _____ skills as well.
8. A neuropsychological test battery for children, developed in part on the basis of Luria's work.
9. It's composed of various kinds of neurons or nerve cells. The part of it referred to as the _____ nervous system consists of neurons that convey messages to and from the rest of the body but excludes the brain and the spinal cord.
11. The phenomenon of _____ control results from the fact that each of the two cerebral hemispheres receives sensory information from the opposite side of the body and also controls motor responses on the opposite side of the body.
12. Organizing, planning, cognitive flexibility, inhibition of impulses, and other activities associated with the frontal and prefrontal lobes of the brain are referred to as _____ functions.
13. It's a group of tests hand-picked by the assessor for the purpose of providing an answer to the referral question. It's referred to as a(n) _____ battery.
14. The Field of Search is an example of a(n) _____ test.
15. A digits-backward task is one way to test it.
17. The branch of medicine that focuses on the nervous system and its disorders is called _____ .
18. The term *organicity* was once synonymous with brain _____ .
20. A puzzle useful as a tool for evaluating executive functioning is the Tower of _____ .

EXERCISE 14-1
MOVIES AND MEASUREMENT

OBJECTIVE

To research a measure of coordination

BACKGROUND

Tests may be used to measure various aspects of neuropsychological functioning. Sometimes finding a test to measure a specific aspect of neuropsychological functioning takes a little research.

The Scarecrow in The Wizard of Oz *evidenced remarkable psychomotor coordination for someone* sans *brain.*

YOUR TASK

Conduct research to identify an instrument designed to measure gross motor coordination. Write a brief review of one such instrument.

EXERCISE 14-2
THE NEUROPSYCHOLOGICAL EXAMINATION

OBJECTIVE

To enhance understanding of and provide firsthand experience with a neurological assessment measure

BACKGROUND

A neuropsychological examination may be undertaken for any number of reasons from general screening purposes to locating the specific site of a neurological lesion. The exact form of the neuropsychological examination (as well as the nature of the tests and measurement procedures employed) will vary as a function of factors such as the purpose of the examination, the thoroughness of the examination, and the neurological intactness of the examinee. In addition to the administration of psychological tests and/or prepackaged test batteries, a history-taking and a physical examination may also be part of the neuropsychological examination. In

Tables 14-1 and 14-2, we have described some of the tests that could be used in a neuropsychological examination; more specifically, these are tests that could be used to evaluate (1) muscle coordination and (2) the intactness of some of the 12 cranial nerves.

YOUR TASK

1. You are a neuropsychologist charged with performing routine neurological screenings on all students in your school who are enrolled in a psychological testing course. Select any three of the four tests described in Table 14-1 and administer these tests to a fellow student in the class.
2. Select any three of the four tests described in Table 14-2 and administer these tests to the same student to whom you had administered the other three tests.
3. Write a brief report of your findings. Include in your report a note about what other tests or prepackaged test batteries you would have also wanted to administer and explain why.
4. Now, trade places—you become the patient and your partner "plays doctor."

TABLE 14-1   *Some Tests Used to Evaluate Muscle Coordination*

Walking-Running-Skipping

If the examiner has not had a chance to watch the patient walk for any distance, he or she may ask the patient to do so as part of the examination. We tend to take walking for granted; but, neurologically speaking, it is a highly complex activity that involves proper integration of many varied components of the nervous system. Sometimes abnormalities in gait may be due to nonneurological causes; if, for example, a severe case of bunions is suspected as the cause of the difficulty, the examiner may ask the patient to remove his or her shoes and socks so that the feet may be physically inspected. Highly trained examiners are additionally sensitive to subtle abnormalities in, for example, arm movements while the patient walks, runs, or skips.

Standing-Still (technically, the Romberg test)

The patient is asked to stand still with feet together, head erect, and eyes open. Whether the patient has arms extended straight out or at his or her side and whether or not the patient is wearing shoes or other clothing will be a matter of the examiner's preference. The patient is next instructed to close his or her eyes. The critical variable is the amount of sway exhibited by the patient once the eyes are closed. Since normal persons may sway somewhat with their eyes closed, experience and training are required to determine when the amount of sway is indicative of pathology.

Nose-Finger-Nose

The patient's task here is to touch his or her nose with the tip of his or her index finger, then touch the examiner's finger, and then touch his or her own nose again. The sequence is repeated many times with each hand. This test, as well as many similar ones (such as the toe-finger test, the finger-nose test, the heel-knee test), is designed to assess, among other things, cerebellar functioning.

Finger Wiggle

The examiner models finger wiggling (that is, playing an imaginary piano or typing), and then the patient is asked to do the same. Typically, the nondominant hand cannot be wiggled as quickly as the dominant hand, but it takes a trained eye to pick up a significant decrease in rate. The experienced examiner will also be looking for abnormalities in the precision of the movements and the rhythm of the movements, "mirror movements" (uncontrolled similar movements in the other hand when instructed to wiggle only one), and other abnormal involuntary movements. Like the nose-finger test, finger wiggling supplies information concerning the quality of involuntary movement and muscular coordination. A related task involves tongue wiggling.

TABLE 14-2 *Some Tests Used in the Assessment of Intactness of the 12 Cranial Nerves*

Cranial Nerve	Test
I (olfactory nerve)	Closing one nostril with a finger, the examiner places some odiferous substance under the nostril being tested and asks whether the smell is perceived. Subjects who perceive it are next asked to identify it. Failure to perceive an odor when one is presented may be indicative of lesions of the olfactory nerve, a brain tumor, or other medical conditions. Of course, failure may be due to other factors, such as oppositional tendencies on the part of the patient or intranasal disease, and such factors must be ruled out as causal.
II (optic nerve)	Assessment of the intactness of the second cranial nerve is a highly complicated procedure, for this is a sensory nerve with functions related to visual acuity and peripheral vision. A Snellen eye chart will therefore be one of the tools used by the physician in assessing optic nerve function. If the subject at a distance of 20 feet from the chart is able to read the small numbers or letters in the line labeled line "20," then the subject is said to have 20/20 vision in the eye being tested. 20/20 vision is only a standard; and while many persons can read only the larger print at higher numbers on the chart (that is, a person who reads the letters on line "40" of the chart would be said to have a distance vision of 20/40), some persons have better than 20/20 vision. An individual who could read the line labeled "15" on the Snellen eye chart would be said to have 20/15 vision.
V (trigeminal nerve)	The trigeminal nerve supplies sensory information from the face, and it supplies motor information to and from the muscles involved in chewing. Information regarding the functioning of this nerve will be examined by the use of tests for facial pain (pinpricks will be made by the physician), facial sensitivity to different temperatures, and other sensations. Another part of the examination will entail having the subject clamp his or her jaw shut. The physician will then feel and inspect the facial muscles for weakness and other abnormalities.
VIII (acoustic nerve)	The acoustic nerve has functions related to the sense of hearing and the sense of balance. Hearing may be formally assessed by the use of an apparatus called the audiometer. More frequently, the routine assessment of hearing will involve the use of a so-called "dollar watch." Provided the examination room is quiet, an individual with normal hearing should be able to hear a dollar watch ticking at a distance of about 40 inches from each ear (30 inches if the room is not very quiet). Other quick tests of hearing involve the placement of a vibrating tuning fork on various portions of the skull. Individuals who complain of dizziness, vertigo, disturbances in balance, and so forth may have their vestibular system examined by means of specific tests.

EXERCISE 14-3

SOME TOOLS OF NEURO-PSYCHOLOGICAL ASSESSMENT USED IN THE *CHAPPLE* CASE

OBJECTIVE

To research and explore information about a tool of neuropsychological assessment

BACKGROUND

The *Chapple* case, as well as the *Daubert* standard applied in that case, is discussed in your text. Let's elaborate on that discussion by listing some of the formal tests and measurement techniques employed by two of the psychologists involved in that case. The flexible battery administered by the clinical psychologist who initially examined the boy included the following tests:

- the Aphasia Screening Test
- the Benton Visual Retention Test
- Knox Cube
- Rey Complex Figure Test
- Seashore Rhythm Test
- Trails
- Wisconsin Card Sorting Test

In addition, the flexible battery included other tests such as Draw a Bicycle, Draw a Clock, Draw a Family, Draw a Person, Category Test, Incomplete Sentences, Lateral Dominance Test, Manual Finger Tapping Test, Peabody Picture Vocabulary Test, subtests of the Woodcock-Johnson, the WISC-R, and the WRAT-R.

The flexible battery administered by the neuropsychologist one year after the auto accident included the following tests and measurement techniques:

- Trails
- Sentence Imitation
- Word Sequence and Oral Direction
  (subtests of the Detroit Test of Learning Aptitude)

- Taylor Complex Figure Test
- Hooper Visual Organization Test
- Attention Capacity
  (subtest of the Auditory Verbal Learning Test)
- Sound and Visual Symbol Recall Test
- Paragraph copy test

Other tests administered by the neuropsychologist included the Kaufman Brief Intelligence Test, the Individual Achievement Test, and the Wechsler Reading Comprehension and Listening Comprehension Test.

YOUR TASK

Select one of the tests or measurement techniques in the bulleted list and write a brief report on it. The focus of the report should be on how such a test or technique might be employed as part of a flexible neuropsychological test battery. Your report should include information about the validity, reliability, and generalizability of the test or technique. Explain how historical and other archival data related to the assessee could help in drawing sound conclusions from the utilization of this test or technique. For the purpose of your report, write about the latest revision of the test chosen.

EXERCISE 14-4
INTERVIEW WITH A NEUROPSYCHOLOGIST

OBJECTIVE

To construct an interview consisting of ten questions you would like to ask a practicing neuropsychologist and then conduct the interview

BACKGROUND

As you read about psychologists in various specialties and the tests and assessment procedures they use in practice, a wealth of questions may arise. Here is your chance to pose any questions you may have about neuropsychological assessment to a practicing neuropsychologist. Your questions may relate to any facet of a neuropsychologist's work—how such work interfaces with medicine, how research is put into practice, and how such a career has its own unique rewards and drawbacks. Check with your instructor before arranging this interview, as it may prove more feasible to have your instructor arrange a class visit by a neuropsychologist.

YOUR TASK

Write your interview questions and be prepared to arrange and conduct the interview upon assignment of this exercise by your instructor.

EXERCISE 14-5
PICK A NEURO-PSYCHOLOGICAL TEST

OBJECTIVE

To learn more about neuropsychological tests not reviewed in the textbook

BACKGROUND

The approach in your textbook is to highlight only a few of the many tests that exist in any given area. For every test covered in your textbook there may well be dozens of other tests designed to measure the same variable or variables.

YOUR TASK

A list of neuropsychological tests, along with a brief description of each, follows in Table 14-3. From this list, select one test that you think you would like to know more about. Then, use all of the resources at your disposal to answer the following:

1. Describe what the test measures.
2. Who would be most apt to use this test? Why? Include in your answer sample questions the test user might hope to answer through the use of this test.
3. Who would be most apt to take this test? Why?
4. Describe the full range of people to whom it would be appropriate to administer this test, including comments about who would be inappropriate.
5. Describe what is known about the test's reliability.
6. Describe what is known about the test's validity.
7. Imagining that you are a measurement consultant, would you recommend this test to clients who are test users? Why or why not?

THE 4-QUESTION CHALLENGE

1. A patient with known damage to brain lobes complains of a severely impaired visual field. Which lobes of the brain have the highest probability of having been damaged?
   a. frontal lobes
   b. temporal lobes
   c. occipital lobes
   d. parietal lobes

2. The term *organicity*
   a. has been used interchangeably with "brain damage."
   b. is not synonymous with "brain damage."
   c. has been used interchangeably with "neurological damage."
   d. all of the above

TABLE 14-3   *Some Neuropsychological Tests and Test Batteries*

Test	*Description*
Neurobehavioral Assessment of the Preterm Infant	For use with preterm infants ranging in conceptual age from 32 weeks to term, this test assesses the effects of medical as well as other complications (such as maternal substance addiction) on preterm infants.
McCarron-Dial System	For ages 3 and up, this test battery is designed to be of particular utility in meeting the therapy needs of handicapped persons.
Children's Category Test	For ages 5 through 16 years, this test is designed to measure complex intellectual functioning, including concept formation and memory.
Portable Tactile Performance Test	For ages 5 and up, this test focuses on the evaluation of tactual performance.
Benton Visual Retention Test	For ages 8 years to adult, this test measures visual perception, memory, and visuoconstructive abilities.
Wisconsin Card Sorting Test Revised	For ages 6.5 through 89, this test is designed to measure several neurological variables, including abstract thinking and perseverative thinking.
Behavior Change Inventory	For children and adults, this test focuses on the evaluation of the effects of head injury.
Ross Information Processing Assessment	For adolescents and adults, this test focuses on the evaluation of communication disorder among people with head injuries.
Boston Diagnostic Aphasia Examination	For adults, this test is designed to focus on the nature of deficits in aphasia as well as common clusters of deficit.
Mini Inventory of Right Brain Injury	For ages 18 and up, this test focuses on the evaluation of deficit due to injury of the right hemisphere of the brain.
Stroop Neuropsychological Screening Test	For ages 18 and up, this is a general neuropsychological screening test designed for individual administration.
Bedside Evaluation and Screening Test of Aphasia	For adults, this is a test of language ability for patients who have suffered neurological damage.
Sklar Aphasia Scale	For adults, this test is designed to measure the nature and severity of language disability following neurological damage.
Cognitive Behavior Rating Scales	For adults and capable of being group-administered, this measure of cognitive impairment and behavioral deficit is completed by informants familiar with the assessee.
Dementia Rating Scale	For adults, this measure is designed to evaluate the cognitive status of an individual with known impairment.
Rivermead Perceptual Assessment Battery	For adults, this test measures nature and degree of visual deficit following stroke or a related injury.

3. Which is *not* a test a neuropsychologist would typically administer to routinely evaluate muscle coordination?
   a. the finger wiggle test
   b. the nose wiggle test
   c. the standing-still test
   d. the walking-running-skipping test

4. The Bender is a test that entails
   a. copying designs.
   b. interpreting proverbs.
   c. connecting dots.
   d. all of the above

CHAPTER 15

The Assessment of People with Disabilities

| Puzzle 15 | **Instructions** Identify what is described, answer a question, or fill in the blank to complete this crossword puzzle based on material presented in Chapter 15 of your textbook. |

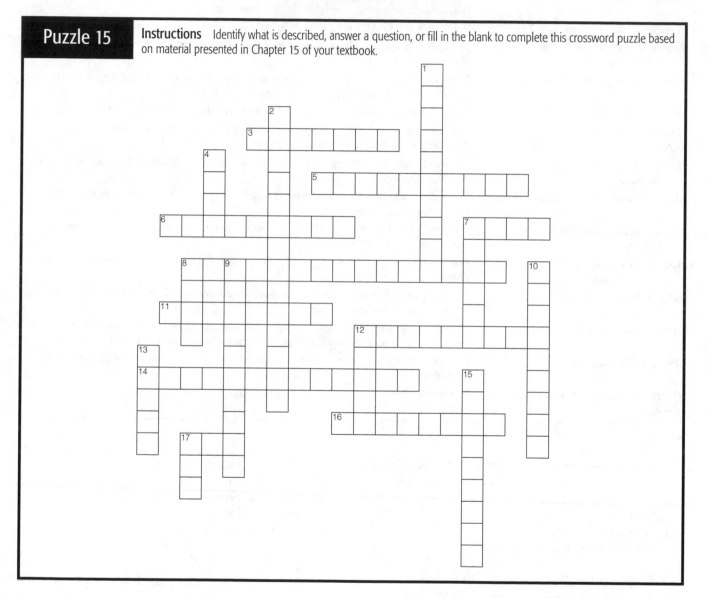

Across

3. The IDEA defined "child with a disability" in two ways, one way for children aged 3 through 9 and the other way for children in _____ .

5. As defined in the Americans with Disabilities Act of 1990, it's a physical or mental impairment that substantially limits one or more of the major life activities of an individual.

6. A claim of discrimination may be brought as a result of a person being regarded as having an impairment and being discriminated against as a result of that perception. This is termed a _____ disability case.

7. The acronym for the Individuals with Disabilities Education Act Amendments of 1997, otherwise known as Public Law 105-17.

8. Variables such as stress, loneliness, and sources of satisfaction are all _____ issues. (Hint: 3 words, hyphenated.)

11. It's a scale of adaptive behavior that placed a city in New Jersey on the map (at least for psychologists and others who have occasion to measure it).

12. _____ disability is a general reference to a broad spectrum of disabling conditions, including various neurological deficits, learning disabilities, autism, and mental retardation.

14. _____ may be defined as the adaptation of a test, procedure, or situation, or the substitution of one test for another, in the interest of making the assessment more suitable for an assessee with exceptional needs.

16. Personal conduct that one is capable of modifying in age-appropriate ways to effectively address needs, demands, and challenges is referred to as _____ behavior.

17. The last word in what PL 94-142 is otherwise known as.

Down

1. It's a condition in which one's ability to perform in some characteristic way (physical, social, or other) has been disrupted. It's called a(n) _____ disability.

2. The _____ Act of 1973 has been dubbed the "Bill of Rights for Handicapped Citizens."

4. An acronym for the organization that has pioneered the classification of persons with mental retardation.

7. According to the IDEA, an at-risk _____ or toddler is an individual under 3 years of age who would be in danger of experiencing a substantial developmental delay if early intervention services were not provided.

8. An acronym that refers to a disabled employee who meets an employer's standards for education, skill, and other job-related qualifications and who can perform the essential functions of the job with or without accommodation in the workplace.

9. The Λ in IDEA.

10. A new classification system for mental retardation employs a qualifier indicative of the _____ of support required across various environments.

12. According to IDEA, a person aged 3 through 9 who is experiencing a developmental delay in physical, cognitive, social, emotional, or adaptive development is a(n) _____ with a disability.

13. Although not expressly defined by the Americans with Disabilities Act of 1990, they are presumed to constitute functions such as caring for oneself, performing manual tasks, walking, seeing, hearing, speaking, breathing, learning, sitting, standing, lifting, reading, reaching, reproducing, and working. Here we speak of _____ life activities.

15. Disability has been conceived of by some as a(n) _____ issue.

17. It's an acronym that has to do with legislation and has nothing whatever to do with the American Dental Association.

EXERCISE 15-1

MOVIES AND MEASUREMENT

OBJECTIVE

To research instruments designed to assess personal adjustment to a disability

BACKGROUND

Some people seem to adjust quite well to a disability. Certainly this was the case for the blind protagonist in *23 Paces to Baker Street* pictured here playing pinball (note the hat obscuring the glass). Other people with disabilities may not be able to adjust quite as well.

Van Johnson as a kind of "pinball wizard" in a film called **23 Paces to Baker Street.**

YOUR TASK

Are there any tests that are used to assess personal adjustment to a disability? Research the literature to answer this question. If you find such as test, write a brief description of it, explaining how and in what contexts it might be used.

ADMINISTERING, SCORING, AND INTERPRETING NONSTANDARDIZED PSYCHOLOGICAL TESTS

OBJECTIVE

To enhance understanding of the problems attendant to the administration and interpretation of psychological tests that have been adapted for use with people with disabling conditions

BACKGROUND

Assessing people with disabling conditions brings with it special problems. For example, in the assessment of people with sensory impairments (such as the visually impaired and the blind and the hearing-impaired and the deaf), there exists the twofold problem of (1) adapting a given test so that it may be administered to the examinee and (2) interpreting the findings in a meaningful way given the absence of norms that would be useful with respect to the nonstandardized test administration.

YOUR TASK

Review the general description of the types of subtests that appear on the Wechsler scales in your textbook. Next, imagine that you are a psychological consultant to a school district that has inquired about modifying tests to make them amenable for administration to people with disabling conditions.

1. Describe the various types of adaptations that might have to be made in each of the subtests in order to adapt the test for administration to (a) a visually impaired individual *or* (b) a hearing-impaired individual.
2. Advise the school district how to proceed after the modified administration of the test to the individual with a sensory impairment; what guidelines for test scoring and interpretation would you suggest?

ASSESSING ADAPTIVE BEHAVIOR

OBJECTIVE

To enhance understanding of and provide firsthand assessment experience with the concept of adaptive behavior

BACKGROUND

Many instruments exist for use in assessing the adaptive behavior of examinees. Two such tests, the Adaptive Behavior Scale (ABS) and the Adaptive Behavior Scale, School Edition (ABSSE), are published by the American Association of Mental Deficiency. A partial listing of some of the general types of items that can be found on these two tests can be found in Table 15-1.

YOUR TASK

1. For each type of item listed in Table 15-1, write one item that could be scored "Correct" or "Incorrect" that you believe would measure the adaptive behavior listed. For example, consider Item IA: "Eating [(use of utensils, table manners, etc.).]" One item that you create might read as follows:

   a. Hand examinee a fork and ask examinee to demonstrate how he or she might eat mashed potatoes. Score "Correct" if fork is held correctly.

2. After you have created your own test of adaptive behavior, administer it to someone—anyone—who will take it. If the examinee does not have a cognitive (or other) disability, a "perfect score" should be obtained. Regardless, on the basis of your (meager) experience, discuss the problems and pitfalls that you can envision one might encounter in (a) devising a test of adaptive behavior, (b) administering such a test, (c) scoring such a test, and

TABLE 15-1   *A Partial Listing of Some of the Types of Items Found on the ABS and the ABSSE*

I. INDEPENDENT FUNCTIONING
   A. Eating
   B. Toilet use
   C. Cleanliness
   D. Appearance
   E. Care of clothing
   F. Dressing/undressing
   G. Travel
   H. Other (such as telephone use)

II. PHYSICAL DEVELOPMENT
   A. Sensory development
   B. Motor development

III. ECONOMIC ACTIVITY
   A. Money handling and budgeting
   B. Shopping skills

IV. LANGUAGE DEVELOPMENT
   A. Expression (such as writing)
   B. Comprehension (including reading)

V. KNOWLEDGE OF NUMBERS AND TIME

VI. RESPONSIBILITY
   A. Care of personal belongings

VII. SOCIALIZATION

(d) interpreting the findings. As an example of (c) and (d) with reference to the "Eating" question above, the question arises, "What is the correct position for holding a fork? *Is* there a correct position for holding a fork?"

EXERCISE 15-4

EVALUATING A TEST OF ADAPTIVE BEHAVIOR

OBJECTIVE

To critically evaluate a test, in this case a test of adaptive behavior

BACKGROUND

A number of resources are available in libraries and on the Internet to help in the evaluation of tests. In this exercise, you will be called upon to use these resources in order to critique a particular test.

YOUR TASK

In its various forms, the Vineland has remained one of the most widely used scales of adaptive behavior. The pros and cons of this test have been discussed in a number of journal articles and other scholarly resources. Using the discussion of the Vineland that follows as a point of departure, locate some additional resources on this measure. Then, write your own brief critique of this test.

PSYCHOMETRIC EVALUATION OF THE VINELAND

Quick quiz before reading on: Based on what you have read about the Vineland to this point, what specific types of reliability and validity do you think are (or should be) available for this test? Check your answer against the discussion that follows.

The manuals for the Vineland provide information about the internal-consistency reliability, test-retest reliability, and inter-rater reliability of the Survey Form of the Interview Edition (Sparrow et al., 1984b) as well as the Classroom Edition (Sparrow et al., 1985). Because no alternate forms of these editions exist, no measure of alternate-forms reliability can be obtained. Few reliability data are available for the Expanded Form (Sparrow et al., 1984a).

In evaluating the test's internal consistency, each domain is conceived of as a homogeneous unit, even though a wide variety of skills is assessed. Internal consistency of the Survey Form was estimated using a split-half proce-

dure, and coefficient alpha was used to estimate the internal consistency of the Classroom Edition. Acceptably high levels of internal consistency were reported for the various domains of both the Survey Form and the Classroom Edition. Additionally, an acceptably high level of internal consistency was reported for the Maladaptive Behavior scale, which is part of the Survey Form only (see the following table). Note that the test authors did not report estimates of internal consistency for the Expanded Form.

Internal Consistency of the Vineland

Area Assessed	Form	
	Survey Form	Classroom Form
Communication domain	.89	.93
Daily living skills domain	.90	.95
Socialization domain	.86	.94
Motor skills domain	.83	.80
Maladaptive behavior scale	.86	NA

The internal consistency of the Adaptive Behavior Composite, a combination of the test's various scales, was calculated to be .89 to .98 (median = .94) for the Survey Form and .96 to .98 (median = .98) for the Classroom Edition. These values are as high as or higher than the reliability estimates for the separate Vineland scales. From this observation, one might suspect that the various scales of the test overlap to measure the same construct or constructs. This hypothesis should be kept in mind when considering the construct validity of the test.

High coefficients of test-retest reliability are typically expected with regard to tests of adaptive functioning. This is so because the construct the test is measuring is presumed to be relatively stable over the short term. The test-retest reliability of the Survey Form was calculated over a two- to four-week retest interval. Over this period, the Adaptive Behavior Composite was found to range from .83 to .93, with a median test-retest reliability of .89. Median test-retest reliabilities for the specific domains also demonstrated stability. The test-retest reliability coefficients reported were .80 (Socialization), .81 (Motor Skills), .86 (Communication), and .85 (Daily Living Skills). The median Maladaptive Behavior test-retest reliability was .87. Test-retest reliability coefficients were not reported for either the Expanded Form or the Classroom Edition.

A third type of reliability relevant to a psychometric evaluation of the Vineland is inter-rater reliability. Although the test manual attempts to provide clear guidelines about how to score particular responses, some examiner judgment is necessary and might contribute to error in the test scores. For example, one of the items in the Communication domain asks whether the assessee "relates experiences in detail when asked" (Sparrow et al., 1984a,

p. 270). A Socialization domain item asks whether the subject "imitates adult phrases heard on previous occasions" (Sparrow et al., 1984a, p. 296). Because of the lack of sufficiently detailed scoring guidelines, there is a danger that the individual judgment of the respondent, and not the quality of the assessee's behavior, will account for a great proportion of the scoring variance. What criterion is used to determine how much detail is sufficient to be scored as "relating experience in detail"? How good must the imitation of a phrase be to be scored satisfactorily on the item that lists imitation of adult phrases as a criterion? These unanswered questions may have the effect of giving interviewers and informants wide latitude in scoring protocols.

Inter-rater reliability data on the Survey Form were gathered through the use of two interviewers, with interviews separated by 1 to 14 days (the average interval of separation between the first and second interview was 8 days). Differences between the conclusions of the two interviewers may be due to differences between the interviewers themselves. Alternatively, differences between the conclusions of the two interviewers may reflect changes in the informant's responses (a finding that could be made as a result of a test-retest reliability study). Inter-rater reliability coefficients would therefore be expected to be smaller than the test-retest reliability coefficients; after all, not only is information being collected twice, but also more variance is being added to the data collection process (because of different interviewers). In fact, the inter-rater reliability coefficients were lower than the test-retest reliability coefficients. Reported inter-rater reliability estimates were .62 (Socialization domain), .72 (Daily Living Skills domain), .72 (Communication domain), and .78 (Motor Skills domain). An inter-rater reliability coefficient of .74 was reported for both the Adaptive Behavior Composite and the Maladaptive Behavior score. Inter-rater reliability was not assessed for the Expanded Form or the Classroom Edition.

Other inter-rater reliability-related questions with regard to a test such as the Vineland concern the reliability not of the interviewers but of the judges or informants. How reliable is a parent's report on the child from one day to the next? How consistent are reports on a particular child from one teacher to the next? The test's manual is silent on such questions, decreasing the possibility of a comprehensive evaluation of the Vineland.

Although no quantitative evidence for the content validity of this test is presented, the authors make their case for the test's content validity on the basis of a rational analysis of the content areas surveyed by the items. Especially with regard to the items in the Expanded Form, efforts to tap the widest possible range of adaptive behaviors are described as having been made. And much like those of its expanded version, the items of the Survey Form were designed to sample broadly from various areas of adaptive behavior. The Classroom Edition was designed to contain items that reflect behavior primarily in the academic setting.

Data relative to the test's criterion-related validity are presented for both the Survey Form and the Classroom Edition, though no such data are presented for the test's Expanded Form. Correlations between the original Vineland and the revised Vineland Survey Form ranged from .55 to .97, according to Sparrow et al. (1984b). However, an independent study of the relationship between these two versions of the Vineland yielded a correlation of only .38 (Raggio & Massingale, 1990). Taken as a whole, these data cast doubt on the expectation that the two versions of the same test are indeed measuring the same thing.

Criterion-related validity evidence can also be gathered from examinations of the relationship between the Vineland and other adaptive behavior scales. These types of studies have yielded correlations between .40 and .70, according to Sparrow et al. (1984b). However, other researchers have observed higher correlations between the Vineland and other adaptive behavior measures. Correlations of between .50 and .95 were reported by Middleton et al. (1990), and correlations of approximately .90 were reported by Roberts et al. (1993). Reported correlations of the Vineland Survey Form with two other parent-report instruments of problem behavior ranged from .46 to .71 (Pearson & Lachar, 1994). Correlations between the Vineland Classroom Edition and other adaptive behavior measures range from .18 to .51 and from .62 to .92 (Harrison, 1985).

Evidence offered in support of the Vineland's construct validity begins with the observation that, in children, adaptive behavior increases with age. If Vineland scores also increased with age, this could be construed as evidence to support the notion that the Vineland is indeed measuring adaptive behavior. Both in the Survey Form and in the Classroom Edition, progressive increases are found in average raw scores for each age group in the standardization samples (Sparrow et al., 1984b, 1985). Another way to examine the construct validity of this test has to do with expected differences for special groups. Children with Down's syndrome tend to develop steadily for the first several years, after which development often slows dramatically. Evidence for the construct validity of the Vineland would be obtained by the observation that scores on the test paralleled this known developmental path. In one study, children with Down's syndrome did show age-related gains in raw score on the Vineland through age 6 or 7. After that, the average raw score no longer increased, and performance became more variable. This pattern of results indicated that some children continued to advance, some stayed the same, and others began to decline (Dykens et al., 1994). In general, the results were deemed supportive of the Vineland's construct validity.

Construct validity evidence may also come from relationships among a test's scales as indicated by factor analysis. Recall that the internal consistency reliability computations indicated that the Vineland, across domains, is internally consistent. Such consistency could be expected to correspond with substantial correlations among the various domain scales. Indeed, as reported by the test's authors, median correlations for pairs of domain scales range from .39 to .55 for the Survey Form and from .43 to .70 for the Classroom Edition. Factor analysis by the test's authors resulted in a single factor that accounts for 55–70 percent of the variance in each age group on the Survey Form. The same single factor was also found to account for 67–80 percent of the variance in each age group on the Classroom Edition. An independent assessment of the factor structure of the Survey Form produced similar findings, with a single factor explaining 75 percent of the variability in test scores (Roberts et al., 1993). These findings suggest that the Vineland is assessing a single underlying construct, which could be labeled "adaptive behavior." The findings may also be construed to support the use of the Adaptive Behavior Composite as an index of level of adaptive behavior.

Evidence concerning the convergent and discriminant validity of the Vineland is also reported in the test manuals. Consistent with the idea of discriminant validity, the Vineland correlates less well with measures of intelligence than it does with other measures of adaptive behavior. Stated another way, the Vineland seems to tap a construct that is somewhat distinct from intelligence. According to Sparrow et al. (1984b), correlations between children's scores on the Vineland's Survey Form Adaptive Behavior Composite and the Kaufman Assessment Battery for Children (K-ABC) Mental Processing Composite ranged from .13 to .41 (median = .22). Correlations between the Survey Form Adaptive Behavior Composite and the Peabody Picture Vocabulary Test, Revised (PPVT-R), ranged from .12 to .37 (median = .21). Somewhat higher correlations were observed between the Vineland Classroom Edition and the K-ABC Mental Processing Composite (range .31 to .53, median .48), as well as the PPVT-R (.20 to .45, median = .31). Communication domain scores tend to correlate most highly with intelligence scales. The skills tapped in the Communication domain may more closely reflect cognitive skills than the other domains of the Vineland (Sparrow et al., 1985).

To demonstrate convergent and discriminant validity, the correlations between the Vineland and other adaptive behavior measures should be greater than the correlations between the Vineland and tests of intelligence. The wide range of discriminant validity coefficients obtained, coupled with the wide range of the criterion-related validity coefficients with which they might be compared, makes such comparisons difficult. For the purposes of clarification, discriminant and convergent validity coefficients within one particular study could be compared. When this is done with the Roberts et al. (1993) data, for instance, evidence of convergent validity (the two adaptive behavior measures correlate .90) and discriminant validity (intelligence correlates with the adaptive behavior measures .26 and .31) can be found.

Now return to the question raised at the very beginning. How did you do? If you were a test reviewer for a scholarly journal, what would you write about the Vineland? Evans and Bradley-Johnson (1988) did scholarly reviews of the Vineland and other adaptive behavior measures. They argue that the moderate levels of test-retest and internal consistency reliability achieved by the Vineland are not as high as they should be for a test of this type. Levels of inter-rater reliability are still lower and are conceptualized only in terms of the reliability of the interviewer. Informant reliability would seem to be an important issue, but it is not considered. Evans and Bradley-Johnson (1988) also conclude that insufficient reliability evidence is available. Only the Survey Form is thoroughly examined relative to reliability issues: No such information is available on the Expanded Form, and only limited reliability information is presented for the Classroom Edition.

Evans and Bradley-Johnson (1988) addressed the validity of the adaptive behavior measures they reviewed as well. They note that none of the measures has very complete information concerning validity, and we concur. Based on the test author's survey of the domains sampled, the test appears to be content-valid, but we would have appreciated some quantitative evidence to support that contention. As it is, our acceptance of the content validity of the test is based more on faith than anything else. Criterion-related validity evidence is so mixed that making relevant comparisons with discriminant validity coefficients is difficult. The range in the magnitude of reported validity coefficients yields a puzzling picture regarding the validity of the Vineland. The fact that the test is not highly correlated with its predecessor and namesake only adds to the mystery. There is some evidence, however, that clearly supports the construct validity of the test. Here we refer to the finding that a single factor underlies scores in the various domains and that expected age-related changes occur for normal and Down's syndrome children.

Clearly, more thorough study of the Vineland is necessary (Evans & Bradley-Johnson, 1988). Until compelling reliability and validity data are published for all versions of the Vineland, the test should not be considered a solid foundation on which to base important decisions about the lives of disabled individuals.

EXERCISE 15-5

PICK A TEST

OBJECTIVE

To learn more about a test for people with disabling conditions that is not reviewed in the textbook

BACKGROUND

The approach in your textbook is to highlight only a few of the many tests that exist in any given area. For every test covered in your textbook, there may well be dozens of other tests designed to measure the same attribute(s).

YOUR TASK

A list of tests for persons with disabling conditions along with a brief description of each follows in Table 15-2. From this list, select one test that you think you would like to know more about. Then, use all of the resources at your disposal to answer the following:

1. Describe what the test measures.
2. Who would be most apt to use this test? Why? Include in your answer sample questions the test user might hope to answer through the use of this test.
3. Who would be most apt to take this test? Why?
4. Describe the full range of people to whom it would be appropriate to administer this test, including comments about who would be inappropriate.
5. Describe what is known about the test's reliability.
6. Describe what is known about the test's validity.

7. Imagining that you are a measurement consultant, would you recommend this test to clients who are test users? Why or why not?

REFERENCES

Harrison, P. L. (1985). *Vineland Adaptive Behavior Scales, Classroom Edition: Manual.* Circle Pines, MN: American Guidance Service.

Middleton, H. A., Keene, R. G., & Brown, G. W. (1990). Convergent and discriminant validities of the Scales of Independent Behavior and the Revised Vineland Adaptive Behavior Scales. *American Journal on Mental Retardation, 31,* 545–547.

Pearson, D. A., & Lachar, D. (1994). Using behavioral questionnaires to identify adaptive deficits in elementary school children. *Journal of School Psychology, 32,* 33–52.

Raggio, D. J., & Massingale, T. W. (1990). Comparability of the Vineland Social Maturity Scale and the Vineland Adaptive Behavior Scale—Survey Form with infants evaluated for developmental delay. *Perceptual and Motor Skills, 71,* 415–418.

Roberts, C., McCoy, M., Reidy, D., & Crucitti, F. (1993). A comparison of methods of assessing adaptive behaviour in preschool children with developmental disabilities. *Australia and New Zealand Journal of Developmental Disabilities, 18,* 261–272.

Sparrow, S. S., Balla, D. A., & Cicchetti, D. V. (1984a). *Vineland Adaptive Behavior Scales, Interview Edition: Expanded form manual.* Circle Pines, MN: American Guidance Service.

TABLE 15-2 *Some Tests for People with Disabling Conditions*

Test	Description
Assessing Linguistic Behaviors: Assessing Prelinguistic and Early Linguistic Behaviors in Developmentally Young Children	For children from birth through a 2-year-old functional level, this test measures children's performance in various areas of cognitive-social and linguistic development such as language comprehension and communicative intentions.
An Adaptation of the Wechsler Preschool and Primary Scale of Intelligence (WPPSI) for Deaf Children	For ages 4 to 6½ years, this is designed to be a general measure of achievement for deaf and hearing-impaired children.
Movement Assessment Battery for Children	For ages 4 through 12, this test is designed to screen and provide management suggestions for children with motor skill disabilities.
Motor Skills Inventory	For children, this is a screening test for impairment in fine and gross motor skills.
CID Phonetic Inventory	For children with hearing impairments, this test evaluates speech ability at the phonetic level.
Living Language	For children, this test is designed to evaluate language skills and impairment.
Behavioral Analysis Language Instrument	For children and adults, this test is designed to identify deficiencies in language.
Employability Maturity Interview	For adult rehabilitation clients, this structured interview is designed to assess readiness for the vocational rehabilitation planning.
Work Personality Profile	For adult rehabilitation clients, this rating scale completed by observers is designed to assess aspects of one's job-related performance deemed to be essential to the achievement and maintenance of employment.
Adaptive Behavior: Street Skills Survival Skills Questionnaire	For developmentally disabled adolescents and adults, this test measures prevocational skills and ability to function independently in the community.

Sparrow, S. S., Balla, D. A., & Cicchetti, D. V. (1984b). *Vineland Adaptive Behavior Scales, Interview Edition: Survey form manual.* Circle Pines, MN: American Guidance Service.

Sparrow, S. S., Balla, D. A., & Cicchetti, D. V. (1985). *Vineland Adaptive Behavior Scales, Classroom Edition manual.* Circle Pines, MN: American Guidance Service.

THE 4-QUESTION CHALLENGE

1. A trend towards altering environments in ways designed to make individuals with handicapping conditions feel less challenged is consistent with
   a. the medical model of disability
   b. the environmental paradigm of disability
   c. the World Health Organization model
   d. the social model of disability

2. Which event was in part responsible for the creation of Regional Centers for Deaf-Blind Youths by the United States Congress?
   a. the discovery of HIV and AIDS
   b. the launching of *Sputnik* by the Soviets
   c. a nationwide epidemic of rubella
   d. a nationwide epidemic of hepatitis

3. If there were a need to learn more about the sexual knowledge and attitudes of a developmentally disabled adolescent, which of the following would probably be most helpful?
   a. the Callier-Azusa Scale
   b. the Socio-Sexual Knowledge and Attitudes Test
   c. the Hand Test
   d. the Southern California Sensory Integration Tests

4. Many tests administered to people with various types of disability do not have norms directly applicable to the testtaker. According to the text, the examiner in such a case may have to
   a. refrain from using the test and use an interview instead.
   b. improvise somewhat in the test administration and interpretation.
   c. contact the APA Committee on Testing for an opinion about how to proceed.
   d. none of the above

CHAPTER 16

Assessment, Careers, and Business

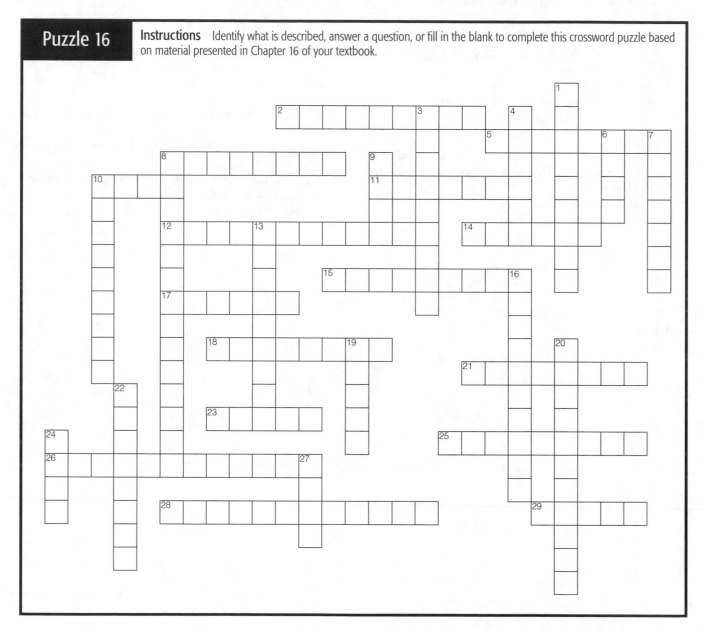

Puzzle 16

Instructions Identify what is described, answer a question, or fill in the blank to complete this crossword puzzle based on material presented in Chapter 16 of your textbook.

Across

2. A screening instrument designed to predict who will and will not be an honest employee is called a(n) _____ test.

5. It's an item format characterized by bipolar adjectives separated by a 7-point rating scale on which respondents select one point to indicate their response. It's called the _____ differential technique.

8. _____ psychology is that branch of social psychology that deals primarily with the development, advertising, and marketing of products and services.

10. It's a type of survey used to record votes which usually contains questions that can be answered with a simple "yes/no" or "for/against" response. Typically used to gauge opinion about issues, it's called a(n) _____ .

11. A psychological syndrome characterized by emotional exhaustion, depersonalization, and reduced personal accomplishment.

12. It's a pleasurable or positive emotional state resulting from the appraisal of one's job or job experiences. It's called job _____ .

14. A fixed list of questions administered orally, in writing, online, or some other way to a selected sample of persons, typically for the purpose of learning about consumers' attitudes, beliefs, opinions, and/or behavior with regard to targeted products, services, or advertising.

15. A state in which the primary force driving an individual comes from an external source (such as salary) and from external contraints (such as job loss) is called _____ motivation.

17. It's a method or procedure that entails the distribution of a predetermined number or percentage of assessees into various categories that describe performance (such as categories that range from "unsatisfactory" to "superior"). It's called a(n) _____ distribution technique.

18. A presumably learned disposition to react in some characteristic manner to a particular stimulus.

21. In workplace settings, it's a method or procedure that entails the recording of employee behaviors evaluated as positive or negative by a supervisor or other rater. It's referred to as the _____ incidents technique.

23. It's a sample of respondents, selected by demographic and other criteria, who have contracted with a consumer or marketing research firm to respond on a periodic basis to surveys, questionnaires, and related research instruments regarding various products, services, and/or advertising or other promotional efforts. It's referred to as a consumer _____ .

25. A relatively superficial process of evaluation based on certain minimal standards, criteria, or requirements.

26. It's the practice of developing norms that are based on the race or ethnic background of testtakers. This controversial practice is referred to as _____ .

28. Output or value yielded relative to work effort made.

29. It's qualitative research conducted with a group of respondents who have typically been screened in some way to qualify for participation in the research. The forum for discussion is referred to as a _____ group.

Down

1. A disposition, transfer, or assignment to a group or category typically made on the basis of a single criterion.

3. It's a state in which the primary force driving an individual comes from within, such as personal satisfaction with one's work. Psychologists refer to it as _____ motivation.

4. It's an organizationally standardized procedure for evaluation that employs a number of assessment techniques. It's referred to as an assessment _____ .

6. Two or more people who interact interdependently toward a common and valued goal. Each member of it has typically been assigned specific roles or functions to perform.

7. The socially transmitted behavior patterns, beliefs, and products of work of a particular population, community, or group of people.

8. Rating, categorizing, or "pigeonholing" with respect to two or more criteria.

9. The acronym for a widely used measure of personality type that was devised by a mother-daughter team of nonpsychologists.

10. _____ assessment is an approach to assessment that employs the evaluation of work samples.

13. A process whereby each person evaluated for a position will be either accepted or rejected for that position.

16. The strength of an individual's identification with and involvement in a particular organization is referred to as organizational _____ .

19. It's a type of consumer group in which the respondents have all agreed to keep diaries regarding their thoughts and/or behavior. In market research, this group is referred to as a _____ panel.

20. It's an adaptation of Lazarus's multimodal clinical approach for use in qualitative research applications, designed to ensure that the research is comprehensive and systematic from a psychological perspective. It's referred to as _____ qualitative research.

22. The Strong is an example of a(n) _____ measure.

24. Laboratory analysis of a urine specimen is used by some employers as a _____ test in screening for new personnel.

27. Based on this acronym, we could envision that F. Scott Fitzgerald would have thought that this general aptitude test battery was just great.

EXERCISE 16-1
MOVIES AND MEASUREMENT

OBJECTIVE

To enhance understanding of and provide firsthand experience with some of the tools of assessment in personnel psychology

BACKGROUND

Some people seem born to pursue certain professions or vocations. Certainly this is the case for Buffy (Sara Michelle Gellar) and her mentor and "watcher," Rupert Giles (Anthony Stewart Head). For most of us, however, identifying an occupation we would like to pursue for life is a bit more complicated. In many instances, psychological tests can provide valuable assistance in making such choices.

Originally a movie and then a television series, Buffy the Vampire Slayer *spins a yarn about natural born slayers.*

YOUR TASK

Imagine that you are a personnel psychologist charged with the responsibility of selecting personnel for a mission to Pluto. Your employer, NASA, has asked you to use your knowledge of psychological tests to identify "natural born astronauts" who will be compatible with each other for this very long mission.

1. Briefly describe the types of tests or measurement procedures that you would employ for the purpose of screening applicants.
2. Briefly describe the types of tests or measurement procedures that you would employ for the purpose of selecting applicants.
3. More specifically, describe the role each of the following variables would (or would not) play in your ultimate selection decision:

   - physical/medical
   - personality
   - intelligence
   - interests
   - cultural factors
   - oral communication skills
   - written communication skills
   - creativity
   - tolerance of ambiguity
   - energy level
   - flexibility
   - decision-making ability
   - ability to delay gratification
   - (insert your own variable here)

4. Beyond the written exercise described above, an in-class exercise would entail one student playing the role of the NASA psychologist screening prospective candidates for the mission (all other class members) by means of a brief interview. All class members then write a paragraph or two on who they felt were the top two choices for the mission and why.
5. Class discussion of each of the above tasks shall take place at the discretion of, and be guided by, "mission control" (the instructor).

EXERCISE 16-2
TEST PROFILES

OBJECTIVE

To enhance understanding of and provide firsthand experience with test profiles and patterns

BACKGROUND

In everyday conversation, the word *profile* is synonymous with a side view of something, most typically a side view of a human head. In the language of psychological testing, the word *profile* generally refers to measurements obtained from a test or tests, most typically (though not necessarily) represented in graphic form. The term probably was derived from the shape of the graphic representation of test data when the graph is of the frequency polygon variety—with the connected lines of the frequency polygon forming a shape reminiscent of a person or object in profile. However, *profile* has generalized in meaning and may also be properly used to refer to measurement data displayed in histogram form or data that are simply listed in tabular form.

Test profiles may be derived from virtually any type of psychological test, be it an intelligence test, a personality test, an educational test, a measure of interest, a measure of attitude . . . the list goes on. One type of test profile makes reference to the subjects (or, in some instances, raw or scaled scores) of a single test. For example, we might speak of a particular child's WISC-IV profile or the profile (or pattern)[1] of test scores obtained by an adult on the WAIS-III. A particular profile of scores (such as one where there are large discrepancies between scores on Verbal and Performance subtests) may be suggestive of neuropsychological impairment. A particular profile or pattern of scores on the MMPI-2 may be suggestive of a particular psychodiagnostic category. And a particular profile of scores on a measure

---
[1]The term *pattern* is, in practice, virtually synonymous with *profile*.

of occupational interest may be suggestive of suitability for one or another profession.

The term *profile* is also used to refer to a pattern of test results with respect to more than one test. For example, the profile of a daycare-center worker who is convicted of child abuse might include (1) average to below-average scores on intelligence tests; (2) scores indicative of maladjustment, particularly in the area of social relations, self-esteem, and sexual adjustment on tests of personality; (3) a higher-than-average incidence of self-report of having been abused as a child.

If a profile is displayed in graphic form, the horizontal axis of the graph will typically list items or subtests or tests, while the vertical axis will typically list scores—expressed as numbers (such as in raw or converted form) or expressed with reference to some qualitative category (such as "low/medium/high").

YOUR TASK

1. Table 16-1 gives the data for John D. Doe's scores expressed as percentiles on the 30 subtests of the "Almost Every Conceivable Aptitude Test" (AECAT), a highly reliable and valid (but entirely hypothetical) measure of high school students' aptitude for entry into various occupations and professions. Graph these data in the space provided on the following page as (a) a frequency polygon and (b) a histogram.

2. You are the high school vocational counselor charged with the responsibility of providing vocational guidance to John D. Doe. What advice might you give the test-taker—a graduating high school senior—on the basis of these data? About what type of career might you suggest that this testtaker learn more?

3. In the space provided on page 243, draw the AECAT profile of an individual who you predict would be ideally suited to enter the field of psychology and specialize in the area of psychometrics. Then, using additional paper if necessary, briefly explain the profile you constructed.

EXERCISE 16-3

ANOTHER DAY, ANOTHER PROFILE

OBJECTIVE

To introduce students to the Differential Aptitude Test and provide additional experience with test profiles

BACKGROUND

The Differential Aptitude Test (DAT) is a vocational aptitude battery that was first published in 1947. It is designed for use with students in grades 7 through 12. The test is based on the idea that people have not one but a variety of measurable vocational aptitudes. It consists of eight subtests, which yield separate scores on eight aptitudes (see Table 16-2, page 243). A ninth score, Scholastic Aptitude, is derived from a combination of the scores on Verbal Reasoning and Numerical Reasoning and is designed to provide an indication of academic ability. With the 1990 revision of this test came the Career Interest Inventory, which combines

TABLE 16-1 *John D. Doe's AECAT Scores*

AECAT Aptitude Codes	Percentile Scores for John D. Doe	AECAT Aptitude Codes	Percentile Scores for John D. Doe
1. Domestic engineering	10	16. Leadership (general)	99
2. Financial planning	30	17. Navigational	80
3. Clerical	50	18. Physical trainer	90
4. Accounting	55	19. Verbal (general)	80
5. College teaching	60	20. Electronics technology	85
6. Food sciences	65	21. Foreign languages	75
7. Computer sciences	70	22. Guidance counseling	90
8. Medical sciences	70	23. Interpersonal skills	75
9. Musical	70	24. Legal	75
10. Political	70	25. Writing (general)	70
11. Agricultural	75	26. Statistical	20
12. Mathematics (general)	80	27. Cosmetology	15
13. Strategic planning	95	28. Artistic	15
14. Military sciences	99	29. Pharmaceutical	10
15. Dental sciences	99	30. Lighthouse keeper	10

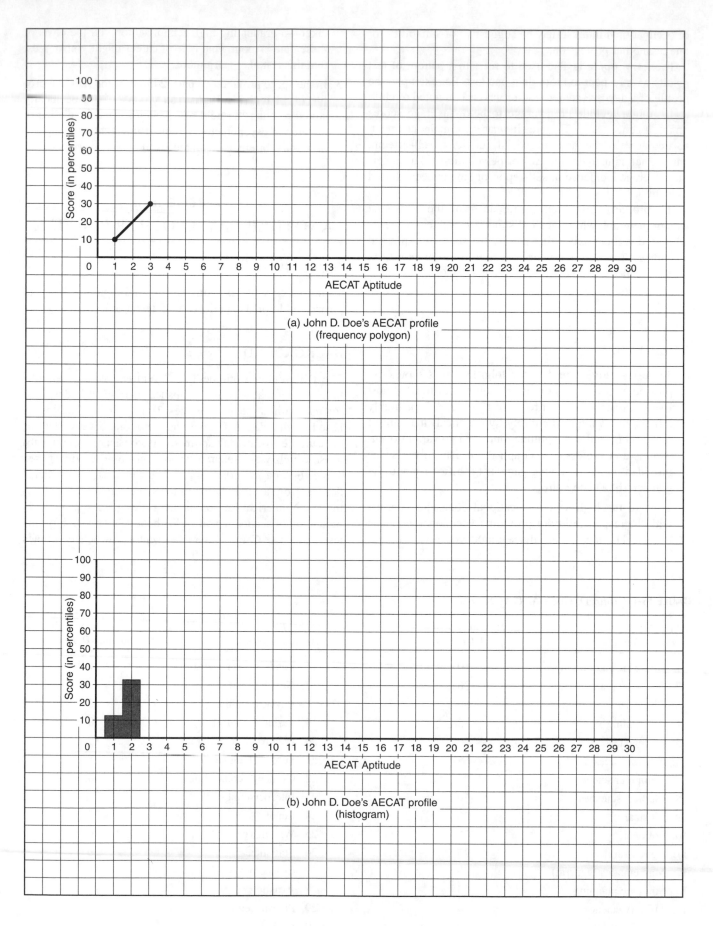

(a) John D. Doe's AECAT profile
(frequency polygon)

(b) John D. Doe's AECAT profile
(histogram)

Explanation of the Profile

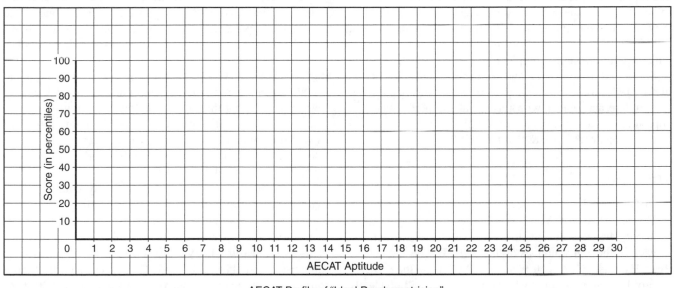

AECAT Profile of "Ideal Psychometrician"

DAT data with data from a supplementary questionnaire tapping interests, educational goals, and preferences. The computerized test report analyzes and discusses the resulting pattern of aptitudes and interests in terms of the appropriateness of various occupational choices.

Approximately 100,000 students from 520 school districts and an additional 22,000 students from research programs participated in the 1990 standardization of the DAT. The sample was stratified on variables such as grade, sex, geographical region, socioeconomic status, ethnicity, and

TABLE 16-2 *The Subtests of the Differential Aptitude Test*

Test	Types of Items
Verbal Reasoning	Double-ended analogies designed in part to test ability to abstract. This type of item requires the testtaker to select the pair of words that best completes the beginning and end of a sentence. An example: _____ is to end, as appetizer is to _____ . 1. beginning __ dessert 2. ending __ appetizing 3. sunset __ dusk 4. final __ midterm 5. fruit cup __ open bar
Numerical Reasoning	Items on this subtest measure computational skills and understanding of numerical relationships.
Abstract Reasoning	The testtaker's task here is to determine which of several alternative figures would logically be next in a series of figures.
Perceptual Speed and Accuracy	Includes tasks resembling those required for clerical jobs (such as filing and coding).
Mechanical Reasoning	Items on this subtest are pictures designed to assess the testtaker's understanding and knowledge of various physical laws and forces affecting activities such as lifting, turning, and pulling.
Space Relations	A two-dimensional picture or pattern is presented, and it is the examinee's task to select which of several alternative pictures or patterns could be produced from the original; this subtest taps the process of visualization—and the ability to mentally rotate objects in space.
Spelling	A word is presented, and the testtaker indicates whether the word is or is not spelled correctly.
Language Usage	Basic language skills such as grammar, punctuation, and capitalization are tapped by this subtest.

urban/rural/suburban residence. Normative data for males and females are presented separately in the manual. Intercorrelations among the subtests are low enough to suggest that they are, in fact, measuring relatively independent areas. Validity evidence comes from research on workers in specific occupations. For example, a composite scale composed of the Verbal, Mechanical, and Numerical Reasoning scales of the DAT, along with a visualization task, has been found to correlate acceptably with the actual job performance of apprentices in the trades, such as plumbing, tool making, and machine repair (Hattrup & Schmitt, 1990).

YOUR TASK

1. In Exercise 16-2, you became acquainted with John D. Doe and his AECAT scores. Based on what you know about Mr. Doe, how would you expect him to score on each of the eight subtests of the DAT? Why?
2. In Exercise 16-3, you were asked to draw the AECAT profile of an individual who you predict would be ideally suited to enter the field of psychology and specialize in the area of psychometrics. How would you expect this individual to score on each of the eight subtests of the DAT? Why?
3. The DAT seems to measure some abilities that overlap with those measured by intelligence tests (Boyle, 1987; Gakhar, 1986). In fact, some DAT subtests have been used as measures of intellectual ability in published research (Landry & McKelvie, 1985; Lynn et al., 1983, 1984). Write a short (one or two paragraphs maximum) argument, taking either a pro or con position on the substitution of subtests of the DAT for a measure of intelligence in a research study.

EXERCISE 16-4

YOUR PERSONALITY SUITS YOU FOR WORK AS . . .

OBJECTIVE

To introduce students to the Guilford-Zimmerman Temperament Survey

BACKGROUND

Is a likeable, dominant, persuasive person better suited for work in sales or work on an assembly line? Clearly such an individual, at least with respect to these personality traits, seems better suited for work in sales. In addition to examining interests and aptitudes, preemployment counseling may also entail the administration of personality tests. Such tests "round out" the vocational assessment by providing additional input. Suppose an individual with an interest in a tele-

vision news career and a high aptitude for writing is weighing the merits of becoming a television news personality or a television news writer. And suppose further that one of the findings in a personality test was that this individual has a very high need for exhibitionism. The personality test findings, combined with other findings, might lead the consulting psychologist to steer the client toward pursuit of an on-air career. Contrariwise, if the findings from personality tests indicated that this client was low in exhibitionism and had a strong need for independence and autonomy combined with little tolerance for relating to authority figures, the client might be asked to consider the merits of freelance work within the field of television news.

Almost any personality test conceivably could be used within the context of vocational counseling. One such test that has enjoyed widespread usage is the Guilford-Zimmerman Temperament Survey (GZTS). This test is a self-report measure that yields scores on the ten personality dimensions listed in Table 16-3. The scores on each of these dimensions or factors are derived from responses to 30 statements that may take the form of "yes," "no," or "?" (uncertain). Interpretation is typically not made with respect to any one score but rather on the basis of all the scores—a profile. Thus, for example, consideration of a high score in General Activity alone might lead the interpreter to suspect that the assessee is one who works quickly. However, if such a score is coupled with a low score on the Restraint dimension, the interpretation might change from "highly energetic" to "highly impulsive," the latter description being more accurate for someone who acts quickly but with little restraint. In addition to the dimension scales, the GZTS has built into it three verification scales designed to detect response sets, intentional faking, and carelessness.

Normative data for the GZTS are based on a college sample of 523 men and 389 women; profiles of patterns of scores for various high school, college, and adult occupational groups are reported in the test manual (Guilford, Zimmerman, & Guilford, 1976). Reliability estimates obtained on each of the different factors were found to range from .75 to .85. Test-retest reliability based on varying intervals of from one to three years tends to lie in the .50s and .60s range. An overview of the extensive amount of research conducted on this test in the years since its publication is presented in the manual. Included are studies exploring scores on the test as a function of variables such as age, education, gender, occupational group, psychiatric diagnosis, socioeconomic status, ethnic group, and political affiliation.

YOUR TASK

1. Create your own GZTS profile by characterizing yourself as either "low," "medium," or "high" with regard to each of the ten dimensions described in Table 16-3.
2. On the basis of the GZTS profile of yourself that you have created, what type of work do you think you are best suited for? Why?

TABLE 16-3 *Guilford-Zimmerman Temperament Survey (GZTS) Personality Dimensions*

Dimension Name	Description
General Activity (G)	A measure of energy level and the rate at which the individual operates. A high scorer would be a person who moves quickly, works at a rapid rate, and is full of vitality.
Restraint (R)	A measure of self-control, persistence, and deliberate action; to some extent this score provides a measure of responsibility. A person scoring low on this scale would be impulsive, spontaneous, and seemingly carefree.
Ascendance (A)	A measure of the degree to which the individual exhibits leadership, initiative, and assertiveness. A low score on this scale reflects submissiveness.
Sociability (S)	The extent to which the individual seeks and develops social contacts.
Emotional Stability (E)	An indication of evenness or fluctuation of moods, optimism, or pessimism, and whether there are feelings of or freedom from feelings of worry, guilt, or loneliness.
Objectivity (O)	A measure of the degree to which the individual is thick-skinned or sensitive.
Friendliness (F)	A measure of congeniality, respect for others, acceptance, and tolerance.
Thoughtfulness (T)	An indication of observation and reflectiveness of self and others.
Personal Reactions (P)	Acceptance and tolerance of others and faith in social institutions.
Masculinity (M)	A measure of the degree to which the individual is interested in masculine activities and exhibits behavior traditionally associated with masculine roles.

3. Create one question that can be answered in a yes/no format to measure each of the ten dimensions of the GZTS. Then describe the process of creating those questions in terms of its ease or difficulty. What obstacles must be overcome in terms of creating such questions?

EXERCISE 16-5
INTRODUCING MYERS AND BRIGGS

OBJECTIVE

To introduce students to the Myers-Briggs Type Indicator (MBTI)

BACKGROUND

Katharine Cook Briggs (1875–1968) and her daughter, Isabel Briggs Myers (1897–1980; see Figure 16-1), are the authors of the Myers-Briggs Type Indicator. Although neither woman had formal training in psychology, both read biographies with great interest. Katharine developed an interest in individual differences in 1915, when she was introduced by her daughter to her future son-in-law, Clarence Myers. For Katharine, Clarence seemed different in fundamental ways from other members of the Briggs family. Owing in part to a desire to better understand those differences, Katharine developed a category of psychological types. After she learned of Carl Jung's work in typology, Katharine studied Jung's writings with her daughter. Years later, Isabel decided to put the ideas she had so long dis-

cussed with her mother to the test—literally. The result was the test now known as the Myers-Briggs Type Indicator.

YOUR TASK

After reading the material on the MBTI that follows, do some research of your own on this test. Then, write a brief review of this test, making sure to touch on the issues related to its validity.

Inspired by the theoretical typology of Carl Jung (1923), the Myers-Briggs Type Indicator (MBTI) was developed by Isabel Briggs Myers and her mother, Katharine Cook Briggs (Myers & Briggs, 1943/1962). In the late 1950s, Educational Testing Service (ETS) marketed the MBTI as a research instrument while the company conducted its own research into the test's psychometric properties. After several years of evaluation, ETS elected to terminate its relationship with the test (Pittenger, 1993). In 1975, Consulting Psychologists Press, Inc. (CPP) published the test along with a wide range of ancillary materials, including interpretive guides and software to create psychological reports. Now available in a children's form, a research form, and a form for personal analysis, the test is represented to have application in contexts ranging from vocational guidance to marriage counseling (Consulting Psychologists Press, 1994).

Consistent with Jung's writings, the MBTI was designed to assess four bipolar dimensions of personality, each dimension believed to be a component of one's psychological type: introversion versus extraversion (with respect to where one focuses one's energy), perceiving versus judgment (with respect to responding to experience; not part of Jung's theory), sensing versus intuition (with respect to

FIGURE 16-1   *A Mother-Daughter Team of Test Developers*
Katharine Cook Briggs (left) and Isabel Briggs Myers (right).

perception), and thinking versus feeling (with respect to making judgments). According to Jung, people can be classified at the extremes of these bipolar dimensions. For example, people who usually make judgments on the basis of feelings will seldom, if ever, make judgments on the basis of thought. This assumption regarding each of these bipolar dimensions is reflected in the way MBTI test items are written (a forced-choice format reflective of opposite poles of dimensions) as well as in the way the test responses are scored and interpreted.

The primary form of the test (Form G) contains a total of 126 forced-choice test items. Based on the testtaker's pattern of response to the items, numerical scores are tabulated. The scores are used to classify the testtaker in one or another of the extreme poles of each of the four dimensions. Ultimately, each testtaker is identified as one of sixteen personality types. There are two poles for each of four dimensions, yielding 16 ($2 \times 2 \times 2 \times 2$) different possible types. A person may be identified, for example, as an extraverted-intuitive-perceiving-feeling type. The two poles for each of four dimensions means, for example, that testtakers may be classified as extraverted if (1) they demonstrate a very strong tendency to be extraverted, or (2) they demonstrate a tendency to be just slightly stronger than the tendency they exhibit to be introverted. These is no middle ground or gray area with regard to the scoring of the four personality dimensions, a feature of the MBTI that has been criticized both for the loss of information entailed and the oversensitivity to responses to single items (Harvey & Murry, 1994; Lorr, 1991). The basic MBTI assumption regarding the bipolarity of the dimensions measured has also been questioned (Girelli & Stake, 1993), as has the reliability of the test; in one study, fully half of all testtakers were found to change in personality type classification over the course of only five weeks (Pittenger, 1993). Many of the validity studies re-

ported in the MBTI manual and elsewhere have been plagued by a variety of methodological difficulties (Martin & Bartol, 1986; Pittenger, 1993), and the four-factor structure of the test has been questioned (Zumbo & Taylor, 1993). Regardless of such psychometric data, the test remains a popular one, perhaps because of its strong intuitive appeal.

EXERCISE 16-6
TASTE TESTS

OBJECTIVE

To obtain firsthand experience with the problems and issues that may arise in conducting a simple consumer experiment such as a taste test

BACKGROUND

"Beer drinkers prefer Brand X to Brand Y by 2 to 1!"

"Take the challenge and you'll see for yourself why the switch is on to Our Cola!"

"A real butter taste, with no cholesterol!"

"It tastes identical to sugar, but with no calories!"

Claims involving taste-test data have by now become quite familiar. Often, it seems simple; a group of consumers of a particular beverage—say, carbonated cola soft drinks—taste-test two or more carbonated cola soft drinks, and a clear preference emerges. But is it really all that simple?

A wealth of literature attests to the fact that there are a number of relatively complex issues that must be dealt with in terms of taste-test administration as well as analysis of taste-test data (Brown, Zatkalik, Treumann, Buehner, & Schmidt, 1984; Buchanan & Morrison, 1984; Day, 1965, 1969; Greenhalgh, 1966; Irwin, 1958; Kuehn, 1962; Luce & Suppes, 1965; Morrison, 1981). In addition, events that may on their face be indicative of taste preferences, may well be due to the operation of other phenomena (Ringold, 1988).

YOUR TASK

1. Simply on the basis of what you know now, design and conduct a taste test to determine which of two brands of carbonated cola drinks is preferred by ten people you know. Write a report of your findings. After you have completed your report, consult references in the professional literature (such as those listed at the end of this chapter) to see if there are any issues in taste-discrimination testing that you may have overlooked. Make a list of these overlooked issues, and be prepared to discuss them in class.

2. Gain experience with conducting in-depth interviews by devising a list of questions to "get at the heart" of why different people you know are loyal to different brands of beer. Identify at least six different people who are loyal to three different beers (two subjects for each beer) and administer your interview. Write a brief report of your findings.

EXERCISE 16-7
PSYCHOGRAPHICS

OBJECTIVE

To acquaint students with the consumer psychology system of "psychographics" and the place of measurement and categorization within that system

BACKGROUND

Demography is the study of characteristics of human populations in terms of variables such as size, growth, density, height, weight, age, and so forth—all referred to by the plural noun *demographics. Psychographics* is a term in marketing, advertising, and consumer psychology (though it may not yet have made it to an English-language dictionary) that refers to the study of psychological characteristics of populations—more specifically, the psychological characteristics of populations of consumers. Why describe groups of consumers in terms of psychological traits? The notion underlying the use of psychographics is that people who share the same or similar personality traits, attitudes, interests, beliefs, and activities will be attracted by the same or similar products and services—and be influenced by the same kinds of advertising and promotion.

Psychographic studies are quantitative studies that tend to employ large numbers of subjects responding to a relatively large number of items. The responses are usually obtained via a format that readily lends itself to quantification (such as Likert scales or semantic differential items), and the data are carefully analyzed in different ways to determine what relationships exist. The object of a typical psychographic study is to identify common psychological and related characteristics of a particular population of people (for example, all people who sent in $400 for a home study course in "How to Get Rich Quick in Real Estate" after exposure to a television commercial). Alternatively, a psychographic study might employ as subjects a large, random group of people on whom many psychological measures have been taken and from whom much consumer information has been obtained; from such information, psychographic profiles of different "types" of consumers might emerge.

Perhaps the best-known and most widely used typology of consumers, one that is based on psychographic research, is the typology developed by the Stanford Research Institute (SRI). The SRI typology is referred to as VALS (an acronym for an ongoing program of Values and Lifestyles). In the VALS taxonomy, nine basic types of consumers have been identified: two types of "need-driven" consumers, three types of "outer-directed" consumers, and four types of "inner-directed" consumers (see Table 16-4). As you read the description of each, try to decide which of these categories best describes yourself, your siblings, and your parents.

The "Outer-Directed" general category of consumer consists of three distinctive groups that, combined, represent two-thirds of the U.S. population—and account for almost 78 percent of all purchases. These groups are concerned with appearance and conformity to established social norms. The *Achievers* within this broad category are the leaders of business, professions, and government. They value efficiency, status, materialism, and creature comforts. They have a high median income and a median age of 42. The *Emulators* are ambitious, upwardly mobile, and status conscious. They are younger than the Achievers, have a lower median income than the Achievers, and aspire to attain the success of the Achievers (some will, but others will fail due to a lack of skills, education, or resources). The *Belongers* are the largest VALS category. They tend to be conservative and traditional, and their lives are focused on the home. They seek to fit in with society rather than stand out.

People who are "Inner-Directed" according to the VALS taxonomy can be characterized by a desire for self-expression and a need to fulfill individual needs. The four groups that make up this category represent about one-fifth of the U.S. population, and they make about 15 percent of the total purchases made in this country. The largest group of Inner-Directeds is the *Socially Conscious* group, a group that places emphasis on simple living, conservation, and environmentalism. The *Experientials* want experience and involvement. They participate in a wide range of activities for the experiences these activities provide. They tend to be

TABLE 16-4 *VALS Lifestyle Segmentation*

Percentage of Population	Consumer Type	Values and Lifestyles	Demographics	Buying Patterns	Spending Power
Need-Driven Consumers					

6	Survivors	Struggle for survival
		Distrustful
		Socially misfitted
		Ruled by appetites
			Poverty-level income
			Little education
			Many minority
			  members
				Price dominant
				Focus on basics
				Buy for immediate
				  needs
					$3 billion

10	Sustainers	Concern with safety,
		  security
		Insecure, compulsive
		Dependent, following
		Want law and order
			Low income
			Low education
			Much unemployment
			Live in country as well
			  as cities
				Price important
				Want warranty
				Cautious buyer
					$32 billion

Outer-Directed Consumers					

32	Belongers	Conforming,
		  conventional
		Unexperimental,
		  traditional, formal
		Nostalgic
			Low to middle income
			Low to average
			  education
			Blue-collar jobs
			Trend toward noncity
			  living
				Family
				Home
				Fads
				Middle to lower
				  market makers
					$230 billion

10	Emulators	Ambitious, show-off
		Status conscious
		Upwardly mobile
		Macho, competitive
			Good to excellent income
			Youngish
			Highly urban
			Traditionally male, but
			  changing
				Conspicuous
				  consumption
				"In" items
				Imitative
				Popular fashion
					$120 billion

28	Achievers	Achievement, success,
		  fame
		Materialism
		Leadership, efficiency
		Comfort
			Excellent incomes
			Leaders in business,
			  politics, etc.
			Good education
			Suburban and city
			  living
				Give evidence of
				  success
				Top of the line
				Luxury and gift markets
				"New and improved"
				  products
					$500 billion

Inner-Directed Consumers					
3	I-Am-Me	Fiercely individualistic Dramatic, impulsive Experimental Volatile	Young Many single Study or starting job Affluent backgrounds	Display one's taste Experimental fads Source of far-out fads Clique buying	$25 billion

5	Experimental	Drive to direct
		  experience
		Active, participative
		Person-centered
		Artistic
			Bimodal incomes
			Mostly under 40
			Many young families
			Good education
				Process over product
				Vigorous, outdoor
				  "sports"
				"Making" home
				  pursuits
				Crafts and introspection
					$56 billion

4	Societally Conscious	Societal responsibility
		Simple living
		Smallness of scale
		Inner growth
			Bimodal low and high
			  incomes
			Excellent education
			Diverse ages and
			  places of residence
			Largely White
				Conservation
				  emphasis
				Simplicity
				Frugality
				Environmental
				  concerns
					$50 billion

2	Integrated	Psychological maturity
		Sense of fittingness
		Tolerant, self-actualizing
		World perspective
			Good to excellent
			  incomes
			Bimodal in age
			Excellent education
			Diverse jobs and
			  residential patterns
				Varied self-expression
				Ethically oriented
				Ecologically aware
				One-of-a-kind items
					$28 billion

hedonistic but often engage in activities such as crafts, building, and do-it-yourself projects because these projects provide opportunities for new experiences. The youngest VALS group is the *I-Am-Me's*. Members of this group are individualistic, impulsive, experimental, and highly energetic. They enjoy faddish items and tend to be innovators, particularly with respect to fashion. Many young adults and students fall into this latter category.

The *Integrated* make up about 2 percent of the population of the United States and spend about $28 billion annually. They are the most highly educated of the groups and have a median age of 40 and a median income of $40,000. This group combines the outward orientation of the outer-directed lifestyle and the sensitivity of the inner-directed. The buying habits of this group revolve around quality, uniqueness, high standards, and ecology. They embrace the values of individualism, tolerance, and a global view.

People who fall into the VALS general category of "Need-Driven" tend to be concerned primarily with security and simply "getting by." Although they represent about 11 percent of the U.S. population, they account for only about 4 percent of total annual purchases in the United States. The *Sustainers* include a large number of females, single heads of household, as well as others who are struggling on the verge of poverty. The *Survivors* are typically older and poor. They tend to be cautious, conservative, authoritarian, and removed from mainstream society.

Members of the different VALS groups do exhibit differences in behavior in the marketplace, and a number of firms have found this taxonomy to be useful in defining their markets. Achievers tend to buy luxury cars; belongers tend to buy family-size cars; the socially conscious buy gas-efficient cars; and the need-driven tend to buy used cars (Capeli, 1984). Timex Medical Products Group focuses its marketing activities for digital thermometers, digital blood pressure monitors, and digital scales on the achievers and socially conscious because consumers in these groups tend to be more concerned with staying healthy, are more highly educated, and are more receptive to innovation than are members of the other groups. Belongers are not considered a viable market for these products because their traditional orientation makes them less receptive to high-tech items ("Timex," 1984).

Critics of the psychographic approach have argued that psychographic categories overlap so much as to be virtually meaningless. It has been further argued that, when all is said and done, psychographic studies reveal nothing that savvy researchers or practitioners do not already know or could not figure out for themselves. Proponents of psychographics concede that there is overlap in defined lifestyle groups but argue that real differences do exist—marginal as they may be in some instances—and may still be quite useful. Proponents of the psychographic approach would further argue that such studies provide insights that cannot be obtained in any other way. Readers interested in more detailed discussions of various aspects of psychographics are referred to the following

sources: Wells (1975); Demby (1974); Veltri & Schiffman (1984); Mitchell (1978); Bearden, Teel, & Durand (1978); Runyon & Stewart (1987); Shim & Bickle (1994).

YOUR TASK

Assuming the role of a consumer psychologist, respond to the following three scenarios with reference to the Stanford Research Institute's VALS taxonomy.

1. A car maker has developed what it boasts is "the mother of all luxury cars." The car has everything from power ashtrays to bucket seats equipped with individual heat and massage units. Describe a research study that could help give you insight on how to market this car.
2. A clothing manufacturer seeks your assistance in marketing a paper-thin, extremely inexpensive fabric that provides superior insulation from the cold. The manufacturer is particularly interested in getting jackets and vests of this material into the hands of the homeless living in cold-weather climates. How could you help?
3. A nationally known distributor of dairy products has developed a new food that is something of a cross between frozen yogurt and chocolate mousse. They consult with you in an effort to determine who, if anyone, is the prime consumer of such a product. What do you say?

EXERCISE 16-8
CREATE A SURVEY

OBJECTIVE

To enhance understanding of and provide firsthand experience with surveys

BACKGROUND

Whether a survey will be conducted face to face, over the telephone, online, or by means of any other medium, the questionnaire must be designed properly. Two key concerns here are effectiveness in terms of fulfilling the objective of the survey and efficiency in terms of making optimal use of the respondent's time.

YOUR TASK

After reading the material on survey design that follows, design a brief survey for administration in face-to-face fashion, by telephone, online, or any other medium you choose. Write a brief essay explaining exactly what you hope to find out with this survey, to whom it should be administered, and why you selected this format for administration. Finally, briefly discuss how you plan to analyze the data and what you plan to do with the findings.

Whether the survey will be conducted face to face or over the telephone, the questionnaire must be designed so that it will not take a substantial amount of a respondent's time. With a mail survey, the length of the questionnaire may be longer; respondents can complete the questionnaire at their convenience and can pace themselves in completing it. However, because the mail survey will be completed at home without the presence of an interviewer to clarify questions, the mail survey must be written very clearly lest the frustration of not understanding the intention of an item prompt the respondent to "forget the whole thing."

Some of the standard items on a survey (such as demographic information) will not require very much talent to prepare, whereas it may require considerable effort to word other questions to best reflect the objective of the question. Two broad approaches to the assessment of attitudes in surveys are referred to as "aggregate scaling" and "multidimensional scaling." We'll also look at the application of the semantic differential technique in the field of consumer psychology.

Aggregate Scaling Methods

Aggregate methods represent the average of some group of people on some measure. The measure may range from an opinion item (such as "Should the death penalty be abolished?") to a self-report of behavior (such as "How often do you eat in a fast-food restaurant each month?"). The federal government and large corporations are among the largest users of aggregate measures; they can be used to take the pulse of a given population on a given issue, determine who buys certain products or services, or assess what customers think of products and services. The user of an aggregate measure is typically keenly interested not only in a measure of central tendency but also in dispersion or variance about the mean; such dispersion will tell whether people tend to be heavily divided with respect to the issue assessed. Attitudes may be based on many factors. For example, consumers may judge an automobile on the basis of its styling, its power, its comfort, its fuel economy, its price, or any number of other attributes. When using aggregate scaling methods, the assumption is made that attitudes toward all these attributes can be combined into a single or composite score.

The simplest aggregative method is the *one-dimensional preference scale,* in which respondents are asked to provide an overall rating for an object, a person, or an institution rather than rating individual attributes. For example, respondents might be asked to use the following scale to rate, say, various brands of canned sardines:

Like	Like Somewhat	Neutral	Dislike Somewhat	Dislike
1	2	3	4	5

The numbers 1 through 5 are assigned to scale values, and ratings can be expressed in quantitative form.

A 5-point preference scale such as that used in this example is an example of the Likert scale. Note that an assumption inherent in the use of such a technique is that respondents can sort out their opinions about the various attributes of the product in question and come up with a valid, overall reaction ranging from "like" to "neutral" to "dislike."

One shortcoming of this form of scaling is that the different ratings are not necessarily interval in nature, and therefore the number of statistical manipulations that can legitimately be performed with such data is limited. A rating of 3 on the scale may not be equally different from ratings of 2 and 4. The scale is an *ordinal* one, and a rating of 3 legitimately may be viewed only as greater than 1. Another limitation inherent in such aggregative data is that there is no assurance that respondents have considered all relevant attributes in arriving at their conclusions. Additionally, the use of an overall rating obscures the possibility that respondents may, indeed, have quite different attitudes toward different attributes of the object being rated.

An alternative approach is to rate each attribute separately and then sum the individual ratings to obtain an overall score. For example, let us assume that respondents are asked to rate a particular brand of sardines on four attributes—flavor, freshness, aroma, and appearance—using the Likert scale. And let's further assume that one respondent has rated a particular brand as follows:

flavor	4
freshness	2
aroma	3
appearance	5

The total rating for these sardines would be 14—obtained by summing the ratings of the individual attributes. This total rating can then be treated in a variety of statistical ways in making comparisons between brands.

Aside from questions about the level of measurement represented in the scaling device, this approach has one major limitation, namely, that each attribute is treated as though it were equally important in arriving at an overall attitude toward the sardines. And although that may be true in some cases, it certainly cannot be presumed to be true all of the time. One way of avoiding this potential pitfall is by employing a variation of the Fishbein-Rosenberg method of scaling. In this approach, respondents are asked two sets of questions. First, they are asked to rate relevant attributes according to their importance. Then, individual objects are rated according to the extent to which they possess each of the attributes in question. Applying this approach to our example, we might find that the attribute of flavor is rated 5 in importance, freshness is also rated 5, and aroma and appearance are rated 4 and 2, respectively. We can now com-

Table 16-5 *Individual Ratings Combined with Attribute Importance*

Attributes	Brand Rating		Attribute Importance		Total
Flavor	4	×	5	=	20
Freshness	2	×	5	=	10
Aroma	3	×	4	=	12
Appearance	5	×	2	=	10
Total				=	**52**

bine the ratings of the individual attribute with the rating of attribute importance as shown in the matrix in Table 16-5. Through the procedure, each attribute rating is multiplied by the importance of the attribute to weight it properly. The weighted results can then be submitted to various statistical treatments for making comparisons between brands.

Another method of aggregate scaling designed to give greater weight to some attributes than to others is an adaptation of Guttman scaling (Guttman, 1944a, 1944b). The Guttman method employs an ordered set of statements about a stimulus object, such as a hypothetical brand of sardines called "Mermaid":

Mermaid Sardines taste good	yes	no
Mermaid Sardines stay fresh	yes	no
Mermaid Sardines have a nice aroma	yes	no
Mermaid Sardines look appetizing	yes	no

The statements are ordered according to their relative importance, with the first statement being most important and the last statement being the least important. The specific statements used and their order are usually determined by interviews with persons familiar with the stimulus object. Often, several orderings are investigated to find the most appropriate one. The global rating is computed by counting the "yes" responses to the ordered question. A "yes" is counted as 1 and a "no" as 0. The preference score is determined by asking the questions in order and adding 1 to the total score for each "yes" answer obtained. When a "no" is encountered, the process stops. The overall rating is a summation of the number of "yes" responses.

A number of other aggregate scaling techniques may be used. Those shown have been introduced to clarify the nature of aggregate scaling and to point up one of the problems of summing attribute ratings—namely, that certain attributes are more important than others and must be weighted in some way to provide a valid rating.

Multidimensional Scaling

Multidimensional scaling (MDS) is a relatively recent development in psychometric research. Unlike aggregate scaling methods, MDS methods reject the notion that attitudes about a stimulus object can be combined into a single score. MDS attempts to locate objects within the framework of an "attribute space" based on perceptions of similarities and differences among the objects.

Figure 16-2 is an example of multidimensional scaling. Several points should be noted about this figure. First, consumer perceptions and preferences for pain relievers can be ordered in a two-dimensional space made up of the two attributes of gentleness and effectiveness. Second, each pain reliever can be located in this space in a position that represents a specific combination of these two attributes. Thus, Tylenol is perceived as very gentle compared with other pain relievers but not as effective as Excedrin. Excedrin, on the other hand, is perceived as somewhat more effective but not at all gentle. Third, different pain relievers may cluster according to their perceived similarity. Bayer, Anacin, and private-label aspirin are perceived as similar in both gentleness and effectiveness. Bufferin, Excedrin, and Tylenol tend to occupy unique positions within the space. The optimal combination of gentleness and effectiveness is represented by the line labeled "Average ideal." Note that different groups of consumers may, in fact, have different ideals. Tylenol is the product most similar to the ideal product for segment one. It is apparent that multidimensional scaling is a useful technique for identifying the position of products in a relevant product space and for relating existing products to the ideal product of consumers.

The construction of a product space through the use of multidimensional scaling is beyond the scope of this text. Essentially, however, it is a computer-based technique that locates products in a space of minimum dimensionality based on perceived similarities and differences. Because MDS is wholly a numerical procedure, it ignores the problem of axis labeling. It is not necessary, therefore, when employing the MDS technique, to specify the attributes on which objects are to be judged. One simply obtains judgments of similarity about the objects being studied in the hope that the most salient attributes will be identified by the ultimate structure obtained in the analysis. By examining the location of objects within the space that is generated, and by being familiar with the characteristics of the objects, the analyst is often able to identify the most salient features on which the data have been mathematically ordered. It is also possible to map attributes onto the derived space to facilitate interpretation of the axes.

Multidimensional scaling, using as input data the naïve perceptions of consumers, appears to have promise as a systematic approach for ordering and analyzing perceptions and preferences (Schiffman et al., 1981). The technique has been used to study a wide variety of consumer (Johnson & Horne, 1992), industrial (DeSarbo & Hoffman, 1987), and corporate (Dowling, 1988) judgments.

The Semantic Differential Technique

The semantic differential is one of the most widely used and versatile scaling techniques employed in marketing research. Originally developed as a clinical tool for defining the meaning of concepts and relating concepts to one another in a "semantic space," the basic technique has undergone modification in its adaptation to a wide range of purposes.

Figure 16-2   *An Illustration of Similarities*

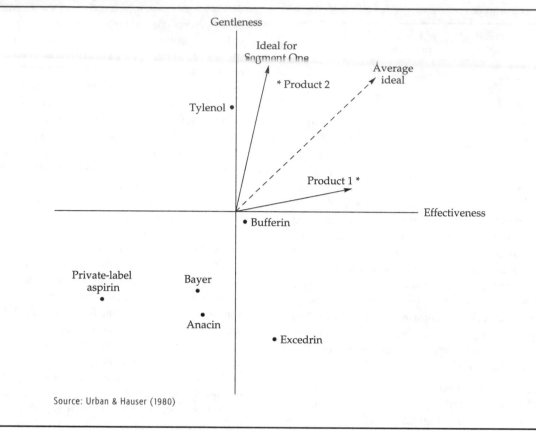

Source: Urban & Hauser (1980)

As initially conceived by Osgood, Suci, and Tannenbaum (1957), the semantic differential involved repeated judgments of a concept using a series of descriptive bipolar adjectives (such as good/bad or strong/weak) on a 7-point scale such as this one:

GOOD ____ / ____ / ____ / ____ / ____ / ____ / ____ / BAD

In the fields of consumer and social psychology, the semantic differential has been used to measure opinions of brands, products, companies, social programs, stores, product users, political candidates, and so forth. A number of modifications in the semantic differential as originally described by Osgood, Suci, and Tannenbaum (1957) are made when this technique is used in consumer-related studies (Mindak, 1961). For example, the bipolar adjective might be replaced by descriptive phrases (such as "something very special" versus "just another drink" with reference to a particular brand of beer).

The semantic differential is a very popular tool in consumer-related research because it provides a relatively simple, efficient way of collecting quantifiable data from large samples and can be used effectively as a before-and-after test (for example, before and after exposure to a commercial or an informational film). It is useful in obtaining an index of attitude that might be difficult to obtain through other approaches, and it can provide a quantifiable benchmark with which competing brands can be compared. Because it requires very little verbal skill, it is quite useful in measuring the attitudes of children and adult respondents who have limited language abilities. Data from the use of this technique also tend to be quite reliable.

Do consumer surveys predict consumer behavior? The validity of surveys purporting to measure consumer satisfaction has been questioned by researchers who argue that the context in which evaluation takes place may be more critical to the response obtained than whatever it is that is being evaluated (Peterson & Wilson, 1992). Still, survey responses predict behavior in the marketplace to varying degrees. One measure of attitudes toward purchasing imported products, called the Consumer Ethnocentric Tendencies Scale, can predict purchasing behavior to the extent that it explains about 30 percent of the variability in automobile purchases (Herche, 1992).

REFERENCES

Beardon, W. O., Teel, J. E., Jr., & Durand, R. M. (1978, Spring). Media usage, psychographic, and demographic dimensions of retail shoppers. *Journal of Retailing*, pp. 65–77.

Boyle, J. P. (1987). Intelligence, reasoning, and language proficiency. *Modern Language Journal, 71,* 277–288.

Brown, C. E., Zatkalik, N. E., Treumann, A. M., Buehner, T. M., & Schmidt, L. A. (1984). The effect of experimenter bias in a cola taste test. *Psychology & Marketing, 1,* 21–26.

Buchanan, B. S., & Morrison, D. G. (1984). Taste tests: Psychophysical issues in comparative test design. *Psychology and Marketing, 1,* 69–91.

Capeli, E. (1984, September). Detroit goes psycho! *Automotive Industries,* pp. 44–48.

Consulting Psychologists Press, Inc. (1994). *1994 catalog.* Palo Alto, CA: Author.

Day, R. L. (1965). Systematic paired comparisons in preference analysis. *Journal of Marketing Research, 2,* 406–412.

Day, R. L. (1969). Position bias in paired product tests. *Journal of Marketing Research, 6,* 98–100.

Demby, E. (1974). Psychographics and from whence it came. In W. D. Wells (Ed.), *Lifestyles and psychographics.* Chicago: American Marketing Association.

DeSarbo, W. S., & Hoffman, D. L. (1987). Constructing MDS joint spaces for binary choice data: A multidimensional unfolding threshold model for marketing research. *Journal of Marketing Research, 24,* 40–54.

Dowling, G. R. (1988). Measuring corporate images: A review of alternative approaches. *Journal of Business Research. Special Issue: Marketing Research, 17,* 27–34.

Gakhar, S. C. (1986). Correctional research—individual differences in intelligence, aptitude, personality, and achievement among science, commerce, and arts students. *Journal of Psychological Researches, 30,* 22–29.

Girelli, S. A., & Stake, J. E. (1993). Bipolarity in Jungian type theory and the Myers-Briggs Type Indicator. *Journal of Personality Assessment, 60,* 290–301.

Greenhalgh, C. (1966). Some techniques and interesting results in discrimination testing. *Journal of the Market Research Society, 8,* 215–235.

Guilford, J. S., Zimmerman, W. S., & Guilford, J. P. (1976). *The Guilford-Zimmerman Temperament Survey handbook.* San Diego: CA: EdITS.

Harvey, R. J., & Murry, W. D. (1994). Scoring the Myers-Briggs Type Indicator: Empirical comparison of preference score versus latent-trait methods. *Journal of Personality Assessment, 62,* 116–129.

Hattrup, K., & Schmitt, N. (1990). Prediction of trades apprentices' performance of job sample criteria. *Personnel Psychology, 43,* 453–466.

Herche, J. (1992). A note on the predictive validity of the CETSCALE. *Journal of the Academy of Marketing Science, 20,* 261–264.

Irwin, F. W. (1958). An analysis of concepts of discrimination and preference. *American Journal of Psychology, 11,* 152–163.

Johnson, M. D., & Horne, D. A. (1992). An examination of the validity of direct product perceptions. *Psychology and Marketing, 9,* 221–235.

Jung, C. G. (1923). *Psychological types.* London: Rutledge & Kegan Paul.

Kuehn, A. A. (1962). Consumer brand choice: A learning process? *Journal of Advertising Research, 2,* 10–17.

Landry, M., & McKelvie, S. J. (1985). Validity of conventional and unbiased intelligence test items for groups differing in age and education. *Psychological Reports, 57,* 975–981.

Lorr, M. (1991). An empirical evaluation of the MBTI typology. *Personality and Individual Differences, 12,* 1141–1145.

Luce, R. D., & Suppes, P. (1965). Preference, utility, and subjective probability. In R. D. Luce, R. R. Bush, & E. Galanter (Eds.), *Handbook of mathematical psychology* (Vol. 3). New York: Wiley.

Lynn, R., Hampson, S. L., & Magee, M. (1983). Determinants of educational achievement at 16+: Intelligence, personality, home background and school. *Personality and Individual Differences, 4,* 473–481.

Lynn, R., Hampson, S. L., & Magee, M. (1984). Home background, intelligence, personality, and education as predictors of unemploy-

ment in young people. *Personality and Individual Differences, 5,* 549–557.

Martin, D. D., & Bartol, K. M. (1986). Holland's Vocational Preference Inventory and the Myers-Briggs Type Indicator as predictors of vocational choice among Master's of Business Administration. *Journal of Vocational Behavior, 29,* 51–65.

Mindak, W. A. (1961). Fitting the semantic differential to the marketing problem. *Journal of Marketing, 25,* 28–33.

Mitchell, A. (1978). *Consumer values: A typology.* Menlo Park, CA: Stanford Research Institute.

Morrison, D. G. (1981). Triangle taste tests: Are subjects who respond correctly lucky or good? *Journal of Marketing, 45,* 111–119.

Myers, I. B., & Briggs, K. C. (1943/1962). The Myers-Briggs Type Indicator. Palo Alto, CA: Consulting Psychologists Press.

Osgood, C. E., Suci, G. J., & Tannenbaum, P. H. (1957). *The measurement of meaning.* Urbana: University of Illinois.

Peterson, R. A., & Wilson, W. R. (1992). Measuring customer satisfaction: Fact and artifact. *Journal of the Academy of Marketing Science, 20,* 61–71.

Pittenger, D. J. (1993). The utility of the Myers-Briggs Type Indicator. *Review of Educational Research, 63,* 467–488.

Ringold, D. J. (1988). Consumer response to product withdrawal: The reformulation of Coca-Cola. *Psychology & Marketing, 5,* 189–210.

Runyon, K., & Stewart, D. W. (1987). *Consumer behavior and the practice of marketing.* Columbus, OH: Merrill.

Schiffman, S. S., Reynolds, M. L., & Young, F. W. (1981). *Introduction to multidimensional scaling: Theory, methods and applications.* New York: Academic Press.

Shim, S., & Bickle, M. C. (1994). Benefit segments of the female apparel market: Psychographics, shopping orientations, and demographics. *Clothing and Textiles Research Journal, 12,* 1–12.

Timex and VALS engineer product launch. (1984, September). *Ad Forum,* 12–14.

Urban, G. L., & Hauser, J. R. (1980). *Design and marketing of new products.* Englewood Cliffs, NJ: Prentice-Hall.

Veltri, J. J., & Schiffman, L. G. (1984). Fifteen years of consumer lifestyle and value research at AT&T. In R. E. Pitts & A. G. Woodside (Eds.), *Personal values and consumer psychology.* Lexington, MA: Lexington.

Wells, W. D. (1975). Psychographics: A critical view. *Journal of Marketing Research, 12,* 195–213.

Zumbo, B. D., & Taylor, S. V. (1993). The construct validity of the Extraversion subscales of the Myers-Briggs Type Indicator. *Canadian Journal of Behavioral Science, 25,* 590–604.

THE 4-QUESTION CHALLENGE

1. In the language of psychometrics, the term "assessment center" refers to
   a. a place where tests are administered.
   b. an organizationally standardized procedure.
   c. the average of a number of assessments.
   d. none of the above

2. The job-seeking factor found to be most important by Champagne in his study of values with male and female unskilled subjects was
   a. working with friends and neighbors.
   b. a job close to home.
   c. a steady job.
   d. vacations and holidays with pay.

3. The expectancy theory of motivation is best associated with
   a. Alderfer.
   b. Mooney.
   c. Vroom.
   d. Vroom-Vroom.

4. In October 1982, the sales of aspirin, Bufferin, Anacin, and Excedrin rose sharply because of
   a. the effectiveness of advertising campaigns for pain relievers.

   b. diligent behavioral observation of consumers shopping in stores.
   c. focus group research that pinpointed consumer "hot buttons."
   d. deaths of people who had consumed a competitive product.

The Midtown Manhattan Practice Personality Inventory (MMPPI)

1. Much like most everyone else, I have my vices.
2. People think I'm a good dancer.
3. I could have breakfast in bed seven days a week.
4. No amount of money can buy happiness.
5. All handguns should be banned.
6. I refrain from taking medication if I can help it.
7. Everyone who meets me likes me.
8. I really should be behind bars or otherwise institutionalized.
9. I am intolerant of just about everything and everyone.
10. I smell things that other people do not.
11. In general, I respect the rights of other people.
12. I feel I am making a statement with my hair.
13. I find myself getting too agitated when driving.
14. I have a fear of snakes.
15. My love of food has led to a real problem with my weight.
16. I enjoy watching soap operas.
17. I experience weakness at the sight of laundry.
18. I tend to be a very outgoing person.
19. One learns more on the street than at school.
20. People consider me to be very adventuresome.
21. I don't feel like I'm being hugged often enough.
22. There is not the slightest shred of bias, prejudice, or ill will toward anybody in myself or any of my close friends.
23. I count miniature golf among my hobbies.
24. I look forward to wearing dentures.
25. I think my body attracts and absorbs heat.
26. In general, the police would be more mellow if they drank more cappuccino and less coffee.
27. I love shopping for shoes and could do it quite often.
28. I am a firm believer in "Child on Board" signs.
29. With regard to my temperament, I experience low "lows" and high "highs."
30. Death is in the very distant future.
31. Satanic cults hold no appeal for me at all.
32. I will only wear sweaters on Tuesdays.
33. I love to wear costumes to work for no occasion at all.
34. I think I would look good in high-heeled shoes.
35. I recently bought tickets to a state-run lottery.
36. I think I am too absorbed in the past.
37. I enjoy traveling on my own.
38. I inevitably have problems with people in authority.
39. I have never considered cosmetic surgery.
40. I take a bubble bath at least once a day, every day.
41. I think I would be very good at gardening.
42. I enjoy hearing the sound of my own voice on tape.
43. I always buckle my seatbelt in a car or van.
44. In many ways, I am very traditional.
45. I have a brother in the federal witness protection program.
46. I organize a party for a friend at least once a year.
47. I enjoy listening to the radio, even if there is only static on.
48. I could stand being a bit more "macho."
49. I wish I had more close friends.
50. People think I'm very neat.
51. I seldom make reservations for restaurants.
52. I have always wanted a pen pal.
53. I consider myself "computer phobic."
54. Few people have anything really important to say.
55. I hear voices commanding me to do certain things.
56. I have a fear of heights.
57. My videotape collection includes over 1000 episodes of *Wheel of Fortune.*
58. Other family members can't believe I'm part of the family.
59. I could take a nap almost anytime, anywhere.
60. I need to take better care of myself.
61. I do not enjoy soap operas.
62. My dreams are probably much like most other people's dreams.
63. I put on pants one leg at a time.
64. I avoid large crowds of people.
65. I find it easy to "tick off" other people.
66. I would never consider getting a tattoo.
67. I feel as if I am in touch with occult phenomena.

68. My thoughts are as pure and as good as can be.
69. I do not consider myself traditional in any way.
70. A supermarket is a good place to meet new people.
71. In comparison to most other people, I am not particularly muscular.
72. I enjoy public speaking.
73. I need to laugh more than I do.
74. Most hunting is unnecessary and should be banned.
75. I sometimes experience strange, unexplainable sensations.
76. I enjoy working with computers.
77. I stutter when I get nervous.
78. I was seen by a physician within the last ten years.
79. I see myself as very different from other people.
80. I have seen *The Rocky Horror Picture Show* more than once.
81. I enjoy sampling new varieties of sushi.
82. I feel uncomfortable at parties.
83. I consider myself a role model for others.
84. I really love when someone sends me flowers.
85. As a youngster, I got along well with other children.
86. I probably watch too much television.
87. The sight of blood has no effect on me.
88. I prefer reading to watching television.
89. I walk away from fights.
90. Only the best is good enough for me.
91. At one time or another, I have considered growing a mustache.
92. I like to drive cars that are faster than most.
93. Happiness is financial security.
94. I do not believe in gun control.
95. There is something frightening about intimacy.
96. I have absolutely no interest in learning to speak French.
97. I think I would enjoy living the rest of my life on some faraway island.
98. The respect of other people is important to me.
99. I frequently order off the menu in restaurants.
100. I look forward to the day when I can just sit home all day and watch television or do whatever else I want.

APPENDIX B

A Glossary of Measurement Terms

Blythe C. Mitchell, Consultant, Test Department, The Psychological Corporation

This glossary of terms used in educational and psychological measurement is primarily for persons with limited training in measurement rather than for the specialist. The terms defined are the more common or basic ones that occur in test manuals and educational journals. In the definitions, certain technicalities and niceties of usage have been sacrificed for the sake of brevity and, it is hoped, clarity.

The definitions are based on the usage of the various terms as given in the current textbooks in educational and psychological measurement and statistics and in certain specialized dictionaries. Where there is not complete uniformity among writers in the measurement field with respect to the meaning of a term, either these variations are noted or the definition offered is the one that the writer judges to represent the "best" usage.

• • •

academic aptitude The combination of native and acquired abilities that are needed for school learning; likelihood of success in mastering academic work, as estimated from measures of the necessary abilities. (Also called *scholastic aptitude, school learning ability, academic potential.*)

achievement test A test that measures the extent to which a person has "achieved" something, acquired certain information, or mastered certain skills—usually as a result of planned instruction or training.

age norms Originally, values representing typical or average performance for persons of various *age* groups; most current usage refers to sets of complete-score interpretive data for appropriate successive age groups. Such norms are generally used in the interpretation of mental ability test scores.

alternate-form reliability The closeness of correspondence or correlation between results on alternate (i.e., equivalent or parallel) forms of a test; thus, a measure of the extent to which the two forms are consistent or reliable in measuring whatever they do measure. The time interval between the two testings must be relatively short so that the examinees themselves are unchanged in the ability being measured. See RELIABILITY, RELIABILITY COEFFICIENT.

anecdotal record A written description of an incident in an individual's behavior that is reported objectively and is considered significant for the understanding of the individual.

aptitude A combination of abilities and other characteristics, whether native or acquired, that are indicative of an individual's ability to learn or to develop proficiency in some particular area if appropriate education or training is provided. Aptitude tests include those of general academic ability (commonly called mental ability or intelligence tests); those of special abilities, such as verbal, numerical, mechanical, or musical; tests assessing "readiness" for learning; and prognostic tests, which measure both ability and previous learning and are used to predict future performance—usually in a specific field, such as a foreign language, shorthand, or nursing.

Some would define "aptitude" in a more comprehensive sense. Thus, "musical aptitude" would refer to the combination not only of physical and mental characteristics but also of motivational factors, interest, and conceivably other characteristics that are conducive to acquiring proficiency in the musical field.

arithmetic mean A kind of average usually referred to as the *mean*. It is obtained by dividing the sum of a set of scores by their number.

average A general term applied to the various measures of central tendency. The three most widely used averages are the arithmetic mean (mean), the median, and the mode. When the term "average" is used without designation as to type, the most likely assumption is that it is the *arithmetic mean*.

battery A group of several tests standardized on the same sample population so that results on the several tests are comparable. (Sometimes loosely applied to any group of tests administered together, even though not standardized on the same subjects.) The most common test batteries are those of school achievement, which include subtests in the separate learning areas.

bivariate chart (bivariate distribution) A diagram in which a tally mark is made to show the scores of one individual on *two variables*. The intersection of lines determined by the horizontal and vertical scales form cells in which the tallies are placed. Such a plot provides frequencies for the two distributions and portrays the relation between the two variables as a basis for computation of the product-moment correlation coefficient.

ceiling   The upper limit of ability that can be measured by a test. When an individual makes a score that is at or near the highest possible score, it is said that the test has too low a "ceiling" for him or her; the individual should be given a higher level of the test.

central tendency   A measure of central tendency provides a single most typical score as representative of a group of scores; the "trend" of a group of measures as indicated by some type of average, usually the *mean* or the *median*.

coefficient of correlation   A measure of the degree of relationship or "going-togetherness" between two sets of measures for the same group of individuals. The correlation coefficient most frequently used in test development and educational research is that known as the Pearson or *product-moment r*. Unless otherwise specified, "correlation" usually refers to this coefficient, but *rank, biserial, tetrachoric,* and other methods are used in special situations. Correlation coefficients range from .00, denoting a complete absence of relationship, to +1.00 and to –1.00, indicating perfect positive or perfect negative correspondence, respectively. See CORRELATION.

composite score   A score that combines several scores, usually by addition; often different weights are applied to the contributing scores to increase or decrease their importance in the composite. Most commonly, such scores are used for *predictive* purposes, and the several weights are derived through multiple regression procedures.

concurrent validity   See VALIDITY (2).

construct validity   See VALIDITY (3).

content validity   See VALIDITY (1).

correction for guessing (correction for chance)   A reduction in score for wrong answers, sometimes applied in scoring true-false or multiple-choice questions. Such scoring formulas (R – W for tests with 2-option response, R – ½W for 3 options, R – ⅓W for 4, etc.) are intended to discourage guessing and to yield more accurate rankings of examinees in terms of their true knowledge. They are used much less today than in the early days of testing.

correlation   Relationship or "going-togetherness" between two sets of scores or measures; tendency of one score to vary concomitantly with the other, as the tendency of students of high IQ to be above average in reading ability. The existence of a strong relationship—i.e., a high correlation—between two variables does not necessarily indicate that one has any causal influence on the other. See COEFFICIENT OF CORRELATION.

criterion   A standard by which a test may be judged or evaluated; a set of scores, ratings, etc., that a test is designed to measure, to predict, or to correlate with. See VALIDITY.

criterion-referenced (content-referenced) test   Terms often used to describe tests designed to provide information on the specific knowledge or skills possessed by a student. Such tests usually cover relatively small units of content and are closely related to instruction. Their scores have meaning in terms of *what* the student knows or can do rather than in their relation to the scores made by some external reference group.

criterion-related validity   See VALIDITY (2).

culture-fair test   So-called culture-fair tests attempt to provide an equal opportunity for success by persons of all cultures and life experiences. Their content must therefore be limited to that which is equally common to all cultures, or to material that is entirely unfamiliar and novel for all persons whatever their cultural background. See CULTURE-FREE TEST.

culture-free test   A test that is free of the impact of all cultural experiences; therefore, a measure reflecting only hereditary abilities. Since culture permeates all of humanity's environmental contacts, the construction of such a test would seem to be an impossibility. Cultural "bias" is not eliminated by the use of nonlanguage or so-called performance tests, although it may be reduced in some instances. In terms of most of the purposes for which tests are used, the validity (value) of a "culture-free" test is questioned; a test designed to be equally applicable to all cultures may be of little or no practical value in any.

curricular validity   See VALIDITY (2).

decile   Any one of the nine points (scores) that divide a distribution into ten parts, each containing one-tenth of all the scores or cases; every tenth percentile. The first decile is the 10th percentile; the eighth decile, the 80th percentile; etc.

deviation   The amount by which a score differs from some reference value such as the mean, the norm, or the score on some other test.

deviation IQ (DIQ)   An age-based index of general mental ability. It is based upon the difference or deviation between a person's score and the typical or average score for persons of his or her chronological age. Deviation IQs from most current scholastic aptitude measures are standard scores with a mean of 100 and a standard deviation of 16 for each defined age group.

diagnostic test   A test used to "diagnose" or analyze; that is, to locate an individual's specific areas of weakness or strength, to determine the nature of his or her weaknesses or deficiencies, and, wherever possible, to suggest their cause. Such a test yields measures of the components or subparts of some larger body of information or skill. Diagnostic achievement tests are most commonly prepared for the skill subjects.

difficulty value   An index that indicates the percent of some specified group, such as students of a given age or grade, who answer a test item correctly.

discriminating power   The ability of a test item to differentiate between persons possessing much or little of some trait.

discrimination index An index that indicates the *discriminating power* of a test item. The most commonly used index is derived from the number passing the item in the highest 27 percent of the group (on total score) and the number passing in the lowest 27 percent.

distractor Any incorrect choice (option) in a test item.

distribution (frequency distribution) A tabulation of the scores (or other attributes) of a group of individuals to show the number (frequency) of each score, or of those within the range of each interval.

equivalent form Any of two or more forms of a test that are closely parallel with respect to the nature of the content and the number and difficulty of the items included and that will yield very similar average scores and measures of variability for a given group. (Also referred to as *alternate, comparable,* or *parallel* form.)

error of measurement See STANDARD ERROR (1).

expectancy table ("expected" achievement) A term with two common usages, related but with some difference:

(1) A table or other device for showing the relation between scores on a predictive test and some related outcome. The outcome, or criterion status, for individuals at each level of predictive score may be expressed as (a) an average on the outcome variable, (b) the percent of cases at successive levels, or (c) the probability of reaching given performance levels. Such tables are commonly used in making predictions of educational or job success.

(2) A table or chart providing an interpretation of a student's obtained score on an achievement test with the score that would be "expected" for those at his or her grade level and with his or her level of scholastic aptitude. Such "expectancies" are based upon actual data from administration of the specified achievement and scholastic aptitude tests to the same student population. The term "anticipated" is also used to denote achievement as differentiated by level of "intellectual status."

extrapolation In general, any process of estimating values of a variable beyond the range of available data. As applied to test norms, the process of extending a norm line into grade or age levels not tested in the standardization program, in order to permit interpretation of extreme scores. Since this extension is usually done graphically, considerable judgment is involved. Extrapolated values are thus to some extent arbitrary; for this and other reasons, they have limited meaning.

f A symbol denoting the *frequency* of a given score or of the scores within an interval grouping.

face validity See VALIDITY.

factor In mental measurement, a hypothetical trait, ability, or component of ability that underlies and influences performance on two or more tests and hence causes scores on the tests to be correlated. The term "factor" strictly refers to a theoretical variable, derived by a process of *factor analysis* from a table of intercorrelations among tests. However, it is also used to denote the psychological interpretation given to the variable—i.e., the mental trait assumed to be represented by the variable, as verbal ability, numerical ability, etc.

factor analysis Any of several methods of analyzing the intercorrelations among a set of variables such as test scores. Factor analysis attempts to account for the interrelationships in terms of some underlying "factors," preferably fewer in number than the original variables, and it reveals how much of the variation in each of the original measures arises from, or is associated with, each of the hypothetical factors. Factor analysis has contributed to an understanding of the organization or components of intelligence, aptitudes, and personality; and it has pointed the way to the development of "purer" tests of the several components.

forced-choice item Broadly, any multiple-choice item in which the examinee is *required* to select one or more of the given choices. The term is most often used to denote a special type of multiple-choice item employed in personality tests in which the options are (1) of equal "preference value," i.e., chosen equally often by a typical group, and (2) such that one of the options discriminates between persons high and low on the factor that this option measures, while the other options measure other factors. Thus, in the *Gordon Personal Profile,* each of four options represents one of the four personality traits measured by the *Profile,* and the examinee must select both the option that describes him or her *most* and the one that describes him or her *least.*

frequency distribution See DISTRIBUTION.

g Denotes *general* intellectual ability; one dimensional measure of "mind," as described by the British psychologist Spearman. A test of "*g*" serves as a general-purpose test of mental ability.

grade equivalent (GE) The grade level for which a given score is the real or estimated average. Grade-equivalent interpretation, most appropriate for elementary level achievement tests, expresses obtained scores in terms of *grade* and *month of grade,* assuming a 10-month school year (e.g., 5.7). Since such tests are usually standardized at only one (or two) point(s) within each grade, grade equivalents between points for which there are data-based scores must be "estimated" by *interpolation.* See EXTRAPOLATION, INTERPOLATION.

grade norms Norms based upon the performance of pupils of given grade placement. See GRADE EQUIVALENT, NORMS, PERCENTILE RANK, STANINE.

group test A test that may be administered to a number of individuals at the same time by one examiner.

individual test A test that can be administered to only one person at a time because of the nature of the test and/or the maturity level of the examinees.

intelligence quotient (IQ) Originally, an index of brightness expressed as the ratio of a person's mental age to his or her chronological age, MA/CA, multiplied by 100 to eliminate the decimal. (More precisely—and particularly for adult ages, at which mental growth is assumed to have ceased—the ratio of mental age to the mental age normal for chronological age.) This quotient IQ has been gradually replaced by the deviation IQ concept.

It is sometimes desired to give additional meaning to IQs by the use of verbal descriptions for the ranges in which they fall. Since the IQ scale is a continuous one, there can be no inflexible line of demarcation between such successive category labels as very superior, superior, above average, average, below average, etc.; any verbal classification system is therefore an arbitrary one. There appears to be, however, rather common use of the term *average* or *normal* to describe IQs from 90–109 inclusive.

An IQ is more definitely "interpreted" by noting the normal percent of IQs within a range that includes the IQ, and/or by indicating its percentile rank or stanine in the total national norming sample. Column 2 of Table 1 shows the normal distribution of IQs for M = 100 and S.D. = 16, showing percentages within successive 10-point intervals. (For IQs whose S.D. is greater than 16, the percentages for the extreme IQ ranges will be larger, and those for IQs near the mean will be smaller, than those shown in the table.) Table 1 indicates that 47 percent, approximately one-half of "all" persons, have IQs in the 20-point range of 90 through 109; an IQ of 140 or above would be considered as extremely high, since fewer than one percent (0.6) of the total population reach this level, and fewer than one percent have IQs below 60. From the cumulative percents given in Column 3, it is noted that 3.1 percent have IQs below 70, usually considered the mentally retarded category. This column may be used to indicate the percentile rank (PR) of certain IQs. Thus an IQ of 119 has a PR of 89, since 89.4 percent of IQs are 119 or below; an IQ of 79 has a PR of 10.6, or 11. See DEVIATION IQ, MENTAL AGE.

internal consistency   Degree of relationship among the items of a test; consistency in content sampling. See SPLIT-HALF RELIABILITY COEFFICIENT.

interpolation   In general, any process of estimating intermediate values between two known points. As applied to test norms, it refers to the procedure used in assigning interpretive values (e.g., grade equivalents) to scores between the successive average scores actually obtained in the standardization process. Also, in reading norm tables it is necessary at times to interpolate to obtain a norm value for a score between two scores given in the table; e.g., in the table shown here, a percentile rank of 83 (from 81 + 1/3 of 6) would be assigned, by *interpolation,* to a score of 46; a score of 50 would correspond to a percentile rank of 94 (obtained as 87 + 2/3 of 10).

Score	Percentile Rank
51	97
48	87
45	81

TABLE 1   *Normal Distribution of IQs with Mean of 100 and Standard Deviation of 16*

(1) IQ Range	(2) Percent of Persons	(3) Cumulative Percent
140 and above	0.6	100.6
130–139	2.5	99.4
120–129	7.5	96.9
110–119	16.0	89.4
100–109	23.4 } 46.8	73.4
90–99	23.4	50.0
80–89	16.0	26.6
70–79	7.5	10.6
60–69	2.5	3.1
Below 60	0.6	0.6
Total	100.0	

inventory   A questionnaire or checklist, usually in the form of a self-report, designed to elicit non-intellective information about an individual. Not tests in the usual sense, inventories are most often concerned with personality traits, interests, attitudes, problems, motivation, etc. See PERSONALITY TEST.

inventory test   An achievement test that attempts to cover rather thoroughly some relatively small unit of specific instruction or training. An inventory test, as the name suggests, is in the nature of a "stock-taking" of an individual's knowledge or skill and is often administered prior to instruction.

item   A single question or exercise in a test.

item analysis   The process of evaluating single test items in respect to certain characteristics. It usually involves determining the difficulty value and the discriminating power of the item and often its correlation with some external criterion.

Kuder-Richardson formula(s)   Formulas for estimating the reliability of a test that are based on *inter-item consistency* and require only a single administration of the test. The one most used, formula 20, requires information based on the number of items in the test, the standard deviation of the total score, and the proportion of examinees passing each item. The Kuder-Richardson formulas are not appropriate for use with speeded tests.

mastery test   A test designed to determine whether a pupil has mastered a given unit of instruction or a single knowledge or skill; a test giving information on *what* a pupil knows, rather than on how his or her performance relates to that of some norm-referenced group. Such tests are used in computer-assisted instruction, where their results are referred to as content- or criterion-referenced information.

mean (M)   See ARITHMETIC MEAN.

median (Md)   The middle score in a distribution or set of ranked scores; the point (score) that divides the group into two equal parts; the 50th percentile. Half of the scores are below the median and half above it, except when the median itself is one of the obtained scores.

mental age (MA)   The age for which a given score on a mental ability test is average or normal. If the average score made by an unselected group of children 6 years, 10 months of age is 55, then a child making a score of 55 is said to have a mental age of 6–10. Since the mental age unit shrinks with increasing (chronological) age, MAs do not have a uniform interpretation throughout all ages. They are therefore most appropriately used at the early age levels where mental growth is relatively rapid.

modal-age norms   Achievement test norms that are based on the performance of pupils of normal age for their respective grades. Norms derived from such age-restricted groups are free from the distorting influence of the scores of under-age and overage pupils.

mode   The score or value that occurs most frequently in a distribution.

multiple-choice item   A test item in which the examinee's task is to choose the correct or best answer from several given answers or options.

N   The symbol commonly used to represent the number of cases in a group.

non-language test   See NON-VERBAL TEST.

non-verbal test   A test that does not require the use of words in the item or in the response to it. (Oral directions may be included in the formulation of the task.) A test cannot, however, be classified as non-verbal simply because it does not require reading on the part of the examinee. The use of non-verbal tasks cannot completely eliminate the effect of culture.

norm line   A smooth curve drawn to best fit (1) the plotted mean or median scores of successive age or grade groups, or (2) the successive percentile points for a single group.

normal distribution   A distribution of scores or measures that in graphic form has a distinctive bell-shaped appearance. Figures 1 and 2 show graphs of such a distribution, known as a *normal, normal probability,* or *Gaussian* curve. (Difference in shape is due to the different variability of the two distributions.) In such a normal distribution, scores or measures are distributed symmetrically about the mean, with as many cases up to various distances above the mean as down to equal distances below it. Cases are concentrated near the mean and decrease in frequency, according to a precise mathematical equation, the farther one departs from the mean. *Mean* and *median* are identical. The assumption that mental and psychological characteristics are distributed normally has been very useful in test development work.

norms   Statistics that supply a frame of reference by which meaning may be given to obtained test scores. Norms are based upon the actual performance of pupils of various grades or ages in the standardization group for the test. Since norms represent average or typical performance, they should

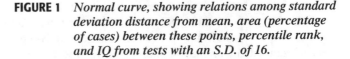

FIGURE 1   *Normal curve, showing relations among standard deviation distance from mean, area (percentage of cases) between these points, percentile rank, and IQ from tests with an S.D. of 16.*

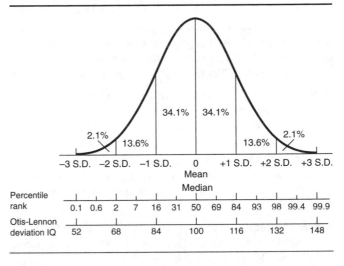

FIGURE 2   *Stanines and the normal curve. Each stanine (except 1 and 9) is one-half S.D. in width.*

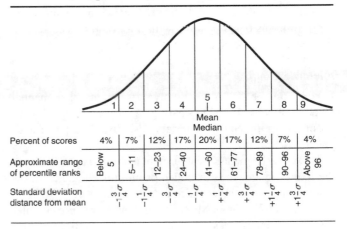

not be regarded as standards or as universally desirable levels of attainment. The most common types of norms are deviation IQ, percentile rank, grade equivalent, and stanine. Reference groups are usually those of specified age or grade.

objective test   A test made up of items for which correct responses may be set up in advance; scores are unaffected by the opinion or judgment of the scorer. Objective keys provide for scoring by clerks or by machine. Such a test is contrasted with a "subjective" test, such as the usual essay examination, to which different persons may assign different scores, ratings, or grades.

omnibus test   A test (1) in which items measuring a variety of mental operations are all combined into a single sequence rather than being grouped together by type of operation, and (2) from which only a single score is derived, rather than separate scores for each operation or function. Omnibus tests make for simplicity of administration, since one set of directions and one overall time limit usually suffice. The Elementary, Intermediate, and Advanced tests in the *Otis-Lennon Mental Ability Test* series are omnibus-type tests, as contrasted with the *Kuhlmann-Anderson Measure of Academic Potential,* in which the items measuring similar operations occur together, each with its own set of directions. In a *spiral-omnibus* test, the easiest items of each type are presented first, followed by the same succession of item types at a higher difficulty level, and so on in a rising spiral.

percentile (P)   A point (score) in a distribution at or below which fall the percent of cases indicated by the percentile. Thus a score coinciding with the 35th percentile (P_{35}) is regarded as equaling or surpassing that of 35 percent of the persons in the group, and such that 65 percent of the performances exceed this score. "Percentile" has nothing to do with the percent of correct answers an examinee makes on a test.

percentile band   An interpretation of a test score that takes account of the measurement error that is involved. The range of such bands, most useful in portraying significant differences in battery profiles, is usually from one standard error of measurement below the obtained score to one standard error of measurement above it.

percentile rank (PR)   The expression of an obtained test score in terms of its position within a group of 100 scores; the percentile rank of a score is the percent of scores equal to or lower than the given score in its own or in some external reference group.

performance test   A test involving some motor or manual response on the examinee's part, generally a manipulation of concrete equipment or materials. Usually *not* a paper-and-pencil test.

(1) A "performance" test of mental ability is one in which the role of language is excluded or minimized and ability is assessed by what the examinee *does* rather than by what he or she says (or writes). Mazes, form boards, picture completion, and other types of items may be used. Examples include certain *Stanford-Binet* tasks, the Performance Scale of *Wechsler Intelligence Scale for Children, Arthur Point Scale of Performance Tests, Raven's Progressive Matrices.*

(2) "Performance" tests include measures of mechanical or manipulative ability where the task itself coincides with the objective of the measurement, as in the *Bennett Hand-Tool Dexterity Test.*

(3) The term "performance" is also used to denote a test that is actually a *work sample;* in this sense it may include paper-and-pencil tests as, for example, a test in bookkeeping, in shorthand, or in proofreading, where no materials other than paper and pencil may be required and where the test response is identical with the behavior about which information is desired. *SRA Typing Skills* is such a test.

The use of the term "performance" to describe a type of test is not very precise, and there are certain "gray areas." Perhaps one should think of "performance" tests as those on which the obtained differences among individuals may *not* be ascribed to differences in ability to use verbal symbols.

personality test   A test intended to measure one or more of the nonintellective aspects of an individual's mental or psychological makeup; an instrument designed to obtain information on the affective characteristics of an individual—emotional, motivational, attitudinal, etc.—as distinguished from his or her abilities. Personality tests include (1) the so-called *personality* and *adjustment inventories* (e.g., *Bernreuter Personality Inventory, Bell Adjustment Inventory, Edwards Personal Preference Schedule*), which seek to measure a person's status on such traits as dominance, sociability, introversion, etc., by means of self-descriptive responses to a series of questions; (2) *rating scales,* which call for rating, by one's self or another, the extent to which a subject possesses certain traits; and (3) *opinion or attitude inventories* (e.g., *Allport-Vernon-Lindzey Study of Values, Minnesota Teacher Attitude Inventory*). Some writers also classify interest, problem, and belief inventories as personality tests (e.g., *Kuder Preference Record, Mooney Problem Check List*). See PROJECTIVE TECHNIQUE.

power test   A test intended to measure level of performance unaffected by speed of response; hence one in which there is either no time limit or a very generous one. Items are usually arranged in order of increasing difficulty.

practice effect   The influence of previous experience with a test on a later administration of the same or a similar test; usually an increased familiarity with the directions, kinds of questions, etc. Practice effect is greatest when the interval between testings is short, when the content of the two tests is identical or very similar, and when the initial testtaking represents a relatively novel experience for the subjects.

predictive validity   See VALIDITY (2).

product-moment coefficient (r)   Also known as the *Pearson r.* See COEFFICIENT OF CORRELATION.

profile   A graphic representation of the results on several tests, for either an individual or a group, when the results have been expressed in some uniform or comparable terms (standard scores, percentile ranks, grade equivalents, etc.). The profile method of presentation permits identification of areas of strength or weakness.

prognosis (prognostic) test   A test used to predict future success in a specific subject or field, as the *Pimsleur Language Aptitude Battery.*

projective technique (projective method)   A method of personality study in which the subject responds as he or she chooses to a series of ambiguous stimuli such as inkblots, pictures, unfinished sentences, etc. It is assumed that under this free-response condition the subject "projects" manifestations of personality characteristics and organization that can, by suitable methods, be scored and interpreted to yield a description of his or her basic personality structure. The *Rorschach* (inkblot) *Technique,* the *Murray Thematic Apperception Test,* and the *Machover Draw-a-Person Test* are commonly used projective methods.

quartile   One of three points that divide the cases in a distribution into four equal groups. The lower quartile (Q_1), or

25th percentile, sets off the lowest fourth of the group; the middle quartile (Q_2) is the same as the 50th percentile, or median, and divides the second fourth of cases from the third; and the third quartile (Q_3), or 75th percentile, sets off the top fourth.

r See COEFFICIENT OF CORRELATION.

random sample A sample of the members of some total population drawn in such a way that every member of the population has an equal chance of being included—that is, in a way that precludes the operation of bias or "selection." The purpose in using a sample free of bias is, of course, the requirement that the cases used be representative of the total population if findings for the sample are to be generalized to that population. In a *stratified* random sample, the drawing of cases is controlled in such a way that those chosen are "representative" also of specified subgroups of the total population. See REPRESENTATIVE SAMPLE.

range For some specified group, the difference between the highest and the lowest obtained score on a test; thus a very rough measure of spread or variability, since it is based upon only two extreme scores. Range is also used in reference to the possible spread of measurement a test provides, which in most instances is the number of items in the test.

raw score The first quantitative result obtained in scoring a test. Usually the number of right answers, number right minus some fraction of number wrong, time required for performance, number of errors, or similar direct, unconverted, uninterpreted measure.

readiness test A test that measures the extent to which an individual has achieved a degree of maturity or acquired certain skills or information needed for successfully undertaking some new learning activity. Thus a *reading readiness* test indicates whether a child has reached a developmental stage where he or she may profitably begin formal reading instruction. *Readiness* tests are classified as *prognostic* tests.

recall item A type of item that requires the examinee to supply the correct answer from his or her own memory or recollection, as contrasted with a *recognition item,* in which he or she need only identify the correct answer.

"Columbus discovered America in the year _____ " is a *recall* (or *completion*) item. See RECOGNITION ITEM.

recognition item An item that requires the examinee to recognize or select the correct answer from among two or more given answers (options).

Columbus discovered America in
  (*a*) 1425   (*b*) 1492   (*c*) 1520   (*d*) 1546

is a *recognition* item.

regression effect Tendency of a predicted score to be nearer to the mean of its distribution than the score from which it is predicted is to its mean. Because of the effects of regression, students making extremely high or extremely low scores on a test tend to make less extreme scores, i.e., closer to the mean, on a second administration of the same test or on some predicted measure.

reliability The extent to which a test is consistent in measuring whatever it does measure; dependability, stability, trustworthiness, relative freedom from errors of measurement. Reliability is usually expressed by some form of *reliability coefficient* or by the *standard error of measurement* derived from it.

reliability coefficient The coefficient of correlation between two forms of a test, between scores on two administrations of the same test, or between halves of a test, properly corrected. The three measure somewhat different aspects of reliability, but all are properly spoken of as reliability coefficients. See ALTERNATE-FORM RELIABILITY, KUDER-RICHARDSON FORMULA(S), SPLIT-HALF RELIABILITY COEFFICIENT, TEST-RETEST RELIABILITY COEFFICIENT.

representative sample A sample that corresponds to or matches the population of which it is a sample with respect to characteristics important for the purposes under investigation. In an achievement test norm sample, such significant aspects might be the proportion of cases of each sex, from various types of schools, different geographical areas, the several socioeconomic levels, etc.

scholastic aptitude See ACADEMIC APTITUDE.

skewed distribution A distribution that departs from symmetry or balance around the mean, i.e., from normality. Scores pile up at one end and trail off at the other.

Spearman-Brown formula A formula giving the relationship between the reliability of a test and its length. The formula permits estimation of the reliability of a test lengthened or shortened by any multiple, from the known reliability of a given test. Its most common application is the estimation of reliability of an entire test from the correlation between its two halves. See SPLIT-HALF RELIABILITY COEFFICIENT.

split-half reliability coefficient A coefficient of reliability obtained by correlating scores on one half of a test with scores on the other half and applying the Spearman-Brown formula to adjust for the doubled length of the total test. Generally, but not necessarily, the two halves consist of the odd-numbered and the even-numbered items. Split-half reliability coefficients are sometimes referred to as measures of the *internal consistency* of a test; they involve content sampling only, not stability over time. This type of reliability coefficient is inappropriate for tests in which speed is an important component.

standard deviation (S.D.) A measure of the variability or dispersion of a distribution of scores. The more the scores cluster around the mean, the smaller the standard deviation. For a normal distribution, approximately two-thirds (68.3 percent) of the scores are within the range from one S.D. below the mean to one S.D. above the mean. Computation of the S.D. is based upon the square of the deviation of each score from the mean. The S.D. is sometimes called "sigma" and is represented by the symbol σ. (See Figure 1.)

standard error (S.E.) A statistic providing an estimate of the possible magnitude of "error" present in some obtained measure, whether (1) an *individual* score or (2) some *group* measure, as a mean or a correlation coefficient.

(1) standard error of measurement (S.E. Meas.): As applied to a single obtained score, the amount by which the score may differ from the hypothetical true score due to errors of measurement. The larger the S.E. Meas., the less reliable the score. The S.E. Meas. is an amount such that in about two-thirds of the cases the obtained score would not differ by more than one S.E. Meas. from the true score. (Theoretically, then, it can be said that the chances are 2:1 that the actual score is within a band extending from *true score minus 1 S.E. Meas.* to *true score plus 1 S.E. Meas.;* but since the true score can never be known, actual practice must reverse the true-obtained relation for an interpretation.) Other probabilities are noted under (2) below. See TRUE SCORE.

(2) standard error: When applied to group averages, standard deviations, correlation coefficients, etc., the S.E. provides an estimate of the "error" that may be involved. The group's size and the S.D. are the factors on which these standard errors are based. The same probability interpretation as for S.E. Meas. is made for the S.E.s of group measures, i.e., 2:1 (2 out of 3) for the 1 S.E. range; 19:1 (95 out of 100) for a 2 S.E. range; 99:1 (99 out of 100) for a 2.6 S.E. range.

standard score   A general term referring to any of a variety of "transformed" scores, in terms of which raw scores may be expressed for reasons of convenience, comparability, ease of interpretation, etc. The simplest type of standard score, known as a *z*-score, is an expression of the *deviation* of a score from the mean score of the group *in relation to* the standard deviation of the scores of the group. Thus:

$$\text{standard score (Z)} = \frac{\text{raw score (X)} - \text{mean (M)}}{\text{standard deviation (S.D.)}}$$

Adjustments may be made in this ratio so that a system of standard scores having any desired mean and standard deviation may be set up. The use of such standard scores does not affect the relative standing of the individuals in the group or change the shape of the original distribution. *T*-scores have an M of 50 and an S.D. of 10. Deviation IQs are standard scores with an M of 100 and some chosen S.D., most often 16; thus a raw score that is 1 S.D. above the M of its distribution would convert to a standard score (deviation IQ) of 100 + 16 = 116. (See Figure 1.)

Standard scores are useful in expressing the raw scores of two forms of a test in comparable terms in instances where tryouts have shown that the two forms are not identical in difficulty; also, successive levels of a test may be linked to form a continuous standard-score scale, making across-battery comparisons possible.

standardized test (standard test)   A test designed to provide a systematic sample of individual performance, administered according to prescribed directions, scored in conformance with definite rules, and interpreted in reference to certain normative information. Some would further restrict the usage of the term "standardized" to those tests for which the items have been chosen on the basis of experimental evaluation and for which data on reliability and validity are provided. Others would add "commercially published" and/or "for general use."

stanine   One of the steps in a nine point scale of standard scores. The stanine (short for *standard-nine*) scale has values from 1 to 9, with a mean of 5 and a standard deviation of 2. Each stanine (except 1 and 9) is 1/2 S.D. in width, with the middle (average) stanine of 5 extending from 1/4 S.D. below to 1/4 S.D. above the mean. (See Figure 2.)

survey test   A test that measures general achievement in a given area, usually with the connotation that the test is intended to assess group status rather than to yield precise measures of individual performance.

t   A critical ratio expressing the relationship of some measure (mean, correlation coefficient, difference, etc.) to its standard error. The size of this ratio is an indication of the significance of the measure. If *t* is as large as 1.96, significance at the .05 level is indicated; if as large as 2.58, at the .01 level. These levels indicate 95 or 99 chances out of 100, respectively.

taxonomy   An embodiment of the principles of classification; a survey, usually in outline form, such as a presentation of the objectives of education.

test-retest reliability coefficient   A type of reliability coefficient obtained by administering the same test a second time, after a short interval, and correlating the two sets of scores. "Same test" was originally understood to mean identical content, i.e., the same form; currently, however, the term "test-retest" is also used to describe the administration of different forms of the same test, in which case this reliability coefficient becomes the same as the alternate-form coefficient. In either case (1) fluctuations over time and in testing situation, and (2) any effect of the first test upon the second are involved. When the time interval between the two testings is considerable, as several months, a test-retest reliability coefficient reflects not only the consistency of measurement provided by the test but also the stability of the examinee trait being measured.

true score   A score entirely free of error; hence, a hypothetical value that can never be obtained by testing, which always involves some measurement error. A "true" score may be thought of as the average score from an infinite number of measurements from the same or exactly equivalent tests, assuming no practice effect or change in the examinee during the testings. The standard deviation of this infinite number of "samplings" is known as the *standard error of measurement*.

validity   The extent to which a test does the job for which it is used. This definition is more satisfactory than the traditional "extent to which a test measures what it is supposed to measure," since the validity of a test is always specific to the purposes for which the test is used. The term *validity,* then, has different connotations for various types of tests, and thus a different kind of validity evidence is appropriate for each.

(1) Content, curricular validity: For achievement tests, validity is the extent to which the *content* of the test represents a balanced and adequate sampling of the outcomes (knowledge, skills, etc.) of the course or instructional program it is intended to cover. It is best evidenced by a comparison of the test content with courses of study, instructional materials, and statements of educational goals; and often by analysis of the processes required in making correct responses to the items. *Face validity,* referring to an observation of what a test appears to measure, is a non-technical type of evidence; apparent relevancy is, however, quite desirable.

(2) Criterion-related validity: The extent to which scores on the test are in agreement with (*concurrent validity*) or predict (*predictive validity*) some given criterion measure. Predictive validity refers to the accuracy with which an aptitude, prognostic, or readiness test indicates future learning success in some area, as evidenced by correlations between scores on the test and future criterion measures of such success (e.g., the relation of score on an academic aptitude test administered in high school to grade point average over four years of college). In concurrent validity, no significant time interval elapses between administration of the test being validated and of the criterion measure. Such validity might be evidenced by *concurrent* measures of academic ability and of achievement, by the relation of a new test to one generally accepted as or known to be valid, or by the correlation between scores on a test and criteria measures that are valid but are less objective and more time-consuming to obtain than a test score would be.

(3) Construct validity: The extent to which a test measures some relatively abstract psychological trait or construct; applicable in evaluating the validity of tests that have been constructed on the basis of an analysis (often factor analysis) of the nature of the trait and its manifestations. Tests of personality, verbal ability, mechanical aptitude, critical thinking, etc., are validated in terms of their construct and the relation of their scores to pertinent external data.

variability   The spread or dispersion of test scores, best indicated by their standard deviation.

variance   For a distribution, the average of the squared deviations from the mean; thus the square of the standard deviation.

Sources

Chapter 2

Malpractice cases excerpted from Ronald Jay Cohen (1979) *Malpractice: A Guide for Mental Health Professionals* published by The Free Press, a division of Macmillan, Inc. © 1979 The Free Press and reproduced by permission.

Chapter 4

"Methods of Expressing Test Scores" by Harold G. Seashore Test Service Notebook #148. Reproduced by permission. The Psychological Corporation, San Antonio, Texas.

"Stanines and Their Computation for Local Use." Test Service Notebook #123. Reproduced by permission. The Psychological Corporation, San Antonio, Texas.

"Interpreting Percentile Scores," "Interpreting Stanine Scores," "Interpreting SAT and ACT Scores" and "Interpreting Grade-Equivalent Scores" from J. R. Hills, *Hills' Handy Hints.* Washington, D.C.: National Council on Measurement in Education, 1986. Reprinted by permission of the National Council on Measurement in Education.

Figure 4-1 Copyright © 1988 Ronald Jay Cohen, Ph.D. All rights reserved. Reproduced by permission of Ronald Jay Cohen, Ph.D.

Chapter 6

Table from "A Quantitative Approach to Content Validity" by C. H. Lawshe, *Personnel Psychology,* 1975, *28,* 563–575. Reprinted by permission of Personnel Psychology, Inc.

"Fairness and the Matter of Bias" by Lois E. Burrill and Ruth Wilson. Test Service Notebook #36. Reproduced by permission. The Psychological Corporation, San Antonio, Texas.

Chapter 7

"Constructing the Puerto Rico Self-Concept Scale: Problems and Prospects" by H. Abadzi and S. Florez, from *Applied Psychological Measurement,* 1981, *5,* 237–243. Copyright 1981 Applied Psychological Measurement, Inc. Reproduced by permission of Applied Psychological Measurement, Inc.

Chapter 8

"Interpreting IQ Scores" from J. R. Hills, *Hills' Handy Hints.* Washington, D.C.: National Council on Measurement in Education, 1986. Reprinted by permission of the National Council on Measurement in Education.

Chapter 10

"Assessing School Ability" by Ruth Wilson. Test Service Notebook #35. Reproduced by permission. The Psychological Corporation, San Antonio, Texas.

"Selection and Provision of Testing Materials" by Roger T. Lennon. Test Service Notebook #99. Reproduced by permission. The Psychological Corporation, San Antonio, Texas.

"Some Things Parents Should Know About Testing." Test Service Notebook #34. Reproduced by permission. The Psychological Corporation, San Antonio, Texas.

"On Telling Parents About Test Results." Test Service Notebook #154. Reproduced by permission. The Psychological Corporation, San Antonio, Texas.

"How a Standardized Achievement Test Is Built" by Lois E. Burrill. Test Service Notebook #125. Reproduced by permission. The Psychological Corporation, San Antonio, Texas.

"Reporting Standardized Achievement Test Results to the Community" by Lois E. Burrill. Test Service Notebook #60. Reproduced by permission. The Psychological Corporation, San Antonio, Texas.

Appendixes

Midtown Manhattan Practice Personality Inventory © 2001 Ronald Jay Cohen. All rights reserved. Reprinted by permission.

"A Glossary of Measurement Terms" by Blythe C. Mitchell. Test Service Notebook #13. Reproduced by permission. The Psychological Corporation, San Antonio, Texas.

Solutions

Chapter 1

ANSWER KEY FOR CROSSWORD PUZZLE

Capitalized terms are "previews" of terms to be presented in coming chapters.

Across

2. rapport
4. VARIANCE
7. scoring
8. test
9. measurement
10. psycinfo
12. VALIDITY
14. ABAP
16. case
17. role
18. testing
21. STANDARD
24. user
25. scale
27. behavioral
29. manuals
30. reliability
31. testtaker

Down

1. psychometrics
3. assessment
5. autopsy
6. alternate
11. NORMS
13. diagnosis
15. portfolio
19. ERROR
20. interview
22. ABPP
23. developer
26. catalogues
28. scaling
29. MMY

THE 4-QUESTION CHALLENGE

1. b   2. a   3. c   4. d

Chapter 2

Across

2. Daubert
7. Jensen
8. Morgan
11. Woodworth
13. Tarasoff
14. Hansen
15. Wechsler
16. Murray
18. Albemarle
19. Griggs
20. Cattell
21. Darwin

Down

1. Hobson
3. Rorschach
4. Wundt
5. Binet
6. Kumho
9. Joiner
10. Diana
12. Witmer
17. Riles
19. Galton

THE 4-QUESTION CHALLENGE

1. d   2. a   3. b   4. c

Chapter 3

Across

1. grouped
4. skewness
8. histogram
11. range
12. ordinal
15. distribution
16. median
17. ratio
19. bimodal
20. stanine
23. variances
25. frequency
27. NC17
28. normal
29. platykurtic
31. nominal
32. bar
34. central
35. zero
36. mesokurtic

Down

2. polygon
3. graph
5. normalized
6. standard
7. interquartile
9. score
10. mean
13. AD
14. interval
16. mode
18. leptokurtic
21. variability
22. ten
24. scale
26. quartile
30. kurtosis
33. semi

EXERCISE 3-5

FIGURE THIS

1. a. 77.9, b. 80, c. 80, d. 50–95, e. 12.574, f. 158.095
2. One frequency distribution option is:

50–59	3
60–69	2
70–79	3
80–89	8
90–99	4

3. .88, −.15, .96, 1.04, .33
4. 31.79, 27.81, 34.97, 42.92, 43.72
5. ratio scale because there is a true zero point and equal intervals
6. Q1=69.25, Q2=80, Q3=88.75

THE 4-QUESTION CHALLENGE

1. a   2. c   3. b   4. d

Chapter 4

Across

1. regression
4. program
7. estimate
8. age
11. local
13. anchor
16. percentile
19. correlation
22. norm
25. incidental
26. purposive
27. fixed
28. multiple
29. user
30. stratified

Down

1. rho
2. sample
3. national
4. Pearson
5. raw
6. meta
9. grade
10. simple
12. outlier
14. standardization
15. norming
17. cut
18. subgroup
19. criterion
20. convenience
21. determination
22. normative
23. race
24. scatterplot

EXERCISE 4-3

STANDARD, STANDARDIZED, AND NORMALIZED STANDARD SCORES

The answers to each of the 10-item true/false tests contained in Exercises 4-3 and 4-4 are provided by Professor John R. Hills of Florida State University.[1]

_____

[1]Reprinted with permission from *Hills' Handy Hints* by John R. Hills, published by the National Council on Measurement in Education (1986).

ANSWERS TO TEST ON PERCENTILE SCORES

Question 8 is true. The others are false.

Explanations

1. Percentile scores indicate the relative standing in a group, not the percentage of items that are correct.
2. Mary's score is a number correct score. One cannot tell whether this is a good score without knowing the performances of others or having a carefully justified cutoff score that reflects mastery. In fact, one cannot be sure that Tim's score, which was a percentile, reflects better-than-average reading without at least knowing the norm group from which his percentile score is obtained.
3. Scores of the 30th percentile are really not far below average. Usually no more than a few percent of a class are failed, say 3 or 4 percent, not anywhere near 30 percent. Besides, a nationally standardized test may not accurately sample the arithmetic skills covered in Susie's class.
4. An increase of 9 percentile units at the top or bottom of the scale represents an improvement of many more items than the same increase near the middle of the scale. On that basis, one could conclude that Bill made much more progress than Jim.
5. Rebecca's score is one standard deviation above the mean. Sally's score is two standard deviations above the mean, and Jeanne's score is three standard deviations above the mean. In terms of score scales such as standard scores, which more accurately reflect the distribution of test scores and differences between them, these students are equally far apart in achievement. The percentile scale distorts the distances between scores.
6. The 50th percentile is near the center of the distribution. If it is to be near the center, some scores must be below it and some above it. It is unrealistic to try to get everyone up to the center. If everyone does improve, or if only the bottom half improve, the median (50th percentile) also increases. While the change in median will not appear on the form of the test now being used, the next time the test is standardized, the median will move up if enough of the students below the median nationally show substantial improvement.
7. The average of percentile ranks is not itself a percentile rank. To get percentile ranks for averages of percentile ranks, one would have to rank the average percentile ranks and get a new set of percentiles for these average ranks.
8. The scores for a class cannot be averaged to evaluate the average score in terms of the norms table for scores of individuals. Class averages can only be evaluated in terms of a norms table for class averages. Some publishers do not provide norms for class averages. In such cases, a comparison between the average score of a class and the average scores of other classes cannot sensibly be made. The spread of class averages is much less than the spread of individual scores.
9. When one considers the standard error of measurement for scores such as those of Rebecca and Helmut, it is possible that those scores could be reversed in position on another testing. The percentile band concept is used to keep from overinterpreting small differences between scores.
10. On most tests the percentile bands near the middle of the score distribution are wide. That signifies that we do not know precisely what a student like Gretchen's reading level really is. Obtaining the percentile rank of her score instead of the percentile band gives the appearance of greater accuracy, but this is only an illusion. There is no practical way to obtain Gretchen's true score, of course.

EXERCISE 4-4

STANINES, SAT/ACT, AND GRADE-EQUIVALENT SCORES

ANSWERS TO TEST ON STANINE SCORES

Explanations:

1. No. Stanine score are numbers from 1 to 9. There is no such thing as a stanine score of zero. A zero score reported as a stanine indicates that an error has been made.
2. Yes and no. Stanine 5 is in the middle of the scale, and in that sense Bill got an average score on the test. However, each stanine represents a band of scores, not a specific score. The 5th stanine

extends from the 40th to the 60th percentile. So Bill might be performing as low as the 40th percentile or as high as the 60th percentile but still receive a stanine of 5. However, because the stanine scale reflects a normal curve, the 40th percentile is usually only a few raw score points lower than the 60th percentile.

3. No. Stanines are represented by the single-digit whole numbers, such as 1, 2, and 3, never by numbers with decimal points. Except for the first and ninth stanines, each stanine represents a narrow band of scores on the test. (The first and ninth stanines may be very wide in terms of raw score points. Each extends to the beginning or end of the test, however far that may be.) Thus, a stanine of 6.5 does not exist. Anyone who uses such a number for a stanine has made an error.

4. No. The ninth stanine is not the 96th percentile. The lower limit of the ninth stanine is the 96th percentile, but the upper limit is plus infinity. Any performance above the 96th percentile is the ninth stanine. Cindy may have scored far above the 96th percentile and received a stanine of 9. The same is true at the other end of the scale for a stanine of 1. A person with a stanine score of 1 may be as high as the 4th percentile, or very much lower.

5. Yes. Three easy landmarks for relating stanines to standard scores are the mean and plus and minus one standard deviation. The mean is in the middle of the fifth stanine. Plus one standard deviation is in the middle of the seventh stanine. Minus one standard deviation is in the middle of the third stanine.

6. Yes. Ms. Billingsley used the *Rule for Four.* With stanines, a close approximation to the distribution of scores can be remembered as starting with 4 percent in either stanine 1 or 9, then adding 4 percent for the next stanine each time up to stanine 5 and then subtracting 4 percent for each to the end of the scale. Thus, the percent of the scores that are assigned 1, 2, 3, . . . 9 are very close to 4, 8, 12, 16, 20, 16, 12, 8, and 4, respectively. So Ms. Billingsley said to herself, "Four percent for stanine 9, 8 percent for stanine 8, and 12 percent for stanine 7." Then she had her answer. She could have started with stanine 5, saying to herself, "Twenty percent in stanine 5, 16 percent in stanine 6, and 12 percent in stanine 7," reaching the same result.

7. No. First, to be correct a decile is a point, not a range. The first decile is the score that separates the lowest scoring 10 percent of scores from the highest scoring 90 percent, for example. The name for the lowest 10 percent is the lowest *tenth,* or the first *tenth,* not the first *decile.* Beyond that, the first tenth is the lowest scoring 10 percent, but the first stanine is the lowest scoring 4 percent, a much lower scoring group, on the average. In general, the only correspondence between tenths of a distribution (or "deciles") and stanines is that tenths and stanines above 5 are high scoring and below 5 are low scoring. The differences between tenths and stanines reflect different assumptions about the distribution of scores. Tenths are based on the assumption that scores have a rectangular or flat distribution. Stanines are based on the more realistic assumption that scores are distributed normally.

8. No. Tests that use stanine scores refer these scores to students in a particular grade, not to subjects in general or to people in general. So a student who regularly receives stanine scores of 5 in a subject from year to year can be assumed to be making normal progress. He stays in the middle of the distribution. Another student who continually makes scores of stanine 7 stays about 1 standard deviation above the mean and makes normal progress also. Normal progress with stanines (or with percentiles or standard scores) is shown by earning the same score over time, not higher scores year by year.

9. No. Mr. Tatnall does not need to worry about a change from one stanine to the adjacent stanine score. One correct question fewer could move a person one stanine down if his score was at the bottom of the range for that stanine. This is one of the problems with stanine scores. A person's performance can be anywhere in a range of scores but receive the same stanine. If Patricia scored at the lower edge of the fifth stanine, a trivial difference in performance could change her score to the next lower stanine.

10. Yes. When scores differ by two stanines, we tend to think of there being a real difference, not an error of measurement. Other things being equal, for tests with satisfactory reliabilities (.90), such differences are expected to occur only about one time in ten. Therefore, differences that large deserve further investigation. Perhaps Elena has benefited from some effective teaching, or she may have become more motivated, or she may have found more time to read, or something in her life that was impeding her progress may have been removed. A difference that large is unlikely to be an accident.

ANSWERS TO TEST ON SAT AND ACT SCORES

Answers:

1. N, 2. N, 3. N, 4. N, 5. N, 6. Y, 7. N, 8. Y, 9. N, 10. N

Explanations:

1. The "average" SAT score depends on whose data are being averaged. The score 500 was the average of 10,654 students who took the SAT in April of 1941. Since then, a process called equating has been used to ensure that the aptitude level represented by 500 in April 1941 is the same level represented by a score of 500 on a SAT taken at any other time. However, in 1983, the mean scores of all college-bound seniors tested were 430 on Verbal and 420 on Mathematics, for boys, and 493 and 445, respectively, for girls. The means for all high school seniors would, of course, be appreciably lower. We know now that mean SAT scores fluctuate from year to year, and until recently they have been declining. The score 500 is probably not the mean for any existing naturally constituted group.
2. Mary must have added together her SAT-V and SAT-M scores to get 900. The highest reported score for either test is 800, so 900 cannot be a score from either section by itself. Susie's scores added together are 900, the same as Mary's scores. The College Board does not advocate adding V and M scores together for any purpose. In fact, if they are to be combined for estimating future success in college, experience indicates that a better general-purpose combination would be 2V + M, with a minimum of 600 and a maximum of 2400.

ANSWERS TO TEST ON GRADE-EQUIVALENT SCORES

Question 1 is true. The others are false.

Explanations:

1. Because GE scores are developed by obtaining the mean or median performance at each of several grade levels on a test whose content covers the several grades, a student who scores above the grade in which he is enrolled has performed above average for students in his grade.
2. A student can obtain a GE score without being able to do the work of students at the grade level indicated by his score. Tim may have obtained a 9.2 score by getting *all* the items that were designed for grades 4, 5, 6, and 7 correct and may not have done particularly well on items designed for grades 8 and 9, if there were any.
3. Often the GEs associated with high or low number-correct scores are obtained by extrapolation. It is possible that no ninth grader was ever tested with the test given Tim.
4. Because Tim could have gotten a GE score of 9.2 by doing well on the easier or lower-level items of the test, one cannot tell from these scores whether he could participate effectively with ninth-graders or not.
5. In most schools, reading is not taught in the ninth grade except perhaps for remediation of ineffective reading skills. So it does not make sense to consider putting Tim into ninth grade instruction in reading. Even if reading (or any subject for which a 9.2 GE was obtained) were taught at the ninth grade, one would not know whether Tim should be put into a higher level of instruction without evaluating whether he had the prerequisite skills. The GE score cannot be relied on to indicate that ninth grade skills have been mastered.
6. The standard deviations of GE scores vary from one subject to another. Tim's score of 9.2 on reading and 7.3 on arithmetic could be equal scores if one used another score scale such as percentiles. The difference between the two GE scores may be due to the fact that students tend to differ less within a grade on arithmetic than on reading. In addition, GE scores above a student's grade do not mean that he has really mastered skills beyond his own grade level.
7. Because the standard deviations for different subjects differ, we cannot tell whether 9.2 in reading is relatively better than 7.3 in arithmetic, and neither necessarily implies that Tim is ahead of his own class.

8. When GE scores have been extrapolated far above or below a student's grade level, it often occurs that even a single additional item correct can change a student's GE score by more than a year. Tim may simply have gotten one or two fewer items correct in the spring than in the fall.

9. The GE score is based on a mean. One dare not expect all students to be at or above grade level on GE scores. In a typical heterogeneous class, about half would obtain GE scores below grade level and half above grade level. Because only 30 percent of Mr. Brown's fifth-graders got GE scores below 5.0, his students may be doing a little better than usual instead of worse.

10. Another peculiar characteristic of GE scores is that the standard deviations get larger year by year. Suppose that a person (or a group average) is at and remains at a given percentile score, say the 16th percentile (which is one standard deviation below the mean). This same percentile each year is translated into a lower GE each year because the standard deviation gets larger from year to year. This can leave the impression that a person (or group) is falling farther behind each year. Similarly, if a student (or group average) is above the mean and stays at the same relative position, he appears to get farther ahead every year in terms of GE scores. This is an illusion created by the GE score system.

EXERCISE 4-6
THE PEARSON r

Final examination data for ten students of the "Home Study School of Elvis Presley Impersonators" are presented along with a record of the actual number of hours each student spent preparing for the examination. Students are asked to (1) create a scatterplot to represent these data, and (2) calculate the Pearson product-moment correlation coefficient (having been provided with formulas, and step-by-step instructions on how to do so). The correct calculations for both the raw score and deviation score Pearson r formulas are presented below.

Calculation of the Pearson r

Raw Data		Deviation Formula Calculations					Raw Score Formula Calculations		
X	Y	$x = X - \bar{X}$	$y = Y - \bar{Y}$	xy	x^2	y^2	XY	X^2	Y^2
23.0	98.0	12.1	22.3	269.83	146.41	497.29	2254	529	9604
16.9	92.0	5.1	16.3	73.13	26.91	265.69	1472	256	8464
.5	45.0	−10.4	−30.7	319.28	108.16	942.49	22.5	.25	2025
12.0	80.0	1.1	4.3	4.73	1.21	18.49	960	144	6400
9.0	76.0	−1.9	.3	−.57	3.61	.09	684	81	5776
10.0	57.0	−.9	−18.7	16.83	.81	349.69	570	100	3249
1.0	61.0	−9.9	−14.7	145.53	98.01	216.09	61	1	3721
14.0	88.0	3.1	12.3	38.13	9.61	151.29	1232	196	7744
8.5	70.0	−2.4	−5.7	13.68	5.76	32.49	595	72.25	4900
15.0	90.0	4.1	14.3	58.63	16.81	204.49	1350	225	8100

EXERCISE 4-7
"HELLO" TO RHO

As an introduction to some facility in calculating Spearman's rho (and subsequently other correlation coefficients) students are presented with a scenario involving ten beauty school students and the following variables: (1) sex, (2) score on a pre-test, (3) score on a post-test, and (4) career disposition. Students are instructed to calculate rho and are asked:

Is there a relationship between the pre-admission score on the qualifying examination and the comprehensive end-of-course examination? If so, how would you describe it?

Having calculated rho for the beauty school problem, the student is then asked to return to the Presley Course data (used earlier to calculate a Pearson r) and calculate rho for it. The computations used to calculate rho in each of these cases follow.

Note in the beauty school problem that rank order of "A" scores proceeded with a rank of 1 being assigned to the score of 91 (the highest score), a rank of 2 being assigned to 88 (the next-highest score), and so forth. The lowest score in the distribution (64) was assigned a rank of 10. The "A" score of 79 had a frequency of 2 and was assigned a rank of 6.5. And since each score of 79 was assigned a rank of 6.5, the next lower score is assigned a rank of 8.

Calculation of Spearman's Rho for the Rankings by Professors Go and Nogo

Student	Professor Go's Rankings	Professor Nogo's Rankings	d	d^2
Tiffany	5	3	2	4
Levelor	1	2	−1	1
Harley	4	4	0	0
Macy	9	7	2	4
Dreyfus	8	8	0	0
Scotch	2	1	1	1
Andersen	10	9	1	1
Visine	7	10	−3	9
Hershey	3	6	−3	9
Chrysler	6	5	1	1

$$\rho_S = 1 - \frac{6\sum d^2}{n^3 - n} = 1 - \frac{6(30)}{10^3 - 10} = 1 - \frac{180}{990}$$

$$\rho_S = 1 - .1818 = .8182$$

Calculation of Spearman's Rho for the Reading Rank-Order Test

Student	First Administration	Second Administration	d	d^2
Kimba	1	3	−2	4
Julep	2	1	1	1
Steve	3	2	1	1
Edie	4	6	−2	4
Nodu	5	7	−2	4
Ike	6	5	1	1
Tina	7	4	3	9

$$\rho_S = 1 - \frac{6\sum d^2}{n^3 - n} = 1 - \frac{6(24)}{7^3 - 7} = 1 - \frac{144}{336}$$

$$\rho_S = 1 - .4286 = .5714$$

EXERCISE 4-8

OTHER COEFFICIENTS OF CORRELATION

Using the beauty school data, students are asked to calculate the coefficient of correlation that expresses the relationship between score on the entry-level test, and sex. Since one variable is continuous in nature and the other is a true dichotomy, the appropriate statistic for the calculation of a correlation coefficient is the point-biserial r. The calculations for the computation of r_{pb} are shown below.

Point Biserial Coefficient of Correlation Problem

Sex of Subject	Score on Entry Level Test	Calculations $(X - \bar{X}^2)$
Male = 0	86	$(86 - 79.7)^2 = 39.69$
Female = 1	91	$(91 - 79.7)^2 = 127.69$
Male = 0	75	$(75 - 79.7)^2 = 22.09$
Female = 1	64	$(64 - 79.7)^2 = 246.49$
Female = 1	73	$(73 - 79.7)^2 = 44.89$
Male = 0	82	$(82 - 79.7)^2 = 5.29$
Male = 0	79	$(79 - 79.7)^2 = .49$
Female = 1	79	$(79 - 79.7)^2 = .49$
Male = 0	88	$(88 - 79.7)^2 = 68.89$
Female = 1	80	$(80 - 79.7)^2 = .09$

Calculating a Point-Biserial r

$$\bar{X}_1 = \frac{\sum X_1}{n_1} = \frac{91 + 64 + 73 + 79 + 80}{5} = \frac{387}{5} = 77.4$$

$$\bar{X}_0 = \frac{\sum X_0}{n_0} = \frac{86 + 75 + 82 + 79 + 88}{5} = \frac{410}{5} = 82$$

$$\bar{X} = \sum X_0 + \sum X_1 = \frac{387 + 410}{10} = \frac{797}{10} = 79.7$$

$$r_{pb} = \sqrt{n_1 n_0} \left(\frac{\bar{X}_1 - \bar{X}_0}{\sqrt{\sum \left(X - \bar{X}^2 \right)}} \right) = \sqrt{\frac{(5)(5)}{10}} \left(\frac{77.4 - 82}{556.1} \right)$$

$$r_{pb} = 1.58(-.195) \cong -.3081$$

The phi coefficient is a coefficient of correlation appropriate for use with two true dichotomies. Again with reference to the beauty school example, the student is asked to calculate the relationship between the variables of occupational entry into the field of beauty (represented in the computations below as X), and sex (represented in the computations below as Y). A 0/1 coding system has also been employed in the present example for both occupational disposition (where 0 = did not enter field of beauty, and 1 = did enter field of beauty) and sex (where 0 = male, and 1 = female).

Calculating a Phi Coefficient

		(X) Entered Beauty Field?		
		No (0)	Yes (1)	Total
(Y) Sex	Male (0)	3	2	5
	Female (1)	2	3	5
Total		5	5	10

$$\phi_{XY} = \frac{p_{(XY)1} - (p_{X1})(p_{Y1})}{\sqrt{(p_{X1})(p_{Y1})(1 - p_{X1})(1 - p_{Y1})}}$$

$$\phi_{XY} = \frac{.30 - (.5)(.5)}{\sqrt{(.5)(1 - .5)(.5)(1 - .5)}} = \frac{.30 - .25}{\sqrt{(.25)(.25)}}$$

$$= \frac{.05}{\sqrt{.065}} = \frac{.05}{.25} = .2$$

$$\phi_{XY} = .2$$

A further word of explanation about the calculations above:

$p_{(XY)1}$ is the proportion of subjects "scoring" 1 on both X and Y; it is equal to 3/10, or .30.

p_{X1} is the proportion of subjects "scoring" 1 on X; it is equal to 5/10, or .5.

p_{Y1} is the proportion of subjects "scoring" 1 on Y; it is equal to 5/10, or .5.

EXERCISE 4-9

AN EXERCISE IN REGRESSION

The calculations are as follows:

X	Y	XY	X^2	Y^2
10	10	100	100	100
30	20	600	900	400
50	30	1500	2500	900
60	40	2400	3600	1600
70	50	3500	4900	2500
80	60	4800	6400	3600

$$n = 6$$
$$\sum XY = 12{,}900$$
$$\sum X \sum Y = 63{,}000$$
$$(\sum X)^2 = 90{,}000$$
$$\sum X^2 = 18{,}400$$

Calculations for the Least-Squares Line

$$\sum X = 300 \qquad\qquad \sum XY = 12900$$
$$(\sum X)^2 = (300)^2 = 90000 \qquad\qquad (\sum X)(\sum Y) = (300)(210)$$
$$\sum X^2 = 18400 \qquad\qquad\qquad = 63000$$
$$\overline{X} = \frac{\sum X}{N} = \frac{300}{6} = 50 \qquad\qquad \overline{Y} = \frac{\sum Y}{N} = \frac{210}{6} = 35$$
$$\hat{y} = a + bX$$
$$b = \frac{\sum XY - N\overline{X}\,\overline{Y}}{\sum X^2 - N\overline{Y}^2} = \frac{12900 - 6(50)(35)}{18400 - 6(50)^2}$$
$$b = \frac{12900 - 10500}{18400 - 6(2500)} = \frac{2400}{18400 - 15000} = \frac{2400}{3400} = .70588$$
$$a = \overline{Y} - b\overline{X}$$
$$a = 35 - .70588(50)$$
$$a = 35 - 35.294$$
$$a = -.294$$

Thus, $\hat{y} = -.294 + .70588X$, and for each unit increase in X, the predicted value for Y would increase by $.70588X$.

$\hat{y} = -.294 + .70588X$, if $X = 78$, the estimated score $\hat{y}$ would be equal to,

$\hat{y} = -.294 + .70588(78)$

$\hat{y} = -.294 + 55.05864$

$\hat{y} = 54.76$

EXERCISE 4-10
FIGURE THIS

1. If the psychologist chooses the "typical" sample then Benito is being compared to an age group that matches his own but one that has no ethnic group that matches his own. If the psychologist chooses the "clinical" sample then Benito would be compared to a same aged peer group that also includes scores from children of his ethnicity. Rosa's age is not represented in either standardization sample so the psychologist doesn't have a viable comparison for her performance on the SPITUP. If the psychologist chooses to use the SPITUP anyway, then Rosa is being compared to children a year older than she with the same caveats as noted for Benito.
2. The psychologist is assuming that the standardization sample that she selects captures those demographic factors that are unique to Benito and Rosa so that discrimination of critical scores on the SPITUP indicate the presence or absence of trauma.
3. This psychologist will have a number of problems explaining why she used the SPITUP with these children: 1) the norm groups don't represent the frequencies of Rosa's and Benito's ethnicity in the USA or New Mexico; 2) the psychologist does not know if the 1% of Hispanic children in the "clinical" sample are bilingual or exposed to Spanish and English in the same way as Rosa and Benito; 3) there is not an appropriate age group to which Rosa may be compared so scores based on SPITUP are suspect; and 4) the norm samples are small for each of the age groups and generally not representative of the ethnic and racial diversity in the USA. As a result of all of these problems, an interpretation of any sort on the SPITUP for either child is suspect.

THE 4-QUESTION CHALLENGE

1. a   2. b   3. c   4. d

Chapter 5

Across

1. generalizability
5. kappa
7. variance
10. true
11. score
14. content
15. homogeneity
18. reliability
20. odd
22. Kuder
26. inflation
27. difference
28. split
29. retest
30. speed
31. Brown
32. judges
33. heterogeneity

Down

2. equivalence
3. alpha
4. stability
6. power
8. Rulon
9. error
10. theory
12. criterion
13. item
16. IRT
17. confidence
19. alternate
21. restriction
23. consistency
24. parallel
25. measurement
26. internal

EXERCISE 5-3

TEST-RETEST AND INTERSCORER RELIABILITY

Here students are asked to calculate coefficients of test-retest and interscorer reliability, using respectively the Pearson *r* and Spearman's rho. The data and the calculations are as follows:

Student	X	Y	Pearson r XY	X²	Y²	R(X) Spearman Rank Order	R(Y)	d	d²
Malcolm	98	84	8232	9604	7056	1	6	–5	25
Heywood	92	97	8924	8464	9409	2	2	0	0
Mervin	45	63	2835	2025	3969	10	10	0	0
Zeke	80	91	7280	6400	8281	5	4	1	1
Sam	76	87	6612	5776	7569	6	5	1	1
Macy	57	92	5244	3249	8464	9	3	6	36
Elvis 2	61	98	5978	3721	9604	8	1	7	49
Jed	88	69	6072	7744	4761	4	9	–5	25
Jeb	70	70	4900	4900	4900	7	8	–1	1
Leroy	90	75	6750	8100	5625	3	7	–4	16

Calculations for Pearson r

$$\sum X = 757$$

$$(\sum X)^2 = (757)^2 = 573049$$

$$\sum X^2 = 59983$$

$$\sum Y = 826$$

$$(\sum Y)^2 = (826)^2 = 682276$$

$$\sum Y^2 = 69638$$

$$\sum XY = 62827$$

$$(\sum X)(\sum Y) = (757)(826) = 625282$$

$$r = \frac{N \sum XY - \sum X \sum Y}{\sqrt{[N \sum X^2 - (\sum X)^2][N \sum Y^2 - (\sum Y)^2]}}$$

$$r = \frac{10(62827) - 625282}{\sqrt{[10(59983) - 573049][10(69638) - 682276]}}$$

$$r = \frac{2988}{\sqrt{[26781][14104]}} = \frac{2988}{19435} = .1537$$

Calculations for Spearman Rank Order Correlation Coefficient rho ρ_S

$$\rho_S = 1 - \frac{6 \sum d^2}{N^3 - N}$$

$$\rho_S = 1 - \frac{6(154)}{10^3 - 10}$$

$$\rho_S = 1 - \frac{924}{990}$$

$$\rho_S = 1 - .933$$

$$\rho_S = .067$$

EXERCISE 5-4
USING THE SPEARMAN-BROWN FORMULA

$$r_{sb} = \frac{n r_{xy}}{1 + (n - 1) r_{xy}}$$

Part 1: Effect on reliability of Reducing the Length of a Test

A reduction from 150 to 100 items would reduce the reliability coefficient from .89 to .84. Thus, if a test developer or user wanted to reduce by 50 the number of items of this test—one that had a pre-existing reliability of .89—it's a good guess that such a reduction can be made without an appreciable loss in reliability of the test.

The solution to Part 1 is as follows.

$$n = \frac{100}{150} = .67$$

$$r_{sb} = \frac{.67(.89)}{1 + (-.33)(.89)} = \frac{.5963}{1 - .2937} = \frac{.5963}{.7063} = .844$$

Part 2: How many items must be added in order to bring a test up to a desired level of reliability?

r = Desired Level of Reliability

r_{xx} = Reliability of the Existing Test

$$r' = \frac{r'(1 - r_{xx})}{r_{xx}(1 - r')}$$

$$\frac{.80(1 - .60)}{.60(1 - .80)} = \frac{(.80)(.40)}{(.60)(.20)} = \frac{3200}{1200} = 2.67$$

The number of items in the test (with an existing reliability of .60) would have to be increased by a factor of 2.7 (2.67 rounded up to 2.7). If the original test contained 100 items with an $r = .60$, the new test would have to contain a total of 270 items (or 2.7 multiplied by a factor of 100) in order to have a reliability of .80.

EXERCISE 5-6
FIGURE THIS

1. a. SEM = 5.81 rounded up to 6
   b. 68% Confidence interval for:

Sam	91–79
Jean	106–94

   c. 95% Confidence interval for:

Byron	138–114
LaKeisha	127–103

   d. 99% Confidence interval for:

Hector	86–50
Hai	163–127

2. Standard Error of Difference between the IQ test and Math Teacher Achievement Test: 7.79
3. Standard Error of Difference between Dexter and LaRonta's scores on the Math Teacher Achievement Test: 6.36

   This standard error of difference (6.36) is then compared to the difference between Dexter's and LaRonta's scores. That difference is 5 points, which is lower than the standard error of difference score of 6.36. This indicates that Dexter's and LaRonta's scores on the Math Teacher Achievement Test are not sufficiently different at the 68th, 95th, or 99th percent confidence intervals to predict, on the basis of their test performances, that one will be a better teacher than the other.

THE 4-QUESTION CHALLENGE

1. a	2. a	3. d	4. c

Chapter 6

Across

1. severity
3. validation
4. face
7. discriminant
9. matrix
10. concurrent
13. construct
14. positive
15. hit
20. confirmatory
22. halo
23. inference
25. tables
28. CVR
30. homogeneity
31. bias
33. rating
34. leniency
35. loading
36. slope
37. generosity

Down

2. validity
5. criterion
6. factor
8. expectancy
11. negative
12. miss
14. predictive
16. intercept
17. local
18. fairness
19. contrasted
21. convergent
23. incremental
24. central
26. base
27. exploratory
29. ranking
32. content

EXERCISE 6-5

THE MULTITRAIT-MULTIMETHOD MATRIX

A The reliability of the anxiety measures is very good, at .95 for the Self-Evaluation measure, and .86 for the Coach's Evaluation measure. The reliability of the skill measures is somewhat lower, at .80 for the Self-Evaluation measure, and .71 for the Coach's Evaluation measure. Convergent validity is represented in the correlations between different measures designed to measure the same construct. Convergent validity is good for the two anxiety measures, at .77, but weak for the two skill measures, at .15. These coefficients should be higher than the remaining correlations in the matrix, which represent discriminant validity. This is true for the anxiety measures, which correlate more highly with each other than with the skill measures; correlations between the anxiety and skill measures range from .10 (self-anxiety with coach-skill) to .40 (self-anxiety with self-skill). Thus the anxiety measures seem to possess good construct validity. However, problems in the construct validity of the skill measures become apparent when their convergent validity coefficient is compared with these same discriminant validity coefficients. For example, we see that the self-evaluation of skill correlates higher with the self-evaluation of anxiety (.40) than it does with the coach's evaluation of skill (.15).

In brief, the reliability and construct validity of the anxiety measures seems to be good. The reliability of the skill measures is not strong, and the construct validity of the skill measures is weak.

B. The reliability coefficients, located on the main diagonal, indicate that (1) both SAT measures are highly reliable, (2) the high school grades are somewhat reliable, and (3) the college grades possess weak reliability.

The three correlations between the various math scores (.77, .73, .78) are relatively high, indicating good convergent validity for the math tests. The three correlations between the various verbal scores (.69, .30, .75) present a more mixed picture. The lowest correlation is between SAT and college scores, indicating that these scores are not closely related.

An evaluation of the discriminant validity coefficients also yields a mixed picture. The situation present with SAT and high school scores is ideal. While correlations are relatively high when SAT math is compared with high school math (.77) and SAT verbal is compared with high school verbal (.69), the correlations are lower between SAT math and high school verbal (.18) and SAT verbal and high school math (.20). These latter values are discriminant validity coefficients. This pattern of convergent validity coefficients that are higher than the discriminant validity coefficients indicates that the two components of the SAT are measuring something specifically related to corresponding components in high school.

The situation with the SAT and college scores is not as clear-cut. Again the convergent validity coefficients (.73 for math, .30 for verbal) are higher than the discriminant validity coefficients (.17 and .10). However, because the convergent validity coefficient for the verbal scores is low, the pattern observed is not as dramatic.

The relationship between the high school and college scores is highly problematic. The convergent validity coefficients (.78 and .75) are both lower than one of the discriminant validity coefficients (.80) and not a lot higher than the other (.66). Thus the high school measures of math and verbal skill are not distinctively related to the college measures of math and verbal skill. This is a construct validity problem.

The only coefficients yet to be discussed are the correlations between verbal and math scores from the same measurement method. SAT verbal and math scores correlate .56, and high school verbal and math scores correlate .55. These coefficients indicate that the two verbal and math scores are not completely distinctive. The fact that these correlations are lower than the convergent validity coefficients is a positive feature. The correlation between college math and verbal scores, at .80, is an anomaly in the matrix provided to challenge the best students. As discussed in Chapter 6 of the text, the correlation between the verbal and math scores, a validity coefficient, is limited by the reliability of the verbal score and the math score. In this case, we see that the validity coefficient is much larger than the reliability coefficients, which is theoretically highly unlikely. It also indicates some important problems for construct validity of the college measures, because verbal and math scores in college correlate better with each other than they do with themselves.

EXERCISE 6-7

FACTOR ANALYSIS II: THE CORRELATION MATRIX

Items for *W*, *X*, and *Y* should be similar while item *Z* should be quite different and should yield answers that arc likely to be unrelated to *W*, *X*, and *Y.* For example:

W: What is your current salary?

X: What was your salary last year?

Y: What do you anticipate your salary will be next year?

Z: On average, how many hours per day do you spend driving to and from work?

EXERCISE 6-8

FACTOR ANALYSIS III: ANALYZING A PUBLISHED ARTICLE

1. Because White and colleagues wanted to understand what the various impulsivity tests are measuring, they chose to include several different impulsivity tests. They selected tests that had published reliability and validity information and seemed interesting from the testtaker's perspective. They purposefully looked for measures that included the viewpoints of various people—while most measures were completed by the subjects of the study, in this case 12- and 13-year-old boys, other tests were designed to be completed about the boys by their teachers, parents, or outside observers. In all, they identified 11 measures of impulsivity.

2. White et al. then selected a sample of 430 boys ages 12 and 13 to complete the test. Because the authors are particularly interested in the relationships between the impulsivity measures and delinquency, approximately half of the boys selected for the study were known to be at high risk for delinquency.

3. If all of the measures mean the same thing by "impulsivity," and if all are valid, then large and positive correlations would be expected between the different measures.

4. The correlations were all between $-.08$ and $+.33$, in what the authors call "the low-to-moderate range" (p. 197). White et al. suggest that these small correlations might indicate the measurement of more than one kind of impulsivity across the different scales.

5. An examination of the factor loadings from the article by White et al. shows that four variables clearly load on the first factor and not on the second factor: impulsivity as rated by the boy, by the parent, and by the teacher, and restlessness as rated by the outside observer. For example, the outside observer's rating of restlessness has a factor loading of .44 on the first factor, but only $-.06$ on the second factor. This indicates that ratings of restlessness reflect whatever constitutes the first factor but are unrelated to the second factor. A similar pattern is evident for each of the three other impulsivity ratings on this factor.

6. Continuing on with the second factor identified by White and colleagues, six variables clearly load on that factor and not on the first factor: the Trail Making Test, the number of Stroop errors, time perception, the number of cards played in a gambling game, ability to delay gratification, and the slowness with which they could trace a circle. All of these were tasks the boys were asked to complete that required the ability and willingness to direct and control one's thought processes.

7. A variety of answers are acceptable here, but should involve the development of a task of cognitive impulsivity that involves the evaluation of others and/or the development of a task of behavioral impulsivity involving observation rather than self-report or other-report. After development, these tasks should be administered to a new group of boys, along with some of the tasks used by White et al. to determine whether, for example, the observational measure of behavioral impulsivity actually correlates with the other measures of behavioral impulsivity used in the White et al. study.

8. First, the authors have clarified the construct of impulsivity. Just two common factors or dimensions seem to underlie the 11 impulsivity measures included in the analysis; there seems to be a behavioral dimension and a cognitive dimension (or, perhaps, a task dimension and a rating

scale dimension). Second, construct validity is demonstrated, particularly for the behavioral dimension of impulsivity, which is related to delinquency in the way that is predicted by relevant theories.

EXERCISE 6-10
FIGURE THIS

1. *Argument for face validity (Professor Lactose):* This test has face validity when I line up my 5 clumsy nieces and nephews and 5 coordinated nieces and nephews in March on my lawn in Madison, Wisconsin; I find a significant difference in the amount of time before ice-cream droppage between the clumsy children and coordinated children.

   Argument against face validity (Florida Professor): I know that this test does not have face validity because when I line up my clumsy nieces and nephews with my coordinated nieces and nephews on my lawn in Miami, Florida in March, they all drop their ice-cream at roughly the same time. I think Professor Lactose is confusing temperature with motor coordination. This would explain his conclusion that children all across the United States are far clumsier than those in the northern states!

2. Clearly, Professor Lactose failed to consider other variables that might explain varied drop-plop ratios for children who live in different climates.

3. If Professor Lactose insists upon using the drop-plop ratio to measure motor coordination in children then he must standardize his sample with different ratio expectations for region of the country, time of year, age of children, type of ice-cream (because some are chunky vs. smooth and may affect the time on the cone), type of cone, size of scoop, scooping device, and so on. Professor Lactose may better serve children if he considers rethinking this item as a measure of motor coordination because too many other factors contribute to the variability in performance.

THE 4-QUESTION CHALLENGE

1. a   2. c   3. d   4. d

Chapter 7

Across

1. qualitative
3. scaling
4. cross-validation
7. co-validation
9. fairness
12. analysis
15. pool
17. class
18. conceptualization
19. tryout
21. endorsement
22. ICC
23. rating
26. selected
27. comparative
28. reliability
29. discrimination

Down

2. Likert
3. shrinkage
5. constructed
6. validity
8. difficulty
10. revision
11. validity
13. guessing
14. sensitivity
15. pilot
16. latent
17. categorical
18. cumulative
20. summative
21. expert
24. Guttman
25. construction

EXERCISE 7-6

ITEM ANALYSIS: QUANTITATIVE METHODS

2. b. The probability of guessing correctly on any single item on the basis of chance alone on a multiple-choice item that contains four alternatives is 1/4, or .25, or 25%

 c. The optimal level of item difficulty for any AHT item can be calculated as follows:

$$\frac{.25+1}{2} = \frac{1.25}{2} = .625$$

 d. If 60 of the 100 examinees were correct in their response to Item 47, the item-difficulty index Item 47 can be calculated as follows:

$$p47 = \frac{60}{100} = .60$$

 e. If 69 of the 100 examinees were correct in their response to Item 93, the item-difficulty index for Item 93 can be calculated as follows:

$$p_{93} = \frac{69}{100} = .69$$

 f. Item 47 was more difficult than Item 93; Item 47 had a lower item-difficulty index than Item 93.

 g. The item-score standard deviations for Items 93 and 47 can be calculated as follows:

$$s_{93} = p_{93}(1 - p_{93}) = .69(1 - .69) = .46$$
$$s_{47} = p_{47}(1 - p_{47}) = .60(1 - .60) = .49$$

 h. The item-reliability index for Item 16 can be calculated as follows:

$$(.40)(.75) = .30$$

 i. The item-discrimination index for Items 1 and 2 can be calculated as follows:

$$d_1 = \frac{25-8}{27} = \frac{17}{27} = .63$$
$$d_2 = \frac{9-14}{27} = \frac{-5}{27} = .185$$

 Item 1 is clearly a better item than Item 2; the item-discrimination index for Item 1 is in the high-middle range while the item-discrimination index for Item 2 is negative (and therefore indicative of a problem).

 j. Without resorting to quantitative analysis and simply "eyeballing" the data, it can be seen that Item 2 is not a good item. More members of the low-scoring (L) than the high-scoring (H) group got the item correct. Distractor choice a seemed to draw a great number of the test-takers in the H group, and one way to begin revising the item might be to discuss it with the members of the H group who believed a to be the correct answer.

 k. Item 1 is a good item to the extent that the ratio of members of group H to group L who got the item right was approximately 3 to 1. However, the item could still be improved; distractor choices b and d fool no one. Also, for the purpose of improving future student learning, the test user might wish to discuss with members of the L group what their thinking was with respect to distractor choice a since so many of the group members selected this incorrect alternative.

EXERCISE 7-11

FIGURE THIS

1. Item 1 difficulty index = .8; item 2 = .1, item 3 = .2, item 4 = .2, and item 5 = .9
2. The average item difficulty for this test is .44. Three items fall below that average and 2 fall above. Overall, the range of item difficulty across the five items suggests that the teacher either

may not have taught all of the concepts she was testing or some other factor contributed to the low overall performance of her class. The teacher may want to use one or more strategies to improve the usefulness of her test: a) She may want to compare her test questions with her lesson to assure that they accurately reflect the instructional content, b) review the test questions and rationales for each with her students, or c) re-teach the lesson upon which the test was based to make certain the test measures the expected mastery of information for each student in the class.

3. Norm-referenced tests allow comparisons of the performance of an individual to that of a reference group. The reference group is based on an important trait or characteristic that you want to measure and report as typical or untypical compared to others who share the same relevant trait or characteristic. You would choose to create a norm referenced test when you plan to compare one individual's performance on the test with other individuals who are in the same category (i.e., age, grade, gender) as the testtaker. Some examples of appropriate norm-referenced tests include: Intelligence, achievement, anxiety rating (or other emotional or behavioral symptoms). If desired outcome is to compare the testtaker with others in a same category, then you will create a norm referenced test.

4. You would choose to create a criterion referenced test when you plan to compare one individual's performance on the test with an established standard that is expected for mastery. An example of this type of test is available in most states where state achievement tests must be passed in order for a student to graduate from high school. Other common examples include tests we take in our coursework to pass a class, exams for drivers licenses, exams to become certified to perform CPR, etc.

THE 4-QUESTION CHALLENGE

1. a   2. b   3. a   4. d

Chapter 8

Across

1. intrapersonal
5. sequential
7. successive
9. cultural
10. interactionism
14. factor-analytic
16. schema
19. crystallized
20. Termites
23. PASS
25. nominating
26. emotional
28. three-stratum
32. vulnerable
34. Flynn
35. temperament
36. giftedness
37. preformationism

Down

1. interpersonal
2. intellect
3. ceiling
4. general
6. information-processing
8. fluid
11. two-factor
12. schemata
13. predeterminism
15. alerting
17. simultaneous
18. orienting
21. maintained
22. age
24. assimilation
27. hierarchical
29. accommodation
30. culture-free
31. intelligence
33. parallel

EXERCISE 8-2

INTERPRETING IQ SCORES

For the answers to this ten-item true/false test we again turn to Professor John R. Hills.[2]

ANSWERS TO TEST ON IQ SCORES

Question 1–5, 7, and 9 are false. Question 8 and 10 are true. The answer to Question 6 is true or false depending on whose opinion you believe, or how you evaluate empirical data, conjecture, opinion, and hope.

Explanations:

1. IQ tests do not measure innate abilities unmodified by environment. It is even questioned whether tests given at birth could be argued to be measures of innate abilities because the fetus is influenced by its environment in many ways.
2. Nearly all IQ scores from current intelligence tests use a deviation IQ based on standard scores with a mean of 100 and a standard deviation of 15 or 16 instead of the ratio IQ score based on MA/CA.
3. Different IQ tests can result in quite different scores for the same person because different IQ tests contain different kinds of items or different relative emphases. Different IQ tests are based on different norms groups, which can also result in different IQs for the same person.
4. IQ scores may change, and sometimes markedly. Cronbach uses as an illustration a person whose IQ changed by 55 points with changes in environment (*Essentials of Psychological Testing,* Third Edition, Harper and Row, p. 232). Other evidence also points to the strong possibility of significant changes in IQ score with changes in the environment or, in the case of older forms of IQ tests, changes in age of the examinee (Ahman & Glock, *Evaluating Pupil Growth,* fourth Edition, Allyn and Bacon, pp. 380–390).
5. Although it is true that blacks on the average score 10 to 15 points lower than whites on IQ tests if the content of the items stresses verbal reasoning, there is no clear evidence that the difference is due to bias in the test or its items. Manny's score of 115 is about a standard deviation above average, or at about the 84th percentile. If he had scored 15 points higher, he would have placed about two standard deviations above average, or at about the 98th percentile. Most likely Manny's performance will correspond to his score of 115, not a higher score. It would be a mistake to predict greater success for Manny than would be associated with his score of 115 or to expect his performance in activities depending on verbal reasoning to be comparable to those of students at the 98th percentile instead of comparable to those of students at the 84th percentile. The same kind of interpretation would apply if Manny had scored a standard deviation below the mean, or at IQ 85. We would then recognize that he has more difficulty with verbal reasoning items than average, and most likely he would then have more than average difficulty with the verbal materials he encountered in school unless something occurred to remedy this weakness.
6. Research support for using IQ scores or part scores on intelligence tests for diagnosis of emotional disorders or brain injury is sketchy at best. For example, read Cronbach, op. cit., pages 248–251, or Tittle's review of WISC-R in the *Eighth Measurements Yearbook,* page 353. However, the manual for WISC-R indicates that it is useful for psychological diagnosis. So, you could reasonably argue that based on what you have read you deserve credit for either T or F.
7. The variety in colleges and their requirements is surprising to those who have not developed a familiarity with the literature on college admissions. Cronbach (op. cit., p. 219) is a handy reference indicating, for example, that among college entrants studied by Wolfle in the 1950s, 18 percent had IQ scores between 100 and 109. Very few colleges are highly selective; most of

---

[2]Reprinted with permission from *Hills' Handy Hints* by John R. Hills, published by the National Council on Measurement in Education (1986).

them reject only students who are below average, that is, below IQ 100, and most colleges admit some of the applicants who are below average.

8. One cannot count on finding predictive validity data in the test manual for IQ tests. A specific example is the WISC-R. Tittle (*Eighth Mental Measurements Yearbook,* p. 353) states that the major weakness of the WISC-R manual is the discussion of validity. Sax (*Principles of Educational and Psychological Measurement and Evaluation,* Second Edition, Wadsworth, pp. 389–391) points out that neither the WISC manual or the WISC-R manual even mentions the word "validity," and he goes on to indicate that the manuals for group intelligence tests similarly fail to provide information about validity (p. 392).

9. One of the mystiques about IQ scores is that the individual should not know what his IQ score is. Any other score is all right, but not the IQ score. Prior to the 1960s, the same mystique applied to College Board SAT scores. I doubt that any educational measurement book espouses such secrecy about any test score. Mehrens and Lehmann (*Measurement and Evaluation in Education and Psychology,* pp. 608–609) firmly state that all achievement and aptitude scores should be disseminated to all professional staff members and to the individuals who were tested, even though they note that according to a study by Goslin, half of teachers surveyed had never given a pupil even a general idea of his intelligence. Remember, IQ scores from modern tests are no more than standard scores on a measure of generalized achievement of cognitive skills and knowledge. They have no special, secret, or magical properties except in the minds of the uninformed.

10. Coaching students for tests of college admission has become an important topic in recent years. Debate continues concerning the effectiveness of coaching for those tests. However, it is often erroneously assumed that IQ tests measure something innate or so fundamental that coaching is ineffective for items on these tests. Some IQ tests include unusual kinds of items for which coaching is beneficial. In fact, some investigators have suggested and demonstrated that IQ scores might be more valid if all children were coached on such items (Cronbach, op. cit., page 245).

THE 4-QUESTION CHALLENGE

1. a   2. c   3. d   4. a

Chapter 9

Across

3. alpha
6. basal
7. Binet
10. anchor
13. ceiling
15. short
17. ratio
18. AFQT
19. point

Down

1. OLSAT
2. deviation
4. ASVAB
5. RAT
6. beta
8. composite
9. limits
11. Wechsler
12. Stanford
14. Terman
16. routing

THE 4-QUESTION CHALLENGE

1. a   2. d   3. b   4. d

Chapter 10

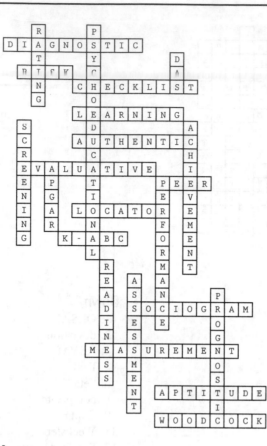

Across

3. diagnostic
5. risk
6. checklist
7. learning
10. authentic
11. evaluative
13. peer
14. locator
15. K-ABC
19. sociogram
20. measurement
21. aptitude
22. Woodcock

Down

1. rating
2. psychoeducational
4. DAS
8. screening
9. achievement
12. Apgar
13. performance
16. readiness
17. assessment
18. prognostic

THE 4-QUESTION CHALLENGE

1. b   2. b   3. b   4. b

Chapter 11

Across

3. ipsative
6. profile
7. nomothetic
9. MMPI
11. structured
14. impression
15. identity
16. sensitive
17. criterion-group
19. forced-choice
24. personality
27. identify
28. halo
29. locus
31. type
34. worldview
36. empirical
37. typeA
38. Q-sort
39. acquiescence

Down

1. generosity
2. acculturation
4. severity
5. trait
8. identification
10. idiographic
12. typeB
13. differential
16. state
18. criterion
20. central
21. self-concept
22. desirable
23. instrumental
25. terminal
26. control
30. self-report
32. style
33. neo
34. Welshcode
35. values

PERSONALITY TEST SCALES

1. MMPPI items scorable on the CR Scale are as follows:
   17. True
   24. True
   32. True
   40. True
   45. True
   47. True
   57. True
   68. False
   78. False

2. Item pairs scorable on the IN Scale, in addition to Item 16 and 61, are as follows:
   Items 4 and 93
   Items 5 and 94
   Items 44 and 69
   Items 53 and 76

3. MMPPI items scorable on the Masculinity/Femininity (M/F) Scale are as follows:
   27. True (Female)   False (Male)
   34. True (Female)   False (Male)
   48. False (Female)   True (Male)
   84. True (Female)   False (Male)
   91. False (Female)   True (Male)

4. If feasible, conduct a study under your instructor's supervision to determine if the scale you created does differentiate members of the target population from nonmembers.

5. Items scorable on the MMPPI Unusual Response Scale (UN-Scale) are as follows:
   10. True
   17. True
   24. True
   25. True
   31. False
   33. True
   40. True
   45. True
   47. True
   57. True
   63. False
   75. True
   78. False

6. Items scorable on the MMPPI Faking Good (FA+) Scale are as follows:
   1. True
   7. True
   9. False
   22. True
   68. True
   Items scorable on the MMPPI Faking Bad (FA−) Scale are as follows:
   8. True
   9. True
   11. False
   31. False
   55. True

THE 4-QUESTION CHALLENGE

1. c   2. c   3. b   4. c

Chapter 12

Across

1. self-monitoring
3. analogue-studies
7. press
8. functional
11. contrast
13. word
14. limits
15. TAT
18. plethysmograph
20. HIT
22. Exner
24. free
25. reactivity
26. objective
27. polygraph

Down

1. sentence
2. need
4. thema
5. unconscious
6. situational
9. unobtrusive
10. inquiry
12. projective
16. apperceive
17. behavioral
19. Machover
21. role
23. scoring

THE 4-QUESTION CHALLENGE

1. d   2. b   3. a   4. a

Chapter 13

Across

3. warn
5. three
7. adressing
11. health
12. ALI
15. custody
16. Barnum
17. insanity
19. neglect
21. abuse
23. evolutionary
24. MAC-R
25. cognitive
26. counseling

Down

1. managed
2. orientation
4. forensic
6. standard
8. Durham
9. status
10. stress
13. competence
14. hypnotic
18. interview
20. clinical
22. DSM

EXERCISE 13-4

THE MULTITRAIT-MULTIMETHOD MATRIX REVISITED

1. Of interest will be those correlations between pairs of scales that are expected to measure the same thing: the correlation between the anxiety scale from the MCMI-II and the anxiety scale from the MMPI, between the depression scale from the MCMI-II and the depression scale from the MMPI, and so on. There are four of these convergent validity coefficients in all, on a downward diagonal in the lower left quadrant of Table 2.

2. The anxiety scales possess high convergent validity, as they correlate .84. The depression and substance abuse scales have a more moderate level of convergent validity, correlating .58 and .40, respectively. Finally, the convergent validity for the two measures of psychotic thought is low, correlating only .19.

3. & 4. All of the remaining coefficients are relevant to discriminant validity. For illustration, consider the MCMI-II anxiety score. In Table 2, this involves the first column of correlations, with the exception of the correlation already examined for convergent validity. Good discriminant validity seems present relative to two of the MMPI scales (substance dependence correlates –.05 and psychotic thought correlates .00). However, the MCMI-II anxiety scale correlates highly with the MCMI-II depression scale (.94), indicating poor discriminant validity in this area. The correlations of the MCMI-II anxiety scale are also higher-than-desired with the MCMI-II sub-

stance dependence measure (.53), the MCMI-II psychosis measure (.75), and the MMPI depression measure (.51). Thus, while the MCMI-II anxiety scale has good convergent validity with the MMPI measure, the scale lacks discriminant validity, indicating (more generally) a problem with construct validity.

Now consider the discriminant validity of the remaining three MCMI-II scales included in Table 2. For each clinical syndrome, there are six discriminant validity coefficients—two for each of the three clinical syndromes different from the one presented on the MCMI-II scale that you are considering. All three remaining MCMI-II scales demonstrate weak discriminant validity, because each correlates more highly with other MCMI-II scales than with the corresponding MMPI scale. For example, the MCMI-II substance dependence scale correlates .53 with the MCMI-II anxiety scale, .56 with the MCMI-II depression scale, and .62 with the MCMI-II psychotic thought scale, all greater than the correlation of .40 with the MMPI measure of substance dependence. The three remaining coefficients relevant to the discriminant validity of the MCMI-II substance dependence scales are the correlations with the MMPI measures of anxiety (.51), depression (.08), and psychosis (.47). Again, two of these three correlations are greater than the convergent validity coefficient for the substance abuse scale. As McCann (1990) notes, these data cast doubt on the construct validity of these MCMI-II scales.

This example illustrates the importance of examining both the discriminant and convergent validity of psychological tests. Often researchers report information about convergent validity, with little or no data about discriminant validity. Although some of the MCMI-II measures have good convergent validity, examination of their discriminant validity leads to questions about the scales' construct validity. The importance of this difficulty becomes clear when we ask about what construct is reflected in a high MCMI-II anxiety score. That score will generally accompany a high MCMI-II depression score, because the two scales are so highly correlated. This makes interpretation difficult: a person with a high anxiety score could be anxious, depressed, or both. The test does not help with making these distinctions. Such psychometric difficulties, then, have practical implications for the use of these measures in understanding testtakers.

THE 4-QUESTION CHALLENGE

1. a   2. c   3. d   4. b

Chapter 14

Across

5. deterioration
6. trail-making
8. neuropsychological
10. pattern
13. fixed
14. perceptual-motor
16. confrontation
19. procedural
21. aphasia
22. central
23. noninvasive

Down

1. Bender
2. organicity
3. declarative
4. history
7. motor
8. NEPSY
9. peripheral
11. contralateral
12. executive
13. flexible
14. perceptual
15. memory
17. neurology
18. damage
20. Hanoi

THE 4-QUESTION CHALLENGE

1. c   2. d   3. b   4. a

Chapter 15

Across

3. general
5. disability
6. perceived
7. IDEA
8. quality-of-life
11. Vineland
12. cognitive
14. accommodation
16. adaptive
17. act

Down

1. functional
2. rehabilitation
4. AAMR
7. infant
8. quid
9. amendments
10. intensity
12. child
13. major
15. diversity
17. ADA

THE 4-QUESTION CHALLENGE

1. d   2. c   3. b   4. b

Chapter 16

Across

2. integrity
5. semantic
8. consumer
10. poll
11. burnout
12. satisfaction
14. survey
15. extrinsic
17. forced
18. attitude
21. critical
23. panel
25. screening
26. race-norming
28. productivity
29. focus

Down

1. placement
3. intrinsic
4. center
6. team
7. culture
8. classification
9. MBTI
10. portfolio
13. selection
16. commitment
19. diary
20. dimensional
22. interest
24. drug
27. GATB

THE 4-QUESTION CHALLENGE

1. b   2. c   3. c   4. d